System Requirements and Tips for the Enclosed DVDs

Georgetown University Press recommends that the DVDs that are provided with the *Al-Kitaab* series be played on a computer rather than a home DVD player, and that the computer has at least the following capabilities:

* **Operating Systems:** Windows 9x/NT4/ME/2000/XP; Mac OS 9 and higher
* **Processors:** Pentium II and higher; Mac G3 and higher
* **Players:** Windows Media Player 10 or higher; or RealPlayer
* **RAM:** 128 MB
* **Monitor Resolution:** 800x600 and higher
* **DVD-ROM drive:** 2x speed
* **Peripherals:** Sound card, video card, speakers, and DVD player software

For optimum DVD performance, use:

* **Windows XP (for PC) or OS X (for Mac), and**
* **Windows Media Player version 10 or higher or the newest version of RealPlayer.**

NOTE: If you are using an earlier version of Windows, you may experience difficulties playing these DVDs. These DVDs are playable as MPEG-2 files, therefore, <u>you must have an MPEG-2 decoder</u>, which is included in the recommended versions of Windows Media Player and RealPlayer.

Windows Media Player is available as a free download in formats for both Macs and PCs at http://www.microsoft.com/downloads. RealPlayer is available for free downloads at http://www.real.com/player.

If you experience any trouble playing the DVDs:

* It is possible that the computer is not equipped to play it. Please try to play it on a different computer that has MPEG-2 capability.
* You may want to allot more memory to virtual memory, or you may restart your computer to refresh the virtual memory. Consult your computer's manual on how to do this.
* Please play **<u>all</u>** the DVDs to check their playability.
* If these tips do not result in your ability to play the DVDs, please ask your bookstore to contact Hopkins Fulfillment Services at 1-800-537-5487 for information on how to acquire replacement DVDs.

Georgetown University Press does not provide person-to-person technical support for the DVDs that come with these books. Please visit our website at http://press.georgetown.edu/arabicfaq.html for more information and navigation tips.

GEORGETOWN UNIVERSITY PRESS
www.press.georgetown.edu

الكتاب
في تعلّم العربية

الجزء الأول

الطبعة الثانية
مع أقراص DVD

Al-Kitaab fii Ta^c^allum al-^c^Arabiyya:

with DVDs

A Textbook for Beginning Arabic

Part One
Second Edition

Kristen Brustad   Mahmoud Al-Batal   Abbas Al-Tonsi

كرستن بروستاد   محمود البطل   عباس التونسي

See the last page for System Requirements for the DVDs accompanying this textbook.

The production of the first edition of this textbook was supported by a grant from the National Endowment for the Humanities, an independent federal agency.

As of January 1, 2007, 13-digit ISBN numbers have replaced the 10-digit system.

13-digit		10-digit	
Paperback:	978-1-58901-104-5	Paperback:	1-58901-104-X

Georgetown University Press, Washington, D.C.

Library of Congress Cataloging-in-Publication Data

Brustad, Kristen.

al-Kitāb fī ta'allum al-'Arabīyah, al-juz' al-awwal / Kristin Brūstād. Mahmūd al-Batal, 'Abbās al-Tūnisī = al-Kitaab fii ta'allum al-'Arabiyya = A textbook for beginning Arabic, part one / Kristen Brustad, Mahmoud Al-Batal, Abbas Al-Tonsi. – 2nd ed.

p. cm.

ISBN 1-58901-104-X (pbk. : alk. paper)

1. Arabic language—Textbooks for foreign speakers—English. I. Title: Kitaab fii ta'allum al-'Arabiyya. II. Title: Textbook for beginning Arabic. III. Al-Batal, Mahmoud. IV. Tūnisī, 'Abbās. V. Title.

PJ6307.B78 2004

492.7'02421 dc22

2004047125

This book is printed on acid-free paper meeting the requirements of the American National Standard for Permanence in Paper for Printed Library Materials.

13 12 11 10 09 08 9 8 7 6

Printed in the United States of America

TABLE OF CONTENTS

Glossaries and Appendices

PREFACE
TO THE SECOND EDITION

Dear Students and Colleagues,

We are pleased to present this second edition of the *Al-Kitaab fii Ta^{c}allum al-^{c}Arabiyya Part I* textbook that comes with DVDs containing all of the audio, video, and cultural materials that accompany the text itself. This edition retains all of the features of the first edition in a sightly revised format and adds some new features as well. Within each chapter, the components are defined in more consistent order than the first edition, following the philosophy outlined in the Arabic introduction. The materials are designed to cover approximately 150 classroom hours, plus 200-300 hours of preparation outside class.

As in the first edition, the twenty chapters in this book are based on the story of Maha and Khalid and their extended family. Each chapter devotes attention to all skills, listening, reading, writing, speaking, and culture, using the basic building blocks of vocabulary and grammar in the format of drills and activities. Many drills are designated as either in-class exercises or homework, and those without designation work well either way. Activities are meant to provide a more open-ended space in which students can push themselves to create with Arabic in speaking and writing, and to comprehend texts slightly beyond their current level in reading and listening. Following are brief descriptions of the major components of each chapter, highlighting changes and additions to the book.

VOCABULARY

The first section of each chapter is devoted to the acquisition and activation of vocabulary. A new feature here is that each vocabulary item is contextualized in a sentence read on the DVD. These sentences are recorded and not written in order to encourage the student to listen to the new vocabulary while studying it at home. The vocabulary section also includes several drills and activities designated for outside or inside the classroom. We have included a new type of exercise, "Find Out," that has been very successful in our classrooms. This exercise helps students activate and personalize new vocabulary by interviewing their classmates in Arabic. Providing students with the questions in English has three benefits: it links the new vocabulary with an English language register they are used to, it precludes the need for English among the students, and it provides the bigger challenge of producing the new vocabulary in context from scratch rather than reading the Arabic words off a page. Another change from the first edition is that the "bank" of vocabulary words is no longer provided in new vocabulary exercises, in order to make these drills more productive. There is thus a substantial amount of grammatical practice that takes place during the time devoted to vocabulary, and this combination ensures more active study and, we believe, faster acquisition.

We suggest that students prepare vocabulary before class by listening, studying with the DVD and doing the drills designated as homework drills before coming to class. Class time should not be spent introducing vocabulary but rather on practicing and activating it through interactive activities such as those suggested in the book. This approach assumes that at least one class hour is spent just on vocabulary activities before tackling the text or any other section. We believe that building vocabulary is the core of building proficiency in Arabic and that the distribution of class time should reflect the importance of activating vocabulary through speaking, reading, writing, and listening activities.

Story

The story of Maha and Khalid remains unchanged, but new actors perform the roles of the characters on the DVD. Unlike the first edition, in which access to the video was restricted, students can now watch the story at home before coming to class. Class time can thus be devoted to interactive work that builds on basic comprehension, expands cultural knowledge, and teaches close attention to structure. Activities such as these are included in many chapters. You will notice that the dictation drill based on the story has been moved to the Review Drills section at the end of the chapter, and that each one contains many more blanks than before. We believe that this new format better serves the philosophy of these materials and the needs of students.

Culture

This new edition includes an expanded cultural component, the key feature of which is a series of short subtitled interviews with Egyptians on questions that arise in the story line. The student can easily watch them at home, or the class can watch them together and discuss, in Arabic as much as possible, what they see. A few chapters have very short visual documentary pieces, such as scenes from a market, a club, and the al-Hussein Mosque.

Grammar

The presentation of grammar remains largely unchanged from the first edition, the major exceptions being the inclusion of non-human plural agreement in Chapter 2 and the introduction of some of the meanings of the verbal forms (awzaan) beginning in Chapter 16. The sequencing of grammar in these materials is not based on a predetermined design, but rather on the story itself, and it takes from that story a natural sequencing of structure in a narrative context that is a hallmark of intermediate language proficiency. In addition, many grammar points are presented more than once at different levels of detail, each time according to the language functions appropriate to students' abilities.

As with vocabulary, we recommend that the students prepare the grammar before coming to class by reading the explanation and writing the specified mechanical drills that will help them internalize the structure. We are confident that the grammar explanations are clear enough for students to understand without lectures or lengthy presentations in class. The explanations are brief and simple, because we believe in the principle of spiralling, in which a concept is introduced more than once, each time with increasing detail according to the students' new level of proficiency. These materials often expose students to structures that they can understand from context well before explaining them. The presentations themselves can thus serve as a synthesis and review of material they have already seen.

This approach also relies on a theory of intergrammar according to which students acquire language by constructing their own internal grammar rather than by internalizing a presentation of grammar to them. It is the goal of this approach to help students build their own grammar, using induction, analogy, and hypothesis formation and testing. Learning a language involves critical thinking no less than memorization. Instructors can help this process along by asking the students questions rather than spoon-feeding them answers: encourage a critical thinking approach to grammar, and use "previews of coming attractions" as a chance to encourage their own evolving understanding of the logic of Arabic grammar.

In this approach, class time is freed up for doing things *with* the grammar rather than talking *about* the grammar. Students do not know the grammar until they can produce it consistently, and this takes constant practice over time. Each grammar point has a mechanical drill designed to be done as homework as well as an in-class activity designed to be done in small groups in class. Of course, grammar practice is part of every class, and belongs in all activities involving structured language production.

Reading Comprehension

We use the term reading comprehension to refer to activities that develop the skills that all fluent readers of Arabic use. We are not concerned here with developing the skill of reading texts aloud, which is unrelated to comprehension and in fact often interferes with it. Reading aloud helps pronunciation and reinforces vocabulary and structure, and we have provided composed texts for just these purposes in the Review Drills section of many of the early chapters. Reading comprehension texts are not meant to be read aloud or translated but rather skimmed, scanned, and analyzed in Arabic as much as possible. Their main purpose is teaching strategies and skills necessary for fluent reading. Of course, focusing on close reading and grammatical details is a crucial part of building fluency in reading. The traditional way to do this is through translation, but we believe that translation of authentic texts at this level is counterproductive because the sheer quantity of unknown vocabulary forces students to process the text in linear fashion.

As in the first edition, each chapter contains at least one authentic text and accompanying activity designed to build strategies for reading comprehension. In this edition, we have tried to increase the amount of attention and sustain with better consistency the development of reading strategies beginning in Chapter 9. Many texts have been replaced with ones we feel provide better opportunities to develop reading skills as well as more cultural content. Texts have been updated as necessary.

These activities include work on both top-down and bottom-up processing skills, as both are essential to developing reading fluency. We recommend that these exercises be done in class as mush as possible, especially at the beginning stages, until students develop confidence both in themselves and in the instructors' expectations of them (and so that well-meaning Arabic speakers do not help them too much!). Many of these exercises work well in pairs, and this cooperative learning approach helps create the desired atmosphere of exploration and discovery that makes reading fun.

Each reading comprehension exercise begins with questions focusing on top-down processing skills, or global comprehension. The key at this stage is to let the students lead by reporting the meanings that they are able to construct. Micromanagement in the form of highly specific questions is counterproductive at this stage. Following the global look at the text, second- and third-round questions ask students to focus on specific sections of the text that present them with "muscle-building" exercises that work on bottom-up processing skills. These questions include guessing the meaning of new words from carefully chosen contexts using contextual and grammatical clues and the Arabic root and pattern system, recognition and accurate processing of grammatical structures in new and authentic contexts, and discourse management, or learning to keep track of large structures, such as how sentences and paragraphs are constructed, identifying parallel construction, paying attention to connectors, and learning to parse long sentences in which the subject and predicate or verb may be located far away from each other.

Because the purpose of these reading exercises is to build these kinds of skills and strategies, we discourage turning reading exercises into vocabulary exercises. Each text here has been carefully chosen so that the students can comprehend a great deal and develop processing skills through reading without any additional vocabulary. Providing lists of all unknown vocabulary in the text will lead students back to linear processing and will not help them develop reading proficiency.

Listening Comprehension

Much of the discussion on reading comprehension applies as well to listening, with a bit of a time lag, since listening comprehension of authentic texts presents additional challenges. In this edition, work with authentic listening passages begins in Chapter 5 but is sporadic until Chapter 16, when the students have acquired enough vocabulary to begin to handle authentic audio-visual materials. It is important to begin these activities by letting the students listen to the entire text a number of times without interruption and posing only general open ended questions that elicit what they understood.

In addition to the authentic texts, we have included on the DVDs in video format a number of composed listening texts, spin-offs of the main story line, that introduce relatives and friends of Maha and Khalid. These texts reinforce the vocabulary and structure students have learned and provide an opportunity to sharpen phonological skills as well as develop their ability to process increasing lengths of text through listening. These passages aim to develop both top-down and bottom-up processing skills.

Writing and Speaking Activities

Work on writing and speaking skills begins on day one of each chapter, when students write vocabulary exercises and interview their classmates in "Find Out" activities, and continues throughout the chapter in the discussion of the story in Arabic, grammar activities, and so forth. The activities that are designated for writing and speaking towards the end of each chapter are meant to be more open-ended and creative to provide the students with opportunities to create in the language—a key aspect of intermediate language proficiency. Many of the ideas for speaking activities in this edition of the book are new, and we hope that they will be a positive addition to your classrooms.

Colloquial

The second edition of *Al-Kitaab Part I* incorporates an Egyptian colloquial component in each chapter. This new addition was part of the original plan of the materials, but logistics prevented us from incorporating it in the fist edition. This colloquial component builds on the situations presented in *Alif Baa*, and prepares the student for more extensive work on colloquial later (this expansion will be continued in the next edition of *Al-Kitaab Part II*). Our goal is not to teach colloquial as a language system, but rather to expose learners to familiar content in a different language register so that they begin to get accustomed to the rhythms of everyday speech and to recognize the connections and similarities between the two registers. While we have chosen the Egyptian colloquial for the reasons outlined in the Arabic introduction, we encourage colleagues who prefer to teach other dialects to do so, and to develop their own materials using this Egyptian set as a model.

Each chapter in this textbook contains two kinds of colloquial situations. The first is an Egyptian colloquial version of the story text, so that students can listen to a colloquial versions of the formal text they heard at the beginning of the chapter. The second is a short scene containing a situation, usually related to the story line. The dose here is meant to be small, and consists of words and expressions, not structures.

Review Drills

A section containing two or three review drills comes at the end of each chapter. The placement of the drills here is designed to give the instructor maximum flexibility. These drills, which include the dictation from the story, can be used as review for a quiz, with a teaching assistant or tutor, or simply left for the students to do on their own. The final section, Remember These Words, provides a summary of all important words that came up in reading, listening and grammar activities throughout the chapter.

We hope that this new edition of the book will serve as a useful learning and teaching tool for Arabic. We apologize for any shortcoming this second edition contains, and hope that the additions and subtractions that we have made will add up to a better set of materials. In the end, it is you, the teacher and the student, who make these materials come alive, and we wish you all a lively and productive journey with them.

To the Student

أهلاً وسهلاً إلى الكتاب في تعلّم العربية !

Now that you have completed learning the alphabet and are beginning to communicate orally in Arabic, you are ready to "jump in" and start reading, writing, listening, and speaking. Before you begin, we would like to tell you about the design of these materials, the goals that we have set for you, and the strategies we suggest for maximum acquisition.

About the Materials

Nobody ever became fluent in a language simply by attending class. You will reach proficiency in Arabic largely through what you teach yourself; hence, these materials are designed to teach you *how to learn*. Your teacher's role is to guide your learning; only you can do the work. This approach thus asks you to do a lot of preparation work outside of class. It assumes college level study skills and the standard 2-3 hours outside of class for every hour of classroom instruction.

The philosophy on which these materials are based places great emphasis on learning aurally (through listening). We have found this to be by far the most effective method in helping students assimilate structure and vocabulary. It will help you to focus on the meaning of phrases and sentences rather than individual words, which means that you will be able to read, listen, speak, and write more quickly, with greater accuracy, and with better comprehension.

These materials will expose you to a large quantity of material. Distinguish between things that you will learn for active control, such as the vocabulary of a new lesson, and those that you are only expected to recognize passively, such as certain grammatical structures. You will also be exposed to a range of what we call language *registers*, a word that refers to the type or level of language used in a given situation. The language registers in these materials range from the everyday colloquial speech of educated Egyptians to the very formal and even classical language of religious texts. Your best strategy in dealing with these different registers is to choose one for active use, and learn to recognize the words, sounds, or forms of the other registers. (This same strategy works well when dealing with more than one dialect.)

These materials are designed to challenge you. (They are not meant to frustrate you, though. If you find yourself becoming frustrated, check to see if you are retaining vocabulary, and see your teacher for help.) Do not expect to understand all of everything you read or hear. Most of the reading texts in this book were written for educated adult native speakers. *Do* expect to understand and learn something from every text you work with: this exposure to "real-life" Arabic can be the most challenging and rewarding exercise you undertake. It helps to approach these texts with an expectation of exploration and discovery: Are there any new words you can guess the meaning of? Can you discover how to say "population," "double room," or "Nobel prize" from the text? Every piece of information you can recognize or extract from authentic texts represents a step forward in building your Arabic language skills.

You will notice that many of the reading and listening exercises in this book ask you to read or listen not once but several times. The time and effort you put into reading and listening in this manner will pay off many times over in increased language skills. Not only will you understand more each time you repeat the activity, but you also need to move through several stages of comprehension. The first phase is that of general or "global" comprehension. The first time reading or listening to a text is usually a quick skim or scan through the text that helps you to pinpoint the context and framework so that in the second and subsequent readings you will be able to guess and fill in from your own knowledge. Beyond global comprehension, you will want to fill in as many details as you can by focusing closer attention on the parts of a text that are most accessible to you. The questions in the reading and listening exercises are designed to help you do this too. The final stage of comprehension is one that the best language learners push themselves to: after understanding as much as possible, go back one more time to concentrate not on *what* is being said but on *how* it is being said.

Because Arabic has a long history and is spoken across a large geographical area, it has an expansive vocabulary. We recommend that you work on this, the biggest challenge of Arabic in our opinion, in a two-pronged approach. First, put as much effort as you can into actively acquiring the vocabulary in each chapter. Second, develop strategies for guessing from context and from your own general knowledge. The reading and listening activities in this book are designed to help you do this. It is a skill that you already have, since you used it to help you learn your own native language. It is helpful to reactivate those same skills and apply them to learning Arabic.

Goals

By the time you have completed this book إن شاء الله you should have achieved solid intermediate proficiency in Arabic. We aim for you to:

1. Be able to read texts on familiar topics and understand the main ideas without using the dictionary,
2. Have confidence in your ability to guess the meaning of new words from context,
3. Be able to speak about yourself, your life, and your environment, and initiate and sustain conversations on a number of daily life topics,
4. Be able to paraphrase if necessary to make yourself understood,
5. Understand native speakers accustomed to dealing with learners of Arabic as a foreign language,
6. Be able to write paragraphs on familiar topics and correspondence connected to daily life,
7. Be able to form and understand all basic sentence structures of Arabic,
8. Be familiar with some of the differences between formal and spoken Arabic, and
9. Be aware of aspects of Arab culture connected to everyday life.

Learning Strategies

We believe the following strategies will help you learn the most from these materials:

In Class

It is the teacher's responsibility to make the classroom a place to practice and work with Arabic in a variety of ways, and it is your responsibility to prepare for those activities by listening to the vocabulary on your DVD and studying it well, by reading grammar or other explanations carefully at home, and by writing out homework exercises with as much effort and concentration as you can. Homework helps you build muscle so that you are ready to play the game in class. Prepare for *active* participation in class. After the first few days, you will be able to predict what kinds of questions will be asked and what kinds of activities will be performed. Be ready for them by guessing what they will be and practicing beforehand.

Class time is limited. To make the most of it, be an active learner by listening to what is being said and how it is being said, and by repeating and correcting things to yourself. Listening does not have to be a passive activity. While your classmates are talking, take the opportunity to concentrate on the vocabulary or structures they are using, and either imitate or try to improve upon their efforts. There is no better drill or practice than to be constantly repeating to yourself correctly formed sentences, and this kind of drill you have to do yourself. If you are not tired by the end of class, you are not learning as much as you can, and you are not taking full advantage of the opportunities it presents.

Active learners ask questions, especially specific questions. When a question occurs to you, ask it, but if you can, try to reason out an educated guess for yourself beforehand. Not only are you more likely to remember the answer, but you will also develop confidence in your own language abilities. The critical thinking skills you bring with you to Arabic can help you be an excellent language learner.

Focus on what you *do* understand rather than on what you do not. The following is an exercise that will show you how much you can understand from a text without having all the pieces. Read the following paragraph and answer for yourself: What can you understand about the topic of this paragraph? Can you fill in a word that makes sense in most or all blanks below? Can you fill in some blanks with more that one word? If so, do the different words you used make a big difference in the meaning? If you could have two of the missing words given to you, which ones would they be, and why? How did your knowledge of English sentence structure help you choose appropriate words to fill in?

> In his short _______ "Children's Heaven," Nobel ________ ________ writer Naguib Mahfouz __________ a parent's _________ on the difficulties of _____________ children. The story ____________ of a ________________ between a father and his daughter about her friend Nadia who goes to a __________ religious class than she. The _____ girl does not ________ why she and Nadia cannot be together during that hour. The father's __________ to explain religious _________ to his daughter fails, but in the end it does not _____ , because although the father has __________ the matter into a philosophical _________, to his daughter it is _______ friendship.

You will use the same knowledge and skills you used here to do many of the reading exercises in this book.

OUTSIDE OF CLASS

Once is not enough. Whether you are pronouncing new vocabulary or reading a text, repeat the activity as many times as you need to until you can do it easily. The Arabic proverb says, Repetition teaches even the donkey (or, in a more polite version, Repetition teaches the smart ones!).

Study out loud. The only way to train your brain and your mouth to speak this language is by doing—thinking about it is not enough! Talking to yourself in Arabic is an excellent way to get extra practice.

Study in pairs or groups if that works well for you, and if you can agree to speak Arabic together as much as you can. This is a good way to prepare for class and review. You can do things together such as ask each other questions, brainstorm about assignments, and practice conjugating verbs.

Read and listen to everything at least one more time *after* you have understood it, so that you can concentrate on form as well as content. You will become fluent in Arabic by paying attention to and imitating the way ideas are expressed, and you will be rewarded later on with the ability to express your own ideas more clearly and accurately.

Resist the temptation to write the meaning of words in English on or near the texts and exercises so that you focus on the Arabic, not the English. Trust your ability to recall meaning with the help of a familiar context. Keep in mind that you will probably forget and relearn a word several times before you retain it, so go ahead and forget, and look it up again if you need to. Forgetting is part of the learning process.

Memorization is central to learning any language. The more you memorize, the more quickly you will learn. If you don't know how to memorize well, ask others how they do it, or ask your teachers for help. Experiment with different techniques—usually a combination of oral and written, active and passive exercises works best. We suggest that you try the following techniques until you find the ones that work best for you: listening to the DVDs and repeating out loud, flashcards, writing out vocabulary by hand over and over, repeating vocabulary out loud, making up your own sentences with new vocabulary, quizzing each other in groups, and word association techniques such as remembering a particular sound or context. It is also important to memorize in chunks or phrases. Memorize all the forms of a word together, such as singular and plural, verb and preposition. The best language learners memorize phrases, sentences, and short, culturally important texts, such as song lyrics, lines of poetry, proverbs, and passages from religious texts. Such cultural references arise often both in readings and in conversation. The definition of culture as the collective *memory* of a people speaks to the importance of this habit.

Finally, we hope that these materials will help make your experience with Arabic enjoyable and rewarding, and we wish you every success!

وبالتوفيق إن شاء الله !

تقديم: في الفلسفة والمنهج

حضرات الزميلات والزملاء :

يسرّنا أن نضع بين ايديكم الطبعة الثانية من «الكتاب في تعلّم العربية الجزء الأول» الذي يمثل الحلقة الثانية في سلسلة كتب لتعليم اللغة العربية لغير الناطقين بها تشمل كتاب «ألف باء : مدخل الى حروف العربية وأصواتها» والجزأين الثاني والثالث من «الكتاب في تعلّم العربية». ونود في هذه الصفحات ان نشرككم معنا في مناقشة الفلسفة التي انطلقنا منها في عملية اعداد الكتاب والمنهج الذي اهتدينا به في تنظيم اجزائه، ذلك اننا نؤمن بأن التدريس الفعّال لأي كتاب لا يستلزم فقط الانطلاق من فلسفته ومنهجه وانما يستلزم ايضاً إثراءه بإبداع المدرس الذي يصب في ذات الاتجاه سواء من خلال دور المدرس «المايسترو» أو من خلال الانشطة التي يؤدّيها الطلاب في الفصل أو من خلال التدريبات والامتحانات.

وقد جاءت محاولة تجديد هذا الكتاب نتيجة للخبرة التي تكونت لدينا نحن والزملاء من تدريس الطبعة الأولى. ورغم التغييرات التي طرأت على شكل الدروس وتوزيع الأنشطة فيها وعلى بعض النصوص إلاّ أن الفلسفة التي قامت عليها الطبعة الأولى لم تتغير بل على العكس، فقد ازددنا إيماناً بها ومن هنا فقد ارتأينا أن نعيد تقديم مبادئ هذه الفلسفة في هذه الصحفات لنؤكد على محورية الفلسفة والمنهج لأي مادة تدريسية وكذلك لأي مدرس أو مدرسة للغة العربية. ولنبدأ بتحديد موقفنا من جملة من القضايا الهامة وأبرزها :

١) قضية«الأصلية»:

إن تجاهل الواقع اللغوي في العالم العربي أو فهم ما يسمى بـ «الازدواجية (أو التعددية) اللغوية» فهما أُحاديا وما يترتب عليه من تطرف إلى هذا الجانب أو ذلك قد أدى ، في رأينا، إلى أن بدت اللغة العربية لغة مستحيلة التعلم لا يتأتى فك طلاسمها إلا لقلة نادرة من الموهوبين ، وهو ما يعني عمليا إلغاء دور العملية التعليمية . إننا مازلنا نخوض معارك «دون كيخوتية» حول الفصحى والعامية تحت وهم أن إحداهما ستقضي على الأخرى، ونلقي باللوم على العامية معتبرين أنها هي السبب في ضعف مستوى الطلاب العرب في الفصحى ، متجاهلين أنها ليست ظاهرة طارئة وأن المشكلة الحقيقية تكمن في تصميمنا على التعامل مع الفصحى والعامية وكأنهما لغتان لا لغة واحدة .

إن جوهر «الأصلية» من وجهة نظرنا يتمثل في التعامل مع واقع اللغة دون وصاية . وإذا كان الهدف الأساسي لهذا الكتاب هو تعلم الطلاب للفصحى فإننا لا نستطيع من أجل هذا الهدف أن نقدم للطالب لغة مصنوعة لا تنتمي للواقع تكريسا لانفصام نَكِد بين الفصحى والعامية . من هنا كان السؤال: بأية لغة سنكتب الخيط القصصي الذي تتبلور حوله مختلف الأنشطة في الكتاب؟ وأية فصحى نريد أن نقدمها لطلابنا ؟ وكيف؟ ووجدنا أن موقف توجّه الشخصيات بالحديث إلى جمهور أو متلقٍ تعرّفه بنفسها وبعالمها يحتمل نوعا من الفصحى المبسطة التي تلتزم مبدأ «سكِّن تَسْلَم»، أما الحوار فمن الطبيعي أن يكون بالعامية لأن أي حوار بالفصحى بين شخصيات القصة سيكون مصطنعا . وهكذا كان الحديث (المونولوج) في الجزء الأول من الكتاب بالفصحى حيث تقدم شخصيات القصة نفسها، أما مواقف الحوار التي جاءت في «ألف باء» وكذلك في هذا الجزء فيجري الحوار فيها طبيعياً بالعامية.

وقد حاولنا في إعداد الخيط القصصي في الكتاب أن تكون اللغة طبيعية قدر الإمكان دون نظر إلى مفردات ينبغي تقديمها أو تراكيب يجب الالتزام بها ، وبعد أن اكتملت كتابة هذا الخيط القصصي بدأنا في تحديد المفردات والتراكيب التي وردت في «القصة» والتي ينبغي تقديمها للطالب ، ومناقشة كيف نراكمها من خلال أنشطة الكتاب المختلفة ، ولم نتدخل في القصة إلا بمحاولة إبطاء إيقاع الحديث عند إعداد مادة الفيديو بحيث يتمكن الطالب من متابعته .

لقد كان موقفنا، حتى في القسم الخاص بالابجدية، أن اختلافات النطق بين الفصحى والعامية ليست مسألة مستحيلة الاستيعاب وليست سرا ينبغي إخفاؤه . ولابد من رفع الوصاية عن الطلاب وأن نقدم لهم صورة لما يجري في واقع اللغة حيث المونولوج في المواقف الرسمية وشبه الرسمية أقرب إلى الفصحى ، أما الديالوج فهو في معظم الأحوال يجري بالعامية . ولم يكن يتفق من وجهة نظرنا أن نجري الحوار بالفصحى ثم نأتي بنصوص مختلفة من الصحف أو الكتابات العربية لنضع ختم الأصلية على المادة المعدة في الكتاب .

إن نصوص القراءة والاستماع في الكتاب امتداد طبيعي للخط القصصي الذي يربط مادة الكتاب بأجزائه كلها وهي ليست مكوّنا إضافيا أو نشاطا ثانويا يمكن التغاضي عنه ، بل إن مادة الكتاب كلٌ لايتجزأ .

وقد التزمنا في نصوص القراءة باستخدام المادة كما هي دون تغيير مفردة أو تبسيط تركيب ، وإن أضطررنا في بعض النصوص التي اخترناها إلى حذف بعض الأجزاء الاستطرادية بحيث يأتي طول النص مناسبا ، وقد ارتأينا أن مثل هذا الحذف أمر طبيعي يلجأ إليه القارىء عندما يقرأ نصا طويلا أو مليئاً بالاستطرادات . وبنهاية الجزء الثاني يكون الطالب نفسه قادرا على القيام بهذا الحذف وعلى إعادة ترتيب النص بعد أن يكون قد تدرّب على هذه العملية على امتداد الكتاب .

٢) قضية العامية والفصحى والعلاقة بينهما :

ان قضية العامية والفصحى ، كما يتضح مما تقدم، وثيقة الصلة بقضية الأصلية وهي تمسّ صلب الفلسفة التي يقوم عليها هذا الكتاب بمختلف أجزائه . وقد ارتأينا ان نعرّض الطالب الى العامية بشكل تدريجي بحيث يفهم طبيعة العلاقة التي تربط بين الفصحى والعامية ويدرك انهما تمثلان امتدادين لواقع لغوي واحد وان بلوغ أي مستوى متقدم من الكفاءة في اللغة العربية لا يمكن ان يتحقق بواحد من هذين المكونين دون الآخر . فبدأنا في «ألف باء» بعدد من الحوارات وعبارات التحية البسيطة وأتبعنا ذلك في هذا الكتاب بمواقف مختلفة تمّ فيها استخدام العامية بهدف تعريض الطالب الى بعض اصوات العامية ومفرداتها . ويهمنا هنا أن نعرض لردنا على بعض الحجج التي تتردد كثيرا في وجه أي محاولة ترفض تكريس الفجوة بين الفصحى والعامية . والحجة الأولى هي أن أي تعامل مع العامية وبأي شكل كان سيتم على حساب الفصحى، وردنا على ذلك بسيط فمهارة الاستماع واحدة سواء كان الاستماع بالفصحى أم العامية ، وإذا وافق الكثيرون على مايذكره دليل الكفاءة من ضرورة معرفة الطالب في المستوى المتفوق بالعامية فهل المُتصوَّر أن تهبط عليه تلك المعرفة فجأة ودون سابق إنذار وأن نفاجئه مرة واحدة بأن نقول له أن ما تعلمته من فصحى خالصة لا يمثل إلا جزءاً من الواقع اللغوي ؟ أو نتركه هو ليكتشف ذلك بمجرد أن تطأ قدمه أرض أي بلد عربي؟ ومن من المثقفين العرب أو المتعلمين يتحدث الفصحى في كل المواقف؟

ثمة حجة أخرى أو سؤال يطرح وهو لماذا العامية المصرية بالتحديد ؟ وما الحل إذا لم يكن المدرس مصريا؟ والإجابة ببساطة وبعيدا عن أية حساسيات قطرية أن العامية المصرية هي أكثر العاميات العربية انتشارا على امتداد العالم العربي ونظرة بسيطة على خريطة برامج الإذاعة والتليفزيون في أي قطر عربي تكشف لنا هذه الحقيقة ، أما مسألة وجود أو عدم وجود مدرس مصري فهي تبدو كما لو كان من الممكن لأي عربي أو مستعرب يقوم بتدريس اللغة العربية أن يزعم أنه لا يفهم هذا المستوى البسيط من العامية المصرية وبالتالي لم يستطع أن يستمتع بأغاني أم كلثوم و عبد الحليم حافظ وعمرو دياب على سبيل المثال أو بأداء فاتن حمامة أو نور الشريف، ولم يشاهد الأفلام والمسلسلات المصرية التي تحفل بها محطات الاذاعة والتلفزيون في شتى أرجاء العالم العربي . ثم اننا لا نرى أي ضير في أن يقوم المدرس الذي يتكلم لهجة من اللهجات الاخرى بتقديم بعض العبارات والمفردات من تلك اللهجة ، فنحن لسنا هنا بصدد فرض أي لهجة على طلابنا وزملائنا ولسنا نرى أي فرق بين أن نعرّض الطلاب الى هذه العامية أو تلك إنما المهم في رأينا هو تزويدهم بجرعة من العامية تسمح لهم بإدراك واقع اللغة والإطار الثقافي الذي تحيا في ظله .

٣) قضية «الكفاءة»:

لقد كان لمعدي هذا الكتاب ، مثل الكثيرين من المشتغلين في المجال، فهم معين تتلخص ملامحه في ما يلي:

أ . ليس معيار نجاحنا في التدريس هو ما يستطيع الطالب أن يفعله في نص ما داخل الفصل ، وإنما المحك هو ما الذي يستطيع أن يقوم به الطالب خارج الفصل في نصوص أخرى أو مهام واقعية . إن نجاح المدرس هو أن يكون الصف إعدادا للطالب لمواجهة واقع اللغة خارج الصف .

ب . إن مثل هذا الإعداد لا يكون بتزويد الطالب بقوائم للمفردات المناسبة في موقف معين ، أو التعبيرات الملائمة لأداء وظيفة معينة مقتطَعة من سياقها الطبيعي ومقلِّصة لدور الطالب إلى مجرد الحفظ والترديد لهذه المفردات والتعبيرات ، وإنما هو في اتاحة الفرصة أمام الطلاب لمراكمة معارفهم ومفرداتهم . إن مثل تلك القوائم قد تكون مفيدة للمراجعة ولكنها ليست بديلا عن هذا التراكم .

ج . إن دور المدرس في حقيقته أقرب إلى دور المرشد أو الموّجه أو المنظّم ، وأن مناط عملية التعلم هو الطالب، وأنه كلما أتاح المدرس للطالب أن يكتشف و يستخدم قدراته ويمارس لغته ويوظف أدواته التي اكتسبها كانت استفادة الطالب أكبر .

د .إن تركيز المنهج التقليدي على القواعد واعتبارها المركز الذي تدور حوله اللغة لاينبغي أن يدفع إلى تطرف مقابل يعتبر القواعد عنصرا هامشيا أو ثانويا لايحظى بعناية كبيرة كيلا يؤثر على انتاج الطالب للغة . إن القواعد ، وإن لم تكن مهارة مستقلة بذاتها، إلا أنها عنصر أساسي يدخل في تكوين وتعزيز كل المهارات ونحن نرى أن محور الخلاف هو في حقيقته طريقة تقديم القواعد وهل تقدَّم من خلال شروح وافية شافية وقواعد محفوظة أم انها حساسية ينبغي أن تُطوَّر من خلال تراكم خبرة الطالب الذاتية في التعامل مع اللغة ثم تأتي عملية التقعيد لتصوغ مثل هذه الخبرة في قوانين عامة . ويتصل بهذا تحديد الأولويات في عملية تقديمها وكذلك طبيعة وحجم الجرعة الضرورية لكل مرحلة . وينطلق موقفنا كذلك من تقديم القواعد الذي سنفصله بعد قليل من التوازن بين أهميتها وجرعتها، بين الحساسية بها أو الأدراك الذاتي لها و تأطيرها ، لذا فقد حرصنا على أن يشمل الكتاب العديد من تمارين القواعد لتمكين الطالب من استخدامها بشكل فعال.

من هنا جاء تقبلنا لحركة الكفاءة وإن تحفظنا على بعض العمليات الإجرائية التي اتخذتها أحيانا من قبيل تحديد الهدف والوظيفة في بداية كل درس فقد شعرنا أن مثل هذا التحديد ينطوي على موقف تعليمي (بمعنى التعليم وليس التعلم) على عكس ما تدعو اليه حركة الكفاءة ، فضلا عن أنه يفقد الطالب جزءا كبيرا من متعة الاكتشاف والتعلم الذاتي، فهو أشبه بالقول «ندرّسك هذا الدرس من أجل هذا الهدف والوظيفة التي عليك أن تصبح قادرا على ادائها بعد الانتهاء من هذا الدرس وهي التعبير عن ...» مما يؤدي الى التعامل مع وظائف اللغة كما لو كانت مصفوفات أو عبوات لا تتداخل وتتراكم وتدوَّر .

وأخيراً فاننا نؤمن بأن نجاح أي صف انما يعتمد بالدرجة الأولى على عطاء المدرس وابداعه وايمانه بطلابه وقدراتهم وتفاعله معهم . وما نقدمه اليكم في هذه الطبعة الجديدة من الكتاب ليس إلا اسهاماً متواضعاً منا في توفير اطار يساعد في اغناء هذا العطاء وتعزيز هذا التفاعل . وأخيرا نرجو أن تغفروا لنا حماسنا إذ لولا إيماننا بما ذكرناه لما كانت هذه المحاولة .

المؤلفون

ACKNOWLEDGMENTS

Production of DVDs by Multimedia Company, Mohammed Shaheen, Director
Production of Video Material by Nashwa Mohsin Zayid
Drawings by Anne Marie Skye, www.amskyeart.com

We would like to express our deep gratitude to all the institutions and individuals who made the production of this book possible. The National Endowment for the Humanities, an independent federal agency, provided the funding for the first edition through a grant to the School of Arabic at Middlebury College, which added matching funds and staff support. The Egyptian Union for Television and Radio graciously provided us with and granted us permission to use some of its programs in support of Arabic teaching in the United States. The contributions of many colleagues and students who tested, critiqued and donated materials to the first edition remain crucial to this new edition as well.

We are grateful to the many people who have helped with different aspects of this project. We set our aspirations high for this edition and have been blessed with the generous and dedicated work of many people.

The staff of Multimedia Company in Cairo Egypt did a phenomenal amount of work to design and construct the DVDs of both *Alif Ba*a and the current volume. These materials are in great debt to both their technical expertise and their sheer determination to make things work.

A special acknowledgment is due Nashwa Mohsin Zayid, director of the video scenes accompanying this book, and the acting and cinematography crew she put together for their dedicated and highly professional work in producing the video materials. Special thanks are also due all the actors who made our characters come to life on the screen. The long days and nights spent filming and editing the visual materials are obvious in the quality of this new product.

The masterful new drawings in this edition are all the work of professional artist Anne Marie Skye. We greatly appreciate her generosity in lending her talents to these materials. Michael Cooperson's original cartoons continue to grace the pages of this new edition.

The Emory College Language Center staff and student assistants have played a key supporting role throughout the work on this project. Thanks to Jose Rodriguez and Juana Clem McGhee for general moral and material support, and special thanks to programming wizard Johnny Wagenner for producing the icons used in this edition. Neil Fried of Chelsea Studios, Atlanta, remains our US-based sound technology expert.

We are grateful to Olla Al-Shalchi for her help in recording audio material here and in *Alif Baa*, and to our friends and colleagues who added their greetings on the *Alif Baa* DVDs.

Our colleagues at Georgetown University Press were instrumental in helping us realize the ambitious additions to this second edition of this book. Special thanks go to Richard Brown, director, and Gail Grella, associate director and acquisitions editor, for continued support of the project. We are grateful to the entire staff for their dedicated and careful work in producing these materials, and for graciously dealing with delays caused by technical problems to get the materials out as fast as humanly possible.

Finally, we would like to express our thanks to all the students and colleagues who have generously provided us with feedback, suggestions and new contributions to the materials, especially Chris Stone, Michael Cooperson, Driss Cherkaoui, Mahmoud Abdallah, Kirk Belnap, Rima Semaan, David Vishanoff, Martha Schulte-Nafeh, and Josie Hendrickson.

We continue to be inspired by the enthusiasm, encouragement, and the generously positive response of many users of these materials. To all of you,

ألف شكر من أعماق قلوبنا !

١. أنا مها

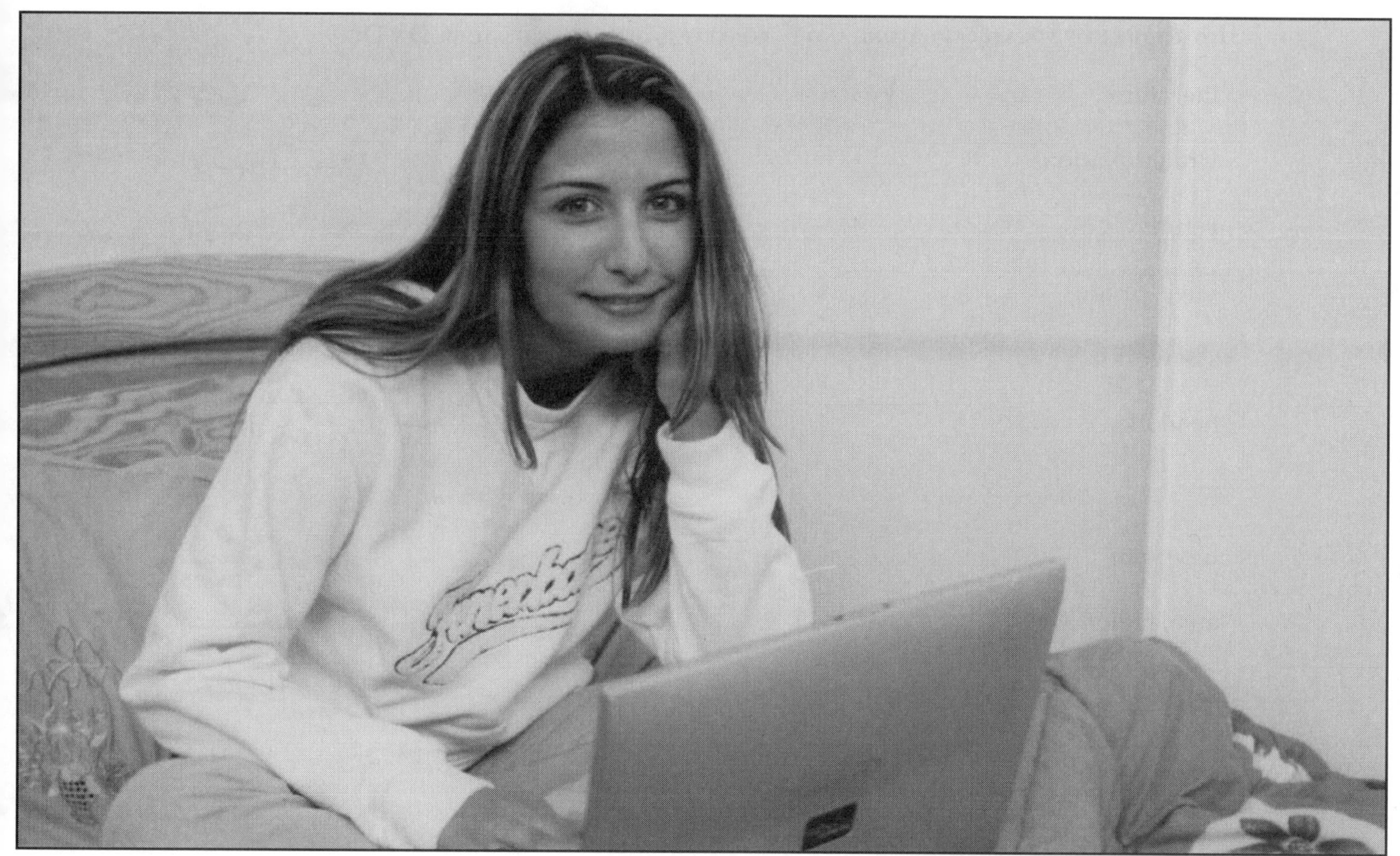

في هذا الدرس:

القصة • مها محمد أبو العلا

الثقافة • الاسم العربي

القواعد • المؤنّث والمذكّر

• الـ

• النّسبة

• السّؤال

الاستماع • الـ

القراءة • نيويورك

العامية • القصة: «انا مها»

• «انتي عربية؟»

المفردات *Vocabulary*

Listen to the new vocabulary alone and in context in sentences on your DVD:

literature	الأَدَب
United Nations	الأُمَم المُتَّحِدة
I study	أَدرُس
I live, reside	أَسكُن
she works	تَعمَل
he works	يَعمَل
in	في
Egyptian	مِصريّ / ة
area, region	مِنطَقة
the same ...	نَفس الـ ...
father	والِد
my father	والِدي
mother	والدة
my mother	والِدَتي

تمرين ١ (في البيت)

On your DVD, listen to the vocabulary and the sentences illustrating its usage. Listen and repeat several times until you can hear and pronounce the words clearly. Write out five (or more) of the sentences. (This is an exercise you can do with every chapter.)

تمرين ٢ (في البيت)

Practice using the vocabulary by giving information about yourself:

١- والدي يعمل __________ .

٢- والدتي تعمل __________ .

٣- أدرس في __________ .

٤- الامم المتحدة في __________ .

٥- أسكن في __________ .

٦- أنا وأنت في __________ الصف.

تمرين ٣ (في الصف)

Ask your classmates questions that will elicit the information requested. Do not translate; rather, formulate direct questions to your classmates, such as "Does your mother (you can say 'the mother') work at home?" Use لا to negate verbs. You can also get information by giving it about yourself and using a "tag" question:

أسكن في منطقة الجامعة. وأنت؟

لا أدرس الأدب. وأنت؟

Find out:

1. Who studies literature?
2. Whose mother is a doctor?
3. Whose mother works at home?
4. Whose father works at a university?
5. Who is a mother or a father?
6. What area do your classmates live in?
7. Who supports (is "with" مع) the UN?

تمرين ٤

Match each word in (أ) with an appropriate word in (ب) to make a phrase or sentence:

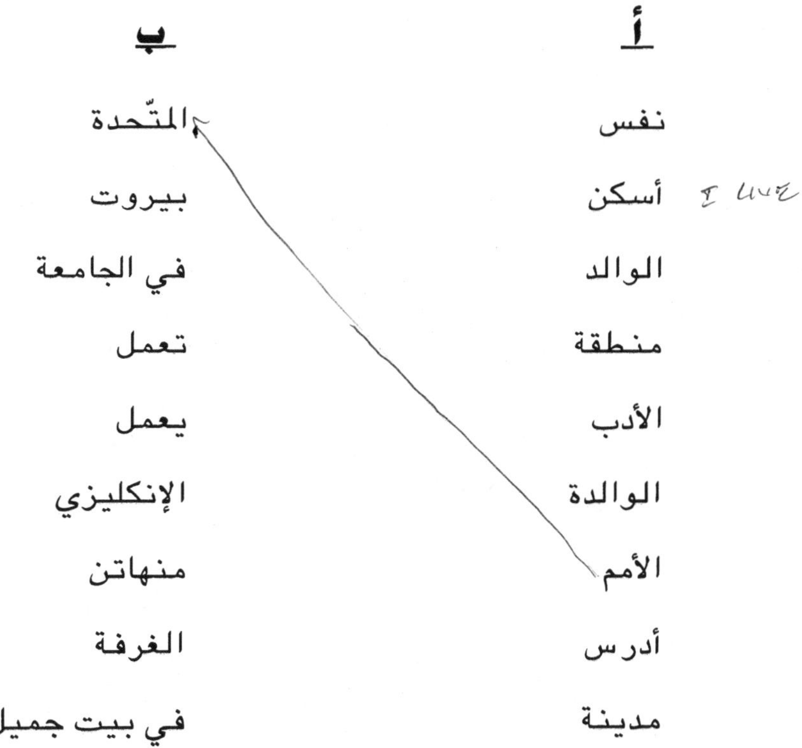

أ	ب
نفس	المتّحدة
أسكن	بيروت
الوالد	في الجامعة
منطقة	تعمل
الأدب	يعمل
الوالدة	الإنكليزي
الأمم	منهاتن
أدرس	الغرفة
مدينة	في بيت جميل

القصة DVD

تمرين ٥ **شاهدوا واستمعوا** *Watch and listen* **(في البيت)**

WATCH AND LISTEN TO القصة ON YOUR DVD UNTIL YOU UNDERSTAND THE MAIN IDEAS, THEN ANSWER IN ARABIC AS MUCH AS YOU CAN:

1. Who is talking?
2. What is the person talking about?

شاهِدوا واسِتَمِعوا مرة ثانية: *Watch and listen again*

WATCH AND LISTEN AGAIN, THEN COMPLETE:

٣ـ الاسم ______________________

٤ـ تسكن في ______________________

٥ـ الوالد ______________________

٦ـ الوالدة ______________________

شاهدوا وخَمّنوا : *Watch and guess*

THIS TIME, TRY TO GUESS THE MEANING OF THE FOLLOWING WORDS, USING CONTEXT AND YOUR OWN GENERAL KNOWLEDGE:

٧ـ فِلَسطينيّة ______________

٨ـ الأدَب الإنجليزيّ (الإنكليزيّ) ______________

9. Study the prefixes of all the verbs you have learned. What patterns can you detect? Use your observations to complete the following:

I	أَدْرُس	أَسْكُن	أَعمَل
he	يسكن	يدرس	يَعمَل
she	تسكن	تدرس	تَعمَل

تمرين ٦ **عن القصة (في الصف)**

IN CLASS, TURN OFF THE SOUND AND WATCH MAHA ON THE DVD WITHOUT IT. WORKING WITH A PARTNER, CREATE A NEW VOICE-OVER FOR THE VIDEO, ONE THAT PRESENTS HER STORY IN THIRD PERSON. PRESENT YOUR VOICE-OVER TO THE CLASS.

الثقافة *Culture*

Arabic Names

An Arab's name tells more about his or her family than an American's name. Arabic names usually take one of two formats, illustrated here by two versions of Maha's name.

(١) مَها مُحمّد أبو العلا

(٢) مها محمد يوسُف

In (١) above, مها is the given name, محمد is her father's first name, and ابو العلا is her family name. The second format is used in official documents in Egypt in particular, and consists of the given name, the father's first name, and the paternal grandfather's first name.

These modern names are shorter versions of the traditional form of Arabic names. An example of the latter, the name of a famous poet of the ninth century, is given below. As you can see, the father's and subsequent ancestral names are separated by ابن *son (of)* (spelled without the alif in between two names). In addition to these genealogical names, people were usually identified by city of birth, by tribe, or by a nickname designating a particular attribute. This poet is known as Ibn al-Rumi, because of his Byzantine background (روميّ means *Byzantine*, from الروم).

عَلي بن العَبّاس بن جريج (ابن الرومي)

Most Arab women do not legally take the name of their husbands when they marry. (In some areas, they may be addressed socially by their husbands' family names.) Maha's mother, مَلَك , retains the name of her father and family for life:

مَلَك طاهِر دَرويش

Also, note that not all female names end in ة . As you learn more names, you will learn to recognize which names are masculine and which are feminine. As in English, a few names may be either gender, such as وَفاء and صَباح .

Stereotypical portrayals of Arabs sometimes include characters named Abdul; however, in Arabic, this is only half a name. The word عَبد *servant of* must be followed by another word, usually an attribute of God, in order to constitute a proper name. You may have heard some of the following examples:

عبد الجَبّار عبد الحَكيم عبد اللّه عبد القادِر

In conversation, Arabs tend to address and refer to each other by their first names, preceded by a title unless they are close friends. For example, Maha's father might be addressed at work as: الدكتور محمد . In introductions and formal settings, both names may be used: الدكتور محمد أبو العلا .

تمرين ٧ | نشاط قراءة

THIS PAGE IS PART OF A SOCIETY SECTION OF AN ARABIC MAGAZINE. READ IT AND FIND:

1. The word for groom :______________
2. The word for bride : ______________
3. Identify for each person her/his given name, father's name, and family name (if given).

العروس / هبة الله نشأت البلتاجي
العريس / وسام سيد عطية

العروس / منال الحناوي
العريس / هشام البطراوي

العروس / هدى عبد الحكيم
العريس/ سامح عبد الرازق

العروس/ اسماء مصطفى محمود
العريس / أشرف عيد حسن

العروس / ريهام الجبيسي
العريس / وليد محمد عبد المنعم

العروس / فوزية السيد محمد
العريس/ ناجح السيد

العروس/ إيمان صبري
العريس / أحمد عبد المنعم

العروس / نيفين إبراهيم عياد
العريس / عصام صادق نصيف

من مجلة «نصف الدنيا» ١٥ يونيو ٢٠٠٣

القواعد Grammar

❁ المؤنث والمذكر Gender

feminine	مُؤَنَّث
masculine	مُذَكَّر

Nouns and adjectives in Arabic always carry gender, either مُذَكَّر or مُؤَنَّث . Arabic distinguishes between two categories of nouns: those that refer to human beings, and those that refer to non-humans. The gender of human nouns, such as أستاذ or صاحبة , including proper nouns, such as مها and محمد , follow the gender of the person. In the category of inanimate objects, each noun has its own gender, which does not change.

There is no neutral, non-gendered word for *it* in Arabic; you must use هو or هي depending on the gender of the noun you are referring to.

The gender of each word must be learned, but the form of the word itself almost always indicates whether it is مُذَكَّر or مُؤَنَّث . In Unit Five of *Alif Baa*, you saw that the letter ة (تاء مَربوطة) usually indicates feminine gender.[1] ة is related to the letter ت , and is sometimes pronounced ت (for example, مها pronounced ة as ت in مدينة نيويورك). In other cases ة is not pronounced, but the فتحة that always precedes it is, as in أنا مصريَّة . You will learn the rule for pronouncing ة as ت soon; meanwhile, pay attention to its pronunciation in the phrases and sentences you learn. **Remember:** ة on a singular noun almost always indicates that the word is مؤنث .

It is important to pay attention to the gender of nouns because the gender of adjectives, pronouns, and (as we will see soon) verbs that refer to them **must agree**, whether in phrases, such as الأدب الإنجليزيّ , in which both the noun and the adjective are مذكر , or in sentences, such as والدتي فلسطينيّة , in which both are مؤنث .

Gender of Proper Place Names DVD

Names of cities are مُؤنّث , following the gender of مدينة . Foreign countries are also مؤنث . The gender of Arab countries must be learned; go to the grammar section of your DVD and click on the map to review the names of Arab countries and learn their gender.

---

[1]Exceptions: a few masculine nouns, generally Classical words with special meanings, take ة ; one is خليفة *Caliph*. Also, a few plurals end in ة . Finally, a handful of nouns are feminine even though they lack ة ; these must be memorized as feminine. One example is شَمس *sun*.

تمرين ٨ مؤنّث ومذكّر (في البيت)

A. Describe these people and objects, as in the example. You may choose from the list of adjectives below or use your own.

مثال: *Example* هذه سيارة كبيرة.

١- أنا طالبة ________ .

٢- والدتي ________ .

٣- نيويورك مدينة ________ .

٤- مها بنت ________ .

٥- هذه منطقة ________ .

٦- أسكن في بيت ________ .

٧- جامعة نيويورك ________ .

٨- والدي ________ .

٩- هذا شارع ________ .

١٠- الأدب ________ .

١١- هذه غرفة ________ .

١٢- هذا مكتب ________ .

١٣- عندي سيارة ________ .

١٤- «بوينغ ٧٧٧» طائرة ________ .

١٥- هذه بناية ________ .

١٦- هذا امتحان ________ .

كبير صغير طويل قصير مريض تعبان

جميل عربي واسع جديد غريب قريب

بعيد صعب مصري لطيف زعلان مصري

جديد طيب فلسطيني انجليزي جوعان جيد

B. Describe as many of the things in your room as you can using nouns and adjectives:

تمرين ٩ **نشاط قراءة**

Below is a partial list of the faculty of the Chemistry Department of جامعة الكويت .

1. Identify the male and female faculty by writing الدكتور or الدكتورة before each name:

قسم الكيمياء

	الاسم	الوظيفة
الدكتور	علي حسن قطريب	أستاذ
	جورج موسى جعنيني	أستاذ
	يحيى عبد الرحمن الطنطاوي	أستاذ مساعد
الدكتورة	فائزة محمد عبد المحسن الخرافي	أستاذ مساعد
	عثمان محمد الدسوقي	أستاذ مساعد
	نجيب عبد المنعم عيسى السالم	أستاذ مساعد
	نجاة ابراهيم الشطي	أستاذ مساعد
	نورية عبد الكريم العوضي	أستاذ مساعد
	محمد يحيى محمد صوان	أستاذ مساعد
	أحمد علي محمد علي كريمي	مدرس
	نادية محمد شعيب محمد شعيب	مدرس
	عبد الهادي عيسى بومليان	مدرس
	فاطمة عبد الله جمعة العمران	مدرس
	صالح محمد عبد الحسين الموسوي	مدرس
	حياة محمد رفيع معرفي	مدرس
	عثمان عبد الله الفليج	مدرس

من «الدليل الدراسي لعام ١٩٨٧–١٩٨٩» ، جامعة الكويت

2. Guess the meaning of the following word from context:

قِسم = ________________

3. For discussion: compare the number of female faculty in Chemistry here with that in your university.

In Unit Eight of *Alif Baa* you learned that the article الـ makes a noun definite; for example, indefinite طالب *a student* corresponds to definite الطالب *the student*. You cannot assume that all words without الـ are indefinite, for some proper names (e.g., [illegible]) as well as nouns in one particular grammatical construction can be definite without it. However, you can assume that all words with الـ are definite.

The use of Arabic الـ differs from that of English *the* in one important respect. In English, singular nouns may be used with **(a)** the indefinite article *a(n)*, as in *a book*, **(b)** the definite article *the*, as in *the teacher*, or **(c)** no article at all, as in *literature*. In general, Arabic uses الـ for **both categories (b)** and **(c).** The following chart summarizes corresponding English and Arabic usages:

a book	كتاب
the teacher	الأستاذ
literature	الأدب

Use this as a **rule of thumb** to determine where you need to use الـ when speaking and writing, and pay attention to the use of الـ as given in new vocabulary.

تمرين ١٠ استماع DVD (في البيت)

LISTEN TO THE FOLLOWING LIST ON DVD AND ADD الـ TO THE WORDS IN WHICH YOU HEAR IT. REMEMBER TO LISTEN FOR الشدّة THAT INDICATES THE ASSIMILATION OF لـ WHEN FOLLOWED BY الحروف الشمسية (FOR REVIEW SEE *ALIF BAA*, UNIT EIGHT).

١- ــــ باب ــــ صغير
٢- ــــ صباح ــــ نور
٣- ــــ جامعة ــــ قاهرة
٤- ــــ شارع ــــ طويل
٥- ــــ رجل ــــ سعودي
٦- ــــ خبز ــــ طيب
٧- ــــ قهوة ــــ تركية
٨- ــــ منطقة ــــ منهاتن
٩- ــــ نفس ــــ طاولة
١٠- ــــ بنك ــــ عربي
١١- ــــ أسرة ــــ مها
١٢- ــــ طالب ــــ مصري

تمرين ١١ الـ (في الصف)

Read the following paragraph and circle all the nouns that you think would take الـ if you translated it into Arabic. Skip possessive nouns (such as *his tribe*).

Poetry holds a central place in Arab culture, and this importance is reflected in the high esteem accorded poets. In ancient times, the poet was among the most important members of his tribe. He recorded the tribe's history and defended its honor through his descriptions of its courage and prowess. Throughout Islamic history, rulers rewarded poets handsomely for their "praise poems." Today, poetry remains a powerful medium of political expression.

❁ النِسبة

the nisba adjective النِّسبة

The word نسبة in grammar refers to a class of adjectives formed from nouns by adding the suffix يّ for مذكّر or يّة for مؤنّث. These adjectives generally indicate origin or affiliation, especially in reference to a place. You have learned several of these already:

مها مصريّة . والدي مصريّ .

والدتي فلسطينيّة . الاستاذة عربيّة .

In formal Arabic, the شدّة on the nisba ending يّ is clearly pronounced, but in spoken Arabic it is not normally pronounced in the masculine. Learn to recognize both variants. Listen to this chart on your DVD and compare: DVD

مذكر spoken/formal	مؤنث
الاستاذ مصريّ / مصري	الاستاذة مصريّة
الاستاذ سوريّ / سوري	الاستاذة سوريّة
الاستاذ لبنانيّ / لبناني	الاستاذة لبنانيّة
الاستاذ مَغربِيّ / مغربي	الاستاذة مغربيّة

Many family names come from nisba adjectives, and refer to the original hometown of the family. Examples include: المصري , البغدادي , التونسي , and الفاسي .

Many nisbas are formed from place names. To form a nisba adjective from a place noun, follow these steps:

(1) **Remove** الـ , ة , and final ا (alif) or يا , if any, from the place name; then

(2) **Add** يّ to make the adjective مذكر , or يـّة to make it مؤنث .

Examples:

أمريكا <-- أمريكـ <-- أمريكيّ / أمريكيّة

جامعة <-- جامعـ <-- جامعيّ / جامعيّة

الأُردُن <-- أُردُنـ <-- أردنيّ / أردنيّة

Now practice by completing the steps for the following:

فَرنسا <-- ________ <-- ________

المَكسيك <-- ________ <-- ________

الصّومال <-- ________ <-- ________

تمرين ١٢ **النسبة (في البيت)**

Identify the nationality or affiliation of the following people, places and things:

مثال: هذه طائرة أمريكية. (أمريكا)

١ـ فاس مدينة ________ . (المغرب)

٢ـ هذه أستاذة ________ . (الجزائر)

٣ـ «نيكول» بنت ________ . (فرنسا)

٤ـ «راج» رجل ________ . (الهند)

٥ـ هذه قهوة ________ . (تُركيا)

٦ـ «ريتشارد» دكتور ________ . (اوستراليا)

٧ـ طوكيو مدينة ________ . (اليابان)

٨ـ سَلمى طالبة ________ . (الباكستان)

٩ـ مها طالبة ________ . (جامعة)

١ـ هذه ساعة ________ . (الصين) *(China)*

تمرين ١٣ النسبة

GIVE THE NATIONALITIES OF THE PEOPLE IN THE MAP:

مثال: ١- حُسَين أُردُني

٢- فَيْصَل ______	٧- عَوَض ______
٣- مُنى ______	٨- عَبد الحَميد ______
٤- خالِدة ______	٩ فاطِمة ______
٥- عَبد اللّه ______	١٠- جَميلة ______
٦- جرجِس ______	١١- إدريس ______

❁ السؤال *Asking Questions*

Arabic has two main types of questions:

1. Questions that require an answer of *yes* or *no*, such as: حضرتك مصرية ؟ .
2. Questions that request information on who, what, where, when, why, and how, such as: أين تسكن مها ؟ .

1. Yes/ No Questions DVD

These are questions that require an answer of either «أيـوه» / نـَعـَم *yes* or لا *no.* Unlike English, which uses auxiliary verbs like *do/does* and *is/are* to form such questions, Arabic forms questions using the same word order and structure as in statements. In other words, there is very little difference between statements and yes/no questions in Arabic. In most varieties of spoken Arabic, this difference is usually signalled by intonation. In formal Arabic, yes/no questions are introduced by the particle هـَل . The following examples illustrate the similar structure of statements and yes/no questions in spoken Arabic. Listen to the difference in intonation on the DVD:

مها مصرية . ——> مها مصرية ؟

أنت طالبة . ——> أنت طالبة ؟

As in many languages, falling intonation generally indicates a statement, whereas rising intonation usually signals a question. The exact intonation of an Arabic sentence or question depends on the dialect region. Listen to and imitate the speech of your teacher and native speakers you know.

هَل ...؟

In formal Arabic, yes/no questions are indicated by the interrogative word هـَل (no English equivalent). Thus in formal contexts you will hear or read the following variants of the examples above:

هـَل مها مصرية ؟

هل أنت طالبة ؟

2. Information Questions DVD

These questions request specific information such as who, what, when, where, and why. Learn the following interrogative particles:

What? (in questions without verbs)	ما ؟
What? (in questions using verbs)	ماذا ؟
Which?	أيّ ؟
Who?	مَن ؟
Where?	أينَ ؟
How?	كَيفَ ؟

Review these prepositions which are often used in asking questions:

with	مَعَ
in	فـي
from	مِن

When interrogative particles are used with prepositions, the prepositions precede in formal Arabic, as the table shows:

From where?	مِن أينَ ؟
In which?	فـي أيّ ..؟
With whom?	مَعَ مَن؟

These examples demonstrate various types of questions: DVD

ما هذا؟ — مَن هي؟

ما هذه؟ — أين تسكن مها؟

ماذا تدرس مها؟ — مِن أين أنتِ؟

في أيّ جامعة تدرس مها؟ — كيف نقول؟

مع مَن تسكن مها؟ — كيفَ الحال؟ *How are things?*

تمرين ١٤ **(في البيت)**

Ask the right question! Choose the appropriate interrogative to complete:

١- ________ أنت يا ماجدة؟ -- أنا من مدينة بغداد.

٢- ________ أنت سوريّة؟ -- لا ، أنا فلسطينيّة.

٣- من فضلك، ________ مكتب الدكتور سامي الخوري؟ -- في هذه البناية.

٤- ________ هي؟ -- هي الاستاذة الجديدة .

٥- ________ تسكن يا علي؟ -- أسكن في شارع بور سعيد.

٦- ________ تدرس في الجامعة؟ -- أدرس الأدب.

٧- ________ هذه؟ -- هذه قهوة عربية.

٨- ________ يعمل والد أحمد ؟ -- هو دكتور.

٩- من فضلك يا أستاذ، ________ نقول "bathroom" بالعربية؟ -- «حَمّام».

تمرين ١٥ نشاط محادثة (في الصف)

ROLE PLAY: YOU ARE IN CAIRO AND HAVE BEEN INVITED TO ATTEND A WEDDING. SINCE YOU WILL MEET MANY PEOPLE WHOM YOU DO NOT KNOW, PRACTICE MAKING POLITE CONVERSATION WITH YOUR CLASSMATES TO PREPARE FOR THE EVENT. USE INTERROGATIVE PARTICLES TO FIND OUT ABOUT THE PEOPLE YOU MEET, AND REMEMBER TO BE POLITE BY USING حضرتك . IF YOU MEET SOMEONE FROM THE BRIDE'S OR GROOM'S FAMILY, BE SURE TO SAY:

congratulations! ! مَبروك

تمرين ١٦ نشاط قراءة (في الصف)

READ THE FOLLOWING ARTICLE IN THREE STEPS AS DIRECTED.

1. Skim the article looking for familiar words and names in boldface. What is this?
2. Skim again and circle everything you recognize.
3. Read through the article as closely as you can looking for the following words. Guess their meaning from the context in which they occur:

جَزيرة ____________ نَهر ____________

الوِلايات المتحدة الأمريكية ____________________

4. For further thought: what could the letters ق , ش , غ , and ج be abbreviations for? Think about the fact that there are four of them. You can check the English-Arabic glossary to see if your guess is correct.

نيـويورك: مـدينة (٩٤٤ كم٢ مع المسطح المائي و٨،٠٨٤،٣١٦ نسـمـة)، ج ق ولاية نيويورك، كبرى مدن الولايات المتحدة الأمريكية، على خليج نيويورك، عند مصب نهر هدسن. تتألف من خمسة اقسام : **منهاتن**، وبرونكس (ش منهاتن)، وكوينز (غ جزيرة لونج ايلند)، وبروكلين، وريتشموند على جزيرة **ستاتن**. وترتبط هذه الأقسام بعدة جسور وأنفاق. وتشمل منطقة الميتروبوليتان (٢١٠٠٠٠٠٠ نسمة)، مناطق صناعية واخرى للاقامة في ج ق نيويورك، و ش ق نيوجرسي، وج غ كونيكتيكيت ، كما تشمل مرفأ فاخرا يعد من اعظم موانئ العالم وعقدة خطوط حديدية وجوية. وهي المركز التجاري والمالي للولايات المتحدة. بها صناعات كثيرة وخاصة السلع الاستهلاكية .

من «الموسوعة الثقافية»، د. حسين سعيد مؤسسة فرانكلين، دار الشعب، القاهرة ١٩٧٢
بتجديد الإحصائيات من U.S. Census Bureau

تمرين ١٧ استمعوا الى مها DVD (في البيت)

Go back and listen to القصة again on your DVD and fill in the blanks below. Write what you hear, but also pay attention to the meaning. Check the spelling of words if necessary.

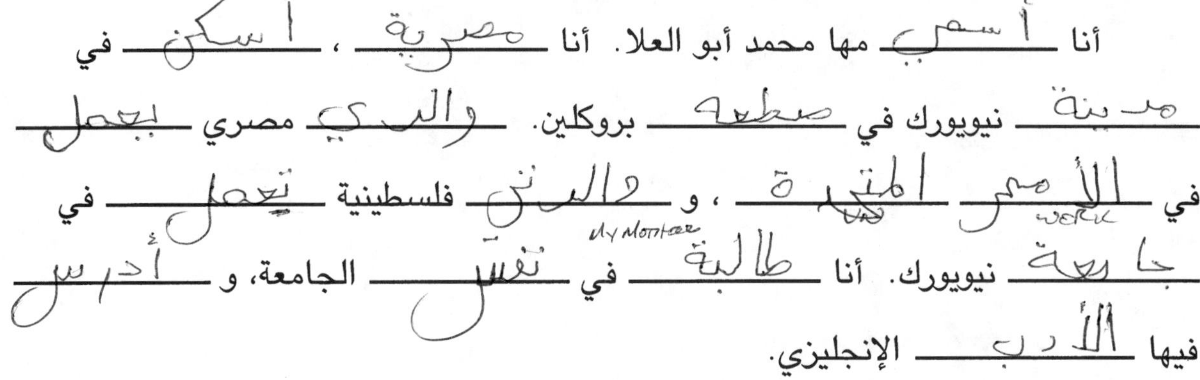

أنا ______ مها محمد أبو العلا. أنا ______ ، ______ في
______ نيويورك في ______ بروكلين. ______ مصري ______
في ______ ______ ، و ______ فلسطينية ______ في
______ نيويورك. أنا ______ في ______ الجامعة، و ______
فيها ______ الإنجليزي.

العامية Colloquial DVD

- القصة: "انا مها"

Listen to Maha tell her story in Egyptian Colloquial on your DVD.

How does she say والدي and والدتي ? How does she pronounce منطقة ?

- "انتي عربية؟"

Watch Maha meet another student at NYU.

تذكروا هذه الكلمات Remember these words

Add these words to your active vocabulary list:

قِسم	الولايات المتحدة الأمريكية	مبروك!
هل ؟	أيّ ؟	مَن ؟
ما ؟	ماذا ؟	كيف ؟
مِن أينَ ؟	مَعَ	مع من؟
في أيّ ؟	الثقافة	القواعد
مذكر	مؤنث	النِسبة

٢ . أنا فعلا وحيدة!

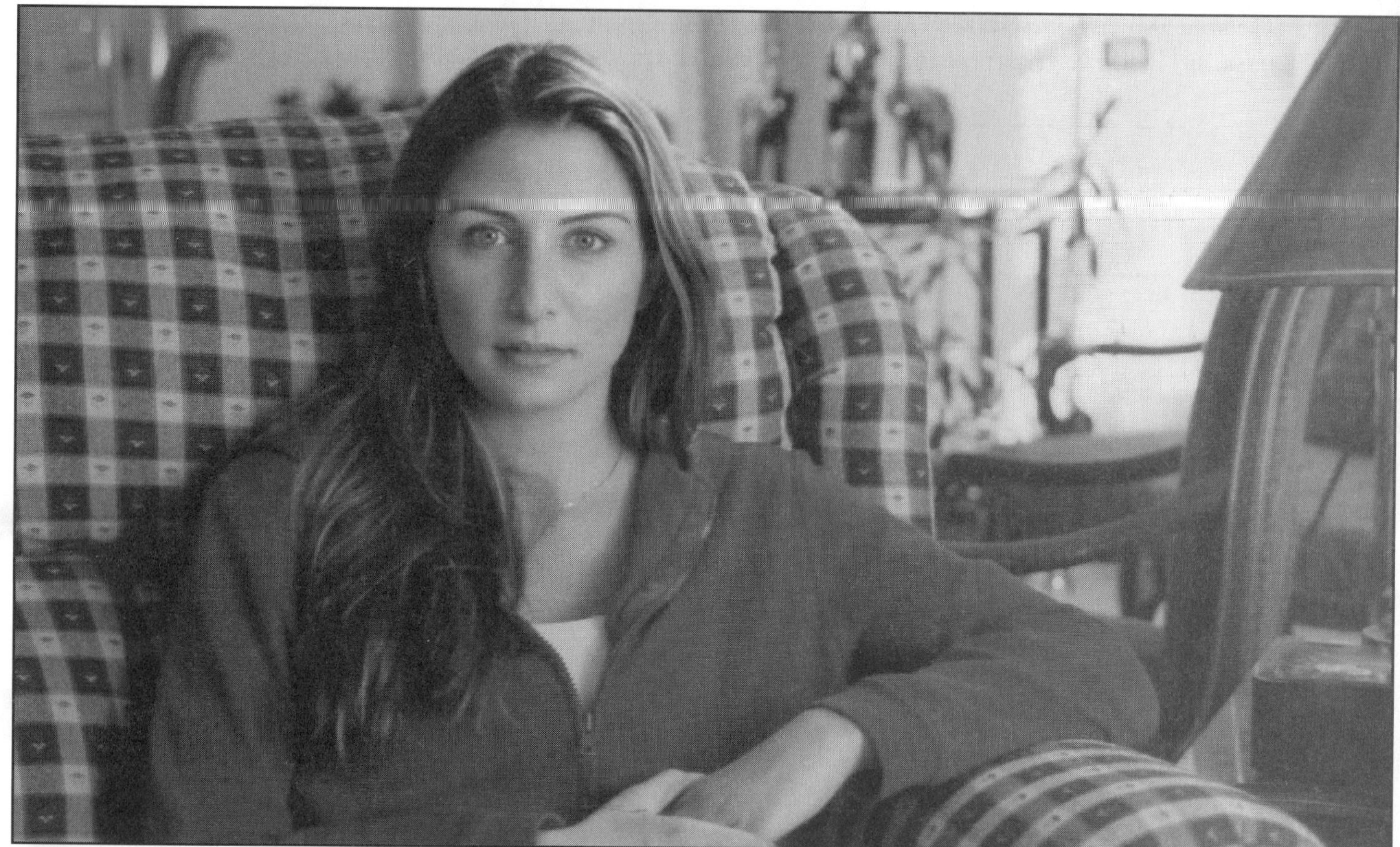

في هذا الدرس:

القصة • أسرة مها

الثقافة • شغل البيت

القواعد • الضمائر *Subject Pronouns*

• الجمع

• الجملة الاسمية: المبتدأ والخبر

القراءة • تعارف

• برامج دراسات الشرق الأوسط

الاستماع • مع العائلة والأصدقاء

العامية • القصة «انا فعلا وحيدة»

• «أخبارك إيه؟»

المفردات DVD

أُسْـرة	family
أيضًا	also
التَـرجَمة (مِن ... إلى)	translation (from ... to)
مُـتَرجِـم / ـة	translator
حَـيثُ	where (**not** in questions)
مُـتَخَـصِّص / ـة في ..	specializing/specialist in
خالـة	maternal aunt
دائـِمًا	always
اِسمُها	her name
الشُـغل (= العَمَـل)	work
مَشغـول / ـة (بـِ)[1]	busy (with)
العَمَـل (= الشُـغل)	work
فِـعلاً	really!, truly
القَبـول	admission(s)
لـِ	belonging to (preposition)
لـي	I have
لِها	Maha has
لُـغة	language
المَساء	evening
النَـهار	daytime
وَحيد / ة	only; lonely [adjective]
مُوَظَّف / ـة	employee

[1]When a preposition is given in parentheses, it is used to give the meaning given in English parentheses. If a preposition is given without parentheses, the preposition must be used.

تمرين ١ الكلمات الجديدة (في البيت)

DESCRIBE YOURSELF. USE THE FOLLOWING SENTENCES AS A STARTING POINT:

١- أسكن في ________ ، حيث ____________ .

٢- ________ في النهار و________ في المساء .

٣- أنا متخصّص / متخصّصة في ____________ .

٤- أنا دائمًا ____________________ .

٥- أنا مشغول/ة ____________________ .

٦- أنا فعلاً ____________________ !

٧- أسرتي ____________________ .

٨- والدتي/والدي ____________________ .

٩- لي ____________________ .

١٠- أنا تعبانة، وصاحبتي ____________ تعبانة!

تمرين ٢ FIND OUT! (في الصف)

USE NEW VOCABULARY TO GET INFORMATION IN ARABIC FROM YOUR CLASSMATES. REMEMBER TO REPHRASE THESE QUESTIONS TO ADDRESS YOUR CLASSMATES ("ARE YOU..."?), AND TO THINK ABOUT HOW TO USE THE NEW WORDS TOGETHER RATHER THAN TRANSLATING WORD-FOR-WORD FROM ENGLISH:

1. Who knows an employee in the admissions office?
2. Who is always in the library, during (=in) the day and evening?
3. Who is majoring in a language? Which language?
4. Who is the only boy/girl in the family?
5. Who has a job on campus?
6. Who has a class in the evening?
7. Who is *really* busy? With what?
8. Who has a maternal aunt or a maternal uncle? [blood relatives only]
   What does he or she do?

القصة DVD

تمرين ٣	شاهدوا واستَمعوا : *Watch and listen*

WATCH AND LISTEN TO القصة ON YOUR DVD UNTIL YOU CAN UNDERSTAND THE MAIN IDEAS, THEN ANSWER THESE QUESTIONS IN ARABIC AS MUCH AS POSSIBLE:

1. What is مها talking about here?
2. What new information have you learned about مها from listening to her this time?

شاهدوا واستَمعوا مَرّة ثانية: *Watch and listen again:*

٣- ماذا يعمل والد مها؟

٤- ماذا تعمل والدة مها؟

٥- مَن نادية؟

٦- أين تسكن نادية؟ ماذا تعمل؟

استَمعوا وخَمّنوا : *Listen and guess*

NOW LISTEN AGAIN, AND GUESS THE MEANING OF THE FOLLOWING FROM CONTEXT:

٧- وِلاية كاليفورنيا ____________________

٨- شغل البيت ____________________

الثقافة

شغل البيت DVD

The workings of individual Arab families differ as much as those of American ones. Either partner may be responsible for day-to-day budgeting and financial management, and it is increasingly common for both husband and wife to work outside the home, while extended families often help with daycare. Marriage is seen as a partnership in both cultures; however, in Arab culture, partners' expectations of each other have not changed as drastically as those in the U.S. have in recent years. In general, the responsibilities of each party remain based on a traditional division of labor (rather than on sharing tasks) in which the wife is responsible for work inside the home, while the husband is expected to be available to run errands, grocery and other, outside it. Watch the interviews on DVD.

"أنا وحيدة"

In Arab culture, spending time by oneself (except to work or study) is generally viewed as undesirable and to be avoided if possible. Close relations and frequent visits among neighbors, members of the extended family, and friends mean that one need rarely be alone for an extended period of time.

القواعد

❁ الضَمائِر Subject Pronouns

Arabic has three sets of personal pronouns: subject, object, and possessive.[1] As is the case in English, there is some overlap among these sets. However, Arabic has more pronouns than English (Formal Arabic has separate categories for masculine and feminine in both second and third person as well as dual pronouns for sets of two; these are not used in most varieties of spoken Arabic. You will learn all of these pronouns over the course of the year). Learn the following most commonly used **subject** pronouns: DVD

we	نَحْنُ	I	أنا
you (plural)	أنتُم	you (مذكر) you (مؤنث)	أنتَ أنتِ
they	هُم	he/it (مذكر) she/it (مؤنث)	هُوَ هِيَ

تمرين ٤ الضمائر (في البيت)

Practice using subject pronouns to talk about people and things by completing the following conversations, as in the example:

مثال: «هل أنتِ أستاذة؟» — «لا أنا طالبة.»

١- «هل ـــــــ جوعان؟» — «نعم، ـــــــ جوعان».

٢- «مِن أين ـــــــ يا شباب؟» — «ـــــــ من مصر».

٣- «هل ـــــــ سورية يا عائشة؟» — «لا، ـــــــ سودانية».

٤- «مَن نادية؟» — «ـــــــ خالة مها».

٥- «أين يعمل والد مها؟» — «ـــــــ يعمل في الامم المتحدة».

٦- أدرس في ميدلبري، و ـــــــ جامعة صغيرة في ولاية ڤيرمونت.

٧- أسكن في منطقة المَزّة، و ـــــــ منطقة قريبة من جامعة دمشق.

---

[1]If you are not familiar with these grammatical terms, think of the English pronouns *I*, *me*, and *my*. *I* is the subject pronoun, as in '*I* live here.' *Me* is the object pronoun, as in 'he saw *me*.' *My* is the possessive pronoun, as in '*my* father.'

❁ الجَمع

singular	مُفرَد (م.)
plural	جَمع (ج.)

English has only one regular plural pattern, the addition of *s* to the singular, as in *students*. Arabic has more than ten regular patterns that you will learn over the course of the year. The first step in acquiring these patterns is to memorize individual words as vocabulary; this will become easier as your vocabulary grows.

Learning plurals in Arabic requires two steps: (1) memorizing the plurals themselves, and (2) mastering the agreement rules, which differ from those of most western languages. In particular, it is useful to distinguish in Arabic between human plurals on one hand and non-human plurals (including animals) on the other.

This chapter introduces you to the plurals of all the nouns you have learned so far. From now on **memorize the singular and plural together as a unit when you first learn a new word.** Vocabulary lists will indicate the plurals of new vocabulary as follows:

word	كَلِمة ج. كَلِمات

Human Plurals

Human plurals in Arabic are of three categories: Broken Plurals, Sound Masculine Plurals, and Sound Feminine Plurals. The charts on the next page show these three groups.

1. Broken Plurals جمع التكسير

These are so-named because the stem of the singular is "broken" by shifting the consonants into different vowel patterns so that the syllabic structure of the word changes. Compare رَجُل to its plural رِجال : both contain the same consonants, ر – ج – ل , but the vowels have changed. This kind of plural is called جمع التَّكسير *broken plural.*

2. Human Sound Masculine Plurals جمع المذكر: -ون / -ين

These plurals, called "sound" because the singular stem remains intact, take a pair of endings that alternate according to grammatical function: in some cases, you will see the ending ونَ and in others, ينَ . The final فتحة on both endings is not usually pronounced except in very formal registers of Arabic. Both forms are used in formal Arabic; learn to recognize both, and choose one to use for now. In spoken Arabic, people use the second form with ين (e.g. مصريين). Almost all نسبة adjectives take this plural, but note the important exception عَرَب .

3. Human Sound Feminine Plurals **جمع المؤنث: -ات**

All nouns and adjectives that refer to human females take the plural ending ـات .

Learn these human plurals: DVD

١ ـ جمع التكسير

رَجُل	رِجال
طالِب	طُلّاب
وَلَد	أوْلاد
خال	أخْوال
صاحِب	أصْحاب
أستاذ	أساتِذة
دُكتور	دَكاتِرة
سَيِّد	سادة
أخ	إِخْوة
جار	جيران
عَرَبِيّ	عَرَب

٢ ـ جمع المُذكَّر

مِصريّ	مِصريّون / مِصريّين
لُبنانِيّ	لُبنانِيّونَ / لُبنانِيّينَ
مُتَرجِم	مُتَرجِمونَ / مُترجِمينَ
مُتَخَصِّص	مُتَخَصِّصونَ / مُتخَصِّصينَ
مَشغول	مَشغولونَ / مَشغولينَ

٣ ـ جمع المؤنث

بِنْت	بَنات
أخت	أخَوات
اِمرَأة	نِساء
طالِبة	طالِبات
أُستاذة	أُستاذات
سَيِّدة	سَيِّدات
خالة	خالات
جارة	جارات
مِصريّة	مِصريّات
فِلَسْطينيّة	فِلَسْطينيّات
مُتَرجِمة	مُتَرجِمات
مُتَخَصِّصة	مُتَخَصِّصات
مَشغولة	مَشغولات

LEARN THESE NON-HUMAN PLURALS: DVD

١ ـ جمع التكسير

As you listen to and memorize these plurals, look for recurring syllabic patterns, such as the initial alif hamza and medial alif of the first four nouns in this chart, and the Damma followed by waaw in the plurals for house, lesson, class, and money [the singular fils refers to an old currency no longer in use].

اِسم	أسماء
عَمَل	أعمال
خَبَر	أخبار
باب	أبواب
كِتاب	كُتُب
مَدينة	مُدُن
أُسرة	أُسَر
غُرفة	غُرَف
قِصّة	قِصَص
بَيت	بُيوت
درس	دُروس
صَفّ	صُفوف
فَصل	فُصول
بَنك	بُنوك
[فِلس]	فُلوس
شارِع	شَوارِع
دَفتَر	دَفاتِر
شُبّاك	شَبابيك
منطقة	مَناطِق
مكتب	مَكاتِب

٢ـ جمع - ات

In addition to human female nouns, which always take -aat plurals, a number of inanimate feminine nouns take -aat as well. However, as we shall see shortly, they take different agreement rules because they fall in the grammatical category of non-human plurals.

جامِعة	جامِعات
طائِرة	طائِرات
سَيّارة	سَيّارات
وِلاية	وِلايات
ساعة	ساعات
لُغة	لُغات
كَلِمة	كَلِمات
صَفحة	صَفَحات
طاوِلة	طاوِلات
وَرَقة	وَرَقات
بِناية	بِنايات
تَرجَمة	تَرجَمات
مَكتَبة	مَكتَبات

❁ الجمع *Non-Human Plural Agreement*

The essential agreement rule of non-human plurals in formal Arabic is that they are always treated as if they were a single group, and they take feminine singular agreement. You saw this when you learned الأمم المتحدة : الأُمَم *nations* is a non-human plural noun and therefore the adjective مُتَّحِدة *united* must be feminine. Remember: in modern formal Arabic, **non-human plural nouns** behave like **feminine singular nouns** in all respects.[1] The following examples demonstrate:

هارفارد وبراون وبرينستون جامعات **أمريكية قديمة.**

هذه ترجمات **جميلة!**

هل الأسر المصرية **كبيرة؟** [Note that *families* is a non-human plural.]

تمرين ٥ الجمع (في البيت)

Describe these groups by using plurals, as in the example:

مثال: نحن طلّاب أمريكيون . (طالب، أمريكي)

١- هم ____________ . (صاحب، لبناني)

٢- الإيطالية والإسبانية والفرنسية ____________ . (لغة، أوروبي)

٣- «هل أنتم ____________؟» (أخ) – «لا، نحن ____________!» (جار)

٤- محمد وعلي وسعيد ____________ . (رجل، يمني)

٥- «هوندا» و«إيسوزو» و«تويوتا» ____________ . (سيارة، ياباني)

٦- هم ____________ في الامم المتحدة . (مترجم، عربي)

٧- نحن دائماً ____________ بالعمل و____________ ! (مشغول، تعبان)

٨- [illegible] وكونيتيكت ____________ . (ولاية، أمريكي)

٩- منهاتن وبروكلين وبرونكس ____________ في نيويورك . (منطقة، صغير)

١٠- الآنسة مُنى والآنسة وفاء والسيدة عبير ____________ . (موظفة، جديد)

١١- «هل أنتم ____________ (فلسطيني)؟» – «لا، نحن ____________ (أردني).»

١٢- «مَن هم؟» – «هم ____________ من جامعة حَلَب.» (أستاذ، سوري)

١٣- الرياض ومكّة وجدّة ____________ (مدينة، سعودي).

---

[1]In spoken and Classical Arabic this rule does not **always** apply.

تمرين ٦ مَن أنتم؟ هل أنت ..؟ (في الصف)

WORK IN GROUPS OF 3 OR 4 AND USE SINGULAR AND PLURAL PRONOUNS. THINK OF AS MANY DIFFFERENT NOUNS AND ADJECTIVES AS YOU CAN THAT MAY DESCRIBE YOUR CLASSMATES, AND ASK THEM QUESTIONS LIKE:

هل أنت حرّان؟ هل أنتم مشغولون؟

AFTER YOU HAVE FINISHED, REPORT ON YOUR FINDINGS.

❁ الجملة الاسمية

sentence	جُملة
noun	اسم
subject (in جملة اسمية)	مُبتَدَأ
predicate	خَبَر

Thus far, most sentences you have seen and heard have a basic sentence structure that is called in Arabic الجُملة الاسمية , from the word اسم , which in grammar means *noun.* الجملة الاسمية is a sentence that **begins with** a noun or pronoun. The following six sentences are all جُمَل اسمية :

١- مها تسكن في نيويورك .

٢- والدتي تعمل في نفس البنك .

٣- أنا من كاليفورنيا.

٤- هم مشغولون بالعمل .

٥- هل الصفوف كبيرة؟

٦- بيروت مدينة جميلة.

Sentences (١) and (٢) contain verbs. They are still considered جمل اسمية because they begin with nouns. Sentences (٣-٦), on the other hand, have no overt verbs, because the verb *to be* in the present tense is understood but not expressed in Arabic. To understand this kind of جملة اسمية , it is necessary to determine where the meaning *am/are/is* belongs in the sentence, what is the subject and what is the predicate. How would you translate sentences (٣-٦) above? Try to identify the placement of *am/are/is.* What clues helped you determine the meaning of each sentence?

The parts of الجملة الاسمية are called المُبتَدَأ *subject* and الخَبَر *predicate* (literally *new information,* i.e., what is being related about the subject). In order to understand this type of sentence, you must first identify its two parts, especially in sentences in which the verb *to be* is understood. As you can see in the examples above, الخبر can be anything:

noun, adjective, verb, prepositional phrase, etc. Look again at the examples above and identify the parts of speech and definiteness/indefiniteness of الخبر in each. Note that الخبر tends to be indefinite when it is a noun or adjective; this clue will help you to identify where the sentence break between the two parts lies. The following diagrams show the breakdown of two جُمَل اسمية :

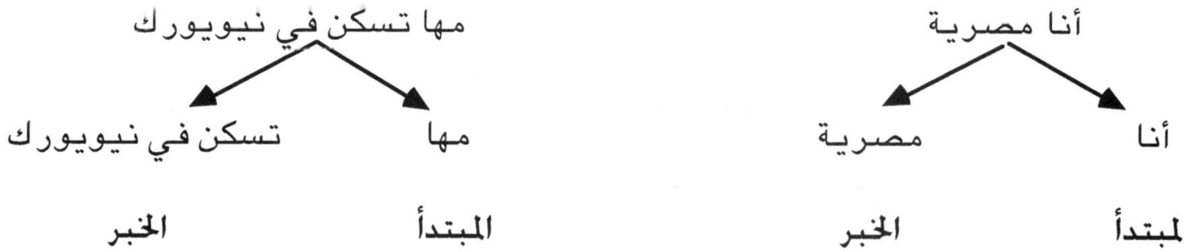

In this type of sentence, nouns and adjectives in both المبتدأ and الخبر must agree in gender (both مذكر or both مؤنث), and number (both مفرد or both جمع , following the agreement rules you just learned), as the following examples show (note, however, that الخبر is often–but not always–indefinite):

الكتب كبيرة.	محمد مترجم .
هي حرّانة.	هم متخصصون في الأدب.
أنتم مشغولون.	الدروس صعبة!

تمرين ٧ الجملة الاسمية (في البيت)

Match each مبتدأ in column أ with an appropriate خبر in column ب . Pay attention to agreement.

أ	ب
١- الطلاّب	متخصصة في الأدب الفرنسي
٢- هو	أساتذه عرب
٣- الدكتورة سامية	طائرات كبيرة
٤- «بوينغ ٧٧٧» و«إيرباص» ٣٠٤ و ٣٨٠	نساء عربيات
٥- مكتب القبول	مشغولون بالامتحانات
٦- ليلى وفاطمة وجميلة	الولد الوحيد في الاسرة
٧- د. علي ود. عايدة ود. سعيد	طالبات أمريكيات
٨- كاثرين وإليزابث وماندي	في هذه البناية

تمرين ٨ الجملة الاسمية (في الصف)

IDENTIFY BOTH المبتدأ AND الخبر IN THESE SENTENCES:

١- سامية ولُبنى وليلى بنات كويتيات.

٢- أخي مشغول بالعمل.

٣- والدتي متخصصة في الكمبيوتر.

٤- هي تدرس اللغة العربية.

٥- هم أساتذة من السودان.

٦- الدروس قصيرة.

٧- هي الامرأة الوحيدة في المكتب.

٨- هذه شوارع واسعة.

تمرين ٩ نشاط محادثة (في البيت وفي الصف)

PLURAL JEOPARDY! PREPARE TO PLAY A GAME OF JEOPARDY IN CLASS IN WHICH THE QUESTIONS CONTAIN PLURAL NOUNS OR ADJECTIVES.

مثال: هوندا وتويوتا وسوزوكي. -> ما هي سيارات يابانية؟

مثال: برونكس وكوينز ومانهاتن وبروكلين. -> ما هي المناطق الكبيرة في نيويورك؟

الاستماع DVD

تمرين ١٠ مع العائلة والاصدقاء (في البيت)

WATCH THE DVD AND ANSWER:

١- من هي؟

٢- أين تسكن؟

٣- ماذا تعمل؟

تمرين ١١ نشاط قراءة (في الصف)

READ OVER THE TEXT ON THE NEXT PAGE: COMPARE THE DIFFERENT ENTRIES AND LOOK FOR ANY INFORMATION YOU CAN FIGURE OUT. GUESS AS MANY NEW WORDS AS YOU CAN. AFTER YOU HAVE FINISHED, WRITE AN ENTRY FOR YOURSELF.

من مجلة «الفرسان» ٢٥ آذار / مارس ١٩٩١

تعارف

الاسم الكامل: فتحي محمد حسين محمد
العمر: ١٨ سنة
المهنة: طالب جامعي
الهواية: القراءة – المراسلة وتبادل الآراء
البلد والعنوان: سوهاج – طهطا – جزيرة الخزندارية – جمهورية مصر العربية

الاسم الكامل: نجم الدين محمد سعيد
العمر: ٢٥ سنة
الهواية: المراسلة – كرة القدم
البلد والعنوان: السودان الشمالية – ارقو الغربية

الاسم الكامل: سليمان عسكر
العمر: ٢٢ سنة
المهنة: طالب – سنة ثانية علوم سياسية
الهواية: المراسلة باللغة العربية والانكليزية – السباحة والتنس
البلد والعنوان: [illegible] – الطريق العام – قرب البنك اللبناني الفرنسي – لبنان

الاسم الكامل: عيسى ابو القاسم ضو
العمر: ٣٥ سنة
الهواية: المراسلة باللغة العربية واليونانية
البلد والعنوان: طرابلس – جنزور – ص.ب ٧٩٢٦ الجماهيرية الليبية

الاسم الكامل: فهد علي
العمر: ٢٣ سنة
الهواية: المراسلة
البلد والعنوان: الدمام – ص.ب ٨١٨٧ المملكة العربية السعودية

الاسم الكامل: محمد رشاد درويش
العمر: ٢٣ سنة
المهنة: موظف
الهواية: المراسلة – السفر – تبادل الآراء والصور والهدايا
البلد والعنوان: محافظة المنوفية – شبين الكوم – مساكن الجلاء البحري – مدخل ٢٠ – شقة ١٩ – مصر

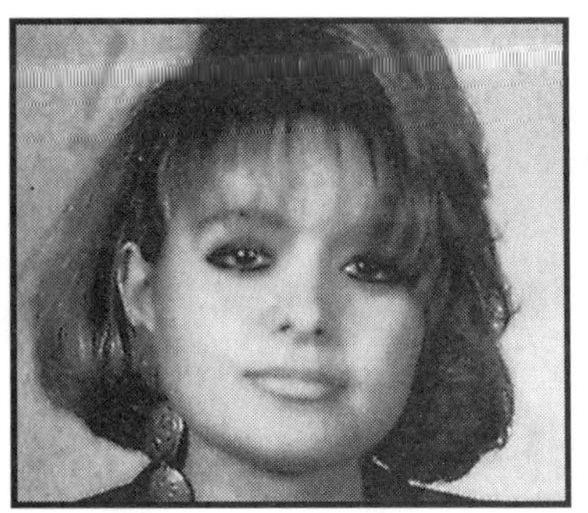

الاسم الكامل: ليلى جبره دبس
العمر: ٢٣ سنة
المهنة: اجازة في الأدب الفرنسي
الهواية: المطالعة – الرياضة – السفر
البلد والعنوان: اللاذقية – مارتقلا – بناء خليل زيدان – طابق ٣ – سوريا

الاسم الكامل: وديع حمزة الرمحي
العمر: ٢١ سنة
المهنة: طالب
الهواية: المراسلة – جمع الصور والطوابع – الرياضة
البلد والعنوان: جامعة الاردن – عمان – ص.ب. ١٣١٧١ – الأردن

تمرين ١٢ **نشاط قراءة (في الصف)**

تعلموا هذه الكلمات:

بَرنامَج	program
قَديم / ة	ancient, old (for things, not people)
الشَّرق الأَوْسَط Middle East	= الشَرق الأدنى Near East

Read and compare the texts below and answer these questions:

1. What do you think these texts are?
2. Find the Arabic words for *center* ____________ and *department* ____________
3. Underline all languages that are listed here. Why are their names all مؤنث?
4. Guess the meaning of:

   بَكالوريوس ____________ ماجِستير ____________ دُكتوراه ____________

5. Find the following words: where and how are they used? Guess their meaning:

   اِبتِدائي ________ مُتَوَسِّط ________ مُتَقَدِّم ________

جامعة نيويورك - نيويورك / نيويورك

New York University
New York, N.Y.

البرنامج : مركز هاقوب كيفوركيان لدراسات الشرق الأدنى، شعبة دراسات لغات وآداب الشرق الأدنى، شعبة الدراسات العبرية واليهودية

Hagop Kevorkian Center for Near Eastern Studies, Department of Near Eastern Languages and Literatures, Department of Hebrew and Judaic Studies

الدرجة العلمية: بكالوريوس، ماجستير، دكتوراه.

لغات الشرق الأوسط : اللغة العربية (ابتدائي، متوسط، متقدم، حلقة دراسية)، التركية (ابتدائي، متوسط، متقدم)، الفارسية (ابتدائي، متوسط، متقدم، حلقة دراسية)، العبرية (ابتدائي، متوسط، متقدم، حلقة دراسية)، الأكادية، الآرامية، سامية الشمال الغربي، المصرية القديمة، الأوجاراتية.

جامعة كاليفورنيا - بيركلي / كاليفورنيا

University of California at Berkeley

Berkeley, CA

البرنامج : مركز دراسات الشرق الأوسط ، شعبة دراسات لغات وآداب الشرق الأدنى، تخصص على مستوى الدراسة الجامعية في دراسات الشرق الأوسط.

Center for Middle Eastern Studies

Department of Near Eastern Studies

Undergraduate Major in Middle Eastern Studies

الدرجة العلمية :

بكالوريوس، ماجستير (في المكتبات ودراسات الشرق الأدنى) دكتوراه (في أديان الشرق الأدنى بالتعاون مع اتحاد طلاب الدراسات العليا في الفكر الديني).

لغات الشرق الأوسط : اللغة العربية (ابتدائي، متوسط، متقدم، حلقة دراسية)، التركية (ابتدائي، متوسط، متقدم)، الفارسية (ابتدائي، متوسط، متقدم، حلقة دراسية)، العبرية (ابتدائي، متوسط، متقدم، حلقة دراسية)، الأكادية، الآرامية ، سامية الشمال الغربي، المصرية القديمة .

من «دليل برامج الدراسات العربية والاسلامية والشرق اوسطية في الجامعات الامريكية»، سفارة المملكة العربية السعودية في واشنطن، الطبعة الثانية، ١٩٩٣، ص. ٥٨ و١٣٩.

تمارين المراجعة *Review Drills*

تمرين ١٣

READ THE FOLLOWING PASSAGE FIRST SILENTLY FOR COMPREHENSION, THEN ALOUD TO PRACTICE PRONUNCIATION:

نادية طاهِر دَرويش خالة مها. السيدة نادية تسكن في مدينة لوس أنجليس في بيت قريب من جامعة كاليفورنيا في لوس انجليس، وتعمل موظفة في بنك كبير وهي متخصّصة في الكمبيوتر.

تمرين ١٤ السؤال

Practice asking and answering questions using old and new vocabulary words:

١ـ «______ هذا الكتاب؟» – «من المكتبة.»

٢ـ «______ عندك صف في المساء؟» – «لا، عندي صف في النهار».

٣ـ «______ تسكن خالتك؟» – «خالتي تسكن في ______.»

٤ـ «______ هذه ؟» – «هذه ترجمة لقصة من الادب العربي.»

٥ـ «______ تدرس في الجامعة ؟» – «أدرس ______ الفرنسية.»

٦ـ «______ هذا الفيلم؟» – «طويل!!»

٧ـ «______ مكتب القبول؟» – «هو في هذه البناية.»

٨ـ «أين السيارة؟» – «______ في شارع قريب.»

٩ـ «______ محمد؟» – محمد مترجم ______ في الامم المتّحدة.»

١٠ـ «هل أنتِ ______ في هذا المكتب؟» – «نعم، أهلا وسهلا! هل عندك سؤال؟»

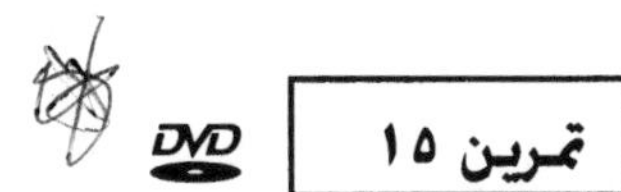

تمرين ١٥

Listen to مها **again on your DVD and fill in the blanks with her exact words:**

والدي ______ ______ في ______ من وإلى ______ ______ والانجليزية و______ ، و______ ______ في مكتب ______ في ______ نيويورك. ______ ______ دائما، ووالدتي ______ ______ بالعمل في ______ وبـ ______ ______ ______ في ______ .

لي ______ ______ نادية ______ في ______ لوس أنجلوس في ولاية كاليفورنيا، ______ ______ في بنك . أنا ______ ______ في ______ وأنا ______ ______ !

العامية Colloquial DVD

- القصّة: "انا فعلا وحيدة"

WATCH مـهـا REPEAT HER STORY IN COLLOQUIAL EGYPTIAN ARABIC.

What expression does Maha use for أيضاً ?

- "أخبارك ايه؟"

WATCH THE DIALOGUE ON THE DVD IN COLLOQUIAL.

Who is Maha talking to and what are they talking about?

تذكروا هذه الكلمات

قَديم / ـة	الشَرق الأوسَط	عُمر
بَرنامَج	سَنة ج. سَنَوات	كلمة ج. كلمات
مفرد	جمع	جملة اسمية
مبتدأ	خبر	بكالوريوس
ماجستير	دكتوراه	

٣ . عائلة والدي

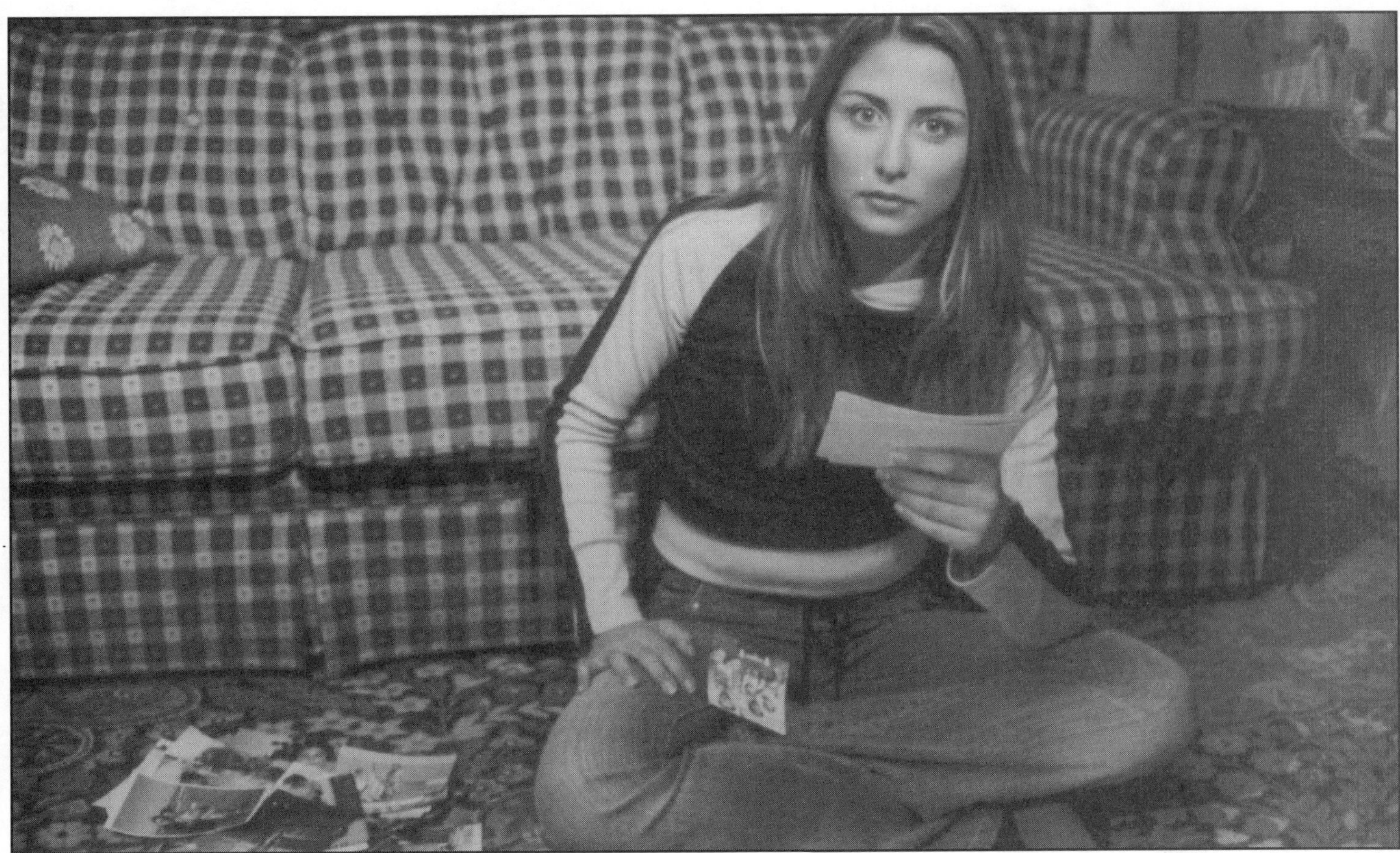

في هذا الدرس:

القصة • عائلة والد مها

الثقافة • «عمّي»

• العائلة العربية

القواعد • الإضافة

• ضمائر الملكية *Possessive pronouns*

الاستماع • مع العائلة والأصدقاء

القراءة • جامعة بيروت العربية وجامعة الجزائر

العامية • القصة: «عيلة والدي»

• «صورة مين دي يا بابا؟»

المفردات

his family	أُسرتُهُ
now	الآن
son	اِبن ج. أبناء
cousin (male, paternal)	اِبن عَمّ ج. أبناء عمّ
army	جَيش ج. جُيوش
actually, in reality	في الحَقيقة
he teaches	يُدَرِّس
letter	رِسالة ج. رَسائِل
husband	زَوج ج. أزواج
her husband	زوجُها
wife	زَوجة ج. زَوجات
picture	صورة ج. صُوَر
officer	ضابِط ج. ضُبّاط
I know	أعرِف
science	عِلم ج. عُلوم
political science	العُلوم السِّياسِيّة
paternal uncle	عَمّ ج. أعمام
my (paternal) uncle	عَمّي
(extended) family	عائِلة ج. عائِلات
relative	قَريب ج. أقارِب
college, school (in a university)	كُلِّيّة ج. كلّيات

تمرين ١ العائلة (في البيت)

A. Arabic has very specific terminology to refer to members of العائلة . You have learned four of these words already: عمّ , عمّة , خالة , and ابن عمّ , and from them you can extrapolate the rest. Use what you know about مذكر and مؤنث to complete the following diagram of the father's and mother's sides of the family, including aunts, uncles, their husbands and wives, and cousins:

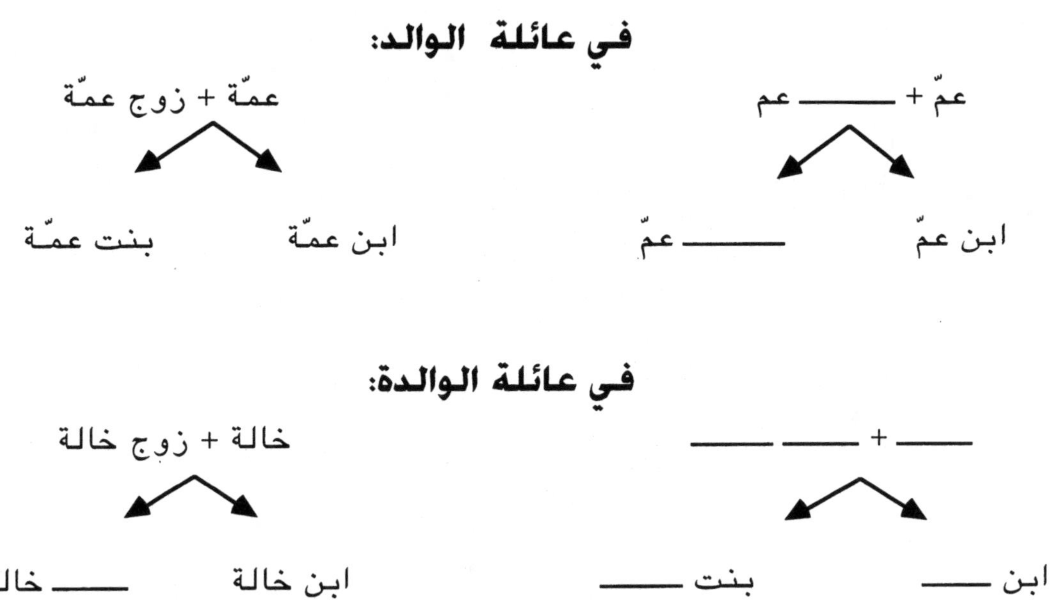

B. Now draw your own family tree, including all your aunts, uncles, and cousins, including the Arabic words for all of your relatives.

تمرين ٢ Find Out! (في الصف)

Find someone in the class:

1. Who has a relative or relatives in the U.S. army (or any army).
2. Who has pictures of her/his family with her/him right now.
3. Lives with a stepmother or أو stepfather [hint: you need to use two words].
4. Knows an officer in the army. Which army?
5. Whose paternal uncle or aunt is a doctor.
6. Is majoring in political science.
7. Writes letters with بـ pen and paper.
8. Whose mother or father teaches.
9. Who doesn't know all of his/her relatives.

تمرين ٣ الكلمات الجديدة (في البيت)

Use old and new vocabulary to write about each picture. Write as much as you can, using all the new vocabulary:

القصة DVD

تمرين ٤ **شاهِدوا واكتبوا:** *Watch and write*

1. Whose pictures is مها holding?

2. Whose names does مها mention?

شاهِدوا مرّة ثانية :

٣- مَن هو مَحمود؟

٤- من هو عادِل؟ ماذا يعمل؟

٥- من هو أحمد؟ أين يعمل الآن؟

٦- من هي فاطمة؟ من في اسرتها؟

شاهدوا وخمّنوا: *Watch and guess*

7. Listen for two uses of the preposition بِـ and guess what it means in this context:

بـجامعة القاهرة and بالإمارات = ________

8. Write the name of the university where أحمد teaches now:

جامعة ______ بالإمارات

تمرين ٥ **عن القصة (في الصف)**

THE FOLLOWING TWO ACTIVITIES ASK YOU TO WATCH THE DVD AGAIN, FIRST WITHOUT SOUND, THEN WITH SOUND, TO FOCUS ON *HOW* MAHA IS SAYING THINGS.

1. With a partner: One of you play Maha and the other an inquisitive new acquaintance who is asking Maha all sorts of questions: What are these pictures? Who are these people?

2. Listen to مها again, and work with a partner to identify the structure of each جملة اسمية you hear in the text. Pick out المبتدأ والخبر . What clues help you identify the separation point between the two parts?

الثقافة

«عَمّي»

You heard مها refer to أحمد as عمّي أحمد even though he is her father's cousin. The words عمّ , عمّة , خالة , and خال may be used to address distant relatives and in-laws, as well as terms of respect for older people outside the family circle. For example, a man who marries into the family may be addressed by younger members of the family as عمّي , mother- and father-in-laws are addressed and referred to as عمّي and زوجة عمّي, and a distant female relative may be called عمّتي. A stepmother may be addressed as خالتي . The exact usage of these terms varies according to regional dialect and local custom.

Relatives by marriage, on the other hand, are specified using terms for *husband* and *wife*. In many dialects, the word امرأة (pronounced in dialect *miraat* or *mart*) is used for *wife* in the following expressions:

aunt (married to عمّ) مراة/ مرة عمّي

aunt (married to خال) مراة/ مرة خالي

By analogy, how can you use the word زوج to specify your aunts' husbands?

It is interesting to note that, while the Arabic language takes great care to specify the exact nature of blood relationships, and even separates terminology for relationships by marriage from that of blood relationships, cultural usage of these terms among speakers of Arabic is more inclusive of non-blood-related people. This difference between "dictionary" and usage is an important one to keep in mind when learning any language.

The word عمّ is also used as a term of respect for an older man of lower social status, or in a joking or intimate manner among close friends (لا يا عمّ!).

العائلة العربية

The concept "family values" in contemporary U.S. society implies a concern with faithful marriage among heterosexuals and a focus on raising happy, healthy children. In Arab culture these values are of equal importance, but they are not part of public discourse, in part because they are not really contested. Arabs usually assume that family values are shared among all members of society.

In general, the extended family plays a somewhat bigger role in Arab society than in American society. Family members visit each other often, in many cases once a week or so if they live in the same city. Many people count their cousins among their friends. However, many people also feel that this general tendency has decreased in recent years.

القواعد

❁ الإضافة

The *iDaafa* (also called "the construct phrase") is one of the fundamental structures of Arabic. Formally, الإضافة consists of two or more **nouns** strung together to form a **relationship of possession or belonging.** You have seen many examples of الاضافة , among them:

جامعة نيويورك　　　　ولاية كاليفورنيا　　　　مكتب القبول

There are three important points to remember about الإضافة :

(1) The relationship between the two (or more) nouns may be thought of as equivalent to the English construction *of.* Arabic has no alternative construction for expressing this relationship between nouns. Thus, to say *the woman's story* in Arabic, you must first reconstruct the phrase to *the story of the woman*: قصة الامرأة . Note that many compound words in English are also expressed using الإضافة , for example:

housework　　　　شغل البيت

(2) **Only the final word in an إضافة can take الـ or a possessive suffix.** In the following examples, note that the first word in each إضافة is definite **by definition, without الـ** . In the final example, note that New York is definite because it is a proper noun.

the family *of* my father = my father's family　　　　عائلة والدي

the office *of* the professor = the professor's office　　　　مكتب الأستاذة

The University *of* New York = New York University　　　　جامعة نيويورك

the notebook *of* the student = the student's notebook　　　　دفتر الطالب

These simple إضافات all consist of two nouns. Complex إضافات , on the other hand, contain more than two, in which case **all non-final nouns** behave like the first and **never take الـ** . Examine the following إضافة , which contains four nouns:

the son *of the* uncle *of the* father *of* Maha= Maha's father's cousin　　　　أحمد ابن عم والد مها

You heard مها use a similar إضافة : «هو ابن عم والدي». Note that only the final noun takes the pronoun suffix. Use the following phrase to remember this rule:

my telephone number　　　　رقم تليفوني

(3) In الإضافة , ة **must always be pronounced as** ت on all words in which it appears except the final word in the إضافة .

Listen to the following words on DVD, read first in isolation, then as the first part of an إضافة , and compare the pronunciations.

DVD

١- مدينة —> مدينة نيويورك	٤- غرفة —> غرفة ابن عمّي
٢- جامعة —> جامعة العين	٥- صورة —> صورة والدتي
٣- عائلة —> عائلة والدي	٦- كلية —> كلية العلوم السياسية

تمرين ٦ الإضافة (في البيت)

MATCH NOUNS IN COLUMNS أ AND ب TO FORM MEANINGFUL إضافات , AND WRITE YOUR COMBINATIONS IN A SENTENCE IN THE THIRD COLUMN. VARIOUS COMBINATIONS ARE POSSIBLE FOR MOST WORDS.

أ	ب		الإضافة
ابن	الطلاب	١-	______________
صورة	العائلة	٢-	______________
مدينة	الجامعة	٣-	______________
ولاية	خالتي	٤-	______________
منطقة	فرجينيا	٥-	______________
عنوان	شيكاغو	٦-	______________
كلية	البنت	٧-	______________
برنامج	الشرق الأوسط	٨-	______________
ضابط	الرجل	٩-	______________
زوج	البوليس	١٠-	______________
مكتب	القبول	١١-	______________
بيوت	المَرْأة (=الاِمْرَأة)	١٢-	______________
سيارات	عمّي	١٣-	______________
زوجة	الاساتذة	١٤-	______________
غرفة	التليفزيون	١٥-	______________

❁ ضمائر الملكية *Possessive Pronouns*

Possessive pronouns in Arabic are suffixes. Those that you have already seen and heard include:

ابنها	اسرته	والدي	اسمها	اسمي
her son	his family	my father	her name	my name

Remember: ة is written and pronounced as ـتـ when a pronoun suffix is added.

The possessive pronouns corresponding to the subject pronouns you know are: DVD

ـنا	(نحن)	ـي	(أنا)
ـكُم	(أنتم)	ـكَ ـكِ	(أنتَ) (أنتِ)
ـهُم	(هم)	ـهُ ـها	(هو) (هي)

Learn to recognize these as the written suffixes. The pronunciation of some of the vowels in these endings varies slightly among different varieties of Arabic. The spoken endings are fixed for each dialect. In formal Arabic, the pronunciation of these endings varies slightly with different grammatical endings. For the present, you are expected to recognize the variants without worrying about the differences. This chart gives one of the three formal endings that you will see and hear: DVD

بيتُنا	(نحن)	بيتي	(أنا)
بيتُكُم	(أنتم)	بيتُكَ بيتُكِ	(أنتَ) (أنتِ)
بيتُهُم	(هم)	بيتُهُ بيتُها	(هو) (هي)

Go to your DVD and click on the third chart to hear the colloquial forms of these pronouns.

تمرين ٧ ضمائر الملكية (في البيت)

For each sentence, show *whose*, as in the example:

مثال: (اسم / أنا) ماري. ⟵ اسمي ماري .

١ـ أين (كُتُب /أنتَ) ؟

٢ـ هل تعمل (والدة /أنتِ) دكتورة ؟

٣ـ هي أردنية و(أقارب /هي) في عمّان .

٤ـ (صورة /هو) جميلة !

٥ـ (بيت /نحن) في هذه المنطقة .

٦ـ هل (عنوان /أنتَ) جديد ؟

٧ـ أين تسكن (عمّة /أنتِ) ؟

٨ـ هل (جامعة /أنتم) قديمة ؟

٩ـ (ابن/أنا) دائمًا مريض !

١٠ـ (رسالة /هو) طويلة !

١١ـ (استاذ /هم) يدرّس في عُمان الآن .

١٢ـ (غرفة /نحن) فعلاً واسعة !

تمرين ٨ ضمائر الملكية (في البيت)

Complete the following about مـهـا using appropriate pronouns, such as هو , هم , ـهـا / هـي .
Remember to rewrite ة as ت where necessary:

مثال: مها طالبة في جامعة نيويورك و**هي** تدرس الأدب الإنجليزي.

مها تسكن في مدينة نيويورك و ــــ طالبة في جامعة نيويورك . والد ــــ مصري،

و ــــ يعمل في الامم المتحدة، ووالدة ــــ فلسطينية و ــــ موظفة في نفس الجامعة.

محمود وعادل وأحمد وفاطمة أقارب مها و ــــ في القاهرة. ونادية خالة ــــ

و ــــ تسكن في كاليفورنيا. عمّ ــــ محمود و أسرة ــــ في الامارات الآن

تمرين ٩ نشاط محادثة (في الصف)

Lost and found: Place books, pencils and other objects you can name in the center of the room. Take turns returning the objects to their owners by asking:

« هل هذا كتابك؟ » « هل هذا دفترك ؟ »

تمرين ١٠ الإضافة (في الصف)

First, skim the list and guess what it is. Then read it again more carefully, with special attention to the grammatical structure of the names. Which contain إضافة ? How can you tell?

الجامعة العربية الدول الأعضاء

- المملكة الأردنية الهاشمية (دولة مؤسسة)
- دولة الإمارات العربية المتحدة
- مملكة البحرين
- الجمهورية التونسية
- الجمهورية الجزائرية الديمقراطية الشعبية الاشتراكية
- جمهورية جيبوتي
- المملكة العربية السعودية (دولة مؤسسة)
- جمهورية السودان
- الجمهورية العربية السورية (دولة مؤسسة)
- جمهورية الصومال
- جمهورية العراق (دولة مؤسسة)
- سلطنة عمان
- دولة فلسطين
- دولة قطر
- جمهورية القمر المتحدة
- دولة الكويت
- الجمهورية اللبنانية (دولة مؤسسة)
- الجماهيرية العربية الليبية الشعبية الاشتراكية العظمى
- جمهورية مصر العربية (دولة مؤسسة)
- المملكة المغربية
- الجمهورية الإسلامية الموريتانية
- الجمهورية اليمنية (دولة مؤسسة)

www.arableagueonline.org

تمرين ١١ الإضافة

Read the following sentences describing مها وعائلتها , first silently, then aloud. Pay special attention to the pronunciation of ة in الإضافات .

١- مها بنت مصرية.

٢- والدة مها مشغولة دائماً.

٣- عائلة والد مها كبيرة.

٤- خالة مها تسكن في مدينة لوس أنجليس في ولاية كاليفورنيا.

٥- والدها من القاهرة، وهي فعلاً مدينة كبيرة!

٦- في الحقيقة، أحمد هو ابن عم والد مها.

٧- حَنان ابنة عمة مها، وهي أستاذة في كلية الترجمة بجامعة الأزهَر في القاهرة.

٨- هذه رسالة من زوجة عمي أحمد، وهذه صورتها هي وأسرتها.

تمرين ١٢ نشاط قراءة (في الصف)

تعلموا هذه الكلمات:

التّاريخ	history	عِلم الإنْسان	anthropology
الحُقوق	law	عِلم الاِجْتِماع	sociology
الدّين	religion	عِلم النَفْس	psychology
الطِّبّ	medicine	الهَنْدَسة	engineering

Below and on the next page you will find some information about جامعة بيروت العربية and جامعة الجزائر . Read through the texts and see how many departments you can recognize with the help of the vocabulary you learned, and how many new words you can guess from your own background knowledge and context. How do these universities compare to each other, and to your own?

جامعة الجزائر

كلية الحقوق

قانون عام
قانون خاص

كلية العلوم الاقتصادية وعلوم التسيير

علوم تجارية
تسيير
علوم اقتصادية

كلية الآداب واللغات

الأدب العربي
اللغة الفرنسية
اللغة الإنجليزية
اللغات الإسبانية والألمانية والروسية
لغات شرقية
ترجمة
لغويات
تعليم مكثف للغات

كلية العلوم السياسية والاتصال

علم الاتصال
علوم سياسية

كلية أصول الدين

الديانات
الشريعة
أصول الدين

كلية الطب

الطب
جراحة الأسنان
الصيدلية

www.univ_alger.dz/arabic/faculte.htm

جامعة بيروت العربية

كلية الآداب

أقسام اللغات

أ - قسم اللغة العربية وآدابها
ب - قسم اللغة الانجليزية وآدابها
جـ - قسم اللغة الفرنسية وآدابها

أقسام العلوم الإنسانية

1. قسم الجغرافيا
2. قسم التاريخ
3. قسم الفلسفة
4. قسم الاجتماع
5. قسم علم النفس
6. قسم الإعلام

كلية الحقوق

1. القانون الخاص
2. القانون العام
3. العلاقات الدولية والديبلوماسية

كلية التجارة

- المحاسبة
- إدارة الأعمال
- الاقتصاد
- الدراسات المالية والجمركية

كلية الهندسة

أ - قسم الرياضيات والفيزياء الهندسية
ب - قسم الهندسة الكهربائية
جـ - قسم الهندسة المدنية
د - قسم الهندسة الميكانيكية

كلية الهندسة المعمارية

كلية العلوم

- قسم الرياضيات
- قسم الفيزياء
- قسم الكيمياء
- قسم العلوم البيولوجية والبيئية

كلية الصيدلة

- قسم الكيمياء الصيدلية
- قسم التكنولوجيا الصيدلية
- قسم العقاقير
- قسم الميكروبيولوجيا الصيدلية

كلية الطب

1. قسم التشريح الآدمي
2. قسم الأنسجة والخلايا (الهستولوجيا)
3. قسم وظائف الأعضاء (الفسيولوجيا)
4. قسم الكيمياء الحيوية الطبية
5. قسم الأمراض (الباثولوجيا)
6. قسم الأدوية (الفارماكولوجيا)
7. قسم الجراثيم والميكروبات الدقيقة (الميكروبيولوجيا) والمناعة
8. قسم طب المجتمع
9. قسم التوليد وأمراض النساء
10. قسم طب الأطفال

www.bau.edu.lb

الثقافة

الجامعات العربية

Many Arab universities show different divisions of fields than are found in American universities, which group most academic departments together in the *School of Arts and Sciences*. Arab universities, on the other hand, generally use smaller divisions such as the *School (or College) of Humanities* كلية الآداب, the *School of Commerce* كلية التجارة, and various science schools. Another difference between the two systems of education is that Medicine and Law are undergraduate, not graduate schools.

The system of education in most Arab countries resembles European models rather than the American "liberal arts" college. By the second year of high school, students must choose to concentrate either in humanities and social sciences or in mathematics and natural sciences. Once that choice is made, the student's choice of college major is limited, so that a humanities major in high school may not enter a science department in college and vice-versa. Each school or department sets its own academic program including all of the courses the students take in each year of study; students are not allowed to choose electives. In many Arab universities, these courses are one year long, and the student's grade is determined solely on the basis of one exam at the end of the year. However, recent years have seen a growth in the number of American-style universities all over the Arab world. If you are interested, do a web search for Arab universities and see what you find.

تمرين ١٣ نشاط كتابة

مكتب القبول في جامعتك HAS ASKED YOU TO HELP PREPARE A HANDOUT IN ARABIC THAT THEY CAN DISTRIBUTE TO الطلاب العرب WHO ARE INTERESTED IN APPLYING TO THE SCHOOL, BUT WHO ARE NOT FAMILIAR WITH THE AMERICAN HIGHER EDUCATIONAL SYSTEM. MAKE AN OUTLINE OF THE STRUCTURE OF YOUR UNIVERSITY

تمرين ١٤ نشاط محادثة

BRING صُوَر OF YOUR FAMILY AND/OR FRIENDS AND PRESENT THEM TO THE CLASS.

تعلموا هذه الكلمة:

grandfather/grandmother (on both sides of the family)	جَدّ / ة

الاستماع DVD

تمرين ١٥ **مع العائلة والأصدقاء**

LISTEN TO THE PASSAGE ON DVD AND IDENTIFY THE SPEAKER:

١- اسمه: ____________

٢- زوجته: ____________

٣- أولاده: ____________

٤- يسكن في ____________

٥- يعمل في ____________

تمارين المراجعة

تمرين ١٦ **الجمع**

LIST ALL OF THE THINGS ONE WOULD FIND IN THE PLACE GIVEN.

مثال: في هذا الكتاب **دروس وكلمات عربية وتمرينات.**

١- في مدينة نيويورك ____________

٢- في البيت ____________

٣- في الجامعة ____________

٤- في عائلة مها ____________

٥- في صفي ____________

٦- في الشارع ____________

٧- في هذا الكتاب ____________ Album

٨- في هذا الكتاب ____________ Mother Goose

تمرين ١٧ استمعوا الى مها

LISTEN TO مها ON TAPE AGAIN AND COMPLETE:

________ والدي ________ ، أعرف ________ من ________ والرسائل.

________ ________ محمد و ________ ، وهذا ________ عادل و ________ ،

________ عادل ________ كبير في ________ . وهذا ________ أحمد و ________

– هو في الحقيقة ________ عم ________ . ________ أحمد ________ في

كلية ________ ________ بجامعة ________ وهو ________ الآن في جامعة

________ بالإمارات ________ ________ . و ________ ________ فاطمة

و ________ وابنها و ________ .

العامية

– القصة: "عيلة بابا كبيرة"

LISTEN TO مها TELL HER STORY IN COLLOQUIAL.

How does she say هذا and هذه in colloquial?

– "صورة مين دي يا بابا؟"

WATCH مها TALK TO HER FATHER.

How does she say مَن؟ in colloquial?

تذكروا هذه الكلمات

الإضافة	جَدّ / ة	التّاريخ
عِلم الإنْسان	الحُقوق	عِلم الاِجْتِماع
الدّين	الطِّبّ	عِلم النَفْس
الهَنْدَسة		

٤ . كيف أحفظ كل الأسماء ؟!

في هذا الدرس:

القصة	• أقارب مها في مصر
الثقافة	• في المدرسة
القواعد	• الفعل المضارع
	• الجملة الفعليّة
	• السؤال
القراءة	• البيت النبوي
	• إعلانات زواج
الاستماع	• مع العائلة والأصدقاء
العامية	• القصة: «ازيّ احفظ كل الاسامي؟!»
	• «انت في قسم إيه؟»

المفردات

first	أَوَّل
primary, elementary	اِبتِدائيّ / ة
I memorize	أَحفَظ
school	مَدرَسة ج. مَدارِس
I remember	أَتَذَكَّر
fourth	رابِع / ة
classmate; colleague (مذكر)	زَميل ج. زُمَلاء
classmate; colleague (مؤنث)	زَميلة ج. زَميلات
traveling[1]	السَّفَر (إلى)
she travels	تُسافِر (إلى)
friend (مؤنث)	صَديقة ج. صَديقات
friend (مذكر)	صَديق ج. أَصدِقاء
childhood	الطُّفولة
individual (person)	فَرد ج. أَفراد
before	قَبْلَ + اسم
all; every	كُلّ + اسم في إضافة
he was	كانَ
I was	كُنتُ

[1]This word is a noun (gerund), not an adjective (participle). It cannot be used in sentences such as "I am travelling" because, as a noun, it cannot express an on-going action.

تمرين ١ الكلمات الجديدة (في البيت)

PRACTICE USING NEW VOCABULARY BY COMPLETING THE SENTENCES:

١- لي ________ اسمه روبرت وهو يدرس العلوم السياسية معي.

٢- هذه صُوَر كل ________ عائلتي: أنا ووالدي ووالدتي وأخي وجدّي وجدّتي.

٣- نحن طلاب في الصف ________ في اللغة العربية.

٤- إليزابث هي ________ي في الجامعة ونحن في نفس الصف.

٥- لا ________ اسم الضابطة الجديدة.

٦- قبل الجامعة، ________ طالبة في المدرسة الامريكية في مدينة عمّان.

٧- هل ________ الطلاب في صفكّم أمريكيون؟

٨- زوجتي ________ الى العراق حيث تسكن عائلتها.

٩- هذا هو الدرس الـ ________ في «الكتاب».

١٠- كيف ________ كل الكلمات قبل الامتحان!؟

١١- كنتُ في المكتبة ________ الصف، حيث كنت أدرس.

١٢- هم يدرّسون في ________ ابتدائية صغيرة.

تمرين ٢ كلمات جديدة (في البيت)

THE NEW VOCABULARY LIST INCLUDES SEVERAL VERBS. USE WHAT YOU HAVE LEARNED SO FAR TO COMPLETE THE CHART. LOOK FOR PATTERNS IN THE PREFIXES AND USE ANALOGY TO FILL IN THE MISSING FORMS:

أنا	أَدرُس	أَعرِف	أُدَرِّس	أَحفَظ	أَتَذَكَّر	
هو	يَدرُس		يُدَرِّس			
هي	تدرُس	تَعرِف				تُسافِر

تمرين ٣ اسألوا زملاءكم FIND OUT (في الصف)

ASK AS MANY زملاء AS YOU CAN AND FIND OUT WHO:

1. Has a friend studying Chinese or Japanese?
2. Whose roommates study in their room or house, and whose do not?
3. Whose father or brother was a student at this university?
4. Was in her or his room before class?
5. Had (=كانَ عندك) a happy childhood?
6. Has a relative who travels a lot by (بـ) plane?
7. Remembers her/his elementary school? Remembers the first grade (= صف)?
8. Is a senior [hint: in which year?] in college?

تمرين ٤ كلمات جديدة وقواعد قديمة (في الصف)

READ THESE SENTENCES, FIRST SILENTLY FOR MEANING, THEN ALOUD TO A PARTNER. PAY ATTENTION TO IDAAFAS.

١- زوجة خالي تُدرّس في مدرسة ابتدائية.

٢- مكتبة الجامعة هي البناية الرابعة في هذا الشارع.

٣- كنت أدرس في مدينة «زوريخ» في سويسرا في طفولتي.

٤- هذه الامرأة تعمل في مكتب السفر في الجامعة الامريكية.

٥- أتذكر هذه المدرسة – هي مدرسة أصدقاء طفولتي.

٦- تسكن أسرتي في البيت الأول في شارع «المنصور».

٧- كنت في غرفة زميلتي قبل الصف.

٨- كيف أحفظ أسماء كل زملائنا الجُدُد؟!

٩- لا أعرف كل أفراد عائلتي الكبيرة.

١٠- والدة صديقي تسافر الى أوروبا دائما.

القصة

| تمرين ٥ | شاهدوا واكتبوا: |

ANSWER بالعربية:

1. Who does مها talk about?
2. مها mentions a trip: إلى أين؟
3. What is the problem she mentions here?

شاهدوا مرة ثانية:

٤- من هي سامية؟

٥- من هو خالد؟

٦- ما اسم زوجة أحمد، عمّ مها؟

٧- هل كان خالد ومها في نفس الصفّ في المدرسة؟

استمعوا وخمّنوا:

٨- كل أفراد العائلة = ____________________

| تمرين ٦ | عن القصة (في الصف) |

WORK WITH A PARTNER ON THESE ACTIVITIES:

1. Tell Maha's story from a third person perspective. What does she remember, and what does she not remember?
2. Listen to مها again and pick out all the إضافة phrases you hear in the text.

الثقافة

في المدرسة

Watch the scenes from Egyptian schools on your DVD. You will see طابور الصباح, the morning line-up. How do the activities and scenes you see compare to your مدرسة ابتدائية?

❁ الفعل المضارع

verb	فِعل ج. أفعال
present or incomplete tense	مُضارِع

By now you have seen and heard a number of verbs, among them:

أسكُن   أحفَظ   أعرِف   أتَذَكَّر   يعمَل   يُدرِّس   تعمَل

These verbs are in المُضارِع , which is sometimes defined as *present tense* and sometimes as *incomplete tense.* المضارع combines both features: it can refer to an incomplete action, usually one taking place in the present, such as *he teaches* or *he is teaching*, or a repeated habitual action, such as *she works at the UN*, or a state such as *I know*. **Remember:** (a) any action that lasts over a period of time or takes place repeatedly will involve المضارع ; and (b) المضارع can express both progressive (*I am studying*) and habitual (*I study*) actions.

In Arabic, the subject of الفعل المضارع is expressed in a prefix or a prefix and a suffix on the verb itself rather than with an independent pronoun. Thus هو يدرس is redundant **unless** the context calls for some kind of contrastive emphasis (such as ***he*** *studies*).

The chart on the next page lists the full conjugations of some of the verbs you have learned so far. When studying the chart, note that:

(a) The prefixes and suffixes that indicate person remain the same for all مضارع verbs, and the stem of each verb remains constant. Once you know the stem of any verb, you can easily derive its conjugation.

(b) Two forms are given for أنتِ , أنتُم , and هُم : one with ن and one without it. Both of these forms are used in formal Arabic; the difference between them is grammatical. For now, learn to recognize both variants and choose one to use; you will learn about the difference later. In most spoken dialects, the form without ن is used, except in Iraq and the Arabian Peninsula, where the form with ن is more common.

(c) An old spelling convention requires that the verb forms for أنتم and هم without ن be written **with a final alif which is not pronounced.**

The following chart highlights the prefixes and suffixes for each person:

to do (used in questions, e.g. "What do you *do*? or What are you *doing*?)

(أنا) أَفْعَل	(نحن) نَفْعَل
(أنتَ) تَفْعَل (أنتِ) تَفْعَلين / تَفْعَلي	(أنتم) تَفْعَلون / تَفْعَلوا
(هو) يَفْعَل (هي) تَفْعَل	(هم) يَفْعَلون / يَفْعَلوا

These charts show the full conjugation of some of the verbs you have seen:

أنا	أَسكُن
أنتَ	تَسكُن
أنتِ	تَسكُنينَ / تَسكُني
هو	يَسكُن
هي	تَسكُن
نحن	نَسكُن
أنتم	تَسكُنونَ / تَسكُنوا
هم	يَسكُنونَ / يَسكُنوا

أنا	أُدَرِّس
أنتَ	تُدَرِّس
أنتِ	تُدَرِّسينَ / تُدَرِّسي
هو	يُدَرِّس
هي	تُدَرِّس
نحن	نُدَرِّس
أنتم	تُدَرِّسونَ / تُدَرِّسوا
هم	يُدَرِّسونَ / يُدَرِّسوا

أنا	أَتَذَكَّر
أنتَ	تَتَذَكَّر
أنتِ	تَتَذَكَّرينَ / تَتَذَكَّري
هو	يَتَذَكَّر
هي	تَتَذَكَّر
نحن	نَتَذَكَّر
أنتم	تَتَذَكَّرونَ / تَتَذَكَّروا
هم	يَتَذَكَّرونَ / يَتَذَكَّروا

❁ نفي الفعل المضارع *Negation*

In formal Arabic, الفعل المضارع is negated with لا , which precedes the verb, as the following examples demonstrate:

she does not remember	لا تتذكّر اسمي
he is not working/ does not work	لا يعمل في المكتب
we do not study/ are not studying	لا ندرس الفرنسية

In formal Arabic, there exists an interrogative particle أ (= هل) that is often used in negative questions:

Don't you know..!?	ألا تعرفين الموظف الجديد؟!
Don't you remember...?!	ألا تتذكّرون اسمي؟!!

The question mark will help you recognize this particle.

تمرين ٧ الفعل المضارع (في البيت)

Describe these people's actions by conjugating the verbs:

١- **مثال:** مها تسكن في نيويورك .

أحمد ــــــــ في الإمارات.

والدة مها ــــــــ في بروكلين .

ــــــــ في بيت الطلاب. (انا)

أقاربي ــــــــ في هذه المنطقة .

أين ــــــــ ؟ (أنتم)

٢- **مثال:** محمود يُدرّس في الجامعة .

زوجته ــــــــ في مدرسة ابتدائية.

هل ــــــــ في الجامعة؟ (أنتَ)

لا ــــــــ في مدرسة. (أنا)

هل ــــــــ في الجامعة؟ (أنتِ)

٣- **مثال:** لا أتذكّر اسمه.

مها لا ــــــــ اسم زوجة عمها.

لا ــــــــ عنوانك. (نحن)

هل ــــــــ أسماء زُملائكم؟ (أنتم)

الطلاب ــــــــ كل الكلمات.

٤- **مثال:** صديقي يعمل في قسم التاريخ.

أصدقائي ــــــــ في مكتبة الجامعة.

هل ــــــــ في الجامعة؟ (أنتِ)

السيدة مريم ــــــــ في مكتب القبول.

أين ــــــــ؟ (أنتم)

تمرين ٨ ماذا يفعلون؟ (في البيت) DVD

A. What are they doing? Listen to and learn these new verbs on your DVD, and write out the sentences you hear.

يُشاهِد   يَكتُب   يَتَكَلَّم   يَقرَأ   تَستَمِع إلى   يأكل   يَشرَب

B. Practice conjugating the new verbs. When studying and learning new verbs, a combination of mechanical and contextual exercises usually works best. Writing out conjugation tables for verbs helps you internalize their forms, and using them in sentences of your own helps you activate your control of them.

تمرين ٩ الفعل المضارع (في البيت)

DESCRIBE THE ACTIONS OF THESE PEOPLE:

١- الدكتورة ليلى ______________ العلوم السياسية . (يدرّس)

٢- كل أفراد عائلتي ______________ في هذه المنطقة . (يسكن)

٣- أخي ______________ هذا الكتاب الآن . (يقرأ)

٤- خالتي ______________ لي رسائل دائماً. (يكتب)

٥- هل ______________ اللغة الإيطالية يا رندة ؟ (يتكلم)

٦- أنتم لا ______________ من هي ؟ (يعرف)

٧- من فضلك ، مَن ______________ في هذا البيت ؟ (يسكن)

٨- أنا وأصدقائي دائمًا ______________ التليفزيون في المساء . (يشاهد)

٩- كيف ______________ كل الكلمات الجديدة ؟! (يحفظ + أنتم)

١٠- يا سامي ، هل ______________ في النهار أو في المساء ؟ (يعمل)

١١- يا سارة، هل ______________ القهوة بالحليب والسكر؟ (يشرب)

١٢- عمّتي وكل أفراد عائلتها لا ______________ الدجاج. (يأكل)

تمرين ١٠ اسألوا زملاءكم (في الصف)

INTERVIEW YOUR زملاء . SEE IF YOU CAN FIND THREE PEOPLE IN THE CLASS WHO:

1. Are always traveling!
2. Whose mothers or fathers teach school.
3. Eat before class.
4. Live with a roommate.
5. Do not know all of their relatives.
6. Remember their elementary school friends.
7. Study with classmates in the evening.
8. Talk to a family member every day (= كلّ يَوْم).
9. Do not watch television every day.
10. Listen to classical music.
11. Do not drink coffee or tea.

❁ الجملة الفعلية

In Chapter 2, you learned about الجملة الاسمية , the sentence that begins with a noun. Arabic has one other sentence pattern, الجملة الفعلية (named for the word فِعل *verb*), which is a sentence that begins with a verb. The subject of this verb is either contained in the verb itself or is expressed as a noun following the verb. Examples of جمل فعلية include:

١- لا أتذكر كل الكلمات الجديدة.   ٣- تستمع زوجتي إلى الراديو في الصباح.

٢- يكتبون رسائل الى أفراد العائلة.   ٤- يعمل والد مها في الامم المتحدة.

In sentences (١–٢) above, the subject of the verb is contained in the verb itself. In sentences (٣–٤), the subject follows the verb.

Most sentences can be expressed either as a جملة اسمية or as a جملة فعلية . The main difference between the two is word order, which does not affect the basic meaning of the sentence. Thus the examples of جمل فعلية given above can also be expressed as جمل اسمية . Compare sentences (٥–٨) below to (١–٤) above:

٥- أنا لا أتذكر كل الكلمات الجديدة.   ٧- زوجتي تستمع إلى الراديو في الصباح.

٦- هم يكتبون رسائل الى أفراد العائلة. ٨- والد مها يعمل في الامم المتحدة.

Both الجملة الاسمية and الجملة الفعلية sentence patterns occur widely in Arabic. The former tends to be more common when there is more than one important topic under discussion, and the latter tends to be more common in the narration of events. Practice identifying both types, الجملة الاسمية والمبتدأ والخبر and الجملة الفعلية and its subject.

تمرين ١١ الجملة الفعلية

How can the meaning of each جملة اسمية be expressed using جملة فعلية ?

مثال: مها تسكن في نيويورك . —> تسكن مها في نيويورك.

١- أستاذنا يُدرِّس الأدب العربي .   ٥- زميلتي سَناء تسافر دائماً.

٢- والدي لا يعرف كل أصدقائي .   ٦- أختي تكتب رسائل إلى أقاربنا.

٣- خالة مها تعمل في بنك كبير.   ٧- والدة مها تتكلم ثلاث لغات.

٤- أخي لا يسكن في بيت الطلاب .   ٨- ابن عمّي لا يشاهد التليفزيون.

More About Questions **السؤال** ❁

In this lesson you heard مـهـا say, لا أعـرف كـيـف أحـفـظ كل الأسـمـاء . This sentence shows that Arabic uses the same format for both direct and indirect questions, unlike English, which allows indirect questions to be phrased with an infinitive verb (e.g., *I don't know how to memorize, I don't remember how to write that*). Thus, in Arabic, the question *How* ***can I*** *memorize all the names?* uses the same word order as the sentence *I don't know how I* ***can*** *memorize all the names.* Other indirect questions in English use the infinitive, such as *I don't know what* ***to study***, لا أعـرف مـاذا أدرس , whereas the Arabic retains exactly the same structure and order as the question *what should I study?* ماذا أدرس ؟ . Note that, in Arabic, intonation and context can often convey the sense of English modals *could, would,* and *should.* How would you translate the following?

كيف أكتب اسمه ؟ <— لا أعرف كيف أكتب اسمه .

أين يسكن صديقنا ؟ <— لا أتذكر أين يسكن صديقنا .

مَن يدرّس التاريخ الإسلامي؟ <— لا أعرف مَن يدرّس التاريخ الاسلامي .

تمرين ١٢ **السؤال**

WHAT DO THESE PEOPLE KNOW OR NOT KNOW? IMITATE THE PATTERN YOU HEARD مـهـا USE:

لا أعرف كيف أحفظ كل الأسماء!

USE THE INTERROGATIVE PARTICLES YOU KNOW: مَن ماذا أين من أين كيف أيّ هل

١- لا أعرف ________________________ .

٢- نعرف ________________________ .

٣- الاستاذ يعرف ________________________ .

٤- لا يعرفون ________________________ .

٥- والدتي لا تعرف ________________________ .

٦- صديقي يعرف ________________________ .

٧- ألا تعرفين ________________________ ؟

٨- ألا تتذكّرون ________________________ ؟

الاستماع DVD

تمرين ١٣ استمعوا واكتبوا:

LISTEN TO THE STATEMENTS ON DVD ONCE TO UNDERSTAND THE GENERAL MEANING, THEN AGAIN AS NECESSARY TO FILL IN THE BLANKS. LISTEN CAREFULLY, BUT ALSO USE THE CONTEXT TO HELP YOU UNDERSTAND THE MEANING AND WRITE WITH GRAMMATICAL ACCURACY.

١- صفّي ________ وأنا لا ________ أسماء كل ________ فيه.

٢- «البنك السعودي» هو البنك ________ في هذا ________ .

٣- أنا الآن في ________ أشاهد التليفزيون وأكتب ________ إلى ابن عمي.

٤- هي فعلاً ________ وتعبانة في ________ .

٥- لي ________ صغيرة وجميلة ________ عبير، وهي الآن في ________ الابتدائية. ________ نيكول فرنسية ، وعبير ________ معي باللغة العربية ومع والدتها بالفرنسية.

٦- قبل ________ إلى الشرق الأوسط، كنت ________ في مكتب للترجمة في ________ واشنطن وكنت ________ اللغة العربية في المساء في مدرسة «بيرليتز» للغات.

تمرين ١٤ مع العائلة والأصدقاء DVD

LISTEN TO THE DVD AS MANY TIMES AS YOU NEED TO ANSWER THE QUESTIONS:

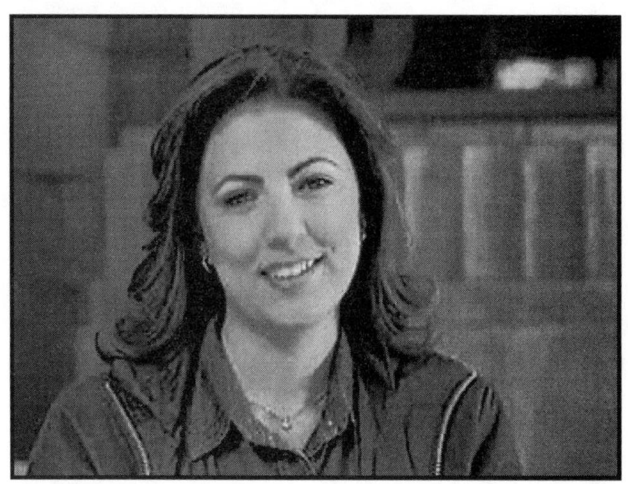

١- مَن يتكلم ؟

٢- كيف تعرف مها ؟

٣- أين تسكن ؟

٤- من في أسرتها ؟

٥- فيمَ (في ماذا) هي متخصصة ؟

الثقافة

عائلة النَّبيّ مُحَمَّد

The chart you are about to read shows the family tree of the Prophet Muhammad and contains many names central to Islamic history. Note when you are reading the names associated with the following Muslim leaders and dynasties, all of whom are related to the Prophet by blood or marriage:

The Four Rightly-Guided Caliphs	الخُلَفاء الرّاشِدون ٦٣٢-٦٦١
The Umayyads, first Islamic dynasty	الأُمَويّون ٦٦١-٧٥٠
The Abbasids, second Islamic dynasty	العَبّاسيّون ٧٥٠ - ١٢٥٨
Revered by Shi'ite Muslims: الشّيعة	عَلي وفاطِمة والحَسَن والحُسَين
The Hashimites, present-day rulers of Jordan	الهاشِميّون

تمرين ١٥ نشاط قراءة (في الصف)

USE THE CHART BELOW TO FIND THESE RELATIONSHIPS AMONG MEMBERS OF THE PROPHET'S FAMILY:

١- النَبي محمد هو ________ عبد الله .

٢- عبّاس وأبو طالب وأبو لهب هم ________ عبد المطّلب .

٣- علي هو ________ النبي محمد .

٤- أولاد النبي محمد هم ________ و________ و________ و________ .

٥- عائشة هي زوجة النبي محمد وهي ________ أبي بكر .

٦- فاطمة الزهراء هي ________ علي .

٧- عباس هو ________ النبي محمد .

٨- النبي محمد هو ________ الحَسَن والحُسين .

٩- رقية هي ________ عُثمان بن عفّان .

١٠- أُم كُلثوم هي ________ الحسن والحسين .

١١- ________ كان أوّل الخلفاء الراشدين .

١٢- عُمَر كان ________ الخلفاء الراشدين .

١٣- ________ كان ثالث الخلفاء الراشدين .

١٤- علي كان ________ الخلفاء الراشدين .

تعلموا هذه الكلمات:

نَبيّ — prophet

خَليفة ج. خُلَفاء — Caliph

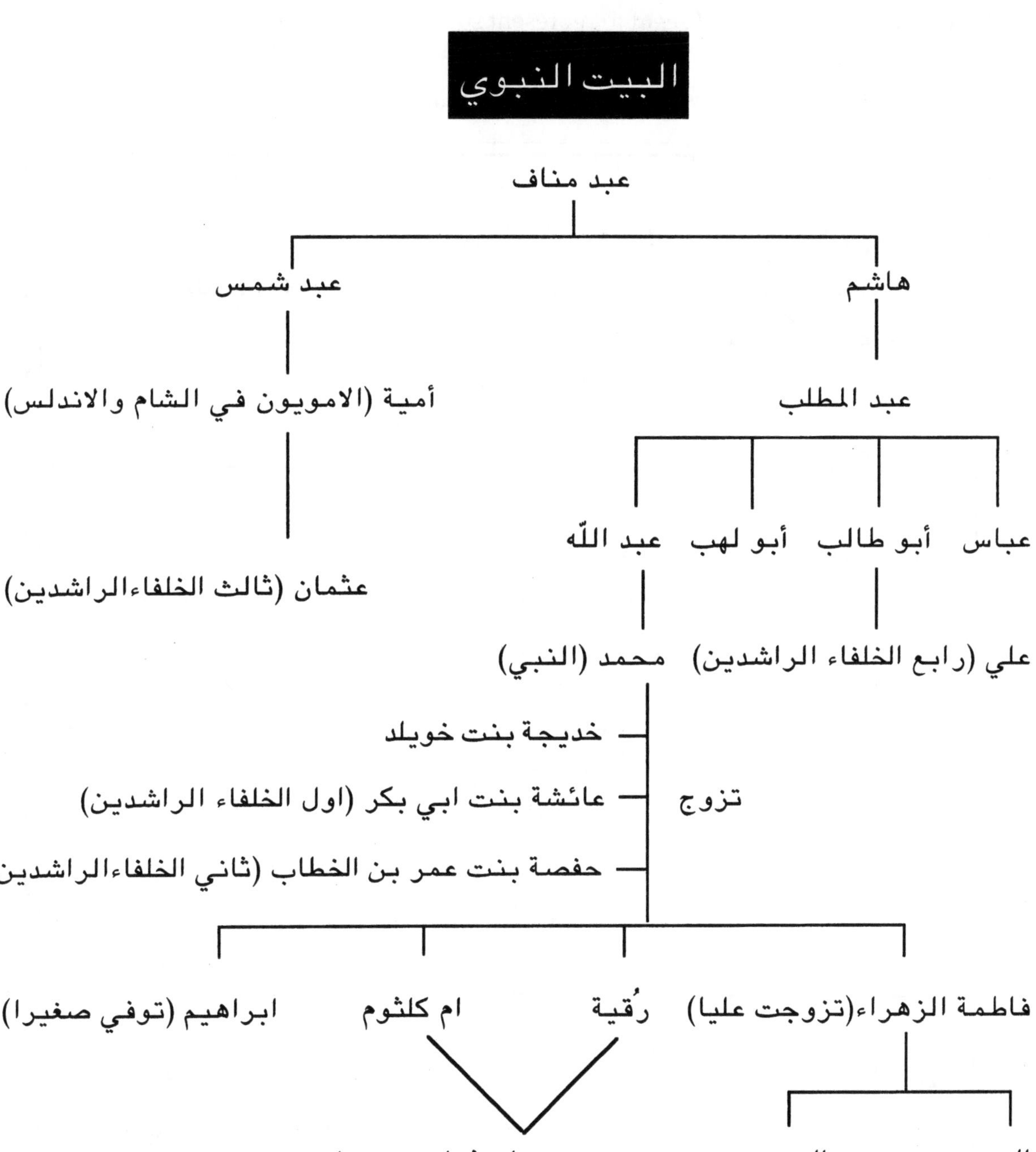

من «المنجد في اللغة والأعلام» ص. ٦٣٧ المكتبة الشرقية بيروت ١٩٨٦

تمرين ١٦ — نشاط قراءة: إعلانات زواج

Below are several personal ads in which the person first describes himself or herself, then describes the qualities he or she seeks in a spouse. Skim, then re-read the ads and answer:

1. Which of these ads were placed by a man and which by a woman? How do you know?
2. Which adjectives recur and seem to represent sought-after qualities?
3. Circle all verbs you can find. How can you identify them?
4. See how many new words whose meanings you can guess from context.

نورة

انا فتاة سعودية ٢٦ سنة من عائلة عريقة في بريدة مطلقة واحمل شهادة جامعية وموظفة جميلة ومثقفة الى ابعد الحدود ارغب بالزواج من انسان طيب وديمقراطي واهم شيء ان يكون رجل اعمال ولا يهم عمره حتى لو كان ١٠٠ سنة المهم موافقته لسفري للدراسة بالخارج ان امكن

للاتصال بالبريد الالكتروني

سالي

انا آنسة مغربية وعمري ٢٧ سنة جميلة مثقفة ومتدينة من اسرة محافظة ارغب بالزواج من انسان يجب ان يكون مسلما وان يكون جادا ولا يهم مكان اقامته او جنسيته لاني مستعدة ان اعيش معه اينما يكون

للاتصال بالبريد الالكتروني

احمد

انا مصري ٢٨ سنة طبيب واعمل بمكة المكرمة مقبول الشكل والطباع على خلق رومانسي جدا جدا ارغب بالزواج من فتاة جامعية على خلق مصرية او سورية مستعدة للسفر جميلة رومانسية جدا جدا

للاتصال بالبريد الالكتروني

ميسون

انا فتاة سودانية ٢١ سنة مقيمة بالسعودية جدة اعمل صحفية وانا جامعية على قدر من الجمال قمحية اللون ارغب بالزواج من رجل ما بين ٢٥-٣٥ لم يسبق له الزواج يقدر الحياة الزوجية ويحترمها اخلاقه حميدة رومانسي وحنون

للاتصال بالبريد الالكتروني

المصدر: www.123Arab.com/6/2003

تمرين ١٧ نشاط كتابة (في البيت) ومحادثة (في الصف)

قبل الصف : On a blank sheet of paper, write as many facts about yourself and your family as you can without revealing your name.

في الصف : Your teacher will collect all the papers and redistribute them randomly. Your goal is to uncover the identity of the person whose paper you hold. Read it, then ask other students questions based on the information you have until you find the right person.

تمارين المراجعة

تمرين ١٨ الإضافة

The sentences below lack a central element. Match words from list أ with words from list ب to form إضافات that will complete the sentences:

أ

منطقة خالة عنوان ولاية
مكتبة اسم كلمات نفس
مكتب عم كلية
مدينة كل أستاذ
زميل زوج صورة

ب

والدتي الجامعة الدرس مها
العلوم الصف أختي البيت
مَنهاتن الحقوق الاستاذ القسم
القاهرة الطالب الكلمات المكتب
ميشيغان الأمريكيين

١- ندرس في ________ ________ .

٢- لا أعرف ________ ________ .

٣- هل ________ ________ يتكلمون اللغة الانجليزية ؟

٤- أحمد أبو العلا ________ ________ وهو ________ ________ السياسية.

٥- أنا وزملائي في الصف نحفظ ________ ________ .

٦- هذه ________ ________ .

٧- أقاربي يسكنون في ________ ________ .

٨- ________ ________ في هذه البناية .

٩- هل تعرفين كيف تكتبين ________ ________ ؟

١٠- مدينة ديترويت في ________ ________ .

١١- أخي طالب في ________ ________ .

١٢- الآنسة ريم موظفة في ________ ________ .

تمرين ١٩ استمعوا الى مها واكتبوا ما تقول: DVD

هذه سامية ________ ________ فاطمة — ________ ________ .

وهذا خالد ________ ________ محمود، ________ في ________

________ ... كان في السف ________ ، و________ في ________

________ . هذه ________ ________ أحمد ... آه ... اسمها ... اسمها ...

في ________ ، لا ________ أسماء ________ ________ ________ .

ولا ________ كيف ________ ________ الأسماء قبل ________

________ القاهرة !

تمرين ٢٠ تمرين قراءة

Read the following text, first silently for comprehension, then practice reading aloud:

سامية محمد صِدقي بنت عمة مها . وكانت صديقة طفولة مها، قبل سفر مها إلى أمريكا. سامية تسكن مع عائلتها في مدينة القاهرة بمنطقة العبّاسية. لها ثلاث أخَوات وأخ واحد وهي البنت الكبيرة في الاسرة. هي الآن طالبة في قسم التاريخ بجامعة عَين شمس حيث تدرس التاريخ المصري القديم .

العامية DVD

- القصة: "ازيّ احفظ كل الاسامي؟!"

Listen to مها tell her story in colloquial.

How does she say كيف ? زوجة عمّي ?

- "إنت في قسم ايه؟"

Watch the scene.

What do we learn about these people?

تذكروا هذه الكلمات

كل يوم	نبي	خليفة	يكتب	يتكلّم	فِعل ج. أفعال
يشرب	يأكل	يستمع إلى	يقرأ	يشاهد	الفعل المضارع

٥. لا أحب مدينة نيويورك!

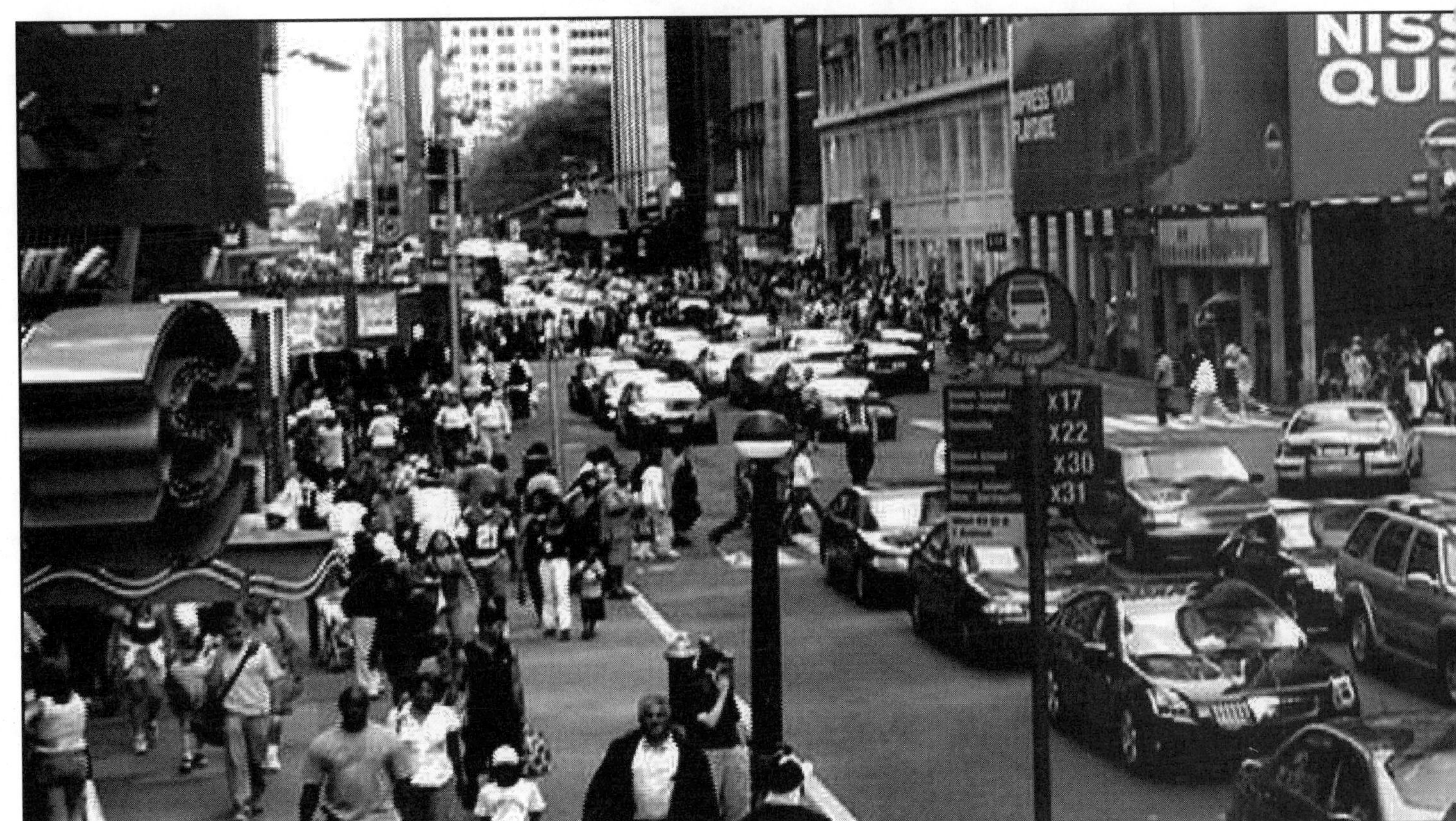

في هذا الدرس:

القصة • الشعور بالوحدة في مدينة نيويورك

القواعد • تنوين الفتح *Adverbs*

• الاسم + الصِّفة

• هذا / هذه

القراءة • الجو اليوم

• وظائف دكتوراه في كليات البنات

الاستماع • الطقس من تليفزيون «الحرة» والتليفزيون السوري

الثقافة • فيروز

العامية • القصة: «ما باحبش مدينة نيويورك»

• «الجو حرّ قوي!»

• «لا .. ولا حاجة»

المفردات

مِـن أَصل + صِـفـة *adjective*	of ... descent
بـارِد / ة	cold (adjective)
جِـدّاً	very
الجَـوّ = الطَّـقـس	weather
أُحِـبّ	I like, love
حـارّ / ة	hot (adjective)
أَحسَن + اسـم مـفـرد indefinite	the best ...
أَحْـيـانـًا	sometimes
الخَـريـف	autumn
دَرَجـة	degree
دَرَجة الحَرارة	temperature
الرَّبيـع	spring (season)
الرُّطوبـة	humidity
الاِزدِحام	crowding, overcrowdedness
بِـسَـبَـب	on account of, because of
الشِّتـاء	winter
أَشعُـر بِـ	I feel, have feelings of
الصَّيـف	summer
الطَّـقـس = الجَـوّ	weather
عالِـيـة	high (مؤنث)
فَصل ج. فُصول	season
فصل دراسيّ	semester
فَـقَـط	only
كَـثـيـرًا	a lot, much (adverb)
كَثير / ة ج. ـون/ين	many (adjective)
بِالنسبة لِـ + اسم / pronoun suffix	as far as (someone) is concerned
الوِحدة	loneliness

DVD

بالنِّسبة لي	بالنِّسبة لَنا
بالنِّسبة لَكَ بالنِّسبة لَكِ	بالنِّسبة لَكُم
بالنِّسبة لَهُ بالنِّسبة لَها	بالنِّسبة لَهُم

تمرين ١ الكلمات الجديدة (في البيت)

COMPLETE THE SENTENCES WITH APPROPRIATE WORDS FROM THE NEW VOCABULARY:

١- عائلتي صغيرة: لي أخت واحدة ________ اسمها لينا.

٢- بالنسبة لي، ________ هو أحسن فصل، وأنتِ ، ما هو أحسن فصل ________ ؟

٣- «رالف نادر» أمريكي ________ ________ عربي .

٤- في السعودية ________ حارّ جداً في الصيف و________ ________ ________ ٤٠° – ٤٥° .

٥- الطقس في العراق ________ جدا في الصيف وبارد في ________ .

٦- (أنا) ________ الشوكولاتة والبيتزا كثيرًا! وأنتم، ماذا ________ ؟

٧- بِناية «إمباير ستيت» في نيويورك ________ جدًا .

٨- لا أحب هذا الشارع الكبير ________ الازدحام .

٩- حبيبته في باريس وهو في لبنان، وهو ________ بالوحدة!

١٠- في جامعتنا ٣ ________ دراسية: الخريف و________ والصيف.

١١- أشاهد التليفزيون في المساء ________ .

١٢- لا أحب السفر الى فلوريدا في الصيف بسبب الجو الـ________ و________ العالية.

١٣- بالنسبة لي ، جامعتي هي ________ جامعة في الولايات المتحدة .

تمرين ٢ اسألوا زملاءكم (في الصف)

Opinion Poll: Ask as many زملاء as you can, then pool your answers:

1. How many زملاء like hot weather? Cold weather?
2. What is their favorite season?
3. How many people can't stand high humidity?
4. How do people feel today? List top 3 states.
5. How many do not like big cities, lots of traffic, and high buildings?
6. Of what descent are الزملاء ?
7. Where is the best coffee on campus?

القصة DVD

تمرين ٣ شاهدوا واكتبوا:

١- هل تُحِبّ مها نيويورك ؟ لماذا / لِماذا لا *Why/why not?*

٢- مَن هي لَيلى؟ ماذا نعرف من مها ؟

شاهدوا مَرّة ثانية:

٣- ما هو أحسن فصل بالنسبة لِمها ؟

٤- مها لا تحب الطقس ________________________ .

٥- كيف تشعُر مها في نيويورك؟ لِماذا؟ *Why*

استمعوا وخمّنوا:

Listen for a particle that signals the explanation of a previous statement (somewhat like a colon in English). مها uses this particle twice. Write what you hear:

٦- أ - لا أحب مدينة نيويورك كثيرًا ، _____ الجو ....

ب - أشعر أحيانًا بالوحدة في هذه المدينة الكبيرة _____ والدي ...

(Remember that one-letter particles are connected to the following word.)

القواعد

❁ تنوين الفتح *Adverbs*

شُكرًا	عَفوًا	دائمًا	فِعلاً
أيضًا	كثيرًا	جِدًا	أحيانًا

These words all share the grammatical ending تنوين الفتح.[1] One of the main functions of this ending is to make a noun or adjective into an adverb (a word that modifies a **verb**). Most adverbs that end in تنوين الفتح are spelled with alif: ـًا. In regular, unvocalized texts, the symbol ـً is often omitted, leaving just ا , as in دائما or جدا . Knowing this helps you identify adverbs in texts: look for words ending in ا . If they are **not** proper nouns, chances are they should be read as تنوين : ـًا. A few words that are commonly used as adverbs end in ـةً ; remember that ة does not take an alif spelling with تنوين الفتح . You will learn some of them later.

Adverb placement is fairly flexible in Arabic and generally corresponds to English word order, except that in Arabic adverbs tend to follow the verb. Adverbs may also follow the object of the verb, or come at the end of the sentence:

والدتي تعمل دائماً   والدي مشغول دائماً .   لا أحبّ نيويورك كثيراً

Like their English equivalents, the adverbs أيضاً , دائماً , and فعلاً may separate المبتدأ and الخبر :

أنا أيضاً تعبانة! *or* أنا تعبانة أيضاً !

هم فعلاً مشغولون. *or* هم مشغولون فعلاً

However, note that the adverb جِداً must follow the adjective it modifies in formal Arabic:

نحن مشغولون جداً!   هي عطشانة جداً!

تعلموا هذه الكلمة:

جَيِّداً	well

هل تتذكرون هذه الكلمات جيداً ؟   لا أدرس جيداً في غرفتي.

---

[1]In addition to its function as an adverb marker discussed here, تنوين الفتح has other functions as well, including marking indefinite direct objects in formal Arabic only. You will occasionally see and hear nouns marked with this ending in formal contexts; for now, you need only recognize it as a grammatical ending. The grammatical roles of تنوين endings are presented in Chapters 16 and 17.

تمرين ٤ نشاط كتابة (في البيت)

Write ten sentences describing what your friends and family members and others do/not do, and how much, often, or well they do it, by using the following verbs and a variety of adverbs.

تتكلم - يعملون - يشعر بـ - تحبّ - يدرس - يقرأون - تكتب - يدرسون

تدرّس - تسافر - يحفظ - يتذكرون - يأكلون - يشرب - تستمع الى

تمرين ٥ تنوين الفتح (في الصف)

The تنوين الفتح ending may be used on many nouns and adjectives that refer to location in time or space. Rephrase the following by making adverbs out of the underlined phrases (remember to drop الـ and use the masculine forms of adjectives).

مثال: زوجي لا يعمل في النهار. —> نهاراً

١- لا أشاهد التليفزيون في الصباح.

٢- أدرس في المساء فقط.

٣- هل تسكنون في بيوت قريبة من الجامعة؟

٤- ندرس ساعات *hours* طويلة كل يوم.

٥- يسافرون الى مدن بعيدة كل صيف.

تمرين ٦ اسألوا زملاءكم (في الصف)

Ask زملاءكم for the following information. Remember to rephrase the questions as second person with أنتِ - أنتَ - أنتم. When you find someone who is like you, say: وأنا أيضاً!.

١- من يكتب رسائل الى اسرته دائما؟

٢- من تعبان جدا؟

٣- من لا يحب هذه المدينة [illegible]؟ لماذا؟

٤- من يسافر بعيداً؟

٥- من يعمل دائما؟

٦- من يشرب الماء دائما؟

٧- من لا يتذكر الكلمات أحيانا؟

٨- من يسكن قريباً من الجامعة؟

٩- أين يدرسون جيداً ؟

❁ الاسم + الصفة *Noun-Adjective Phrases*

noun	اِسم ج. أسماء
adjective	صِفة ج. صِفات

In Arabic, noun-adjective phrases and جمل اسمية resemble each other closely. Only the presence or absence of the definite article الـ distinguishes one from the other. In fact, الـ is one of the most important particles in Arabic, and paying attention to its usage can make a big difference in comprehension. Consider the three sets below. One of them contains جمل اسمية and the other two contain noun-adjective phrases:

٣		٢		١	
a big class	صفّ كبير	*the big class*	الصّف الكبير	*The class is big*	الصّف كبير
a big city	مدينة كبيرة	*the big city*	المدينة الكبيرة	*The city is big*	المدينة كبيرة

Set (١) contains جمل اسمية , set (٢) contains definite noun-adjective phrases, and set (٣) contains indefinite noun-adjective phrases. Notice where الـ is placed in each set. In (١), the fact that الصف and المدينة are **definite**, while كبير and كبيرة are **indefinite**, makes these **complete sentences.** In (٢), the fact that both words are **definite** makes these **definite noun-adjective phrases.** In (٣), the fact that both words are **indefinite** makes these **indefinite noun-adjective phrases.**

Remember: a definite noun phrase, such as *the new car*, must be **completely definite** in Arabic, which means that both the noun and its adjective must be definite. An indefinite noun-adjective phrase, such as *a big city*, must likewise be **completely indefinite.** A noun and adjective that do **not** agree in definiteness constitute a **complete sentence.**

Remember that **possessive suffixes** make nouns **definite without** الـ . For example, صديقي , أقاربها , and مدينتنا are all definite. Therefore, in a definite noun phrase, the adjective must also be definite, with الـ :

my Egyptian friend	صديقي المصري
her Palestinian relatives	أقاربها الفلسطينيّون
our beautiful city	مدينتنا الجميلة

تمرين ٧ الاسم + الصفة (في البيت)

Complete the sentences below with noun-adjective phrases by matching the nouns and adjectives from the lists below. Remember to make the adjective agree with their nouns and to use الـ where needed. Some sentences will require plural forms.

أسماء			صفات		
صديق/ة	ابن/بنت	زميل/ة	لبناني	بارد	ابتدائي
موظف/ة	جامعة	بناية	وحيد	جميل	كبير
استاذ/ة	طالب/ة	مدرسة	عربي	جديد	صغير
منطقة	طقس	رجل	متخصص	أمريكي	مصري

١- هل تسكنين في هذه ________ ________ ؟

٢- هل تعرفون ________ ________ في الأدب العربي ؟

٣- ________ ________ تدرّس في كلية الحقوق .

٤- ________ ________ يشعر بالوحدة .

٥- ________ ________ تتكلم ٣ لغات .

٦- ________ ________ لا يحبون شغل البيت .

٧- ________ ________ من عائلة كبيرة .

٨- لا نحب ________ ________ في الشتاء !

٩- أختي الصغيرة تدرس في ________ ________ .

تمرين ٨ اسم + صفة أو إضافة؟

Determine whether each of the following phrases is إضافة or اسم + صفة :

١- رجل طويل ________

٢- غرفة الصف ________

٣- طقس نيويورك ________

٤- (من) أصل سوري ________

٥- الرطوبة العالية ________

٦- اللغة العربية ________

٧- أوتوبيس المدرسة ________

٨- الولايات المتحدة ________

٩- بنت عمّها ________

١٠- أختي الكبيرة ________

❁ هذا / هذه

The demonstratives هذا and هذه are used in both sentences (*This is ...*) and phrases (*this ...*). By now you have seen هذه / هذا used in three different ways:

This is a city.	١- هذه مدينة .
this city	٢- هذه المدينة
This is the city.	٣- هذه هي المدينة .

Note that (١) and (٣) are sentences, whereas (٢) is a phrase. Memorize these patterns and use them as models for other nouns.

(a) Sentence (١) above represents the construction *This is a....* Other examples:

هذا اسم عربي　　هذه طائرة جديدة　　هذا بيت جميل　　هذه صورة قديمة

(b) هذا/هذه followed by a **definite noun** will always be a phrase, *this....* Other examples:

هذا الفصل　　هذه الجامعة　　هذا الصيف　　هذا المكتب　　هذه البنت

(c) Sentence (٢) represents the construction *This is the....* Other examples:

هذا هو الصف الأول　　هذه هي الامم المتحدة　　هذا هو صفّ العربية

تمرين ٩　**ترجِموا إلى اللغة العربية : كيف نقول؟**

1. The old (كبير) man is tired.
2. Is this test hard?
3. This is the old school.
4. This is a long class!
5. Is this your new roommate?
6. This is a hot summer!
7. Cairo is a very big city.
8. Is this our new room?
9. The new library is very cold.
10. The short woman is Saudi.
11. Their new car is beautiful.
12. I live on (في) a wide street.
13. The new student is French.
14. This is her new friend.
15. This weather is hot!
16. This is the new building.

تمرين ١٠ الاسم + الصفة / الإضافة (في الصف)

WITH A PARTNER, COMBINE THE FOLLOWING PAIRS OF WORDS INTO A PHRASE AND USE EACH IN A SENTENCE. THINK ABOUT WHETHER YOU WANT TO USE إضافة OR اسم + صفة AND THINK ABOUT THE RULES FOR EACH.

١- مدرسة + وحيد
٢- طقس + ربيع
٣- عائلة + صديقة
٤- زميل + جديد
٥- أخ + كبير
٦- صف + إسباني
٧- كلية + علوم
٨- رسالة + طويل
٩- صورة + حبيب
١٠- جيش + العراق

الاستماع DVD

تمرين ١١ نشاط استماع: كيف الطقس؟

قبل الاستماع، تعلموا هذه الكلمات:

غائم
مُمطِر/ماطِر
ثَلج
مُشمِس

NOW WATCH THE WEATHER REPORTS ON YOUR DVD SEVERAL TIMES AND ANSWER ORALLY:

1. What cities and countries are mentioned?
2. Which season is this? How can you tell?
3. Do the weather reports talk about نفس الفصل ? How can you tell?

تمرين ١٢ نشاط قراءة (في الصف)

تعلموا هذه الكلمة:

عاصِمة ج. عَواصِم	capital (city)

READ THE WEATHER FORECAST BELOW AND ANSWER IN ARABIC:

1. What areas does this forecast cover? What is the prevailing weather in each area?

2. You are travelling to Montreal, London, and Rome. Find out how the weather will be in each city.

3. Find and underline the verbs in each sentence, and see if you can identify the subject of each one (remember to look for الجملة الفعلية). Can you recognize any new words that share consonants with weather vocabulary you know?

الجو اليوم

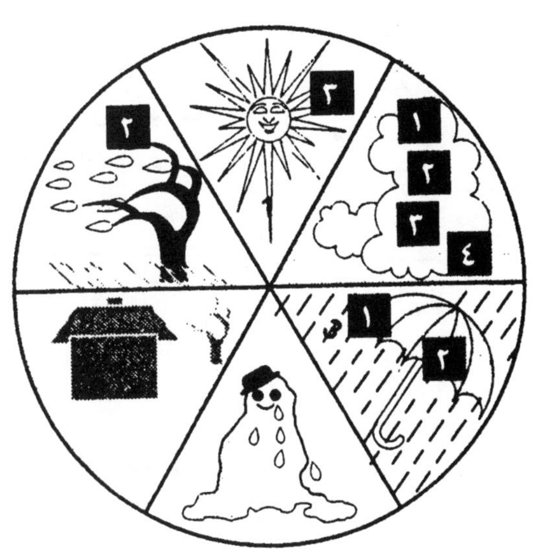

١ أوروبا:

الجو ممطر على بودابست ودبلن ولندن ووارسو، غائم على بقية العواصم.

٢ أمريكا:

في الشمال تهب عواصف مصحوبة بثلوج خفيفة على شيكاغو مونتريال وتورنتو وتسقط الأمطار على سياتل ويكون الجو غائما على نيويورك وواشنطن ، أما في الجنوب فتهب عواصف رعدية على معظم العواصم.

٣ آسيا:

الجو غائم على معظم العواصم باستثناء سنغافورة فالجو فيها صحو.

٤ البلاد العربية:

تغطي الغيوم معظم العواصم العربية وتظهر السحب المنخفضة والعالية.

من جريدة «العالم اليوم»، ١٩٩١/١١/٢٦

تمرين ١٣ نشاط قراءة (في الصف)

Read this article from the Saudi paper عُكاظ and look for answers to these questions:

1. Who wrote the article? In what city? Try to find the name of an official who is quoted.
2. Underline all the fields of study mentioned in the article.
3. Note the word وظيفة (related to ة/و ظ ف), meaning عمل/شغل . What is its plural?
4. Guess the meaning of at least one new word you have not seen before.
5. Find in the text at least one example of:

إضافة اسم + صفة فعل مضارع جمع مؤنث non-human plural agreement

١٤١٦ وظيفة «دكتوراه» في كليات البنات

باسمة مراد (جدة)

أعلنت كليات البنات عن توفر ١٤١٦ وظيفة اكاديمية من حاملات الدكتوراه وذكر عبد الله الحصين الوكيل العام لكليات البنات ان الوظائف المعلنة تتوزع في كافة المناطق في مختلف التخصصات في الدراسات الاسلامية واللغة العربية ورياض الاطفال والمكتبات والجغرافيا والتاريخ واللغة الانجليزية والرياضيات والحاسب الآلي والفيزياء والكيمياء والاقتصاد المنزلي وعلم الحيوان وعلم النبات والتربية وعلم النفس وعلم الاجتماع وطرق التدريس.

من جريدة «عكاظ» السعودية ٥/٦/٢٠٠٣

تمرين ١٤ نشاط كتابة ومحادثة (في الصف)

You have heard مها introduce and describe new people twice so far:

لي خالة اسمها نادية . لي صديقة اسمها ليلى .

This kind of sentence can be used to introduce and describe any new person:

لي عمه تسكن في مدينة واشنطن. لي أخت تدرس في كلية دارتموث.

On small cards or pieces of paper, introduce and describe people in your life in sentences based on these models. Write one sentence on each card. Your teacher will then collect the cards and put them in a central location. Take a card from the pile and find its owner by asking questions, e.g.,

هل لك أخت تعمل في واشنطن؟ هل لك عمّ يُدرّس في جامعة تكساس؟

الثقافة

فَيروز

فـيــروز is a Lebanese singer, one of the most famous and popular in the Arab East today among all generations because of her beautiful voice and the many different musical genres that she sings. These genres range from Classical poetry to folk songs to modern "Arabicized jazz." Her career began in the late 1950s, and was launched mainly by the musical plays that her husband, عاصي الرَحباني, and his brother منصور wrote. Many of her most famous songs, including the following, come from those musicals. The الرحـبـانـي brothers were themselves very influential in the field of modern Arabic music, and created a "school" of songwriting that combined elements from folklore, the Classical Arabic tradition, and western music. More recently, her son, زياد الرحـبـانـي, has written songs for her that show the influence of jazz and other western musical genres while retaining Arabic elements.

فـيــروز sings the following song—one of her most famous—in the Lebanese dialect, which differs from formal Arabic in some of its sounds and vocabulary. Notice, for example, that the word الشِتاء is pronounced الشِتي in Lebanese. Listen and sing along:

«حَبّيتك بالصَيف»

حَبَّيتك بالصَيف — حَبَّيتك بالشّتي

نَطَرتَك بالصيف — نَطَرتَك بالشتي

وعيونَك الصيف — وعيوني الشتي

وملآنا يا حبيبي — خَلف الصيف

وخلف الشتي

نَطَرتَك	*I waited for you*	مَلآنا	*our meeting*
عُيون	*eyes*	خَلف	*behind, beyond*

تمارين المراجعة

تمرين ١٥ **(في البيت)**

MAKE IT PERSONAL! USE PRONOUNS TO PERSONALIZE THESE WORDS AND COMPLETE THE SENTENCES. YOU MAY NEED TO USE THE PLURALS OF SOME OF THE NOUNS:

١ ـها تسكن في نيويورك و ــــــــــ يسكنون في القاهرة
و ــــــــــ عادل ضابط في الجيش .(قريب ، عم)

٢- نتذكر ــــــــــ جيدًا . (طفولة)

٣- زملائي يدرسون في ــــــــــ أحيانًا. (بيت)

٤- أخي ــــــــــ صالِح وأختي ــــــــــ سَحَر . (اسم)

٥- يحبون كل ــــــــــ كثيرًا . (ولد)

٦- هل هذه ــــــــــ ؟ (صورة)

٧- ــــــــــ الابتدائية كانت صغيرة جدا، أنا أتذكر كل ــــــــــ .
(مدرسة) (صديق)

تمرين ١٦ **استمعوا إلى مها واكتبوا :** DVD

لا ــــــ مدينة نيويورك ــــــ ــــــ ــــــ و ــــــ ،

فـ ــــــ ــــــ جدًا في ــــــ و ــــــ الرطوبة ــــــ ،

و ــــــ جدًا في ــــــ . ــــــ ــــــ ــــــ

لي هو ــــــ .

ــــــ أحيانًا بـ ــــــ في هذه ــــــ ــــــ ، فَـ ــــــ

و ــــــ مشغولان ــــــ ، ولي ــــــ ــــــ فقط ــــــ ليلى

و ــــــ أمريكية ــــــ ــــــ ــــــ .

العامية DVD

- القصة: "ما باحبش مدينة نيويورك"

LISTEN AS مها TELLS HER STORY IN COLLOQUIAL.

- "الجو حرّ قوي!"

WATCH محمد AND ملك .

What word do they use for جداً ?

- "لا .. ولا حاجة"

WATCH THE DIALOGUE.

What is going on?

تذكروا هذه الكلمات

اسم ج. أسماء صِفة ج. -ات جيّداً لماذا ؟

عاصِمة ج. عَواصِم مُمطِر/ماطِر مُشمِس ثَلج غائِم

٦. أنا خالد

في هذا الدرس:

القصة
- خالد محمود أبو العلا

الثقافة
- مَن هو المعيد؟
- ماذا تفعل كل يوم؟
- الأكل العربي

القواعد
- المصدر
- لماذا؟

القراءة
- مطعم البراسيري
- مطعم مروش

العامية
- القصة: «انا خالد»
- «تشربوا حاجة الأول؟»

المفردات

commerce, trade	التِّجارة
I get, obtain	أَحصُل على
to get/getting, to obtain/obtaining	الحُصول على
lecture	مُحاضَرة ج. مُحاضَرات
I graduated from	تَخَرَّجْتُ مِن
business administration	إدارة الأعمال
that [thing] (demonstrative, corresponds to هذا/هذه)	ذٰلِكَ (مؤنث : تِلكَ)
I go to	أذهَب إلى
week	أُسْبوع ج. أسابيع
year	سَنة ج. سَنَوات
graduate fellow; teaching assistant	مُعيد ج. ون /ين
in order to	لِـ [1]
why?	لِماذا ؟
because	لِأنَّ + جملة اسمية
so, thus, for this reason	لِذٰلِك
since, ago (meaning depends on verb tense)	مُنذُ
have been .. ing ... since/for	فعل مضارع + منذ
two years ago	منذ سَنَتَيْن
day	يَوم ج. أيّام
today	اليَوم

[1]Remember the rule for writing لِـ with الـ: لِلـ. You have seen لِـ in the phrase بالنسبة لِـ and in the possessive لي ; in this chapter you will learn another function of لِـ with verbs.

يوم الجُمْعة	يوم الخَميس	يوم الأرْبِعاء	يوم الثُلاثاء	يوم الاِثنَين	يوم الأحَد	يوم السَبت

Determine the correspondence between the names of the days in Arabic and English. (Hints: one of the names is a cognate of *Sabbath*, and the *first* day of the week is Sunday.)

تمرين ١ الكلمات الجديدة (في البيت)

COMPLETE USING NEW VOCABULARY, WITH SPECIAL ATTENTION TO THE GRAMMATICAL INFORMATION GIVEN IN THE WORD LIST:

١. بنت عمتي نورا ________ في القسم الإنكليزي بالجامعة .

٢. يوم الأربعاء عندي ________ من الصباح الى المساء .

٣. ________ الى الكلية كل يوم .

٤. تخرّجت من الجامعة ________ ثلاث سنوات .

٥. مها هي البنت الوحيدة في أسرتها، و ________ هي تشعر بالوحدة .

٦. الآن، بعد ________ على البكالوريوس، يعمل زميلي أحمد في الجيش .

٧. لا أحب فصل الصيف ________ الجو فيه حار جداً ودرجة الرطوبة عالية .

٨. بالنسبة لي ، يوم الجمعة أحسن يوم في ________ .

٩. أختي تدرس الآن للحصول على الماجستير في ________ .

١٠. ________ من الجامعة في سنة ٢٠٠٤ .

١١- صديقتي تدرس في المساء فقط لأنّها تعمل قبل ________ .

١٢- الطلاب في كلية الطب يدرسون ٣ ________ بعد الحصول على البكالوريوس.

تمرين ٢ اسألوا زملاءكم (في الصف)

FIND AS MANY زملاء AS YOU CAN WHO:

1. Graduated from college, are graduate fellows now, and are studying to get a دكتوراه .
2. Graduated from المدرسة 1 year ago / 2 years ago / 3 years ago.
3. Whose parent(s) or sibling(s) have a Master's ماجستير in Business Administration.
4. Go to الكافتيريا in the morning before their classes.
5. Does not have classes five days a week.
6. For whom this is his/her only class today.
7. Go to lectures in the evening (not for a class)
8. Remember how the weather was a week ago. How was it?
9. Are majoring in business.

تمرين ٣ أيام الأسبوع (في البيت)

FILL IN THE TABLE WITH YOUR CLASS SCHEDULE. WRITE OUT THE NAMES OF THE DAYS AND YOUR CLASSES AND LECTURES USING AS MUCH ARABIC AS YOU CAN. WRITE THE TIMES AS SHOWN:

				يوم الاثنين	الساعة
					٩,٠٠

الثقافة

من هو المعيد؟ DVD

Watch the interview on your DVD with a معيدة مصرية as she explains the معيد system.

ماذا تفعل كل يوم؟ DVD

Watch as a طالب جامعي مصري tells us about his daily schedule.

القصة DVD

تمرين ٤ **شاهدوا واكتبوا\ (في البيت)**

١- من يَتَكَلَّم؟

٢- ماذا يعمل؟

٣- ماذا وأين يدرس؟

شاهدوا مرة ثانية:

٤- مَتى *when* تخَرَّجَ؟

٥- في أيّ كلّية يدرس؟ وفي أيّ جامعة؟

٦- فيمَ (= في ماذا) هو متخصص؟

٧- هل هو يدرّس؟ لماذا / لماذا لا؟

استمعوا وخمّنوا:

٨- في أيّ أيام يذهب خالد إلى الجامعة؟ Check off the days:

السَبت	الأحَد	الاِثنَين	الثُلاثاء	الأرْبِعاء	الخَميس	الجُمْعة

تمرين ٥ **عن القصة (في الصف)**

WITH A PARTNER, LISTEN FOR THE "GLUE" THAT HOLDS THE TEXT TOGETHER, THE "LITTLE" WORDS (LITTLE IN SIZE BUT IMPORTANT TO THE COHESION OF THE TEXT!) SUCH AS و , لِـ , لأنّ , لذلك , AND PREPOSITIONS. WHAT QUESTIONS DO THESE WORDS ANSWER? WHAT IMPLIED QUESTIONS DOES KHALID ANSWER IN THIS NARRATIVE? WRITE OUT THE QUESTIONS بالعربية .

القواعد

❁ الـمَصدَر

Review the meanings of السّفر and الحُصول على . Formally, these words are nouns that are closely related to verbs, and often function as infinitive verbs. The Arabic term for this grammatical category is مَصدَر (ج. مَصادِر) . In addition to its use as an infinitive, المصدر can also be used to express the abstract concept of the action; you have seen السفر used this way in the phrase قبل السفر إلى القاهرة.[1] Note that المصدر will almost always be **definite,** either with الـ or as the first word in an إضافة . Remember that the first word in an إضافة never takes الـ.

Each verb has its own مَصدَر . The مصدر forms of the verbs you have learned so far are given below. Beginning in Chapter 7, the مصدر form will be given for each new verb so that you can memorize both المضارع and المصدر **together**. (It is much easier to learn them at the same time.) For now, you must memorize each مصدر individually; however, like the plural patterns, many مصادر share the same syllabic structure. You will gradually become familiar with these patterns, and eventually learn to predict many مصادر .

الفعل	المصدر	الفعل	المصدر
يذهَب إلى	الذّهاب إلى	يشرَب	الشُّرب
يحفَظ	الحفظ	يأكُل	الأكل
يدرُس	الدِّراسة	يُدَرِّس	التَّدْريس
يكتُب	الكتابة	يُشاهِد	المُشاهَدة
يقرَأ	القراءة	يُسافِر إلى	السَّفَر إلى
يشعُر بـ	الشُّعور بـ	يُحِبّ	الحُبّ
يحصُل على	الحُصول على	يتخرَّج	التَّخرُّج
يعرف	المَعرِفة	يتَذكَّر	التَّذَكُّر
يَعمَل	العَمَل	يَتَكَلَّم	الكَلام
يَسكُن	السَّكَن	يَستَمِع إلى	الاستِماع إلى

[1]Note that المصدر is a **noun**, not an adjective: in English we use the suffix *-ing* for both, as in *I am traveling* and *Traveling is fun*. The مصدر can only be used for the **latter**; it corresponds to what is called in English grammar *gerund*.

The مـصـدر is usually used (a) after a main verb to give the meaning of the infinitive or (b) as an abstract noun. Below are some examples of contexts in which you can use المصدر . Note that all of the مصادر are definite, but the ones in (٣) and (٤) do not have الـ because each is the first term of an إضافة :

١ـ أدرس قبل الذهاب الى الصف .

٢ـ <u>السفر</u> بالأوتوبيس صعب!

٣ـ أحبّ <u>دراسة</u> اللغات .

٤ـ لا أحب <u>مشاهدة</u> التليفزيون .

تمرين ٦   المصدر (في البيت)

READ THE FOLLOWING SENTENCES AND FOR EACH (A) UNDERLINE المصدر AND (B) DETERMINE HOW IT IS BEING USED AS IN THE EXAMPLE. PAY ATTENTION TO iDAAFAS.

مثال: لا أحب <u>كتابة</u> الرسائل. *to write letters (literally, the writing of letters)*

١ـ هل تحبّين السَّكَن في نيويورك ؟

٢ـ أستمع إلى الكلمات قبل قراءتها.

٣ـ صديقتي مشغولة بكتابة الواجب.

٤ـ أذهب الى المكتبة لقراءة الأخبار.

٥ـ الشُعور بالوحدة صعب جداً.

٦ـ هل تدرس للحصول على الدكتوراه؟

٧ـ والد مها يحب العَمَل في الامم المتحدة.

٨ـ أستاذتنا لا تحبّ التّدريس في الصباح.

٩ـ شرب القهوة في الصباح جميل!

١٠ـ هل تحبّون مُشاهَدة الأفلام العربية ؟

تمرين ٧   المصدر والفعل المضارع (في الصف)

HOW WOULD YOU EXPRESS THE FOLLOWING IN ARABIC? IN SOME CASES YOU WILL USE المصدر AND IN OTHERS فعل مضارع ; DETERMINE WHICH IS CORRECT FOR EACH CONTEXT AND TRANSLATE:

1. I like to travel.
2. We like studying Arabic.
3. He is working now, before obtaining a degree.
4. I sometimes study at home, but studying at the library is best.
5. My mother doesn't like to write letters.
6. When are you graduating?
7. She likes to speak Arabic.
8. Do you like to go to the movies (السينما)?
9. All of us like to watch movies.
10. Are you traveling this week?

تمرين ٨ ماذا يحبون / لا يحبون ؟ (في الصف)

USE المصدر TO EXPRESS WHAT YOU DO/NOT LIKE TO DO. ASK YOUR زملاء WHAT THEY LIKE (TO DO) AND WRITE THE BEST ANSWERS HERE:

١- ____ .

٢- ____ .

٣- ____ .

٤- ____ .

٥- ____ .

٦- ____ .

٧- ____ .

٨- ____ .

❁ لماذا؟

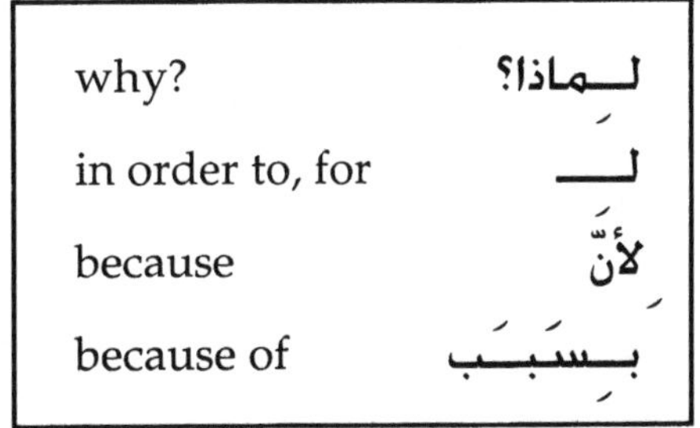

why?	لماذا؟
in order to, for	لِـ
because	لأنَّ
because of	بِسَبَب

For the first time in this chapter, we will begin working with complex sentences, that is, sentences that contain more than one clause. As we move beyond simple sentence patterns, it will become increasingly important for you to think grammatically about sentence construction. The structures of Arabic sentences are easy to understand and produce if you learn to think according to step-by-step construction, in which each "piece" of the sentence will tell you what kind of grammatical structure comes next. This information will be given to you in the vocabulary lists and grammar sections of each chapter. For example, in this chapter you saw: بسبب + اسم في إضافة . This explanation tells you what needs to follow بسبب in any sentence you construct.

You now know three ways to answer the question, لماذا ؟ *why?*, or to give information about reasons or purposes. However, while the meanings of these particles are similar, their grammatical usages are quite distinct. Memorize the way in which each word or particle is used in context in addition to its dictionary meaning.

١ـ لِـ + المصدر / المضارع *in order to*

لِـ is used to express a reason/purpose for doing something, and corresponds to the English *in order to* or *for*.[1] In this construction لـ may be followed by a مصدر, which should be **definite**, either with الـ or in إضافة, or it may be followed by a فعل مضارع. Both constructions mean the same thing; المصدر tends to be a bit more formal in style than المضارع. The following pairs of examples are equivalent in meaning:

أدرس للحصول على بكالوريوس .	=	أدرس لأحصُل على بكالوريوس .
يذهبون إلى المكتبة للدراسة .	=	يذهبون إلى المكتبة ليدرسوا .
تستمع إلى الـ DVD لحِفظ الكلمات .	=	تستمع إلى الـ DVD لتحفظ الكلمات .

٢ـ بسبب (في إضافة) *because of*

بِسَبَب followed by a noun or noun phrase forms an إضافة (سَبَب *reason* is the first noun of الإضافة):

أمثلة: لا أحب نيويورك بسبب الازدحام. *because of the overcrowding*

نحب الصيف بسبب الجو الجميل. *because of the beautiful weather*

Remember that بسبب cannot be followed by a sentence.

٣ـ لأنّ + جملة اسمية *because*

لأنّ is used to give an explanation that requires a full sentence, such as *the weather is cold* or *she is sick*. This construction corresponds to English *because* and must be followed by a جملة اسمية.

أمثلة: لا أحب بوسطن لأنّ الجو فيها بارد في الشتاء. *because the weather there is cold*

لا تذهب إلى الكلية هذا الأسبوع لأنّها مريضة. *because she is sick*

Note that, if الجملة الاسمية that follows لأنّ begins with a pronoun, as the second example immediately above shows, **the pronoun must be attached to** لأنّ as the following chart shows:

---

[1] **Do not confuse** *in order to* **with infinitive** *to* in phrases such as *I like to read*. Always ask yourself: does this *to* answer the question لماذا؟ .

because I ...	لأِنّي / لأِنَّني	لأنّ + أنا <--
because you...	لأِنَّكَ ، لأِنَّكِ	لأنّ + أنتَ ِ <--
because he/it...	لأِنَّهُ	لأنّ + هو <--
because she/it...	لأِنَّها	لأنّ + هي <--
because we...	لأِنَّنا	لأنّ + نحن <--
because you...	لأِنَّكُم	لأنّ + أنتم <--
because they...	لأِنَّهُم	لأنّ + هم <--

تمرين ٩ لماذا؟ (في البيت)

GIVE REASONS FOR THE FOLLOWING USING لـ , لأنّ OR بسبب :

١- زوجي دائمًا تعبان ______ شغل البيت .

٢- لا يحب الصيف ______ الجو فيه دائمًا حارّ .

٣- لا أعمل الآن ______ عندي امتحانات هذا الاسبوع .

٤- أختي تدرس ______ الحصول على الدكتوراه .

٥- نحب السفر إلى الشرق الأوسط ______ الدراسة .

٦- مها تشعر بالوحدة ______ والدها ووالدتها مشغولان دائمًا .

٧- لا أتذكر أسماء كل أقاربي ______ عائلتي كبيرة .

٨- لا يذهبون إلى السينما ______ مشغولون بالدراسة .

٩- أحب هذه المنطقة ______ طقسها الجميل .

١٠- نذهب إلى غرفة صديقتي ______ مشاهدة برنامج «الأصدقاء» .

تمرين ١٠ لماذا؟ (في الصف)

DECIDE WHICH CONSTRUCTION (لـِ , لأنّ , OR بسبب) TO USE TO EXPRESS THE REASON FOR OR PURPOSE OF EACH ACTION, THEN TRANSLATE AS MUCH OF THE SENTENCE AS YOU CAN INTO ARABIC.

1. I'm studying Arabic to speak with Arabs. ____________________
2. I like her because she's a nice woman. ____________________
3. They are going to the library to watch the video. ____________________
4. We like Arabic because it's so easy. ____________________
5. Maha doesn't like New York because of its weather. ____________________
6. Do you drink coffee to study at night? ____________________
7. He married her because of her money. ____________________
8. Are you writing these words to memorize them? ____________________
9. We will go by car because the restaurant is quite far. ____________________
10. She is not going because she is busy with her friends. ____________________

تمرين ١١ لماذا؟ (في البيت)

COMPLETE, GIVING REASONS OR PURPOSES FOR THE FOLLOWING:

١- أشعر أحياناً بالوحدة ____________________ .

٢- خالد لا يذهب إلى الجامعة كل يوم ____________________ .

٣- مها تدرس في جامعة نيويورك ____________________ .

٤- لا أتذكر كل الكلمات ____________________ .

٥- أحب الربيع ____________________ .

٦- أدرس العربية ____________________ .

٧- احبّ جامعتي ____________________ .

٨- لا أسكن في بيت عائلتي الآن ____________________ .

٩- مها تحب السفر إلى مصر ____________________ .

تمرين ١٢ نشاط كتابة أو محادثة (في الصف)

WOULD YOU RECOMMEND YOUR SCHOOL TO A PROSPECTIVE STUDENT FROM AN ARAB COUNTRY? DRAFT A "TOP TEN" LIST GIVING AS MANY REASONS AS YOU CAN لماذا / لماذا لا .

تمرين ١٣ كتابة

WRITE A STORY ABOUT THE WOMAN IN THESE PICTURES (GO RIGHT TO LEFT). USE AS MANY VERBS AS YOU CAN.

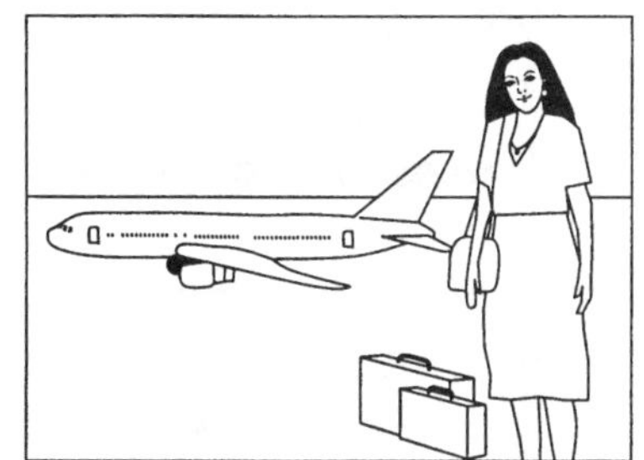

تمرين ١٤ نشاط قراءة

تعلموا هذه الكلمات:

مَطعَم ج. مَطاعِم	restaurant
عَشاء	dinner
بَرنامَج ج. بَرامِج	program

أسئلة :

١- اسم المطعم وعنوانه: ______________________

٢- أيام الاسبوع it is open ______________________

٣- الأكل served ______________________

البرنـــامج اليومــى
فى
مطعم البراسيرى
يومياً ... بوفيه جديد
السبت
ليالى الـ ستيك الأمريكي
عشاء فقط
الثلاثـاء
ليالى الشرق الأقصى
عشاء فقط
الأحـد
ليالى لبنانية
عشاء فقط
الأربعـاء
ليالى إيطالية
عشاء فقط
الإثنيـن
أسماك ومأكولات بحرية
عشاء فقط
الخميس
ليالى مصرية
عشاء فقط
الجمعة
بوفيه البرانش للعائلة
مع برنامج خاص للأطفال
س ١١ صباحاً إلى ٣ مساءاً
مريديان
القاهرة
كورنيش النيل - جاردن سيتي - تليفون : ٣٦٢١٧١٧

الثقافة

الأكل العربي DVD

The rich regional cuisines of the Arab world reflect the long history of civilization in the Middle East and the Mediterranean, and include contributions from Persian, Turkish, and indigenous cultures. Rice in the Gulf and rice and/or bread in Egypt and the Levant are part of every meal, except in North Africa, where couscous and bread are staples. You have probably eaten حُمُّص , كَباب and تَبّولة in a Middle Eastern restaurant. Other popular dishes include salads, vegetable stews flavored with beef or lamb, rice and meat, and various beans and legumes. Most dishes are spiced with garlic, onion, lemon, parsley, and/or and cumin. Listen to your DVD to learn some basic terms.

تمرين ١٥ نشاط قراءة ومحادثة

The next two pages contain excerpts from a menu from Maroush, a Lebanese restaurant in Cairo. Take a couple of your زملاء to this restaurant and order a complete meal for everyone, including drinks, appetizers, main dishes and desserts. Your teacher will be your waiter and will be able to explain some of the dishes if you ask. See if you can guess the meaning of abbreviations ص and ك.

ساندوتشات مروش

*شيش طاووق ———— ٥و٢٥
*شاورمة لحم ———— ٤و٠٠
*شاورمة دجاج ———— ٤و٥٠
*كبدة مروش ———— ٤و٠٠
*فلافل ———— ٢و٥٠
*لبنة ———— ٣و٠٠
*كلوب ساندوتش ————
- لحم /دجاج ———— ١٢و٥٠
- جبنة حارة ———— ٨و٠٠

الطلبات الخاصة (بالطلب)

*ديك رومي مع الأرز والمكسرات ———— ٣٥/٣٠ للكيلو
*سمك حار بالطحينة والمكسرات ———— ٤٥ / للكيلو
*كبة بالصينية مع الزبادي ———— ١٨ / للطلب

المشروبات الساخنة

*قهوة تركي /قهوة لبناني ———— ٢و٧٥
*قهوة بيضاء ———— ١و٧٥
*شاي ———— ٢و٧٥
*نعناع ———— ١و٧٥
*كابتشينو /نسكافيه /كاكاو باللبن ———— ٤و٠٠
*سحلب بالمكسرات ———— ٤و٧٥

المشروبات المثلجة والعصائر

*كوكتيل مروش ———— ٦و٠٠
*عصير ليمون /عصير برتقال ———— ٣و٥٠
*عصير موز باللبن /عصائر فواكه الموسم ———— ٤و٥٠
*عيران ———— ٤و٥٠
*تمر هندي /كركديه ———— ٢و٥٠
*المشروبات الغازية بأنواعها (كولا /شويبس /صودا /تونيك)
- زجاجة ———— ٢و٠٠
- علبة ———— ٣و٧٥
*مياه معدنية (ص /ك) ———— ١و٧٥/٢و٧٥

الحلو

*ارز باللبن والمكسرات ———— ٤و٥٠
*كريم كرامل ———— ٥و٠٠
*شعيبيات ———— ٤و٠٠
*أم علي ———— ٦و٥٠
*ليالي لبنان ———— ٦و٥٠

شيشة مروش ———— ٤,٠٠

٦٤ ميدان لبنان - المهندسين - الجيزة

تليفون / ٣٤٦٦٨٩١ / ٣٤٦٦٨٩١ / فاكس / ٣٠٤٦٩٨٠

مطعم مروش

السلطات اللبنانية والمقبلات

*حمص - متبل - بابا غنوج - تبولة - فتوش - لبنة - محمرة
لبن زبادي بالخيار - كبيس وزيتون - شنكليش - خضرة طازجة ٤و٧٥
*محشي ورق عنب بالزيت (بارد) ———— ٥و٠٠
*كبة نية ———— ٢و٠٠
*حمص مروش باللحم ———— ٨و٠٠
*كبة مقلية ———— ٢و٠٠
*فول /فلافل مروش ———— ٥و٠٠
* حمص بليلة ———— ٣و٢٥

المعجنات

*السمبوسك (لحم - جبن - سبانخ) ———— ١و٨٥
*فطائر (مروش - جبنة-سبانخ) ———— ٤و٠
*مناقيش (بالزعتر /بالجبن) ———— ٤و٠٠
*صفيحة - لحم بعجين ———— ٤و٧٥
*لبنة بخبز على الصاج ———— ٤و٠٠
*بيتزا مروش
حجم وسط ———— ٧و٠٠
حجم كبير ———— ١٢و٠٠
*خبز مروش ———— ٥٠و

أطباق ساخنة ومشويات من مطبخ مروش

*مقانق مروش ———— ١٨و٠٠
*كبدة مروش ———— ١٦و٠٠
*قطع دجاج مروش بالمشروم ———— ٢٢و٠٠
*كبة لبنية مع الأرز ———— ١٨و٠٠
*خضروات الموسم بالموزة مع الأرز ———— ١٨و٠٠
*فيليه لحم مع صلصة المشروم /الفلفل ———— ٢٢و٠٠
*محشي ورق عنب ساخن ———— ١٢و٠٠
*فتة موزة - فتة ملوخية - فتة كوارع - فتة دجاج ———— ١٨و٠٠
*فتة حمص ———— ٨و٠٠
*اسكالوب دجاج (يقدم مع الأرز والبطاطس المحمرة) ———— ٢٠و٠٠
*أرز بالكبد والكلاوي ———— ٦و٥٠
*مكرونة بصلصة بولونيز /نابوليتان ———— ٦و٥٠
*بطاطس محمرة ———— ٣و٠٠

أطباق المشويات على الفحم

*كفتة ———— ١٨و٠٠
*شيش طاووق ———— ٢٠و٠٠
*فيليه لحم ———— ٢٢و٠٠
*حمام مشوي (عدد ٢) ———— ٢٠و٠٠
*دجاج مشوي (١/٢ دجاجة) ———— ١٢و٥٠
*شاورمة لحم (ص /ك) ———— ١٠و٠٠ / ١٦و٠٠
*شاورمة دجاج (ص /ك) ———— ١٢و٠٠ / ٢٠و٠٠

تمارين المراجعة

تمرين ١٦ مفردات *Vocabulary*

In each group, cross out the word that does not fit:

١-	الاحد	الاثنين	الخريف	الخميس
٢-	مترجم	ضابط	معيد	صديق
٣-	زميل	ابن	زوج	بنت
٤-	جو	ازدحام	رطوبة	طقس
٥-	كلية	جامعة	مدرسة	دبلوم
٦-	لأنّ	لذلك	بالنسبة لِـ	بسبب
٧-	فعلاً	نهارًا	صباحاً	مساءً
٨-	أتذكر	أحفظ	أعرف	أسكن
٩-	كلية	منطقة	مدينة	شارع
١٠-	مشمس	مشغول	ممطر	غائم

تمرين ١٧ هذا/هذه

Complete the sentences with the Arabic equivalent of the phrases in parentheses.

١- لا أحبّ السكن في ______________ . *(This old house)*

٢- ______________ الأسبوع الرابع. *(This is)*

٣- ______________ قهوة عربية؟ *(Is this?)*

٤- ______________ تدرّس التاريخ الأوروبي. *(This new professor)*

٥- ماذا تدرسون في ______________ ؟ *(this college)*

٦- ______________ عندي صفوف صعبة جداً! *(This semester)*

٧- في ______________ ٧ طلاب فقط. *(this small class)*

٨- ______________ المكتبة؟ *(Is this)*

٩- أحبّ الأكل في ______________ . *(This excellent restaurant)*

١٠- زملائي يسكنون في ______________ . *(This area)*

تمرين ١٨ | استمعوا إلى خالد واكتبوا : DVD

أنا خالد ______________ أبو العلا ، ______________ في كلية ______________

بجامعة القاهرة، تخرّجت ______________ ______________ وأدرس الآن ______________

______________ ماجستير في إدارة ______________ . ______________ ______________

ثلاثة ______________ فقط في ______________ ، ولا ______________ ______________

______________ في كليتنا لا ______________ ، لذلك ______________ ______________

الكلية أيام ______________ و______________ و______________ فقط .

العامية DVD

- القصة: "انا خالد"

WATCH خالد INTRODUCE HIMSELF IN COLLOQUIAL.

What word does he use for فقط ?

- "تشربوا حاجة الأول؟"

WATCH THE SCENE IN A RESTAURANT.

What phrase do you hear repeated?

تذكروا هذه الكلمات

السكن	المعرفة	الدراسة	القراءة	الكتابة
الحصول على	المشاهدة	الحبّ	التخرج	الكلام
الاستماع الى	الشعور بـ	برنامج	عشاء	دَجاج
مطعم ج. مطاعِم	سَمَك	لحَم	سَلَطة	شوربة
أرُز	زَيت	خُضار	فَواكِه	

٧. أنا أكبرهم

في هذا الدرس:

القصة
- أسرة خالد

الثقافة
- الثانوية العامة
- العملات العربية
- ما هي هواياتك؟ ، كرة القدم

القواعد
- لِـ وعند ومع
- الجملة الاسمية: الخبر المقدم
- كان
- كم ؟ بكم ؟ الأعداد ١-١٠

القراءة
- وفاة
- أصدقاء المراسلة

الاستماع
- مع العائلة والأصدقاء

العامية
- القصة: «انا اكبرهم»
- «حاموت من الجوع»

المفردات DVD

first	أُولى (مؤنث ؛ مذكر: أوّل)
secondary	ثانَوِيّ / ة
Baccalaureate (see below in الثقافة)	الثّانَويّة العامّة
grandfather (plural: ancestors)	جَدّ ج. أجداد
grandmother	جَدّة ج. -ات
accident	حادِث ج. حَوادِث
preparatory (school, = junior high)	إعْداديّ
general, public (adjective)	عامّ / ة
(she) lives	تَعيش
economics, economy	الاِقتِصاد
the biggest or oldest	أكبر + اسم في إضافة
the oldest of them	أكْبَرهم
she/it was	كانَت
(she) died	ماتَت
ministry	وِزارة ج. -ات

تمرين ١ كلمات جديدة (في الصف)

You have learned two words that have superlative meaning: أحسن (فصل) and أكبر (وَلَد). Note that these words share a pattern. The following sentences give you similar words; expand your vocabulary by using analogy to determine the meaning of these sentences.

١- خالد أكبَر ولد في أسرته.

٢- بالنسبة لي، «سان فرانسيسكو» أجمَل مدينة في أمريكا.

٣- «هارفارد» أقدَم جامعة أمريكية .

٤- الأحد هو أوّل يوم في الاسبوع .

٥- أبْرَد طقس في أمريكا في آلاسكا.

تمرين ٢ الكلمات الجديدة (في البيت)

Practice using new vocabulary. Remember to put each word in its correct form.

١- والدتي تدرّس اللغة الفرنسية في مدرسة ____________ .

٢- أنا ____________ ولد في الاسرة ولي أخ صغير وأخت صغيرة.

٣- مات أمريكيون كثيرون في ____________ سيارات هذه السنة .

٤- نسكن في البناية ____________ في هذا الشارع .

٥- ____________ صديقتي هُدى تسكن معي في نفس البيت قبل سفرها إلى السعودية.

٦- في أيام الطفولة، كنت ____________ مع جدي وجدتي في الصيف .

٧- أحب دراسة ____________ لكنه صعب !

٨- طلاب السنة ____________ في الجامعة يسكنون في هذه البيوت .

٩- ____________ زوجته منذ سنة، ولذلك فهو يشعر بالوحدة الآن .

١٠- النبي محمد والد السيدة فاطمة و____________ الحَسَن والحُسين .

١١- في مدينة نيويورك مكتبة ____________ كبيرة وممتازة فيها كتب بلغات كثيرة.

١٢- زوج عمّتي موظف كبير في ____________ العمل *Labor* في واشنطن دي سي.

تمرين ٣ اسألوا زملاءكم (في الصف)

A. Find out from زملاءك :

1. Whose car died this year?
2. Who was in a car accident this year? Where? Was it a big one?
3. With whom do they live?
4. How is the U.S. economy [doing] now in their opinion?
5. Who knows where the Department of Labor (=Ministry of Work) is?
6. Who is in their first year of college?
7. Where do their grandparents live?
8. Where are their ancestors from?
9. Do they go to the public library in their hometown?

B. With a partner, list in Arabic the full names of all the schools you both studied in. Think about how you would order the nouns and adjectives.

الثقافة

ما هي الثانويّة العامّة بالنسبة لك؟ DVD

In many Arab countries, الثانوية العامّة refers to both the last year of high school and the set of examinations students take at the end of that year. The exams are cumulative, covering all subjects studied throughout high school, and students' scores on these exams determine whether or not they will graduate, and in what college they may enroll. Cut-off scores are very high for Medicine, Engineering, and the sciences in general. Students face tremendous pressure to perform well on these exams, and this pressure can affect the entire family. Watch the interviews on your DVD to hear people describe what it is like.

القصة DVD

تمرين ٤ **شاهدوا واكتبوا:**

١- من يتكلّم ؟

٢- عَمَّ (=عن ماذا، *about what*) يتكلم ؟

شاهدوا مرة ثانية:

٣- مَن في اسرة خالد ؟ من يعيش معهم ؟

٤- من ماتَ ؟ منذ كَم *how many* سنة ؟

٥- ماذا نعرف عن والد خالد ؟

٦- أين يدرس إخوة خالد؟ اكتبوا :

الأخ	الاسم	المدرسة
١		
٢		
٣		

استمعوا وخمّنوا:

٧- لماذا يَقول *say* خالد « الله يَرحَمها »؟ What do you think this means?

8. The English equivalent of مُنذُ depends on the tense of the verbs that precede and follow it. Translate:

أ - والدتي ماتَت منذ ثلاث سنوات ____________________

ب - جدتي تعيش معنا منذ ماتت والدتي ____________________

القواعد

❁ لِـ وعِند ومع + الضمائر

The pronoun forms used with prepositions are essentially the same as the possessive forms given in Chapter 3. The following charts give these endings with prepositions denoting possession. Listen and repeat: DVD

مَعَنا	مَعي
مَعَكُم	مَعَكَ مَعَكِ
مَعَهُم	مَعَهُ مَعَها

عِندَنا	عِندي
عِندَكُم	عِندَكَ عِندَكِ
عِندَهُم	عِندَهُ عِندَها

لَنا	لي
لَكُم	لَكَ لَكِ
لَهُم	لَهُ لَها

As its meaning implies, مع indicates physical possession of a thing at the time of speaking:

Do you have ... with you? معكم قلم؟ معك دولار؟

While لـ and عِند overlap a great deal in spoken Arabic, each of these prepositions has a slightly different connotation in formal Arabic: لِـ is used to describe human relationships or possession of highly abstract entities one cannot physically possess, such as *a past* or *a future*, while عند denotes straightforward possession. Some speakers of Arabic use عند for human relationships as well.

(she/he) has ... لها أصدقاء كثيرون. خالد له ثلاثة أخوة.

Do you have ... عندك سيارة؟ عندك كمبيوتر في البيت؟

Note that these prepositions are not used to describe places or institutions, as in phrases like *the university* or *our house has.*[1] Rather, Arabic uses the preposition في to express non-human "possession:"

في بيتنا ثلاث غرف كبيرة. الجامعة فيها خمس كليات.

---

[1]However, لِـ may be used to attribute highly abstract qualities to things, such as:

الجامعة لها تاريخ طويل.

For now, focus on using في when describing inanimate objects.

In modern formal Arabic, this kind of sentence is negated with the verb لَيسَ , which you will learn in Chapter 8. In spoken Arabic, many dialects negate these prepositions with ما . For example:

I don't have ...	ما معي قلم .	ما معي دولار .
I don't have ...	ما عندي سيارة .	ما عندي كمبيوتر .

تمرين ٥ عند ولـ ومع (في البيت)

USE THESE PREPOSITIONS TO EXPRESS RELATIONSHIPS OF POSSESSION, ASSOCIATION, AND ACCOMPANIMENT AMONG HUMANS AND OBJECTS:

١- والده ــــــــــــــ فلوس كثيرة . (عند + هو)

٢- ــــــــــــــ أقارب في عمّان . (لـ + نحن)

٣- يا ريما! هل كتابك ــــــــــــــ ؟ (مع + انتِ)

٤- ليلى ــــــــــــــ أربعة أولاد . (لـ + هي)

٥- ــــــــــــــ واجبات كثيرة اليوم ! (عند + نحن)

٦- هل ــــــــــــــ سؤال ؟ (عند + انتم)

٧- كنتُ ــــــــــــــ في نفس المدرسة . (مع + هم)

٨- ما هو أحسن عمل بالنسبة ــــــــــــــ ؟ (لـ + انتَ)

٩- ــــــــــــــ ١٠ دولارات فقط . (مع + أنا)

١٠- سامي ــــــــــــــ خال يعمل في الجيش . (لـ + هو)

NOW WRITE SENTENCES OF YOUR OWN USING لـ , مع , AND عند WITH PRONOUNS:

١١- ــ .

١٢- ــ .

١٣- ــ .

١٤- ــ .

Fronted Predicate ❁ الجملة الاسمية: الخبر المقدم

You have seen both عند and لـ used to indicate possession, as in:

لي خالة اسمها نادية .　　　　　عندي سيّارة .

These words are used to express a verbal concept, *to have*, but are not themselves verbs. Grammatically, they are prepositional phrases, and the sentences in which they occur are جمل اسمية.[1] In this kind of الجملة الاسمية, the order of المبتدأ and الخبر is reversed and الخبر is fronted. In the examples above, عند and لـ begin the sentences even though they belong to الخبر. This word order must be maintained because **an Arabic sentence may not begin with an indefinite noun.**

there; there is/are	هُناكَ

In Arabic, the reversed جملة اسمية is often used to express the concept *to have* and the English construction *there is/there are*. In these kinds of sentences, الخبر usually consists of a prepositional phrase (with لِـ , عند , في or مع) or the word هُناكَ *there*, as the following examples demonstrate:

There are many students in this class.	في هذا الصف طلاب كثيرون .
There is only one daughter/girl in my family.	في أسرتي بنت واحدة فقط .
There are many Egyptians in the Emirates.	هناك مصريون كثيرون في الإمارات .

The following diagrams show the grammatical structure of reversed جملة اسمية :

في هذا الصف طلاب كثيرون. <—— في هذا الصف (الخبر) طلاب كثيرون (المبتدأ).

في أسرتي بنت واحدة فقط. <—— في أسرتي (الخبر) بنت واحدة (المبتدأ) فقط.

هناك مصريون كثيرون في الإمارات. <—— هناك (الخبر) مصريون كثيرون (المبتدأ) في الإمارات.

[1]To understand how this kind of sentence works, think of a "grammatical translation" for the two examples given: *An aunt named Nadia is belonging-to-me* and *A car is at-me.*

تمرين ٦ الجملة الاسمية (في الصف)

IDENTIFY المبتدأ والخبر IN THE FOLLOWING SENTENCES (IGNORE ADJECTIVES AND ADVERBS):

١ـ له صديق واحد فقط .

٢ـ في اسرتي خمسة أولاد .

٣ـ عندهم محاضرات اليوم .

٤ـ هل عندك صفّ الآن ؟

٥ـ هناك ٢٥ جامعة وكلية في مدينة بوسطن .

٦ـ لنا أصدقاء لبنانيون وفلسطينيون .

٧ـ في هذا البيت غرفة كبيرة جدا .

٨ـ في مدرستنا خمس طالبات فرنسيات .

٩ـ في هذه الصورة كل أفراد عائلتي .

تمرين ٧ الجملة الاسمية (في البيت)

ASSIGN THE FOLLOWING TO PEOPLE AS YOU SEE FIT:

مثال: صديقة واحدة فقط —> مها لها صديقة واحدة فقط .

١ـ واجبات وامتحانات كثيرة: ______________________ .

٢ـ مكتب واسع: ______________________ .

٣ـ صفوف صعبة: ______________________ .

٤ـ أعمام وأخوال: ______________________ .

٥ـ محاضرات كل يوم: ______________________ .

٦ـ أقارب يعيشون في لبنان: ______________________ .

٧ـ زملاء عرب: ______________________ .

❁ كان

The verb كانَ is used to situate actions and states in the past, as these examples show:

I was	كُنتُ طالبة .	<—	أنا طالبة .
she was	كانَت استاذة .	<—	هي استاذة .
we used to	كُنّا ندرس اللغة الألمانية .	<—	ندرس اللغة الألمانية .

In all of these examples, the effect of كانَ is to place the action or state into the past. Note that كان in conjugated according to its subject. Learn the conjugation of this verb:

DVD

(نحن) كُنّا	(أنا) كُنتُ
(أنتم) كُنْتُم	(أنتَ) كُنْتَ (أنتِ) كُنْتِ
(هم) كانوا	(هو) كانَ (هي) كانَت

When the verb كانَ is used to put possessive and *there is/are* sentences in the past, it is often used as an impersonal verb that puts the sentence **as a whole** into the past. In these cases it precedes everything and remains **fixed** as كـان , not agreeing with anything in the sentence.[1] Examples:

كان معي ١٠ دولارات!	<—	معي ١٠ دولارات.
كان في هذه المنطقة مدرسة واحدة فقط.	<—	في هذه المنطقة مدرسة واحدة فقط.

Memorize these phrases: كان هناك – كان عند .. – كان لـ .. – كان معـ ..

---

[1]In formal Arabic, you will find another variation of agreement in which the verb كان agrees with the grammatical مبتدأ of the sentence, which is not the possessor but the thing possessed. Study the example, in which كانت agrees not with logical English subject *I*, but with the grammatical Arabic subject سيارة (*A car was at-me*). Remember that سيارة, not عندي, is المبتدأ.

I had	كانَت عندي سيارة .	<—	عندي سيارة .

The verb كان may be negated using ما , as these examples demonstrate:

we did not have ما كان عندنا كمبيوتر منذ سنة.

were you not لماذا ما كُنتَ في الصف يوم الجمعة؟

تمرين ٨

SITUATE THESE ACTIONS AND STATES IN THE PAST BY USING THE CORRECT FORM OF كان :

١- ــــــــ أسكن في تلك البناية منذ سنتين.

٢- يا ليلى، أين ــــــــ صباح اليوم ؟

٣- والدتها ــــــــ موظفة كبيرة في الامم المتحدة .

٤- أنا وزملائي ــــــــ نستمع إلى المحاضرة، وقبل ذلك ــــــــ نأكل في الكافتيريا.

٥- ــــــــ الازدحام في هذا الشارع كبيراً جداً اليوم .

٦- يوم السبت ويوم الأحد ــــــــ عندي شغل كثير.

٧- ما ــــــــ الجو بارداً قبل أسبوع .

٨- هل ــــــــ تدرسون اللغة الاسبانية؟

٩- ــــــــ يذهبون إلى السينما كثيراً.

١٠- ــــــــ الرسالة على مكتبي في الصباح.

١١- ــــــــ عندنا امتحان كبير منذ أسبوع.

تمرين ٩ **اسألوا زملاءكم: (في الصف)**

FIND OUT FROM YOUR CLASSMATES:

1. Where they were on Saturday.
2. Whether they had a car in high school.
3. Whether they had a lot of friends in high school.
4. What they used to like.
5. Where they used to live.
6. What they used to watch on television.

❁ كم ؟ ١-١٠

How many...? كَـم ؟ + المفرد

You have learned the numbers from one to ten. Now learn the following rules for requesting and giving quantities with these numbers:

أ ـ كم ؟

The interrogative particle كم؟ followed by a **singular noun** is used to ask about quantity. In formal Arabic, the noun is marked with تنوين الفتح .

أمثلة : كم يومًا في الاسبوع ؟ — كم فصلاً في السنة ؟

كم طالبًا في الصف ؟ — كم طالبةً في الصف ؟

ب ـ كم ؟ ١

The number واحـد/ة **is not used as a number** in counting objects. To express the quantity (١), the noun is used alone:

one girl بنت — *one school* مدرسة

واحد / واحدة may only be used as an **adjective** to emphasize **one and only one:**

عندي صديقة واحدة فقط . — معي دولار واحد فقط .

In this case, واحد / ة must **agree with and follow the noun.**

جـ ـ كم ؟ ٢

the dual المُـثـَنّى

The number اثنان/ اثنين is not used to count objects. To express the quantity *two,* you must add the ending ان / ـَيـْن to the singular noun.[1] This is called the dual, or المُـثـَنّى (from the word اثنان).

بنت ⟵ بنتانِ / بنتَيْنِ — فصل ⟵ فصلانِ / فصلَيْنِ

بيت ⟵ بيتانِ / بيتَيْنِ — صديقة ⟵ صديقتانِ / صديقتَيْنِ

جامعة ⟵ جامعتانِ / جامعتَيْنِ — سيّارة ⟵ سيّارتانِ / سيّارتَينِ

---

[1]In spoken Arabic, only ـَيـْن is used; learn to recognize انِ as a formal variant. The final kasra is pronounced only in formal contexts.

Remember that ة always changes to تـ when the مـثـنـى ending is added to it. Look at the words جامعة , صديقة , and سيارة above and note their مثنى forms, جامعتان/ جامعتين , صديقتان/صديقتين , and سيارتان/سيارتين , respectively.

Note that there exists a special form of المُثَنّى for أخ :

أخ —> أخَوان / أخَوَيْن

د ـ كم ؟ ٣-١٠

Numbers from three to ten take الجمع , as in the following:[1]

ثلاث بنات	أربعة فصول	ستّة أصدقاء
سبع جامعات	تسعة أسماء	خمس محاضرات

هـ ـ بِكم ؟

How much? (price)	بِكَم ؟

To ask about price, use بِـكَـم ؟ . In the response, the price itself is also given with the preposition بِـ :

بكم هذا الدفتر؟ — بدولارَيْن فقط!

بكم كيلو اللحم؟ — بثلاث دولارات.

بكم الهامبورغر مع البطاطس؟ — بثمانية دولارات.

الثقافة

العُملات العربية

Each Arab country has its own currency, and, although some of the names are common to several countries, the values of the currencies themselves differ. The names of these currencies are all foreign in origin. Some were borrowed from Greek and Latin, and date from the eighth century, when the Umayyad Caliph عَبد المَلك بن مَروان ordered the first Islamic coins minted. Others are more recent, reflecting European colonization of some Arab countries in the nineteenth and twentieth centuries. Go to your DVD and look at the pictures of currencies from various Arab countries. Identify the name and country of each, and look for any other information you can find.

---

[1]In formal Arabic, there are special rules for the form of the number, such that sometimes it is مذكر and other times مؤنث . For now, concentrate on using the plural noun with these numbers; you will learn the agreement rules later.

تمرين ١٠ بكم؟ (في الصف)

HAVE A (PRETEND) GARAGE SALE IN CLASS. BRING SOME ITEMS TO CLASS. IN TEAMS, WRITE OUT PRICE TAGS FOR ITEMS. IN SOME CASES YOU MAY WANT TO PRICE SMALL THINGS IN GROUPS, SUCH AS ثلاثة بدولار .

تمرين ١١ كم ؟ (في البيت)

SHOW HOW MANY:

مثال: أختي لها ٣ بنات . (بنت)

١- في هذا الفصل نقرأ ٧ ________ ________ . (كتاب، قصير)

٢- تسكن ١٠ ________ ________ في هذه البناية . (عائلة، عربي)

٣- في أسرة خالد ٤ ________ . (ولد)

٤- في لبنان ٤ ________ ________ . (مدينة، كبير)

٥- عندها ________ . (٢ ابن)

٦- في هذه الكلية ٩ ________ و٥ ________ . (استاذ، أستاذة)

٧- زوجة أحمد تتكلم ________ . (٢ لغة)

٨- في هذه المنطقة ٥ ________ ابتدائية . (مدرسة)

٩- أعمل في المكتبة مع ٣ ________ (زميل) و٥ ________ . (زميلة)

١٠- في السنة ٤ ________ : الربيع والصيف والخريف والشتاء . (فصل)

١١- كم ________ عندك اليوم ؟ (صف)

١٢- أعمل في المكتبة ٣ ________ في الاسبوع . (يوم)

١٣- لهذه البناية ٣ ________ . (باب)

١٤- هناك ٩ ________ و٧ ________ يعملون في هذا المكتب. (امرأة، رجل)

١٥- كم ________ تعرفون؟ (جار)

تمرين ١٢ **نشاط قراءة**

SKIM THE NEWS ARTICLE BELOW, LOOK FOR WORDS YOU KNOW, AND ANSWER AS WELL AS YOU CAN:

١- مَن؟ __________ أين؟ __________ متى *when*؟ __________

2. Skim the text and circle all instances of المثنّى (ignore the unrelated word ان).
   (Hint: check the plural of ضابط before you start.)
3. Find and underline five noun-adjective phrases, and bracket three إضافات .

فرنسا تعلن عن فقد ضابطين في الكويت

باريس: **رويتر** • قالت فرنسا امس الاول ان ضابطين من السلاح الجوي الفرنسي يخدمان في الكويت مفقودان وانها طلبت من العراق معلومات عنهما .

وقالت وزارة الدفاع في تصريح ان الرجلين مفقودان منذ مغادرتهما مدينة الكويت يوم الثلاثاء الماضي .

وقالت الوزارة : تشير الشواهد الى انهما ربما كانا في المنطقة الحدودية بين الكويت والعراق . وقد أجريت اتصالات دبلوماسية مع السلطات العراقية بهدف الحصول على معلومات عنهما.

والضابطان مساعدان فنيان للسلاح الجوي الكويتي .

من جريدة «عكاظ» السعودية، ١٩٩١

الاستماع DVD

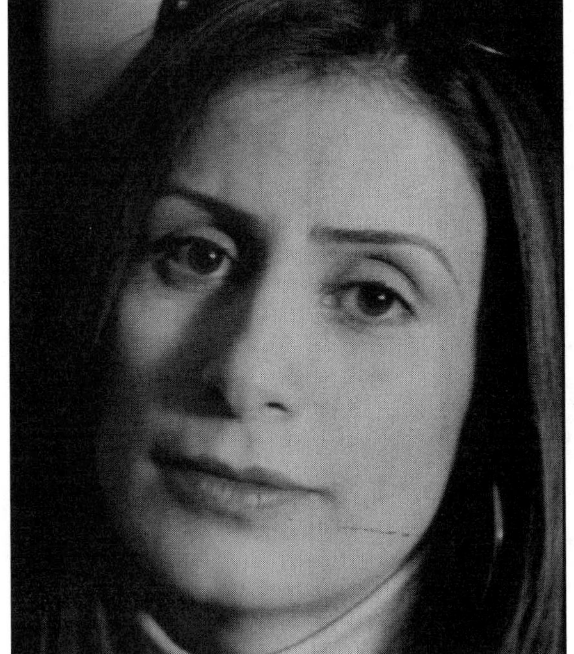

تمرين ١٣ **مع العائلة والاصدقاء**

خَجول / ة — shy
هـٰكَذا — in such a way

أسئلة:

١- من يتكلم؟ الاسم: __________
العمل: __________
عائلتها: __________

٢- كيف تعرف مها؟ وماذا تقول *say* عن مها؟

تعلموا هذه الكلمات:

هِـوايـة ج. ـات	hobby
الرِياضة	sports

الهوايات

كُرة السَّلّة

كُرة القَدَم

الكُرة الطائرة

الجَري

التَّزَلُّج

السِّباحة

الرَّقص

الموسيقى

القراءة

السينما

الرَّسم

التَّصوير

الثقافة DVD

ما هواياتك؟

Listen to interviews with some شباب مصريين about their هوايات on your DVD.

كُرة القَدَم

Soccer enjoys tremendous popularity throughout the Arab world. Since the sport requires little equipment, children can play it in the street or an empty lot using a ball or even a tin can. Regional, national, and international matches and playoffs are televised to national audiences. Watch your DVD for some scenes from soccer games in Arabic.

تمرين ١٤ نشاط قراءة

MANY ARABIC MAGAZINES PROVIDE A PEN PAL LISTING SERVICE LIKE THE ONE ON THE FOLLOWING PAGE.

1. Look at the title of the page:

أصدقاء المراسلة

What does المراسلة mean?

SKIM THE ENTRIES ON THE FOLLOWING PAGE AND ANSWER:

2. What are the most popular هوايات ?

3. What is the range of ages and educational backgrounds?

4. Find as many female names as you can. Look for ى and ا in addition to ة . (There will be several others that do not have any of those letters; your teacher will help you find those.) Do هوايات البنات seem different in any way from هوايات الشباب ?

مجلة «كلمتنا» ٢٠٠٢/١١

الاسم	السن	الهوايات	الدراسة	العنوان
حسين ممدوح حسين	١٥	كرة السلة، الموسيقى الاجنبية	١ ثانوي	٣ ش حفني الطردي للنيل، القاهرة، ش٣
رفعت يونس	١٢	كرة القدم، السلة، المراسلة	٢ إعدادي	٥٠ ش السلام من السكة – ص.ب. ٣١١١١، طنطا
محمود محمد جميل	١٧	مشاهدة كرة القدم، الكمبيوتر	كلية الحقوق	ش سعد زغلول بجوار السجل المدني–دمنهور
هالة عادل سعد	١٧	الرسم، سماع الأغاني	٣ ثانوي	١٣ ش ابن الفرات، شبرا – مصر
نشوى حامد عبد اللطيف	١٧	القراءة، المراسلة، سماع الأغاني	ثانوية عامة	٣٩ ش خليفة – روض الفرج
رشا ممدوح حافظ	٢١	الموسيقى، القراءة	بكالوريوس تجارة	ش ٢٣ يوليو – مجمع السلام – مكتب ٥٢–٥٦ بور سعيد
أحمد محمد شاهين	١٧	المراسلة، الإنترنت، الشطرنج	حاسبات القاهرة	محافظة الغربية–قطور– بتاج – الرمز البريدي٣١٧٢٧
داليا محمد إبراهيم	١٦	سماع الأغاني والموسيقى والقراءة	الثالث الثانوي	الشرقية–إبراهيمية–الحبش–خلف مدرسة عمرو بن العاص
ريم أحمد محمود ملوخية	١٧	الإسكواش، السباحة، البيانو	ثالثة ثانوي	٢١ ش ملك حفني، فيكتوريا، الإسكندرية
سمر محمد خميس	١٦	مراسلة البنات فقط، الكمبيوتر	ثانوي	١٥ ش مصطفى كامل – سموحة – شقة٤٠٢ – الإسكندرية
أحمد محمد الشناوي	١٧	سماع الموسيقى، النت	ثانوية عامة	١٧ ش عبد المنعم حداد – كفر الزيات– الغربية–أمام مدرسة الثانوية بنين
هند محمد عطية	٢٠	القراءة، النت، سماع الموسيقى	فنون جميلة	٧٢ ش مصطفى كامل– طلمنج – برج التحرير– الإسكندرية
أيمن محمد زكي	٢٠	الموسيقى، القراءة	كلية العلوم	١٢ م ش عفان محرم اللاسلكي، الهرم
محمد زكريا عامر	٢٠	السينما، الرياضة، الموسيقى	تجارة	٤٣٦ ش جمال عبد الناصر–المندرة بحري– الإسكندرية
محمود أحمد سليمان	٢٥	جمع العملات، المراسلة، كرة القدم	دبلوم صنايع	الدقهلية – ميت سلسيل–قرية المباحث
محمد صلاح سالم	١٩	القراءة في مجال السياسة، الدين		كفر الشيخ – دسوق– ش الجيش – الكشلة –عمارة رفاعي عطوان
مي عبد المنعم خاطر	٢٠	الرحلات، النت، المراسلة	خدمة اجتماعية	١ سكة سندوب –مشعل – منزل أبو نمرة رقم ١ – المنصورة
فاطمة صبري رشيدي	٢٤	القراءة الدينية والأدبية والشعر	معهد إدارة وسكرتارية	قنطرة غمرة–رقم٥٦١ – غمرة – القاهرة كود بريد ١٢٧١
فريد صقر سيد	٨	الرسم، الكمبيوتر، القراءة	الثاني الابتدائي	٣ ش حمد ياسين، فيصل – مدينة النور–القاهرة
محمود محمد أحمد	١٧	سباق الدراجات، الرسم، السباحة	ثانوية عامة لغات	٩ ش جامع خضر، طوسون، شبرا
شريف كمال محمد	٣٠	سماع الموسيقى الهادئة	دراسات عليا ك. التربية	الإسكندرية، سموحة، ميدان مصطفى كامل، عمارة ١٣، ش ١٠
نهى أحمد السيد	١٨	القراءة، المراسلة، سماع الأغاني	كلية الآداب	٧٦ ش عمربن أبي ربيعة الحضرة القبلية–الإسكندرية
ثريا محمد جمال	١٨	الرسم، سماع الأغاني	كلية التجارة	ش جمال عبد الناصر القبلي، شبين الكوم–المنوفية
محمد صبري	١٨	المراسلة، الرسم، الموسيقى	كلية الهندسة	العزيزة – المنزلة – دقهلية
مؤمن درويش	٢٢	المراسلة، السفر، الرياضة		أسيوط ٧١١١١ – ص.ب ١٣٤
باسم حسن حامد	١٤	الكمبيوتر، التنس	١ ثانوي	٣٣ ش الشرفا، أحمد سعيد
هبة الله مصطفى	٢٢	القراءة، سماع الأغاني، المراسلة	ليسانس آداب	٣٦ ش د.أحمد إبراهيم– مدينة نصر– الدور ٣
محمد حسين جاد	١٩	القيادة، سماع الأغاني	كلية التجارة	السويس، ش بنك مصر– الدور ٣ – شقة ٥

تمرين ١٥ نشاط قراءة

كلمات مُفيدة *helpful* :

مَـرحوم /ة = فَـقيـد / ة	deceased
أَمْس	yesterday
شَقيق / ة	= أخ / أخت
حَـرَم	= زوجة
الحاجّ / الحاجّـة	title of respect for someone who has completed the pilgrimage to Mecca, الحجّ

A. Read the following text, taken from the obituaries, and find:

١- اسم المرحومة ____________________

٢- اسم زوج المرحومة ____________________

B. List two family names and three place names that recur in the text. (Look for a preposition that can indicate place.)

٣- أسماء عائلات: أ- ____________ ب- ____________

٤- أسماء مدن : أ - ____________ ب - ____________ جـ - ____________

5. When did the funeral take place?

C. Now go through the text again and examine the two uses of و : (a) instead of a comma, to list things, and (b) instead of a period, to mark the beginning of a new sentence. To distinguish between these uses, you must look carefully at the context. First, look for lists of names (e.g., a list of brothers and sisters), and bracket each list. Second, look for words that indicate familial relationships and use their grammatical context, i.e., جملة اسمية and إضافة , to help with the meaning. Find:

6. كم ابنًا وبنتًا لها ؟ Underline their names and titles.

7. Bracket the names of the grandchildren.

البقاء لله

إنتقلت الى رحمة الله تعالى امس

الحاجة

إنصاف إبراهيم الدسوقى

حرم

الحاج محمد السمنودى

والدة

المهندس مجدى السمنودى

صاحب مؤسسة السمنودى

للقوى الكهربائية بالقاهرة

ورئيس مجلس إدارة

الشركة الدولية للقوى الكهربائية

بالعاشر من رمضان

والمهندس محسن السمنودى بالسعودية والمهندس ماهر السمنودى ببلقاس والدكتورة موعظه السمنودى بجامعة عين شمس والسيدة مرفت السمنودى المحاسب بادارة مصر للبترول حرم المقدم محمد السيد ومديحة السمنودى حرم شوقى شلبى بادارة المقاولون العرب بالاسكندرية والمهندسة مؤمنة السمنودى بتليفونات المنصورة حرم المهندس قدرى ابو السعد ومكارم السمنودى حرم المرحوم محمد عبد الفتاح ببلقاس والفقيدة شقيقة المرحوم محمد فائق الدسوقى المدير العام بوزارة الرى والمرحوم المقدم السيد الدسوقى والمرحوم الدسوقى ابراهيم بالمجمعات الاستهلاكية بالقاهرة والمرحومة حرم الحاج على السمنودى وحرم على أبو المعاطى المقاول وخالة الدكتور عادل السمنودى المدرس بطب بنها وعلاء وعاطف وعصام وعناية على السمنودى ببلقاس وجدة مدحت مجدى السمنودى بتجارة القاهرة ومحمد واحمد مجدى السمنودى بعباس العقاد للغات واشرف شوقى بهندسة الأسكندرية ومحمد وهانى شوقى بالأسكندرية ودينا ودعاء محمد السيد بالمعادى واحمد ومدحت وايمن محمد عبد الفتاح وأحمد أبو المعاطى ببلقاس والفقيدة عمة المقدم محمد السيد الدسوقى ومحمود ومختار السيد الدسوقى بالقاهرة وصفوت محمد فائق الدسوقى بوزارة العدل بالكويت وهانى محمد فائق الدسوقى بادارة مستشفى بلقاس وحرم أشرف امام الجواهرجى وابراهيم الدسوقى بمؤسسة السمنودى بالقاهرة والسيد الدسوقى المدرس بالقاهرة والفقيدة قريبة ونسيبة عائلات خيره بالمنصورة بناروه ومشرع براس الخليج ومحجوب والطناحى بسمنود وابو المعاطى وابو السعد والبراوى وإسام ببلقاس

وقد شيعت الجنازة أمس الاثنين

تلغرافيا

بلقاس دقهلية

من: جريدة الاهرام ١٧/٣/١٩٩٢

تمارين المراجعة

تمرين ١٦ **مفردات**

COMPLETE, USING ANY APPROPRIATE WORD:

١- في الاسبوع سبعة ________ .

٢- سمير استاذ في ________ ثانوية .

٣- أنا ________ أسماء كل الطلاب في الصف .

٤- هذه الاستاذة ________ في اللغة المصرية القديمة .

٥- ________ من الجامعة منذ سنتين .

٦- صديقي رشيد أمريكي من ________ عربي .

٧- تكساس ________ كبيرة جدا .

٨- مها تذهب كل سنة إلى كاليفورنيا ________ تسكن خالتها .

٩- أحسن يوم بالنسبة لي هو ________ .

١٠- ________ خالتي -- الله يرحمها -- في سنة ١٩٩٩ .

١١- أنا ________ جدا اليوم بسبب الدراسة والعمل .

١٢- عم صديقي ________ كبير في ________ الحقوق بجامعة دمشق .

١٣- هذه رسالة من مكتب ________ بالجامعة .

١٤- الرطوبة في مدينة واشنطن ________ جدا في الصيف .

١٥- في اسرة خالد أربعة أبناء وخالد ________ .

تمرين ١٧ **تمرين قراءة**

ريم عَلوان طالبة في جامعة نيويورك حيث تدرس الكيمياء . ريم زميلة مها، وهي تعرف مها من الجامعة حيث كانت تدرس معها في صف تاريخ الشرق الأوسط. ريم لا تعرف مها جيّداً لأن مها لا تتكلم مع الطلاب في الجامعة كثيراً وتذهب الى بيتها بعد المحاضرات كل يوم.

والد ريم ووالدتها عراقيان، والدها من مدينة بغداد ووالدتها من مدينة الموصل. ريم تحب مدينة نيويورك كثيراً لأنها تسكن فيها منذ طفولتها.

تمرين ١٨ **ماذا يفعلون ؟**

USE THE VERBS YOU KNOW TO DESCRIBE WHAT THESE PEOPLE ARE DOING. REMEMBER TO MAKE THE VERB AGREE WITH ITS SUBJECT.

يعمل يسكن يدرّس يعيش يدرس يحبّ يشعر يحفظ يشاهد يستمع يقرأ يذهب

مثال: والدة مها تعمل في جامعة نيويورك .

١- زملائي في البيت ________ التليفزيون كثيرا.

٢- كنا ________ في هذه المنطقة منذ سنة .

٣- عمها أحمد الآن ________ العلوم السياسية في جامعة العين.

٤- ثلاثة من أصدقائي ________ في مطعم «ماكدونالد».

٥- هل تذهب إلى المغرب لِـ ________ اللغة العربية يا مارك؟

٦- في الصيف، ________ مع والدي ووالدتي في بيتنا في ميشيغان.

٧- يا مُنى ، هل ________ إلى الجامعة بالاوتوبيس؟

٨- هل ________ أستاذكم الجديد؟

٩- مَن يعرف كيف ________ الكلمات ؟

١٠- سَلمى ________ بالوحدة بسبب سفر أسرتها.

١١- خالد وأسرته ________ إلى القرآن في الراديو يوم الجمعة.

١٢- في صف الأدب، ________ كتابا جديدا كل اسبوع.

تمرين ١٩ **استمعوا إلى خالد واكتبوا ما يقول:** DVD

والدي ________ في ________ ________ ووالدتي، الله يرحمها، كانت

________ في ________ . ________ ي ________ ________ ________ ، أنا

________ ؛ عادل طالب في ________ ________، ووليد طالب في

________ ________ بـ ________ ________ وعبد المنعم طالب في

________ ________ بـ ________ ________ . ________ ________

معنا ________ ________ والدتي، الله يرحمها، في ________

________ ثلاث ________ .

العامية DVD

- القصة: "انا أكبرهم"

WATCH خالد TALK ABOUT HIS FAMILY IN COLLOQUIAL .

What word does he use for يعمل ?

- "حاموت من الجوع!"

WATCH وليد وعبد المنعم COME HOME FROM المدرسة .

What do they ask الجدة ? What do you think the title of this scene means?

تذكروا هذه الكلمات

عمَّ (= عن ماذا)	هُناك	كم؟ + المفرد	المُثَنّى (اثنين)
بِكَم؟	مرحوم / ة	أمس	الحاجّ / ة
هواية ج. ات	الرياضة	السباحة	الرَسم
الرَقص	الجَري	كرة القَدَم	كرة السَلّة
الكرة الطائرة	الموسيقى	التصوير	

٨. المستقبل للتجارة

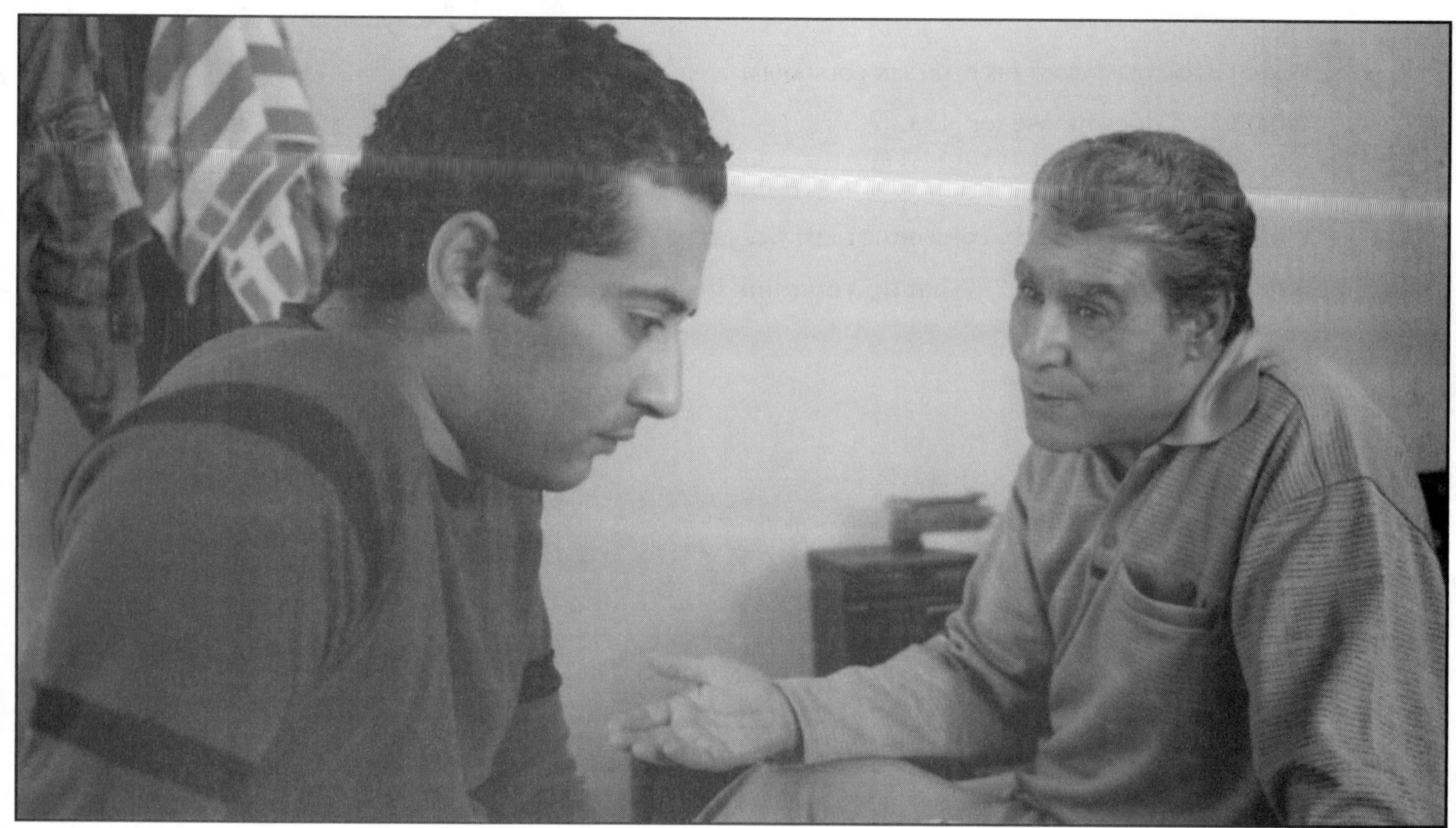

في هذا الدرس:

القصة
- خالد يتكلم عن دراسته

القواعد
- الفعل الماضي
- الجذر والوزن
- القاموس العربي
- الاعداد ١١-١٠٠

القراءة
- شركة بحاجة الى موظفين
- استمارة الالتحاق بوحدة اللغة العربية

الاستماع
- مع العائلة والاصدقاء

العامية
- القصة: «المستقبل للتجارة»
- «الأدب مالوش مستقبل»
- «اسرتي»

المفردات DVD

أُمّ ج. أُمَّهات	والدة
بَعْدَ	≠ قبل
حصلتُ على	I got, obtained
دخلتُ	I entered
أدخُل ، الدُّخول (إلى)	I enter
أُذاكِر	I study (go over lessons, review)
المُذاكَرة (مصدر)	الدراسة (reviewing lessons, doing homework)
رَأي ج. آراء	opinion
في رأيِهِ	in his opinion
رَفَضَ + المصدر	he refused
أرفُض + المصدر	I refuse
أَرادَ أنْ + **فعل مضارع**	he wanted to
أُريد أنْ + **فعل مضارع**	I want to
المُساعَدة (مصدر)	help, helping
أُساعِد .. في + مصدر	I help (someone) to/in (doing)
طِوال	throughout (time period)
بِفَضل + اسم	thanks to
مُسْتَقبَل	future
كَما + **فعل**	as
أَلْتَحِق بِـ	I join, enter (school, army political party, government service)
لَيْسَ	(he/it) is not
ليس هناك	there is not
لَيسَ له / لَها	she/he/it does not have
لَيسَ فيهِ / فيها	it does not have (for places, institutions, etc.)
مِثلَ	like
نَجَحْتُ في	I succeeded in, passed
أنجَح في ، النَجاح في	I succeed in, pass

تمرين ١ **الكلمات الجديدة**

PRACTICE USING NEW VOCABULARY. REMEMBER TO PUT THE NEW WORDS IN CORRECT GRAMMATICAL FORM:

١- لا ______ أنْ أسكن في هذه المنطقة بسبب الازدحام!

٢- أحب صديقي مروان ______ أخي .

٣- والدي ______ العمل في الوزارة لأنه لا يريد أن يسافر كثيراً.

٤- ______ الجامعة منذ سنة وأنا الآن طالب في السنة الثانية.

٥- هل تعرفون ماذا تريدون أن تعملوا في الـ ______ بعد التخرّج؟

٦- ______ على البكالوريوس منذ سنتين والآن أدرس للحصول على الماجستير.

٧- في ______ مها، الطقس في نيويورك بارد جداً في الشتاء.

٨- كما تعرفون، مها بنت وحيدة، ______ لها أخ ولا أخت .

٩- هي موظفة و ______ لأربعة أولاد .

١٠- أحب أن ______ الكلمات والقواعد مع زملائي في المكتبة بعد الصفوف.

١١- بعد تخرّجي من الجامعة أريد أنْ ______ بكلية الحقوق إن شاء الله .

١٢- الحمد لله! ______ في امتحان الاقتصاد!

١٣- نحن تعبانون لأننا كنا ندرس ______ النهار والمساء .

١٤- والدي لا يحب ______ أمّي في شغل البيت .

١٥- الحمد لله، نجحت في الدراسة ______ المذاكرة الكثيرة.

تمرين ٢ **اسألوا زملاءكم :**

PRACTICE USING THE NEW VOCABULARY:

1. Do they help their mother with (= في) housework? Did they used to help?
2. Do they help their classmates with homework? Who do they ask when they want help ?
3. How many hours do they study (review) in the evening?
4. What do they want in the future?
5. Who is studying for (= لِـ) entrance exams for law school or medical school?
6. What is their opinion about (= في) women joining the army?
7. Where do they go after class?
8. What do they refuse to eat?
9. Are they like their siblings? Are they like their mother or their father?

تمرين ٣ **كلمات جديدة وقواعد قديمة (في الصف)**

WITH A PARTNER, DESIGN AN OPINION POLL FOR YOUR CLASS. FOCUS ON USING AS MANY MASDARS AS YOU CAN, AND REMEMBER TO USE إضافة WHERE NECESSARY. HERE ARE SOME IDEAS TO GET YOU STARTED:

ما رأيهم في ... **مثال:** ما رأيهم في الالتحاق بالجيش؟

ماذا يرفضون؟ **مثال:** هل يرفضون مشاهدة كرة القدم؟

ماذا (لا) يحبون؟ **مثال:** هل يحبون المذاكرة؟

القصة DVD

تمرين ٤ **شاهدوا واكتبوا:**

١- من يتكلّم؟

٢- عمَّ (عن ماذا) يتكلم؟ عمّن (عن مَن) يتكلم؟

استمعوا وشاهدوا مرة ثانية:

٣- ماذا أراد خالد أن يدرس؟ ماذا أراد والده؟

٤- ما رأي والد خالد في دراسة الادب؟ وما رأيه في دراسة التجارة ؟

٥- من كان يُساعِد خالد في المذاكرة؟

شاهدوا وتعلّموا :

تَقْدير evaluation: an evaluation of a student's overall performance based on comprehensive exams given at the end of the school year. Scores are given for exams in each subject, then a تَقدير is given based on the exam scores, ranging from مُمتاز *excellent* to جَيِّد جداً *very good* to جيّد *good* to مَقبول *acceptable* (i.e., passing), to the failing grades of ضَعيف *weak* or ضعيف جداً.

٦- ماذا كان تقدير خالد في الدراسة؟ لماذا حَصَلَ خالد على هذا التقدير؟

تمرين ٥ **عن القصة (في الصفّ)**

ROLE PLAY: KHALID AND HIS PARENTS, OR KHALID AND HIS FRIENDS, DISCUSS HIS FUTURE.

القواعد

❁ الفعل الماضي

past	الماضي

In Chapter 4, you learned that الفعل المضارع describes incomplete and habitual actions, similar to the English present tense. To describe past completed actions and events, Arabic uses الفعل الماضي , of which you have seen several examples:

والدي رفض ذلك　　　تخرّجتُ منذ سنتين　　　ماتَت والدتي ، الله يرحمها

Note that الماضي is conjugated with suffixes, and that most verbs have similar, but not identical stems for the two tenses. You must memorize both stems, المضارع and الماضي , for each verb. As you learn more verbs, you will see that they follow certain patterns, and you will be able to derive new verb stems based on these patterns. To work towards that goal, start paying attention to the syllabic structure of both المضارع and الماضي verbs. Beginning with this chapter, stems for both المضارع and الماضي will be given for each new verb. Make it a habit to learn both stems **together.** The following chart shows the conjugation of الماضي using the verb فَعَلَ *to do*:

الفعل الماضي DVD

(أنا)	فَعَلْتُ	(نحن)	فَعَلْنا
(أنتَ) (أنتِ)	فَعَلْتَ فَعَلْتِ	(أنتم)	فَعَلْتُم
(هو) (هي)	فَعَلَ فَعَلَتْ	(هم)	فَعَلوا

Note that the alif on the plural ending وا for هم is a spelling convention only and **it is not pronounced** (like the alif on the مضارع suffix وا , as in يفعلوا) .

Remember that you learned to conjugate the past verb كان with two stems, كـان – and كُـنـ – . The verb أراد also has two stems in الماضي , as shown in the following chart. **Memorize:**

DVD

(أنا) أَرَدْتُ	(نحن) أَرَدْنا
(أنتَ) أَرَدْتَ (أنتِ) أَرَدْتِ	(أنتم) أَرَدْتُم
(هو) أَرادَ (هي) أَرادَتْ	(هم) أَرادوا

❁ نفي الماضي *Negation*

المضارع and الماضي are negated differently in formal Arabic. In Chapter 4, you learned to negate المضارع with لا , as in لا اعرف . There are two ways to negate the past tense in formal Arabic; the one we will use for now is ما + الماضي . The following examples demonstrate:

I did not graduate	ما تخرجتُ من الجامعة.
why were you not	لماذا ما كنتَ في الفصل؟
she did not enter (go to)	جدتي ما دخلَت الجامعة.

❁ دراسة الفعل: الماضي والمضارع والمصدر

Whenever you learn a new verb, memorize المضارع , الماضي , and المصدر together **as a set**. All three will be given in new vocabulary lists in third masculine singular (هو) , which is the convention used in dictionaries, e.g.,

to enter	دَخَلَ ، يَدخُل ، الدُّخول

Note that *to enter* is not a translation of دَخَلَ , just a way of listing the meaning of the stem. The vocabulary lists will give you the stems, but then you must do the real work of learning to use the verbs in context. The following chart contains all the verbs you have learned.

As you listen to the chart, pay attention to similarities of syllable patterns, especially long and short vowels. There are a limited number of these patterns in Arabic, and you can use them to help you remember how to pronounce verbs. Associate maSdars that sound alike together. It is most helpful to listen to the stems and repeat them aloud until you can summon up the way they sound in your ear.

المصدر	المضارع	الماضي
السَّكَن	يَسكُن	سَكَنَ
الدِّراسة	يَدرُس	دَرَسَ
الكِتابة	يَكتُب	كَتَبَ
الشُّعور بـ	يَشعُر بـ	شَعَرَ بِـ
الحُصول على	يَحصُل على	حَصَلَ على
الدُّخول	يَدخُل	دَخَلَ
الرَّفض	يَرفُض	رَفَضَ
الأكل	يَأكُل	أَكَلَ
الشُّرب	يَشرَب	شَرِبَ
الذَّهاب إلى	يَذهَب إلى	ذَهَبَ الى
النَّجاح	يَنجَح	نَجَحَ
القِراءة	يَقرَأ	قَرَأَ
العَمَل	يَعمَل	عَمِلَ
الفِعل	يَفعَل	فَعَلَ
الحِفظ	يَحفَظ	حَفِظَ
المَعرِفة	يَعرِف	عَرَفَ
الكَون	يَكون[1]	كان / كُنت
القَول	يَقول	قالَ / قُلْتُ
المَوت	يَموت	ماتَ / مِتُّ
العَيْش	يَعيش	عاشَ /عِشتُ

[1]The مضارع of كان is used in future and infinitive contexts (*will be* and *to be*), which will be introduced soon.

The verbs in this chart have different patterns, involving the addition of a shadda or a long vowel or taa. Three of these patterns have a Damma vowel in the present stem prefix. When you memorize these verbs, you are memorizing important patterns that will help you understand and take advantage of the verb system in Arabic.

دَرَّسَ	يُدَرِّس	التَّدريس
شاهَدَ	يُشاهِد	المُشاهَدة
ساعَدَ	يُساعِد	المساعَدة
ذاكَرَ	يُذاكِر	المُذاكَرة
سافَرَ الى	يُسافِر إلى	السَّفَر الى
أَحَبَّ	يُحِبّ	الحُبّ
أراد (أرَدتُ)	يُريد	الإرادة
تَذَكَّرَ	يَتَذَكَّر	التَّذَكُّر
تَكَلَّمَ	يَتَكَلَّم	التَّكَلُّم/الكَلام
تَخَرَّجَ	يَتَخَرَّج	التَّخَرُّج
اِستَمَعَ الى	يَستَمِع الى	الاِستِماع الى
اِلتَحَقَ بـ	يَلتَحِق بـ	الاِلْتِحاق بـ

تمرين ٦ **ماذا فعلوا؟ (في البيت)**

PRACTICE NARRATING AND DESCRIBING PAST EVENTS USING THE FOLLOWING VERBS:

١- الحمد لله! ________ أختي في كل امتحاناتها. (نجح)

٢- بعد التخرج من الجامعة ________ ابن خالي بالجيش. (التحق)

٣- كم سنة ________ الأدب الفرنسي يا سميرة؟ (درس)

٤- هل ________ مع أصدقائكم إلى المطعم الجديد؟ (ذهب)

٥- ________ المدرسة الابتدائية وعمري ٦ سنوات. (دخل)

٦- كيف ________ عنوان بيتنا يا سامية؟ (عرف)

٧- أمس ، أنا وزملائي ________ طوال النهار. (عمل)

٨- في الحقيقة ، أنا ما ________ معها منذ أسبوعين. (تكلم)

٩- ________ ابن عمّي السفر إلى تونس ولكن والدته ________ . (أراد، رفض)

١٠- الموظفون ما ________ في مكاتبهم يوم الجمعة. (كان)

تمرين ٧   اسألوا زملاءكم: ماذا فعلوا؟ (في الصف)

PRACTICE TALKING ABOUT PAST EVENTS BY ASKING YOUR CLASSMATES THESE QUESTIONS. THEN REPORT WHAT YOU FOUND OUT TO THE CLASS.

١ـ هل حَفِظوا الكلمات الجديدة ؟

٢ـ مع مَن تَكَلَّموا بالتليفون ؟

٣ـ من أيّ مدرسة تخرجوا ؟

٤ـ منذ كم سنة دَخَلوا الجامعة ؟

٥ـ ماذا / أين عملوا الصيف الماضي ؟

٦ـ هل شاهَدوا فيلمًا في الأسبوعَيْن الماضيين ؟

٧ـ إلى مَن كَتَبوا رسالة ؟

٨ـ هل دَرَسوا كثيرًا أمس ؟

٩ـ هل اِستَمَعوا إلى الراديو هذا الصباح ؟

١٠ـ أيّ كتاب قَرَأوا هذا الأسبوع ؟

تمرين ٨   نشاط كتابة: لماذا فعلت هذا؟

GIVE REASONS OR PURPOSES FOR THE FOLLOWING ACTIONS AND SITUATIONS IN LONG SENTENCES:

١ـ لماذا اِلتحقت بهذه الجامعة؟ ولماذا دخلت هذا الصف؟

٢ـ لماذا (ما) سافرت هذه السنة؟

٣ـ هل كنت في الصف أمس؟ لماذا / لماذا لا؟

٤ـ هل ساعدت زملاءك في كتابة الواجب؟ لماذا / لماذا لا؟

٥ـ أي لغة درست في المدرسة الثانوية؟ لماذا؟

❁ الجذر والوزن

root	جَذر
pattern	وَزن

You have noticed that, in Arabic, words that are related in meaning tend to be related in form as well, in that they contain the same core group of consonants. For example, think of the words you know having to do with books and writing:

> كَتَبَ /يكتب، الكِتابة، مكتب ج. مكاتب، مكتبة ج. مكتبات، كتاب ج. كُتُب

Likewise, you know several words that have to do with studying:

> دَرَسَ /يدرس، الدراسة، يُدرّس، التدريس، مَدْرسة ج. مدارس، دَرْس ج. دروس

Each group of words above shares three consonants: the first group shares ك–ت–ب and the second, د–ر–س . This core group of consonants that gives the basic meaning to a family of words is called the **root**, or الجَذر . الجـــذر is not a word, but a group of consonants, usually three in number (in rare cases, two or four). One of the consonants in a root may be a و or ي , as in يوم or بيت . Alif can never be part of الجذر , but hamza can, as in the root ق–ر–ء that has to do with *reading*. The order of these consonants is critical to the integrity of الجـذر : د–ر–س is not equivalent to س–ر–د , and ك–ت–ب is different from ك–ب–ت .

To identify الجـــذر , look for three "core" consonants. The following cases are straightforward:

الكلمة:	دُخول	مِثل	بارِد	وِزارة	أكْبَر
الجذر:	د - خ - ل	م - ث - ل	ب - ر - د	و - ز - ر	ك - ب - ر

The جذر of other words may be less obvious. How can you identify الجذر of the following words, which have more than three consonants?

مشغول   مستقبل   يلتحق   الاقتصاد

First, eliminate any prefixes and suffixes and الـ . Second, look for long vowels —especially alif—and the consonants ت , س , م , and ن . These letters are often not part of الجذر but rather belong to الوزن , or pattern, which we will see shortly. Eliminating these letters from the previous words, we are left with الجذر :

الاقتصاد	يلتحق	مستقبل	مشغول
ق–ص–د	ل–ح–ق	ق–ب–ل	ش–غ–ل

Keep two final points in mind. First, if in looking for الجــذر you see only two consonants, the second consonant may have a شـدّة . This is called a *doubled* (or *geminate*) *root*. For example, الجــذر of the word عمّ is ع–م–م , and that of صفّ is ص–ف–ف .[1] Second, sometimes the plural of a noun or المضـارع of a verb will clarify a missing letter of its جذر . For example, only two consonants appear in the word خال . However, the plural, أخـوال , shows a third root letter, و . Similarly, the جـذر of the verb يعـيش (ع–ي–ش) is visible in المضارع but not in عاش (الماضي) .

Learning to identify الجذر is important for two reasons. First, having an idea about the basic meaning of a جـذر will often help you guess the meanings of related words, thus increasing your vocabulary and comprehension. In addition, the vast majority of Arabic dictionaries do not list words alphabetically, but rather by الجذر . For example, to find the word مـشـغـول , you must know to look it up under ش–غ–ل . Identifying الجـذر is a skill that takes practice. You can develop this skill by identifying الجذر of new and old vocabulary, or by looking up words you already know in an Arabic-English dictionary (not the glossary).

In Arabic word formation, the consonants of a جـذر fit into slots of a **pattern**, or وَزن (ج. أوزان) . A وزن is a skeletal structure of vowels and consonants that gives the syllabic structure of a word. Every word in Arabic has both a جذر and a وزن . In Arabic grammar, أوزان are given using the consonants ف–ع–ل as a neutral جذر . For example, the وزن of the word طالِب is فاعِل . You can see that the consonants ط–ا–ب can be fit into this وزن in place of the consonants ف–ع–ل to form the word طالب . The following أوزان are familiar to you from your vocabulary:

وزن يَـفْـعُــل:	يَدرُس	يَحصُل	يَدخُل	يَرفُض
وزن فَـعيــل:	جَميل	كَبير	صَغير	وَحيد
وزن فِـعــالــة:	دِراسة	تِجارة	وِزارة	سِياسة

[1]Do not confuse the شـدّة here with شـدّة in words like يدرّس , which already have three clear root consonants. The latter شدّة is part of الوزن (see below).

When a specific جذر intersects with a specific وزن , an individual word is formed. This is the process of word derivation in Arabic. Theoretically, all combinations are possible; in practice, however, only some are used. The chart below gives you a partial overview of this process using some examples:

مَفْعول	افْتَعَلَ	فَعَّلَ	فَعَلَ/فَعِلَ	الوزن / الجذر
مَدْروس (something) studied	----	دَرَّسَ he taught	دَرَسَ he studied	د–ر–س
مَشْغول occupied	اشْتَغَلَ he worked	شَغَّلَ he made to work	شَغَلَ it occupied	ش–غ–ل
مَسْموع heard, audible	اسْتَمَعَ he listened	سَمَّعَ he made to hear	سَمِعَ he heard	س–م–ع

Arabic has many أوزان , some commonly used for المفرد , others for الجمع , others for المصدر , and a set of verbal أوزان (more on these later). Some أوزان have more syllables than others (such as many plural أوزان). Longer أوزان are derived from shorter ones and expanded using certain consonants. The extra letters used to make up longer أوزان include شدّة , long vowels, and the consonants م, س , ت , أ , and occasionally ن . The following are some of the أوزان that contain these letters:

مَشْغول	وزن مَفْعول	طالِب	وزن فاعِل
مُسْتَقْبَل	وزن مُسْتَفْعَل	يُدَرِّس	وزن يُفَعِّل
امْتِحان	وزن افْتِعال	انْشَغَلَ	وزن انْفَعَلَ

Most longer أوزان are related to verbs; we will return to them later. When you study vocabulary, note which words have the same وزن , and practice saying them out loud; this will help your pronunciation, reading, spelling and vocabulary retention by making it easier to remember the exact shape and sound of a word.

تمرين ٩ الجذر (في البيت)

IDENTIFY الجذر OF THE FOLLOWING WORDS:

التجارة	— — —	مساعدة	— — —	تقدير	— — —
المرحومة	— — —	منطقة	— — —	وحيد	— — —
الحقيقة	— — —	المذاكرة	— — —	الاعدادية	— — —
متخصص	— — —	أقارب	— — —	أسرة	— — —

تمرين ١٠ الوزن (في البيت)

CLASSIFY THE WORDS LISTED BELOW UNDER THEIR وزن. WHAT PATTERNS CAN YOU PICK OUT? FOR EXAMPLE, DO ANY أوزان SEEM TO INCLUDE WORDS OF A PARTICULAR GRAMMATICAL CATEGORY?

فَعْل	أفعال	فُعول	فَعيل	فِعالة	فاعِل	فَعلان

جميل	أعمام	الشعور	تعبان	القراءة	فصل
أفلام	الكتابة	والد	طويل	جيوش	زعلان
بَنك	التجارة	حادث	فصول	ضابط	الطقس
أزواج	لطيف	الدراسة	بردان	علوم	حران
أعمال	بنوك	صفوف	أفراد	بارد	واسع

❁ القاموس العربي The Arabic Dictionary

Arabic dictionaries list words according to الجذر. The consonants of الجذر are listed in alphabetical order, with alif representing the consonant ء (remember that the vowel alif cannot be part of a root). Thus, in the dictionary, the root أ–ب–ر precedes ب–ر–د which in turn precedes ب–ر–ز. Doubled roots, such as ح–ق–ق of حقيقة, are usually listed according to the alphabetical order of the first two letters only, such that ح–ق–ق precedes ح–ق–ب. Make sure you know the order of the alphabet, because to find the جذر you are looking for, you must look up **each letter** in turn in that جذر.

Each dictionary entry presents one جـذر. Within this entry, the first section lists the verbs. (We will discuss this section in more detail in Chapter 14.) Skip down to the next sub-entry, and you will find a noun, usually of the « فَعْل » وزن, followed by other nouns and then adjectives, all listed by وزن. In some dictionaries, internal vowels are given in transliteration (English letters). Each noun entry should give a plural, and good dictionaries will give prepositions and idiomatic expressions as well. It is important to pay attention to these when looking up the meaning of a word.

تمرين ١١ مع القاموس (في الصف)

Practice using القاموس by looking up the following words with a partner. First, identify their جـذر. (If it is familiar, think about what the approximate meaning of the new word will be.) Then arrange the words in alphabetical order by الجـذر and write both in the space provided. Finally, look up the words in alphabetical order and write the meaning:

شُعور	مُساعِد	مَعْمَل	حَقّ	أديب
تَبادُل	تَفْسير	سُرعة	ضَيف	مُراسِل

الكلمة	الجذر	Meaning
١- ________	— — —	________________
٢- ________	— — —	________________
٣- ________	— — —	________________
٤- ________	— — —	________________
٥- ________	— — —	________________
٦- ________	— — —	________________
٧- ________	— — —	________________
٨- ________	— — —	________________
٩- ________	— — —	________________
١٠- ________	— — —	________________

❁ الاعداد ١١-١٠٠

Learn the numbers from eleven to one hundred: DVD

أَحَد عَشَر	١١	ثَلاثون/ثَلاثين	٣٠
اِثنا عَشَر	١٢	أربَعون/أربعين	٤٠
ثَلاثة عشر	١٣	خَمسون/خَمسين	٥٠
أربَعة عشر	١٤	سِتّون/سِتّين	٦٠
خَمسَة عَشَر	١٥	سَبعون/سَبعين	٧٠
سِتّة عشر	١٦	ثَمانون/ثَمانين	٨٠
سَبعة عشر	١٧	تِسعون/تِسعين	٩٠
ثَمانِية عشر	١٨	مِئة (مائة)[1]	١٠٠
تِسعة عشر	١٩		
عِشرون/عِشرين	٢٠		
واحد وعشرون	٢١		
اثنان وعشرون	٢٢		
ثلاثة وعشرون	٢٣		

Unlike the numbers from 3-10, which are followed by a plural noun, the numbers from 11-100 must be followed by a singular noun.[2] **In formal Arabic, you will see nouns** following numbers 11-99 written with تنوين الفتح ending. Study the following examples:

قرأت ٢٠ (عشرين) كتابًا .

في فبراير ٢٨ (ثمانية وعشرون) يومًا .

عمري ١٩ (تسع عشرة) سنةً وجدتي عمرها ٨٦ (ست وثمانون) سنةً.

---

[1]The alternate (older) spelling مائة for مئة does not affect its pronunciation.

[2]Formal Arabic imposes agreement rules that affect the gender of the numeral. You will learn these rules later. Spoken Arabic uses fixed forms that vary slightly from dialect to dialect, but are easily understood once you know the basic underlying form presented here.

تمرين ١٢ (في البيت)

Listen to the tape and circle the number you hear in each line:

١-	٦١	٧١	٢١
٢-	٩٦	٦٩	٩٧
٣-	١٥	٢٥	٥١
٤-	٣٢	٢٣	٢٢
٥-	٢٧	٧٢	١٧
٦-	١٥٥	١١٥	١٠٠
٧-	٨٨	٧٨	٨٧
٨-	١٢	١٨	٢٨
٩-	٦٥	٥٦	٥٧
١٠-	٤٤	١٤	٤٠

تمرين ١٣ (في البيت)

An American publisher needs help in ordering pages that fell out of an Arabic manuscript. Order all of the following page numbers in sequence, and show where to insert them by giving the previous page number for each page or series of pages:

٦٢	٥١	٧٧	٨٩	٨١	٩٤	٨٤	٩٢
٧٣	٧٥	٤٥	٨٨	٩٨	٩٩	٨٦	٨٠
٦٦	٧٢	٧٦	٤٤	٨٢	٦٣	٨٧	٤٨

تمرين ١٤ بينغو! (في الصف)

Play Bingo! Draw up Bingo sheets with five rows and five columns containing numbers from 1-99. One person at a time acts as the caller, calling out numbers randomly, and the others check off the numbers they have. The first person to get five straight across or diagonally wins the round.

تمرين ١٥ نشـاط قراءة (في الصف)

تعلموا هذه الكلمات:

شَرِكة ج. شَرِكات	company
بِـحـاجـة إلى	in need of

Read the following advertisement to find the information requested:

1. Who placed this ad? What do they need? Whom would they prefer to hire?
2. Find the section which lists educational requirements. What are they?
3. Find the section which indicates experience desired. Name two.
4. Where are the benefits described? Name one benefit given.
5. For practice, choose two words to look up in your dictionary. Choose well: identify words you think are key to understanding a certain part of the text. Before opening your dictionary, have a sense of what kind of meaning you are looking for, e.g., a noun, an adjective, or something to do with a particular field. Then identify الجذر and look it up.

الأفضلية للسعوديين

شركة وطنية كبرى

بحاجـة إلـــى : **سكرتير أول ومدير مكتب**

المؤهلات المطلوبة :

١ ـ بكالوريوس أو دبلوم في إدارة الأعمال أو السكرتارية .

٢ ـ بكالوريوس لغة إنجليزية .

الخبرة

١ ـ خبرة لا تقل عن خمس سنوات كسكرتير أول لمدير تنفيذي سابقاً.

٢ ـ إستعمال الحاسوب والطباعة عليه IBM أو آبل ماكنتوش.

٣ ـ لديه القدرة على الطباعة والترجمة من اللغة العربية إلى الإنجليزية وبالعكس وبسرعة جيدة.

٤ ـ يفضل من لديه خبرة سابقه لدى إحدى البنوك أو دوائر الاستثمار أو إحدى مكاتب الترجمة.

المـــــيـزات

راتب يحدد حسب المقابلات الشخصية – السكن المناسب – علاج طبي

الأولوية للسعوديين أو من لديه إقامة قابلة للتحويل

فمن يجد لديه الكفاءة الاتصال على **هاتف: ٤٧٩٣٧٠٠ – تحويلة – ٢١٢ أو ٢١٣**

من جريدة الشرق الأوسط ١٩٩٢/٦/٢٩

الاستماع DVD

تمرين ١٦ مع العائلة والاصدقاء DVD

تعلموا هذه الكلمات:

إذا + الماضي	if
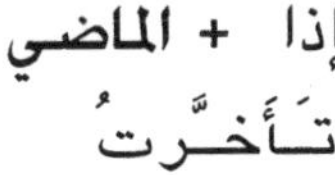 تَـأَخَّـرتُ	I was late, fell behind

أسئلة:

١- من يتكلم؟ من هو بالنسبة لخالد؟

٢- أين يدرس؟ أين يدرس أصدقاؤه؟

٣- ماذا يريد أن يدرس في الجامعة؟

٤- ماذا يريد أن يعمل بعد التخرج؟

٥- ماذا يحب أن يشاهد في التليفزيون؟

تمرين ١٧ نشاط كتابة

WRITE A SHORT قصه ABOUT EACH SET OF PICTURES (GO FROM RIGHT TO LEFT). USE AS MANY VERBS IN الماضي AS YOU CAN. A TIME FRAME IS GIVEN FOR EACH SET OF PICTURES.

١- يوم السبت الماضي

٢- الفصل الدراسي الماضي

٣- السنة الماضية

تمرين ١٨ نشاط قراءة ومحادثة وكتابة

You may be interested in studying in an Arab country. The following is an application to one such program. Read through it with a partner, and as you do so, fill out the form for her/him by asking questions (in Arabic, of course). Guess what you can from context and الجذر , and skip the questions for which you cannot make a reasonable guess.

بسم الله الرحمن الرحيم

المملكة العربية السعودية

جامعة الملك سعود

معهد اللغة العربية

ص. ب ٤٢٧٤ ـ الرياض ١١٤٩١

استمارة ترشيح بوحدة اللغة والثقافة بمعهد اللغة العربية

١ ـ اسم الطالب (مطابقًا لجواز السفر) : ....

٢ ـ الجنسية .... ٣ – الديانـة: ....

٤ ـ أ) تاريخ الميلاد: .... ب) العمر: ....

٥ مكان الميلاد .... ٦ – الحالة الاجتماعية: ☐ متزوج ☐ أعزب

٧ ـ الجنس: .... ٨ – المهنـة: ....

٩ ـ العمل الحالي: ....

١٠ ـ إذا كنت قد درست في بلاد عربية من قبل فاذكر:

ا ـ اسم البلـد: ....

ب ـ اسم المدرسة أو الجامعة: ....

جـ ـ تاريخ التخرج: ....

١١ ـ اذكـر اللغات التي تعـرفهـا ومدى معرفتك بهـا من ناحية فهـم الكـلام، والتحدث، والقراءة، والكتابة، مع ذكر المستوى إذا كان ممتازًا أو جيِّدًا أو متوسطًا .

ا ـ لغتك الام : ....

ب ـ لغات اخرى:

اللغة	فهم الكلام	التحدث	القراءة	الكتابة
	ممتاز جيد متوسط	ممتاز جيد متوسط	ممتاز جيد متوسط	ممتاز جيد متوسط

١٢ ـ اذكر مؤهلاتك العلمية :

اسم المدرسة ، المعهد ، الكلية ، أو الجامعة	تاريخ الالتحاق	تاريخ التخرج	مدة الدراسة	التخصص	المؤهل العلمي	التقدير العام

تمارين المراجعة

تمرين ١٩ **كلمات جديدة وقواعد قديمة**

DEFINITE OR INDEFINITE? DETERMINE HOW EACH OF THESE NOUNS FITS INTO THE CONTEXT. REMEMBER TO LOOK FOR الإضافة:

١- ________ الكلمات الجديدة كل يوم تساعد في حفظها. (المذاكرة)

٢- أحسن هواية بالنسبة لها هي ________ . (القراءة)

٣- هل تعرفين اسم الموظفة ________ ؟ (جديد)

٤- أريد أن أتكلم العربية مثل أصدقائي ________ . (عرب)

٥- دخلت كلية الطب بفضل ________ أسرتي وأساتذتي. (المساعدة)

٦- من فضلك ، هل مكتب الدكتور صالح مصطفى في هذه ________ ؟ (بناية)

٧- ________ ممطر ولذلك أريد ________ البيت . (جو، يدخل)

٨- لا أحب ________ في هذا ________ . (السكن ، بيت)

٩- أمس كانت خالتي في الوزارة طوال ________ . (يوم)

١٠- أختي فاتن متخصصة في ________ الشرق الأوسط . (التاريخ)

تمرين ٢٠ **تمرين قراءة**

اسمه عادل محمود ابو العلا وهو أخو خالد. عادل طالب في الثانوية العامة ولكنه، مثل كل الشباب، لا يحب المذاكرة! عادل يريد الالتحاق بالجامعة ليكون مع أصدقائه، فأصدقاؤه دخلوا الجامعة منذ سنة، أمّا هو، فما نجح في السنة التي ماتت فيها أمه، الله يرحمها، ولذلك ما تخرّج السنة الماضية.

عادل يريد أن يدخل كلية التجارة مثل خالد، إذا نجح في الثانوية العامة، ويريد أيضاً أن يعمل في شركة أمريكية بعد التخرّج. ولذلك يدرس اللغة الانجليزية ويحب مشاهدة البرامج التليفزيونية باللغة الانجليزية.

تمرين ٢١ استمعوا إلى خالد واكتبوا ما يقول :

All verb forms have been removed from the text. Focus your attention on following the thread of narration by listening for verbs. In addition, listen for المصدر and note how it is used.

بعد ______ ي على ______ ______ ، ______ ______

أن ______ كلية الآداب ______ ______ محمد، لكن والدي ______

ذلك، و______ أن ______ بكلية ______ ______ و______

والدتي، ______ دراسة ______ في رأيهِ ______ لها ______

و______ ______ . فَـ ______ كلية ______ كما ______

هو والمرحومة ______ ، و______ والحمد لله في ______

و______ على تقدير ______ جدًا ______ ______ الدراسة

______ الله و______ ______ ______ لي في ______ .

العامية DVD

- القصة: "المستقبل للتجارة"

Watch خالد tell his story in colloquial.

Listen for the colloquial of مثل and أريد .

-"الادب مالوش مستقبل"

-"أسرتي"

Listen to several شباب tell us about their families.

What can you understand?

تذكروا هذه الكلمات

إذا [+ الماضي] تَأَخَّرَ الماضي شَرِكة ج. ات

بحاجة الى الجذر الوزن الأعداد ١١-١٠٠

٩ . جدتي توقظني في السادسة والنصف

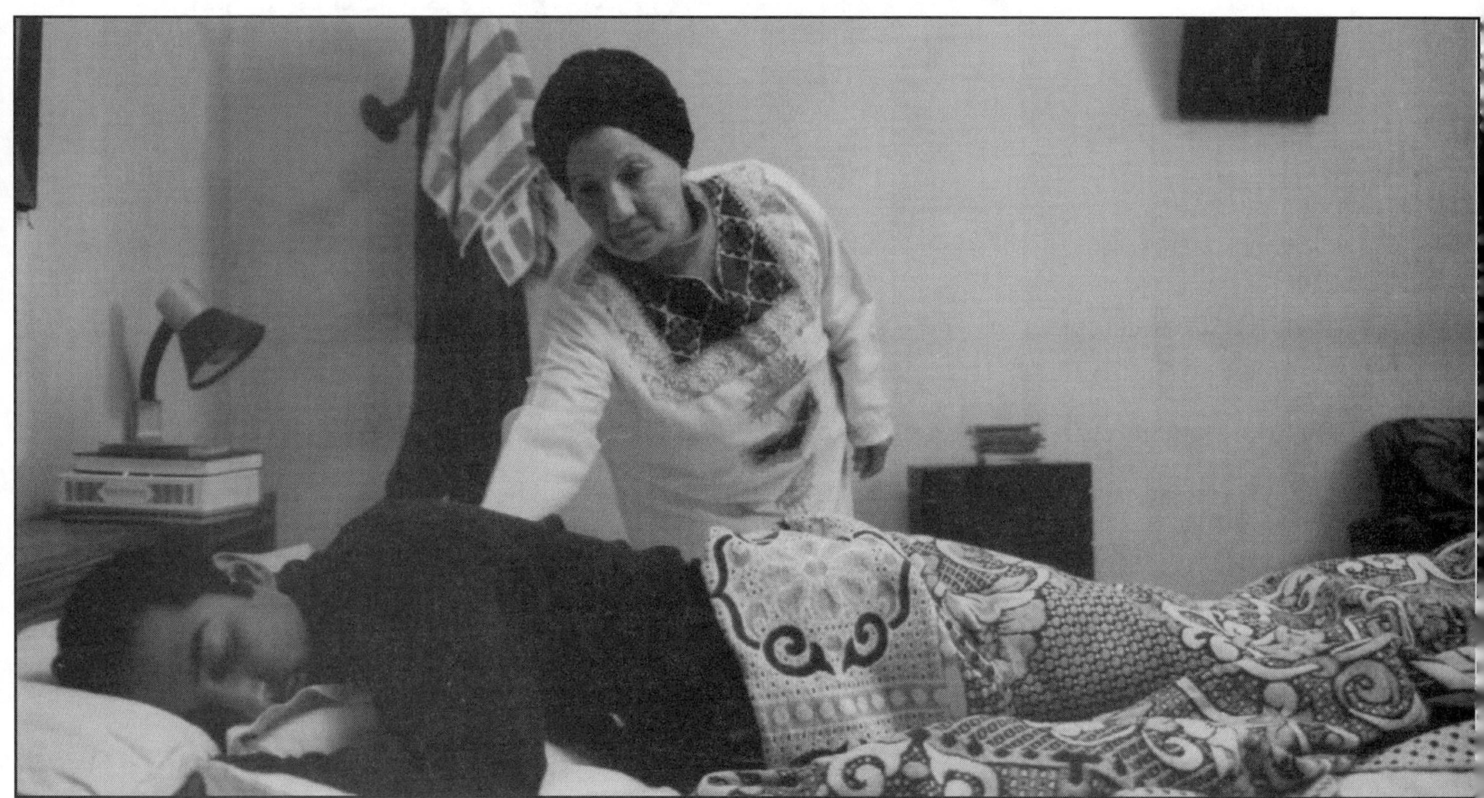

في هذا الدرس:

القصة • برنامج خالد اليومي

الثقافة • النادي

• هل تدخّنون أمام الأسرة؟

القواعد • ليس + الجملة الاسمية

• الأعداد الترتيبية

• كم الساعة ؟

القراءة • مواطنة تحصل على الماجستير

• برامج التليفزيون

الاستماع • مع العائلة والأصدقاء

العامية • القصة: «جدتي بتصحيني الساعة ستة ونص»

• «صباح الفلّ يا حاجّة»

المفردات DVD

آخَر ، مؤنث: أُخرى ، ج. آخَرون	other
أو	or
بَدَأَ ، يَبدَأ ، البَدء	to begin
بَعض ا اسم جمع في اضافة	some (of)
ثُمَّ	then, بعد ذلك
جَريدة ج. جَرائِد	newspaper
جَلَسَ ، يَجلِس ، الجُلوس	to sit
حَوالَيْ	approximately, about (a certain time)
خَرَجَ من ، يَخرُج من ، الخُروج من	to leave (a place, e.g., room, house)
خاصّ	special; (its) own; private (adjective)
دَخَّنَ ، يُدَخِّن ، التَّدخين	to smoke
سادِس	sixth (adjective)
ساعة ج. -ات	hour; o'clock; clock, watch
الشَطَرَنْج	chess
اِستَطاعَ أنْ ، يَستَطيع أنْ *or* + المصدر	to be able to
بَعدَ الظُّهْر	afternoon
عادَ الى ، يَعود الى ، العَوْدة الى	to return
عَيْن ج. عُيون	eye
الغَداء	lunch
فَطَرَ ، يَفطُر ، الفُطور	to eat breakfast
قليلاً	≠ كثيراً
لَعِبَ ، يَلعَب ، اللَّعِب	to play
النادي ج. النَوادي	club (e.g., sports, social; see الثقافة)
نَزَلَ من ، يَنْزِل من ، النُّزول من	to leave (the house); literally: to descend
نِصف	half
يوقِظ	to wake (someone) up (مضارع)
ـــ ني	me (object of verb)

تعلموا هذين الفعلين:

In this new section of each chapter you will be given one or two new verbs to memorize whose جذر contains و or ي . As you know from learning كان , these verbs have two stems for الماضي . By memorizing a couple of verbs at a time, you will gradually acquire all of the stem patterns of the Arabic verb system.

الماضي

عُدتُ	عُدنا
عُدتَ عُدتِ	عُدتُم
عادَ عادَت	عادوا

المضارع

أعود	نَعود
تَعود تَعودين/تَعودي	تَعودون/تَعودوا
يَعود تَعود	يَعودون/يَعودوا

الماضي

اِسْتَطَعتُ	اِستَطَعنا
اِستَطَعتَ اِستَطَعتِ	اِستَطَعتُم
اِستَطاعَ اِستَطاعَت	اِستَطاعوا

المضارع

أستَطيع	نَستَطيع
تَستَطيع تَستَطيعين/تَستَطيعي	تَستَطيعون/تَستَطيعوا
يَستَطيع تَستَطيع	يَستَطيعون/يستطيعوا

تمرين ١ استطاع وأراد (في البيت)

Use the verbs أراد and استطاع to complete the following. Note the use of المصدر to express the infinitive verb:

١- أنا لا ________ شُرب القهوة قبل الفطور.

٢- الطلاب ________ حِفظ الكلمات.

٣- صديقتنا ________ الذهاب معنا إلى السينما لكنها لا ________ .

٤- أنت طالب جديد هنا؟! (نحن) ________ مساعدتك!

٥- الطقس اليوم ممطر وبارد جدا - هل (أنتم) ________ الخروج فيه؟

٦- الأسبوع الماضي ما ________ الخروج من البيت بسبب الثلج.

تمرين ٢ المفردات الجديدة (في البيت)

اكتبوا كلمات جديدة في الجمل:

١- كان عمّي، الله يرحمه، ________ حوالي ٣٠ سيجارة كل يوم .

٢- أنا وزوجي نقرأ ________ ونشرب القهوة كل صباح .

٣ يوم الأحد الماضي ________ كرة السلة مع ________ أصدقائي .

٤- لا ________ الجلوس في الشمس كثيراً.

٥- يوم الجمعة لا ________ من البيت قبل الساعة الواحدة ________ .

٦- أمي تعبانة وتريد أن ________ قليلاً .

٧- ابنة عمّي دكتورة متخصّصة في أمراض *diseases* ________ .

٨- تخرجتْ من كلية إدارة الأعمال ________ التحقت بشركة «سوني» حيث تعمل الآن.

٩- صديقي لا يأكل الدجاج ________ اللحم .

١٠- لا نستطيع أن ندخل إلى هذا النادي لأنّه ________ .

١١- في الصباح لا ________ ولكنّي أشرب قليلاً من القهوة .

١٢- لا أريد قراءة هذا الكتاب، أريد قراءة كتاب ________ .

١٣- ________ دراسة اللغة العربية في الخريف الماضي ونستطيع الآن القراءة والكتابة والكلام بها!

تمرين ٣ اسألوا زملاءكم :

1. Who leaves their house/room before eating breakfast? [Remember to use قبل + المصدر]
2. Who reads the paper every day? Which paper/s?
3. How many hours per week do they play sports?
4. Do they smoke? Did they ever smoke?
5. Who has joined a student club? Which one?
6. Who gets (= returns) home late in the evening?
7. Who begins studying (doing homework) in the afternoon?
8. Whose classes begin before noon?
9. Is there a special room or building they like to sit in to study?
10. Who wakes up his/her roommate in the morning?

القصة DVD

تمرين ٤ **شاهدوا واكتبوا: (في البيت)**

1. Mention something خالد does:

أ - في الصباح ______________________________

ب - بعد الظهر ______________________________

جـ - في المساء ______________________________

استمعوا مرة ثانية:

2. Order the following activities according to what خالد does:

___ أفطر	___ أعود الى البيت	___ جدتي توقظني
___ أقرأ الجرائد	___ أخرج من البيت	___ ألعب الشطرنج
___ آكل الغداء	___ أدرس في المكتبة	___ ينزل والدي وإخوتي

استمعوا وشاهدوا مرة ثالثة :

٣- متى يخرج خالد من البيت؟

٤- متى تبدأ محاضراته في الجامعة؟

٥- ماذا يفعل بعد الخروج من البيت وقبل أن تبدأ المحاضرات؟

٦- ماذا يعمل في المساء؟

7. Khalid used a formal verb to talk about eating lunch. Write what you hear:

لِـ __________ الغداء

This verb is used mainly in formal Arabic, and must be mentioned with a meal:

أتناول الفطور / الغداء / العشاء

8. خالد introduces a new topic, يوم الجمعة , using the topic switched:

as for ... , ... أمّا ... ، فَـ ...

ماذا يَقول خالد عن يوم الجمعة؟ ______________________________

9. Guess the meaning and explain the grammar of this phrase:

لنلعب الشطرنج هوايتي المُفَضّلة ______________________________

تمرين ٥ عن القصة (في الصف)

WITH A PARTNER, COMPARE YOUR SCHEDULES TO THAT OF خـالد BY COMPLETING THE CHART BELOW. ADD TIMES AS YOU NEED THEM.

نحن	خالد	الساعة
		٦,٣٠
		١٠,٠٠
		٣,٠٠

الثقافة

ما هو النادي؟ ماذا تفعلون في النادي؟ DVD

In Egypt, النـوادي offer social and recreational facilities to those who can afford them, much like American country clubs. The three largest in Cairo are نـادي الجَــزيـرة , نـادي الزَمـالك , and النـادي الأهلي . The latter two have كـرة القـدم teams that enjoy a large following and a fierce rivalry. In addition to these private clubs, some large companies, professional associations, and government agencies offer نـوادي to employees and their families, such as نـادي الضُـبّـاط . These clubs are more social than recreational, offering places to eat, drink coffee, socialize, and host events such as weddings. Watch as members of نـادي هليوبوليس talk about what role it plays in their lives.

هل تدخّنون أمام الأسرة؟ DVD

Is Khalid's refusal to smoke in front of family members unusual? Watch the interviews on your DVD to hear the opinions of some other young smokers.

القواعد

❁ ليس + الجملة الاسمية

You have learned how to use الجملة الاسمية with a fronted خبر to express the concepts of possession, accompaniment, and *there is / there are*. You should be able to understand and analyze the following examples of this construction:

(١) عندي كمبيوتر .　　　(٣) في كل غرفة طالبان .

(٢) معي دولار .　　　(٤) له مستقبل .

In formal Arabic, these kinds of sentences may be negated using لَيسَ.[1] Compare sentences 1-4 above with counterparts 1a-4a:

(١ أ) لَيسَ عندي كمبيوتر .　　　(٣ أ) لَيسَ في كل غرفة طالبان .

(٢ أ) لَيسَ معي دولار .　　　(٤ أ) لَيسَ له مستقبل .

Note that ليس must come at the beginning of the sentence, preceding both المبتدأ and الخبر .

These جمل اسمية may be put in the past with كان or negative past with ما كان . As you saw in Chapter 7, كان should not be conjugated for the logical subject (the possessor) but rather may be thought of as a fixed expression. Like ليس , كان precedes both المبتدأ and الخبر .

كان عندي سيارة ولكن ليس عندي سيارة الآن.

ما كان عندنا صفوف اليوم بسبب الثلج.

هل كان لكم أصدقاء كثيرون في المدرسة الثانوية؟

When describing places or institutions, do not use عند , which refers to people. Instead, use في for physical possessions and لِـ for abstract ones:

جامعتنا ليس فيها كلية طب.

هذه المدينة ليس لها تاريخ طويل.

However, the abstract word وَقت *time* is usually used with عند :

ليس عندي وقت!!　　　*I don't have time!*

---

[1]Earlier we noted that عند may be negated with ما in spoken Arabic, as in ما عندي كمبيوتر . Here we present the formal negation with ليس . These two constructions differ in usage, not in meaning.

تمرين ٦ ترجموا إلى اللغة العربية (في الصف)

1. There are no students of Arab descent in our class.
2. Last Friday, there was no traffic (overcrowding) in the streets!
3. She refused to talk with us because she had no time.
4. This area does not have many restaurants.
5. Does this club have special programs for kids?
6. In his childhood, Beirut did not have McDonald's restaurants, and now it has seven.
7. Last week we had a very hard test.
8. They had two sons and three daughters, but the oldest son died.
9. I don't have an opinion but I would like to listen to yours.

تمرين ٧ ليس + جملة اسمية (في البيت)

WHAT DO OR DID THESE PEOPLE AND PLACES *NOT* HAVE?:

مثال: الطلاب في مصر <u>ليس عندهم محاضرات يوم الجمعة</u> .

١- هذا النادي ____________________ .

٢- خالد ____________________ .

٣- أمس أنا وأصدقائي ____________________ .

٤- غرفة صفنا ____________________ .

٥- «يا طلاب، لماذا ____________________ في الأسبوع الماضي؟»

٦- «لماذا ____________________ ؟» (أنتِ)

٧- إخوتي ____________________ .

٨- هذه الجامعة ____________________ .

٩- السنة الماضية، ____________________ .

❁ الأعداد الترتيبية *Ordinal Numbers*

You have learned the cardinal (counting) numbers from 1-100. Arabic also has ordinal numbers that are easily derivable from the cardinal numbers through the وزن and جذر system. The جذر of the cardinal number is put into the pattern «فاعِل» (feminine فاعِلة). This combination produces ordinal numbers from 2-10 (2-9 are also used in combinations above 20). Listen to and learn the مؤنث and مذكر forms: DVD

العدد	مذكر	مؤنث
واحد/ة	الأوّل	الأُولى
اِثنان/اِثنَيْن اِثنَتان/اِثنَتَيْن	الثاني	الثّانِية
ثَلاث/ة	الثّالِث	الثّالِثة
أربَع/ة	الرّابِع	الرّابِعة
خَمس/ة	الخامِس	الخامِسة
سِتّ/ة	السّادِس	السّادِسة
سَبع/ة	السّابِع	السّابِعة
ثَماني/ة	الثّامِن	الثّامِنة
تِسع/ة	التّاسِع	التّاسِعة
عَشَر/عَشْرة	العاشِر	العاشِرة
أَحَد عَشَر إحدى عَشْرة	الحادي عَشَر	الحادِية عشرة
اِثنا عَشَر اِثنَتا عَشْرة	الثاني عَشَر	الثّانِية عشرة
ثَلاثة عَشَر ثَلاث عَشْرة	الثالِث عَشَر	الثّالِثة عشرة

Notes: أوّل *first* is derived from a different جذر than that of واحد *one* (just as English *first* and *one* do not resemble each other). The difference between ستّة and السادس is historical in origin: الجذر of *six* is really س-د-س and not س-ت-ت, which reflects a later development of the counting number 6. Cardinal numbers in Arabic have masculine and feminine forms. Classical Arabic has complex rules for using these numbers with nouns that you will learn later.

أمثلة: نحن في الأسبوع الخامس من هذا الفصل الدراسي.

أسكن في غرفة ٤١٣ وهي الغرفة الثانية بعد غرفة الجلوس.

معظم الموظفين يخرجون من مكاتبهم للغداء في الساعة الثانية عشرة.

تمرين ٨ **(في البيت)**

Use an ordinal number to designate which one:

١- بعض زملائي طلاب في السنة ________ في الجامعة.

٢- ما كانت سعيدة مع زوجها ________، ولكنها سعيدة الآن مع زوجها ________

٣- اللغة العربية هي لغتي ________.

٤- في طفولتها، عاشت مها في مصر وكانت طالبة في الصف ________.

٥- يوم الخميس هو اليوم ________ في الأسبوع.

❁ كم الساعة؟ *What Time Is It?*

تعلموا هذه الكلمات: DVD

Listen to these words and sentences demonstrating their use on your DVD:

وَقت	time (as an abstract entity)
رُبع	quarter
ثُلث	third
إلاّ	less (literally: except)
١٢.٥٥ = الساعة الواحدة إلاّ خمسة	
دَقيقة ج. دَقائِق	minute
في أيّ ساعة ... ؟	At what time...?

In formal Arabic, ordinal numbers are used to tell time. In spoken Arabic, cardinal numbers are used to tell time: الساعة خمسة , الساعة ستّة and so forth. **Remember:** in telling time, الساعة الواحدة (**not** الساعة الأولى) is used for 1:00.

أمثلة: ١.١٥ = الساعة الواحدة والرُبع ٥.٢٠ = الساعة الخامسة والثُلث

Now go back to the DVD to hear and compare times given in spoken and in formal Arabic.

تمرين ٩ **اسألوا زملاءكم: في أي ساعة ... ؟**

ASK زملاءك IF THEY DO THESE ACTIVITIES AT THE TIMES SHOWN. IF NOT, WHAT TIME? BE SURE TO SPECIFY صباحاً , بعد الظهر , OR مساءً .

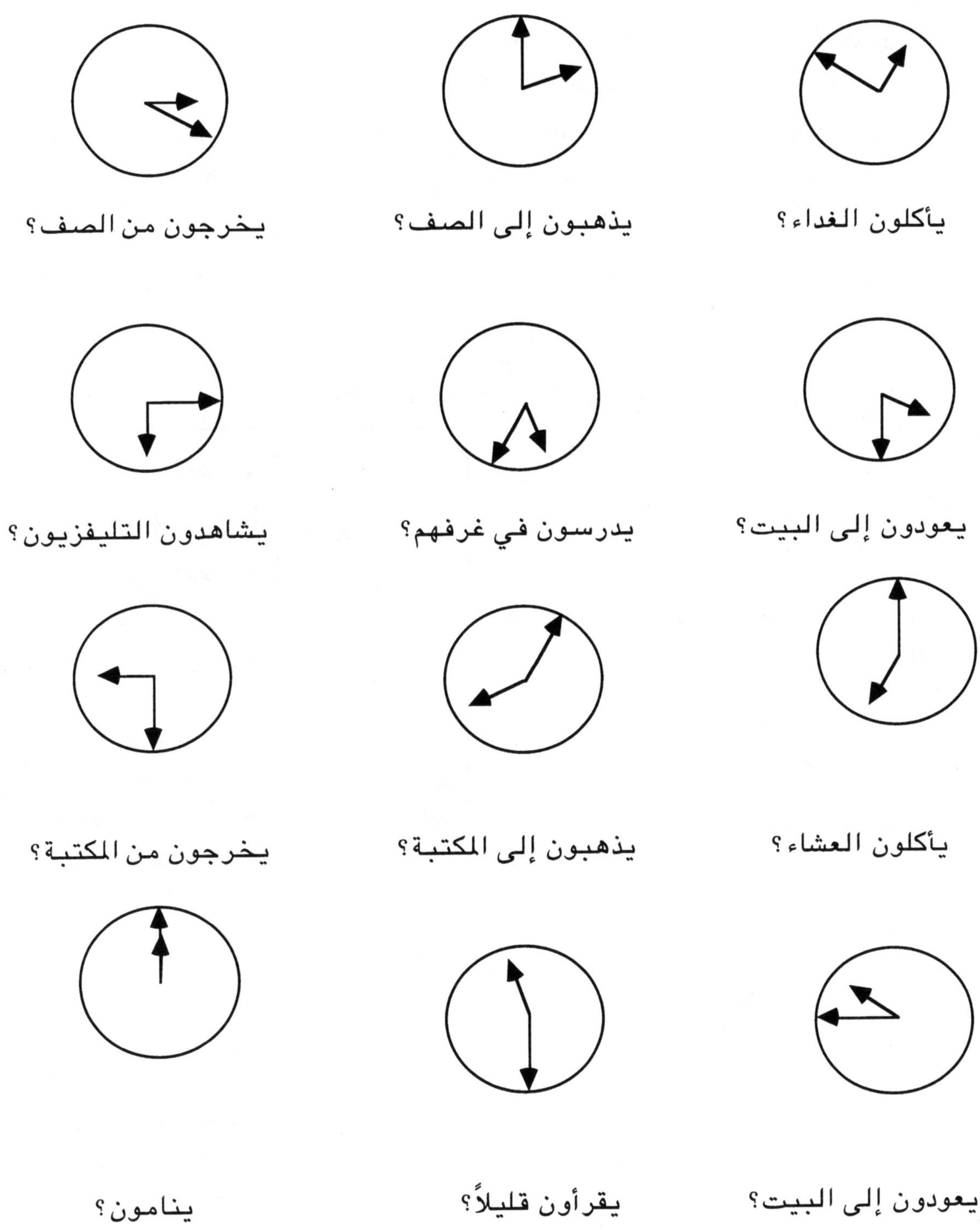

B. DID THEY DO ANY OF THESE THINGS AT ANOTHER TIME YESTERDAY أمس ?

تمرين ١٠ **نشاط قراءة**

تعلموا هذه الكلمة:

المُناقَشة (مصدر) — discussion, to discuss

أسئلة:

READ THE FOLLOWING NEWS ARTICLE ACCORDING TO THE STEPS OUTLINED HERE. THESE STEPS ARE DESIGNED TO HELP YOU DEVELOP READING STRATEGIES FOR READING NEWS ARTICLES IN PARTICULAR.

1. First, scan the article to get a sense of its overall structure. News articles usually have a predominance of الجملة الفعلية ; use this information to help you identify how many sentences this news article contains.

2. Find the basic information of the article in the first sentence:

من؟ ماذا؟ أين؟ متى؟

Look carefully at the structure of the sentence. In what order do the pieces of information appear?

3. Identify all و as either "new sentence" و or the و that marks lists, and bracket all lists.

4. Bracket all proper noun phrases. What helps you identify them?

5. Find three different adverbs.

6 Choose the word you think is the most important one you do not know and look it up.

مواطنة تحصل على الماجستير في الفقه الإسلامي

حصلت امس الطالبة ماجدة محمد يوسف العوضي على درجة الماجستير في الشريعة الاسلامية تخصص الفقه الاسلامي في كلية الدراسات الاسلامية والعربية بدبي حول رسالتها بعنوان «تحقيق مخطوط الحاوي الصغير القزويني من اول الكتاب حتى نهاية باب الجعالة»، وضمت لجنة المناقشة كلا من الدكتور رجب سعيد شعبان استاذ الدراسات العليا بالكلية مشرفا، والدكتور محمد الزحيلي استاذ الفقه وعميد كلية الشريعة والدراسات الاسلامية بجامعة الشارقة مناقشا خارجيا والاستاذ الدكتور ابراهيم محمد سلقيني من قسم الشريعة بكلية الدراسات الاسلامية والعربية بدبي مناقشا.

من جريدة الاتحاد (الإمارات) ٢٠٠٣/٦/١٢

الاستماع DVD

تمرين ١١ **مع العائلة والأصدقاء**

أسئلة:

١- من هو سامي ؟

٢- ماذا يعمل ؟

٣- لماذا يذهب إلى الجامعة كل يوم ؟

٤- ما هواية سامي المفضّلة ؟

٥- خمّنوا: رسالة الماجستير = __________

تمرين ١٢ **نشاط قراءة (في الصف)**

تعلموا هذه الكلمة:

العالَم	the world

أسئلة:

Read البرامج التليفزيونية and look for the information requested. Watch for جذور you know. How many new words can you guess from context? What clues help you identify foreign names that you will recognize if you sound them out?

١- خمّنوا: مُسَلسَل (أو سلسلة) = __________ قناة = __________

٢- أين ومتى هناك برامج إسلامية؟ برامج رياضية؟ برامج نسائية؟

٣- أين ومتى هناك برامج أمريكية؟

٤- أين هناك برنامج تاريخي؟

٥- أين ومتى نستطيع أن نعرف الطقس؟

٦- أي قناة تحبون أن تشاهدوا، ولماذا؟

قناة المستقبل (لبنان)

06.30 عالم الصباح 09.00 سيدتي مسلسل مكسيكي مدبلج 10.07 مسلسل العمة نور 11.00 مسلسل ذكريات الزمن القادم 12.00 المطبخ 13.00 مسلسل رحيل الطيور 14.00 نفحات إسلامية 14.30 آذان المغرب 14.45 مسابقة القرآن الكريم 15.30 وراك وراك كاميرا خفية 16.00 مسلسل العمة نور-إ 17.30 برنامج رادار 18.00 مسلسل رجل الأقدار 19.00 برنامج ست الحبايب 19.30 مسلسل ذكريات الزمن القادم-إ 20.30 برنامج بيني وبينك 21.30 برنامج الأغنية رقم واحد 23.30 برنامج سوبر ستار-إ 01.30 برنامج ست الحبايب-إ 02.00 قرآن كريم وتسابيح 02.10 آذان الفجر 02.20 نفحات إسلامية-إ 02.30 برنامج ديني 03.00 مسلسل رجل الأقدار-إ Honey I Shrunk The Kids 04.00

الجزيرة (قطر)

السبت 21 يونيو

10.05 منبر الجزيرة ـ إعادة 10.55 دقيقة رياضة 11.00 الأخبار 11.35 أكثر من رأي ـ إعادة 13.00 الجزيرة منتصف اليوم 14.30 أخبار الرياضة 14.45 النشرة الجوية 14.50 حديث الصور 15.00 الأخبار 15.30 السينما في أسبوع 17.00 الأخبار 17.25 الملف الأسبوعي ـ مباشر 18.00 الأخبار 18.35 حوار في الرياضة 20.00 حصاد اليوم

الأحد 22 يونيو

3.15 النشرة الجوية 3.20 برنامج وثائقي 4.05 تاريخ الماء 4.50 حديث الصور 5.00 الجزيرة هذا الصباح 7.15 من واشنطن ـ إعادة 9.45 مرآة الصحافة 10.05 زيارة خاصة ـ إعادة 11.35 حوار في الرياضة ـ إعادة 14.02 نشرة الجزيرة الاقتصادية 14.30 حديث الصور 15.30 مدن من العالم 16.40 أخبار الرياضة 16.45 نشرة الجزيرة الاقتصادية ـ 18.35 الشريعة والحياة ـ مباشر 20.00 حصاد اليوم.

الإثنين 23 يونيو

3.20 برنامج وثائقي 3.30 مدن من العالم ـ إعادة 4.00 الأخبار 4.50 حديث الصور 5.00 الجزيرة هذا الصباح 6.05 شاهد على العصر ـ إعادة 7.25 الملف الأسبوعي ـ إعادة 9.30 أخبار الرياضة 10.05 مراسلو الجزيرة ـ إعادة 11.35 الشريعة والحياة ـ إعادة 14.05 نشرة الجزيرة الاقتصادية 14.30 أخبار الرياضة 14.50 حديث الصور 15.30 الرياضة العربية ـ مباشر 17.25 فن الخدع السينمائية 19.05 للنساء فقط.

قناة MBC (دبي)

09.10 صلاة الجمعة من مكة المكرمة نقل مباشر 10.10 برنامج يرد على الأسئلة الدينية: الإفتاء 13.05 عالم دريد 13.35 شباب اون لاين 14.05 على ورق 15.05 اكشن 18.30 من سيربح المليون 19.30 صدى الملاعب 21.30 مسلسل عربي: امرؤ القيس 22.20 مسلسل خليجي: سهم الغدر 00.05 مسلسل عربي: زمن عاد الدين

قناة Parramount

01.00 ويل وجريس - سلسلة كوميدية ممتازة 01.30 برنامج هذا المساء - حوارات مع نجوم 02.00 هلا بطفلي- مسلسل كوميدي 09.30 بانسون 10.00 المستشفى العسكري المنتقل - مسلسل درامي 10.30 نساء مصممات - سلسلة كوميدية 11.00 مورفي براون 11.30 أقل من الكمال 12.00 بيكير - برنامج فكاهي 12.30 عائلة باركرز - مسلسل كوميدي 13.30 هلا بطفلي - مسلسل كوميدي 14.00 فراندز (الأصدقاء) - مسلسل كوميدي 14.30 مجنون بحبك - مسلسل كوميدي 15.30 حسب قول جيم - مسلسل كوميدي 16.30 مثبت مدى الحياة - مسلسل كوميدي 18.00 سهرة مع جاي لينو - حوارات مع النجوم 19.00 سهرة مع كونان أوبرين - برنامج حوارات 20.00 اقتلني - كوميديا ممتازة 22.00 برنامج السهرة مع دايفد لاترمان

القناة الأولى (مصر)

٧,٠٠ صباح الخيريا مصر	**الأصدقاء** إخراج
١٠,٠٥ كارتون للأطفال	إسماعيل عبد الحافظ
١٠,٤٥ المخترع الصغير	٨,٥٥ حديث الروح
١٢,٣٠ ربيع العمر	٩,٠٠ نشرة الأخبار
١,١٠ الفيلم العربي	١١,٠٠ يوم ورا يوم
الدخيل	١٢,١٥ نادي السينما
٢,٤٥ فترة مفتوحة	٣,٠٠ برنامج ثنائيات
٢,٠٠ برنامج دنيا	٤,٢٠ عرض خاص
٤,٠٠ برنامج يللا بينا	٥,١٠ رجال ونساء
٥,٥٥ في مثل هذا اليوم	... من القرآن الكريم
٧,٣٠ المسلسل العربي	٥,٢٥ القرآن الكريم

الاهرام العربي TV 21 يونيو 2003 م
ومجلة «ستالايت» نوفمبر ٢٠٠٣

تمرين ١٣ نشاط محادثة (في الصف)

A tray of بقلاوة is missing and believed stolen from the department office. Investigators from each class will interrogate everyone. With a partner, construct your alibi for the past 24 hours. Make sure you both know your story, because you will be interrogated separately!

تمرين ١٤ نشاط كتابة (في البيت)

Write a story describing هذه الصور . You can write one story for the entire set or break them up into shorter stories.

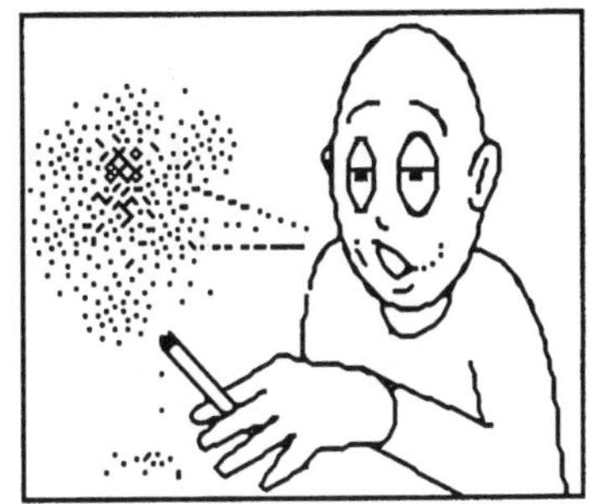

الرسم: الدكتور مايكل كوبرسون

تمارين المراجعة

تمرين ١٥ **مفردات**

اكتبوا أحسن كلمة في كل جملة:

١ـ أولادي دائمًا ______ أسهم في شغل البيت .
أ ـ يعملون ب ـ يساعدون جـ ـ يذاكرون

٢ـ ______ جدّي منذ سنة .
أ ـ عاش ب ـ مات جـ ـ شعر

٣ـ ______ من المدرسة الثانوية ثم التحقت بالجامعة .
أ ـ تناولت ب ـ نزلت جـ ـ تخرجت

٤ـ ______ بنت عمتي على الدكتوراه في الاقتصاد .
أ ـ حصلت ب ـ استطاعت جـ ـ نجحت

٥ـ ______ كرة القدم مع اصدقائي كل يوم جمعة .
أ ـ أدخل ب ـ ألعب جـ ـ أعود

٦ـ أتناول ______ مع عائلتي في الساعة السابعة صباحًا .
أ ـ العشاء ب ـ الفطور جـ ـ الغداء

٧ـ في المساء ، جلست في النادي ______ ثمّ ذهبت إلى البيت .
أ ـ قليلاً ب ـ أحيانًا جـ ـ دائمًا

٨ـ جامعة "برينستون" جامعة ______ .
أ ـ وحيدة ب ـ ثانوية جـ ـ خاصّة

٩ـ لا ______ قراءة بعض الكلمات في هذه الرسالة .
أ ـ أستطيع ب ـ أتكلّم جـ ـ أستمع

١٠ـ ______ المفضلة هي الموسيقى .
أ ـ درجتي ب ـ هوايتي جـ ـ مذاكرتي

١١ـ نجح أحمد في كل الامتحانات وحصل على ______ «جيد».
أ ـ برنامج ب ـ مستقبل جـ ـ تقدير

١٢- عشت في منطقة «أكدال» في الرباط ــــــــ سنوات طفولتي.
أ - طوال ب - حوالي جـ - حيث

١٣- أنا ــــــــ ، وأريد قليلاً من الماء .
أ - عطشان ب - جوعان جـ - بردان

١٤- يوم ــــــــ لا يذهب خالد إلى الجامعة .
أ - الجمعة ب - الاثنين جـ - السبت

١٥- ــــــــ في الذهاب إلى الفصل بسبب الازدحام في الشارع .
أ - تذكرت ب - تأخّرت جـ - خرجت

١٦- ــــــــ السنة الدراسية في سبتمبر في بعض الجامعات الأمريكية.
أ - تبدأ ب - تدخل جـ - تنزل

تمرين ١٦ **كم؟**

SPECIFY HOW MANY, USING THE CORRECT FORM OF THE NOUN. REVIEW THE RULES FOR USING NOUNS WITH NUMBERS IN CHAPTERS 7 AND 8 IF YOU NEED TO.

١- من فضلك، بكم كيلو البطاطس؟ — الكيلو بـ ٥٠ ــــــــ . (ليرة)

٢- كم ــــــــ يدخّن خالد كل يوم؟ (سيجارة)

٣- لماذا عادوا من سفرهم بعد ــــــــ فقط؟ (٢ يوم)

٤- الجيش بحاجة إلى حوالي ١٠٠ ــــــــ جديد . (ضابط)

٥- الطقس اليوم حار جداً، فالحرارة ٣٩ ــــــــ . (درجة)

٦- ليس عنده إلاّ ستة ــــــــ قبل امتحان الثانوية العامة. (أسبوع)

٧- ابني سالم عمره ١١ ــــــــ وبنتي سلوى عمرها ٩ ــــــــ . (سنة)

٨- لا تستطيعون أن تجلسوا في الشمس أكثر من ٣٠ ــــــــ . (دقيقة)

٩- خالد له ثلاثة ــــــــ وخمسة ــــــــ . (أخ، صديق)

١٠- في السنة الماضية كان في هذا الشارع ١٠٠ ــــــــ ! (حادث)

١١- لا أستطيع الدراسة في المكتبة ثلاث ــــــــ ! (ساعة)

تمرين ١٧ **تمرين قراءة**

سامي زميل خالد في الجامعة حيث هو معيد في قسم الاقتصاد . ليس عنده محاضرات لأنّه يكتب رسالة الماجستير هذه السنة، ولكن يذهب الى الجامعة كل يوم – إلاّ يوم الجمعة – ويدرس ويكتب في المكتبة لأنه لا يحب الدراسة في البيت.

سامي يذهب مع خالد إلى النادي يوم الاربعاء بعد محاضرات خالد. خالد يحب الشطرنج كثيراً، أمّا سامي، فهو يحب شُرْب القهوة والكلام مع البنات!

تمرين ١٨ **استمعوا إلى خالد واكتبوا ما يقول** DVD

في الأيام التي ______ فيها إلى الجامعة، ______ ______ البيت ______ الساعة ______ صباحًا، لكن ______ توقظني ______ ______ في ______ و ______ لـِ ______ ______ . بعد أن ______ ______ و ______ ، ______ ______ في الفراندة ______ ______ القهوة و ______ سيجارة ______ عن ______ ______ وأقرأ ______ .

______ ______ في الثالثة ______ ______ ، لذلك ______ قبلها ______ في ______ ______ أو ثلاث ثمّ أتناول ______ . وبعد ______ ______ مع بعض ______ ______ ______ القهوة لـ ______ الشطرنج، ______ المفضلة، ثم ______ إلى البيت و ______ إخوتي ______ في ______ . في الأيام ______ ، أذهب إلى ______ صباحًا و ______ في ______ . أمّا ______ ______ ، فله ______ ______ .

العامية DVD

- القصة "جدتي بتصحّيني الساعة ستة ونص"

WATCH خالد TELL HIS STORY IN COLLOQUIAL.

Listen for the way he says بعد ذلك .

- "صباح الفل يا حاجّة"

WATCH الجدة TRY TO WAKE UP خالد .

What verb does she repeat, and what does it seem to mean?

Pay attention to her hand gestures. What do they signal?

تذكروا هذه الكلمات

وقت ج. أوقات	إلاّ	رُبع	ثُلث
دقيقة ج. دقائق	أمّا .. فَـ	أمس	العالَم
المناقشة			

١٠ . بيت العائلة

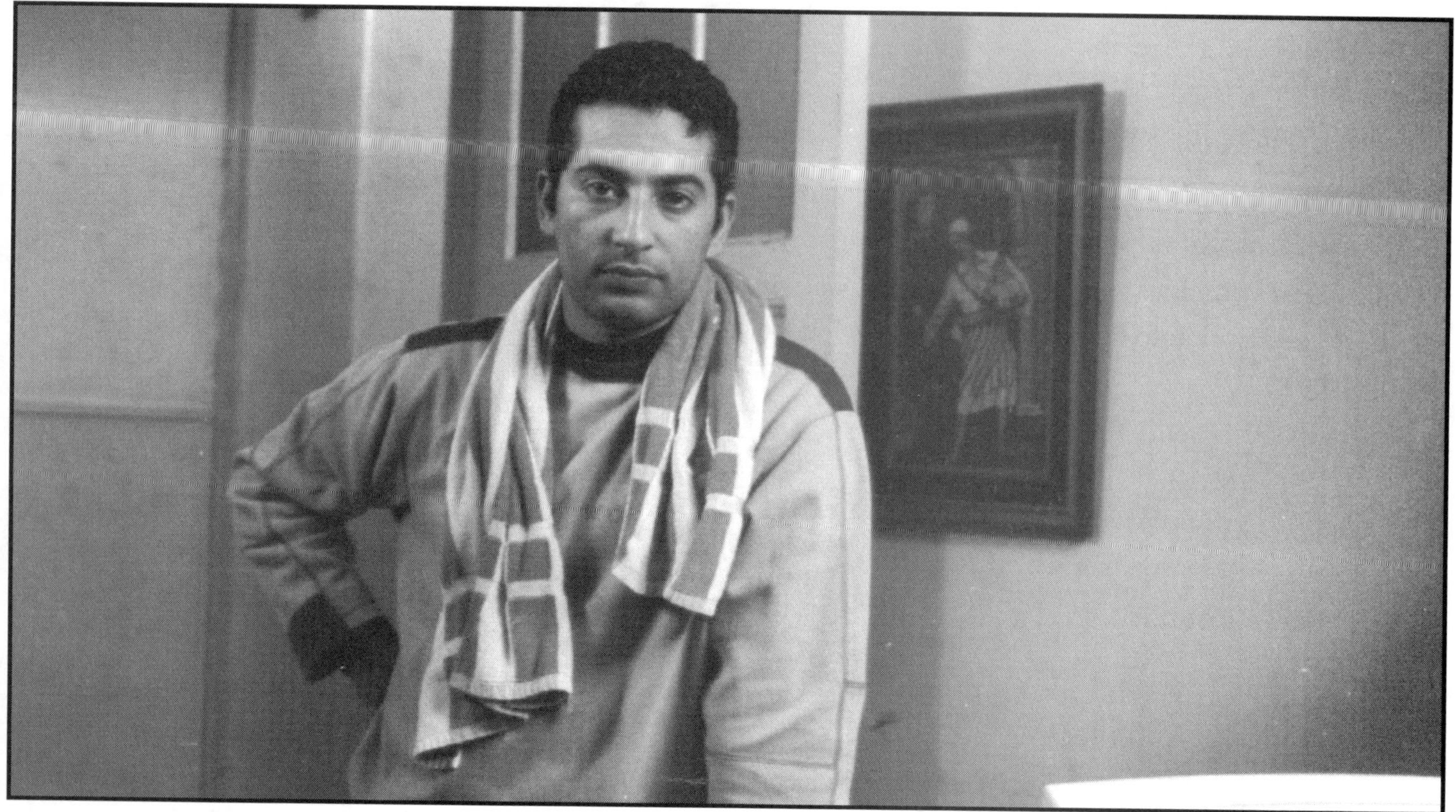

في هذا الدرس:

القصة • برنامج خالد يوم الجمعة

الثقافة • ما هو بيت العائلة بالنسبة لك؟

• ماذا تفعلون في نهاية الأسبوع؟

• جامع الحسين

القواعد • المضارع المنصوب

• إلى وعلى + الضمائر

• ضمائر النصب

القراءة • معيشة جلالة الملك

الاستماع • من برامج راديو «صوت العرب»

العامية • «بيت العيلة»

• «يلاّ يا ولاد!»

المفردات DVD

مُتَأَخِّر ج. ـون/ين	late
الَّتي	that, which (definite, مؤنث)
مُبَاراة ج. مُبَارَيات	match, game (sports)
جامِع ج. جَوامِع	mosque
جاءَ (جِئتُ) إلى ، يَجيء إلى ، المَجيء الى	to come
بِسُرعة	quickly (lit. *with quickness*)
سَهِرَ ، يَسْهَر ، السَّهَر	to stay up late
أصبَحَ ، يُصْبِح	to become
صَحا (صحَوتُ) ، يَصحو	to wake up
الصَّلاة	prayer
عادةً	usually
فَهِمَ ، يَفْهَم ، الفَهم	to understand
أقامَ (أقَمْتُ) ، يُقيم ، الإقامة	to reside, take up residence (hotel also)
أكثَر	more
لَيلة ج. ليالي / لَيالٍ	night
اللَّيلة	tonight
باللَّيْل	at night
اِستَمْتَعَ بـ ، يستَمْتِع بـ ، الاِسْتِمتاع بـ	to enjoy
يُمْكِن أنْ + **فعل مضارع**	it is possible to
يُمكِنُني أنْ (يُمكِنُكَ أن ، يُمكِنُهُ أن ..)	I can (literally: it is possible for me to...)
نامَ (نِمْتُ) ، يَنام ، النَّوم	to sleep, go to sleep
مَوعِد ج. مَواعيد	(fixed) time, appointment

تعلموا هذه الأفعال: DVD

LISTEN TO THESE VERBS ON YOUR DVD AND REPEAT UNTIL YOU CAN PRONOUNCE THEM EASILY. THEN PRACTICE BY MAKING UP QUESTIONS AND ANSWERS BY YOURSELF OR WITH A STUDY PARTNER.

الماضي

نِمنا	نِمتُ
نِمتُم	نِمتَ نِمتِ
ناموا	نامَ نامَت

المضارع

نَنام	أنام
تَنامونَ / تَناموا	تَنام تَنامينَ / تَنامي
يَنامونَ / يَناموا	يَنام تَنام

الماضي

جِئنا	جِئتُ
جِئتُم	جِئتَ جِئتِ
جاءوا (جاؤوا)	جاءَ جاءَت

المضارع

نَجيء	أجيء
تَجيئونَ / تَجيئوا	تَجيء تَجيئينَ / تَجيئي
يَجيئونَ / يَجيئوا	يَجيء تَجيء

الماضي

صَحَوْنا	صَحَوْتُ
صَحَوْتُم	صَحَوْتَ صَحَوْتِ
صَحَوا	صَحا صَحَت

المضارع

نَصحو	أصحو
تَصحونَ / تَصحوا	تَصحو تَصحينَ / تَصحي
يَصحونَ / يَصحوا	يَصحو تَصحو

تمرين ١ كلمات جديدة وقواعد قديمة (في البيت)

WRITE THE WORDS IN THE CORRECT FORM:

١- زميلتي ________ ضابطة في الجيش. (أصبح)

٢- ________ هذا الصباح متأخراً ولذلك ما ________ إلى المحاضرة. (أنا)
(صحا) (جاء)

٣- هل ________ المحاضرة ليلة أمس يا سارة؟ (يستمتع بـ)

٤- بعد التخرج أريد ________ في مدينة عربية مثل بيروت أو عمّان. (أقام)

٥- يمكنكم أن تشاهدوا ________ ________ طوال النهار والليل في ESPN.
(مباراة) (رياضي)

٦- هل ________ أن ________ أكثر بالعربية الآن؟ (يستطيع، يفهم)

٧- صفوفي ________ في الساعة ٩,٠٠ صباحاً .ولذلك لا ________ عادةً.
(بدأ) (فطر)

٨- ليلة الجمعة، الطلاب عادةً ________ مع أصدقائهم و________ الى ساعة ________ (خرج، سهر، متأخّر)

٩- هل يمكنكَ أن ________ الى بيتي للعشاء ؟ (جاء)

١٠- في هذه المدينة هناك ١٠٠ ________ أو أكثر. (جامع)

١١- عندي ثلاثة ________ مع أساتذتي هذا الاسبوع. (موعد)

تمرين ٢ اسألوا زملاءكم (في الصف)

1. Whether they resided outside خارِج the U.S. during their childhood.
2. What time they come to campus usually.
3. If friends come to their room or house a lot, and whether someone came over last night.
4. Whether they slept well last night, and whether they stayed up late in order to study.
5. Whether they enjoy more watching basketball, football, or soccer games.
6. What time they usually wake up in the morning and go to sleep at night.
7. When they became a college student.

تمرين ٣ الجذر والوزن (في الصف)

Expand your vocabulary: use الجذر of words you know to guess the meaning of these words:

١- يستطيع المسلم أن يُصَلّي في المسجد أو في البيت.

٢- السفر والسينما هوايات مُمتِعة!

٣- أخي مُقيم في فرنسا الآن

٤- كانت الـ «كونكورد» طائرة سَريعة جداً.

٥- هل التدخين مُمكِن في مطعم الجامعة؟

تمرين ٤ اكتبوا وزن كل كلمة من هذه الكلمات: (فَعَلَ ، فَعيل ، فاعِل ...)

الكلمة	الوزن	الكلمة	الوزن	الكلمة	الوزن
جامِع	________	أصبَحَ	________	أكثَر	________
يَفهَم	________	مَوعِد	________	يُمكِن	________
سَهِرَ	________	يَستَمْتِع	________	مُتَأَخِّر	________

تمرين ٥ كلمات جديدة + المصدر (في البيت)

Use المصدر to list things you do and do not enjoy and can and cannot do (use this exercise to review old vocabulary):

أستمتع بـ	لا أستمتع بـ
١- ٢- ٣-	١- ٢- ٣-
يمكنني ١- ٢- ٣-	لا يمكنني ١- ٢- ٣-

القصة DVD

تمرين ٦ **شاهدوا واكتبوا: (في البيت)**

١- ماذا يعمل خالد ليلة الخميس ؟ أ -

ب -

٢- إلى أين يذهب خالد يوم الجمعة ؟ من يذهب معه ؟

٣- ماذا يحب خالد ؟ أ - ب -

شاهدوا مرة ثانية:

٤- لماذا لا يخرج خالد من البيت مساء الجمعة ؟

٥- لماذا برنامج يوم الجمعة خاص بالنسبة لخالد؟

أ -

ب -

جـ -

٦- إلى أيّ جامع يذهب خالد للصلاة؟ جامع ________________

شاهدوا وخمّنوا:

٧- أستمتع أكثر <u>بالجَلسة</u> مع أصدقائي =____________

٨- هل تفهمون <u>ما أقصِد</u> ؟ = ________________

تمرين ٧ **نشاط عن القصة (في الصف)**

١- **للمناقشة:** ماذا يقصد خالد بـ «بيت العائلة»؟

٢- Compare يوم الجمعة بالنسبة لخالد ويوم السبت ويوم الأحد بالنسبة لكم:
ماذا يفعل وماذا تفعلون؟

الثقافة

ما هو بيت العائلة بالنسبة لك؟ DVD

Watch the interviews on your DVD about بيت العائلة . To what extent do people's experiences and situations differ? Are the differences comparable to those you would find in this country?

ماذا تفعلون في نهاية الأسبوع؟ DVD

How do الشباب المصريون spend their weekend? Watch the interviews on your DVD to find out.

جامع الحُسَين DVD

جامع الحسين جامع كبير في مدينة القاهرة في منطقة اسمها «الحسين»، وهي منطقة قريبة من جامع الأزهر. والحسين هو ابن علي بن أبي طالب، الخليفة الرابع، وفاطمة بنت النبي محمد. عاش الحسين في «المدينة» ومات في سنة ٦٨٠ في مدينة كَربلاء في العراق. يمكنكم أن تشاهدوا جامع الحسين في الـDVD .

Hussein's importance to Muslims lies in his opposition to the rule of the Umayyad dynasty and his assassination at the hands of Umayyad soldiers. Shi'ites (الشيعة) commemorate his assassination every year on عاشوراء , the tenth day of the Islamic month مُحَرَّم . Shi'ities consider الحسين to be the third إمام , or leader, after his father الإمام علي and his older brother الإمام الحَسَن .

الإمام الحسين:

ابن الإمام علي (ابن عم النبي محمد) والسيدة فاطمة (بنت النبي محمد)

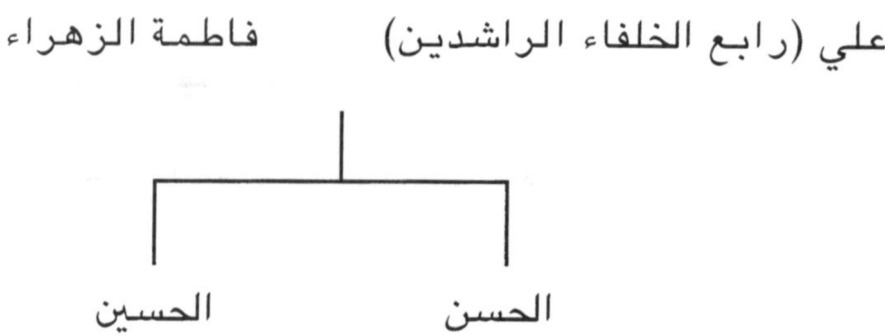

القواعد

❁ المضارع المنصوب

المُضارِع المَنصوب[1]	one of three forms of الفعل المضارع

You have seen المصدر used to express the infinitive verb in constructions like:

لا يمكننا الخروج   أستطيع الدراسة

and with لِـ to express *in order to,* as in:

أذهب الى المكتبة للدراسة   يدرس للحصول على دبلوم

This same meaning may also be expressed by أنْ followed by الفعل المضارع , as you have seen in:

يمكننا أن نسهر   كنت أريد أن أدخل كلية الآداب

Likewise, the infinitive in the phrase *in order to* may also be expressed using لِـ followed by المضارع , as in:

نعود إلى البيت لنأكل الغداء   نسهر لنشاهد التليفزيون

Note that these constructions are equivalent in meaning:

المصدر = أنْ + المضارع المنصوب

While المصدر tends to be more formal than المضارع , both constructions are widely used in formal Arabic. Study these examples:

كنت أريد أن أدخل كلية الآداب .   =   كنت أريد دخول كلية الآداب .

نسهر لنشاهد التليفزيون .   =   نسهر لمشاهدة التليفزيون .

أستطيع أن أدرس في المكتبة .   =   أستطيع الدراسة في المكتبة .

When المضارع is used with لِـ or أنْ , it takes a form called المضارع المنصوب . In unvocalized texts, you will not notice anything different about المضارع المنصوب , **except** in the forms for persons انتِ, انتم, and هم . When we introduced the مضارع conjugation in

---

[1]This form of the verb is often called *the subjunctive* in English treatments of Arabic grammar, and it shares some semantic features of subjunctives in other languages. It mainly serves as a subordinate, non-finite verb form.

Chapter 4, we noted that the forms for these persons include two variants: one with ن , and one without it:

أنتِ :	تفعلين	تفعلي
أنتم :	تفعلون	تفعلوا
هم :	يفعلون	يفعلوا

The forms on the left, the ones **without** ن , are the المضارع المنصوب forms. The مضارع منصوب forms for the other persons take a final فتحة vowel, which is indicated only in fully vocalized texts. Study and listen to the chart on your DVD and note the differences of the أنتِ , أنتم and هم forms as main verb and infinitive verb:

المضارع المنصوب DVD

أريد أنْ أذهبَ	نريد أنْ نذهبَ
تريد أنْ تذهبَ تريدين أنْ تذهبي	تريدون أنْ تذهبوا
يريد أنْ يذهبَ تريد أنْ تذهبَ	يريدون أنْ يذهبوا

It is also important to begin learning when to use أنْ + المضارع المنصوب . This construction usually parallels the English infinitive or gerund, with one important exception: Arabic does not use أنْ with verbs that delimit the time frame of an action, such as بدأ :

بدأتُ أدرس اللغة العربية في الخريف الماضي .

The verbs you know that can be followed by either المصدر or أنْ + المضارع المنصوب are:

استطاع   يمكن   يحبّ   أراد   رفض

Finally, **remember** that قبل and بعد **must** be followed by either المصدر or أنْ :

قبل السفر	*before traveling*	=	قبل أن نُسافِرَ	*before we travel*
بعد التخرّج	*after graduating*	=	بعد أن نتخرّجَ	*after we graduate*

تمرين ٨ اسألوا زملاءكم: قبل أو بعد؟ (في الصف)

WHAT DO YOU DO FIRST? ORDER THESE ACTIVITIES, USING قبل أن OR بعد أن : THEN ASK زملاءك WHAT THEY DO FIRST.

مثال: آكل الغداء - أذهب إلى الصف —> آكل قبل أن أذهب إلى الصف .
—> أذهب إلى الصف بعد أن آكل .

١- أقرأ - أنام
٢- ندرس الكلمات الجديدة - نشاهد الفيديو
٣- أخرج من البيت - يخرج زميلي من البيت
٤- آكل العشاء - أذهب إلى المكتبة
٥- أعود إلى البيت - تعود والدتي
٦- أصحو - أشرب القهوة
٧- أفطر - أستمع إلى الأخبار

تمرين ٩ من المصدر الى المضارع المنصوب (في البيت)

READ EACH SENTENCE AND IDENTIFY المصدر , THEN REWRITE USING المضارع المنصوب . WRITE ALL THE VOWELS ON المضارع المنصوب VERBS:

١- أحبّ السّفر إلى الشرق الاوسط.
٢- لا يمكنني الذهاب إلى النادي اليوم.
٣- يريدون السكن بعيداً عن هذه المنطقة.
٤- لماذا لا تستطيعين الخروج معنا؟
٥- لا أريد التأخّر عن موعدي!
٦- لماذا ترفضون مشاهدة هذا الفيلم ؟
٧- يريد كتابة رسالة إلى أمه .
٨- نستطيع حفظ كل هذه الكلمات.
٩- هل يمكنك مساعدتنا؟
١٠- تريد العمل في الوزارة بعد التخرُّج.
١١- خالد يدخّن بعد نزول والده.

❁ إلى وعلى + الضمائر

Listen to and learn the combinations of the prepositions إلى and على with pronouns:

على DVD

عَلَيْنا	عَلَيَّ
عَلَيْكُم	عَلَيْكَ عَلَيْكِ
عَلَيْهِم	عَلَيْهِ عَلَيْها

إلى DVD

إلَيْنا	إلَيَّ
إلَيْكُم	إلَيْكَ إلَيْكِ
إلَيْهِم	إلَيْهِ إلَيْها

In formal Arabic, the pronunciation of possessive pronoun endings ـهُ and ـهُم shifts to ـهِ and ـهِم when immediately preceded by a kasra or ي .

أمثلة: يجيئون إلى بيتنا كثيراً. ←— يجيئون إلَيْهِ كثيراً.

استمعنا إلى هذه الموسيقى. ←— استمعنا إلَيْها .

كتبتُ الكلمات على الدفتر. ←— كتبت الكلمات علَيْهِ .

تمرين ١٠ **(في البيت)**

COMPLETE THE SENTENCES WITH A PREPOSITION AND A PRONOUN (YOU NEED TO IDENTIFY THE NOUN THAT THE PREPOSITION REFERS TO IN ORDER TO DETERMINE WHICH PRONOUN TO USE).

١- لا أحبهم ولا أريد أن أستمع __________ .

٢- عندها دكتوراه، وحصلت __________ في سنة ٢٠٠٤.

٣- لا أفهم لماذا جئتم __________ (أنا) للكلام عن هذا!

٤- بيروت مدينة جميلة يذهب __________ كثير من العرب كل صيف.

٥- هذا الكرسي قديم ولا أريد أن أجلس __________ .

٦- أذهب الى المكتبة للدراسة أحياناً وأجلس إلى الطاولة لأبدأ الدراسة ولكن بعد وقت قصير أنام __________ !

Object Pronouns ❁ ضمائر النصب

You have learned to use subject pronouns (...هي ، أنت ، أنا) and possessive pronouns (... ـها ، ـك ، ـي). The third and final set of personal pronouns are those that indicate the object of a verb, as in: جدتي توقظني and الله يرحمها . The following chart gives the pronoun forms that are used as objects of verbs. As you can see, most of them match the possessive pronouns:[1]

us	ـنا	me	ـني
you (pl.)	ـكُم	you (m.) you (f.)	ـكَ ـكِ
them	ـهُم	him, it her, it, them[2]	ـهُ ـها

Now study the pronoun object suffixes in the context سَاعَدَ *he helped (me/you/etc.)*:

ساعَدَنا	ساعَدَني
ساعَدَكُم	ساعَدَكَ ساعَدَكِ
ساعَدَهُم	ساعَدَهُ ساعَدَها

Note: when pronouns are affixed to verbs ending in the plural suffix وا , the alif drops:

أمثلة: أقاربي تذكّروا + أنا —> أقاربي تذكّروني .

تريدون أن تقرأوا + هو —> هل تريدون أن تقرأوه ؟

---

[1]In spoken Arabic, the suffixes for أنتَ and أنتِ are often pronounced ـكَ and ـكِ respectively. In formal Arabic, the suffix تُم gets a helping vowel when object pronouns attach to it: شاهدتُموني .

[2]For non-human plurals.

تمرين ١١ **ضمائر النصب (في البيت)**

Put the verb in the correct form, then add the correct pronoun to show *whom*:

مثال: أنا أتذكرها . (يتذكر + هي)

١ـ الاستاذة ــــــــــــ أن نذاكر جيداً. (يريد + نحن)

٢ـ أقاربي ــــــــــــ كثيراً. (يحبّ + انا)

٣ـ أمها ــــــــــــ في كتابة الرسالة. (ساعد + هي)

٤ـ أنتم لا ــــــــــــ ! (يفهم + انا)

٥ـ جدّتنا ــــــــــــ كل صباح. (يوقظ + نحن)

٦ـ مَن ــــــــــــ الكيمياء؟ (يدرّس + انتم)

٧ـ متى ــــــــــــ الخروج معنا؟ (يمكن + انتِ)

٨ـ هل (انتم) ــــــــــــ جيّداً؟ (يعرف + هو)

٩ـ لماذا ــــــــــــ مكتب القبول؟ (رفض + انتَ)

١٠ـ لا أعرف إذا كانوا ــــــــــــ . (يتذكر + انا)

تمرين ١٢ **اسألوا زملاءكم (في الصف)**

مثال: هل ذاكرت الكلمات؟ – نعم، ذاكرتها / لا ، ما ذاكرتها .

١ـ هل ساعدوا زملاءهم؟

٢ـ هل شاهدوا مباراة كرة السلة؟

٣ـ هل فهموا قراءة الدرس الماضي؟

٤ـ هل ذهبوا الى صفوفهم أمس؟

٥ـ هل يستمعون إلى الأخبار؟

٦ـ من يُدرّسهم الأدب/العلوم السياسية؟

٧ـ هل يستمتعون بصفوفهم؟

٨ـ هل أكلوا الفطور/الغداء؟

تمرين ١٣ نشاط محادثة (في الصف)

WITH A PARTNER, ASSUME THE ROLES OF A JOURNALIST AND AN ARAB CELEBRITY. THE JOURNALIST INTERVIEWS THE CELEBRITY ABOUT HIS OR HER LIFESTYLE. USE AS MANY VERBS AS YOU CAN, AND REPORT ON:

برنامجه/ها اليومي – هواياته/ها – أين عاش/ت

سفره/ها – رأيه في أمريكا – ماذا يريد/تريد أن يفعل/تفعل هذه السنة

استماع DVD

تمرين ١٤ نشاط استماع

LISTEN TO THE ANNOUNCEMENT OF DAILY PROGRAMMING FROM THE RADIO STATION صوت العرب. BELOW IS A LIST OF PROGRAMS WE WOULD LIKE TO RECORD AND NEED TO CHECK THE TIMES THEY WILL BE BROADCAST:

البرنامج	الموعد
"المرأة العربية"	
"العالم اليوم"	
"قصة مخطوط"	
"ليالي الشرق"	
"أسماء في الأخبار"	
"معاني وأسامي"	
"الدنيا بخير"	
"أنت وطفلك"	

Also list here any religious programs and songs you can identify and the broadcast times:

تمرين ١٥ نشاط كتابة (في البيت)

USE YOUR IMAGINATION TO WRITE A STORY ABOUT THE FOLLOWING SEQUENCE OF PICTURES:

رمسيس
موقف
الأوتوبيس

الرسم: الدكتور مايكل كوبرسون

تمرين ١٦ **نشاط قراءة (في الصف)**

تعلموا هذه الكلمات:

مَـلِك ج. مُـلوك	king
جَلالـة المَلِك	his majesty the king
حَمّام ج. -ات	bathroom, bath
اِستَقبَلَ ، قابَلَ	to receive, meet (people)

THE FOLLOWING TEXT IS AN EXCERPT FROM A **1931** OFFICIAL BIOGRAPHY OF KING FUAD OF EGYPT. THE LANGUAGE IS SOMEWHAT FLOWERY, BUT VERY ACCESSIBLE. FOLLOW HIS MAJESTY'S MAIN ACTIVITIES BY LOOKING FOR WORDS YOU KNOW AND CAN GUESS THE MEANING OF FROM الجـذر OR CONTEXT. REMEMBER THAT THE FINAL ي IN EGYPTIAN WRITING AND PRINTING OMITS THE DOTS.

معيشة جلالة الملك اليومية

قال جلالة الملك فؤاد مرة لجماعة من أخصائه : «انى أستيقظ عادة الساعة الخامسة صباحا ولكنى لا أغادر الجناح الخاص بى الا بعد ذلك بوقت طويل».

وبعد الاستيقاظ يدخل جلالة الملك الحمام ، ويرتدى ملابسه على الاثر ، ثم يقوم ببعض الحركات الرياضية ، ويجلس بعد ذلك الى المائدة ليفطر فطوراً خفيفا جداً ، وبعد الفراغ من الاكل يعكف جلالته على العمل فيجلس فى احدى قاعات الجناح الخاص به ويبدأ في تصفح الجرائد والمجلات ، ومن البديهى ان الجرائد المصرية هى التى تهمه أكثر من غيرها. فيؤتى لجلالته بالجرائد اليومية العربية والافرنجية حال صدورها .

ويتلقى جلالة الملك عشر جرائد يومية ونحو عشرين مجلة فرنسية وأربع أو خمس جرائد يومية ونحو عشرين مجلة انجليزية ، وكثيراً من الجرائد والمجلات الايطالية . وبهذه الطريقة يتمكن جلالة الملك من متابعة الحالة العامة فى العالم كله كما انه بمطالعته للجرائد اليومية المحلية يقف على جميع دقائق الحالة السياسية والادبية والاجتماعية فى مملكته .

وفى منتصف الساعة الحادية عشرة يبدأ جلالة الملك باستقبال الزائرين وكثيراً ما تدوم المقابلات والتشريفات حتى الساعة الثانية بعد الظهر بلا انقطاع ويستقبل جلالته الزائرين عادة في مكتبه الواسع الذى يشرف على سراى عابدين .

وبعد انتهاء المقابلات يتناول جلالة الملك طعام الغداء ثم يستقبل فى الحال رؤساء الديوان الملكى ويدرس معهم المسائل التى يعرضونها عليه فيصدر اليهم تعليماته ويوقع المراسيم والاوامر حتى منتصف الساعة الرابعة بعد الظهر إذ يعود جلالته الى مقابلاته الرسمية .

وبعد انتهاء المقابلات الرسمية يجتمع جلالة الملك بكبار موظفى السراى ويشتغل معهم حتى ساعة متأخرة ، وكثيراً ما يظل جلالته حتى الساعة الثامنة فى مكتبه ... ثم يدخل جلالة الملك جناحه الخاص ليتعشى عشاء خفيفاً وليمضى فترة من الزمان مع أفراد أسرته الكريمة .

من كتاب «جلالة الملك بين مصر واوروبا» لكريم ثابت، دار الهلال ، القاهرة ، ١٩٣١

تمارين المراجعة

تمرين ١٧ ترجموا إلى اللغة العربية

1. My grandfather used to have beautiful pictures of old Kuwait.
2. Did you have an exam this week?
3. There are no classes today because of the snow!
4. She doesn't have any time today, so we can't sit and chat with her.
5. The members of my family do not have opinions like mine.
6. Do you have any news from your family in Yemen?
7. My new roommate has a sister who works for the Ministry of Labor.
8. I don't like this job because it has no future.
9. There are good Chinese restaurants in this area.

تمرين ١٨ استمعوا إلى خالد واكتبوا ما يقول DVD (في البيت)

________ الخميس ________ أن ________ لـ ________ التليفزيون أو

أن ________ مع أصدقائنا، لذلك ________ ________ يوم الجمعة، فـ ________

________ والحمد لله هو ________ . ________ مع والدي و ________

________ الجمعة في ________ الحسين ، ثم ________ ________ إلى

البيت لـنتناول ________ قبل أن ________ ________ كرة القدم التي

________ ها ________ في التليفزيون يوم ________ . وفي ________ التي

ليست فيها ________ ، ________ ________ و ________ أو ساعتين بعد

________ . أما في المساء فلا ________ ________ لأن بيتنا، منذ ________

معنا ________ ________ بيت ________ ، ________ ________ كل

يوم جمعة كل أفراد العائلة. في ________ أحب ________ ولكني ________

________ بالجلسة مع أصدقائي. هل ________ ما أقصد؟

العامية DVD

-القصة: "بيت العيلة"

شاهدوا خالد يتكلم.

How does خالد say يمكنني and أصحو in colloquial?

-"يلّا يا ولاد !"

شاهدوا محمود والأولاد يتكلمون مع حنّا.

What topics are included in a friendly and polite greeting among neighbors?

تذكروا هذه الكلمات

مَلِك ج. مُلوك　　حمّام ج. ات　　اِستَقبَلَ　　المضارع المنصوب

١١ ـ أشعر بالخجل أحيانا

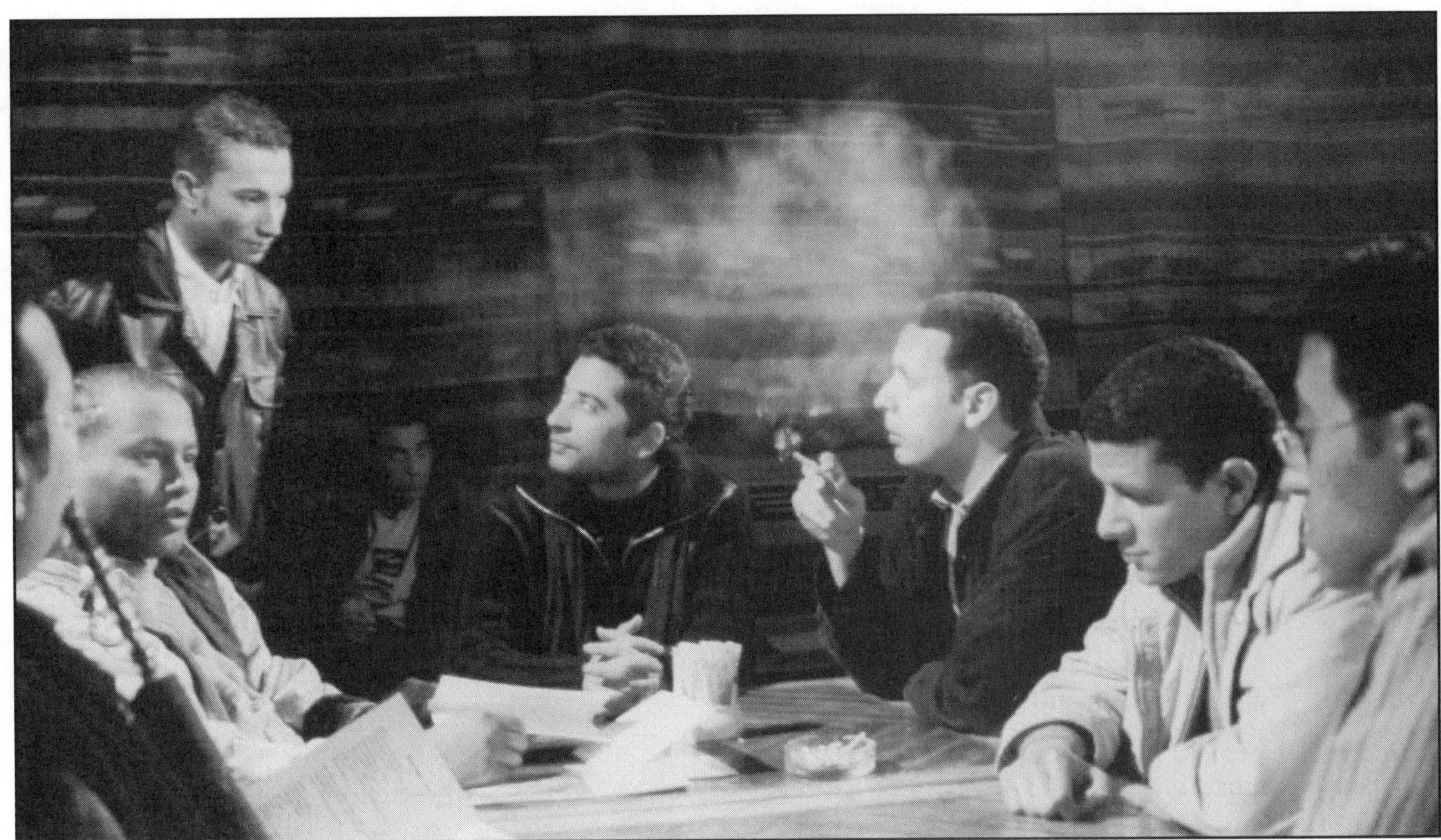

في هذا الدرس:

القصة • خالد وأصدقاؤه

الثقافة • كيف هي صداقاتك وعلاقاتك؟

القواعد • المضارع المرفوع

• جملة الصفة

• كل، بعض، معظم، عدّة *Quantifiers*

القراءة • دليلك الى الفنادق في عمان

• مقالة أخبار

الاستماع • مع العائلة والأصدقاء

العامية • القصة: «باحس بالخجل أحيانا»

• «عايزة أقولك حاجة»

المفردات

to exchange	تَبادَلَ ، يَتَبَادَل ، التَّبـادُل
(an) experience	تَجْرِبة ج. تَجارِب
shyness, embarrassment	الخَجَل
she got engaged to	خُطِبَت لِـ
tourism	السِّياحة
pharmacy	صَيْدَلِيّة ج. -ات
several	عِدّة + اسم جمع indefinite
to get to know, meet	تَعَرَّفَ على ، يَتَعَرَّف على ، التَّعَرُّف على
emotional; romantic	عاطِفيّ
most (of)	مُعظَم + اسم جمع في إضافة
relationship; (plural) relations (between)	عَلاقة ج. -ات (بَيْنَ)
when (non-interrogative)	عِندما + فعل
hotel	فُندُق ج. فَنادِق
to be cut off	اِنْقَطَعَ ، يَنْقَطِع ، الاِنْقِطاع
once, (one) time	مَرّة ج. -ات
together	مَعًا
of, among (to specify part of a group)	مِن
engineer	مُهَنْدِس ج. -ون/ين

تمرين ١ كلمات جديدة وقواعد قديمة (في البيت)

DESCRIBE THESE PEOPLE AND THINGS BY USING THE APPROPRIATE FORM OF THE WORDS GIVEN:

١- عندما ______ على زملاء جُدُد، ______ معهم عنوان الـ email.
(تعرّف) (تبادل)

٢- كل أعمامي ______ يعملون في مصر والسعودية . (مهندس)

٣- معظم ______ ______ بالخجل قليلاً في أول السنة الدراسية. (طالب، يشعر)

٤- كم ______ في الاسبوع تخرجون معاً؟ (مرة)

٥- واحدة من ______ خطبت لرجل يعمل في وزارة السياحة ويتكلم خمس ______ .
(زميلة) (لغة)

٦- في المنطقة التي نسكن فيها عدّة ______ ______ . (صيدلية، صغير)

٧- من هواياته ______ الرسم و______ الرسائل الإلكترونية.
(مفضّل) (تبادل)

٨- استمتعنا بهذه ______ ولكننا نريد دخول ______ ______ دائماً.
(تجربة) (تجربة) (آخر)

٩- من منكم يستمتع بمشاهدة الأفلام ______ ؟ (عاطفي)

تمرين ٢ اسألوا زملاءكم (في الصف)

1. What the best hotel in this area is.
2. How many times per week they exchange emails with their family.
3. How/when/where they met their husband/wife/girlfriend/boyfriend/best friend.
4. Whether they are enjoying their college experience.
5. Whether they like to read romantic stories.
6. What they would do if their college money was cut off.
7. Whether in their opinion relations between Europe and the U.S. are better than last year.
8. Whether they like the experience of travelling to other countries, and why or why not.
9. Whether they are more often lonely or shy.

تمرين ٣ الكلمات الجديدة (في البيت)

COMPLETE WITH AN APPROPRIATE WORD من الكلمات الجديدة :

١ـ صديقتي وفاء تعمل في مكتب لِـ ________ والسفر.

٢ـ أحبِ أن أذهب الى السينما ________ كل اسبوع .

٣ـ عندما سافرت صديقتي إلى القاهرة أقامت في ________ «هيلتون» .

٤ـ أشعر بـ ________ أحياناً عندما أتكلم في الصفّ .

٥ـ زميلي متخصص في العلوم السياسية وهو يدرس ________ العربية-الأمريكية.

٦ـ «روميو وجولييت» قصّة ________ .

٧ـ شاهدت فيلم «كاسابلانكا» ٤ ________

٨ـ الصيف الماضي عملتُ في الامم المتحدة وكانت هذه ________ ممتازة.

٩ـ أقامت في السعودية ________ سنوات بعد زواجها.

١٠ـ مها وعائلتها ________ الرسائل والاخبار مع أقاربهم في مصر.

١١ـ ________ العلاقة بين الحبيبيْن بسبب سفره إلى أمريكا.

١٢ـ ________ بنت عمّي لِزميل يعمل معها في نفس الشركة.

١٣ـ ________ عليهم منذ أربع سنوات، ونحن أصدقاء منذ ذلك الوقت.

١٤ـ كل يوم، ننزل أنا ووالدتي ________ من البيت في السابعة صباحا.

تمرين ٤ الوزن (فَعَّلَ ، مَفعول ، فاعِل) اكتبوا وزن هذه الكلمات:

الكلمة	الوزن	الكلمة	الوزن	الكلمة	الوزن
تَبادُل	________	يَتَعَرَّف	________	اِنْقَطَعَ	________
عَلاقة	________	مُعظَم	________	تَجارِب	________

القصة DVD

تمرين ٥ شاهدوا واكتبوا:

١- عمّن/ عمَّ يتكلم خالد؟

أ-

ب -

شاهدوا مرة ثانية:

٢- من أي كليات تخرّج أصدقاء خالد؟ Circle:

العلوم السياسية	الصيدلة	الاقتصاد	الهندسة
السياحة والفنادق	الحقوق	التجارة	الآداب

٣- متى يجلس خالد مع أصدقائه؟ عمَّ يتكلمون؟

٤- من هي البنت التي تعرّف عليها خالد؟ ماذا حَدَثَ *happened* لِلعلاقة؟

٥- كيف يشعر خالد عندما يتكلم مع أصدقائه؟ لماذا؟

شاهدوا وخمّنوا :

٦- اثنان منهم تخرّجا — What do you think the ending on this verb refers to? (Think about the subject of the verb.)

٧- قصص الحُبّ = ______________________

8. You know the word صيدلية . Khalid uses a related word here. Listen for it, write the phrase in which it occurs and guess the meaning: ______________________

تمرين ٦ عن القصة (في الصف)

1. Role Play: Create a scene for either خالد والبنت or خالد وأصدقائه in which the parties discuss العلاقة وانقطاعها .

2. Listen to خالد again and focus on his use of و to mark new sentences and lists. Identify each و and the two or more phrases or sentences it connects.

الثقافة DVD

كيف هي صداقاتك وعلاقاتك؟

Watch the interviews on your DVD with بعض الشباب المصريين about their friendships. How do their ideas compare to your own?

القواعد

❁ المضارع المرفوع

In Chapter 4, you learned to recognize various endings of الفعل المضارع . In Chapter 10, you learned about one of these endings, المضارع المنصوب , the form of المضارع used in formal Arabic after أنْ and لِـ . A second form of المضارع , which is considered to be the basic or "default" form, is called المضارع المرفوع , and is used in most cases. When المضارع is the main verb in its sentence or clause, it usually takes this form. It is the form you learned about in Chapter 4 with the ن endings.

All of the forms of المضارع share the same stem; the only difference between them is the ending. You know that المضارع المنصوب takes a final فتحة on most persons, and does not take the final ن on أنتِ , أنتم and هم (to review see the chart in Chapter 10). In contrast, المضارع المرفوع takes a ضمّة on most persons and retains the final ن on أنتِ , أنتم and هم . The final ضمة vowel will not appear in unvocalized texts, and you will only hear it spoken in very formal contexts. This chart gives the endings of المضارع المرفوع using the verb يفعل as a model:

المُضارع المَرفوع DVD

أفعلُ	نفعلُ
تفعلُ تفعلينَ	تَفعَلونَ
يفعلُ تفعلُ	يفعلونْ

تمرين ٧ في البيت

Mechanical practice will help you master the verb endings. Choose 3 or 4 verbs and draw up charts for them showing both المضارع المرفوع and المضارع المنصوب endings. Say them out loud as you write them out, and think about how you would use them in a context.

تمرين ٨ المضارع المنصوب والمرفوع (في البيت)

Decide whether each فعل مضارع should be مرفوع or منصوب and write the correct form:

١- خالد ــــــــــ من النادي حوالي الساعة الثامنة مساء . (يعود)

٢- لماذا لا ــــــــــ مع زملائكم ؟ (يجلس)

٣- أنا لا ــــــــــ أن ــــــــــ كلامها . (يستطيع ، يفهم)

٤- متى ــــــــــ عادةً يا ريما ؟ (ينام)

٥- أقاربي ــــــــــ إلى بيتنا مرةً كل اسبوع . (يجيء)

٦- هل ــــــــــ أن ــــــــــ معنا يا رندة ؟ (يحب ، يأكل)

٧- نحن ــــــــــ أن ــــــــــ الرسائل مع زملاء من العالم العربي. (يريد، يتبادل)

٨- يا أحمد، في أي ساعة ــــــــــ يوم الجمعة ؟ (يصحو)

٩- لا يمكنني أن ــــــــــ معكم لأنّ عندي امتحانين كبيرين يوم الأربعاء. (يسهر)

١٠- هو دائماً ــــــــــ من بيته في السادسة والربع صباحاً ! (يخرج)

١١- ــــــــــ كم أن ــــــــــ معي في أي وقت . (يمكن، يتكلم)

١٢- أولادي ــــــــــ أن ــــــــــ قبل أن ــــــــــ . (يحبّ ، يقرأ ، ينام)

١٣- يا نورا ، هل ــــــــــ أن ــــــــــ ني ؟ (يمكن، يساعد)

تمرين ٩ اسألوا زملاءكم (في الصف)

In answering, use المرفوع endings, and use a pronoun instead of the underlined noun:

مثال: هل تحبينَ الجامعة؟ - نعم أحبُّها

١- هل يحبون السياحة؟

٢- هل يشاهدون مباريات كرة السلة عادة؟

٣- هل يفهمون الاساتذة عادةً؟

٤- هل يأكلون العشاء في الجامعة؟

٥- هل يتذكرون بيت طفولتهم؟

٦- هل يقرأون القصص العاطفية؟

٧- هل يستمعون الى أمهم عندما تتكلم؟

٨- هل يتبادلون الأخبار عن تجاربهم مع أفراد اسرتهم؟

٩- هل يستمتعون بمشاهدة المباريات الرياضية في التليفزيون؟

❁ جملة الصفة

In Chapter 5 you practiced introducing and describing friends and relatives with sentences like these:

لي صديقة اسمها ليلى.

لي صديق يدرس تاريخ الشرق الاوسط.

In this chapter, خالد uses a similar sentence to explain the end of his relationship:

خُطِبَت لِمهندس يعمل في السعودية.

These sentences introduce and describe new entities (people or things). Since they are at first unknown to the reader/listener, these nouns are indefinite: *a friend, a girl, a professor,* etc. The phrases that further identify and describe them are joined to the noun directly, just like an indefinite **adjective** (= صفة); hence the name, جملة الصفة.[1] These phrases often begin with a verb, as you can see from the examples above and below:

صديقي حامد استاذ يدرّس الادب العربي في جامعة القاهرة .

تعرّف على امرأة تعمل في قسم اللغات .

The sentences that describe the indefinite noun are **complete sentences** that could stand on their own. The noun they describe is the topic of جملة الصفة , but is not part of the structure of the sentence, and so its place in جملة الصفة must be filled by a pronoun that refers back to it as follows:

(1) If the noun being described is the subject of the verb, the pronoun is expressed in the verb. In the following example, the subject of the verb تعمل is هي , which refers to امرأة :

...a woman *[who] (she) works* تعرّف على امرأة تعمل في قسم اللغات.

(2) If the noun being described is the object of the verb, in a possessive relationship, or the object of a preposition, a matching pronoun must fill its slot in the sentence:

...a film *[that] I watched (it)* تكلمت عن فيلم شاهدته.

...a son *whose name is (who his name is)* لها ابن اسمه طارق.

...a game *[that] I enjoyed (it)* شاهدت مباراة استمتعت بها.

It is important to learn to recognize this structure, especially when reading. Pay attention to indefinite nouns and what follows them, and watch for pronouns that refer back to them.

---

[1]In English, the words *who, that* and *which* are used in these kinds of sentences; Arabic has no such words. Learn to think about the structure and meaning of what you are saying, and avoid translating word-for-word.

تمرين ١٠ **جملة الصفة (في البيت)**

A. Match phrases from أ with ones from ب to form sentences containing جملة الصفة :

	أ	ب
١-	تعرّفَ على بنت	ينجحون دائمًا في الامتحانات
٢-	لي زميلة	استمتعتُ به كثيرًا
٣-	أعرف مصريين	تدرس معه في الكلية
٤-	شاهدت فيلمًا	اسمه طارق
٥-	هم طلاّب	يسكنون في مدينة هيوستن
٦-	هم زملاء	أصبحت موظفة كبيرة في الوزارة
٧-	هو صديق	يعمل فيها خالي
٨-	أعرف امرأة	تدرس الصيدلة
٩-	هذه شركة	أحبه كثيرًا
١٠-	أكلنا في مطعم	تتكلم ٦ لغات
١١-	لها بنت	اسمه «مطعم علي بابا»
١٢-	لي صديق طفولة	أجلس معهم في النادي

B. Now complete the following sentences, writing your own جملة الصفة :

١٣- لنا استاذة ____ .

١٤- هذه جامعة ____ .

١٥- أمس تعرّفت على رجل ________________________________ .

١٦- قرأت قصة ____ .

١٧- لها اخت ____ .

١٨- عندما كانوا في دمشق، أقاموا في فندق ____________________ .

تمرين ١١ جملة الصفة: ترجمة (في الصف)

Familiarize yourself with the structure of جملة الصفة in Arabic by changing the structure of the following English sentences to an Arabic structure as in the example. Remember to use pronouns that refer back to the noun being described when needed.

Example: I saw a movie I didn't like. → I saw a movie I didn't like **it**.

1. He's in love with a girl he met last year.
2. I've watched every game they played this year.
3. I remember that from a book I read.
4. Last year I had a roommate who used to sleep all the time.
5. I enjoy every lecture I go to.
6. She is busy with friends who came Thursday night.
7. I have an appointment I want to go to.
8. I live in an area that has good schools.
9. She got engaged to a man who lives in Morocco.
10. They're talking about a new story she wrote.

والآن ترجموا هذه الجمل إلى اللغة العربية.

تمرين ١٢ أين جملة الصفة؟ (في الصف)

اقرأوا للفهم أولاً ، ثم لمعرفة أين جمل الصفة:

Underline all جمل صفة you can find:

هل تريدون أن تسمعوا الى قصة تحبونها؟ عندي صديق يعيش في مدينة بوسطن حيث يدرس في جامعة تعرفونها جيداً. وهذا الصديق يسكن في بيت ليس فيه «كاراج»، وعنده سيارة لا تعمل جيداً، ولكنه يحب أن يذهب بسيارته الى السوق البعيد. ومرّة، عندما كان في السوق، وأراد أن يعود الى بيته، ماتت سيارته. الحمد لله، شاهدته امرأة تعمل في السوق، وساعدته في الكلام مع AAA . بعد ذلك، تكلّم صديقي مع المرأة التي ساعدته بالتليفون وبدآ يخرجان معاً . -- هل هذه بداية علاقة عاطفية؟ لا نعرف!

❁ كل / بعض / معظم /عدّة *Quantifiers*

no one, none (of)	لا أحَد (من الـ ..)
people (plural)	الناس
all	كل الـ + الجمع
each, every	كل + مفرد indefinite
several	عِدّة + جمع indefinite

Learn the rules for using these quantifying expressions in Arabic by remembering whether they are followed by a definite or indefinite, plural or singular noun phrase, and which ones use من to signal *part of* a group. The examples below give you models.

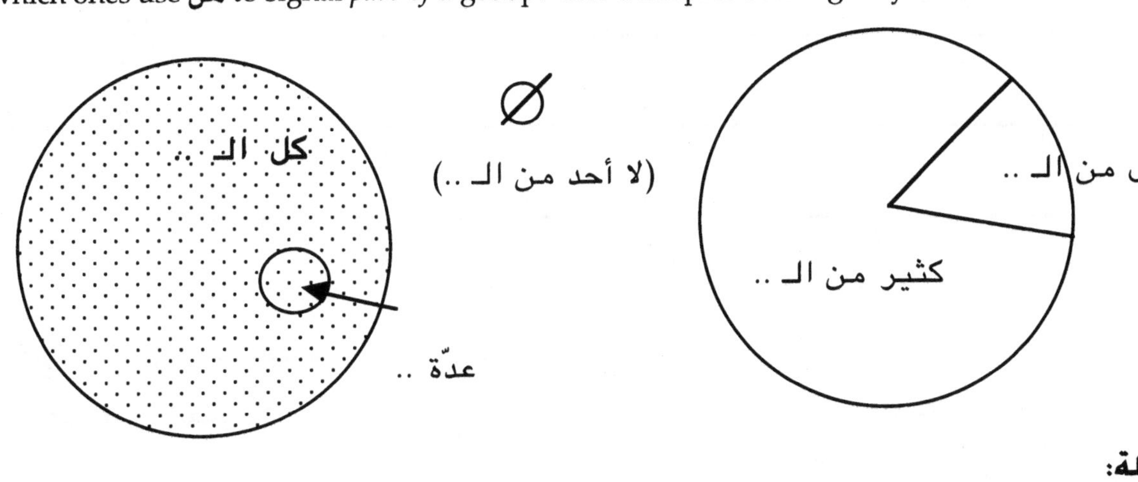

أمثلة:

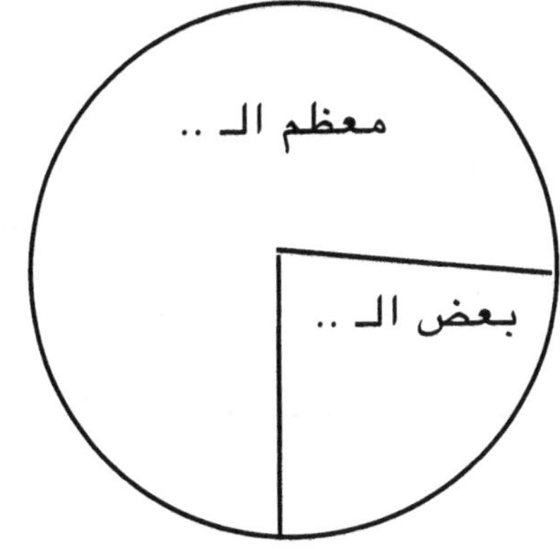

كل الناس يحبون السينما!

أسهر **كل ليلة** الى حوالي الساعة الواحدة.

معظم أفراد عائلتي دخلوا الجامعة.

كثير من الفنادق في هذه المنطقة قديمة.

قليل من الطلاب ينامون قبل نصف الليل!

بعض الصيدليات في هذه المنطقة تعمل ٢٤ ساعة.

لا أحد من أصدقائي يدخّن. (Note the singular verb here.)

هذه السنة تعرّفت على **عدّة طلاب** جُدُد. (Note the indefinite plural here.)

تمرين ١٣ **من يفعل /لا يفعل هذا؟ (في البيت)**

DEFINE WHO DOES THESE THINGS USING QUANTIFIERS, AS IN THE EXAMPLE:

مثال: يحبّ الواجب . —> معظم الطلاب لا يحبّون الواجب .

١- يحب أن يقرأ القصص العاطفية ________________ .

٢- يحب أن يصحو في الساعة ٦,٠٠ صباحًا ________________ .

٣- يشعر بالخجل عندما يتكلم مع ناس لا يعرفهم ________________ .

٤- يحب يوم الاثنين ________________ .

٥- يشاهد التليفزيون ٣ أو ٤ ساعات كل يوم ________________ .

٦- يرفض العمل يوم الأحد ________________ .

٧- يموت في حوادث سيّارات ________________ .

تمرين ١٤ **نشاط قراءة (في الصف)**

تعلّموا هذه الكلمات:

عَدَد ج. أعداد	number (of)
سَرير	bed

أسئلة:

١- في أي مدينة عربية هذه الفنادق؟ ما هي اسماء بعض المناطق؟

٢- اكتبوا كل الكلمات الجديدة التي استطعتم أن تعرفوا معناها *meaning* من الـ context:

٣- ماذا عرفتم عن الفنادق في هذه المدينة؟ اكتبوا بعض الجمل:

مثال: كل الفنادق فيها مطاعم.

كلمات اخرى: بعض، معظم، عدّة، واحد/اثنان/ثلاثة ...

من «دليلك المفصل في عمّان» ، دار عمان للنشر ، آذار (مارس) ١٩٩٤

دليلك المفصل إلى

الفنــــــادق

مجموع عدد الغرف	مكيف هواء	بركة سباحة خارجية
عدد الغرف بسرير واحد	خدمة تنظيف الملابس	بركة سباحة داخلية
عدد الغرف بسريرين	مطاعم	استعدادات خاصة للأطفال
حمام في الغرفة	صالون تجميل	مكتب تأجير سيارات
حمام خارج الغرفة	حمام ساونا	موقف سيارات مكشوف
هاتف في كل غرفة	ملاعب تنس	موقف سيارات مغطى
تلفزيون في كل غرفة	غرفة ألعاب داخلية	بطاقات التسليف مقبولة
راديو في كل غرفة	قاعة اجتماعات ومؤتمرات	١)أميركان إكسبرس ٤)ماستر كارد
عرض أفلام في الغرف	فرقة ترفيهية	٢)كارت بلانش ٥)داينرز كلوب
تدفئة مركزية	ديسكو	٣)فيزا ٦)يورب كارد

★★★★★ فنادق الخمس نجوم

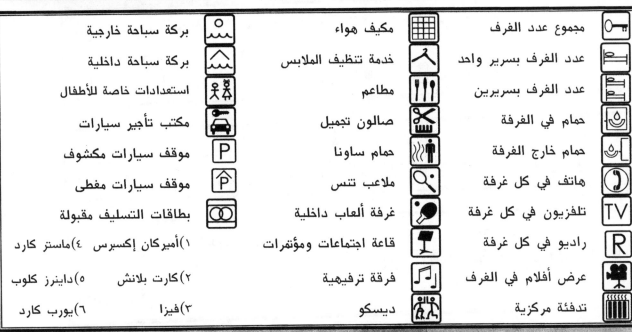

إنتركونتننتال الأردن ، جبل عمان ، الدوار الثالث هاتف: ٦٤١٣٦١ ، فاكس ٦٤٥٢١٧، ص.ب ٣٥٠١٤ عمان
٣٨١ ٨٢ ٢٧٠ و ٢٨ جناح، بالاضافة إلى جناح ملكي
١ ، ٢، ٣ ، ٤ ، ٥

عمان ماريوت ، الشميساني ، هاتف: ٦٠٧٦٠٧ ، فاكس ٦٧٠١٠٠، ص.ب ٩٢٦٣٣٣ ٢٩٤ ٤٢
٢٢٦ و ٢٦ جناح ملون ثلاجة
١ ، ٢ ، ٣ ، ٤ ، ٥

فورتي جراند عمان ، الشميساني ،هاتف: ٦٩٦٥١١ ، فاكس ٦٧٤٢٦١، ص.ب ٩٥٠٦٢٩ عمان ٣٠٣
٣٢ ٢٣٢ و ٣٩ جناح ملكي
١ ، ٢ ، ٣ ، ٤ ، ٥

★★★★ فنادق الاربع نجوم

عمرة ، جبل عمان ، الدوار السادس ، هاتف: ٨١٥٠٧١ ، ص.ب ٩٥٠٥٥٥، عمان .
٢٧٤ ٦٠ ٢٠١ و ١٣ جناح
١ ، ٢ ، ٣ ، ٤ ، ٥

★★★ فنادق الثلاث نجوم

شبرد ، شارع زيد بن حارثة ، خلف الكلية العلمية الإسلامية ، جبل عمان ، هاتف: ٦٣٩١٩٧/٨/٦٤٢٤٠١، فاكس ٦٣٩١٩٨ ، ص.ب ٢٠٢٠ .
٤٤ ٦ ٣٨ ملون ثلاجة ١ ، ٢

عمان انترناشيونال ، شارع الجامعة الأردنية ، هاتف: ٨٤١٧١٢/٨٤١٧١٣، فاكس ٨٤١٧١٤ ، ص.ب ٢٥٠٠
٣٧ ٨ ٢٤ و ٥ أجنحة ١ ، ٣ ، ٤ ، ٥

جراند بالاس ، طريق المدينة الرياضية ، شارع الملكة علياء ، هاتف ٦٩١١٣١، فاكس ٦٩٥١٤٣ ، ص.ب ٩٢٢٤٤٤. ١٦٠ ١٠ ١٥٠
١ ، ٣ ، ٥

كراون ، شارع الإذاعة والتلفزيون ، هاتف ٧٥٨١٨٠/١، فاكس ٦٤٨٠٥٠ ، ص.ب ١٣١٨
٧٥ ٧٢ و ٣ أجنحة
١ ، ٣

الشرق الأوسط ، الشميساني ، هاتف ٦٠٧١١٥/ ٦٠٧١٦٠ / ٦٠٧١١٩/ ٦٠٧٤٢٣ ، فاكس ٦٦٧٤٢٢ ،
ص.ب ١٩٢٢٤ ٩٩ ١٤ ٧٠ و ١٥ جناح ملون ثلاجة
١ ، ٣ ، ٥

إمبسادور ، الشميساني ، هاتف ٦٠٥١٦١/ ٦٨٦١٦١ / ٦٧١٢٦١/ ٦٠٧١٩٥ / ٦٠٧٢١٥، فاكس ٦٨١١٠١،
ص.ب ٩٢٥٣٩٠ ١٠٠ ٨٨ و١٢ جناح ثلاجة
١ ، ٣ ، ٤ ، ٥

تمرين ١٥ **نشاط قراءة**

تعلموا هذه الكلمات:

سَفير ج. سُفَراء	ambassador
الصِحّة	health

اقرأوا الخبر من جريدة سعودية واكتبوا:

١- ما هو الخبر؟ من؟ __________ و__________

ماذا؟ __________________________

أين؟ __________ متى؟ __________

2. In the first sentence, identify and label these grammatical elements: subject—verb—object—adverb of time–prepositional phrase indicating place.
3. Look at the phrase معالي الوزير and guess from الجذر what it means.
4. Knowing the source of the article, guess the meaning of the word المَلَكة .
5. In the second sentence, find all cases of المصدر . Why do some **not** have الـ ? See how many cases of إضافة and صفة + اسم you can find.

د. المانع استقبل السفير الصيني

الرياض - واس:

استقبل معالي وزير الصحة الدكتور حمد بن عبد الله المانع بمكتبه بالوزارة أمس سفير جمهورية الصين لدى المملكة سي كي وو. وقد تم خلال الاستقبال تبادل الأحاديث الودية ومناقشة سبل تدعيم التعاون الصحي بين البلدين.

من جريدة «الجزيرة» السعودية ١٢/٦/٢٠٠٣

تمرين ١٦ **نشاط كتابة**

Write about أصدقائك , from any standpoint you wish. Title your piece «أصدقائي». Remember to use connectors such as و , لذلك , and كما .

الاستماع

تمرين ١٧ المصدر

LISTEN TO THE SENTENCES ON YOUR DVD AND WRITE المصدر THAT YOU HEAR. REMEMBER TO LISTEN FOR الشدّة THAT RESULTS FROM SUN LETTERS + الـ , AND BE ON THE LOOKOUT FOR الإضافة :

١ـ لا أحبّ ــــــــــــــــ في الصباح .

٢ـ بدأت ــــــــــــــــ الطبّ منذ سنتين .

٣ـ نجحت في الامتحان بفضل ــــــــــــــــ والدي ووالدتي .

٤ـ هوايتها ــــــــــــــــ الصور والرسائل .

٥ـ لا أستطيع ــــــــــــــــ عندما أكون جوعانة .

٦ـ خرجت من البيت بعد ــــــــــــــــ أولادها من المدرسة .

٧ـ ما تزوّجَتْه بسبب ــــــــــــــــ عائلتها .

٨ـ أقامت جدّتي معنا بعد ــــــــــــــــ جدّي .

٩ـ أنا وأصدقائي نستمتع بـ ــــــــــــــــ .

١٠ـ لا يمكنني ــــــــــــــــ الدرس قبل ــــــــــــــــ الكلمات الجديدة.

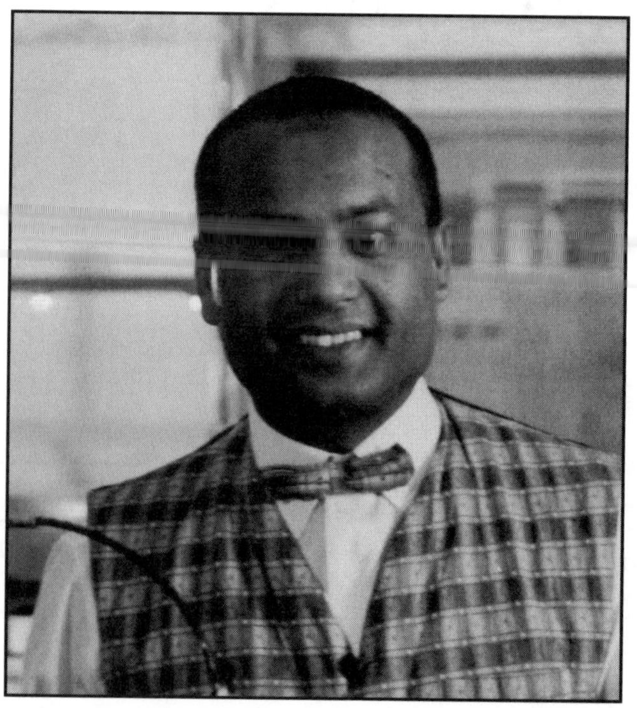

تمرين ١٨ مع العائلة والأصدقاء

شاهدوا الـ DVD واكتبوا:

١ـ من يتكلم؟ من هو بالنسبة لخالد؟

٢ـ ماذا يعمل؟ أين يعمل ؟

٣ـ ما برنامجه اليومي ؟

٤ـ ماذا يفعل يوم الاثنين ؟

٥ـ هل هو مثل خالد؟ لماذا/لماذا لا؟

تمارين المراجعة

تمرين ١٩

THESE SENTENCES ARE MEANINGLESS WITHOUT THE RIGHT PREPOSITION. COMPLETE THEM:

١- التحق عمّي ـــــــ الجيش منذ عشر سنوات .

٢- ننزل ـــــــ البيت عادةً ـــــــ الساعة السابعة والنصف .

٣- تريد أختي أن تحصل ـــــــ الماجستير ـــــــ إدارة الأعمال .

٤- لا يمكنني أن أصحو ـــــــ النوم قبل الساعة التاسعة .

٥- عادل يشعر ـــــــ الوحدة بعد أن ماتت زوجته .

٦- جدة خالد تسكن ـــــــهم في البيت .

٧- أستمتع كثيراً ـــــــ قراءة الجريدة صباح الأحد .

٨- تعرفت ـــــــ معظم أصدقائي في النادي .

٩- عاد أخي الصغير ـــــــ المدرسة ودخل ـــــــ غرفته .

١٠- تكلمت الأستاذة ـــــــ محاضرتها ـــــــ العلاقات الأوروبية - العربية .

١١- لا أحب أن أستمع ـــــــ الأخبار لأني لا أحب السياسة .

تمرين ٢٠ تمرين قراءة

اسمه طارق، وهو واحد من أصدقاء خالد. تخرّج من كلية السياحة والفنادق منذ سنتين ثم حصل على عمل في فندق «رَمسيس هيلتون»، في مطعم الفندق. طارق يعمل ستة أيام في الاسبوع من الساعة السادسة صباحًا الى الساعة الرابعة بعد الظهر. لذلك يومه يبدأ في الساعة الرابعة عندما يصحو من النوم، ثم ينزل من البيت في الخامسة. يعود طارق إلى البيت في الساعة الخامسة بعد الظهر بعد يوم طويل ويشاهد التليفزيون بعد أن يأكل الغداء وقبل أن ينام.

في يوم الاثنين طارق لا يعمل، ولذلك يذهب مع خالد والأصدقاء الآخرين إلى النادي حيث يلعبون ويتكلمون عن أخبارهم. طارق يحب خالد كثيراً ولكن، في رأيه، خالد خجول جداً ولا يريد أن يدخل تجربة اخرى بعد انقطاع العلاقة مع البنت التي كان يخرج معها. أما طارق، فهو يحب التجارب العاطفية ويستمتع بها كثيراً.

تمرين ٢١ **استمعوا إلى خالد واكتبوا ما يقول**

________ ________ الآن كانوا ________ في ________

الثانوية، ________ ________ تخرّجا من كلية ________ ، وواحد من ________

________ ، وواحد من ________ ________ ، وواحد من ________ ________

و ________ . نجلس ________ ________ كل ________ لـ

________ ________ و ________ ________ . أشعر ________

أحيانا لأنه ليست لي ________ ________ مثلهم . ________

________ طالبا في ________ ________ ، ________ على طالبة في

السنة ________ و ________ معا ________ ________ ، ثم

________ ________ بعد أن خطبت لـِ ________ ________

بالسعودية .

العامية

- القصة: "باحسّ بالخجل أحيانا"

شاهدوا خالد يتكلم عن أصدقائه وعلاقته.

Listen to the way he says ليست لي تجارب عاطفية and انقطعت علاقتنا .

- "عايزة أقولك حاجة"

شاهدوا خالد وصديقته.

How does the girl say "there is someone" in colloquial?

تذكروا هذه الكلمات

المضارع المرفوع	جملة الصفِة	لا أحد	الناس
عدد ج. أعداد	سفير ج. سُفَراء	سَرير	الصِحّة

١٢. أصعب قرار في حياتي

في هذا الدرس:

القصة	• محمد أبو العلا
القواعد	• أَفعَل التفضيل *The Superlative*
	• المستقبل
	• الجملة الفعلية *Subject-Verb Agreement*
القراءة	• وفاة ادوارد سعيد
	• مقالة أخبار
الاستماع	• عن جامعة عربية
العامية	• القصة: «أصعب قرار في حياتي»
	• أغنية «زوروني كل سنة مرّة»

المفردات

أخَذَ ، يَأخُذ ، الأخْذ	to take
آخِر + اسم مفرد indefinite	the last...
بَقِيَ ، يَبْقى ، البَقاء	to stay, remain
جَميعًا	all together
إجازة ج. -ات (= عُطْلة)	vacation
الحَياة	life
زارَ ، يَزور ، الزِّيارة	to visit
سَـ (سَوفَ) + المضارع المرفوع	(future marker)
لم تُسافِر	= ما سافَرْتَ
أصْعَب + اسم مفرد indefinite	the most difficult...
بالإضافة إلى	in addition to
طَبْعًا	of course, naturally
عُطلة ج. عُطَل	day off, = إجازة
عَلِمَ بـ ، يَعْلَم بـ ، العِلم بـ	to learn of
عُيِّنْتُ	I was appointed
تَغَيَّبَ عن ، يَتَغَيَّب عن ، التَّغَيُّب عن	to be absent from, miss
قَرَّرَ ، يُقَرِّر + أنْ + المضارع المنصوب / المصدر	to decide to
قَرار ج. -ات	decision
مُقارَن	comparative (adjective.)
قَضى ، يَقْضي ، القَضاء	to spend (+ **time**)
مِنْحة ج. مِنَح	scholarship award, grant, fellowship
هُنا	here
وَفاة	= مَوت

تعلموا هذه الأفعال: DVD

الماضي

زُرتُ	زُرنا
زُرتَ زُرتِ	زُرتُم
زارَ زارَت	زاروا

المضارع

أزور	نَزور
تَزور تَزورينَ	تَزورونَ
يَزور تَزور	يَزورونَ

بَقيتُ	بَقينا
بَقيتَ بَقيتِ	بَقيتُم
بَقِيَ بَقِيَتْ	بَقوا

أبقى	نَبقى
تَبقى تَبقَيْنَ	تَبقَوْنَ
يَبقى تَبقى	يَبْقَوْنَ

قَضَيْتُ	قَضَيْنا
قَضَيْتَ قَضَيْتِ	قَضَيْتُم
قَضى قَضَت	قَضَوا

أَقضي	نَقضي
تَقضي تَقضينَ	تَقضونَ
يَقضي تَقضي	يَقضونَ

تمرين ١ **الوزن والجذر (في الصف)**

Name الجذر والوزن of these كلمات جديدة :

أَخَذَ   مُقارَن   تَغَيَّبَ   يُقَرِّرَ   أصعَب   عُطلة

تمرين ٢ المفردات الجديدة (في البيت)

COMPLETE THE SENTENCES USING NEW VOCABULARY:

١- كانت مريضة ولذلك ________ في السرير كل اليوم.

٢- بعد حصولي على الدكتوراه ________ استاذة في قسم اللغة الفرنسية وآدابها.

٣- معظم طلاب الجامعات والمدارس يأخذون ________ طويلة في الصيف.

٤- ________ منطقة الشرق الأوسط منذ ثلاث سنوات.

٥- هل ________ بخبر زواج سمير وسامية؟!

٦- فاطمة ________ أولادها إلى المدرسة كل يوم صباحاً.

٧- كانت ________نا إلى عمّان قصيرة جداً - ثلاثة أيام فقط.

٨- استاذتي متخصصة في الادب ________.

٩- بعض الطلاب ________ عن المحاضرات بسبب الطقس المثلج.

١٠- جدة خالد تعيش معهم منذ ________ والدته.

١١- ستسافر اختي إلى اوروبا حيث ________ اجازتها السنوية.

١٢- ________ والدتي العودة إلى العمل بعد الانقطاع عنه سنوات طويلة.

١٣- سنصحو في السابعة صباحا ثم سننزل ________ لنفطر في الكافتيريا.

١٤- حصلت على ________ من جامعة جورجتاون لدراسة الاقتصاد السياسي.

١٥- ليلى تتكلم اللغتين الانكليزية والفرنسية ________ اللغة العربية.

تمرين ٣ ماذا فعلوا أو سيفعلون؟

USE EACH SET OF WORDS TO WRITE جملة طويلة WITH AT LEAST ONE "NEW SENTENCE" و. FOCUS ON USING NEW VOCABULARY AND THINK ABOUT THE TENSE OF THE VERBS.

١- أخي وأصدقاؤه / بعد أسبوعيْن / زار / قضى / بالإضافة الى

٢- بنت عمّتي / الاسبوع الماضي / قضى / قرّر / علم بـ / وفاة

٣- أنا وبعض زملائي/ يوم الخميس الماضي / تغيّب عن / زار / قرّر / طبعاً / جميعاً

٤- يا شباب! / لماذا؟ / أخذ / بقي / عندما

تمرين ٤ كلمات جديدة + قواعد قديمة (في البيت)

COMPLETE THESE SENTENCES USING AT LEAST ONE NEW كلمة IN EACH SENTENCE. REMEMBER TO PAY ATTENTION TO THE GRAMMATICAL STRUCTURES YOU NEED TO USE WITH أن , سـ , لأنّ , AND بسبب .

١- لماذا قررتم أن ________________________________ ؟

٢- زملاؤنا يريدون أن ________________________________ .

٣- هل علمتم بـ ________________________________ ؟

٤- من فضلك، هل يمكنك أن ________________________________ ؟

٥- صديقي يشعر بالخجل لأنّ ________________________________ .

٦- انقطعت العلاقات بيننا بسبب ________________________________ .

٧- لا نستطيع أن ________________ لأنّ ________________ .

٨- في المستقبل سـ ________________________________ .

تمرين ٥ اسألوا زملاءكم (في الصف)

1. Who visited them and whom did they visit on their last vacation?
   How many times في a semester do they visit their families?
2. How many hours per day do they spend في studying? reading?
3. Do they stay here on campus on the weekends?
4. What was the best decision they ever made (=decided OR took) in their lives?
5. Do they remember where they were when they learned of 9/11?
6. What was the hardest class they have taken/took in college?
7. Do they spend time (= وقت) with friends every day?
8. Do they miss class or work often? Why/why not?
9. Do they know of any scholarships for summer language study?

القصة DVD

تمرين ٦ **شاهدوا واكتبوا:**

١- من يتكلّم ؟

٢ - عمَّ يتكلم ؟ أ-

ب -

شاهدوا مرة ثانية:

٣- من أين تخرّج؟

٤- إلى أين سافر بعد ذلك؟

٥- فيمَ (في ماذا) كان متخصصاً؟

٦- ماذا يقول عن البقاء في أمريكا؟

٧- متى زار مصر آخر مرّة؟

٨- من سيسافر معه إلى القاهرة هذه المرّة؟

٩- كم أسبوعًا سيقضون في القاهرة؟

استمعوا وخمّنوا:

خمّنوا معنى هذه الكلمات :

١٠- عرفتم الكثير عني من مها = ____________

١١- أخذنا إجازتنا السنوية = ____________

تمرين ٧ **عن القصة (في الصف)** Role Play

قبل قرار السفر الى مصر، مها ومحمد وملك يتكلمون عن الإجازة. ومحمد يقول" أريد أن نقضي الإجازة في القاهرة جميعاً". ماذا تقول مها وملك؟

القواعد

❁ أفعَل التفضيل *The Superlative*

You have seen several examples of the superlative:

أحسن فصل　　　　　　أصعب قرار　　　　　　آخر مرّة

The superlative adjective, named أفعَل التفضيل after its وزن , is formed from a simple adjective by putting the جذر of the adjective into وزن أفْعَل.[1] Listen to the أفعل forms of these adjectives on the DVD and complete the chart. (You can see that adjectives whose جذر contains a doubled consonant, like حارّ and جديد , take a modified form; learn the ones given here.) DVD

بارد -> أبْرَد	جميل -> أجْمَل	(حَسَن) -> أحْسَن
صغير -> ______	كبير -> ______	حارّ -> أحَرّ
قليل -> أقَلّ	قريب -> ______	بعيد -> ______
طويل -> ______	قصير -> ______	كثير -> ______
جديد -> أجَدّ	سهل -> ______	صعب -> ______
واسع -> أوْسَع	عالي -> أعلى	قديم -> ______

Remember that these words are fixed in form and cannot take ة . **Remember** also that the superlatives *first* and *last* take special forms: DVD

أوّل	آخِر

The أفعل adjective can be used to form superlative phrases like the ones you have seen. In this case, the adjective acts as a noun and is used in a kind of إضافة with an indefinite noun.

the kindest man — أطْيَب رجل

the nicest woman — ألْطَف امرأة

the strangest movie — أغْرَب فيلم

---

[1]In general, نسبة adjectives and adjectives with longer أوزان like مقارن , متأخر or مفضّل (i.e., those with extra consonants) **cannot** be made superlative by using this وزن .

The most important thing to remember about this superlative construction is that **although its English equivalent is definite, the Arabic is indefinite.** When used in a sentence, it acts just like an indefinite noun, and often occurs in جملة الصفة (see Chapter 11):

١) القاهرة أكبر مدينة مصرية. ٢) آخِر فيلم شاهدناه كان جيّدًا.

In the first sentence, note that the adjective مصرية is indefinite, because it modifies the indefinite phrase أكبر مدينة . In the second sentence, the phrase آخر فيلم is modified by جملة الصفة , which describes an indefinite noun.

The superlatives أوّل and آخِر often occur in contexts like the one you heard in the text:

The last time [in which] ... آخر مرّة زرت مصر فيها كانت منذ ثلاث سنوات .

Note the use of فيها to complete جملة الصفة . The preposition في indicates location in both time and space in Arabic, and you will see and hear it in such contexts often.

تمرين ٨ **أفعل التفضيل (في البيت)**

Describe these things using superlatives:

مثال: نيويورك أكبر مدينة في أمريكا

١- اللغة العربية هي ________ ________ درستها.

٢- البحرين ________ ________ عربي والسعودية ________ ________ ________ .

٣- فندق «فور سيزونز» -________ ________ في العالم.

٤- ________ ________ دخلها خالد انقطعت لأن البنت خطبت لمهندس، ولا يريد أن يبدأ علاقة اخرى الآن.

٥- يوم ١/١ ________ ________ في السنة ويوم ١٢/٣١ ________ ________ ________ .

٦- ________ ________ شاهدت فيها فيلمًا كانت منذ أسبوع .

٧- ________ ________ في حياتي كان الالتحاق بهذه الجامعة.

٨- أسبوع الامتحانات هو ________ ________ في السنة!

٩- والدتي دكتورة وهي تقضي يومها كله مع المرضى، و________ ________ يبدأ عادة في الساعة الثامنة صباحاً و________ ________ في حوالي الساعة السادسة.

تمرين ٩ نشاط محادثة (في الصف)

WORK WITH A PARTNER TO WRITE ENTRIES FOR A "GUINNESS BOOK OF WORLD RECORDS" FOR THE CLASS. USE AS MANY DIFFERENT أفعل WORDS AND VOCABULARY AS YOU CAN.

❁ المُستَقبَل

In formal Arabic, المُستَقبَل *the future* is formed by adding the prefix سَـ or its long form سَوف to المضارع المرفوع . The following chart shows the conjugation of المستقبل using the verb يفعل as an example: DVD

سَأفعَلُ / سَوفَ أفعَلُ	سَنَفعَلُ / سَوفَ نَفعَلُ
سَتَفعَلُ / سَوفَ تَفعَلُ سَتَفعَلينَ / سَوفَ تَفعَلينَ	سَتَفعَلونَ / سَوفَ تَفعَلونَ
سَيَفعَلُ / سَوفَ يَفعَلُ سَتَفعَلُ / سَوفَ تَفعَلُ	سَيَفعَلونَ / سَوفَ يَفعَلونَ

❁ لَن

In formal Arabic, the particle لَن (**without** س/سوف) is used to negate the future. لن is followed by المضارع المنصوب . The following chart shows future negation using the verb يفعل as an example: DVD

لَن أفعَلَ	لَن نَفعَلَ
لَن تَفعَلَ لَن تَفعَلي	لَن تَفعَلوا
لَن يَفعَلَ لَن تَفعَلَ	لَن يَفعَلوا

Memorize the future forms of the verb كان :

سَنَكونُ	سَأكونُ
سَتَكونونَ	سَتَكونُ سَتَكونينَ
سَيَكونونَ	سَيَكونُ سَتَكونُ

لن نَكونَ	لن أكونَ
لن تَكونوا	لَن تَكونَ لَن تكوني
لَن يَكونوا	لَن يَكونَ لَن تَكونَ

تعلموا هذه الكلمات:

غَدًا	tomorrow
القادِم /ة	next, coming

أمثلة: سوف نأخذ اجازتنا في الاسبوع القادم إن شاء الله .

السنة القادمة سأكون معكم إن شاء الله .

غداً، لن أكون في البيت ، سأكون في الجامعة.

الثقافة

The expression إن شاء الله *God willing,* is often used when talking about the future to express the hope or wish that something will happen, much the way American English speakers use the phrase *hopefully*.

أمثلة: سوف أتخرّج بعد سنة إن شاء الله .

سأسافر إلى [illegible] السنة القادمة إن شاء الله .

تمرين ١٠ نشاط محادثة: قراءة المستقبل (في الصف)

In Arab culture, fortunes are told in several ways. One of the most common is the "reading" of the coffee grounds left in the cup, الفِنجان , after drinking Arabic/Turkish coffee. Have a cup of coffee if you can and tell the fortunes of your classmates as they read yours for you.

تمرين ١١ **ماذا سيفعلون أو لن يفعلوا؟ (في البيت)**

Fill in the blanks using المستقبل or its negative according to the sentence, as in the two examples. Write all vowels on all verbs.

مثال: أصدقائي سَيَذهَبون إلى السينما اليوم. (ذهبوا)

١- ــــــــــ أختي من الجامعة بعد ثلاث سنوات إن شاء الله. (تخرّجَت)

٢- هل ــــــــــ في المباراة في كرة القدم غداً بعد الظهر يا أحمد؟ (لعِبتَ)

٣- هل ــــــــــ خالد إلى أمريكا في الصيف القادم؟ (سافر)

٤- لن ــــــــــ مرّة اخرى كما سهرنا أمس!! (سهِرنا)

٥- ــــــــــ بالوحدة إذا عِشتِ بعيداً عن عائلتك وأصدقائك. (شعرتِ بـ)

٦- غداً ، ــــــــــ إخوتي في المذاكرة ثم ــــــــــ إلى النادي.
(ساعدتُ) (ذهبتُ)

٧- لن ــــــــــ إلى تلك المدينة مرّة أخرى! (عُدنا)

٨- صديقتي ــــــــــ الجامعة في أوّل السنة القادمة إن شاء الله. (دخلت)

٩- في أيّ ساعة ــــــــــ من البيت غدا؟ (نزلتم)

١٠- ــــــــــ على زميلتي الجديدة عندما تجيء الى الغرفة اليوم. (تعرّفتُ)

١١- أختي لن ــــــــــ ني اليوم لأنّ ابنها مريض. (زارت)

١٢- عندما أتخرج إن شاء الله، ــــــــــ ماذا أريد أن أعمل. (قرّرتُ)

١٣- هو تعبان جدا، ولذلك لن ــــــــــ في المكتب كل اليوم! (بقِيَ)

١٤- لن ــــــــــ قبل الساعة الحادية عشرة يوم السبت! (صحَوتُ)

١٥- عندما يسافرون الى عمّان، ــــــــــ في فندق «عمان ماريوت». (أقاموا)

١٦- أنتم تعملون كثيراً جداً، وإن شاء الله ــــــــــ إجازة قريباً! (أخذتم)

١٧- لن ــــــــــ السفر إلى مصر هذه السنة. (استطعنا)

Subject-Verb Agreement **الجملة الفعلية**

By now you have seen many examples of الجملة الفعلية , sentences that begin with verbs. In some جمل فعلية , the subject of the verb is contained in the verb itself, as in:

أسكن في مدينة نيويورك .

نسهر لنشاهد التليفزيون .

هل تفهمون ما أقصد ؟

In other جمل فعلية , the subject, الفاعِل , is expressed independently and **follows** the verb:

١- لم يسافر **الأولاد** مع أمهم .

٢- يجيء **كل أفراد العائلة** إلى البيت.

٣- استمتع **الطلاب** بالمحاضرة أمس.[1]

٤- حصل **سمير ورشيد وابراهيم** على البكالوريوس من جامعة صنعاء.

Note that the verbs in these sentences are singular, even though the subjects are plural. This is because **whenever a verb precedes its subject**, and that subject is a separate noun (i.e., not part of the verb), **the verb must always be singular**. It **must agree with the subject in gender,** مؤنّث or مذكّر . Compare sentences ١, ٢, ٣, and ٤ above with the following :

٥- **الأولاد** لم يسافروا مع أمهم .

٦- **كل أفراد العائلة** يجيئون إلى البيت .

٧- **الطلاب** استمتعوا بالمحاضرة أمس .

٨- **سمير ورشيد وابراهيم** حصلوا على البكالوريوس من جامعة صنعاء.

The verbs in sentences ١–٤ precede their subjects, while those in ٥–٨ follow their subjects. The first four are جمل فعلية ; the last four are جمل اسمية .

When the subject of a جملة فعلية is a non human plural or a human feminine plural the verb is feminine singular (هي):

ستسافر ملك ومها مع محمد.

حصلت بعض الطالبات على منح للدراسة في الجامعة.

تبادلتْ السعودية والصين رسائل دبلوماسية.

Remember: a verb that precedes its subject must be singular.

---

[1]Notice the placement of the subject in these sentences: when the verb phrase includes a preposition, the subject normally occurs **between** the verb and its preposition.

تمرين ١٢ الجملة الاسمية والجملة الفعلية (في البيت)

أ ـ غيّروا *change* **من جمل فعلية إلى جمل اسمية :**

مثال: يسكن بعض أصدقائي في واشنطن. ——> بعض أصدقائي يسكنون في واشنطن .

١ـ يعيش معظم أقارب مها في مصر .

٢ـ يتبادل الأصدقاء الصور والرسائل .

٣ـ حصل بعض الطلاب على مِنَح دراسية .

٤ـ يذهب خالد ووالده وإخوته للصلاة في المسجد .

٥ـ يزور الناس في العالم العربي أقاربهم كثيراً .

٦ـ سيقضي عبد الله وأولاده عدّة أيام معنا .

ب ـ غيّروا *change* **من جمل اسمية إلى جمل فعلية :**

٧ـ إخوة خالد يريدون دخول الجامعة مثله.

٨ـ معظم الموظفين تغيّبوا عن العمل أمس بسبب الجو.

٩ـ زملائي علموا بقصة حبي لها.

١٠ـ رشيد وأيمن ونبيل سهروا معنا ليلة الخميس.

١١ـ بعض الناس يستمتعون بشرب القهوة.

١٢ـ الاساتذة تكلموا مع المعيدين عن الامتحانات.

تمرين ١٣ نشاط كتابة (في البيت)

Write about your favorite vacation. You may want to address the following points:

متى أخذت العطلة ؟   من كان معك ؟   أين قضيت العطلة ؟   لماذا استمتعت بها ؟

Try using جملة فعلية and as many connectors as you can when you write:

و	should begin all related sentences (except those beginning with ثم or فـ)
فَـ	(to signal explanation or elucidation of a main point)
كما	as; as well as (connects two related actions)
وبالإضافة الى ذلك ...	(connects related sentences)

تمرين ١٤	نشاط قراءة

اقرأوا الخبر واكتبوا:

١ـ ما هو الخبر؟ ماذا نعرف عن هذا الرجل؟

2. How should we read the verb يدرس? How do you know?

3. You have seen the verb تناول used with meals: أتناول الغداء/العشاء . Here you see it in a new context. الكتب تناولت . What could it mean here?

4. Circle all the new words whose جذر you know. Which ones can you guess the meaning of by looking at the grammatical form?

وفاة ادوارد سعيد

عكاظ . وكالات (نيويورك)

توفي أمس الخميس في نيويورك المفكر الفلسطيني المعروف عالمياً ادوارد سعيد بعد ان كان يعاني من مرض السرطان على ما أفاد مصدر في جامعة كولومبيا حيث كان يدرس .

ولد ادوارد سعيد في ١٩٣٥ في القدس وصدر له العديد من الكتب التي تناولت النزاع في الشرق الاوسط .

وقد كان متخصصاً في الموسيقى وكان يدرس الادب الانكليزي المقارن في جامعة كولومبيا .

من جريدة عكاظ ٢٠٠٣/٩/٢٦

تمرين ١٥ **نشاط قراءة**

تعلموا هذه الكلمة:

رَئيس ج. رُؤَساء — president

اقرأوا الخبر واكتبوا:

١- ما هو الخبر؟ من؟ __________ ماذا؟ __________

متى؟ __________ لماذا؟ __________

2. Identify all sentences as either جملة اسمية or جملة فعلية . Find the subjects of all verbs.
3. Underline the words that tell you the topics under consideration.
4. Find the pair of expressions that mean *in general* and *in particular*.
5. What does the final sentence tell you about هذه الزيارة ?

مبارك يزور أنقرة اليوم

أنقرة ـ أ. ف. ب: يصل الى أنقرة اليوم الرئيس المصري حسني مبارك في زيارة عمل تستغرق 24 ساعة. وقالت وزارة الخارجية التركية ان زيارة الرئيس المصري تركز بشكل خاص على عملية السلام في الشرق الاوسط والمفاوضات الفلسطينية ـ الاسرائيلية الاخيرة.

وأضافت الوزارة ان الرئيس مبارك والرئيس التركي سليمان ديميريل سيستعرضان ايضا جملة من القضايا ذات الصلة بالمنطقة والعلاقات الدولية بشكل عام. ولم تتوفر معلومات أخرى أمس عن هذه الزيارة التي لم تكن مقررة للرئيس المصري.

من جريدة «الشرق الاوسط» ١٩٩٤/٢/١

الاستماع DVD

تمرين ١٦ **مع العائلة والاصدقاء**

تعلموا هذه الكلمات:

مُدير	director, manager
مُشكِلة ج مَشاكِل	problem

شاهدوا الـ DVD واكتبوا:

١- من يتكلم؟ من هو؟

٢- ماذا يعمل؟ أين؟

٣- ما هي مشكلة شغله؟

٤- ماذا يقول عن محمد؟

٥- كيف العلاقة بين محمد ومحمود؟

تمرين ١٧ **نشاط استماع** DVD

شاهدوا البرنامج عن جامعة عربية واكتبوا:

١- يتكلم هذا البرنامج عن: ______________________

٢- أول كلية في الجامعة كانت ______________________

شاهدوا الفيديو مرّة ثانية واكتبوا:

٣- اكتبوا أسماء ٤ من الكليات والتخصصات التي يتكلم عنها البرنامج:

أ - ________ ب - ________ جـ - ________ د - ________

٤- في الماضي، كان لهذه الجامعة أسماء أخرى، اكتبوا واحداً منها: ______________

تمارين المراجعة

تمرين ١٨

COMPLETE THESE SENTENCES WITH THE CORRECT PREPOSITIONS AND ANY NECESSARY PRONOUNS:

١- يا أولاد ! هل ______ واجبات كثيرة اليوم؟
٢- غرفتك كبيرة ويمكننا أن نجلس ______ جميعًا .
٣- هذه مدرسة كبيرة تخرج ______ ٣٠٠ طالب وطالبة.
٤- ما كانت تحبه عندما خُطبت ______ .
٥- لا أحب هذه الموسيقى ولا أريد أن أستمع ______ !
٦- كانت المحاضرة ممتازة ولكن كثيرًا من الطلاب تغيّبوا ______ .
٧- – متى تعرّفت ______؟ – قبل سنة عندما جاءوا ليسكنوا في ذلك البيت.
٨- منحة فولبرايت منحة أكاديمية يحصل ______ طلاب وأساتذة أمريكيون.
٩- أحب أفراد عائلتي كثيرا ولا أريد أن أعيش بعيدًا ______ .
١٠- «نادي الجزيرة» من أكبر النوادي في القاهرة ويذهب ______ كثير من الناس.

تمرين ١٩

NEGATE THE SENTENCES USING لا , لن , OR ليس . REMEMBER TO WRITE THE CORRECT مرفوع OR منصوب ENDINGS AND ALSO REMEMBER THAT ليس NORMALLY COMES AT THE BEGINNING OF THE SENTENCE IT NEGATES.

١- هذا أخي.
٢- هذا أول كتاب أقرأه باللغة العربية.
٣- سيكون عندنا عطلة طويلة في الربيع وسأسافر فيها الى لبنان.
٤- يحب معظم الأولاد أن يأكلوا الخضار والفواكه.
٥- سيزورني كل أفراد عائلتي عندما أسافر للدراسة في مصر السنة القادمة.
٦- يحصل خالد على تقدير «ممتاز» دائماً.
٧- ستبقى جدتي معنا إلى آخر هذا الاسبوع.
٨- أستطيع السهر كل يوم لأن أول صف لي يبدأ في الساعة التاسعة.
٩- لي أعمام كثيرون يعيشون في هذا البلد.
١٠- تتغيّب مريم عن صفوفها أحيانًا بسبب ابنها الصغير.
١١- سنسافر هذه السنة إلى الجزائر ان شاء الله.
١٢- يخرجون من البيت قبل الساعة السابعة صباحًا.
١٣- في غرفة صفّنا شبابيك كثيرة.
١٤- السفر من بيروت إلى دمشق يأخذ وقتًا طويلاً.

تمرين ٢٠ استماع : الـ

Listen to the sentences on your DVD and write in each blank الـ if you hear it and X if you do not. Listen for شدة on words that begin with حروف شمسية and think about the meaning and grammar of each sentence.

١ـ فصل ـــ خريف هو فصلي ـــ مفضل لأنّ ـــ دراسة تبدأ فيه وهذا يعني ـــ عودة إلى ـــ أصدقاء و ـــ زملاء ، وأيضًا لأنّ ـــ جو فيه يكون جميلاً .

٢ـ ـــ لغة ـــ عربية هي ـــ لغة ـــ عرب في جميع ـــ بلادهم ، وهي كذلك ـــ لغة ـــ قرآن ـــ كريم ولغة ـــ أدب و ـــ ثقافة ـــ عربية .

٣ـ في ـــ اسبوع ـــ ماضي ذهبت مع ـــ عدد من ـــ أصدقائي إلى ـــ مطعم ـــ عربي ـــ جديد اسمه « ـــ ليالي ـــ شرق » حيث أكلنا ـــ حمص و ـــ تبولة و ـــ فتوش و ـــ فلافل وطبعًا ـــ بقلاوة ـــ لذيذة .

٤ـ صباح ـــ يوم ، صحوت في ـــ سادسة و ـــ نصف ـــ صباحًا وشربت ـــ قهوة أنا وزوجتي ثم أكلت ـــ فطور وقرأت ـــ جرائد ـــ صباح واستمعت إلى ـــ أخبار ، وفي ـــ ساعة ـــ ثامنة نزلت من ـــ بيت . ركبت ـــ أوتوبيس لأنّ زوجتي دائمًا تأخذ ـــ سيارة ـــ يوم ـــ اثنين ، وتأخرت في ـــ وصول إلى ـــ مكتب بسبب ـــ ازدحام . ـــ ازدحام ، ـــ ازدحام ، ـــ ازدحام ، ... نفس ـــ قصة ـــ كل ـــ يوم .

تمرين ٢١ استمعوا إلى محمد واكتبوا ما يقول:

أنا اسمي ـــــ أبو العلا، ـــــ ـــــ الكثير ـــــ ـــــ مها، ـــــ

ـــــ قسم ـــــ ـــــ ـــــ بـ ـــــ و ـــــ معيدًا ـــــ ـالقسم،

وـــــ الماجستير ـــــ ـــــ ـــــ ـــــ للدكتوراه ـــــ جامعة كاليفورنيا في

سانتا باربرا. بعد ـــــ ـــــ الدكتوراه في ـــــ ـــــ ـــــ ـــــ البقاء

ـــــ . ـــــ كان هذا ـــــ ـــــ في ـــــ ، فأنا ـــــ

ـــــ ـــــ عائلتي و ـــــ . ـــــ مرّة ـــــ فيها مصر ـــــ ـــــ

ثلاث ـــــ عندما ـــــ بـ ـــــ وفاة ـــــ ـــــ محمود، وكانت ـــــ

ـــــ جدا، ولم ـــــ ملك و مها معي. هذه ـــــ سـ ـــــ جميعًا، وسـ ـــــ

ـــــ في القاهرة، أنا وملك ـــــ ـــــ السنوية، ومها ـــــ أسبوعًا ـــــ

محاضراتها ـــــ ـــــ ـــــ الربيع .

العامية DVD

- القصة: "أصعب قرار في حياتي"

شاهدوا محمد يتكلم.

Colloquial Arabic uses a different prefix for المستقبل , see if you can hear what it is.

- أُغنية "زوروني" لِـفيروز

WATCH AND LISTEN TO فيروز SING THE FAMOUS SONG زوروني :

زوروني كل سنة مرّة	حَرام تِنْسوني بالمرّة
زوروني كل سنة مرّة	حرام تنسوني بالمرّة
يا خوفي والهَوى نَظرة	تِجي وتروح بالمرّة
حبيبي فُرقتك مُرّة	حرام تنسونا بالمرّة

كلمات جديدة:

بالمَرّة	completely
حَرام	expression meaning: Shame (on you)! It's not right!
تنسوا	you forget
تجي	تجيء
تروح	تذهب

تذكروا هذه الكلمات

مُدير	مُشكلة ج. مَشاكِل	لن	حَرام!
غَداً	(الـ)قادِم/ة	رئيس ج. رُؤَساء	

١٣. لماذا قررت البقاء في أمريكا؟

في هذا الدرس :

القصة
- محمد يتكلم عن حياته

القواعد
- لم + المضارع المجزوم
- أنّ
- ما زال

القراءة
- أنهيت برنامج الماجستير
- مقالة أخبار

الاستماع
- مع العائلة والأصدقاء

العامية
- القصة: «ليه قررت أعيش في أمريكا؟»
- «حضرتك مين؟»

المفردات DVD

أخيرًا	finally, at last
أمامَ	in front of, before
مَجَلّة ج. ‑ات	magazine, journal
حَضَرَ إلى ، يَحضُر إلى ، الحُضورإلى	to come to
حَضَرَ ، يَحضُر ، الحُضور	to attend (e.g., a lecture)
رَجَعَ ، يَرجِع ، الرُّجوع من/إلى	= عاد ، يعود
رَغِبَ في ، يَرغَب في ، الرَّغبة في	to desire, wish to
ما زِلتُ	I continue to (be), still (be/do)
شَجَّعَ على ، يُشَجِّع على ، التَّشْجيع على	to encourage (someone) to
ظَنَّ أنّ (ظَنَنْتُ أنّ) ، يَظُنّ أنّ ، الظَّنّ	to think that
يَعني	it means
الغُربة	longing for one's native land; feeling of being a stranger
فُرْصة ج. فُرَص	opportunity, chance
فَشِلَ ، يَفْشَل ، الفَشَل (في)	to fail
فَصَلَ ، يَفصِل ، الفَصْل	to dismiss, fire (from a job)
اِسْتَقَرَّ ، يَسْتَقِرّ ، الاِستِقرار	to settle down, become stable
مَقالة ج. ‑ات	article (e.g., in a newspaper)
كَذٰلِك	likewise, also
مُناسِب	appropriate, suitable
اِنْتَهى مِن ، ينتَهي من ، الاِنْتِهاء مِن	to finish (something)
وَجَدَ ، يَجِد	to find
لم أجِد = ما وَجَدتُ	I did not find
وَظيفة ج. وَظائف	position, job

تعلموا هذه الأفعال: DVD

الماضي

ظَنَنْتُ أنّ	ظَنَنّا أنّ
ظَنَنْتَ أنّ ظَنَنْتِ أنّ	ظَنَنْتُم أنّ
ظَنَّ أنّ ظَنَّت أنّ	ظَنّوا أنّ

وَجَدْتُ	وَجَدْنا
وَجَدْتَ وَجَدْتِ	وَجَدْتُم
وَجَدَ وَجَدَت	وَجَدوا

اِنْتَهَيْتُ من	اِنْتَهَيْنا من
اِنْتَهَيْتَ من اِنْتَهَيْتِ من	اِنْتَهَيْتُم من
اِنْتَهى من اِنْتَهَتْ من	اِنْتَهَوْا من

المضارع

أظُنّ أنّ	نَظُنّ أنّ
تَظُنّ أنّ تَظُنّينَ أنّ	تَظُنّونَ أنّ
يَظُنّ أنّ تَظُنّ أنّ	يَظُنّونَ أنّ

أجِد	نَجِد
تَجِد تَجِدينَ	تَجِدونَ
يَجِد تَجِد	يَجِدونَ

أنْتَهي من	نَنْتَهي من
تَنْتَهي من تَنْتَهينَ من	تَنْتَهونَ من
يَنْتَهي من تَنْتَهي من	يَنْتَهونَ من

الثقافة

"فرصة سعيدة"

When you meet someone new, it is polite to use تشرّفنا to first greet her or him, and فرصة سعيدة *it was nice meeting you* or *nice to have met you* when saying good-bye.

"يعني"

You will often hear native speakers use يعني in conversation as a "filler" similar to the English *you know* or *like.*

تمرين ١ **المفردات الجديدة (في البيت)**

اكتبوا كلمة من الكلمات الجديدة في كل جملة:

١- في جريدة اليوم ــــــــــ جيّدة عن السياحة في تونس .

٢- بعد أنْ ــــــــــ من المذاكرة سنذهب إلى النادي لنأكل العشاء .

٣- حصل ابن عمّي سعيد على ــــــــــ ممتازة في وزارة الاقتصاد .

٤- لم أشعر بـ ــــــــــ طوال إقامتي في أوروبا .

٥- ــــــــــ في زيارة الشرق الأوسط في الصيف القادم .

٦- هل هذا الفيلم ــــــــــ للأولاد ؟

٧- كانت والدتي - الله يرحمها - دائماً ــــــــــ ـني على الدراسة .

٨- يوم الثلاثاء سَـ ــــــــــ من العمل في ساعة متأخرة.

٩- لم أجد الـ ــــــــــ التي أريدها في المكتبة ، لكني وجدت بعض الكتب.

١٠- كانت له علاقات عاطفية كثيرة ولكنّه أخيراً تَزَوَّجَ و ــــــــــ .

١١- مكتب القبول ــــــــــ كلية الحقوق .

١٢- ليس أمامه ــــــــــ عمل كثيرة لأنّه ما حصل على البكالوريوس .

١٣- أصدقائي ــــــــــ إلى بيتنا لتناول الغداء أمس .

١٤- ــــــــــ ـه الشركة لأنّه كان دائماً يتأخر في الحضور إلى العمل .

تمرين ٢ الأفعال الجديدة (في البيت)

اكتبوا الأفعال الجديدة في هذه الجمل:

١- أحياناً أشعر أنّي لن ______ من واجباتي!! أمس ______ منها

في الساعة الثانية بعد نصف الليل!

٢- يا شباب، هل ______ أنّ الطقس سيكون أحسن غداً؟

٣- ______ وظيفة جيدة للصيف القادم، الحمد لله! وأنت يا كريم،

هل ______ وظيفة للصيف؟

٤- يا سامية، هل ______ الكتب التي كنت بحاجة اليها؟

٥- هل ______ أنّ جامعتكم أحسن جامعة ؟

تمرين ٣ الوزن والجذر (في الصف)

اكتبوا الجذر والوزن لهذه الكلمات ثم اكتبوا كلمة اخرى من نفس الجذر:

مثال: حضر: ح ض ر فَعَلَ محاضرة

١- مقالة --- ______ ______ ٤- وظيفة --- ______ ______

٢- الاستقرار --- ______ ______ ٥- الغربة --- ______ ______

٣- فَصَلَ --- ______ ______ ٦- مناسب --- ______ ______

تمرين ٤ اسألوا زملاءكم:

Now that you are acquiring some synonyms, we will italicize the words that you should use from your new vocabulary. Find out who:

1. Had a *job* she or he would like to *return* to next summer.
2. Has friends or relatives who are *encouraging him/her to* marry and *settle down.*
3. Knows someone (أحد) who has *failed* (في) a physical education (=sports) class.
4. Knows someone who feels *like a stranger* in this country. Why?
5. Has some tough decisions *ahead of* her or him this year.
6. *Thinks that firing* an employee who misses work a lot is *appropriate.*
7. Knows where you can *find* good *articles* about U.S.-Arab relations.
8. *Thinks that* job *opportunities* will be plentiful when they *finish* their studies.

القصة DVD

تمرين ٥ **شاهدوا واكتبوا:**

١- متى حضر محمد ابو العلا إلى أمريكا ؟

٢- ماذا كان محمد يعمل في القاهرة قبل سفره إلى أمريكا؟

٣- ما الوظيفة التي حصل عليها في أمريكا ؟

٤- كيف يشعر في حياته في أمريكا الآن ؟

شاهدوا مرة ثانية:

٥- ماذا كان يريد أن يفعل بعد الانتهاء من الدراسة في أمريكا؟

٦- لماذا قرّر محمد البقاء في أمريكا؟

أ -

ب -

٧- لماذا ما رجع محمد إلى مصر عندما لم يجد وظيفة مناسبة ؟

استمعوا وخمّنوا: DVD

Notice the word ألاّ (أنْ + لا). Figure out its meaning from the sentence (hint: think about the grammar of قرّر):

٨- قررّت ألاّ أرجع = ______________

٩- اكتبوا ما يقول محمد:

«كنت أرغب في الانتهاء من دراستي والعودة إلى مصر، ________ كنت ...»

«لم أستطع الرجوع، _____ فصلتني الجامعة»

Guess what this word means: _______

تمرين ٦ **عن القصة (في الصف)**

PREPARE A FORMAL INTRODUCTION OF محمد أبو العلا AS IF HE WERE GIVING A LECTURE AT YOUR SCHOOL. INCLUDE PERTINENT AND INTERESTING INFORMATION ABOUT HIM FOR THE AUDIENCE. FORMAL INTRODUCTIONS OFTEN INCLUDE:

سيّداتي وسادتي ladies and gentlemen

أُقَدِّم لكم ... I present to you

القواعد

❁ نفي الماضي: لم + المضارع المجزوم

You know how to negate الماضي with ما , as in: ما شربت قهوة اليوم . Using ما is the most common way to negate in spoken Arabic. In formal, written Arabic, however, الماضي is more commonly negated with لم + المضارع :

She did not work.	=	ما عَمِلَت	=	لم تَعمَل
he did not find	=	ما وَجَدَ	=	لم يَجِد

In this case, المضارع takes a form called المُضارع المَجزوم , which is the third and final class of المضارع . The chart below shows the endings of المجزوم , some of which it shares with المضارع المنصوب. In particular, note that the verb forms for the persons انتِ, انتم, and هم do not carry the final ن . The final سكون on the other persons appears only in fully vocalized texts. Learn to recognize these endings when you see them, but be aware that it is the particle لم that signals the negation of the past. The following chart shows the endings of المضارع المجزوم on the verb يفعل :

المُضارع المَجزوم DVD

لم نَفعَلْ	لم أفعَلْ
لم تَفعَلوا	لم تَفعَلْ لم تَفعَلي
لم يَفعَلوا	لم يَفعَلْ لم تَفعَلْ

Remember: ما + الماضي and لم + المضارع المجزوم convey the same meaning in modern Arabic. The difference between these two forms lies in their usage:

spoken Arabic, less formal : ما+ الماضي

formal Arabic : لم + المضارع المجزوم

You should now begin to use لم + المضارع المجزوم form in writing.

تمرين ٧

Negate the following sentences using لم + المضارع المجزوم.

مثال: سافرتُ إلى لبنان . —> لم أسافرْ إلى لبنان .

١- سهرنا طوال الليل.

٢- جلسَتْ في الفراندة.

٣- استمتعتَ بالجلسة.

٤- التحقوا بالجيش.

٥- نزلتم معًا في الصباح.

٦- قرأوا القصّة الجديدة.

٧- حصلتِ على وظيفة مناسبة.

٨- شاهدتُ مباراة كرة السلة.

٩- حضر الرئيس المصري إلى اليمن.

١٠- رجعوا من المحاضرة.

❁ المضارع المرفوع والمنصوب والمجزوم

Review once more the rules for using المضارع endings. Remember that the default form of المضارع is المرفوع . In other cases, the following rules apply:

المضارع المجزوم occurs after:	المضارع المنصوب occurs after:	المضارع المرفوع occurs after:
لَمْ	أنْ لِـ لَن	سـ / سوف

تمرين ٨ المضارع المرفوع والمنصوب والمجزوم (في البيت)

COMPLETE, USING APPROPRIATE المرفوع , المنصوب , OR المجزوم ENDINGS:

١- قال سليم إنّه لن ______ بالاستقرار إلاّ بعد أنْ ______ على وظيفة.
(شعر) (حصل)

٢- قرّروا ألاّ ______ على شركة طيران الشرق الأوسط . (سافر)

٣- اختي لا ______ في الزواج الآن لأنّها ______ صغيرة .
(رغب) (ما زال)

٤- أنزل من البيت عادةً في الثامنة صباحًا و______ في الرابعة بعد الظهر.
(عاد)

٥- أقاربي لا ______ أنّ الشركة فصلتني من العمل . (عرف)

٦- كانت مشغولة جدًا ولذلك لم ______ موعدها مع الدكتور. (تذكّر)

٧- لماذا لم ______ يا وفاء؟ ظننت أنّك جوعانة ! (أكل)

٨- متى سـ______ لزيارتنا ؟ (جاء + أنتم)

٩- لماذا ______ أنْ ______ مع عائلتكِ ؟
(رفض) (سكن)

١٠- سـ______ إلى النادي بعد الانتهاء من المذاكرة إن شاء الله . (ذهب + أنا)

١١- لم ______ بخبر وفاة عمّتهم إلاّ بعد ٣ أسابيع . (علم)

١٢- قالت هِند إنّها سوف ______ اجازتها السنوية في باريس هذه السنة. (قضي)

١٣- لن ______ أنْ ______ معكم طويلاً اليوم .
(استطاع) (جلس)

١٤- خالد لا ______ من البيت قبل الساعة العاشرة صباحاً. (نزل)

❁ أنّ

In English, verbs used to report information and opinions take sentence complements with the conjunction *that*, such as: [1]

Mike thinks *that history is interesting.*
Mary knows *that she wants to go to law school.*
Susan says *that she's not coming.*
I read *that the economy is doing better.*

The Arabic counterpart of *that* in these contexts is أنّ . You heard محمد say:

ظننتُ أنّ فرص النجاح أمامي هنا كثيرة .

However, this conjunction is frequently omitted in spoken English, so take a few minutes to imagine hearing the examples above without *that*. It is important to remember that the function of *that* to introduce sentence complements (italicized above) **must** be expressed in Arabic with أنّ .

In addition to ظنّ , the following verbs you know can also take أنّ . The best way to learn how to use أنّ is to memorize these verb phrases as units:

يعرف أنّ	أعرف أنّ الحصول على الدكتوراه سيأخذ ٥ سنوات .
قرأ أنّ	قرأتُ أنّ فرص العمل كثيرة في الإمارات .
شعر بأنّ	يشعر بأنّ والده لا يشجعه على دراسة الادب .
فهم أنّ	فهمت أنّ العودة إلى بلدها تعني انقطاع العلاقة .
تذكّر أنّ	لم نتذكر أنّ الامتحان اليوم !!
يعني أنّ	الطقس مثلج ، وهذا يعني أنّ الطائرة ستتأخر .
علم أنّ	هل شعرتَ بالوحدة عندما علمتَ أنّها لن ترجع؟

Note that the verb قال/يقول *to say* takes a special form, إنّ :

قال إنّ	الجرائد تقول إنّ الطقس سيبقى باردًا لِعدّة أيام .

---

[1]**Do not confuse** *that* here with *that* in sentences like: the homework *that is due tomorrow* or I want *that one.* English uses the word *that* for three different grammmatical functions, each corresponding to a diffferent word in Arabic. Here we are only concerned with *that* following a verb, as the examples show.

Grammatically, أنّ behaves like another conjunction you have learned, لأنّ , in that it **must be followed by** a جملة اسمية . This جملة اسمية can begin with a pronoun, which **must be attached to it.** The following chart shows أنّ with the pronoun suffixes:

that I ...	أنّي	أنّ + أنا ⟵
that you...	أنّكِ	أنّ + أنتِ ⟵
that he/ it...	أنّهُ	أنّ + هو ⟵
that she/ it...	أنّها	أنّ + هي ⟵
that we...	أنّنا	أنّ + نحن ⟵
that you...	أنّكم	أنّ + أنتم ⟵
that they...	أنّهم	أنّ + هم ⟵

Finally, remember that in print, أنّ will usually not carry shadda and will resemble أنْ . However, these two particles are used and pronounced differently. How can you tell them apart, and how can you tell which one to use in a given context? First, you must learn which verbs take أنْ and which verbs take أنّ . Memorize this list of the verbs you know:

(verb) that أنّ (فعل)	(verb) to أنْ (فعل)
أنّ + جملة اسمية	أنْ + جملة فعلية
ظنّ أنّ	أراد أنْ
عرف أنّ	استطاع أنْ
قرأ أنّ	رغب في أنْ
علم أنّ	رفض أنْ
شعر بأنّ/شعر أنّ	يحب أنْ
تذكّر أنّ	قرر أنْ
كتب أنّ	شجع على أنْ
فهم أنّ	يمكن أنْ
(هذا) يعني أنّ	

Second, it is important to pay attention to what **follows** أن . Remember that أنْ must be followed by المضارع المنصوب , while أنّ must be followed by جملة اسمية . Study these examples:

أردت أنْ أعيش معهم.	أظنّ أنّهم استقرّوا في حياتهم .
أرغب في أنْ أجلس مع أصدقائي.	أشعر بأنّها ليست سعيدة في وظيفتها .
رفضنا أنْ نأكل في الكافتيريا.	يقول إنّكِ لم تنتهي من كتابة المقالة .
لا يحب الناس أنْ يفشلوا.	قرأتُ في الجريدة أنّه مات، الله يرحمه.
زوجي شجّعني على أنْ أدرس أكثر.	تذكرتُ أنّهم لن يكونوا في البيت .

تمرين ٩ **أنّ (في البيت)**

WHAT INFORMATION OR OPINIONS WOULD YOU LIKE TO REPORT?

١- الجو ممطر وهذا يعني أنّ ______ .

٢ ظنّت امّي أن ______ .

٣- أشعر بأنّ ______ .

٤- هل تعرفين أنّ ______ .

٥- قرأت في الجريدة أنّ ______ .

٦- الاستاذ يقول إنّ ______ .

٧- أنتم لا تعلمون أنّ ______ .

٨- كلنا نفهم أنّ ______ .

٩- لا أحد يعرف أنّ ______ .

١٠- اليوم في الصباح تذكرت أنّ ______ .

❁ ما زال

In Arabic, the concept *still* as in *Do you* ***still*** *go to the club every week,* is expressed by the verb ما زالَ.[1] In this chapter, you heard محمد say:

I still feel... ما زِلتُ أشعر بالغربة هنا .

Since ما زلت is a verb, it must be conjugated for person. The following chart gives the conjugation of the verb ما زالَ :

ما زال DVD

ما زِلتُ	ما زِلنا
ما زِلتَ ما زِلتِ	ما زِلتُم
ما زالَ ما زالَت	ما زالوا

أمثلة:

أ - مها ما زالت طالبة.

ب - أختي ما زالت مريضة.

ج - هل ما زِلتم تسكنون هنا؟

د - ما زالوا يشعرون بالوحدة.

Notice that ما زال behaves like the verb كان : it can be followed by either a noun or adjective, as in أ and ب above, or a مضارع مرفوع , as in جـ and د . Compare the uses and meanings of these two verbs in the following examples:

I used to play... كنت ألعب كرة القدم السنة الماضية .

I still play... ما زلت ألعب كرة القدم هذه السنة .

They used to exchange... كانوا يتبادلون الرسائل .

They still exchange... ما زالوا يتبادلون الرسائل .

The verb بدأ also functions like كان and ما زال in that it may be followed by either an object (in this case usually a مصدر) or a مضارع مرفوع verb:

I began/have begun to attend ... بدأت أحضر المحاضرات عن الأدب.

They began to be absent from ... بدأوا يتغيّبون عن العمل.

Have you all started smoking?! هل بدأتم التدخين؟!

---

[1] This idiom is actually composed of the verb زال and the negative ما (lit. *to not cease*).

تمرين ١٠ **كان وما زال وبدأ**

USE EITHER ما زال , كان , OR بدأ TO CREATE A TIME FRAME OF THE FOLLOWING SENTENCES:

مثال: أدرس اللغة العربية . —> ما زلت أدرس اللغة العربية .

١- تعيش مع جدّتها .

٢- نشاهد فيلماً مرّة كل اسبوع .

٣- يشعر بالخجل .

٤- أصحو في الساعة السابعة صباحاً .

٥- يساعد زوجته في شغل البيت .

٦- يتغيّبون عن الصف كثيراً .

٧- أريد أن أصبح دكتوراً .

٨- تلعب التنس ثلاث مرات في الاسبوع .

٩- نحب أن نجلس في الكافتيريا .

١٠- أزور عائلتي كل أسبوعين أو ثلاثة .

NOW COMPLETE: WHAT DO YOU THINK THESE PEOPLE USED TO DO/ARE STILL DOING?

١١- تزوّجت البنت من رجل آخر ، ولكن خالد ________ ـها .

١٢- عندما كان محمد طالباً في جامعة القاهرة ________ .

١٣- مها تعيش في أمريكا ، لكنها ________ اللغة العربية في البيت .

١٤- أختي الصغيرة ________ .

١٥- ________ مع أصدقائي من المدرسة الثانوية .

تمرين ١١ **نشاط محادثة: كان/ما زال (في الصف)**

TO WHAT EXTENT HAVE YOUR LIVES CHANGED? ASK A PARTNER ABOUT THE THINGS SHE OR HE USED TO DO IN THE PAST, STILL DOES NOW, AND WHAT SHE OR HE HAS BEGUN TO DO RECENTLY.

مثال: هل كنت تذهب الى السينما كل أسبوع، وهل ما زلت تفعل هذا الآن؟

تمرين ١٢ نشاط قراءة

اقرأوا الخبر واكتبوا

١ـ من هو رئيس الفلبين؟ ومن هو رئيس الإمارات العربية المتحدة؟

٢ـ عمَّ سيتكلم رئيس الفلبين مع رئيس الامارات؟

3. Pick out أنّ in this article. What kinds of verbs can you expect in news articles that would take أنّ ? Guess the general meaning of these verbs:

وصل إلى ______________

سيناقش ______________

أضافَ = ______________

(Hint: think of بالإضافة إلى)

رئيس الفلبين يزور أبوظبي

أبوظبي – وكالات الأنباء: وصل الى أبوظبي امس فيدل راموس رئيس الفلبين في زيارة رسمية قصيرة، واستقبله في المطار رئيس دولة الامارات العربية المتحدة الشيخ زايد بن سلطان آل نهيان.

وقال روي سنيرز سفير الفلبين لدى الامارات إن راموس سيناقش العلاقات التجارية وقضايا سياسية مع الشيخ زايد .

واضاف : ان الرئيس الفلبيني يأمل بتشجيع الصادرات الفلبينية الى الامارات واستثمار الامارات في الفلبين.

واضاف : انه سيكون نقاشا عاما.

من جريدة الشرق الأوسط، ١٩٩٥/٣/٦

تمرين ١٣ نشاط قراءة (في الصف)

تعلموا هذه الكلمات:

أحتاج إلى	= أنا بحاجة إلى
أجنَبيّ ج. أجانِب	foreign, foreigner
مُؤَسَّسة	foundation
عُنوان ج. عَناوين	address

READ THE FOLLOWING LETTER TO مجلة «الوطن العربي» AND ANSWER:

١ـ ما اسم الطالب الذي كتب الرسالة؟ ومن أين هو؟

٢ أين بدأ الدراسة؟ أين يدرس الآن؟ لماذا ذهب إلى جامعة اخرى؟

٣ـ من أي جامعة حصل على البكالوريوس؟ والماجستير؟ ما كان تقديره؟

٤ـ ما هي المشكلة التي يتكلم عنها؟

٥ـ أي مساعدة يريد من المجلّة؟

انهيت برنامج الماجستير بمعدل مائة في المائة واحتاج الى منحة

انا شاب فلسطيني من غزة بدأت دراستي الجامعية في كلية الهندسة الكهربائية في جامعة بيرزيت حيث انهيت عامين فيها بمعدل ٩٣ بالمائة. ونظرا لظروف الانتفاضة التي لا تخفى عليكم حولت الى جامعة الشرق الاوسط التقنية في انقرة. وانهيت البكالوريوس هناك بتقدير امتياز مع مرتبة الشرف بمعدل ٩٩.٥ في المائة وعينت معيدا في الكلية وانجزت برنامج الماجستير وانهيت المواد المطلوبة بمعدل ١٠٠ في المائة، ولم يبق عليّ سوى انهاء البحث الذي اتوقع انجازه في اواخر شباط (فبراير) القادم.

مشكلتي بدأت منذ حوالي ثلاثة اشهر، اذ تمّ فصل كل المعيدين الاجانب في تركيا، وذلك لاعتبارات لا اعرفها.

وداومت على عملي في الجامعة بصورة غير رسمية، اذ يصرف لي نصف مرتبي من ميزانية الكلية، واحاول جاهدا الاكتفاء به وتحمل الظروف حتى انهي بحث الماجستير في شباط (فبراير) القادم.

اريد ان ترسلوا لي عناوين الشركات والمؤسسات العربية والاجنبية التي تقدم منحا او قروضا مشروطة للطلاب الذين هم في وضعي حتى اتمكن من الالتحاق ببرنامج الدكتوراه في احدى الجامعات الاميركية او اية جامعة تتمتع بمستوى علمي مرتفع وتدرس باللغة الانجليزية. مع العلم بان الحصول على قبول في جامعة معروفة امر سهل بالنسبة لي، ولكن تبقى المشكلة في تغطية النفقات المالية للسنة الاولى، لأن بمقدوري الحصول على مساعدة تعليمية من الجامعة بعد ان اثبت لها مقدرتي باذن الله.

محمد عبد العاطي - انقرة (تركيا)

١ - ليست هناك شركات عربية واجنبية تقدم منحا او قروضا للطلبة العرب.

اما بالنسبة للمؤسسات فهناك المؤسسة العالمية لمساعدة الطلبة العرب (وقد قمت بمراسلتهم فلم تحصل على نتيجة ايجابية منها) وهناك مؤسسة الحريري وهي تختص بالطلبة اللبنانيين.

٢ - هناك عدة جامعات اميركية تقدم منحا ومساعدات تعليمية لطلبة الدراسات العليا الاجانب المتفوقين.

وسوف نذكر لك كل المنح والمساعدات التي تقدمها الجامعات الاميركية لطلبة الدراسات الهندسية العليا الاجانب، مع شروط اعطائها:

أ - جامعة ولاية كولورادو: تقدم مساعدات تعليمية:

GRADUATE TEACHING ASSISTANTSHIP

ومساعدات ابحاث:

GRADUATE RESEARCH ASSISTANTSHIP

لطلبة الدراسات الهندسية العليا الاجانب المتفوقين في دراستهم.

ومدة المساعدة سنة واحدة. وقيمتها غير محددة. ويقدم الطلب بشأنها قبل الاول من آذار (مارس) من كل عام الى هذا العنوان:

GRADUATE ADMISSION OFFICER
GRADUATE SCHOOL
OFFICE OF INTERNATIONAL EDUCATION
COLORADO STATE UNIVERSITY
315 AYLESWORTH HALL
FORT COLLINS , COLORADO 80523
U.S.A.

ب - جامعة بورديو تقدم مساعدات تعليمية ومساعدات بحث لطلبة الدراسات الهندسية العليا الاجانب المقبولين للدراسة فيها.

ويقدم طلب الحصول على المساعدة قبل ستة اشهر (على الاقل) من الموعد المحدد لبدء الدراسة وذلك الى العنوان التالي:

THE GRADUATE SCHOOL
GRADUATE HOUSE EAST
ROOM 130
PURDUE UNIVERSITY
WEST LAFAYETTE, INDIANA 47907
U.S.A.

جـ - جامعة ستانفرد العريقة تقدم زمالات ومساعدات تدريسيةلطلبة الدراسات العليا المتفوقين.

وتقدم الطلبات بشأنها بين الاول من تشرين الاول (اكتوبر) والاول من كانون الثاني (يناير) الى هذا العنوان:

OFFICE OF GRADUATE ADMISSIONS
STANFORD UNIVERSITY

من مجلة الوطن العربي - العدد ٢٣٤ - ٧٦٠ الجمعة ١٩٩١/٩/٢٧

الاستماع DVD

تمرين ١٤ **مع العائلة والاصدقاء**

كلمات تساعد على الفهم:

لَو ... لَـ	if ... then (hypothetical)
أَرى	I see
بِدون	without

أسئلة:

١- من يتكلم؟ ماذا نعرف عن حياتها؟
ماذا فهمت عن قصة زواجها؟

٢- ما رأيها في بقاء محمد في أمريكا؟

٣- ما رأيها في ملك، زوجة محمد؟ لماذا؟

٤- ماذا تريد لِخالد؟

تمرين ١٥ **نشاط كتابة**

A university in an Arab country has announced a new program for foreign students to study the language and culture. Write a letter of application to the program, using these formulaic opening and closing phrases:

حضرة الاستاذ الدكتور...	It is appropriate to address the letter to:
تَحيّة طيّبة وبعد ، فـ ...	*Warm greetings* (formulaic opening for letters)
وتفضّلوا بقبول شكري واحترامي ،	*Please accept my thanks and respect* (closing)

تمارين المراجعة

تمرين ١٦ **كم ؟**

١- عمري الآن ــــــ وعندما أتخرج إن شاء الله سيكون عمري ــــــ . (سنة)

٢- لي ــــــ و ــــــ و ــــــ . (أخ، أخت، عمّ، خال)

٣- في عطلة الصيف سأذهب لزيارة عائلتي وسأبقى هناك ــــــ . (أسبوع)

٤- أنا بحاجة إلى ـــــــ من النوم يومياً. (ساعة)

٥- عائلتي ما زالت تسكن في نفس البيت منذ ـــــــ . (سنة)

٦- في صفنا ـــــــ وـــــــ وـــــــ وـــــــ وـــــــ .
(طالبة) (طالب) (كرسي) (باب) (طاولة)

٧- فيلمي المفضل هو «ـــــــ» وشاهدته ـــــــ . (مرة)

٨- أكبر صف درست فيه في الجامعة كان فيه ـــــــ . (طالب)

٩- في هذه المدينة ـــــــ . (جامعة)

تمرين ١٧ **استمعوا إلى محمد واكتبوا ما يقول:** DVD

LISTEN FOR PARALLEL STRUCTURES HERE. WHENEVER YOU HEAR و YOU SHOULD BE THINKING ABOUT WHAT TWO OR MORE THINGS ARE BEING CONNECTED AND USUALLY, THIS PARALLELISM INVOLVES A REPEATED GRAMMATICAL FORM, SUCH AS A PAIR OF مصدر OR فعل مضارع , ETC.

لماذا ـــــــ ـــــــ في أمريكا؟ ـــــــ ـــــــ إلى ـــــــ

ـــــــ خمس عشرة ـــــــ ، ـــــــ ـــــــ في ـــــــ من

دراستي و ـــــــ إلى مصر، إذ ـــــــ ـــــــ ـــــــ في جامعة

القاهرة، و ـــــــ كذلك ـــــــ بعض ـــــــ في ـــــــ «المسرح»،

ولكن بعد ـــــــ ـــــــ الدكتوراه، ـــــــ ـــــــ ـــــــ النجاح

ـــــــ هنا ـــــــ ، و ـــــــ ـــــــ ـــــــ .

و ـــــــ ملك على ـــــــ ـــــــ ، لانها كانت ـــــــ هنا، ولكني

ـــــــ أجد ـــــــ ـــــــ ، و ـــــــ أستطع أيضاً ـــــــ ، إذ

ـــــــ الجامعة، و ـــــــ ـــــــ يعني ـــــــ . الحمد لله،

ـــــــ ـــــــ مترجماً في الامم ـــــــ ، و ـــــــ حياتنا

ـــــــ ، ولكني ـــــــ ـــــــ أشعر بـ ـــــــ هنا .

العامية DVD

ـ القصة: "ليه قررت أعيش في أمريكا؟"

شاهدوا محمد يتكلم.

كيف يقول «سعيدة»؟ كيف يقول «قررت ألاّ أرجع»؟

ـ "حضرتك مين؟"

شاهدوا مها تتكلم بالتليفون.

ماذا تقول مها لوالدها؟

تذكروا هذه الكلمات

المضارع المجزوم	ألا (أنْ + لا)	المَسرَح	أحتاج الى
أجنَبيّ ج. أجانِب	أرى	بِدون	

١٤ ـ أتمنى ألا نترك هذا البيت

في هذا الدرس:

القصة • بيت مها

القواعد • الجملة الاسمية: وصف الأماكن

• الإضافة *Definite and Indefinite*

• أوزان الفعل والقاموس

القراءة • فرص عمل

• مالك بن نبي

الاستماع • مي زيادة

العامية • القصة: «أتمنى مانسيبش البيت دا»

• «فيه شقة فاضية؟»

المفردات

اِستَأجَرَ ، يَستَأجِر ، الاِستِئْجار	to rent
تَرَكَ ، يَترُك ، التَّرك	to leave (someone or something)
حَدَثَ ، يَحْدُث	to happen
حَديقة ج. حَدائق	garden, yard
حديقة عامّة	public park
حَمّام ج. ـات	bathroom, bath
حَمّام سِباحة	swimming pool
ذَكَرَ ، يَذْكُر ، الذِّكر	to recall; to mention
راحة	comfort, ease
السُّفرة	dining (room)
شَقّة ج. شِقَق / شُقَق	apartment
مَطبَخ ج. مَطابِخ	kitchen
طابِق ج. طَوابِق	floor, story
أعَدَّ ، يُعِدّ ، الإعْداد	to prepare, make (something) ready
غُرفة ج. غُرَف	room
اِسْتَقبَلَ ، يَستَقبِل ، الاِستِقبال	to receive, to welcome
مِن قَبل	previously, before
تَكَوَّن من ، يَتَكَوَّن من	to consist of, to be made up of
مَكان ج. أماكِن	place
تَمَنّى أنْ ، يتَمَنّى أنْ	to hope, wish (for someone) to
اِنْتَقَلَ إلى ، يَنْتَقِل إلى ، الاِنتِقال إلى	to move to

تعلّموا هذا الفعل: DVD

أتَمَنّى أنْ	نَتَمَنّى أنْ
تَتَمَنّى أنْ تَتَمَنَّين أنْ	تَتَمَنَّونَ أنْ
يَتَمَنّى أنْ تَتَمَنّى أنْ	يَتَمَنَّونَ أنْ

تعلّموا "في" و"بـ" + الضمائر: DVD

في

فِيَّ	فينا
فيكَ فيكِ	فيكُم
فيهِ فيها	فيهِم

بـ

بي	بِنا
بِكَ بِكِ	بِكُم
بِهِ بِها	بِهِم

تمرين ١ نشاط محادثة في الصف DVD

Go to the section المفردات on your DVD and find تمرين ١ . Here we will pay a virtual visit to شقة عائلة خالد . Create a voiceover for the tour using old and new vocabulary. Remember to use فيه/فيها (not عنده/عندها) to list what شقة خالد has.

تمرين ٢ المفردات الجديدة (في البيت)

PRACTICE USING NEW VOCABULARY:

١- ________ شقّة ممتازة فيها غرف كبيرة ومشمسة. ليس فيها سفرة ولكن ________ واسع جدا وهناك مكان فيه لطاولة آكل عليها.

٢- في نيويورك ________ كبيره وجميله اسمها «سنترال بارك».

٣- ________ والدتي الفطور لنا في الصباح.

٤- ________ أن أجد وظيفة مناسبة بعد التخرّج!

٥- احبّ هذا البيانو ولكن ليس في شقّتي ________ له.

٦- أقمنا في هذا الفندق عدّة أيام ثمّ ________ إلى فندق أحسن.

٧- في الأيام الحارّة في الصيف أقضي معظم وقتي أمام ________ .

٨- ________ نيويورك من خمس مناطق منها «منهاتن» و«بروكلين».

٩- الحمد لله! انتهيت من كل امتحاناتي، لذلك أشعر بـ ________ كبيرة.

١٠- يسكنون في شقة في ________ الثالث في هذه البناية.

١١- ________ المقالة أنّ الملك الأردني سيحضر الى القاهرة الأسبوع القادم وإنّ الرئيس المصري سـ________ـه في مطار القاهرة.

١٢- ماذا ________ لكم؟! لماذا تأخّرتم؟!

١٣- ________ زوجها عندما علمت أنّ له علاقة بامرأة اخرى.

١٤- لم يزوروا العالم العربي ________ ________ ، وهذه أول زيارة لهم الى المنطقة.

تمرين ٣ مفردات جديدة وقواعد قديمة (في البيت)

COMPLETE THESE SENTENCES USING AT LEAST ONE NEW VERB IN EACH:

١- هل تعرفون ________________________ .

٢- تقول المقالة إنّ ________________________ .

٣- في رأيي، قليل من ________________________ .

٤- علمنا من صديقنا ________________________ .

٥- مدير الشركة يظن ________________________ .

تمرين ٤ اسألوا زملاءكم (في الصف)

AFTER YOU FINISH INTERVIEWING, REPORT YOUR FINDINGS TO THE CLASS USING قال/قالت إنّ :

1. Who has *moved* more than three times in the past five years?
   Who *wishes* to *move* to another city after graduation?
2. Where is the best *place* to *rent* a car?
3. In their opinion, is it better to *rent* an *apartment* or live in the dorm?
   What do most student *apartments consist of*?
4. Who *prepares* her/his food at home and who eats in the cafeteria?
5. Do they *recall* the first word they read in Arabic?
6. What usually *happens* in the first class of the semester?
   Do they usually feel *comfortable* on that day? Why /not?
7. What is the most beautiful *place* they have ever visited?
   What do they *recall* about their visit there?
8. Can you *leave* books in the library and know that they will be there when you get back?
9. Where do they *hope* to settle down? What do they *hope* to have?

تمرين٥ الوزن والجذر

AS YOU READ THE FOLLOWING SENTENCES, IDENTIFY الجذر OF THE UNDERLINED WORDS AND GIVE THE RELATED WORD FROM الكلمات الجديدة . GUESS THE MEANING OF THE NEW WORD FROM CONTEXT AND COMPARE THE MEANINGS OF THE OLD AND NEW WORDS: WHAT IS DIFFERENT?

١- هذا الكرسي مُريح جداً --ليس مثل الكراسي العادية!

٢- أريد أن أنقُل هذه الطاولة من السفرة الى المطبخ، فهل يمكن أن تساعدوني؟

٣- تقول صديقتي إنها تريد أن تتزوج لتُكَوِّن أسرة ويصبح لها أولاد.

٤- البيت كبير وكل أولادهم تخرجوا وتزوّجوا ولذلك يريدون أن يُؤجِّروا واحدة من الغرف لطالبة أجنبية تدرس هنا.

٥- أنا وزوجي نحب أن نطبُخ ، ونحن نعدّ العشاء معاً معظم الوقت.

القصة DVD

تمرين ٦ **شاهدوا واكتبوا:**

١- عمَّ تتكلم مها هنا ؟

٢- متى حضرت مها إلى أمريكا ؟

٣- أين كانت مها تسكن السنة الماضية ؟ أين تسكن مها واسرتها الآن ؟

شاهدوا مرة ثانية:

٤- كم غرفة تذكر مها في الطابق الاول ؟ وكم غرفة في الطابق الثاني ؟

(Hint: listen for the connector و to signal each new item in a list.)

٥- أين غرفة مها؟ أين مكتب والدها ؟

٦- ماذا أمام البيت ؟

٧- كيف تشعر مها في بيتها الآن ؟ هل تريد أن تنتقل إلى بيت آخر ؟

٨- لماذا لا تتذكر مها كيف كانت شقتهم في مصر ؟

استمعوا وخمّنوا :

What are these rooms? Do they correspond to rooms in your house?

٩- غرفة المَعيشة ______________ غرفة الاستقبال ______________

غرفة النَوم ______________

استمعوا وتعلّموا :

Now that you have understood the meaning of the text, listen again to understand the structure. In other words, after understanding what Maha says, you need to pay attention to how she says it. Write exactly what Maha says:

١٠- «عندما جئنا إلى أمريكا ______________ .»

١١- «في الطابق الثاني غرفة النوم وغرفة ______________ .»

القواعد

❀ الجملة الاسمية: وصف الأماكن *Describing Places*

Notice that مها uses الجملة الاسمية with reversed مبتدأ وخبر to describe the house in which she lives:

أمام البيت حديقة صغيرة .

في الطابق الأول غرفة الاستقبال وغرفة المعيشة والمطبخ وحمّام صغير .

You have learned that the order of المبتدأ and الخبر is reversed in this kind of الجملة الاسمية because المبتدأ is **indefinite**, and thus cannot begin a sentence. In the second example above, المبتدأ contains a list of items some of which are indefinite; therefore the same principle must apply. Notice also that في (**not** عند) is used to ascribe "possession" to a place (English *it has*):

This area has... في هذه المنطقة فنادق كثيرة . = هذه المنطقة فيها فنادق كثيرة .

This house has... في هذا البيت ثلاثة طوابق. = هذا البيت فيه ثلاثة طوابق .

This kind of sentence is often used in describing spatial relationships as well as possession and association. The preposition أمام *in front of, before*, refers both to spatial location and abstract choices or obligations:

أمامي فرص كثيرة للنجاح . المستقبل ما زال أمامنا .

Remember that this kind of sentence is negated with ليس , which must directly precede الخبر , and that the tense can be shifted by using كان / سيكون , which must also precede الخبر . These prepositions will help you describe location:

تعلّموا هذه الكلمات:

بَيْنَ	between
تَحتَ	below, underneath
بِجانِب	next to, beside
فَوقَ	above, on top of
وَراءَ	behind

أمثلة : ليس وراء بيتنا حديقة كبيرة. سيكون بجانب الفندق الجديد حمام سباحة.

كان بينه وبينها علاقة خاصة. فوق الطاولة كتب ومجلات.

تمرين ٧ **جملة اسمية خبر مقدم (في البيت)**

Assign these items to appropriate places or people, using the structure you learned and a variety of prepositions.

أمثلة: حمّام كبير -> ليس في هذه الشقة حمّام كبير.

فرص كثيرة -> أمام [illegible] فرص كثيرة .

محاضرة ١- ____________________

ملعب «تنس» ٢- ____________________

شقق جديدة ٣ ____________________

علاقة حبّ ٤- ____________________

خمسة إخوة وأخوات ٥- ____________________

شقة اخرى ٦- ____________________

سيارة جميلة ٧- ____________________

مدرسة خاصة ٨- ____________________

حمّام سباحة ٩- ____________________

مسارح كثيرة ١٠- ____________________

تجربة جميلة في اليمن ١١- ____________________

قرارات صعبة ١٢- ____________________

حديقة جميلة ١٣- ____________________

مقالات ممتازة ١٤- ____________________

حوالي ١٠ كيلومترات ١٥- ____________________

❁ الإضافة *Definite and Indefinite*

You know that the following phrases are examples of الإضافة :

the bedroom	غرفة النوم
the parlor, receiving room	غرفة الاستقبال
the living/family room	غرفة المعيشة

Note that these phrases are all definite. How, then, are the concepts *my bedroom* and *a bedroom* expressed in Arabic?

First, remember that only the last noun in an إضافة can be marked definite. Thus the possessive pronoun suffix must come at the **end** of the إضافة :

my bedroom	غرفة نومي
their parlor	غرفة استقبالهم

Second, a distinction is made between definite and indefinite إضافة . The examples above, and most of the إضافات that you have seen so far are definite, because **the last word in the إضافة is definite.** An indefinite إضافة is one in which **the last word is indefinite.** Compare the definite examples above to their corresponding indefinite إضافة :

a bedroom	غرفة نوم
a parlor	غرفة استقبال
a living/family room	غرفة معيشة

Since these are indefinite phrases, they behave just like any indefinite noun. For example, adjectives modifying them are indefinite:

أريد غرفة نوم كبيرة

هذه غرفة استقبال جميلة.

Note that the adjectives كبيرة and جميلة are مؤنث because they modify غرفة .

Other rules for definite إضافات apply as well to indefinite ones. In particular, **remember to pronounce** ة on all non-final words of any إضافة .

تمرين ٨ نشاط كتابة ومحادثة (في البيت ثم في الصف)

في البيت : FIND OR DRAW A PICTURE OF A PLACE YOU CAN DESCRIBE AND PREPARE A DESCRIPTION OF IT, MENTIONING AS MANY DETAILS AS YOU CAN.

في الصف : PRESENT YOUR DESCRIPTION WITHOUT SHOWING THE PICTURE WHILE A PARTNER DRAWS HIS/HER IMPRESSION OF THE PICTURE YOU ARE DESCRIBING. WHEN HE/SHE HAS FINISHED, COMPARE PICTURES.

تمرين ٩ الإضافة (في البيت) DVD

YOU WILL HEAR A LIST OF PHRASES READ ON THE DVD. WRITE DOWN EACH ITEM, AND CIRCLE ALL OCCURRENCES OF إضافة, THEN IDENTIFY WHICH إضافات ARE DEFINITE AND WHICH ARE INDEFINITE. REMEMBER TO LISTEN FOR الشدّة THAT INDICATES الـ ON WORDS BEGINNING WITH SUN LETTERS.

١- ________		٩- ________	
٢- ________		١٠- ________	
٣- ________		١١- ________	
٤- ________		١٢- ________	
٥- ________		١٣- ________	
٦- ________		١٤- ________	
٧- ________		١٥- ________	
٨- ________		١٦- ________	

❁ أوزان الفعل

When we introduced الوزن والجذر in Chapter 8, we mentioned that there exists a special set of أوزان for الفعل . Learning these أوزان not only enables you to use the dictionary, but also to understand and pronounce correctly a variety of related nouns and adjectives derived from them.

Arabic has ten basic verb أوزان. In the most commonly used Arabic-English dictionaries, these are numbered I-X with Roman numerals by convention. The Arabic tradition, by contrast, does not number them, but refers to them by وزن with the representative جذر : ف-ع-ل . These three letters act as symbols that stand for the three letters that make up a root: ف represents the first letter of the root, ع represents the second letter, and ل the third. **You must learn both the number and ف-ع-ل** representations.

الوزن الأول, or Form I, is considered to be the basic form that gives the core meaning from which others are derived. The other أوزان build upon that basic meaning, each in a particular way, for example, by making it transitive or passive. It will take some practice to develop a sense of the meanings of the derived أوزان ; for now, focus on learning the forms.

The chart below lists the أوزان both by number and by وزن . Remember that the consonants أ , س , ت , and ن as well as shadda often (but not always!) serve as part of الوزن rather than الجذر , and that alif is **never** part of الجذر . As you memorize the أوزان , learn which extra letters mark each وزن .

أوزان الفعل DVD

The internal vowels and المصدر of Form I are not stable and must be memorized for each verb.

The short vowels and المصدر of Forms II-X remain fixed, with a few مصدر exceptions.

We have listed المصدر forms without الـ here so that you can focus on their forms.

Form IX is quite rare. It is included here only to complete the overall picture.

المصدر	المضارع	الماضي	الوزن
(varies)	يَفْعَل/يَفْعُل/يَفْعِل	فَعَلَ/فَعُلَ/فَعِلَ	I
تَفْعيل	يُفَعِّل	فَعَّلَ	II
مُفاعَلة	يُفاعِل	فاعَلَ	III
إِفْعال	يُفْعِل	أَفْعَلَ	IV
تَفَعُّل	يَتَفَعَّل	تَفَعَّلَ	V
تَفاعُل	يَتَفاعَل	تَفاعَلَ	VI
اِنْفِعال	يَنْفَعِل	اِنْفَعَلَ	VII
اِفْتِعال	يَفْتَعِل	اِفْتَعَلَ	VIII
اِفْعِلال	يَفْعَلّ	اِفْعَلَّ	IX
اِسْتِفْعال	يَسْتَفْعِل	اِسْتَفْعَلَ	X

Now let us look at a concrete example of how this system works. You know the verb انقَطَعَ, whose root is ق-ط-ع , and you can see by looking at the chart that it is Form VII, or وزن انفَعَلَ . This same root ق-ط-ع combines with other أوزان as well, as the chart below demonstrates. Note that the meanings of all these verbs are related in some way to the basic meaning, *to cut*, which is the meaning of الوزن الأول . Each other وزن adds something to this basic meaning.

The root ق-ط-ع was chosen to demonstrate this system because it happens that most of the theoretically possible forms can be derived from it. In other words, ق-ط-ع has an actual verb for each possible وزن (except IX). Most roots do not make use of all of the theoretically possible أوزان and thus have verbs corresponding to only some of them, as you will see when you practice looking up verbs in the dictionary.

المعنى	المصدر	المضارع	الماضي	الوزن
to cut	القَطْع	يَقْطَع	قَطَعَ	I
to chop up	التَّقْطيع	يُقَطِّع	قَطَّعَ	II
to cut off	المُقاطَعة	يُقاطِع	قاطَعَ	III
to divide up (land)	الإقْطاع	يُقْطِع	أَقْطَعَ	IV
to be chopped up	التَّقَطُّع	يَتَقَطَّع	تَقَطَّعَ	V
to intersect	التَّقاطُع	يَتَقاطَع	تَقاطَعَ	VI
to be cut off	الاِنْقِطاع	يَنْقَطِع	اِنْقَطَعَ	VII
to take a cut of	الاِقْتِطاع	يَقْتَطِع	اِقْتَطَعَ	VIII
--	--	--	--	IX
to deduct	الاِسْتِقْطاع	يَسْتَقْطِع	اِسْتَقْطَعَ	X

If you look at the meanings of these verbs, you can see that they are all related to the basic meaning of وزن , *to cut*. Arab grammarians have a saying that the more letters you add to the basic وزن , the more you add to the meaning, so that the higher أوزان are longer and also tend to have more complex or abstract meanings. Some of these meanings involve passive and reflexive meanings (to be X-ed or to X oneself). When you have more vocabulary to work with, you will learn to predict the basic meaning of many of the أوزان when you know the basic meaning of الجذر .

Recognizing الجذر takes practice. Knowing the patterns of the أوزان helps a great deal. The best way to learn the أوزان is to choose one verb from each وزن that you know well and use it as a reference. We suggest the following (but use others if you prefer):

المصدر	المضارع	الماضي	الوزن
الدِّراسة	يَدرُس	دَرَسَ	I
الجُلوس	يَجلِس	جَلَسَ	
العَمَل	يَعمَل	عَمِلَ	
التَّدريس	يُدَرِّس	دَرَّسَ	II
المُشاهَدة	يُشاهِد	شاهَدَ	III
الإمْكان	يُمكِن	أَمْكَنَ	IV
التَّذَكُّر	يَتَذَكَّر	تَذَكَّرَ	V
التَّبادُل	يَتَبادَل	تَبادَلَ	VI
الاِنْقِطاع	يَنْقَطِع	اِنْقَطَعَ	VII
الاِسْتِماع	يَسْتَمِع	اِسْتَمَعَ	VIII
الاِسْتِقْبال	يَسْتَقْبِل	اِسْتَقْبَلَ	X

Remember that همزة, whether written ء , أ , ئـ , or ؤ, **is a consonant, and can be a part of any** جذر. For example, the جذر of استأجر is ء-ج-ر , and that of قرأ is ق-ر-أ . The dictionary lists the consonant ء as أ in the place of the long vowel الف (ا), which cannot be part of a جذر because it is always a vowel.

Recognizing الجذر والوزن of verbs whose roots contain و or ي takes a bit of practice. (Remember that alif cannot be a part of a جذر. و and ي can be part of a جذر because they function as consonants as well as vowels.) In verbal أوزان , و and ي alternate between consonants and vowels depending on الوزن. Knowing the derived أوزان, including all the short vowels, will allow you to recognize these verbs. You already know verbs that can serve as models for the أوزان in which these letters turn into vowels; these are summarized in the next chart. Use these model verbs as references for recognizing the جذر and وزن of verbs that have و or ي as part of their roots.

المصدر	المضارع	الماضي	الجذر	الوزن
الكَوْن	يَكون	كانَ	ك-و-ن	I
المَجيء	يَجيء	جاءَ	ج-ي-ء	I
البَقاء	يَبقى	بَقِيَ	ب-ق-ي	I
الصَّحو	يَصحو	صَحا	ص-ح-و	I
الإِرادة	يُريد	أرادَ	ر-و-د	IV
الإِقامة	يُقيم	أَقامَ	ق-و-م	IV
الاِنْتِهاء	يَنْتَهي	اِنْتَهى	ن- هـ - ي	VIII
الاِسْتِطاعة	يَسْتَطيع	اِسْتَطاعَ	ط-و-ع	X

Make it a habit to identify the وزن of each new verb you learn, and practice manipulating its مصدر ، ماضي and مضارع forms.

تمرين ١٠ في البيت

Fill in the missing information in the chart below:

المصدر	المضارع	الماضي	الوزن
		فَهِمَ	I فَعَلَ
		شَجَّعَ (على)	
المُساعدة			III فاعَلَ
	يَتَكَوَّن من		
	يَسْتَمِع الى		
العَودة			
التَّبادُل			
		اِلْتَحَقَ بـ	

❁ القاموس

In Chapter 8, you practiced using the dictionary to look up nouns and adjectives. Now that you have learned about أوزان الفعل , you can begin to look up verbs as well. You will find verbs listed in the first subsection of an entry, listed by the root. The first part of the entry gives the Form I or الوزن الأوّل verb **if it exists,** listed in الماضي . Further information that you need to be able to conjugate and use the verb is given as well. Look up a verb you know by its جذر in your dictionary and look for the following pieces of information:
(a) At the beginning of the entry, right after الجذر , you will find the Form I verb in Latin letters showing how to pronounce it, followed by a single vowel, *a, u,* or *i.* This vowel represents the internal vowel for the Form I مضارع , fatHa, Damma, or kasra, since these vowels vary (e.g., يشرَب , يجلِس , or يحصُل). In some dictionaries, this information is given in Arabic.
(b) The next piece of information is the Form I مصدر (also unpredictable), which may be given both in Arabic script and Latin letters.
(c) Listed in numerical order, the أوزان from II-IX that exist for this جذر . Arabic-English dictionaries generally assume that you can derive the actual verbs for these أوزان on your own according to pattern, so only the number is given.

تمرين ١١ مع القاموس (في الصف)

THIS EXERCISE IS MEANT AS AN EXPLORATION OF THE VERB ENTRIES IN YOUR DICTIONARY AND THE MEANINGS OF الأوزان WITH SOME FAMILIAR ROOTS. LOOK UP THE ROOT ع – ل – م IN YOUR DICTIONARY AND COMPLETE:

ع - ل - م

المعنى	المصدر	المضارع	الماضي	الوزن
	العِلم			I فَعَلَ
to teach				II
		يَتَعَلَّم		
			تَعالَمَ	
				X

REPEAT THIS EXERCISE WITH EACH جذر LISTED BELOW AND SEE WHICH أوزان ARE GIVEN.

١- بدل ٢- ذكر ٣- خرج

تمرين ١٢ أوزان الفعل (في الصف)

READ EACH SENTENCE AND FIND A NEW VERB THAT HAS A FAMILIAR جذر . IDENTIFY ITS وزن AND WRITE IN THE INTERNAL VOWELS ON THE STEM ACCORDING TO THE PATTERN. GUESS THE APPROXIMATE MEANING FROM THE CONTEXT AND THEN LOOK IT UP IN YOUR قاموس TO CHECK:

١- غدا سيحاضر الاستاذ الدكتور أمين عبد المعطي عن الاقتصاد السعودي .

٢- نرغب في أن نتراسل مع بعض الطلاب العرب .

٣- انفصلت عن زوجها بعد أن فشلت العلاقة الزوجية.

٤- أريد أن أراجع كل الدروس قبل الامتحان.

٥- أحب السياحة والسفر، وأحب أن أصوّر المدن والمناطق التي أزورها.

تمرين ١٣ نشاط قراءة

ON THE NEXT PAGE ARE TWO SETS OF PERSONAL ADVERTISEMENTS OF PEOPLE SEEKING WORK.

تعلموا هذه الكلمات:

خِبرة	experience
الخَليج	the (Persian/Arabian) Gulf

أسئلة:

١- What information is included in each ad?

٢- في أي بلاد يريدون أن يعملوا ؟

٣- خمّنوا معنى:

كاتِب = ____________ عامِل = ____________

حاصِلة على = ____________

٤- مُحَرِّر = ____________ Guess the meaning from context, then look up to check:

5. What differences do you notice between the two sets of ads?

عامل في مطعم أو فندق

الاسم الكامل: رامز محمد الغاشي
العمر: ٢٤ سنة
الجنسية: سوري
المؤهلات: الثانوية العامة - شهادة حدادة إفرنجية
الخبرة: غير متوفرة
العمل المطلوب: عامل في مطعم أو فندق عربي
مكانه: فرنسا
العنوان: اللاذقية - حي الأزهري-دار والدة-سوريا.

عامل سياحي

الاسم الكامل: عبد العزيز توفيق النايلي
العمر: ٢٤ سنة
الجنسية: ليبي
المؤهلات: ثالثة معلمين - بائع في المنتزهات السياحية
الخبرة: سنة واحدة
العمل المطلوب: عامل في احد المرافق السياحية
مكانه: الخليج العربي
العنوان: بنغازي - بريد العروبة - ص.ب.١٠٠٧٣ - ليبيا

محرر

الاسم الكامل: عصام سعيد سعد
العمر: ٤٤ سنة
الجنسية: لبناني
المؤهلات: طالب في الدكتوراه قسم العلوم السياسية
الخبرة: كاتب في مجلة «الهدف» وجريدة «السفير» و«القبس» وجريدة «الحياة»
العمل المطلوب: محرر
مكانه: باريس - العالم العربي - افريقيا
العنوان: SAAD ISSAM
44 - 50 Bd . VICTOR - HUGO
92110 CLICHY - FRANCE
Tel : 47 56 10 29

من مجلة الفرسان ١٩٩١/٩/٢٣ و ١٩٩٢/١/٢٠

عمل

• الآنسة مونية نمروك (٢٣ سنة)، جامعية، حاصلة على دبلوم في المطبخ المغربي، تطلب فرصة عمل، العنوان: ٩٨ شارع النصر، حي الرياض، طريق عين السمن ٣٠٠٠٠ ، فاس، المغرب .

• الآنسة فاطمة أحمين (٢٨ سنة)، حاصلة على دبلوم الكفاءة التربوية لتربية الأطفال، تطلب عملاً، العنوان: حي جميلة ٤، الزنقة ١٠٢ ، الرقم ٧، قرية الجماعة، الدار البيضاء، المغرب .

• الآنسة فاتن موايزي (٣٣ سنة)، حاصلة على دبلوم لتعليم اللغة العربية، لديها تجربة ثلاث سنوات في هذا الميدان، تطلب عملاً في دولة خليجية كمدرسة، العنوان: ٣٥ طريق بالشاطر عند يوسف الجربي، وادي المرج ، بنزرت ٧٠٠٠ ، الجمهورية التونسية.

• الآنسة عواطف مفلح (٣٢ سنة)، حاصلة على دبلوم في تربية وتمريض الأطفال، لديها خبرة سبع سنوات في هذا الميدان، تطلب فرصة عمل في دولة عربية، العنوان: زنقة القائد العيدي، ٣٠٩ المحمدية، المغرب .

• الآنسة جميلة حجري (٢٢ سنة) متخصصة في المحاسبة، تطلب عملاً في دولة خليجية، العنوان: رقم ١٨٩ ، الحزام الكبير، الحي المحمدي، الدار البيضاء - المغرب.

من مجلة الوطن العربي العدد ١٣ ١٣٧١/٦/٣ ٢٠٠

تمرين ١٤ نشاط قراءة

اقــرأوا المقــالــة عن المُفكّر *thinker* الجزائري «مالِك بن نبي» لتتعرفوا عليه وعلى حياته:

أسئلة

١ـ ما هي الاماكن التي عاش فيها ؟

أين؟	متى؟

٢ـ أين درس ؟

المدرسة	البلد	السنوات

٣ـ بعض الناس الذين تعرف عليهم:

4. Find two sentences in which the connector لـ signals a cause and effect relationship.

5. Follow the narration of Malik Bin Nabi's life by identifying all the verbs that describe his own actions (remember to look for جمل فعلية and the و that often signals a new sentence.) As you find each verb, identify its وزن and read it out loud, takng care to put the all the short vowels according to the patterns you have learned.

6. For discussion: What changed in Algeria during Bin Nabi's lifetime, and how is that change reflected in his life?

مالك بن نبي : محطات في سيرته

– ولد في قسنطينة سنة ١٩٠٥ من أسرة فقيرة.

– تعلم في طفولته قراءة القرآن الكريم في «مدرسة الكتّاب» ثم انتسب الى مدرسة فرنسية.

– اقام في تبسه حتى١٩١٨ وانهى فيها دروسه الاعدادية.

– نال منحة لاكمال دراسته الثانوية وعاد الى قسنطينة فانتسب الى المدرسة الفرنسية وفي الوقت نفسه واصل دروسه العربية والقرآنية على يد الشيخ عبد المجيد في الجامع الكبير.

– دخل المدرسة الثانوية في ١٩٢٠ وهناك تعرف على بعض تلامذة الشيخ عبد المجيد بن باديس.

– انهى دراسته الثانوية في ١٩٢٥ وسافر الى مرسيليا وليون وباريس بحثاً عن عمل... وفشل في سعيه فعاد الى الجزائر.

– عين كاتباً في المحاكم في منطقة وهران (أفلو) في١٩٢٧ واخذ يطلع على جريدة «الشهاب» التي يصدرها ابن باديس.

– عاد في١٩٢٨ الى قسنطينة واختلف مع كاتب المحكمة الفرنسي فاستقال من وظيفته.

– عاد الى قريته تبسه واشتغل في مطحنة للقمح وفشل المشروع في١٩٢٩ .

– سافر ثانية الى فرنسا في١٩٣٠ طلباً للعلم وتسجل في معهد الدراسات الشرقية ولم تقبله الادارة فدخل مدرسة للاسلكي (هندسة الكهرباء).

– تزوج من فرنسية (اشهرت اسلامها) في١٩٣١ .

– في باريس التقى المستشرق ماسينيون واختلف معه. وقابل المهاتما غاندي الذي زار فرنسا عام ١٩٣٢ .

– التقى فريد زين الدين (نائب وزير خارجية «الجمهورية العربية المتحدة» لاحقا) ومنه تعرف على افكار شكيب ارسلان الذي كان يعيش يومها لاجئاً في جنيف.

– اخذ يتنقل بين الجزائر وفرنسا، والتقى في١٩٣٦ بعثات ازهرية في فرنسا بينها بعثة برئاسة الشيخ محمد عبد الله درّاز.

– التقى في١٩٣٦ الوفد الجزائري الذي جاء الى فرنسا ليطالب الحكومة بالمشاركة البرلمانية وكان في عداد الوفد ابن باديس والشيخ البشير الابراهيمي.

– حاول تأسيس معهد تعليم في قسنطينة في١٩٣٦فرفض الحاكم الفرنسي، وعمد الى تأسيس مدرسة للأميين في مرسيليا في١٩٣٨–١٩٣٩ فاقفلتها البلدية فعاد الى قريته.

– انفجرت الحرب العالمية الثانية في١٩٣٩ فترك الجزائر الى فرنسا وبقي هناك الى ان انتقل الى القاهرة في١٩٥٦ ، ولم يعد الى فرنسا نهائياً، واستمرت علاقته مع زوجته بالمراسلة.

– في القاهرة اتصل بالرئيس جمال عبد الناصر وخصصت له الحكومة مرتباً شهرياً وتفرغ للعمل الفكري. وتزوج ثانية وانجب بنتين توأمين.

– عاش في مصر الى العام١٩٦٣ وعاد الى الجزائر بعد استقلالها واصبح مديراً للتعليم العالي حتى العام١٩٦٧ .

– تفرغ بن نبي للاصلاح والدعوة الى ان توفي في سنة١٩٧٣ .

– معظم مؤلفاته باللغة الفرنسية. وبدأ منذ ١٩٦٠ التأليف بالعربية فكانت محاولته الاولى كتابه «الصراع الفكري في البلاد المستعمرة».

من جريدة الحياة ١٢/١٠/١٩٩٢

تمرين ١٥ نشاط كتابة

The article on مالك بن نبي contains the names of several famous people. Choose one to look up further information on and write about. Give a basic سيرة *biography* of the person on the model of the article you read.

الاستماع DVD

تمرين ١٦ نشاط استماع

A. Skim, then read the following text, focusing on the information given. B. Watch the selection on your DVD as many times as you need until you can underline everything in the text that matches the information given in the video.

* * *

١٦ – مي زيادة : (١٨٨٦ – ١٩٤١)

اسمها ماري الياس زيادة، وعرفت بمي: كاتبة أديبة لبنانية. كان والدها من أهل كسروان بلبنان، وأقام مدة في الناصرة بفلسطين، وبها ولدت ماري، وتعلمت في إحدى مدارسها الابتدائية، ثم تعلمت بمدرسة عينطورة بلبنان. وفيما بعد انتقلت مع والديها إلى مصر، وأخذت تكتب المقالات في جريدة «المحروسة» وفي مجلة «الزهور». وكانت تحسن اللغات الأجنبية: الفرنسية والإنجليزية والإيطالية والألمانية.

* * *

من «مختارات من النثر العربي» د. وداد القاضي،

المؤسسة العربية للدراسات والنشر، بيروت ١٩٨٣

تمارين المراجعة

تمرين ١٧

Complete using an appropriate form of the right verb. Use what you know about أنْ and أنّ to help you find the correct words. Remember to think about agreement rules and tense, and write in the correct مضارع ending.

ذكر	تمنى	انتقل	ما زال	ترك	تكلم
رغب	جاء	حصل	تغيب	شجع	زار
قرر	رفض	أكل	استأجر	فهم	حدث

١- ________ الجرائد أنّ الرئيس المصري ________ الولايات المتحدة قريباً.

٢- ________ كثير من الناس أنْ ________ وظائفهم و________ إلى وظائف اخرى لأنّهم ليسوا سعداء في وظائفهم.

٣- بدأت أكتب رسالة الدكتوراه منذ سنة ونصف والى الآن ________ أعمل عليها.

٤- ________ كثير من المهندسين الأجانب إلى أمريكا كل سنة ليعملوا و________ على خبرة .

٥- ________ صديقتي وأختها عن المحاضرات يومين بسبب مشكلة عائلية.

٦- في الأوّل، لم ________نـي أفراد عائلتي على الالتحاق بكلية الموسيقى لأنهم كانوا ________ في أن أدرس الهندسة ولكنهم أخيراً ________ أنّ الموسيقى هي حبي الأول والأخير وأنّ لها مستقبل!

٧- ________ أصدقائي أنْ ________ سيارة للسفر الى ولاية فليوريدا لعطلة الربيع.

٨- ________ بعض الناس أنْ ________ السَلَطة والخضار عندما يسافرون لأنّهم لا يريدون أن يمرضوا.

تمرين ١٨ استمعوا إلى مها واكتبوا ما تقول : DVD

مصر ... لا ــــــ الكثير ــــــ . ــــــ ــــــ ــــــ إلى أمريكا
ــــــ ــــــ ــــــ سنوات، ــــــ ــــــ كيف ــــــ
ــــــ في مصر. في السنة ــــــ ــــــ ــــــ صغيرة في
بروكلين، هذه ــــــ ــــــ بيتا في ــــــ ــــــ ، ــــــ
من ــــــ و ــــــ ــــــ صغيرة، ــــــ كبيرا و ــــــ
ــــــ ــــــ ــــــ مثل بيت ليلى، لكنه جميل و ــــــ ــــــ
بـ ــــــ ــــــ . في ــــــ ــــــ غرفة ــــــ
و ــــــ و ــــــ و ــــــ ــــــ و ــــــ ــــــ ــــــ .
في ــــــ ــــــ غرفة ــــــ وغرفة ــــــ ها والدي مكتبا
ــــــ ، و ــــــ ، و ــــــ . ــــــ ألا ــــــ هذا البيت بعد
ــــــ أو ثلاث لـ ــــــ إلى ــــــ ــــــ كما ــــــ من قبل .

العامية DVD

- القصة: "أتمنى مانسيبش البيت دا"

شاهدوا مها تتكلم.

كيف تقول «غرفة»؟

- "فيه شقة فاضية؟"

شاهدوا السيدة الأجنبية تتكلم مع الرجل أمام البناية.

ماذا تريد أن تعرف؟ ماذا تأخذ من الرجل؟

تذكروا هذه الكلمات

غرفة المَعيشة	غرفة نوم	خبرة	الخليج	فَوقَ
غرفة الاستقبال	بِجانِب	بَيْنَ	تَحتَ	وراء

١٥ . لست مصرية ولست أمريكية

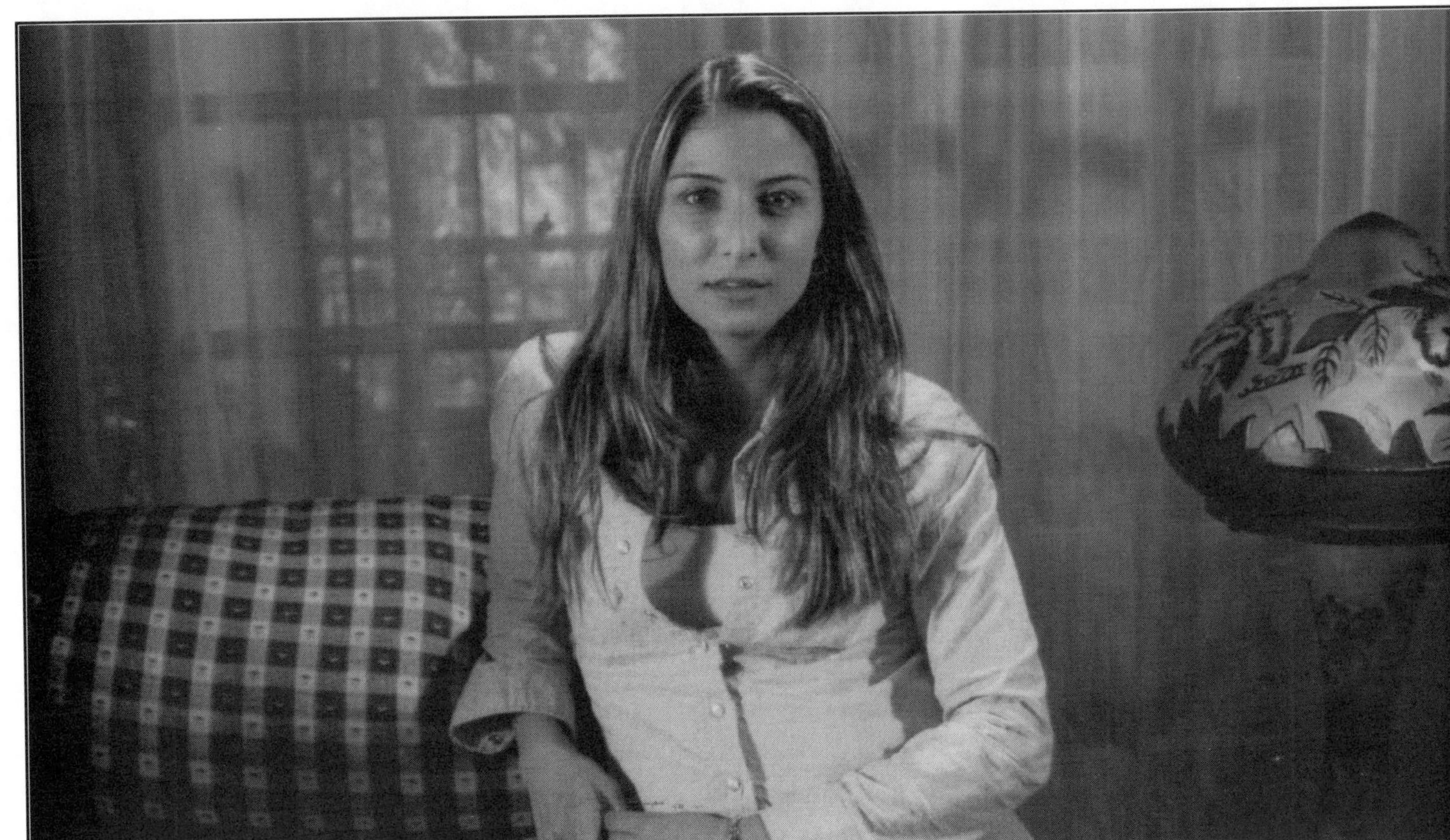

في هذا الدرس:

القصة
- علاقة مها بوالدتها وبليلى

الثقافة
- «هل الاولاد عندهم حرية أكثر من البنات؟»

القواعد
- الاسم الموصول
- مراجعة النفي
- الشرط : إذا ، إنْ ، لو

القراءة
- مشكلتي
- تونس

الاستماع
- مع العائلة والأصدقاء

العامية
- القصة: «انا مش مصرية ومش أمريكية»
- «كنتي فين؟!»

المفردات

إلاّ	except
(لا / ليس /لن / لم ...) إلاّ	(with preceding negative) only
الّذي ، مؤنث: الّتي ، ج. الّذينَ	which, that (as in *the* ... *that* ...) (definite)
مَجْموعة من ج. -ات	(a) group of
حَدَّدَ ، يُحَدِّد ، التَّحديد	to determine, set (e.g., a time, topic)
الحُرِّيّة	freedom
سَمَحَ لِـ بِـ + أنْ/المصدر ، يَسْمَح لِـ بِـ ، السَّماح لِـ بِـ	to permit someone to
شَخْص ج. أشْخاص	person
اِشتَرَكَ في ، يَشْتَرِك في ، الاشتِراك في	to share, have in common, participate in
مَشغول عن ج. -ون	too busy (to have time) for
شَيء ج. أشْياء	thing
صاحِب /ة ج. أصْحاب	friend; boyfriend/girlfriend
العامِّيّة	colloquial or spoken Arabic
غَضِبَ من ، يَغْضَب من ، الغَضَب من	to get angry
الفُصْحى	formal or Classical Arabic
كَـ + اسم	like, as = مثل
لَبِسَ ، يَلبَس ، اللُّبس	to wear, put on (clothes)
لَسْتُ	I am not
مَلَكَ ، يَمْلِك ، المِلك	he owns, possesses
نَوى + أنْ/المصدر ، يَنوي ، النِّيّة	to intend to
هُما	they, both of them (مُثَنّى)
مَوضوع ج. -ات / مَواضيع	subject, topic
وُلِدَت	she was born

تعلموا هذا الفعل: DVD

we are not	لَسْنا	I am not	لَسْتُ
you (pl.) are not	لَسْتُم	you (m.) are not you (f.) are not	لَسْتَ لَسْتِ
they are not	لَيسوا	he/ it is not she/ it is not	لَيسَ لَيسَت

أمثلة : هل أنت لبنانية؟ -- لا، لست لبنانية ، أنا سورية .

نحن مشغولون، ولكن لسنا مشغولين عنك !

لماذا ترفضون مساعدتهم ؟ أليسوا ناساً مثلكم ؟!

تمرين ١ **الملابس** DVD

Go to your DVD and click on the pictures to learn words for items of clothing. Remember that pants and shoes are plural in English but in Arabic we refer to a <u>single pair</u> of each with المفرد.

بَدلة ج. بِدَل	جاكيت ج. -ات	بلوزة ج، -ات	قَميص ج. قُمصان
كرافات ج. -ات	بَنطَلون ج. -ات	بيجاما ج. -ات	بلوفر ج. -ات
تي شيرت ج. -ات	شورت ج. -ات	بُرنيطة ج. بَرانيط	مَلابِس داخلية
فُستان ج. فَساتين	تَنّورة ج. تنانير/ جيب ج. -ات		جَلاّ بيّة ج. جَلاليب
عَباءة ج. -ات	كوفيّة ج. -ات	حِذاء ج. أَحذية	نَظّارات

في الصف : Use this new vocabulary to answer:

١- ماذا تحب/ين أن تلبس/ي في الطقس الحار ؟ وفي الطقس البارد؟

٢- ما أجمل ملابس لبستها في حياتك، وأين ومتى كان ذلك؟

٣- سنسافر الى الشرق الاوسط لأسبوعيْن. ما هي الملابس التي ستأخذ/ينها معك ؟

٤- هل درست في مدرسة تحدد للطلاب الملابس التي يلبسونها؟ ما رأيك في هذا؟

تمرين ٢ **المفردات الجديدة (في البيت)**

اكتبوا كلمات جديدة مناسبة في كل جملة:

١ـ ______ النبي محمد (صلى الله عليه وسلم) في مكة سنة ٥٧٠ ومات في المدينة سنة ٦٣٢.

٢ـ بعد الحصول على شهادة الطب إن شاء الله ______ خطيبتي أن تتخصص في أمراض العيون .

٣ـ في الصيف أحب أن ______ البنطلونات القصيرة (الشورتات) .

٤ـ ______ والدتها منها لأنها رفضت مساعدة أختها في إعداد العشاء .

٥ـ هل تعرفون متى سـ ______ الجامعة مواعيد امتحانات الدخول ؟

٦ـ لم أترجم الكتاب وحدي ولكن ______ معي في ترجمته بعض طلابي المعيدين.

٧ـ انتقالنا إلى شيكاغو كان صعباً جداً علينا لأننا أصبحنا بعيدين عن ______ نا .

٨ـ غرفة السفرة في شقتي صغيرة ولا يمكن أن يجلس فيها أكثر من ٥ ______ .

٩ـ كانت خالتي في أول ______ من النساء التحقت بجامعة الكويت .

١٠ـ -هل تعرف ماذا سيكون ______ محاضرتها الليلة ؟

– أظنّ أنها ستتكلم عن «المرأة العربية بين الماضي والمستقبل».

١١ـ ______ المديرة لي بأن أترك المكتب بعد الظهر لآخذ ابني إلى الدكتور.

١٢ـ في العالم العربي يقرأ الناس ويكتبون بالعربية ______ ولكنهم يتكلمون بـ ______ في حياتهم اليومية .

١٣ـ نشعر بأنك دائماً ______ عنا ولا تريد أن تقضي أي وقت معنا .

١٤ـ لا ______ أي شيء في هذا البيت إلا الكرسي الذي أجلس عليه !!

١٥- ما هي ________ التي سنكون بحاجة إليها في سفرنا ؟

١٦- الناس في كل بلاد العالم يحبون ________ ويتمنّون أن يستمتعوا بها .

تمرين ٣ **ليس (في البيت)**

COMPLETE, USING THE CORRECT FORM OF ليس , AND GIVE A REASON.

مثال: صديقتي غادة ليست سعيدة في حياتها لأنها لم تحصلْ على وظيفة مناسبة.

١- أنا الآن ________________________ .

٢- كثير من الأمريكيين ________________________ .

٣- معظم الناس في هذه المنطقة ________________________ .

٤- يا محمد، لماذا ________________________ .

٥- زوجته ________________________ .

٦- أنا وإخوتي ________________________ .

٧- ظننتُ أنّكم ________________________ .

٨- موضوع الشرق الاوسط ________________________ .

تمرين ٤ **اسألوا زملاءكم :**

1. Who *participates in* student clubs? Which ones? What are *the things that* the club does?
2. Where *were they born*?
3. When are they *too busy to* go out with their *friends*?

   Do their *friends get angry* at them because of that?
4. What do they *intend* to do after graduation?
5. Do they *have* (possess) the *freedom that* they want?
6. Do they think the university should *allow* students *to set* the time of their exams?

   Why or why not?
7. Do they know *a person* who does not *own* a car?
8. Do they feel shy when they talk in front of a large *group of* people?

9. What are their favorite *subjects*?

القصة

تمرين ٥ **شاهدوا واكتبوا:**

١- ما هي الأشياء الجديدة التي نعرفها عن ليلى الآن؟

أ - ____________ جـ - ____________

ب - ____________ د - ____________

٢- ماذا تقول مها عن العلاقة بينها وبين ليلى ؟

شاهدوا مرة ثانية :

٣- ماذا تستطيع مها أنْ تفعل؟ ماذا لا تستطيع أنْ تفعل؟

٤- ماذا تفعل والدة مها إذا تأخّرت مها في الرجوع الى البيت؟

٥- كيف تشعر مها بالنسبة لهُوِيّتها *her identity*؟

٦- لماذا تقول مها إنّ ليلى تملك حرّيتها؟

استمعوا وتعلموا:

7. Listen to how مها expresses her restrictions. Write exactly what she says:

«والدتي تسمح لي بـ__________ أريد .... ولكنها لا تسمح ____________»

8. You know أي؟ *which* as an interrogative; here مها uses it with a different meaning. In the first part of the sentence in question (7), she compares herself with someone. Complete:

«والدتي تسمح لي ____ كـ______ ____ ____ أسريكية»

The word أي can also function as a noun meaning *any*, as in أي شخص *any person*. أيّ is normally used in its مذكر form, but in formal registers it may occur in the مؤنث form when it precedes a مؤنث noun: لا تتكلم أية لغة اخرى .

9. What does مها say about Layla's parents? Write what you hear. What endings are used and why?

«هما ________ شركة تجارية ____________ عنها.

تمرين ٦ نشاط محادثة

WHEN INTERPERSONAL PROBLEMS OCCUR IN ARAB CULTURE, A FAMILY MEMBER OR CLOSE FRIEND OFTEN ASSUMES THE ROLE OF THE INTERMEDIARY, RATHER THAN A PROFESSIONAL COUNSELOR. IN A ROLE PLAY, IN GROUPS OF THREE OR FOUR, ACT OUT A SCENE IN WHICH مها ووالدتها TRY TO RESOLVE THEIR CONFLICTS.

الثقافة

هل الأولاد عندهم حرية أكثر من البنات؟ DVD

شاهدوا الـ DVD واستمعوا الى أراء بعض الشباب المصريين في حرية البنت وحرية الولد!

القواعد

❁ الاسم الموصول: الَّذي ، الَّتي ، الَّذين

الَّذي (مذكر)	الَّتي (مؤنث)	الَّذينَ (جمع human)

In Chapter 11 you learned how to recognize and form جملة الصفة, a sentence that modifies an **indefinite** noun, as in the examples:

١- لي صديق أتكلّم معه عن كل شيء .

٢- تعرّفتُ على بنت تجلس بجانبي في الصف .

٣- مَن هم؟ هم زملاء أعرفهم من العمل .

The same structure is used to form sentences that modify **definite** nouns, with one difference: definite nouns are followed by a **definite** pronoun called الاسم المَوْصول that introduces the modifying sentence (similar to English *which* or *that*). These relative pronouns must agree in gender with the noun they modify. Compare ١, ٢ and ٣ above with corresponding sentences ٤ , ٥ and ٦ below, which modify definite nouns:

٤- محمد هو الصديق الذي أتكلم معه عن كل شيء .

٥- تعرفتُ على البنت التي تجلس بجانبي في الصف .

٦- من هم؟ هم الزملاء الذين أعرفهم من العمل .

The nouns in 1, 2 and 3 are **indefinite**, so **no connector** is used. The nouns in 4, 5 and 6 are **definite**, so the **definite** relative pronoun, الاسم الموصول , is used. **Remember** that the relative pronouns must agree in gender and number with the nouns they modify:

الصديق الذي البنت التي الزملاء الذين

❁ ما ومَن

The pronouns ما *what/whatever* and مَن *who/whoever* also function as relative pronouns. You heard Maha use ما in the following sentences, in which it functions like the phrase الأشياء التي or الشيء الذي :

ليلى تفهم ما أشعر به . = ليلى تفهم **الشيء الذي** أشعر **به**.

والدتي تسمح لي بأن ألبس **ما** اريد. = والدتي تسمح لي بأن ألبس **الأشياء التي** أريد**ها**.

Similarly, مَن functions like الشخص الذي or الأشخاص الذين :

ليلى تخرج مع **مَن** تريد . = ليلى تخرج مع **الشخص الذي** تريد أن تخرج **معه**.

Although they function like الشيء الذي and الشخص الذي , both ما and مَن tend to be used when the speaker wants to be general, not specific, in contrast to the former phrases, which refer to very specific entities. Contrast what Maha says about Layla:

صديقتي ليلى هي **الشخص** الوحيد **الذي** أتكلم **معه** عن كل شيء.

with what she might say about an unspecified person: أنا لا أجد مَن يفهمني في أسرتي.

The following statements with ما and من are general in meaning:

لا أحب **ما** يقول.　　　　لم أجد في المكتب **مَن** يساعدني.

Note that ما and من do not always require a pronoun that refers back to them, except on a preposition, as the first sentence above shows: تفهم ما أشعر به .[1] For now, you are expected to recognize ما and من when you see them.

تمرين ٧　**ما ومَن (في الصف)**

CHANGE THESE UNSPECIFIC SENTENCES WITH ما AND من TO MORE SPECIFIC ONES WITH الشيء الذي OR الأشياء التي OR الشخص الذي OR الأشخاص الذين :

١ـ هل تفهمون ما أقصد؟

٢ـ هل تذكرين من منهم بقي هنا ومن سافر؟

٣ـ أظنّ أنكم تعرفون جيداً ما أريده من كل واحد منكم!

٤ـ من يرغب في الحصول على هذه الوظيفة يحتاج الى ٣ سنوات من الخبرة.

٥ـ كيف يمكنك ألاّ تشعري بنفس ما أشعر به؟

---

[1] The optional use of a referent object pronoun with ما clauses may have to do with the degree of specificity, in that the less specific the reference, the less likely there is to be a referent object pronoun.

تمرين ٨ الاسم الموصول (في الصف)

PRACTICE USING THE STRUCTURE OF DEFINITE RELATIVE CLAUSES IN ARABIC BY RE-FORMING THE FOLLOWING SENTENCES IN ENGLISH TO PARALLEL THE ARABIC STRUCTURE, THEN TRANSLATE THE SENTENCES INTO ARABIC. IN THE EXAMPLE, THE HIGHLIGHTED WORDS *THE*, *THAT*, AND *IT* REMIND YOU OF THE IMPORTANT ELEMENTS IN ARABIC STRUCTURE.

Example: I didn't like the movie I saw. —> I didn't like **the** movie **which/that** I saw **it**.

1. Do the students you know study a lot?
2. The years they lived in the Middle East were happy [ones].
3. The apartment I lived in last year was too small.
4. I didn't find the books I wanted (=want) in the library.
5. When I went to the place I usually sit in I found a person sitting there.
6. Some people do not possess the freedom you enjoy in America.
7. We felt very comfortable in the hotel we stayed at in Cairo.
8. She's busy with her friends who are visiting her.
9. The woman who usually helps me is not in her office.
10. My favorite vacation was the vacation I spent in Canada.

تمرين ٩ الذي /التي/الذين (في البيت)

DESCRIBE THESE PEOPLE AND PLACES BY USING الذي , التي OR الذين WHERE NEEDED. IF NO اسم موصول SHOULD BE USED, LEAVE BLANK.

١- هذا هو البيت ________ وُلدت فيه .

٢- المكتبة مكان ________ نذهب إليه للدراسة .

٣- أين المجلة ________ قرأتِ فيها تلك المقالة؟

٤- هل تشعر بالراحة في السرير ________ في غرفتك ؟

٥- في هذا الشارع بناية عالية ________ تتكون من ٢٥ طابقاً .

٦- بالنسبة لي ، هذه كانت أجمل اجازة ________ أخذتها في حياتي.

٧- أنا دائماً أتبادل الرسائل مع أصدقائي ________ يسكنون خارج مصر.

٨- «سِنْدباد» قصة ________ يحبها الأولاد في كل بلاد العالم.

٩- هذه وظيفة ________ لا يمكنني الحصول عليها.

١٠- المدن ________ زرناها في العالم العربي هي مراكش ودمشق والقاهرة .

١١- هل تعرفون طلابا آخرين ________ يدرسون العربية؟

تمرين ١٠

Specify the people or places you mean using a sentence with الاسم الموصول :

١- مَن هو الاستاذ ________________________ ؟

٢- من هم الناس ________________________ ؟

٣- تعرّفت على المرأة ________________________ .

٤- هذا هو الرجل ________________________ .

٥- ما هي الموضوعات ________________________ ؟

٦- الاثنين والأربعاء والجمعة هي الأيام ________________________ .

٧- ما اسم الشركة ________________________ ؟

❁ مراجعة النَفي *Negation*

Review the negation particles in formal Arabic:

Particle	Negates	القواعد
لا	الفعل المضارع	+ المضارع المرفوع
ما	الفعل الماضي	+ الماضي
لن	المستقبل	+ المضارع المنصوب
لم	الماضي	+ المضارع المجزوم
ليس	جملة اسمية	agrees with subject

Negation is one aspect of Arabic grammar that shows notable differences between the formal and informal registers, mostly in the particles used. Formal Arabic uses the specialized negation particles that you see above. In spoken Arabic, ما is more commonly used. You have also heard مش used in colloquial Arabic for ليس .

تمرين ١١

ANSWER THESE أسـئلة PRETENDING YOU FEEL LIKE SAYING "NO!" TO EVERYTHING TODAY. USE AS MANY DIFFERENT NEGATION FORMS AS YOU CAN, AND WRITE IN ALL THE مرفوع , منصوب AND مجزوم ENDINGS ON THE VERBS:

١- هل في هذه المنطقة حدائق جميلة؟

٢- هل عرفت أنه يقيم في الكويت الآن؟

٣- في رأيك ، هل الفشل هو أصعب شيء في الحياة؟

٤- كنت مريضاً/مريضة أمس ، فهل أنت أحسن اليوم؟

٥- هل قرّرت الخروج مع مجموعة من الأصدقاء بالليل؟

٦- هل هذه أول مرة تدخّن/ين فيها؟

٧- هل تملك عائلة صاحبتك/صاحبك بناية في هذه المنطقة؟

٨- هل تذكّرت اسم الشخص الذي كان يتكلم معك؟

٩- هل عندكم اجازة في الأسبوع القادم؟

١٠- هل هناك علاقة بينهما؟

١١- هل قرأت الرسالة التي كتبتها لك ؟

١٢- هل تريد/ين أن تشترك/ي معنا في العمل على الواجب؟

١٣- هل يسمح لك والدك بأخذ السيارة عندما تريد/ين؟

١٤- هل ستقضي/ن العطلة مع عائلتك؟

١٥- هل حددت موعد سفرك؟

Conditionals ❁ الشـرط

There are three words for *if* in Arabic: إذا , إنْ , and لَـو .

إذا is the most commonly used conditional particle. Remember that إذا **must be followed by** الماضي no matter what the meaning of the sentence (past, present or future), and that a result clause (if ... then ...) following إذا is usually introduced by فَـ .

أمثلة:

إذا نجحتُ في الثانوية العامة إن شاء الله ، فأريد أن أدخل كلية التجارة .	*if I pass*
إذا كان الطقس جميلاً فسأذهب إلى النادي وإذا كان ممطراً فسأبقى في البيت .	*if it is*
والدة مها تغضب إذا تأخّرت في العودة إلى البيت .	*if she is late*

You already know **إنْ** from the expression إنْ شـاء الله , *if God wills*. It may take a verb either in الماضي , as you can see from the verb شـاء , or المضـارع المجـزوم . It tends to be more formal than إذا , and usually occurs in proverbs and expressions.

لَـو introduces a condition that is untrue or impossible to fulfill, such as *If I were you....* The result clause is introduced by لَـ , and **both** clauses must be in الماضي .

أمثلة:

لو كنت الرئيس لَساعدت كل الناس .	*If I were ...*
لو كان عندي مليون دولار لَسافرت إلى كل بلاد العالم .	*If I had ...*

الرسم: الدكتور مايكل كوبرسون

تمرين ١٢ اسألوا زملاءكم ماذا سيفعلون إذا / لو :

FIND OUT WHAT YOUR CLASSMATES WOULD DO IF:

1. They got a scholarship to study in the Middle East.
2. They do not find a decent job after graduation.
3. They find out there is an exam tomorrow.
4. They had a vacation now.
5. They were a "مليونير" .
6. The weather is sunny and warm tomorrow.
7. They owned a private plane.
8. They were not in class now!

تمرين ١٣ ماذا سيحدث إذا / لو ...؟

SPECULATE:

١- إذا نجحتُ في دراستي فـ ______________ .

٢- إذا لم أستطع أن أفهم الدرس فـ ______________ .

٣- إذا كنتَ مشغولاً فـ ______________ .

٤- لو كنت أعرف أنّك ستحضرين لَـ ______________ .

٥- ______________ فأنوي أن أدخل كلية الحقوق إن شاء الله .

٦- ______________ فستغضب صديقتي .

٧- ______________ فسنذهب إلى السينما .

٨- أنا سأساعدك إذا ______________ .

٩- ______________ لَسهرت معكم إلى آخر الليل !

١٠- لو______________ لَـ ______________ .

١١- إذا ______________ ، فـ ______________ .

تمرين ١٤ نشاط قراءة (في الصف ثم في البيت)

كلمة تساعد على الفهم:

لا أدري = لا أعرف

أ ـ القراءة الاولى

READ THIS LETTER FROM AN ADVICE COLUMN ONCE THROUGH WITHOUT STOPPING AND ANSWER AS BEST YOU CAN:

١ـ ماذا عرفت عن الشابة التي كتبت هذه الرسالة؟

عمرها وماذا تفعل: ______________________________

من في أسرتها: ______________________________

كيف علاقتها بزوجها: ______________________________

ب ـ القراءة الثانية

THIS TIME, LOOK FOR WORDS WHOSE جذر YOU RECOGNIZE AND TRY TO PIECE TOGETHER NEW INFORMATION.

٢ـ لماذا ليست مع زوجها الآن؟ ______________________________

جـ القراءة في البيت

ON THE THIRD READING (NOT BEFORE) USE THE DICTIONARY, BUT DO NOT LOOK UP EVERY WORD. LOOK UP JUST ENOUGH TO ENSURE THAT YOU HAVE UNDERSTOOD THE ESSENTIAL POINTS. CHOOSE 3 WORDS THAT RECUR OR SEEM PARTICULARLY IMPORTANT TO THE STORY, AND LOOK THEM UP IN YOUR قاموس .

٣ـ نشاط كتابة أو محادثة:

RESPOND TO THIS LETTER EITHER IN WRITING OR IN A RADIO TALK SHOW FORMAT. GIVE HER THE BEST ADVICE YOU CAN!

مشكلتى

سيدتى[1]

في الحقيقة لا أدرى كيف أبدأ رسالتى لتوضيح المشكلة. فأنا فتاة في العشرين من عمرى، أحببت شابا طيباً حنونا وجدت فيه صفات فارس أحلامى، وتزوجنا بعد قصة حب جميلة استمرت حوالى خمس سنوات ومضى على زواجنا ما يقارب السنة والنصف، ونحن نعيش فى سعادة وهناء. ولكن الدنيا لا تبتسم دائما، فقد بدأت مشكلتى منذ أن قرر زوجى العزيز أن يواصل دراسته في الطيران، مما يلزمه بالابتعاد عنى، في البداية لم استطع السفر معه بسبب الحمل. وسافر هو قرابة ٦ شهور، ولم يحضر سوى شهر واحد وذلك ليكون معى فى الولادة، وسافر بعدها. وقد مضى على سفره ٩ شهور، ومع الاسف لم يتمكن من الحضور لظروف دراسته. ولأنى طالبة ايضا بالكلية ولا اريد ترك الدراسة، فلن اتمكن من الذهاب إليه مع انه يلح بذلك. بصراحة لا ادرى ماذا افعل وإلى متى سيستمر هذا الحال؟ فقد تعبت من مواجهة الحياة وحدى. فهل اترك الدراسة أو اؤجلها وذلك بأخذ اجازة إلى أن يكمل زوجى دراسته وأكون معه ام اواصل دراستى واتحمل عذاب الفراق ومسئولية ابنتى؟

الحائرة أم يوسف

من «مشاكل البنات»، فوزية سلامة، الجزء الثالث، ص. ١٣٤، مكتبة مدبولي الصغير، القاهرة، ٢٠٠٠

[1]The name of the women's magazine that publishes this advice column.

تمرين ١٥ **نشاط قراءة**

تعلموا هذه الكلمات:

بَحر ج. بِحار	sea
جَزيرة ج. جُزُر	island

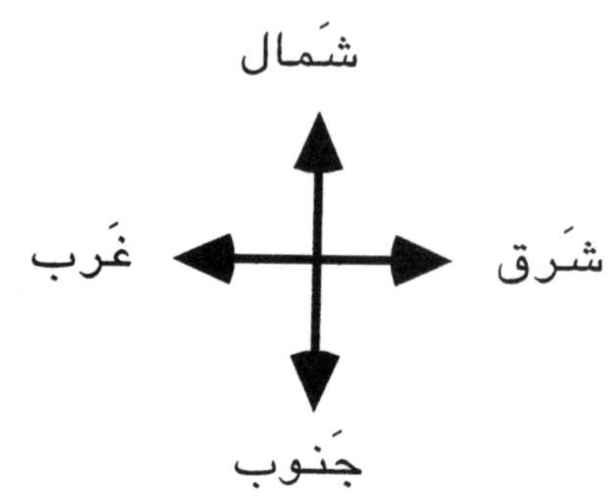

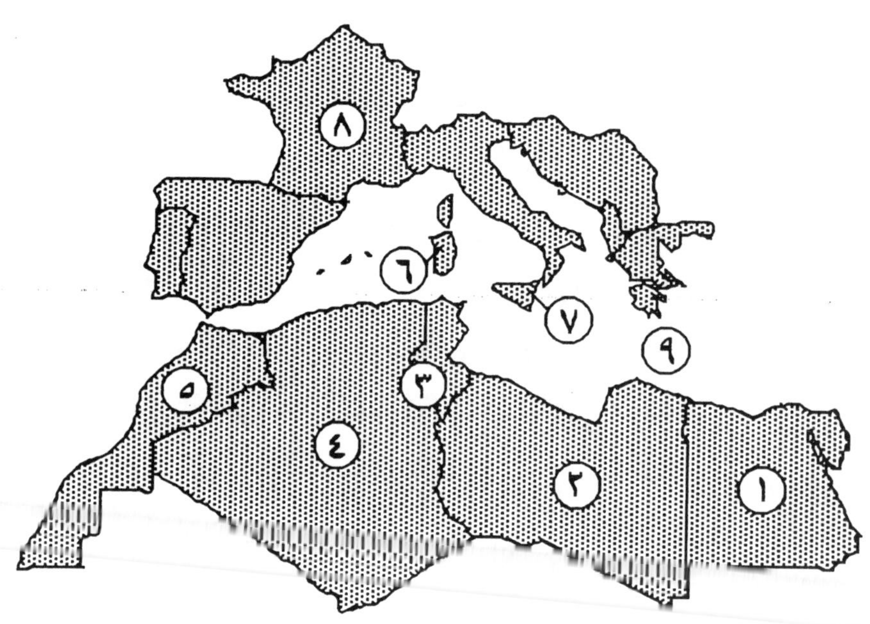

أين تونس في هذه الخريطة *map* ؟ ما هي أسماء البلاد والمناطق الاخرى؟

١-____________ ٤-____________ ٧-____________

٢-____________ ٥-____________ ٨-____________

٣-____________ ٦-____________ ٩-____________

اقرأوا المقالة واكتبوا:

١- ما معنى كلمة «مَوقِع» في «الموقع الجغرافي»؟ ________________

خمّنوا معنى: القارة الأفريقية = ________________

٢- كان عدد السكان في تونس حوالي ________________ مليون في سنة ١٩٨٨.

٣- اللغات التي تذكرها المقالة هي ________________________ .

خمّنوا معنى : اللغة الرسمية = ________________

٤- الدين في تونس هو ____________ ومعظم السكان في تونس مسلمون، ولكن

هناك قليل من ______________ و______________ .

الكلمة العربية التي تعني minorities هي ________________ .

٥- الطقس في تونس ____________ في الصيف و____________ في الشتاء .

٦- ما معنى كلمة «توقيت»؟ ______________ (الجذر = ___ ___ ___)

٧- أيام العمل في المكاتب هي من يوم ____________ الى يوم ____________ .

٨- هل مواعيد العمل في الصيف هي نفس مواعيد العمل في الشتاء؟ لماذا؟

تــــونــس بيـــــن يديــــك

اعداد : الدكتور مصطفى علي

الموقع الجغرافي: تقع تونس في شمال القارة الافريقية .

المساحة: تبلغ مساحة الاراضي التونسية ١٦٣,٦١٠ الف كيلومتر مربع (٦٣,١٧٠ الف ميل مربع).

السكان: يبلغ عدد سكان تونس ٧,٨٠٩,٠٠٠ مليون نسمة حسب تقديرات الامم المتحدة لعام ١٩٨٨ .

العاصمة التونسية: العاصمة التونسية هي مدينة «تونس» ويبلغ عدد سكانها ٥٩٦,٦٥٤ الف نسمة حسب احصائيات عام ١٩٨٤.

الموقع الجغرافي: تقع الجمهورية التونسية على السواحل الافريقية للبحر الابيض المتوسط، وتقع على بعد ١٣٠ كيلومتراً (٨٠ ميل) جنوب غرب جزيرة صقلية، وتبعد ١٦٠ كيلومتراً (١٠٠ ميل) عن جنوب جزيرة ساردينيا .

اللغة المستعملة: اللغة العربية هي اللغة الرسمية والمستعملة في تونس. وتدرس اللغة الفرنسية في المدارس التونسية كلغة ثانية، اما اللغة الانكليزية فهناك من يحسن تكلمها في المدن التونسية الكبرى.

الديانة: الدين الاسلامي هو دين الدولة التونسية، حيث غالبية التونسيين يدينون بالدين الاسلامي وهناك بعض الاقليات من الكاثوليك والبروتستانت.

ساعات العمل في المكاتب: في فصل الشتاء: من الساعة ٨ صباحاً حتى ١٢,٣٠ ظهراً ومن الساعة ٢,٣٠ ظهراً وحتى الساعة ٦ مساءً. طيلة ايام العمل الاسبوعية (من يوم الاثنين حتى يوم الجمعة) . اما يوم السبت فيكون الدوام من الساعة ٨ صباحاً حتى الساعة ١٢ ظهراً.

التوقيت : ان التوقيت في تونس هو (+ ساعة عن توقيت غرينتش) في الشتاء (+ ساعتين عن توقيت غرينتش) [للفترة من ١ مايو وحتى ٢٩ سبتمبر].

اما في فصل الصيف نفس الساعة ٧ صباحاً حتى ١ ظهراً من يوم الاثنين حتى يوم السبت من كل اسبوع. وللحصول على معلومات تجارية يمكن الاتصال بمكتب غرفة التجارة التونسية في مدينة تونس العاصمة.

المناخ في تونس : تتصف تونس بمناخ دافئ طيلة ايام السنة. واكثر فصول السنة اعتدالاً هو فصل الربيع والخريف. في فصل الصيف ترتفع درجات الحرارة عالياً وخاصة في المناطق الداخلية من الاراضي التونسية. اما في فصل الشتاء فالمناخ معتدل وتسقط فيه الامطار بكثرة.

بطاقات الاعتماد : تقبل بصورة واسعة بطاقات الاعتماد التالية بطاقة الاكسس - الماستر كارد - الاميركان اكسبرس - داينرزكلوب - والفيزا كارد.

من مجلة الحياة السياحية - عدد يناير ١٩٩٢

الاستماع DVD

تمرين ١٦ **مع العائلة والأصدقاء**

تعلموا هذه الكلمات::

كنيسة ج. كنائِس	church
الرَّبّ (ربّنا)	God, Lord

شاهدوا واكتبوا:

١ـ ماذا قال حنا عن العلاقة بينه وبين خالد؟

أ ـ كيف بدأت ؟

ب ـ كيف هي الآن ؟

جـ ـ في اي أشياء كان حنا وخالد يشتركان؟ وفي أي أشياء لا يشتركان؟

٢ـ ماذا ينوي حنا ان يفعل في المستقبل؟

٣ـ هل تظن/ين ان حنا يشعر بالسَعادة في حياته؟ لماذا/لماذا لا؟

٤ـ اذكروا شيئين آخرين عرفناهما عن حنا:

أ ـ

ب ـ

تمارين المراجعة

تمرين ١٧ | الجملة الاسمية والجملة الفعلية

غيّروا الجمل الاسمية إلى جمل فعلية والجمل الفعلية الى جمل اسمية كما في المثال:

THIS EXERCISE REVIEWS الجملة الاسمية والجملة الفعلية , BUT ALSO ASKS YOU TO THINK ABOUT THE DIFFERENT GRAMMATICAL CONTEXTS IN WHICH WE USE EACH ONE. FOR EACH SENTENCE BELOW, CHANGE THE WORD ORDER FROM الجملة الفعلية TO الجملة الاسمية OR VICE-VERSA, AND PUT EACH NEW SENTENCE INTO A GRAMMATICAL CONTEXT YOU CREATE IN ORDER TO GIVE A GRAMMATICAL "REASON" FOR REVERSING THE ORDER. IN OTHER WORDS, YOU WILL NEED TO ADD SOMETHING TO THE SENTENCE THAT REQUIRES THE WORD ORDER THAT YOU WILL USE, SUCH AS أنْ , WHICH REQUIRES A FOLLOWING VERB, OR أنّ , WHICH NEEDS A NOUN. THE TWO EXAMPLES DEMONSTRATE:

مثال: محمد وملك ومها سيسافرون معاً إلى القاهرة.

<- قبل أنْ يسافر محمد وملك ومها معاً الى القاهرة، سيكونون مشغولين جدا.

مثال: سيسافر محمد وملك ومها معاً إلى القاهرة.

<- نعرف أنّ محمد وملك ومها سيسافرون معاً الى القاهرة.

١- إخوتي يتأخرون في الرجوع إلى البيت .

٢- يسكن معظم الموظفين الذين يعملون في الجريدة في هذه المنطقة .

٣- تغيّبت زميلتي عن العمل بسبب وفاة جدّها .

٤- زميلاتي قرّروا ان يسافروا إلى فلوريدا في العطله .

٥- انتهوا من امتحاناتهم ويرغبون في أخذ اجازة طويلة للراحة.

٦- (هل) أنتم ستقيمون في فندق «حياة» عندما تسافرون الى المغرب؟

٧- حدّدت المدرسة يوم ٧ سبتمبر كآخر موعد لقبول الطلاب الجُدُد.

تمرين ١٨ كانت سنة !!

WRITE ABOUT YOUR (REAL OR FICTIONAL) TERRIBLE FIRST YEAR, USING مضارع مجزوم ENDINGS:

أول سنة قضيتها في هذه الجامعة كانت سنة صعبة بالنسبة لي لأنني

لم ____ ،

ولم ____ ،

ولأن اساتذتي لم ____ ،

وأصدقائي لم ____ ،

وزميلي/زميلتي في الغرفة لم ____________________________ ،

ولكن، الحمد لله ، كل شيء أصبح أحسن الآن !

تمرين ١٩ استمعوا إلى مها واكتبوا ما تقول: DVD

______ ليلى هي ______ ______ ______ الذي ______ ______ ______ عن ______

______ ، وهي التي ______ ما ______ به . ______ أني ______ ______ مصرية

و ______ ______ ______ . والدتي ______ ______ ب ______ ______ ______ ما

______ كأية ______ ______ ، ولكنها لا ______ ______ ______ بِ ______

إلا لـ ______ ليلى أو مع ______ ______ ______ الزملاء ، و ______ لي ______

______ إلى البيت و ______ ______ ______ ______ . ______ ______

______ مثل ______ أو ______ ليلى . ______ ______ ______ ______

ووالدتها ______ ، وهما ______ ______ ______ يعملان بها . هما

______ ______ ______ ، لكنها ______ ______ ______ . ليلى تدرس في

______ ______ ______ ، ولكننا ______ في ______ ______ ______

______ . وهي ______ ______ ______ اللغة ______ ______ ______ ______ في

______ ، لكنها ______ ______ ______ تدرس العربية ______ في الجامعة .

العامية

- القصة: انا مش مصرية ومش أمريكية"

شاهدوا مها تتكلم بالعامية.

كيف تقول مها بالعامية:

«الذي»؟

«تغضب إذا تأخرت»؟

«ليس لي صاحب»؟

- "كنتي فين؟!"

شاهدوا مها تعود الى البيت.

ماذا تقول لها أمها؟ وماذا تقول مها؟

تذكروا هذه الكلمات

جزيرة ج. جُزُر	غَرب	جَنوب	شَمال
بَحر ج. بِحار	أيّ / أيّة	الربّ / ربّنا	كَنيسة ج. كَنائس
بَدلة ج. بِدَل	جاكيت ج. ـات	بلوزة ج، ـات	قَميص ج. قُمصان
كرافات ج. ـات	بَنطَلون ج. ـات	بيجاما ج. ـات	بلوفر ج. ـات
تي شيرت ج. ـات	بُرنيطة ج. بَرانيط	شورت ج. ـات	ملابِس داخلية
فُستان ج. فَساتين	تَنّورة ج. تنانير/ جيب ج. ـات		جَلاّبيّة ج. جَلاليب
عَباءة ج. ـات	كوفيّة ج. ـات	حِذاء ج. أحذية	نَظّارات

١٦. رسالة من عمي

في هذا الدرس:

القصة
- الاستعداد لزيارة مها وأسرتها

الثقافة
- شهور السنة
- «رسالة من تحت الماء» عبد الحليم حافظ، نزار قباني»
- الأسواق

القواعد
- أفعل التفضيل *The Comparative*
- من الـ ... أنْ
- مقدمة الى معاني أوزان الفعل: فَعَّلَ وأَفْعَلَ
- مقدمة الى إعراب الاسم المرفوع والمنصوب والمجرور

القراءة
- من الكتاب المقدس
- رسالة من محمد

الاستماع
- كوليت خوري

العامية
- القصة: «رسالة من عمّي»
- «عايزة حاجة تاني؟»

المفردات DVD

أَيْ	i.e.
يا تُرى ... ؟! + سؤال (هل/أين/من ...)	I wonder (fixed expression)
رَتَّبَ ، يُرَتِّب ، التَّرتيب	to arrange
أرسَل ، يُرسِل ، الإرسال	to send
رَسَمَ ، يَرسُم ، الرَّسْم	to draw
اِشْتَرى ، يَشْتَري ، الشِراء	to buy, purchase
شَهْر ج. أشهُر ، شُهور	month
أَصْلَحَ ، يُصْلِح ، الإصلاح	to repair, repairing
اِسْتَعَدَّ لِـ ، يَستَعِدّ لِـ ، الاِستِعداد لِـ	to prepare for
غَيَّرَ ، يُغَيِّر ، التَّغيير	to change (something) (+ DIRECT OBJECT)
فوطة ج. فُوَط	towel
أقَلّ مِن	less than
مِن اللازِم أنْ	it is necessary to (impersonal)
مِلاية ج. ـات	(bed)sheet
مُنْتَصَف	middle
يَجِب أن / المصدر = من اللازم أن	(impersonal verb, does not conjugate)
وَصَلَ الى ، يَصِل الى ، الوُصول الى	to arrive

تمرين ١ **أوزان الأفعال الجديدة (في البيت)**

FOR EACH NEW VERB, IDENTIFY الوزن والجذر.

تعلموا هذين الفعلين: DVD

الماضي

وَصَلتُ	وَصَلنا
وَصَلتَ وَصَلتِ	وَصَلتُم
وَصَلَ وَصَلَتْ	وَصَلوا

المضارع

أَصِل	نَصِل
تَصِل تَصِلينَ	تَصِلونَ
يَصِل تَصِل	يَصِلونَ

اِشْتَرَيْتُ	اِشْتَرَيْنا
اِشْتَرَيْتَ اِشْتَرَيْتِ	اِشْتَرَيْتُم
اِشْتَرى اِشْتَرَتْ	اِشْتَرَوا

أَشْتَري	نَشْتَري
تَشْتَري تَشْتَرينَ	تَشْتَرونَ
يَشْتَري تَشْتَري	يَشْتَرونَ

تمرين ٢ اسألوا زملاءكم :

1. How much time do they spend (in) *preparing fo*r class?
2. Who is *less than* 21 years old [remember to use عمر]?
3. What needs *fixing* in their apartment/room?
   How often do they *straighten up* their room/apartment?
   How often do they *change* their *sheets*?
   Do they think *it is necessary to change* them every week?
4. Do they know someone who knows how to *draw* well?
5. *Did they get* the message (=letter) the teacher sent last night?
   [Hint: you must rephrase to "Did the message..."]
6. Where do they usually *buy* their clothes?
   Do they *buy* anything from Target, K-Mart, or Walmart? Why or why not?
7. What are they usually doing at *midnight*?
8. Do they usually *get to* class on time (= في وقته)?
9. To whom do *they have to send* an email message (=electronic letter) today?

الثقافة

شهور السنة DVD

I. الشهور الميلاديّة

لكل شهر ميلادي اسمان باللغة العربية: اسم يُستَعمَل *is used* في المَشرِق العربي (سوريا ولبنان والأردن والعراق وفلسطين) واسم يُستعمل في مصر والمغرب العربي (شمال أفريقيا) كما في الجدول. ويستعمل الاسمان في منطقة الخليج العربي، بالإضافة الى الشهور الهِجرية أو الإسلامية.

II. الشهور الهجريّة :

التاريخ الهَجري يبدأ من هِجرة *migration* النبي محمد من مكّة إلى المدينة في سنة ٦٢٢ ميلادية . والسنة الهجرية قَمَرية تتكوّن من ٣٥٤ أو ٣٥٥ يومًا و كل شهر فيها يتكوّن من ٢٩ أو ٣٠ يومًا .

في مصر والمغرب العربي		في المشرق العربي
يناير	=	كانون الثاني
فِبراير	=	شُباط
مارِس	=	آذار
أبريل	=	نيسان
مايو	=	أيّار
يونيو	=	حَزيران
يوليو	=	تَمّوز
أغُسطُس	=	آب
سبتَمبر	=	أيلول
أكتوبَر	=	تِشرين الأوّل
نوفَمبر	=	تِشرين الثاني
ديسَمبر	=	كانون الأوّل

شهور السنة الهجرية
١- مُحَرَّم
٢- صَفَر
٣- رَبيع الأوّل
٤- رَبيع الثاني/الآخِر
٥- جُمادى الأولى
٦- جُمادى الآخِرة
٧- رَجَب
٨- شَعبان
٩- رَمَضان
١٠- شَوّال
١١- ذو القَعْدة
١٢- ذو الحِجّة

These different calendars are often used side by side, especially in newspapers and magazines, as you can see in the example:.

السبت ٥ حزيران (يونيو) ٢٠٠٤ الموافق ١٧ ربيع الآخر ١٤٢٥ هـ

تمرين ٣ نشاط محادثة أو كتابة: حدث/يحدث في مثل هذا الشهر

For each month, describe either an important historical event or an annual event, such as:

الشهر الذي نتذكر فيه الأمّهات - حصول البلد على الحرية - بدء وانتهاء السنة - الشهور الهجرية التي تحدث فيها أشياء خاصة - عيد الشكر - بدء فصول السنة

عيد ج. أعياد — holiday, day of celebration

تمرين ٤ اكتبوا كلمة مناسبة من الكلمات الجديدة: (في البيت)

١- الجو في نيويورك بارد في فصل الشتاء وخاصةً في ———— ديسمبر .

٢- يجب أن نترك البيت الآن إذا أردنا أن نصل الى المطار لأن عندنا ———— من ساعة فقط قبل موعد طائرتك.

٣- هذه صورة جميلة ————ها «بيكاسو» وهي في رأيي من أجمل صوره.

٤- ستبدأ الامتحانات بعد اسبوع، لذلك يجب أن ———— لها جيداً .

٥- بنطلوناتي وبلوفراتي أصبحت قديمة ولذلك أريد أن ———— ملابس جديدة للشتاء.

٦- يجب أن أساعد زميلي في ———— الشقة قبل أن يصل والده ووالدته الليلة.

٧- التكنولوجيا الجديدة ———— حياتنا كثيراً .

٨- في بعض المناطق في أمريكا، تبدأ الدراسة في المدارس الابتدائية والإعدادية والثانوية في ———— شهر أغسطس.

٩- ———— الرسالة إلى مكتب القبول بـ«فيديرال إكسبريس».

١٠- المطبخ في البيت الذي نريد أن نستأجره قديم جدا وأظن أنه يحتاج إلى ———— قبل أن نسكن هناك.

١١- غيّرت لك الملايات وتركت لك ———— في الحمّام الصغير .

١٢- نزلنا من البيت في الساعة الواحدة و———— إلى الكنيسة في الواحدة والنصف.

١٣- ———— ماذا حدث لأصدقائي من أيام الطفولة وأين أصبحوا الآن؟

القصة DVD

تمرين ٥

قبل المشاهدة: من محمد بالنسبة لخالد؟ ماذا نعرف عن سفر محمد وأسرته؟

شاهدوا واكتبوا:

٢- عمّ يتكلم خالد هنا؟ أ -

ب -

جـ -

شاهدوا مرة ثانية:

٣- متى سيصل محمد واسرته إلى القاهرة؟ أين سيقيمون؟

٤- ماذا يجب على خالد وعائلته أنْ يعملوا لترتيب الشقة؟

أ-

ب -

٥- متى رَأى *saw* خالد مها آخر مرة؟

٦- ماذا نعرف عن العلاقة بينهما؟

٧- ماذا يسأل خالد عن مها؟

استمعوا وتعلّموا:

٨- ترجموا: «كانت ما تزال صغيرة» = ______________________

9. Notice how خالد lists the things his family must do. Write what he says. What grammatical structure is repeated that helps you identify the list?

«يجب أن نبدأ من الآن في ______________ و ______________.»

«يجب ______________ و______________.»

تمرين ٦ **عن القصة (في الصف)**

Role play: خالد وجدته meet to plan and delegate the work of الاستعداد لزيارة مها. Give assignments to محمود وعادل ووليد وعبد المنعم. (The grandmother might also bring up the topic of Maha to Khalid.)

القواعد

❁ «أفعل» التفضيل *The Comparative*

You have seen comparative and superlative constructions in Arabic using the « أفعل » pattern, called أفعل التفضيل , such as:

أحسن فصل بالنسبة لي　　　أنا أكبرهم　　　سيأخذ عمي غرفتي لأنها أكبر

The وزن أفعَل can give either a superlative or a comparative meaning depending on how it is used grammatically. We are concerned here with contrasting the form and meaning of the two most common grammatical constructions in which أفعَل occurs:

أ - (الخريف هو) **أحسن فصل**　　　ب - (غرفتي) **أكبر من** (غرفة أخي)

In Chapter 12, you learned how to form superlative phrases like the one in (أ) above. It is important to remember that the superlative meaning here comes from the use of أفعَل as a noun that acts as the first word in an **indefinite** إضافة (even though English expresses this concept with a definite phrase, it remains indefinite in Arabic). In other words, it **precedes** the noun it modifies.

The comparative meaning, on the other hand, is indicated through the use of أفعَل as an adjective in an اسم + صفة construction. In other words, it **follows** the noun it modifies. However, it differs from other adjectives in that it **does not agree in gender** with its noun, but rather remains fixed in form.

more freedom	ليلى عندها حرية **أكثر** من مها .
a smaller city	أريد أن أسكن في مدينة **أصغر**.
a better university	أريد أنْ أترك جامعتي وألتحق **بجامعة أحسن** .

Remember this difference in form and meaning by memorizing one phrase for each meaning to serve as a model, something like the following:

a bigger room　**غرفة أكبر**　　　*the best season*　**أحسن فصل**

When أفعل is used to compare two entities, it is usually followed by مِن :

bigger than	مدينة نيويورك **أكبَر مِن** مدينة شيكاغو.
better than	جامعتي **أحسَن مِن** جامعتك .
taller than	أنا **أطوَل مِن** اختي .

However, the comparison can be implied (as in English):

«أستمتع **أكثر** بالجلسة مع أصدقائي.»

تعلموا هذه الصفات:

FORM أفعَل ADJECTIVES FROM THESE ADJECTIVES AND LEARN BOTH FORMS:

غالي (غالٍ) *expensive* --> ____________

رَخيص *cheap, inexpensive* --> ____________

مَشهور ج. -ون/ين *famous* --> ____________

تمرين ٧ نشاط كتابة

COMPARE THE FOLLOWING, USING AS MANY DIFFERENT ADJECTIVES AS YOU CAN IN أفعل التفضيل.
CHOOSE TWO TO EXPAND INTO A PARAGRAPH. USE CONNECTORS فـ , وكذلك , بالإضافة الى ذلك.

١- أنا — أخي/اختي

٢- السكن في شقة — السكن في بيت أو في بيت الطلاب

٣- الحياة في الشرق الاوسط — الحياة في أمريكا

٤- الجو في الخريف — الجو في الصيف

٥- عطلة الربيع — اجازة الصيف

٦- التاريخ العربي — التاريخ الامريكي

تمرين ٨ اسألوا زملاءكم :

1. What would they do if they had more time? Is more time better than more money?
2. What would they buy if they had a bigger room?
3. What is the most expensive thing they own?
4. What is the place in which they feel more comfortable?
5. Do they live in a better room or apartment this year than the one they lived in last year?
6. Who is the most famous person they know personally (شخصياً)?
7. Do they think Middle Eastern food is more tasty than American food?
8. Who are the nicest people they know?

❁ من الـ ... أنْ

Statements that are meant to be accepted without argument are often phrased in an impersonal way to make the content more authoritative. The impersonal construction *It is ... to,* as in the phrases *it is necessary to, it is difficult to,* and *it is important to* and is expressed in Arabic by using the construction من الـ ... أنْ with an adjective following الـ :

من اللازم أنْ نستعدّ للسفر.　　　　من الـمُمكِن أنْ نبقى هنا ساعتين .

To shift the tense to past or future, use كـان and سـيكون respectively. To negate these expressions, use لم يَكُنْ (=ما كان) , ليس and لن يَكون . Read the following examples:

كان من الصعب أنْ أنام بسبب الامتحان.　　　　سيكون من اللازم أنْ أرتّب كل شيء.

ما كان من الممكن أنْ أجيء أمس.　　　　ليس من المناسب أن تقول لهم ذلك .

تعلموا هاتين الصفتين:

مُمِلّ	boring
مُمتِع	enjoyable, fun

تمرين ٩　**من الـ ... أنْ (في البيت)**

أكملوا *complete* **الجمل بالفعل الذي بين () كما في المثال:**

مثال: ليس من السهل أنْ أغيّر موعدي مع الدكتور الآن. (غيّر)

١- من الـ ______ أنْ ______ محمد ______________ . (ترك)

٢- من الـ ______ أنْ ______ مها ______________ . (لبس)

٣- من الـ ______ أنْ ______ خالد ______________ . (انتهى من)

٤- هل من الـ ______ أنْ ______________ شقة هنا؟ (استأجر)

٥- لم يكُن من الـ ______ أنْ ______________ . (اشترى)

٦- كان من الـ ______ أنْ ______________ . (استعدّ لـ)

٧- من الـ ______ أنْ ______________ . (أصلح)

٨- ليس من الـ ______ أنْ ______________ . (غضب)

٩- سيكون من الـ ______ أنْ ______________ . (رتّب)

١٠- من الـ ______ أنْ ______________ . (حدّد)

❁ أوزان الفعل

As you work towards gaining full control of أوزان الفعل and learning to recognize and produce each wazn in any of its ماضي , مضارع , or مصدر forms, we will be introducing some of the meanings of the derived أوزان (II-X) one at a time. In this system, the meaning of a given wazn depends on the meaning of the base form, الوزن الأوّل (I). That base meaning then takes on a new aspect in the derived awzaan. Keep in mind that the meaning of أوزان الفعل is not an exact science, and that it is more useful to think of relationships between two أوزان than it is to think of any particular wazn on its own or in the abstract.

In order to understand how the meanings of the various أوزان relate to each other, you need to understand and recognize three basic grammatical concepts that we use in talking about verbs in any language: transitivity, intransitivity, and reflexivity. A verb is *transitive* if it takes a direct object, like *to read* and *to write*. One *reads* ***a book*** and *writes* ***a paper***. A verb is *intransitive* if it cannot take a direct object, like *to sleep*. One does not *sleep* ***something***. A verb is *reflexive* if it refers back to the subject's *self*, such as *to wake oneself up*, or *to prepare oneself (for something)*.

The distinction between transitive and intransitive is central to understanding how the meanings of أوزان الفعل function. English makes this distinction too, but in English we often use the same verb for both transitive and intransitive meanings and simply add a direct object to make an intransitive verb transitive. For example, in the two sentences *She walks every day* and *I walk the dog*, the verb in the first is intransitive, since the complete action is expressed in the subject and the verb, while the verb in the second is transitive, because the action is not complete without the object, *the dog*. In Arabic, these two meanings are expressed by different أوزان of the same جذر . Similarly, the verb *to change* can be either transitive or intransitive in English; in Arabic, you have learned the transitive form, غيَّر *to change (something)*, but if you want to say *to change* (in and of itself, e.g. *the weather changed*, or *my life has changed*) you need a different وزن , in this case, تغيَّر . In general, the shorter أوزان that number from II-IV tend to be transitive, while the longer أوزان that number V-X tend to be intransitive and often reflexive. We will gradually introduce you to these pairs and the meanings of الأوزان as you acquire more verbs.

فَعَّلَ وأفْعَلَ

These two forms are transitive ones that take the meaning of the basic وزن فَعَلَ and add transitivity and a direct object to it. Recent new vocabulary includes several verbs of the فَعَّلَ and أفعَلَ forms. Note that all of them take a direct object:

فَعَّلَ		أفعَلَ	
غَيَّرَ	to change (something)	أرسَلَ	to send (something)
رَتَّبَ	to arrange (something)	أصلَحَ	to repair (something)
شَجَّعَ	to encourage (someone)	أعَدَّ	to prepare (something)

There is no way to predict whether a given جـذر or وزن فـعَّل will have an actively used transitive verb in one or the other, or both, of these وزنين. (You will find many forms listed in dictionaries that are not commonly used, even though they exist in theory as part of the Arabic verb system.) Rather, understanding the general transitive meaning of these two forms helps you to predict the meaning of new verbs you come across, especially if you know their جذر.

Some جذور have verbs in فـعَّلَ, some in أفعَلَ, and some in both. There can be some overlap between the two forms, but usually each one takes a slightly different meaning or is used in a different register. In general, وزن أفـعَلَ tends to be more prevalent in الفصحى while وزن فـعَّلَ tends to be used more in العامية. Thus the verb أصلَحَ is used in formal Arabic, but in colloquial you are more likely to hear صلَّحَ with the same meaning. The verb وَصَلَ is another good example:

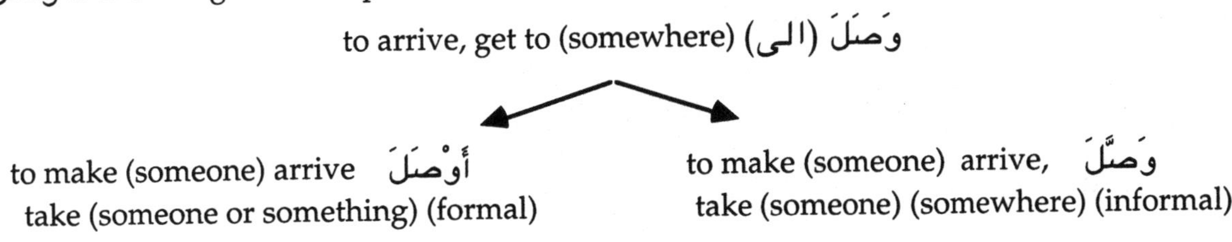

In other cases, each of these two forms takes a slightly distinct extension of the basic meaning of الجذر. The following sets of verbs will demonstrate:

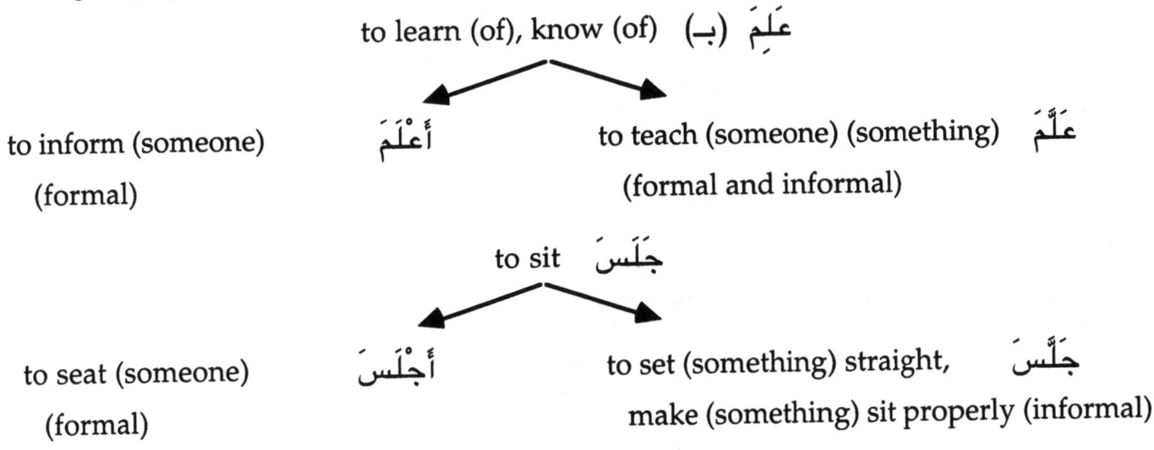

It is possible to derive وزن أفعَلَ verbs from وزن فَعَلَ (though in practice they may not be in active usage). Consider the following examples:

to make (someone) angry	أَغْضَبَ	to be/become angry	غَضِبَ
to make (someone) happy	أَسْعَدَ	to be happy	سَعيد: سَعُدَ
to dress (someone)	أَلْبس	to wear, put on	لَبِسَ

However, while the system allows you to derive verbs in this fashion, and Arabic speakers themselves do this occasionally, keep in mind that some verbs may not be idiomatic in usage. If you would like to try your hand at deriving new verbs as you practice the أوزان system by all means do so, just check with your teacher, or a good dictionary, or an educated speaker of Arabic to make sure you are saying what you intended.

تمرين ١٠ فَعَّلَ وأفعَلَ

PRACTICE USING SOME OF THE VERBS YOU SAW OF وزن فَعَّلَ AND وزن أفعَلَ IN CONTEXT. CHOOSE THE MOST APPROPRIATE وزن FOR EACH جذر IN EACH SENTENCE.

١- اليوم أستاذ التاريخ ________ نا أشياء جديدة عن تاريخ آسيا الوسطى القديم. (ع-ل-م)

٢- يجب أن ________ الولد في الكرسي الخاص به في السيارة. (ج-ل-س)

٣- ________ ني أن أساعدكم في كل ما تريدونه! (س-ع-د)

٤- المدير ________ الموظفين أنه من اللازم أن يعملوا ساعات أطول في الأسبوع القادم. (ع-ل-م)

٥- الكلام الذي تقولينه ________ ني أحياناً!! (غ-ض-ب)

٦- يا صديقي، سيارتي لا تعمل وأخذتها عند الميكانيكي. وهو قال لي إنه سـ ________ ها (ص-ل-ح) في اليومين القادمين. فهل من الممكن أن ________ ني الى الجامعة غداً وبعد غد؟ (و-ص-ل)

٧- الأم ما زالت ________ ابنها كل يوم وعمره ٧ سنوات!! (ل-ب-س)

❁ إعراب الاسم: المرفوع والمنصوب والمجرور

case marking الإعراب

Now that you know the main sentence structures of Arabic, it is time to learn about the case-marking system. When you learned the alphabet, you saw these endings:

ـُ	ـٌ	ـَ	ـًا	ـِ	ـٍ

and you learned that they indicate the sentence roles that nouns and adjectives play in formal Arabic. You have already learned one of these endings, ـًا , and you know that one of its functions is to mark adverbs. Although these case endings do not play an important role in native speakers' comprehension of most prose writing, they are essential to reading poetry and Classical literature, and they are an integral part of the language of religious texts. They also lie at the core of what Arabs consider to be one of the most important parts of their cultural heritage: العربية الفصحى . The Arabic name for the case-marking system is الإعراب : literally, *making it proper Arabic.*

The concept of case marking on nouns and adjectives is parallel to that of the endings that المضارع verbs take: المرفوع والمنصوب والمجزوم . Remember that المضارع takes different endings depending on how it is used. Similarly, nouns take different endings depending on their roles in a particular sentence.

Case marking on nouns is similar to the system of endings on المضارع in two ways. First, notice that nouns take three types of case endings: المرفوع , المنصوب , and المجرور , parallel to the three endings that المضارع takes. Second, notice that two of the three noun endings share the same name as two المضارع endings: المرفوع and المنصوب . This is because they share the same vowel; in the case of المرفوع , that vowel is ضمّة , and in the case of المنصوب , it is فتحة .

In this chapter, we will present an overview of the case system and the writing of the endings. You will learn more about how each case functions in Chapter 17. Before we turn to the endings themselves, you should be aware of three general features of the case system:

1. In general, case marking differs depending on whether a noun is definite or indefinite. Remember that a noun is definite when it has الـ or a possessive pronoun, or when it is the first or any non-final word in an إضافة .
2. Both nouns and adjectives take these endings. In noun-adjective phrases, the adjective always agrees with its noun in case, just as it agrees in gender and number.

3. Some types of nouns, which we will call "special cases," take slightly different endings, and have only two instead of three, one for المرفوع and one that functions as both المنصوب and المجرور . When we introduced these kinds of nouns and adjectives, we noted that the difference between the endings ون and ين for plurals and ان and يْنِ for duals is grammatical. Now you will see how, and begin to learn when to use each ending.

1. Definite Endings

المَرفوع : ـُ	المَنصوب : ـَ	المَجرور: ـِ

A definite noun or adjective in a formal context will have one of the above endings. For example, the words الطالب , الطالبة , and الطلاب may appear with any of the following endings, depending on their role in the sentence:

المرفوع	المنصوب	المجرور
الطالبُ	الطالبَ	الطالبِ
الطالبةُ	الطالبةَ	الطالبةِ
الطلابُ	الطلابَ	الطلابِ

The next chart shows these endings on nouns with the possessive pronoun ـهُ . In this situation, the case marking comes **between** the noun and the pronoun. Note that the kasra vowel of المجرور affects the vowel of the pronoun ـهُ, shifting it to ـهِ This shift is caused by the vowel كسرة (and parallels the vowel shift that occurs with prepositions بِـ and في).

المرفوع	المنصوب	المجرور
طالبُهُ	طالبَهُ	طالبِهِ
طالبتُهُ	طالبتَهُ	طالبتِهِ
طلابُهُ	طلابَهُ	طلابِهِ

The كسرة vowel has this effect on pronouns that begin with ـهُ: ـهُ, ـهُما and ـهُم:

المجرور:	طلابِهِ	طلابِهِما	طلابِهِم

Finally, note that the pronoun ـي *my* ... "swallows" the case endings so that no marking occurs. Thus words like والدي and غرفتي do not change.

2. Indefinite Endings:

المَرفوع : ـٌ	المَنصوب : ـً ، ـاً	المَجرور: ـٍ

Indefinite nouns and adjectives are marked with تنوين . Thus the words طالب , طالبة , and طلاب may appear in fully vocalized texts as:

المرفوع	المنصوب	المجرور
طالبٌ	طالباً	طالبٍ
طالبةٌ	طالبةً	طالبةٍ
طلابٌ	طلاباً	طلابٍ

3. Special Categories: المثنى and جمع المذكر والمؤنث

Several categories of nouns have a slightly different set of case endings: one ending for المرفوع and another that serves as both المنصوب and المجرور . The nouns and adjectives that fall in this category include dual endings ان/يَن and masculine and feminine plural endings ون/ين and ات .[1] The final chart shows the case designations of these endings. Note also that dual and masculine human plural nouns and adjectives take the same endings whether they are definite or indefinite, whereas feminine plurals take separate endings like the "regular" nouns and adjectives.

Remember also that the kasra and fatHa on the ن of dual and masculine plural endings respectively are not case endings but rather fixed vowels that do not change. They are only pronounced in formal contexts.

	المرفوع	المنصوب والمجرور
المثنّى	(الـ)طالبانِ	(الـ)طالبَيْنِ
جمع المذكر	(الـ)مصريّونَ	(الـ)مصريّينَ
جمع المؤنث	الطالباتُ	الطالباتِ
جمع المؤنث	طالباتٌ	طالباتٍ

[1]This category also has another subset that includes certain word patterns (أوزان) and proper nouns; you will learn about this group later.

تمرين ١١	نشاط قراءة

تعلموا هذه الكلمة:

sign (from God)	آية ج. ـات
sky, heaven	السَّماء

Read the following excerpt from the Bible الكتاب المُقَدَّس **as the questions direct you.**

1. The name of the book from which this passage is taken is التكوين . Which وزن and جذر does the name come from? Can you guess what it means? Which words do you recognize? Look for the plural of نور and a verb that comes from the same جذر . Can you identify الوزن and guess the meaning?
2. On your second read, identify the case endings of the words you know and see if you can identify the grammatical category of words you do not know. Practice naming the case markings as definite or indefinite, مرفوع , منصوب or مجرور . Which case ending is used after prepositions? See if you can pick out the case ending that indicates the subject of a sentence.
3. Look at the way the text is structured. What role does repetition play here? Where can you see parallel words and phrases joined by و ?

التكوين ١:١٤–١٩

١٤ وَقَالَ ٱللهُ : «لِتَكُنْ أَنْوَارٌ فِي جَلَدِ ٱلسَّمَاءِ لِتَفْصِلَ بَيْنَ ٱلنَّهَارِ وَٱللَّيْلِ،
وَتَكُونَ لِآيَاتٍ وَأَوْقَاتٍ وَأَيَّامٍ وَسِنِينٍ. ١٥ وَتَكُونَ أَنْوَارٌ فِي جَلَدِ ٱلسَّمَاءِ لِتُنِيرَ عَلَى
ٱلأَرْضِ». وَكَانَ كَذلِكَ. ١٦ فَعَمِلَ ٱللهُ ٱلنُّورَيْنِ ٱلْعَظِيمَيْنِ: ٱلنُّورَ ٱلأَكْبَرَ لِحُكْمِ
ٱلنَّهَارِ، وَٱلنُّورَ ٱلأَصْغَرَ لِحُكْمِ ٱللَّيلِ ، وَٱلنُّجُومَ. ١٧ وَجَعَلَهَا ٱللهُ فِي جَلَدِ ٱلسَّمَاءِ
لِتُنِيرَ عَلَى ٱلأَرْضِ، ١٨ وَلِتَحْكُمَ عَلَى ٱلنَّهَارِ وَٱللَّيْلِ، وَلِتَفْصِلَ بَيْنَ ٱلنُّورِ وَٱلظُّلْمَةِ.
وَرَأَى ٱللهُ ذلِكَ أَنَّهُ حَسَنٌ. ١٩ وَكَانَ مَسَاءٌ وَكَانَ صَبَاحٌ يَوْمًا رَابِعًا.

من الكتاب المقدس، سفر التكوين

تمرين ١٢ نشاط قراءة

The letter on the next page is handwritten in Egyptian style, which means that the final shapes of some letters vary slightly from the print you are accustomed to. In particular, the letters ن , ق , and ض , when written by hand, take a different "tail" shape here and do not take their normal dots, and remember that final ي is written without dots as well. Your teacher will help you identify these letters and get you started. Look for words you know and note how they are written. Reading might go slowly at first, but you will soon become accustomed to the differences and pick up speed.

تعلموا هذه الكلمات:

أرجو (المصدر: الرجاء) + أن / المصدر	I hope; please
أرجو أنْ تكون	I hope you are
تَتَّصِل بِـ	you contact, call, get in touch with (someone)

أسئلة:

١- مَن كتب الرسالة وإلى مَن كتبها؟

٢- اذكروا خمسة أشياء كتب عنها:

أ-

ب -

جـ -

د -

هـ -

تمرين ١٣ نشاط كتابة

Write a response from خالد to عمه محمد . Ask about مها and ملك , confirm arrival date and time, and tell him your (Khalid's) news and whether you would like anything from the U.S. Imitate رسالة محمد as much as you can and use the following letter formulae:

عمّي الحبيب ، (أو) عمّي العزيز ،

تَحِيّاتي وأشواقي	*greetings and longings (to see you)*
سَلامي لِـ / إلى	*my best to...*

بسم الله الرحمن الرحيم

أخي العزيز محمود :

تحياتي وأشواقي لكم جميعاً وسلامي الخاص وقبلاتي للوالدة الغالية. إزيّها وازيّ صحتها ؟ أرجو ان تكون بخير وكذلك أرجو ان تكون انت والأولاد جميعاً بأحسن صحة وحال.

نحن جميعاً بخير والحمد لله وملك ومها بصحة جيدة وهما ترسلان لكم اطيب السلام. نحن مشتاقون اليكم جميعاً والى الجلوس بينكم والحديث اليكم واتمنّى من الله تعالى ان يجمعنا كلنا في اقرب فرصة. والله " وحشتوني " يا محمود ووحشتني مصر واهلها. كم نحن سعداء بأننا سنراكم قريباً ونقضي اياماً من رمضان والعيد معكم. كل سنة وانتم طيّبين.

أخي محمود ،

أرجو منك إخبار كل أفراد العائلة اننا سنصل الى القاهرة إن شاء الله يوم الخميس ٨ مارس على طائرة شركة مصر للطيران. أرجو ان لا تتعبوا انفسكم بالذهاب الى المطار فنحن سنأخذ تاكسي من المطار الى البيت ونراكم هناك بإذن الله. وأرجو منك ان تتصل بصديقي مجدي وتخبره بموعد وصولنا.

سلامي لعادل واولاده وفاطمة وزوجها واولادها وسلامي لأحمد واسرته ومرة أخرى، قبلاتي للحاجة من نراكم جميعاً إن شاء الله بعد ٢ أسابيع.

أخوك

محمد

ملحوظة :

أرجو ان تتصل بي تليفونياً اذا كان هناك أي شئ تريدونه من هنا. سأحضر معي بعض الفيتامينات للوالدة. اذا كان خالد بحاجة الى أي كتب أو برامج للكومبيوتر من هنا فيمكنه ان يكتب لي كل طلباته ويرسلها لي بال e-mail ، وكذلك أرجو إخباري بطلباتك انت والأولاد.

الاستماع DVD

تمرين ١٤ **نشاط استماع: كوليت خوري**

الاستماع الأول

As you listen for general comprehension, focus on recognizing familiar words that have case endings, especially indefinite tanwiin endings.

استمعوا مرة اخرى واكتبوا:

١- كوليت خوري هي ________________________________

٢- ولدت في ________________________________

٣- والدها ________________________________

٤- جدها ________________________________

٥- أولادها ________________________________

٦- في أي جامعة درست؟ وفيمَ كانت متخصصة؟ ________________

استمعوا أكثر واكتبوا:

٧- لماذا تركت كوليت خوري الجامعة؟ ________________

٨- عندما عملت كوليت خوري أستاذة، درّست ________________

٩- من الكتب التي كتبتها كوليت خوري أ - ____________ ب - ____________

١٠- ماذا حدث في سنة ١٩٥٩؟ ________________________

Write the new verb you hear in this sentence, guess its meaning and identify its وزن وجذر, then look it up to check.

الثقافة

نزار قباني ، شاعِر الحبّ

ولد نزار قباني في مدينة دمشق في سَوريا سنة ١٩٢٣، وبعد إتمام دراسته الثانوية التحق بكلية الحقوق بجامعة دمشق وحصل منها على البكالوريوس، وبعد ذلك عمل ديبلوماسيًا في عدة عواصم أوروبية وآسيوية. بدأ نزار قباني يكتب الشِعر *poetry* عندما كان طالباً، وكتب أول كتاب له بعنوان «قالت لي السمراء» وهو في التاسعة عشرة من عمره. ومن أعماله «قصائد من نزار قباني» و«كتاب الحب» و«مئة رسالة حب». وبالإضافة إلى موضوع الحب ، يكتب نزار قباني عن مواضيع سياسية واجتماعية *social* وعن المرأة. ويقرأ شعره ملايين من العرب في كل البلاد العربية.

Nizar Qabbani is perhaps the most widely known and read poet throughout the Arab world. His popularity is due in part to his simple style, and in part to the topics he addresses. Known as شاعِر الحب *poet of love*, he writes mostly الشِعر الحُرّ *free verse*, which differs from Classical poetry in its lack of strict adherence to a single meter and rhyme. Some of his poems, including the following, were put to music and became popular songs. This poem was sung by عَبد الحَليم حافظ (الله يرحمه) , an Egyptian singer known as العَندَليب الأسمَر *the dark-complexioned nightingale*, himself immensely popular. While you are reading and listening, note the role the case endings play in form as well as content: they lend rhythm to the lines and are essential to the meter.

رسالة من تحتِ الماء

DVD

إنْ كنتَ حبيبي .. ساعِدْني
كي أرحلَ عنكْ
أو كنتَ طبيبي .. ساعِدْني
كي أشفى منكْ
لو أنّي أعرفُ أنّ الحبَّ خطيرٌ جدًا ..
ما أحبَبتْ
لو أني أعرفُ أنّ البحرَ عميقٌ جِدًا
ما أبحَرْتْ
لو أني أعرفُ خاتمتي
ما كنتُ بدأتْ

من ديوان «أحلى قصائدي»، نزار قباني، منشورات نزار قباني، بيروت د.ت.

مفردات تساعد على الفهم:

كَيْ	= لِـ =
أرحَل	= أسافر
أُشفى	be cured
خَطير	dangerous
عميق	deep

تمارين المراجعة

تمرين ١٥

COMPLETE THIS PASSAGE USING THESE WORDS, CHANGING THEIR GRAMMATICAL FORM AS NECESSARY TO FIT:

الماضي	يشعر	قسم	الحصول	وقت	يملك
فرص	شقة	أقارب	رفض	الخجل	أسهل
وُلدتْ	تعرّف	السياحة	ترك	قرّر	بدأ
حضر	تكلم	زار	رغب	وحيد	عاش

السلام عليكم !

اسمي بلهادي بكّوش وأنا والد ليلى . أنا تونسي من مدينة سوسة ولكنّي ______ هنا في الولايات المتحدة منذ ٢٦ سنة . أظنّ أنكم تعرفون أننا أنا وزوجتي ______ شركة صغيرة في منهاتن نعمل بها .

عندما ______ إلى أمريكا كنت ______ في ______ على البكالوريوس في الاقتصاد ولكنني ، بعد ______ قصير من الدراسة فقط ، قرّرت أنْ ______ الجامعة لأنني لم ______ بالراحة في دراستي ولأنني وجدت أنّ ______ العمل في التجارة هنا في نيويورك كثيرة .

تجربتي في التجارة ______ بالعمل في مكتب لِبيع البيوت و______ .

عملت في ذلك المكتب ٥ سنوات ، وفي ذلك الوقت ______ على «ليز» التي كانت تعمل في مكتب لِـ ______ والسفر في منهاتن. علاقتي بـ "ليز" كانت علاقة صداقة في البداية لأنني كنت ______ الزواج من أمريكية ، ولكن بعد أن تعرفت عليها أكثر أحببتها فَـ ______ أنْ نتزوج . وبعد ٤ سنوات من زواجنا ______ ابنتنا ______ ليلى.

ليلى الآن طالبة جامعية تدرس في ______ علم الإنسان في جامعة نيويورك. ______ معها بالعربية أحياناً ولكني أجد الكلام بالإنكليزية ______ .

عندما ______ عائلتي في تونس في السنة ______ شعرت بـ ______ لأنّ ليلى لم تستطع أن تتكلم مع ______ بالعربية. ولكن ماذا يمكنني أن أفعل؟! لا أعرف كيف أشجع ليلى على أن تتعرف أكثر على أصلها العربي؟

تمرين ١٦ | استمعوا إلى خالد واكتبوا ما يقول: DVD

MAKE SURE TO LISTEN FOR PRONOUNS AS OBJECTS ON SOME OF THE VERBS.

_______ أمس، _______ من عمي محمد _______ _______ _______ سـ _______ في

_______ _______ القادم، أي _______ _______ _______ ثلاثة _______ .

_______ أن _______ من الآن في _______ لزيارتهم و _______

_______ . يجب _______ _______ الملايات و _______ _______

، و _______ _______ الثاني . و _______ من _______ أن _______ إلى

_______ عادل لـ _______ عمي وزوجته _______ _______ _______ .

_______ مها فـ _______ مع جدتي في _______ . كانت _______ _______

صغيرة _______ _______ آخر مرة ... _______ _______ _______ في

الثالثة عشرة من _______ . هل ما _______ _______ ؟ كنت _______ لها بعض

_______ وكانت _______ _______ بعض _______ التي _______ ، يا ترى

_______ _______ _______ في أمريكا ؟

العامية DVD

- القصة: "رسالة من عمّي"

شاهدوا خالد يقول القصة بالعامية.

كيف يقول خالد:

«أمس»

«في منتصف الشهر القادم»

«من اللازم أنْ أنتقل»؟

«كانت في الثالثة عشرة من عمرها»

- **"عايزة حاجة تاني؟"**

شاهدوا خالد يتكلم مع جدته.

ماذا تريد الجدة أن يشتري خالد لها؟

ماذا قال خالد للرجل في المَحَلّ *store* ؟

الثقافة DVD

الأسواق

Watch the DVD for a short visual portrayal of a Cairo market .

تذكروا هذه الكلمات

مُمِلّ	مُمتِع	مَشهور ج. -ون	كَيْ (= لِـ)
آية ج. -ات	الإعراب	رخيص	أرجو أنْ (تكون)
سلامي لِـ	غالي (غالٍ)	عَلَّمَ ، يُعَلِّم ، التَّعليم	عيد ج. أعياد
السَّماء	اتَّصَلَ بـ ، يَتَّصِل بـ ، الاتِّصال بـ		

١٧. كلُّ عامٍ وأنتم بخير

في هذا الدرس:

القصة • برنامج خالد في رمضان

الثقافة • الصيام عند المسيحيين الأقباط

القواعد • أوزان الفعل: اِنفَعَلَ واِفتَعَلَ

• إعراب الاسم المرفوع والمنصوب والمجرور

القراءة • القرآن الكريم والحديث النبوي

• «تساؤلات»

الاستماع • التعليم في الإسلام

العامية • القصة: «كل سنة وانتو طيّبين!»

• أغنية «رمضان جانا»

المفردات DVD

يَبدو أنّ	it appears, seems that
بَقِيّة	(the) rest, remainder of (noun)
اِجْتَمَعَ ، يجْتَمِع ، الاِجْتِماع (بـ / مع)	to meet, gather (with)
حَتّى	until
اِختَلَفَ عن ، يَخْتَلِف عن ، الاِختِلاف عن	to differ from
بِخَير	well, fine (said of people only)
السُّحور	meal eaten before dawn during رمضان
مُسَلْسَل ج. -ات	series, serial (on television)
أشْرَفَ على ، يُشرِف على ، الإشراف على	to supervise
اِنْشَغَلَ بِـ ، يَنْشغِل بـ ، الانشِغال بـ	to be/become (pre)occupied with
صَحيفة ج. صُحُف	= جريدة
طَبَخَ ، يَطبُخ ، الطَبْخ	to cook
اِعْتادَ (على) + أنْ/المصدر ، يَعتاد (على)	to get used to, accustomed to
عام ج. أعوام	= سنة
كل عام وأنتم بخير	(greeting used on holidays, birthdays, etc.)
الإفطار	meal breaking fast in رمضان, breakfast
قَمَر الدّين	rolled dried apricots, or a sweet drink or pudding made from them
مَقهَى ج. مقاهٍ / المقاهي	cafe
قامَ ، يَقوم ، القِيام	to get up
الكُنافة	a kind of Middle Eastern pastry
تَولّى ، يَتَولّى ، التَّولّي	to undertake, assume (a task or position)

تعلموا هذا الفعل: DVD

المضارع		الماضي	
نَعتاد	أعتاد	اِعتَدْنا	اِعتَدْتُ
تَعتادونَ	تَعتاد تَعتادينَ	اِعتَدْتُم	اِعتَدْتَ اِعتَدْتِ
يَعتادونَ	يَعتاد تَعتاد	اِعتادوا	اِعتادَ اِعتادَت

تمرين ١ **أوزان الأفعال الجديدة وجذورها (في البيت)**

IDENTIFY الوزن OF ALL NEW VERBS. WHICH ONES COME FROM جذور YOU KNOW? LIST THE WORDS YOU KNOW FROM EACH FAMILIAR جذر. HERE IS SOME HELP WITH A جذر THAT IS NOT READILY TRANSPARENT:

قام يقوم القيام *to get up* I ← أقام ، يُقيم ، الإقامة *to set up (something)*, IV *to set up house, residence*

تمرين ٢ **المفردات الجديدة**

ONE OF THE BIGGEST CHALLENGES IN LEARNING ARABIC IS ACQUIRING ITS RICH VOCABULARY, WHICH INCLUDES A LARGE NUMBER OF SYNONYMS. TO PRACTICE ACTIVATING SOME NEW SYNONYMS, REWRITE THE FOLLOWING PARAGRAPH REPLACING THE UNDERLINED WORDS WITH NEW ONES AND MAKING ANY NECESSARY CHANGES:

طوال السنوات الماضية كنت أستيقظ من النوم كل يوم في حوالي الساعة السابعة صباحاً وكان أول شيء أفعله هو أن أشرب القهوة وأقرأ الجرائد. وبعد ذلك كنت ألبس وأخرج من البيت وأذهب الى الجامعة وأبقى خارج البيت الى الساعة الثامنة او التاسعة مساءً، ولذلك لم أكُن أعِدّ الغداء او العشاء في البيت. كنت مشغولاً بالتدريس والاجتماعات. ولكن أظنّ أنّ برنامجي في السنة القادمة لن يكون كما كان، لأني حصلت على منحة وسأبدأ بكتابة كتاب جديد، ولذلك سأستطيع أن أسافر الى المغرب لستة شهور إن شاء الله وبعد ذلك أنوي أن أعود الى بيتي وأقضي فيه الشهور الاخرى في السنة في الكتابة والقراءة.

تمرين ٣ **المفردات الجديدة (في البيت)**

اكتبوا الكلمة المناسبة في كل جملة:

١- من المقرّر أن ينتهي بناء المكتبة الجديدة في منتصف ______ ٢٠٠٩ .

٢- جدتي تحب مشاهدة ______ التليفزيونية المصرية والسورية في رمضان.

٣- سهرت كثيراً ليلة أمس ولذلك ______ من النوم في ساعة متأخرة هذا الصباح.

٤- ______ العربية الفصحى عن العامّية في بعض الكلمات والقواعد.

٥- والدتي مشغولة جداً في العمل هذه الأيام ولذلك قرّرت أنْ أساعدها في ______ وشغل البيت .

٦- بعد سنة من الدراسة، الطلاب ______ على الكلام والقراءة باللغة العربية.

٧- ______ أنهم سعداء وأنّ حياتهم بدأت تستقرّ أخيراً .

٨- في شهر رمضان أعود الى البيت في الساعة الثالثة بعد الظهر وأنام قليلاً قبل موعد ______ في حوالي الخامسة والنصف.

٩- كل يوم، ينزل جدي إلى ______ حيث يشرب قهوته ويقضي الصباح في قراءة ______ والمجلات .

١٠- طوال الاسبوع الماضي ______ بالاستعداد للانتقال إلى الشقة الجديدة.

١١- في كل سنة، ______ كل أفراد عائلتنا معاً في شهر أغسطس حيث نقضي أسبوعين على البحر في ولاية كارولاينا الشمالية.

١٢- اليوم سنسهر ______ الساعة الواحدة صباحاً لنشاهد المباراة النهائية لـ«كأس العالم» في كرة القدم في التليفزيون.

١٣- يوم الجمعة يصحو خالد في الساعة العاشرة صباحًا، أما في ______ الايام فهو يصحو في السادسة والنصف .

١٤- يجب أن أتكلم مع الاستاذة التي ______ على دراستي لأناقش معها برنامجي الأكاديمي للعام القادم.

١٥- سمعت أن والدتك كانت مريضة، أرجو أن تكون ______ الآن!

١٦- من اللازم أن نقرر من سـ ______ إعداد الأكل طوال هذا الأسبوع.

تمرين ٤ اسألوا زملاءكم :

1. When do they think a woman will *assume* the presidency (الرئاسة) of the U.S.?
2. Would they like to have a job in which they *supervise* other people? Have they ever had someone *supervising* them they didn't like? What did they do?
3. Does it *seem* to them that the *newspapers* they read *differ* from each other in anything? How do they *differ*?
4. Do they watch *cooking* shows on television? What *soap operas* do they watch? Which comedy (كوميدي)or drama (دراما) *series* do they watch?
5. Is it difficult [for them] to *get used to* a new place of residence or new roommates?
6. If they *get up* tired, do they stay tired for *the rest of* the day?
7. Who *meets* with their teachers/classmates outside of class? Where do they *meet*? Is there a *cafe* around here that study groups *meet* in?
8. Do they ever *get engrossed in* studying *until* late at night and don't remember to eat?
9. (Ask Muslim classmates who fast:) What do they eat to *break the fast*? For the *dawn meal*?
   Who *cooks* or prepares the meals?
   (Ask other students who fast:) When do they fast? (يَصوم، الصَّوم/الصِّيام)
   How do they *break the fast*?

الثقافة DVD

ماذا يعني الصيام عند المسيحيين الأقباط؟

Muslims are not the only Middle Easterners who fast, of course. Arab Christians (المَسيحيّون) follow a variety of fasting practices. Watch the interview on your DVD to learn more about Egyptian Coptic fasting.

القصة DVD

تمرين ٥ **شاهدوا وأجيبوا:**

١- لماذا يقول خالد «كل عام وانتم بخير»؟

٢- ماذا تفعل العائلة كل سنة في رمضان؟

شاهدوا مرة ثانية:

٣- مَن يذكُر خالد هنا؟ ماذا يفعلون؟

أ- ______________ ________________________

ب - ______________ ________________________

جـ - ______________ ________________________

٤- ما هو برنامج خالد في رمضان؟

أ - __________________ هـ - __________________

ب - __________________ و - __________________

جـ - __________________ ز - ينام__________________

د - __________________

٥- في رأيك، لماذا يقول خالد إنّه لن يستطيع أن يخرج مع أصدقائه في رمضان هذه السنة؟

استمعوا وتعلّموا:

6. Write the connectors that خالد uses in this sentence:

_____ زوجة عمي أحمد _____ وصل من أبو ظبي منذ ثلاثة أيام، _____ تولّت إعداد قمر الدين والكنافة.

Remember that the connector أمـا .. فـ signals a change of topic. What is the new topic here? You also heard the word قَد, which is a particle used in الفصحى to emphasize that an event has taken place. قد is followed by الماضي when it functions this way and may be preceded by فـ or لَـ (a formal emphatic particle). Other examples:

لقد تغيّرت حياتنا كثيراً في السنوات الأخيرة.

كانت الحفلة فعلاً جميلة! فقد رقصنا وأكلنا وسهرنا حتى الصباح.

القواعد

❁ أوزان الفعل: اِنْفَعَلَ وافْتَعَلَ

In Chapter 16, we worked with some of the transitive أوزان . Here we will take a brief look at two of the longer أوزان . One of them is highly predictable in meaning; the other is not. Our goal for now is for you to recognize them when you see them.

The form انفَعَلَ is one of the most predictable of all أوزان in meaning: it is almost always a simple passive of فَعَلَ . You have learned two verbs of this form. Compare these verbs with their corresponding فَعَلَ forms:

to be occupied, preoccupied with	اِنْشَغَلَ بـ	← *to occupy, preoccupy*	شَغَلَ
to be cut (off)	اِنقَطَعَ	← *to cut (something)*	قَطَعَ

The انفَعَلَ form is also one of the least common because of its very specialized meaning, since many verbs cannot be put into a passive voice.[1]

The form افتَعَلَ is less transparent. In the Arabic system, it is a reflexive form, having to do with oneself, but it is not the only form that has reflexive meaning and the exact kind of reflexive meaning it takes is difficult to predict. For now, focus on recognizing this وزن and identifying الجذر when you come across it. Following are examples from words you know that will help you see the relationship between the فَعَلَ and افتَعَلَ forms in context:

١- أ - عندما كنت صغيرة كانت هوايتي المفضلة جَمع الصور. *to collect, gather*

ب - أحب أن أجتَمِع مع أساتذتي خارج الصف. *to get oneself together with* → *to meet*

٢- أ - أقوم من النوم عادةً في الثامنة صباحاً. *usually* or *habitually*

ب - كل صيف نعود إلى نفس المنطقة لقضاء عطلتنا. *to go back to*

ج - متى ستعتاد على الكلام والقراءة بالعربية؟ *to take as a habit for oneself,*

to have oneself go back to over and over again → *to get used to*

٣- أ - هل من الممكن أن تساعدني في نَقل هذه الطاولات الى غرفة أخرى؟

to move (something)

ب - مها لا تريد أن تَنتَقِل الى بيت آخر. *to move (oneself)*

---

[1]You have also seen another way to express the passive voice in Arabic, one that involves a change of internal vowels, as in: وُلِدَت, خُطِبَت , and عُيِّنَت . The difference between these two passives is that the one that is formed through vowel shifts implies an agent that is not mentioned, while انفعل has no agent.

The root ش–غ–ل gives a good view of both of these forms:

أ - أنا مهندسة، وأحب شغلي كثيراً. *occupation, work*

ب - تغيبت لأني اِنشَغَلت بوالدتي، فهي مريضة. *to be occupied with*

جـ - أين تَشتَغِلين ؟ – أَشتَغِل في مكتب سياحة. *to (put oneself to) work, to take as an occupation (for oneself)*

تمرين ٦ مع أوزان الفعل (في الصف)

FORM انـفَـعَـلَ AND افـتَـعَـلَ VERBS AS INDICATED USING الجـذر OF THE UNDERLINED WORD IN THE FIRST SENTENCE. NOTE THAT IN 4 AND 5 THE DIFFERENCE IN MEANING BETWEEN THE TWO FORMS IS HIGHLY NUANCED.

١- فصلت الشركة ١٠٠ موظف وموظفة. *to dismiss or separate (someone or something)*

_______ الزوجان بعد سنة واحدة فقط من الزواج.

(اِنفَعَلَ) *to be separated*

٢- قضينا وقتاً جميلاً على البحر أمس.

_______ الوقت بسرعة !!

(اِنفَعَلَ) *to be spent (of time), to pass by*

٣- محمد ما زال يشعر بالغربة في أمريكا.

محمد سافر الى أمريكا و_______ .

(اِفتَعَلَ) *to make oneself a stranger take oneself to a foreign country*

٤- مها لا تشعر أنها تملك حريتها.

عائلة ليلى _______ شركة تجارية صغيرة.

(اِفتَعَلَ) *to possess (for oneself), have ownership of (material possession)*

٥- يبدو أن الصيف بدأ ، فالرطوبة أصبحت عالية جداً.

_______ حَرَكَة *movement* الحقوق المَدنيّة مع مارتن لوثر كينغ الابن وآخرون.

(اِفتَعَلَ) *to begin, get (oneself/itself) started, commence*

❁ الإعراب

In this section, we will examine the functions of the cases المرفـوع , المجـرور , and المنصـوب and practice identifying nouns that are marked with them in written texts. You are not expected to digest all of this information at once, but you will learn best by practicing, so we will lay out here all of the rules you need to know to begin and then start you practicing the endings in contexts of sentences. For the present, we will ignore all proper nouns and avoid marking plurals of certain أوزان because the rules for marking them differ slightly. We will also ignore nouns that end in long vowels ا or ى , since they do not take these endings. Like final ي in the possessive pronoun ـي *my...*, these vowels swallow up the case endings.

We will begin with الاسم المجـرور because it has the highest frequency among the three cases, and also because its rules take precedence over the rules of the other two cases in any situation where a conflict might arise (this will be explained further in the following sections). Before reading further, make sure you know the basic grammatical terms and concepts that the case-markings indicate:

preposition	حرف جَر
subject of a جملة اسمية	مبتدأ
predicate of a جملة اسمية	خبر
subject of a جملة فعلية	الفاعل
object of a جملة فعلية	المفعول بِهِ

Pronouns, including هذا – هذه – ذلك – تلك , do not take إعراب endings

❁ الاسم المجرور

تذكروا: الطالبِ طالبِهِ طالبٍ الطالباتِ (الـ)طالبَيْنِ (الـ)مصريّينَ

The first grammatical case that we will examine is called الجَرّ , and a noun that is so marked is called الاسم المجـرور.[1] A noun that is مـجـرور takes one of the endings listed above depending on whether it is definite, indefinite, جمع مذكر , or مثنى . Review these مجرور endings, and remember the effect of ـِ on pronoun suffixes containing ـهُ . This case ending marks two functions:

[1] جر/مجرور is referred to as *the genitive* in English treatments of Arabic grammar.

(1) the object of a preposition, and

(2) the possessive relationship of one noun to another, on all nouns in an إضافة **except** the first.

Thus, all nouns and adjectives in prepositional phrases, and all nouns **except the first** in an إضافة take this ending. (The first noun in an إضافة takes its case according to what precedes it or what role it plays in the sentence; thus it **can** be مجرور if preceded by a preposition.) Study the following examples of nouns and adjectives marked as مجرور and see if you can give the reason for each ending:

١- سأجتمعُ مع بقيةِ الطلابِ في صفِ تاريخِ الشرقِ الأوسطِ في الساعةِ التاسعةِ.

٢- ستجد مقهى صغيراً في الطابقِ الأولِ من هذه البنايةِ .

٣- أمس تعرّفتُ على شخصٍ لطيفٍ في مطعمِ الجامعةِ .

٤- خالد يستمتعُ بوقتِهِ مع أصدقائِهِ .

٥- أنا وزملائي نجتمعُ عادةً في المكتبةِ .

تمرين ٧ **الاسم المجرور (في البيت)**

IDENTIFY WHICH WORDS ARE مجرور AND MARK THE CORRECT ENDING WHERE APPROPRIATE:

١- سينتقل خالد إلى غرفة عادل .

٢- هل تعرفت على الطلاب القطريين الذين يسكنون هنا؟

٣- زوجة عمّي تولّت إعداد قمر الدين والكنافة .

٤- لا تسمح لِبنتها بالذهاب إلى بيت زميلها .

٥- برنامجي في الصيف يختلف عن برنامجي في الشتاء .

٦- انتقلوا إلى منطقة سكَنيّة جميلة في مدينة تونس .

٧- بعد الانتهاء من عمله ذهب إلى النادي مع اثنين من أصدقائه .

٨- يشعرون بالغربة في هذا المكان .

٩- في الساعة الرابعة سأكون أمامَ حمّام السباحة .

❁ الاسم المرفوع

تذكروا : الطالبُ   طالبٌ   (الـ)طالبانِ   (الـ)مصريونَ

٨ .[1] This case is called الرَّفع , and a noun that is so marked is called مرفوع . A noun that is مرفوع takes one of the endings listed above depending on whether it is definite, indefinite, مثنى or جمع مذكر . This case is used to mark:

(1) الفاعِل in الجملة الفعلية , and

(2) Both المبتدأ والخبر in الجملة الاسمية
except when الخبر consists of a prepositional phrase, such as في الجامعة , because, as you saw above, prepositional phrases are marked مجرور .

Study the following examples of الاسم المرفوع and figure out the reason for each ending:

١ـ زوجتُهُ لبنانيةٌ.   ٢ـ والدُها مديرٌ كبيرٌ في تلك الشركة.

٣ـ تسمح لنا والدتُنا بالخروج.   ٤ـ تكلم الاستاذُ أمس عن تجربته في التدريس.

Identifying nouns in المجرور case is relatively easy, because all you need to look for is prepositions and إضافات . In order to identify المرفوع , however, you must pay attention to the **structure of the entire sentence** in order to find الفاعل or المبتدأ and الخبر .

تمرين ٨ الجملة الاسمية (في البيت)

REVIEW THE STRUCTURE OF الجملة الاسمية BY IDENTIFYING المبتدأ AND الخبر IN EACH SENTENCE. WRITE ALL مرفوع ENDINGS:

١ـ معظم الصور التي رسمتها جيدة.

٢ـ كرة القدم واحدة من هواياتي المفضّلة.

٣ـ البيت الذي كنت أسكن فيه عندما كنت صغيرة واسع.

٤ـ في الطابق الثاني من هذه البناية شركات تجارية.

٥ـ في هذه الصحيفة مقالة جيدة عن اجتماع الرئيسين.

٦ـ كثير من العرب الذين يقيمون في ولاية ميشيغان يمنيّون.

---

[1]In English treatments of Arabic, this case is called *the nominative.*

تمرين ٩ الاسم المرفوع والمجرور (في الصف)

IDENTIFY THE STRUCTURES OF THESE SENTENCES, THEN MARK ALL OF THE APPROPRIATE مرفوع AND مجرور ENDINGS IN THESE SENTENCES:

١- يجيء أقاربنا لزيارتنا كل عام في رأس السنة (يوم ١/١).

٢- أمامك فرص كثيرة !

٣- تبدأ الأجازة الصيفية بعد أسبوع .

٤- هل يمكنني أن أجتمع معك بعد المحاضرة؟

٥- حديقة بيتهم كبيرة وواسعة وأحب أن أجلس فيها وأستمتع بمشاهدتها.

٦- انشغل أخي وزوجته بإعداد شقتهما الجديدة التي سينتقلان إليها بعد شهر.

٧- العربية الفصحى هي لغة القرآن واللغة التي يدرسها الطلاب العرب في المدارس، وهي أيضاً لغة الأدب والجرائد والمجلات.

٨- انقطعَت العلاقة بينهم بعد وقت قصير بسبب علاقاته مع صديقته القديمة.

٩- من الأشياء التي سأنشغل بها في بداية العام القادم اجتماعات في النادي الذي أشترك فيه.

١٠- انتهيْنا من ترتيب الكتب والاوراق والآن يجب ترتيب بقية الشقة.

١١- لا يختلف هذا المسلسل عن بقية المسلسلات التليفزيونية التي نشاهدها في تلفزيونات بلاد الخليج .

١٢- لها ابن عم يسكن في الكويت وبنت عم تعمل في إيطاليا وأولاد خال في أوستراليا.

١٣- تتكوّن مدينة فاس في الحقيقة من مدينتين، المدينة القديمة وهي عربية والمدينة الجديدة التي بَناها الفرنسيون.

❁ الاسم المنصوب

تذكروا: الطالبَ طالباً طالبةً (الـ)طالبَين (الـ)مصريين

The third and final case is called النَّصب , and a noun or adjective in this case is called منصوب .[1] You know that this case marks adverbs such as عادةً and أحياناً . A noun or adjective that is منصوب takes one of the endings listed above, depending on whether it is definite, indefinite, مثنى , or جمع مذكر . This case marks:

(1) the direct object of a verb المفعول به , and

(2) adverbs.[2]

It may be useful to think of المنصوب as signalling the answer to the questions ماذا؟ كيف؟ and متى؟: In the following sentences, the words طالباً , السمكَ , طالباً , and يومَ are all منصوب because their function in the sentences is to answer one of these three questions:

ماذا كنتَ ؟	<---	كنتُ طالباً .
ماذا أكلتِ ؟	<---	أكلتُ السمكَ .
كيف جاء محمد الى أمريكا؟	<---	جاء الى أمريكا طالباً .
متى يشاهد المباريات؟	<---	يشاهد المباريات يومَ الجمعةِ .

But within this framework, remember that الإضافة and prepositional phrases **override** the case المنصوب . For example, in the last sentence above, the logical answer to متى is actually the إضافة phrase يوم الجمعة , but only يوم takes المنصوب , because الجمعة is the second word in الإضافة and therefore is مجرور . In the following sentences, the words لعب , طائرة , كلية , and المساء answer the questions ماذا , متى or كيف , but they all take المجرور endings because they are the objects of prepositions, and the مجرور case of prepositions takes precedence over المنصوب .

أستمتع بلعبِ الشطرنج . سافرت على طائرةٍ كبيرةٍ .

التحق خالد بكليةِ الآداب . أدرس في المساءِ .

---

[1]This case is called *the accusative* in English.

[2]Arabic treats adverbs as belonging to several different grammatical categories, each of which has its own name, although they all share the منصوب case. You will learn the names and types of adverbs later.

تمرين ١٠ الإعراب (في البيت)

A. Circle each إعراب ending, name the case, and give the reason for each marking using Arabic terminology as much as possible:

١- عملَت استاذةً السنةَ الماضيةَ .

٢- تخرّجَ كلُ طلابِ القسمِ وأصبحوا مهندسين .

٣- اجتمع كلُ طلابِ الصفِ ليلةَ أمسِ .

٤- خالد كان طالباً في المدرسةِ الابتدائيةِ ومها كانت زميلتَهُ .

٥- شاهدنا فيلمَيْنِ جديديْن الأسبوعَ الماضي.

٦- بيتُنا ليس كبيراً ولكنّي أحبُه لأنّه قريبٌ من البحرِ.

B. Mark إعراب endings on all nouns and adjectives:

١- ليلة الخميس يمكننا أن نشاهد المسلسل العربي .

٢- بيتنا أصبح بيت العائلة .

٣- خالد يحبّ عائلته كثيرا .

٤- تصحو متأخرة وتنزل من البيت في الساعة الواحدة بعد الظهر.

٥- أدرس ساعتين في المكتبة .

٦- في الصباح نشرب القهوة ونقرأ الصحف .

٧- حفظت كل الكلمات الجديدة .

٨- رفضوا مساعدته في ترتيب المكتب.

٩- تريد أنْ تشتري سيارة جديدة .

١٠- ما استطعتُ أن أنتهي من قراءة القصّة .

تمرين ١١ **الإعراب (في الصف)**

اكتبوا الإعراب على كل الأسماء والصفات:

١ـ محمد آخِرِ الأنبياء في الإسلام .

٢ـ مها زميلة ليلى .

٣ـ جون كان طالبا في جامعة أخرى قبلَ أنْ يلتحق بهذه الجامعة .

٤ـ لا أعرف هذا الاستاذ – هل هو جديد هنا ؟

٥ـ أعرف موظفين يعملان بالجريدة .

٦ـ سميرة وأيمن طالبان جديدان في قسمنا .

٧ـ ليس في هذا الصف طلاب كثيرون .

٨ـ تبدأ صلاة الجمعة في الساعة الواحدة بعد الظهرِ ، لذلك يجب انْ ننزل من البيت قبل ذلك بحوالي نصف ساعة .

٩ـ هذه مقالة ممتازة تدرس موضوع العلاقة بين الدين والسياسة في الشرق الأوسط.

١٠ـ قرّرت الشركة فصله من العمل لأنّه رفض الانتقال الى مكان عمله الجديد.

١١ـ خُطبت ابنة عمي «لينا» لضابط كبير بالجيش يملك شقّة بمنطقة «المعادي» في القاهرة.

١٢ـ غضبت زوجته منه لأنّه عاد الى البيت متأخّرا ليلة أمسِ وعندما وصل الى البيت، لم تقلْ له شيئا ولكن دخلت الى غرفتها ونامت .

الثقافة

القرآن الكريم *The Holy Quran*

تعلموا هذه الكلمات:

سورة ج. سُوَر	chapter (of the Quran)
آية ج. آيات	verse

القرآن هو كتاب الله ، أنْزَلَه إلى النبي محمد والمسلمين . وللقرآن أسماء أخرى أيضًا منها: «الكتاب» و«التَنزيل»، و«المُصحَف». والقرآن يتكوّن من ١١٤ سورة وكل سورة تتكون من آيات. وترتيب القرآن هو: السور الطويلة أولاً، وبعدها السور القصيرة. ومعظم السور الطويلة نزلت متأخرةً، بعد هِجرة محمد والمسلمين إلى المدينة وتُسمّى هذه السور «السُوَر المدنية». ومعظم السور القصيرة نزلت عندما كان محمد والمسلمون لا يزالون في مكّة، وهذه السور تُسمّى «السور المكّية».

القرآن is considered to be the highest stylistic model for العربية الفصحى, as well as a model for the codification for its grammar. Read the following verses with your teacher:

كلمات تساعد على فهم الآيات:

يا أيّها	= يا
أعبُد	I worship

آيات من القرآن:

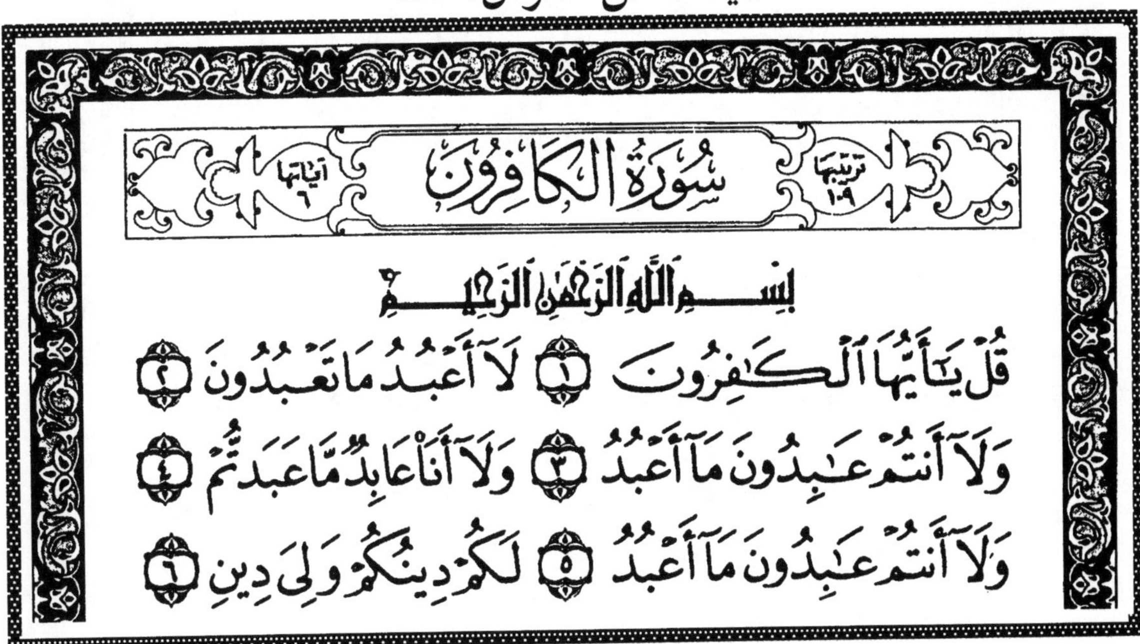
سُورَةُ الكَافِرُونَ
ترتيبها ١٠٩ آياتها ٦
بِسْمِ اللَّهِ الرَّحْمَٰنِ الرَّحِيمِ
قُلْ يَا أَيُّهَا الْكَافِرُونَ (١) لَا أَعْبُدُ مَا تَعْبُدُونَ (٢)
وَلَا أَنتُمْ عَابِدُونَ مَا أَعْبُدُ (٣) وَلَا أَنَا عَابِدٌ مَّا عَبَدتُّمْ (٤)
وَلَا أَنتُمْ عَابِدُونَ مَا أَعْبُدُ (٥) لَكُمْ دِينُكُمْ وَلِيَ دِينِ (٦)

كلمات تساعد على فهم الآيات:

آمَن ، يُؤمِن ، الإيمان	to believe
كُتِبَ	it was written (as law)
الصِّيام (صامَ ، يصوم)	fasting, to fast
اليُسر	= السهل
العُسر	= الصعب

من سورة البقرة

﴿١٨٢﴾ يَـٰٓأَيُّهَا ٱلَّذِينَ ءَامَنُوا۟ كُتِبَ
عَلَيْكُمُ ٱلصِّيَامُ كَمَا كُتِبَ عَلَى ٱلَّذِينَ مِن قَبْلِكُمْ
لَعَلَّكُمْ تَتَّقُونَ ﴿١٨٣﴾ أَيَّامًا مَّعْدُودَٰتٍ ۚ فَمَن كَانَ مِنكُم
مَّرِيضًا أَوْ عَلَىٰ سَفَرٍ فَعِدَّةٌ مِّنْ أَيَّامٍ أُخَرَ ۚ وَعَلَى ٱلَّذِينَ
يُطِيقُونَهُۥ فِدْيَةٌ طَعَامُ مِسْكِينٍ ۖ فَمَن تَطَوَّعَ خَيْرًا فَهُوَ خَيْرٌ
لَّهُۥ ۚ وَأَن تَصُومُوا۟ خَيْرٌ لَّكُمْ ۖ إِن كُنتُمْ تَعْلَمُونَ ﴿١٨٤﴾ شَهْرُ
رَمَضَانَ ٱلَّذِىٓ أُنزِلَ فِيهِ ٱلْقُرْءَانُ هُدًى لِّلنَّاسِ
وَبَيِّنَـٰتٍ مِّنَ ٱلْهُدَىٰ وَٱلْفُرْقَانِ ۚ فَمَن شَهِدَ مِنكُمُ ٱلشَّهْرَ
فَلْيَصُمْهُ ۖ وَمَن كَانَ مَرِيضًا أَوْ عَلَىٰ سَفَرٍ فَعِدَّةٌ مِّنْ
أَيَّامٍ أُخَرَ ۗ يُرِيدُ ٱللَّهُ بِكُمُ ٱلْيُسْرَ وَلَا يُرِيدُ بِكُمُ
ٱلْعُسْرَ وَلِتُكْمِلُوا۟ ٱلْعِدَّةَ وَلِتُكَبِّرُوا۟ ٱللَّهَ عَلَىٰ مَا
هَدَىٰكُمْ وَلَعَلَّكُمْ تَشْكُرُونَ ﴿١٨٥﴾

تمرين ١٢ **نشاط قراءة**

كلمات تساعد على الفهم:

حَديث (نَبَويّ) ج. أحاديث — Hadith (sayings and deeds of the Prophet)

صَلّى الله عليه وسَلَّم — God bless him and grant him salvation (of the Prophet)

رَضِيَ الله عنه — May God be pleased with him (said of the Companions of the Prophet, الصَّحابة)

الحديث النبوي

كما تعلمون، الحديث النبوي بالنسبة لكثير من المسلمين ليس مصدراً †*source*من مصادر الشريعة الإسلامية فقط ولكنه أيضاً مصدر من المصادر التي يرجع اليها المسلم ليجد الإرشاد †*guidance*الذي يحتاج اليه في حياته. والحديث يتكوّن من مجموعة كبيرة من الأقوال التي وصلتنا من النبي محمد صلّى الله عليه وسلّم ومن الصَّحابة عنه. وفي كتب الأحاديث، يبدأ كل حديث بكلمة «عن .... (+ اسم شخص)» ويذكر اسم الشخص أو الأشخاص الذين نَقَلوا الحديث عن النبي صلى الله عليه وسلم.

عن أَنَس رَضِيَ اللّه عنه عن النبيّ صلّى الله عليه وسلّم قال «لا يُؤْمِنُ أَحَدُكُم حَتَّى يُحِبَّ لأَخيهِ ما يُحِبُّ لِنَفْسه».

الاستماع DVD

تمرين ١٣ **نشاط استماع: استمعوا واكتبوا**

١- ما موضوع هذا البرنامج؟

٢- اكتبوا ما تسمعون:

.. فكانت أول ________ و ________ ________ ________ ________

________ «اقرأ» و ________ حتى ________ ________ ________

________ و ________ ________ ________ أُنزِلَ ________

________ .

.. فالأب ________ ________ و ________ ________ ________

و ________ ________ ________ ________ .

تمرين ١٤ نشاط قراءة

مواعيـــد الدراســـة بجامعة القاهرة في رمضان

قـررت جـامعة القـاهرة تأخير بـدء المحـاضرات لمدة ساعـة يومـيا طـوال شـهر رمضـان المبارك وتخفيض زمن كل محاضرة ، وتحديد السـاعة الثالثة بعـد الظهر كآخر مـوعد للمحـاضرات حـتى يتاح للطلاب والعاملين فسحة من الوقت قبل حلول موعد الافطار.

من جريدة الجمهورية ١٩٩٢/٣/٥

أسئلة:

١- ماذا قررت جامعة القاهرة ؟

٢- وما سبب هذا القرار ؟

٣- ماذا يقول الخبر عن آخر موعد للمحاضرات ؟

٤- خمنوا معنى: العاملين = ______________

5. Parallel structure is extremely important in formal Arabic. You know to look for parallel phrases and clauses joined by و . This text offers a good example of how exact parallel structure often is. Find the list of things that Cairo University decided to do. How do they match? Think about parts of speech and الوزن .

تمرين ١٥ نشاط محادثة

YOU AND YOUR زملاء ARE STUDYING ABROAD IN DAMASCUS. AT HOLIDAY TIME, YOU WANT TO CELEBRATE TOGETHER, SINCE YOU ARE FAR FROM YOUR FAMILIES. PLAN WHAT YOU WILL DO TO CELEBRATE TOGETHER.

كلمات جيدة:

يجتمع   يتولّى   يطبخ   يعدّ

يساعد   يشتري   يرتّب   يشرف على

تمرين ١٦ **نشاط قراءة**

كلمات تساعد على الفهم:

لا يتجاوز = لا يزيد عن = ليس أكثر من

أُغادِر = أترك

فَكَّر في ، يُفَكِّر في ، التَّفكير to think about

القراءة الاولى: الأفكار الرئيسية

١- عمَّن تتكلم هذه المقالة؟

2. In the paragraph that begins: .. استيقظ في الصباح , follow the husband's account of how they spend the day by finding and underlining the main verbs of the narration.

القراءة الثانية

٣- أين الزوج والزوجة؟ ماذا يفعلان ؟

٤- منذ كم سنة تزوّجا ؟

٥- لماذا يقول الزوج «قضينا ثلاث سنوات معًا» ؟

٦- خمّنوا معنى هذه الكلمات :

أستيقظ في الصباح = __________ (تذكروا : توقظ)

حياة بِلا عمل = __________

In the paragraph that begins لا أقول ذلك :

ما يتبقى من الوقت = __________

في الاقتراب من = __________

أَحِبّائنا وأقاربنا وأصدقائنا = __________

القراءة الثالثة: مع القاموس

7. Choose three important words to look up that will give you new pieces of information to answer: ماذا يريد الزوج أن يقول؟

تسـاؤلات ..؟

◆ على مائدة الافطار حيث يلتقي الزوجان يوميا.

الزوج ـ أتعرفين كم من الوقت الحقيقي قضينا معا؟

الزوجة ـ ما هذا السؤال ـ خمسة وعشرون عاما . عمر زواجنا .

ـ أبدا يا عزيزتي إنه لا يزيد كثيرا عن ثلاث سنوات .

ـ شكرا ، يبدو أنك لم تشعر بوقتك معي هذا رائع .

ـ (يضحك) لم أقصد ذلك ، ولكني حسبت الوقت الحقيقي .

ـ ماذا تقول ؟

ـ تعالي نحسبها .

استيقظ في الصباح وأستعد للعمل ، أقضي معك مدة لا تتجاوز عشر دقائق على مائدة الافطار أغادر الى العمل أعود في الثانية نلتقي الى الغداء ثم أنصرف لقراءة ما لم أقرأ من صحف الصباح ثم أنام قليلا . استيقظ ولا أكاد أراك لأنك إما مشغولة مع الأولاد أو لسبب آخر ، أغادر إلى العمل ، أعود مساء ، نشاهد التلفزيون لا نكاد نتحدث إلا قليلا .. وعليه لو حسبت كم من الوقت الحقيقي أقضي معك ستجدينه لا يتجاوز ساعة يوميا في أحسن الأحوال ، بمعنى (١٢) يوما في السنة .. أي ثلاث سنوات وتزيد قليلا في الخمسة والعشرين سنة الماضية .

ـ فإذا أسقطنا ساعات النكد يا عزيزي ، كم يتبقى من لحظات السعادة ؟

ـ لقد وصلت لما أردت أن أقول : نعم كم من الوقت في عمرنا كله نقضيه سعداء ، نقضيه كما نريد ، كما يجب ؟ كم من الوقت نقضيه بلا لهاث وإرهاق وعمل ؟ كم من الوقت نقضيه حقا لذواتنا ؟

ـ ولكن العمل مطلوب ، ولا أظنك تقصد حياة بلا عمل ؟

ـ لا أقول ذلك ، ولكن أقول ما يتبقى من الوقت كيف نقضيه ؟ كم من الوقت نقضيه في نزهة جميلة مع أبنائنا في الاقتراب من احبائنا وأقاربنا وأصدقائنا ؟ كم من الوقت نستغله لنعرف كيف نعيش السعادة ؟

غادر الزوج ،

وبقيت الزوجة تفكر ..

في كلام الزوج كثير من الحقيقة ..

فلماذا لا نفكر في نمط الحياة التي نعيش ؟

ألا يمكن أن يقود التفكير إلى التغيير ؟

د. كافية رمضان

من مجلة « أسرتي » ١٩٨٦/١١/١

تمارين المراجعة

تمرين ١٧

FILL IN THE BLANKS USING THE CORRECT PARTICLE FROM THE LIST:

أنّ إنّ الذي التي الذين أنْ

OR, IF YOU THINK NO PARTICLE SHOULD BE USED, WRITE Ø .

١- لن أستطيع ـــــــ أذهب معكم إذا لم يسمح لي والدي بذلك.

٢- ما زالت تحب نفس الأشياء ـــــــ كانت تحبها من قبل .

٣- تتكون ولاية «هاواي» من عدة جزر ـــــــ أكبرها جزيرة «أواهو».

٤- الشيء الوحيد ـــــــ أعرفه عنهم هو ـــــــ هم انتقلوا من بيتهم القديم.

٥- هل تحبون ـــــــ تذهبوا معنا إلى النادي؟

٦- هل تتذكرين الموضوع ـــــــ تكلمنا عنه في الاسبوع الماضي؟

٧- «سنترال بارك» حديقة كبيرة ـــــــ يذهب إليها كثير من الناس ـــــــ يزورون نيويورك.

٨- في جامعتنا طلاب أجانب كثيرون ـــــــ يدرسون الهندسة.

٩- ماذا تنوي ـــــــ تدرس في المستقبل؟

١٠- قرأت خبراً ـــــ يقول ـــــ الرئيس الامريكي سيزور الشرق الأوسط هذا الشهر.

١١- هذا أغلى مطعم ـــــــ أكلت فيه ، ولكن الطعام ـــــــ أكلته لم يكُن ممتازاً.

١٢- هل تظنّون ـــــــ هذا الفيلم مناسب للأولاد الصِغار ؟

١٣- أوّل مرّة ـــــــ زرت مصر فيها كانت منذ عشر سنوات.

١٤- من فضلك ، هل يمكن ـــــــ تشتري لي جريدة عندما تنزل؟

١٥- معظم الناس ـــــــ أعرفهم يقولون ـــــــ هم ليسوا سعداء في حياتهم.

تمرين ١٨

Part of the "glue" that holds these sentences together is missing. Complete:

١ـ هل يختلف الطقس في الأردن ــــ الطقس في لبنان؟

٢ـ أنا عادة آكل في المطاعم لأن وقتي لا يسمح لي ــــ الطبخ.

٣ـ أظن أنه أصبح ــــ اللازم أن تبدأوا بالاستعداد ــــ السفر.

٤ـ لا أفهم لماذا يرفضون الاشتراك ــــ نا ــــ إصلاح الشقة ؟! خاصة أنني تكلمت ــــ هم ــــ هذا الموضوع ــــ قبل!

٥ـ كان والدي دائما يشجعني ــــ أن أقول رأيي ــــ كل شيء ــــ حرية.

٦ـ من الاساتذة الذين يشرفون ــــ رسالتك ــــ الدكتوراه ؟

٧ـ يتكون المتحف المصري ــــ عدة أقسام ، أكبرها قسم التاريخ الفرعوني القديم.

٨ـ لم أعلم ــــ انتقاله ــــ وظيفة اخرى إلاّ قبل يومين فقط.

٩ـ لا يمكنني التغيب ــــ الصف هذه المرة لأن الاستاذ سيغضب ــــ ي !

تمرين ١٩ استمعوا إلى خالد واكتبوا ما يقول:

كل ــــ وأنتم بـ ــــ ! أمس كان ــــ ــــ ــــ ــــ رمضان

الذي ــــ ــــ له منذ ــــ ــــ أسبوع. ــــ كل العائلة على

ــــ كما ــــ ــــ ــــ ــــ كل سنة، ــــ جدتي على ــــ كل شيء.

ــــ عمتي فاطمة و ــــ عمي عادل منذ ــــ بـ ــــ ، أما ــــ

ــــ أحمد الذي ــــ ــــ ــــ أبو ظبي منذ ثلاثة ــــ ، فقد ــــ

ــــ قمر الدين والكنافة. ــــ في رمضان ــــ عن ــــ

ــــ السنة، إذ ــــ ــــ من النوم و ــــ ــــ بعد الظهر.

بعد ــــ نشاهد ــــ التليفزيوني، ثم ــــ لـ ــــ ــــ ــــ

ــــ في الحسين أو ــــ ــــ حتى ــــ . بعد ــــ أقرأ

ــــ و أنام، لكن ــــ لن استطيع هذا العام ــــ

و ــــ مع أصدقائي.

العامية DVD

- القصة بالعامية: "كل سنة وانتو طيبين"

شاهدوا خالد يتكلم بالعامية.

كيف يقول خالد بالعامية:

«بدأنا الاستعداد له منذ أكثر من أسبوع» ؟

«لن أستطيع الخروج والسهر مع أصدقائي» ؟

«زوجة عمّي» ؟

- أغنية "رمضان جانا"

استمعوا الى هذه الأُغنيّة *song* الرمضانية المشهورة.

ماذا تستطيعون أن تفهموا؟

تذكروا هذه الكلمات

صام ، يَصوم ، الصَّوم /الصِّيام	مَسيحيّ ج. -ون	فكَّر في
حديث ج. أحاديث	سورة ج. سُوَر	آية ج. آيات
حَرف جَرّ	الفاعِل	المَفعول به
أُغنِيّة ج. أغاني (أغانٍ)		

١٨. المهمّ هو رأي خالد ومها ...

في هذا الدرس:

القصة
- محمد يتكلم عن أصدقائه وشبابه وأحلامه

الثقافة
- جمال عبد الناصر وأم كلثوم وعبد الحليم حافظ
- عبارات فيها ألوان وأعضاء الجسم

القواعد
- المثنى
- الألوان
- وزنا فعَّلَ وتَفَعَّلَ
- الإعراب : إنّ / أنّ

القراءة
- الأخوان رايت
- النصف الآخر

الاستماع
- طه حسين

العامية
- القصة: «المهم رأي خالد ومها»
- «مالك؟»

المفردات DVD

بَريد	mail, post
بِطاقة ج. -ات	card
جُزء (مِن) ج. أجزاء	part (of)
حَقيقِيّ ج. -ون	real, actual, true
حُلم ج. أحلام	dream
مُختَلِف (عن) ج. -ون	different (from)
أخلاق (جمع)	morals
ذَكِيّ ج. أذكِياء	smart, intelligent
رُبَّما	perhaps, maybe
رَحَّبَ بِـ ، يُرَحِّب بِـ ، التَرحيب بِـ	to welcome
شابّ ج. شَباب / شُبّان	young man
الشَباب	youth (abstract or collective)
شَغَلَ ، يَشْغَل ، الشُّغل	to occupy, preoccupy
شَكْل ج. أشكال	form, shape
صَداقة ج. -ات	friendship
اِعتَبَرَ ، يَعْتَبِر ، الاعتِبار	to consider (someone/something to be ...)
مَعنى ج. المعاني / معانٍ	meaning
فِكْرة ج. أفكار	idea, thought
مُتَفَوِّق ج. -ون	superior, outstanding
لَمَّحَ (إلى) أنّ ، يُلَمِّح ، التَّلميح	to hint that
مُهِمّ ج، -ون	important
المُهِمّ هو	the important thing (is)

تعلموا هذه الكلمات: DVD

الجِسم

الرسم للدكتور مايكل كوبرسون

تمرين ١ **نشاط محادثة**

PLAY "SIMON SAYS" WITH زملائك TO PRACTICE THE NAMES OF THE BODY PARTS.

تمرين ٢ **اكتبوا كلمة مناسبة من المفردات الجديدة في كل جملة: (في البيت)**

١- حصلت على منحة لأنّها كانت ______ في الدراسة وتخرّجت بتقدير «ممتاز».

٢- هي جميلة ولطيفة و______ .

٣- بعد أنْ وصلت إلى الفندق جلست وكتبت بعض ______ البريدية لأصدقائي وأفراد عائلتي .

٤- قبل أنْ يبدأ دراسة العربية، ما كان عنده أيّ ______ عن العرب أو عن الشرق الأوسط .

٥- يا بنتي! ليس ______ في الشابّ فلوسه أو سيارته أو عائلته ولكن ______ هو أخلاقه ! (نفس الكلمة × ٢ use)

٦- نحن أصدقاء ، و______نا بدأت منذ أيام المدرسة الابتدائية .

٧- كلمة «ذَهَبَ» لها نفس شكل كلمة «ذَهَب» *gold* ولكن كل واحدة لها ______ مختلف.

٨- الإسلام كان وما زال ______ مهمًا من الثقافة العربية .

٩- هل تظنّون أنّ القصّة في هذا المسلسل التليفزيوني ______ ؟

١٠- ______ها أنْ تصبح كاتبة قصص مشهورة.

١١- سأتخرّج بعد شهرين إن شاء الله ولكن موضوع الحصول على وظيفة مناسبة ______ني كثيرًا الآن!

١٢- في رأيي، ليست الحياة هنا ______ عن الحياة في أي بلد آخر.

١٣- ______ رئيس الشركة في كلامه أنّ الشركة ربّما تفصل عددًا من الموظفين والعمّال في نهاية السنة.

١٤- من اللازم أنْ أذهب إلى مكتب ______ لإرسال كل هذه الرسائل والبطاقات.

١٥- جدّي الآن كبير ويقضي معظم وقته في البيت ، ولكنّه كان لاعِب كرة قدم ممتاز في أيام ______ .

١٦- كل الناس يحبّونه لأنّه لطيف و______ عالية .

١٧- قال أخي لي في رسالته إنّه تعرّف على ______ فلسطيني يدرس معه في الجامعة وإنّهما يدرسان ويقضيان معظم الوقت معًا.

١٨- عندما زرتهم، استقبلوني و______ بي .

١٩- أنا لا ______كَ صديقًا فقط ولكن ______كَ أخًا لي. (نفس الكلمة)

تمرين ٣ نشاط كتابة

Make five بطاقات **for people you know. Wish them happy birthday, holidays, have a nice day, and other good wishes using** الكلمات الجديدة **and these expressions:**

أتمنّى [illegible] (+ مصدر/أنْ)   أرجو أن تكون/تكوني ...   بخير   مبروك على ...

تمرين ٤ اسألوا زملاءكم (في الصف)

1. Are *looks* (=*the form*) *more important* than *morals* in a relationship? In politics?
   Do they think that *intelligent people* usually have high *morals* too?
   Are the same things *important* in relationships and *friendships*? Why or why not?
2. What are their *thoughts* on (في) the *meaning* of life?
3. Do they think *youth* today are different from *youth* in the past?
   If so, how?
4. If they could, would they change any *part* of their *body*? What part(s)?
5. What *preoccupies* them these days?
6. Which class do they *consider* the *most important* class they are taking now?
7. Do they buy birthday and holiday *cards*? Do they buy *postcards* when they travel?
   Why or why not?
8. What are their *dreams* for the future?
9. Do they usually like to read or watch *true* stories?

تمرين ٥ الوزن والجذر (في الصف)

These pairs of words share a جذر. **What can you extrapolate about the relationship of their** أوزان**?**

١ـ يختلف عن – مختلف عن	٤ـ فوق – متفوّق
٢ـ مرحباً – رحّب بـ	٥ـ يعني – معنى
٣ـ فكّر في – فكرة	٦ـ صديق – صداقة

القصة DVD

تمرين ٦ **شاهدوا محمد وأجيبوا:**

١- ماذا يقول محمد عن أصدقائه في أمريكا؟ وماذا يقول عن أصدقائه في مصر؟

٢- ما هو شكل الصداقة في أمريكا ، في رأي محمد؟

شاهدوا مرّة ثانية:

٣- ماذا يشغل محمد؟

٤- أ - إلى ماذا لمّح محمود في رسالته؟

ب - ما رأي ملك في هذا؟

جـ - ما رأي محمد في هذا؟

د - ما رأي خالد ومها في هذا؟

٦- ماذا يقول محمد عن خالد؟

شاهدوا وخمّنوا المعنى:

٧- المُكالمات التليفونية = ________________

٨- لمّح محمود في إحدى رسائله = ________________

(Hint: remember أحد . What do you think the relationship between the two words is?)

٩- قلت لها نَفس ما قلتهُ لمحمود = ________________

٩- المهمّ هو رأي خالد ومها اللذين ... ________________

١٠- كيف قال محمد « email » بالعربية؟ ________________

تمرين ٧ **للمناقشة في الصف:**

لماذا ، في رأيكم ، لمّح محمود أنه يريد أن يخطب مها لخالد؟

ما رأيكم في ما قاله محمد عن الصداقة في أمريكا؟

الثقافة

جَمال عبد الناصر وأم كُلثوم وعبد الحليم حافظ

While watching القصة on the DVD, you saw pictures of three Egyptian cultural and political icons who were widely popular throughout the Arab world from the late fifties to the mid seventies: the late president, جمال عبد الناصر , the famous singer أم كلثوم , and the heartthrob singer/actor عبد الحَليم حافظ (who sang رسالة من تحت الماء in Chapter 16). The first two in particular symbolized to millions of Arabs their hopes for unity and progress.

ولد جمال عبد الناصر في مصر عام ١٩١٨ وقضى طفولته في مدينة الاسكندرية حيث عمل أبوه في مكتب البريد، وعندما ماتت أمه، أرسله أبوه إلى القاهرة عند عمه. وبعد أن تخرج من المدرسة الثانوية التحق بالجيش المصري وأصبح ضابطًا فيه، وهو ومجموعة من الضبّاط الشبان اسمها «الضبّاط الأحرار» أخرجوا الملك فاروق من مصر في ٢٣ يوليو سنة ١٩٥٢ وأصبحت مصر بذلك جمهورية. وفي سنة ١٩٥٤ أصبح عبد الناصر أول رئيس لمصر، وبقي رئيسًا حتى وفاته عام ١٩٧٠، وبعده تولّى أنور السادات رئاسة مصر.

Nasser's most noted achievements include:

The nationalization of the Suez Canal — تَأميم قَناة السُوَيس (١٩٥٦)

The United Arab Republic — الجمهورية العربية المتحدة: الوِحدة مع سوريا (١٩٥٨–١٩٦١)

The High Dam in Aswan — السَّدّ العالي

أُم كُلثوم , also known as كوكب الشرق, *Star of the East* and سيّدة الغناء العربي *First Lady of Arabic Singing*, ranked as Egypt's premier singer for decades until her death in 1975. Named after one of the Prophet's daughters, she studied the Quran as a little girl and began singing at *mawlids* مَوالِد , or celebrations of the birth of the Prophet and other holy figures. She used to give monthly concerts that were broadcast on radio to millions of listeners, and she also made several movies. Even now, some thirty years after her death, her songs are heard daily on the radio from Morocco to the Gulf. Among the most famous are أنت عمري , الأطلال , ليلة الحب , and ألف ليلة وليلة .

القواعد

❁ الألـوان

color	لَـون ج. ألـوان

There are two kinds of adjectives for color in Arabic: ordinary adjectives, most of which are نسبة adjectives, and adjectives of the «أفْعَل» وزن.[1] Common نسبة colors include: DVD

grey	رَماديّ / ة	brown	بُنّيّ / ة
gold	ذَهَبيّ / ة	purple	بَنَفْسَجيّ / ة
silver	فِضّيّ / ة	pink	زَهريّ / ة

DVD

Basic colors have a special set of أوزان unique to them with a specific وزن for feminine and human plural. These colors and their أوزان are listed in the facing chart. Note that المؤنث has a different وزن than المذكر, as does الجمع, but remember that الجمع † is only used for **human** plurals.

المعنى	الجمع	المؤنث	المذكر
blue	زُرق	زَرقاء	أزرَق
red	حُمر	حَمراء	أحمَر
white	بيض	بَيضاء	أبيَض
black	سود	سَوداء	أسوَد
green	خُضر	خَضراء	أخضَر
yellow	صُفر	صَفراء	أصفَر

You have already begun to see that Arabic and English differ in the ways they use possession to describe people and things. In English, we tend to use possession in describing people physically, as in *They have green eyes*, *She has black hair*, and so forth. In Arabic, however, things that are part of you are not "possessed," so we use patterns like the following:

عيونهم خضراء مثل أمهم.   شعرها أسود وطويل.

في أيام شبابي، شعري كان بنياً .

[1]There is no relationship between أفعل التفضيل and أفعل of colors, or between either of these and the «أفعل» وزن of verbs.

In addition to colors, أفعل is used for certain physical characteristics of human beings such as the following:[1]

DVD

المعنى	الجمع	المؤنث	المذكر
dark-complexioned	سُمر	سَمْراء	أسْمَر
blond, fair-complexioned	شُقر	شَقْراء	أشْقَر
grey/white-haired	شيب	—	أشْيَب
bald	صُلع	—	أصْلَع
blind	عُمي	عَمْياء	أعْمى

الثقافة

أبو الطيّب المُتَنَبّي (٩١٥-٩٦٥)

يُعتبر المتنبي من أشهر الشُعَراء *poets* العرب الكلاسيكيين، ويدرس الطلاب شِعره *poetry* في المدرسة وفي الجامعة. ومن أشهر أبيات *lines* شِعره:

أنا الّذي نَظَرَ الأعمى إلى أدَبي وأسْمَعَتْ كَلِماتي مَن بِهِ صَمَمُ

الألوان في الجغرافيا

نجد في الشرق الأوسط: مدينة **الدار البيضاء** في المغرب و**البحر الأبيض المُتَوَسِّط** بين أفريقيا وآسيا وأوروبا و**البحر الأحمر** بين مصر والسعودية واليمن و**البحر الأسود** في آسيا. كما تُعرف تونس بـ«**تونس الخضراء**» ومدينة مراكش بـ"**مرّاكش الحمراء**" بسبب بيوتها وبناياتها الحمراء الكثيرة.

---

[1]When we presented the أوزان in Chapter 14, we mentioned that Form IX is rare. This form is actually used for these types of color and physical attribute adjectives. Here are two examples so that you can see how it works and recognize it if you see it:

اِحْمَرَّ ، يَحْمَرّ ، الاِحْمِرار	to become red	اِحْمَرَّت عيونهم بعد السهر الطويل للمذاكرة.
اِسْوَدَّ ، يَسْوَدّ ، الاِسْوِداد	to become black	اِسْوَدَّت يدي من هذا القلم الرخيص!

عبارات فيها ألوان وأعضاء الجسم DVD

SAY IT WITH COLOR! ARAB POPULAR CULTURE IS RICH IN EXPRESSIONS USING COLORS AND PARTS OF THE BODY. THE EXPRESSIONS LISTED BELOW ARE NORMALLY USED IN THE COLLOQUIAL REGISTER IN THE CENTRAL REGIONS OF THE ARAB MIDDLE EAST.

١- قلبه أبيض	kind or good hearted
٢- بطنه كبير = كِرشُه كبير	(figuratively, of doctors and lawyers) charges too much
٣- نَفسه خضرا [خضراء]	(of older men) he is still interested in women
اللون الأخضر	a positive color in Arabic, associated with life, vitality, and hope
٤- عينه حمرا [حمراء]	= غاضب جداً
٥- من عينيّ الاثنين!	to say "I'd be happy to" in response to a request
= على عيني وراسي [رأسي]	
٦- لسانه طويل	talks back, insults or criticizes people
٧- إيده [يده] طويلة	said of someone who steals
٨- دمه ثقيل *heavy*	unpleasant, obnoxious
٩- دمه خفيف *light*	good-humored, funny, fun to be with
١٠- يا خَبَر اسود !! / يا نهار اسود !!	said to express shock upon hearing bad news
١١- يا خبر أبيض !	said to express surprise, or as a euphemism for يا خبر اسود

تمرين ٨ نشاط محادثة في مجموعات صغيرة DVD

FASHION SHOW: YOU ARE WORKING AS A MARKETING CONSULTANT FOR A GROUP OF FASHION DESIGNERS. LOOK AT THE PICTURES ON YOUR DVD AND PREPARE A PRESENTATION FOR RETAIL STORES ON THE CLOTHES AND COLORS YOU WANT TO SELL.

تمرين ٩ **الألوان: اكتبوا ألوانًا مناسبة كما في المثال:**

مثال: الألوان في شقتي هي الأحمر والأصفر والبرتقالي.

١- لوني المفضل هو (اللون) ________ .

٢- الألوان التي ألبسها كثيراً هي ________ و________ و________ .

٣- الرئيس الأمريكي يسكن في البيت ________ .

٤- أحب العيون ________ .

٥- شاهدتها في النادي وكان معها شابّ ________ .

٦- ________ في أمريكا يريدون فرصًا أكثر للدراسة والعمل والنجاح.

٧- معظم أفلام «تشارلي شابلين» بـ ________ و________ .

٨- أمي ________ ووالدي ________ وأنا ________ .

٩- أتمنى أنْ أملك سيارة ________ .

١٠- ألوان جامعتنا هي ________ و________ .

١١- معظم العرب ________ ولكنك تستطيع أن تجد بعض الـ ________ في سوريا ولبنان والاردن وحتى في شمال أفريقيا.

١٢- إذا رسمت صورة فسأرسمها بـ ________ و________ .

١٣- بيت أحلامي سيكون فيه غرفة نوم ________ و________ و________ .

❁ المُثَنّى

In الفصحى , the quantity *two* of anything is expressed with المثنى . You know that the dual of any word is formed from the singular by adding the suffix انِ or ـَيْـنِ , which represent case endings. You have also seen that dual agreement extends to adjectives and verb endings. You have heard and seen sentences like:

هما مشغولان عنها　　　　هما يملكانِ شركة تجارية يعملانِ بها .

المهم هو رأي خالد ومها اللذين لا يعرفان اي شيء عن الموضوع.

These sentences illustrate the basic rules for المثنى , which we will outline here.

First, all nouns, pronouns, adjectives, and verbs that refer to *two* of anything must take المثنى in formal Arabic.[1] Thus, الفصحى has dual pronouns أنتُما *you two, both of you;* and هُما *they two, both of them.* Both pronouns serve as مذكر and مؤنث .

Second, remember that the gender of the singular noun determines its gender as dual:

كتاب (مذكر) —> كتابان —> هما (مذكر)

غرفة (مؤنث) —> غرفتان —> هما (مؤنث)

Parts of the body that come in pairs are feminine: عين , يد , and رجل .

Words in المثنى are easy to form if you remember one simple rule: **derive the مثنى from the مفرد .** (If the gender of the two parties differs, هو is the default gender). Study the following derivations and note that ان or ا is just added to the stem of the singular verb.

المضارع

الضمير	المفرد starting point	المثنى ->
هما (علي وأحمد) / هما (ماجدة وخليل)	(هو) يفعل	يفعلان / أنْ يفعلا
هما (ماجدة وعزيزة)	(هي) تفعل	تفعلان / أنْ تفعلا
أنتما	(أنت) تفعل	تفعلان / أن تفعلا

[1]In spoken Arabic, many dialects use the dual ending on nouns, which then take plural agreement in the pronouns, adjectives, and verbs that refer to them.

الماضي

الضمير	المفرد starting point	-ا المثنى
هما (علي وأحمد) / هما (ماجدة وخليل)	(هو) فَعَلَ	فَعَلا
هما (ماجدة وعزيزة)	(هي) فعلَت	فَعَلَتا
أنتما	rhymes with pronoun	فَعَلْتُما

The next chart summarizes all the verb endings for المثنى forms. Listen on DVD:

المثنّى: الفعل والضمائر

الضمير	الماضي	المضارع المرفوع	المنصوب والمجزوم
أنتُما	فَعَلتُما	تَفعَلانِ	تَفعَلا
هُما (مذكر)	فَعَلا	يَفعَلانِ	يَفعَلا
هُما (مؤنث)	فَعَلَتا	تَفعَلانِ	تَفعَلا

Dual agreement also includes demonstrative pronouns and الاسم الموصول. All مثنى forms show case endings, and all pronouns, verbs, and adjectives must agree with the noun in gender and case. DVD

The demonstrative and relative pronouns forms are given in the facing chart.

الضمير	المرفوع	المنصوب والمجرور
هما – مذكر	اللَّذانِ	اللَّذَيْنِ
هما – مؤنث	اللَّتانِ	اللَّتَيْنِ
هما – مذكر	هٰذانِ	هٰذَيْنِ
هما – مؤنث	هاتانِ	هاتَيْنِ

There is one final rule for المثنى that we will mention in passing: the ن of a dual noun drops whenever it is the first (or non-final) word in an إضافة , or has a possessive pronoun suffix. We will activate this rule later; for now learn to recognize these forms and memorize the forms for *my parents* and parts of the body.

المثنى في الإضافة

الكلمة	مرفوع	منصوب ومجرور
والدان:	والدا + اسم / pronoun	والدَيْ + اسم / pronoun — *parents*
عينان:	عينا + اسم / pronoun	عينَيْ + اسم / pronoun — *eyes*

أمثلة: أحبّ والدَيّ كثيراً. عيناه جميلتان! هل هما والداها؟

تمرين ١٠ المثنى (في الصف)

THE FOLLOWING SENTENCES DEMONSTRATE ALL ASPECTS OF مثنى AGREEMENT. READ THEM, IDENTIFY ALL مثنى FORMS AND WRITE ALL CASE ENDINGS:

١- يوما السبت والأحد هما يوما عطلة نهاية الأسبوع هنا، وهما يوماي المفضّلان.

٢- الأختان الصغيرتان كانتا تسكنان في بيت جميل ولكنهما لم تكونا سعيدتين.

٣- إذا تزوج خالد ومها، فأين سيعيشان؟ وهل سيكونان سعيدين؟

٤- محمد وملك قرّرا أن يبقيا في أمريكا بعيدين عن عائلتيهما.

تمرين ١١ ماذا فعلا / يفعلان؟ (في البيت)

١- عمتي وزوجها ــــــــ من نفس الكلية في نفس السنة. (تخرّج)

٢- مها وليلى لن ــــــــ من الغرفة قبل انتهاء المحاضرة. (خرج)

٣- ماهر وأخوه سـ ــــــــ معنا في المباراة. (اشترك)

٤- ــــــــ الزميلان إلى الشقة في العاشرة مساءً . (عاد)

٥- الرئيسان السوري واللبناني ــــــــ الزيارات كثيراً. (تبادل)

٦- أنا غاضبة منكما لأنكما لم ــــــــ لزيارتي منذ وقت طويل! (حضر)

٧- أظنّ أنكما لا ــــــــ أن ــــــــ إلى رأيي في الموضوع. (أراد، استمع)

٨- بعد أن ــــــــ عبد المنعم ووليد من المذاكرة ــــــــ من البيت و ــــــــ إلى مطعم قريب حيث ــــــــ ساندويشات فلافل. (انتهى، نزل، ذهب، أكل)

تمرين ١٢	نشاط قراءة

كلمات تساعد على الفهم:

صَمَّمَ	to design
مُحَرِّك	engine

اقرأوا المقالة مرة لفهم الافكار العامة، ثم مرة ثانية مع القاموس للعمل على الاوزان.

١- تذكر هذه المقالة القصيرة رجليْن مشهورين: من هما؟
ماذا تذكر المقالة عن حياتهما؟

2. Circle all مثنى forms you see.
3. Find in the text, and use your grammatical and historical knowledge to guess and your قاموس to confirm:
   a. a مصدر of وزن افتَعَلَ whose جذر you recognize
   b. the meaning of the phrase صانعي درّاجات . Can you explain the ending on صانع ?
   c. the information given about the flight in the last sentence.

من هما؟
الأخوان رايت

مهندسان أمريكيان صمما ونفذا وطارا بأول طائرة ذات محرك، وذلك في العام ١٩٠٣ . ولد الأخوان «أورفيل» (١٨٧١-١٩٤٨) و«ويلبور رايت» (١٨٦٧-١٩٢١) في ولاية «أوهايو» حيث تابعا دراستهما الإبتدائية والثانوية، ولم يتلق الأخوان «رايت» أي دراسة في الهندسة، وكل ما كانا يعرفانه عن الموضوع بعض المعلومات البسيطة من الكتب، ومن تجربتهما كصانعي دراجات. إلا أن اهتمامهما بالطيران جعلهما يصممان أول محرك طائرة بطاقة ١٢ حصاناً. ومن ثم صمما الهيكل الخارجي، وأخيراً الأجنحة. وفي السابع من ديسمبر عام ١٩٠٣ قاما بأول محاولة طيران وذلك في ولاية «نورث كارولاينا» ودامت الرحلة ١٢ ثانية وغطت ١٢٠ قدماً فقط.

❁ وزنا فَعَّلَ وتَفَعَّلَ

In Chapter 16, you learned that وزن فَعَّلَ normally has a transitive meaning (*to do X to someone or something*) compared to the meaning of base I وزن . Here we will discuss the relationship between the two forms II فَعَّلَ and V تَفَعَّلَ . The similarity in form between these two verbs is obvious, and points to a relationship in meaning as well. In this pair, وزن فَعَّلَ is the transitive wazn, while وزن تَفَعَّلَ turns the meaning into a reflexive one. Some examples will clarify:

غَيَّرَ	*to change something/someone*	الحياة في أمريكا غيّرتْ مها.
تَغَيَّرَ	*to change (by itself)*	مها تَغَيَّرَت بسبب الحياة في أمريكا.
ذَكَّرَ	*to remind (someone)*	الـ palm pilot يُذَكِّرني بكل مواعيدي.
تَذَكَّرَ	*to remind oneself, remember, recall*	من الصعب أن أتذكّر كل مواعيدي.
أَخَّرَ	*to make someone or something late*	الازدحامُ أخَّرَني!
تَأَخَّرَ	*to be late*	تَأَخَّرتُ بسبب الازدحام!

You can see that the difference between these two forms is that فَعَّلَ is transitive and تَفَعَّلَ is reflexive. The choice of وزن is one of agency: who is the actor, or the agent, of the action, and if there is an object of that action. Of course, not all جذور are used in both of these forms, but in general, the two forms constitute a fairly predictable pair.

تمرين ١٣ أوزان الفعل (في الصف)

FOR EACH PAIR OF SENTENCES, CHOOSE THE CORRECT وزن FOR EACH SENTENCE. LOOK TO SEE WHETHER OR NOT THERE IS AN OBJECT THAT INDICATES وزن فَعَّلَ .

١- غيّر – تغيّر

أ - أحب أن أخرج معكم ولكني أريد أن ________ ملابسي أولاً.

ب - مطر، مطر، مطر! إذا لم ________ الطقس قريباً فلا أعرف ماذا سأفعل!

٢- أخّر – تأخّر

أ - الازدحام في الشوارع ________ ني عن الموعد.

ب - إذا ________ أكثر من خمس دقائق فلا تستطيع أن تدخل الى الصف.

٣- حقيقة، حقيقي ← حَقَّق to realize, make real ، تَحَقَّق to be realized

أ - أرجو أن ________ أحلامكم!

ب - أتمنّى أن ________ كلُّ أحلامي في الحياة!

تمرين ١٤ نشاط قراءة ومحادثة

اقرأوا الإعلانات *ads* مع زميل أو زميل:

١ـ ماذا تريد النساء في الزوج؟ اكتبوا ٥ صِفات *attributes* :

٢ـ ماذا يريد الرجال في الزوجة؟ اكتبوا ٥ صفات:

٣ـ أين يقيمون ويعملون؟ اكتبوا أسماء البلاد:

٤ـ لماذا تقول T488 «السيدة» وتقول النساء الأخريات «الآنسة»؟

5. Find several instances of desired age: What verb is used? ________________

   Give الوزن والجذر and guess the meaning from context: ________________

6. Find the words meaning: divorced = __________ complexion = __________

   and another word for يرغب في = ________________

7. Identify الجذور of the following words and use them to guess the meaning.

لا يَهُمّه =	________________	خَلوق =	________________
مُتديِّن =	________________	مُثقَّف =	________________
مَقبول الشكل =	________________	رَبّة بيت =	________________

٨ـ للمناقشة في الصف

THIS TEXT CONTAINS A LOT OF SOCIAL DATA THAT YOU CAN ANALYZE TOGETHER بالعربية.

- ✦ لماذا يقول بعض الناس فقط إنهم مسلمون؟
- ✦ ماذا نستطيع أن نقول عن الناس الذين كتبوا هذه الإعلانات *ads* ؟
- ✦ ما هي أهم الأشياء في الزوج/ة بالنسبة للرجال والنساء هنا؟
- ✦ من هذه القراءة، هل تظنون أن الأفكار عن الزواج عند الناس الذين كتبوا هذه الإعلانات مختلفة عن أفكاركم؟ لماذا؟

النصف الآخر

T481 الآنسة «ب .هـ» تونسية من العاصمة، ٢٦ سنة، على قدر وافر من الجمال والأناقة، من أسرة محافظة، ومتدينة، ربة بيت ممتازة، تحترم الحياة الزوجية، تود الزواج من شاب عربى مسلم، صادق، خلوق، لديه عمل ثابت، يكون مقيما فى دولة أوروبية.

T482 الآنسة «ن.ر». مغربية تقيم فى فرنسا، ٣٠ سنة. مقبولة الجمال، خلوقة، طموحة، تودّ الزواج من شاب عربى مسلم، خلوق، متواضع، متفهم وقادر على تحمّل أعباء الحياة الزوجية.

T483 الآنسة «أ.أ» مغربية من بنى ملال، ٢٦ سنة، جامعية، جميلة، جذابة، أنيقة، محجبة، خلوقة، ترغب فى الزواج من شاب عربى مسلم، متدين، لا يتجاوز عمره ٥٠ سنة، تفضله سعودياً أو خليجياً.

T485 الآنسة «ع.ف» مغربية من الدار البيضاء، ٣٧ سنة، جامعية ، صاحبة مدرسة للأطفال، حسنة الشكل، أنيقة، متواضعة، تودّ الزواج من رجل عربى مسلم لا يقل عمره عن ٥٠ سنة، يحترم المرأة، ويقدر الحياة الزوجية.

T487 الآنسة «أ.أ» لبنانية مسلمة من العاصمة، ١٩ سنة، متعلمة، جميلة، من أسرة محافظة، متدينة، ترغب فى الزواج من شاب عربى مسلم، تفضله لبنانياً، متديناً، شريفاً، ويقيم فى أوروبا أو فى أميركا، وألا يتجاوز عمره ٣٠ سنة.

T488 السيدة «م.س» تونسية تقيم فى سويسرا، مطلقة، جامعية، حسنة المظهر، أنيقة، ٣٩ سنة، تودّ الزواج من رجل عربى مسلم، مثقف، لا يتجاوز عمره ٤٥ سنة، لديه رغبة صادقة فى تكوين أسرة، ويقبل العيش معها فى المهجر.

T489 الآنسة «س.س»، عراقية تقيم فى تركيا، ٢٩ سنة، محجبة، جميلة الخلق والأخلاق، طويلة القامة، رشيقة، مثقفة، تودّ الزواج من شاب عربى مسلم، متدين، خلوق، مثقف، لديه عمل محترم، مقبول الشكل، وصادق فى رغبته بالزواج.

T490 الآنسة «م.ف»، مغربية من تطوان، ٣١ سنة، جامعية محاسبة، مقبولة الجمال، بيضاء البشرة، محجبة، تودّ الزواج من شاب مغربى، تفضله مقيماً فى هولندا، صادق وطيب القلب.

T491 «م.ل» جزائرى، يقيم ويعمل فى إيطاليا، ٤٨ سنة، عازب، مستوى مهنى رفيع، حسن المظهر والأخلاق، يودّ الزواج-صادقاً-من آنسة أو سيدة عربية مسلمة، ولا يهمه مكان إقامتها.

T492 «ن.ع» إماراتى، ٣٧ سنة، موظف، خلوق، يودّ الزواج من آنسة أو سيدة عربية مسلمة، بيضاء البشرة، جميلة القوام، ولا يهمه مكان إقامتها.

T493 «ب.ع» مغربى يقيم ويعمل فى فرنسا، ٣٨ سنة، يرغب فى الزواج من آنسة أو سيدة عربية مسلمة، لا يمانع إن كان لديها أبناء، حسنة الشكل، ذات أخلاق حميدة، ويفضلها مقيمة فى أوروبا.

T494 «م.د» فلسطينى مسلم، يقيم فى لبنان، ٢٧ سنة، لم يسبق له الزواج، يرغب فى الزواج من آنسة أو سيدة عربية، يفضلها مقيمة فى المهجر، حنونة، خلوقة، مقبولة الجمال، ولا يتجاوز عمرها ٢٤ سنة.

T495 «م.د» مغربى يقيم ويعمل فى ألمانيا، ٣٣ سنة، لديه عمل محترم وثابت، خلوق، يرغب فى الزواج من آنسة عربية مسلمة، جميلة الشكل، حنونة، خلوقة، ولديها رغبة صادقة فى الزواج والاستقرار، وترضى بالعيش فى ألمانيا، ولا يزيد عمرها على ٢٨ سنة.

T498 «ق.ق» أردنى مسلم من جرش، ٣٢ سنة، موظف حكومى، ميسور الحال، حسن المظهر، يودّ الزواج من آنسة عربية مسلمة، خلوقة، حسنة الشكل، وتقدس الحياة الزوجية.

T499 «ب.أ» مغربى يقيم ويعمل فى فرنسا، ٣٦ سنة، لديه عمل ثابت ومحترم، يود الزواج من آنسة مغربية، لا يتجاوز عمرها ٣٢ سنة، تحترم الزوج، وتتمتع بأخلاق رفيعة، وتعرف اللغة الفرنسية.

T500 «م.هـ» سورى مسلم، يقيم ويعمل فى إسبانيا، ٣٨ سنة، طبيب أسنان، طويل القامة، رصين، جاد، يرغب فى الزواج من آنسة عربية مسلمة، طويلة القامة، جميلة الشكل، بيضاء البشرة، ولا يزيد عمرها على ٣٠ سنة، وترغب – صادقة – فى بناء أسرة سعيدة.

من مجلة «الوطن العربي» العدد ١٣٧١ ٢٠٠٣/٦/١٣

تمرين ١٥ **نشاط كتابة**

A. The following poetic description was written by one of your fellow students of Arabic. Read his poem and pick out the images (صُوَر) you like best:

امرأة أرسمها

حبيبة مثل كل الألوان .
هي بنّيه مثل الأرض التي ولدتها .
هي بنفسجية مثل ملابس الملكة .
هي زهرية مثل الغَمائم في المساء .
هي ذهبية مثل الشمس في شعرها .
هي زرقاء مثل الماء الضروري للحياة .
هي بيضاء مثل الثلج الجديد .
هي سوداء مثل الليلة المُغرية .
هي خضراء مثل عيون القطّ الجميل .

ستيفن كاوفمان
كلية وليم اند ماري ، ١٩٩٣

ب – من هو رجل أحلامك / امرأة أحلامك؟ اكتب/ي وَصفاً *description* **له / لها.**

You can write it in poetry or prose. Begin by making a list of the new and old vocabulary you want to use.

الاستماع DVD

تمرين ١٦ **نشاط استماع**

١- يتكلم هذا البرنامج عن الدكتور طه حسين. ماذا عرفتم عن:

أ - دراسته؟

ب - الوظائف التي عمل بها؟

جـ - كتاباته؟

2. Identify and write in the passage a noun that has المنصوب ending. Listen to the context and give the reason for المنصوب .

٣- استمعوا واكتبوا بقية الكلمات :

يُعتبر ________ ________ طه حسين من أوائل ________ ________

حركة ________ في مصر.

❁ الإعراب: إنّ / أنّ

In Chapter 17 you learned most of the basic إعـراب rules. There remain additional rules, such as certain categories of nouns that take a modified set of endings, that you will learn gradually. One additional rule that we want you to learn now is the rule that إنّ , أنّ , and لأنّ require the noun or noun phrase that follows them to take المنصوب ending, and if a pronoun follows, it is attached. The خـبـر of the sentence after انّ is not affected and remains مرفوع .

أمثلة: قلتُ لهم إنّ شبابَنا متفوّقون َوإنّهم سينجحون إن شاء الله.
اشترَوا البيتَ لأنّ ألوانَهُ جميلةٌ وحديقتَهُ كبيرةٌ.
ذَكَرَ الرئيسُ الأمريكيُّ أنَّ السلامَ في الشرقِ الأوسطِ مهمٌّ للسلامِ العالميّ.

تمرين ١٧ **القراءة بالفصحى**

YOU READ THE ARTICLE BELOW FOR GENERAL COMPREHENSION IN CHAPTER 12. HERE YOUR TASK WILL BE TO PREPARE THIS NEWS ITEM FOR ORAL PRESENTATION ON A BROADCAST, WHICH MEANS PUTTING إعـراب ENDINGS ON ALL WORDS EXCEPT THE FINAL WORD IN A SENTENCE (IGNORE PROPER NOUNS). EVEN NATIVE SPEAKERS PREPARE TEXTS BEFORE READING THEM ALOUD, BECAUSE IT IS DIFFICULT TO SPEAK OR READ SPONTANEOUSLY WITH FULL CASE ENDINGS. REREAD THE ITEM AND USE YOUR KNOWLEDGE OF أوزان TO GUIDE YOU IN THE VOWELING AND PRONUNCIATION OF UNFAMILIAR VERBS. (LOOK THEM UP IF YOU CANNOT GUESS THEIR MEANING.) AFTER YOU HAVE PREPARED THE TEXT, READ IT ALOUD OR RECORD IT FOR YOUR TEACHER.

مبارك يزور أنقرة اليوم

أنقرة ـ أ. ف. ب: يصل الى أنقرة اليوم الرئيس المصري حسني مبارك في زيارة عمل تستغرق 24 ساعة. وقالت وزارة الخارجية التركية ان زيارة الرئيس المصري تركز بشكل خاص على عملية السلام في الشرق الاوسط والمفاوضات الفلسطينية ـ الاسرائيلية الاخيرة.

وأضافت الوزارة ان الرئيس مبارك والرئيس التركي سليمان ديميريل سيستعرضان ايضا جملة من القضايا ذات الصلة بالمنطقة والعلاقات الدولية بشكل عام. ولم تتوفر معلومات أخرى أمس عن هذه الزيارة التي لم تكن مقررة للرئيس المصري.

من جريدة «الشرق الاوسط» ١٩٩٤/٢/١

تمارين المراجعة

تمرين ١٨ **اكتبوا أي كلمة مناسبة في كل جملة:**

١- ـــــــــ مرّة زرت فيها عائلتي كانت منذ شهرين .

٢- نحن ـــــــــ دائماً وليس عندنا وقت لـ ـــــــــ ، ولذلك، فنحن نأكل في المطاعم معظم الأوقات.

٣- والدتي ـــــــــ أنْ ترجع إلى العمل وألاّ تجلس في البيت.

٤- ـــــــــ أنّ الطقس اليوم سيكون مثل الطقس أمس.

٥- ـــــــــ اختي الصغيرة ندى في سنة ١٩٩٨.

٦- لم ـــــــــ له والدته بالذهاب إلى النادي لأنه لم يساعدها في شغل البيت.

٧- هل عندك ـــــــــ «أميريكان أكسبريس»؟

٨- لا أشعر بـ ـــــــــ في هذه المدينة بسبب كبرها والازدحام الدائم فيها.

٩- من اللازم أن ـــــــــ مع الاساتذة الذين يشرفون على دراستي هذا الاسبوع.

١٠- كتبت لها رسالة و ـــــــــ ها بالبريد قبل أكثر من شهر ولكنها لم ـــــــــ إلى الآن.

١١- ربّما نذهب إلى السوق بعد ظهر اليوم ، فهل تريدين أي ـــــــــ من هناك؟

١٢- ـــــــــ والدي مني لأنني أخذت السيارة ولم أسأله.

١٣- سأبدأ بإعداد العشاء بعد ـــــــــ من مشاهدة هذا المسلسل.

١٤- في السنة القادمة سـ ـــــــــ من هذه الشقة إلى شقة ـــــــــ .

١٥- غداً سيكون يوماً طويلاً وصعباً ولذلك ـــــــــ أنْ أنام جيداً الليلة.

١٦- أنا واختي ـــــــــ في بعض الأشياء ونختلف في بعض الأشياء الاخرى.

١٧- أنوي أن ـــــــــ سيارة أسافر بها إلى واشنطن لزيارة أختي.

تمرين ١٩ **اكتبوا الشكل المناسب للكلمة كما في المثال:**

ADD ANY MISSING PRONOUNS AND الـ AS NECESSARY, AND PAY ATTENTION TO AGREEMENT.

مثال: ناقشوا في الاجتماع عدة موضوعات اقتصادية. (موضوع ، اقتصادي)

١- أحب ______ ______ ______ . (شاهد، مسلسل، أجنبي)

٢- إذا ذهبت الى القاموس فستجد كل ______ ______ لهذه الكلمة. (معنى، مختلف)

٣- لن يكون من الممكن ______ السيارة قبل أول الشهر. (أصلح)

٤- زرنا كثيراً من ______ ______ في سوريا. (مكان، سياحي)

٥- ما مشكلتك؟ لماذا كل هذه ______ ______ ؟! (فكرة، أسود)

٦- هل ______ ______ في نفس الوظيفة يا رانيا؟ (ما زال، عمل)

٧- هذه المقالات ______ ويجب عليكم جميعًا أن ______ . (مهمّ ، قرأ)

٨- أين ______ أنْ ______ اجازتكم السنوية ؟ (يرغب، يقضي)

٩- في هذه الصورة ______ وألوان ______ . (شكل، جميل)

١٠- الحمد لله! بدأنا نشعر بـ ______ بعد سنوات ______ من السفر والانتقال من مكان إلى مكان. (استقرّ، طويل)

١١- أظنّ أنهم سـ ______ هناك عدة ______ . (بقي، يوم)

١٢- معظم ______ ______ ______ في فرنسا هم من المغرب والجزائر. (عربي، الذي، يعمل)

١٣- كتبت الكاتبة السورية غادة السمان عدداً كبيراً من ______ ______ . (قصة، قصير)

١٤- اعتاد جدّي، الله يرحمه، أنْ ______ في هذا ______ كل يوم مساءً. (جلس، مقهى)

١٥- من الصعب أن ______ الطلاب من ______ قبل الساعة الثامنة. (قام، نام)

تمرين ٢٠ **استمعوا إلى محمد واكتبوا ما يقول:** DVD

لي كثير من ______ هنا، ولكن من ______ أن ______ علاقتي بهم ______

______ كما كانت ______ في مصر، ربما لأن ______ الصداقة هنا ______ ، ___

______ هنا ______ ______ ______ التليفونية أو ______ ______ ، أو

______ الإلكترونية ، الـ email ، ______ لأن ______ في مصر ______ ______

حياتي و ______ و ______ . ______ أحيانا ______ أريد ______ ______ كل

______ هنا و ______ ______ مصر. ______ ـني ______ مها بعد ______ ، ______

محمود في إحدى ______ ______ يريد أن ______ ـها لخالد. خالد ______ ______ و

______ و ______ ممتازة، ولكن ملك لا ______ ______ ______ . ______ ______

نفس ______ ______ لمحمود وهو ______ ______ هو ______ خالد ومها اللذين لا

______ ______ شيء ______ ______ .

العامية DVD

- القصة: "المهم هو رأي خالد ومها"

شاهدوا محمد يتكلم بالعامية.

كيف يقول محمد: «أحياناً أشعر»؟

«خالد ومها اللذين لا يعرفان أي شيء عن الموضوع»؟

- "مالك؟"

تعلموا هذه العبارة:

«الجواز قِسمة ونَصيب» الزواج is a matter of luck and fate

شاهدوا خالد يتكلم مع صاحبه سامي.

كيف يبدو خالد هنا؟ لماذا؟

ماذا قال سامي لخالد؟

تذكروا هذه الكلمات

رأس	شَعر	يَد	لِسان
بَطن	رِجل	قَلب	دَم
لَون ج. أَلوان	بُنّي	بَنَفسَجيّ	زَهريّ
رَمادي ّ	ذَهَبيّ	فِضّيّ	
أزرَق ، زَرقاء	أحمر، حَمراء	أَخضَر، خَضراء	أَصفَر، صَفراء
أَخضَر، خَضراء	أَصفَر، صَفراء	أبيَض ، بَيضاء ، بيض	
أَسوَد ، سَوداء ، سود		أَسمَر، سَمراء ، سُمر	
أَشقَر، شَقراء ، شُقر		أصلع	أشيَب
أعمى	حَقَّقَ	تَغَيَّرَ	أَخَّرَ

١٩ـ ماذا يقصدان بكلمة مناسبة؟!

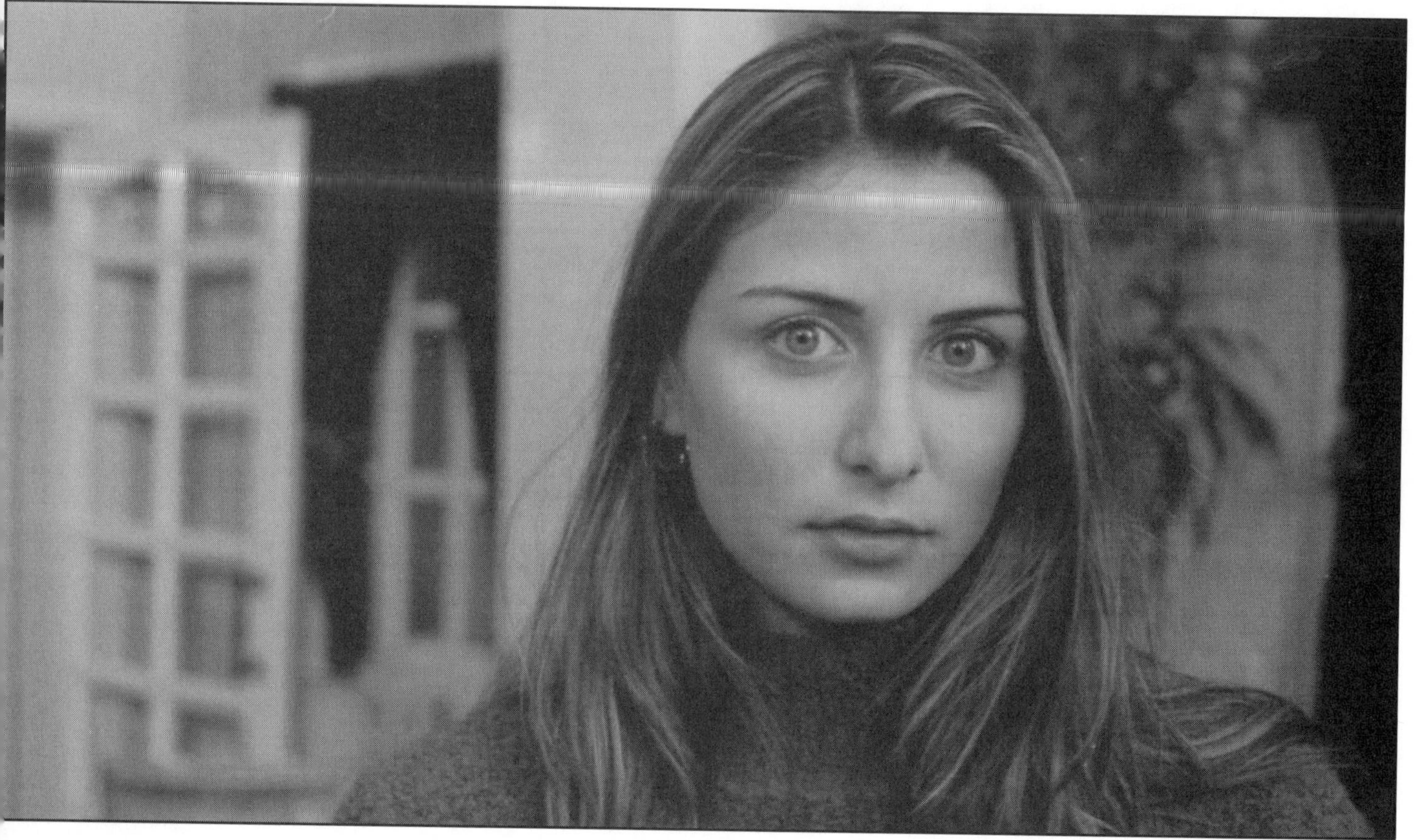

في هذا الدرس:

القصة • ترتيبات السفر إلى القاهرة

القواعد • كـ ، مثل ، كما ، كأنّ *Similarity*

• جمع المؤنث

• أب وأخ

الثقافة • الكُنية

القراءة • دروس للسيدات في الجامعة الأهلية

• نجيب محفوظ

الاستماع • آنسات النادي الأهلي

العامية • القصة: «يعني ايه كلمة مناسبة؟!»

• «اشتريتي ايه؟»

المفردات DVD

أَب ج. آباء	= والد
اِستَأنَفَ ، يَستَأنِف ، الاِستِئناف	to resume
حَتّى + المضارع المنصوب	= لِـ
اِختارَ ، يَختار ، الاِختِيار	to choose
تَرتيب ج. تَرتيبات	arrangement
سُلوك	behavior, way of acting (general)
تَصَرُّف ج. تَصَرُّفات	act, action (of behavior)
ضَروريّ	necessary
طِفل /ة ج. أَطفال	child
طَلَبَ من (أنْ) ، يطلُب من (أن) ، الطَّلَب من (أن)	to ask of (someone to)
غابَ (عن) ، يَغيب (عن) ، الغِياب (عن)	= تَغَيَّب (عن)
قابَلَ ، يُقابِل ، المُقابَلة	to meet (someone)
مُقابَلة ج. مُقابَلات	interview
قَصَدَ ، يَقصِد ، القَصد	to mean, intend
كَأَنّ + جملة اسمية	as if
مَرَّ (بِـ) ، يَمُرّ (بـ) ، المُرور (بـ)	to pass (by), drop by
نَصيحة ج. نَصائِح	(piece of) advice
تَوَقَّفَ (عن) ، يَتَوَقَّف (عن) ، التَوَقُّف (عن)	to stop
هَدِيّة ج. هَدايا	gift, present

تعلموا هذين الفعلين : DVD

الماضي

مَرَرْنا بـ	مَرَرْتُ بـ
مَرَرْتُم بـ	مَرَرْتَ بـ مَرَرْتِ بـ
مَرّوا بـ	مَرَّ بـ مَرّتْ بـ

المضارع

نَمُرّ بـ	أَمُرّ بـ
تَمُرّون بـ	تَمُرّ بـ تَمُرّينَ بـ
يَمُرّونَ بـ	يَمُرّ بـ تَمُرّ بـ

أمثلة: - كل يوم أمرّ بالكافتيريا قبل الذهاب إلى الصف .

- هل يمكنك أن تمرّي بمكتب البريد وترسلي لي هذه الرسالة ؟

اِخْتَرْنا	اِخْتَرْتُ
اِخْتَرْتُم	اِخْتَرْتَ اِخْتَرْتِ
اِخْتاروا	اِخْتارَ اِخْتارَت

نَخْتار	أَخْتار
تَخْتارونَ	تَخْتار تَخْتارينَ
يَخْتارونَ	يَخْتار تَخْتار

تمرين ١ المصدر كاسم

You are adept at using المصدر in its verbal sense. You have also seen that المصدر can function as a noun as well (with no verbal meaning). In this usage المصدر usually takes a plural of ـات , as you saw in مقابلات .مقابله ج and ترتيبات .ترتيب ج . Expand your vocabulary by using مصادر from new and old vocabulary to make nouns, and use each one in a sentence:

choice(s)	absence(s)
request(s)	consideration(s)
hint(s)	preparation(s)
repair(s)/reform(s)	meeting(s)
difference(s)	changes (choose the best وزن for your meaning)

تمرين ٢ **المفردات الجديدة (في البيت)**

اكتبوا الكلمة المناسبة في كل جملة:

PRACTICE YOUR إعراب : WRITE ALL ENDINGS ON جمل ١–٧ .

١- الحمد لله! انتهيت من امتحان الدكتوراه والآن أصبح من اللازم أنْ ______ موضوعًا لرسالة الدكتوراه .

٢- عندما تزوجتْ سلمى اشترى لها زملاؤها في الشركة ______ جميلة.

٣- عمره ٢٦ سنة ولكنه يتصرّف ______ ـه ولد صغير .

٤- قرّر البلدان ______ العلاقات الديبلوماسية بينهما بعد انقطاع طويل.

٥- ______ الرئيس صباح اليوم بعض ضبّاط الجيش .

٦- ______ الاستاذ منّا أنْ نترك كل كتبنا خارج الصفّ للامتحان.

٧- معرفة اللغة العربية ______ لكل الذين يرغبون في فهم الثقافة العربية.

٨- كان الطقس ممطرًا جدًا في الصباح ولكن المطر ______ في المساء.

٩- قرّرت المدرسة فصل خمسة من الطلاب بسبب ______ .

١٠- إذا سافرت من القاهرة إلى السعودية فسوف ______ فوق البحر الأحمر.

١١- سوف ______ عن الصف بعد ظهر اليوم لأنّ عندي مقابلة في مكتب القبول.

١٢- هل تعرف أنّ أحمد تزوج وأصبح أبًا لثلاثة ______ ؟!

١٣- عندي مشكلة وأريد أن أطلب ______ من أحد ولكن لا أعرف من؟

تمرين ٣ **نشاط كتابة بالمفردات الجديدة والقديمة**

بعد تجربتكم في دراسة اللغة العربية إلى الآن، أصبحت لكم بعض الآراء في كيفية دراسة لغة ثانية بنجاح. وصلت لكم رسالة من طالبة عربية تدرس اللغة الانجليزية وتريد منكم نصائحكم في كيف يجب أن تدرس. فماذا ستقولون لها؟

INCLUDE AS MANY OF الكلمات الجديدة AS YOU CAN, AND USE CONNECTORS TO MAKE YOUR LETTER FLOW:

و أمّا .. فـ بالإضافة إلى كذلك بالنسبة لـ

إذا ... فـ يجب أن من اللازم أن أظنّ أنّ في رأيي

تمرين ٤ اسألوا زملاءكم

1. Who feels that their parents talk to them and *behave* with them *as if* they are adults? Do they still *ask* their parents *to* do things for them? What?
2. What would they do if a friend *stopped acting* like he/she usually acts and began to *act* strangely (= بشكل غريب)?
3. Do they find it difficult to *resume* studying after a long *absence*? What do they do *in order to get started again* quickly?
4. Do they do well (= succeed) in *interviews*? Is it *necessary* to dress up for interviews?
5. Do they know a good place to buy small *gifts*? What kinds of *gifts* can one buy there?
6. Have they *chosen* their classes for next term? What *advice* would they offer freshmen who are *choosing* classes for the first time?
7. Do they and their friends *drop by* (=*pass by*) each others' rooms without a موعد ?
8. Do they think that watching some television shows changes *children's behavior*? What should *parents* (= *fathers* and mothers) do?
9. Do they always say what they *mean*?

تمرين ٥ أوزان الفعل :

PRACTICE WHAT YOU HAVE LEARNED ABOUT فَعَلَ , فَعَّلَ , AND تَفَعَّلَ . READ THE SENTENCES, IDENTIFY الأوزان , AND EXPLAIN THE MEANING OF EACH ONE WITH THE HELP OF THE CONTEXT.

١- (أ) لا أفهم لماذا يَغيب هذا الموظف كثيراً عن العمل – هل عنده مشكلة؟

(ب) الغيوم clouds غَيَّبَت الشمس اليوم.

(جـ) يجب أن أتغيّب عن الصفوف الأسبوع القادم بسبب سفري.

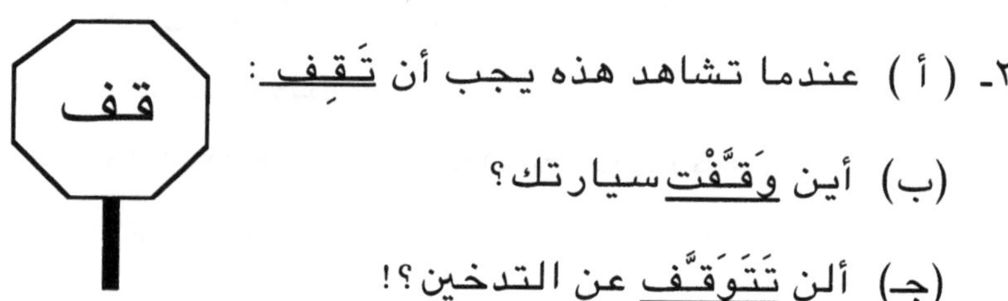

٢- (أ) عندما تشاهد هذه يجب أن تَقِف:

(ب) أين وَقَّفْت سيارتك؟

(جـ) ألن تَتَوَقَّف عن التدخين؟!

القصة DVD

تمرين ٦ **شاهدوا الفيديو وأجيبوا:**

١- عمَّ تتكلم مها هنا؟

٢- متى سيسافرون؟

٣- ماذا يريد والد مها؟

٤- ماذا تريد أمها ؟ أ -

ب -

شاهدوا مرّة ثانية:

٥- ماذا يجب على مها أن تفعل قبل السفر؟

٦- ماذا يقول أبو مها وامها لها؟ كيف تشعر مها بالنسبة لهذا؟

شاهدوا وخمّنوا

اكتبوا ما تقوله مها:

٧- «سآخذ معي بعض الكتب ______________________ الدراسة».

خمنوا معنى كلمة «مُستعدّة» = ______________

للمناقشة في الصف:

لماذا، في رأيكم، يُعطي *give* أبو مها وأمها نصائح كثيرة عن تصرفات مها في مصر؟

القواعد

❁ مثل ، كـ ، كما ، كأنّ *Similarity*

The four particles كَـ , مِثل , كَما , and كَأَنَّ all express similarity or likeness, but their usage differs slightly in both meaning and grammar. Learn the following rules:

مثل ، كـ + اسم

مِثل *like* is a noun that occurs as the first term of an إضافة and can take pronoun suffixes:

أمثلة: أخي طويل وأشقر **مثلَ** أبي. أريد أن أصبح مهندساً **مثلك**.

كَـ *like, as* is a preposition and must be followed by a **noun** (**never** by a **pronoun**):

أمثلة: القهوة العربية ليست **كالقهوة** الأمريكية.

أريد أن ألبس فستاناً جميلاً **كـفستانك** الأسود.

كـ and **مثل** overlap a great deal in meaning and usage, except that **only** مثل may be used with pronoun suffixes, while كـ tends to be more literary, and is used in similes:[1]

أمثلة: لستُ مثلك، يا صديقي! سلوكه **كسلوك** الأطفال.

أنا بِلا حبيبي **كليلة** بلا قمر أو **ككتاب** بلا صور.

كما + جملة فعلية

كما *as, just as* introduces a **sentence** and must be followed immediately by a verb:

أمثلة: أنوي أنْ آكل **كما** أريد! **كما** تعلمون، من المهم ألاّ تغيبوا عن الصف.

Note also that when كما links two identical or similar verbs, it means *also*:

مثال: اشتريت بعض الأشياء للبيت، **كما** اشتريت صحيفة وبعض المجلات .

(و)كأنّ + جمله اسميه

كأنّ or **وكأنّ** *as if* introduces an idea that might seem **as if** it is true but is not. It must be followed by a جملة اسمية :

أمثلة: مرّت هذه السنة (و)**كـأنّـها** شهر! (= السنة مرّت بسرعة، مثل شهر)

شعرت بسعادة كبيرة (و)**كأنني** أعيش حلماً جميلاً.

---

[1] In Classical usage, كـ is also used to cite examples, meaning *such as*.

تمرين ٧ **كـ ، مثل ، كما ، كأنّ (في البيت)**

أ ـ اختاروا الكلمة المناسبة من : كـ أو مثل أو كأنّ أو كما .

YOU MAY NEED TO ADD A PRONOUN IN SOME CASES, AND THERE MAY BE MORE THAN ONE POSSIBLE ANSWER.

مثال: هل تتصرّف مها كأنّها طفلة ؟!

١ـ لون شعرها ـــــ لون شعري .

٢ـ هم من الآباء والامّهات الذين يتركون أطفالهم يلعبون ـــــ يريدون .

٣ـ أتمنّى أن أجد سيارة جيدة ورخيصة ـــــ سيارتك .

٤ـ لم يفهموا أي شيء قلتُه لهم، ـــــ كنتُ أتكلم معهم بلغة أجنبية .

٥ـ فرص العمل في السعودية ـــــ فرص العمل في الإمارات.

٦ـ هي ترفض أن تعيش ـــــ عاشت امها .

٧ـ بعد الحادث شعرَت ـــــ وُلِدت من جديد .

٨ـ تشعر بالخجل كثيرًا ـــــ أي بنت في عمرها .

٩ـ أنا - ـــــ تعرفون - لا أحب النصائح .

١٠ـ لم أعرفه عندما شاهدته آخر مرّة ـــــ أصبح شخصًا آخر .

تمرين ٨ **اسألوا زملاءكم (في الصف)**

١ـ هل علاقتهم بوالدَيْهم الآن كما كانت من قبل؟ هل هي كما يريدون أن تكون ؟

٢ـ هم مثل من، وليسوا مثل من، في عائلتهم؟

٣ـ من هم الاشخاص الذين يريدون ان يكونوا مثلهم؟

٤ـ كيف يشعرون عندما ينجحون في شيء ؟ وعندما يفشلون ؟

٥ـ ما رأيهم في حياة نُجوم (★★★) السينما وتصرّفاتهم؟

٦ـ كيف يبدو الجو اليوم؟

❁ جمع المؤنث

You know that the feminine human plural marker for nouns and adjectives is ـات . In addition to this marker, formal Arabic has special human plural forms for verbs and other pronouns.[1] These forms are:

الضمائر DVD

Object and Possessive	Independent
ـكُنَّ	أنْتُنَّ
ـهُنَّ (ـهِنَّ)	هُنَّ

أمثلة:

هل أنتنّ طالبات هنا؟ — هل هذا بيتكُنّ ؟

هنّ زميلاتي في الجامعة. — أنا صديقتهُنّ .

لم أشاهدكنّ في المحاضرة. — أظنّ أنهُنّ في بيتهِنّ .

Verb conjugations for أنتُنّ and هُنّ have only one form that functions for all three مضارع forms, مرفوع ومنصوب ومجزوم .

الأفعال DVD

	الماضي	المضارع
أنتُنَّ	فَعَلْتُنَّ	تَفْعَلْنَ
هُنَّ	فَعَلْنَ	يَفْعَلْنَ

أمثلة: ظننتُ أنّكنّ أردتنّ أنْ تجلسْنَ معنا.

تكلّمْنَ معنا عن موضوع دراسات النساء .

The relative pronoun for feminine human plurals can take either of these forms (there is no difference in meaning, but اللائي is more formal and literary):

اللَّواتي or اللائي

---

[1]The group must be entirely female; if even one member is male, the gender of the group is masculine. In spoken Arabic, these feminine pronouns and verb forms are used mostly in Bedouin dialects.

One demonstrative pronoun serves both **male** and **female humans**:

those	هـٰؤُلاء

أمثلة: هؤلاء الرجال جاءوا مع هؤلاء النساء.

من سيتولّى اختيار البنات **اللواتي** سيشتركن في المباراة النهائية؟

Human feminine plural agreement thus appears on all adjectives, verbs and pronouns.

You saw in passing in Chapter 16 that the ending ـات has only two grammatical endings, one for المرفوع and one for both المنصوب and المجرور , shown in the chart below on the noun طالبات . Remember that the ending ـات never takes فتحة or تنوين فتحة as a case ending.

الإعراب

المرفوع	**المنصوب والمجرور**
طالباتٌ	طالباتٍ
الطالباتُ	الطالباتِ

تمرين ٩ **جمع المؤنث (في الصف)**

READ SILENTLY THEN ALOUD THE FOLLOWING SENTENCES AND IDENTIFY ALL جمع مؤنث FORMS IN THEM. MARK ALL GRAMMATICAL ENDINGS.

١- معظم البنات الامريكيات يلبسن ما يُرِدنَ ويخرجن كثيراً.

٢- هل كنتنّ طالبات في نفس الكلية؟

٣- هذا بيت الطالبات وصديقاتي يسكنّ فيه.

٤- لي ٣ خالات وكلُهنّ متزوجات وعندهنّ أولاد.

٥- زميلاتي يرغبن في التعرّف على أخي.

٦- هل تعْرفن أي شيء عن هذا الموضوع؟

٧- هل البنات المصريات لا يلبسن البنطلونات؟!

٨- الاستاذات الجديدات عندهنّ اجتماع مع رئيس الجامعة بعد الظهر.

٩- هل أنتنّ مُستعِدّات للذهاب إلى المسرح؟

تمرين ١٠ **غيّروا هذه الجمل إلى الجمع المؤنث كما في المثال: (في البيت)**

CHANGE THE NOUNS IN THESE SENTENCES FROM SINGULAR TO PLURAL, MARK ALL CASE ENDINGS ON NOUNS AND ADJECTIVES, AND VOWEL ALL VERBS:

مثال: هي مصرية . —> هنّ مصرياتٌ.

١- صديقتي لبنانيّة وهي بنت ذكيّة ومثقّفة وأخلاقها عالية .

٢- هل ستنزلين من البيت غداً لتخرجي مع صاحبتك؟

٣- تخرّجت منذ سنتين ولكنها لم تجد عملاً مناسباً حتى الآن .

٤- يبدو أنّها غيّرت رأيها بالنسبة لموضوع الوظيفة .

٥- عمّتي طبخت هذه الأكلة .

٦- زميلتها تعمل معيدة في قسم علم الإنسان .

تمرين ١١ **نشاط محادثة: الرجال جاءوا من المِرّيخ** *Mars* **والنساء جئنَ من الزُّهرة** *Venus*.

ما هي الصور النَمَطية *stereotypes* **الامريكية عن النساء والرجال؟**

مفردات لها علاقة بهذا الموضوع:

طلب من أنْ	يبدو أنّ	اختار	شغل/انشغل بـ	اختلف	غيّر
توقّف عن	قصد	تصرّف	تفوّق	اعتبر	اشترى

الاستماع DVD

تمرين ١٢ **نشاط استماع**

بُطولة championship

الأندية = النوادي (م. النادي)

١- هذا البرنامج يتكلم عن مباراة في ________ ________ لبطولة الأندية ________ .

٢- ما هي الكلمات التي تعني : won = ________ team= ________

٣- ماذا كانت النَتيجة *score* من المباراة؟ ________

٤- اكتبوا الكلمة التي تسمعونها: انّهن قادرات على ________ افريقيا».

Think about الوزن والجذر . What could it mean?

تمرين ١٣ **تشـاط قـراءة**

اقرأوا ثلاث مرات واكتبوا:

القراءة الأولى: ما موضوع هذه المقالة؟ ما بعض أسماء النساء اللواتي ذكرتهن المقالة؟

القراءة الثانية: Find all جمع المؤنث forms.

القراءة الثالثة Choose 3 words to look up to help you understand more of the passage.

بدعم كبير من الأميرة فاطمة اسماعيل، افتتحت الجامعة الأهلية في ديسمبر سنة ١٩٠٨ (مكان الجامعة الأمريكية الحالية) وكانت الجامعة مختلطة وبها استراحة مكتوب على بابها

محجوز للسيدات

وكان العدد حوالي ٢٢ طالبة منهن نبوية موسى ومي زيادة وعدد من المصريات الأجنبيات يحضرن المحاضرات جنبا الى جنب زملائهن الرجال.

بداية من يوم الجمعة ١٥ يناير سنة ١٩٠٩ تم تخصيص محاضرات خاصة بالنساء يوم الإجازة الأسبوعية الخاصة بالجامعة. وتجاوز عدد الحاضرات ٦٠ سيدة.

كانت أول محاضرة «درس النسائيات» يوم الجمعة في مقر الجامعة المصرية، ألقتها مدموازيل مارجريت كليمان وهي من أبرز الداعيات لحصول المرأة الفرنسية على حق الانتخاب. وقد كانت المحاضرة بدعوى من السيدة هدى شعراوي وتحت رئاسة الأميرة عين الحياة. ونشرت مجلة «الجريدة» نص المحاضرة بتاريخ ٢٠ يناير ١٩٠٩ تحت عنوان:

«خطبة مدموازيل كليمان في تحرير المرأة.»

من: «مدخل الى قضايا المرأة في سطور وصور»، هدى الصدة (محررة)، أميمة أبو بكر، رانيا عبد الرحمن، سحر صبحي، هالة كمال، هدى السعدي، ملتقى المرأة والذاكرة، القاهرة، ٢٠٠٢

❁ أب وأخ

The two nouns أخ and أب belong to a very small group of nouns (six total) that show their case endings as long vowels when they have possessive pronoun suffixes or are in an إضافة . You know the forms for *my brother* and *my father*, أخي and أبي , these forms do not show any case endings because the pronoun ـي swallows them. The following chart shows the forms of these nouns with case endings and gives examples:[1]

المرفوع:	أخو .. / أبو ..	هل هذا أخوك؟	هذا أبو خالد؟
المنصوب:	أخا .. / أبا ..	لا أعرف أخاها.	أعرف أبا صديقتي.
المجرور:	أخي .. / أبي ..	هل تكلمت مع أخيك؟	تكلمنا مع أبيه.

الثقافة

الكُنية

It is common in many parts of the Arab world for family members, friends, and neighbors to address each other by their كُنية , a name formed by adding the name of the oldest son to أبو or امّ . For example, محمود أبو العلا may be addressed as أبو خالد and his wife would have been called امّ خالد . Some family names, such as أبو العلا , originally came from a كنية . If there are no sons, the name of the oldest daughter may be used. What would your father's and mother's كنية be?

تمرين ١٤ **اكتبوا الشكل المناسب للكلمات:**

مثال: هل أخوك في المدرسة الإعدادية يا علي؟ (أخ)

١- هل سيجيء ــــــــ معك؟ (أخ)

٢- ستسافر مها مع أمها وــــــــها. (أب)

٣- يساعد خالد ــــــــه الصغير في مذاكرته. (أخ)

٤- هل وصلتك رسالة من ــــــــك؟ (أخ)

٥- هل هو فعلاً ــــــــ هذه البنت؟ (أب)

٦- عندما قابل الشاب ــــــــ البنت، طلب منه يد بنته في الزواج. (أب)

[1]Since spoken Arabic does not have case endings, the spoken forms for these words are fixed within each dialect. For example, the forms used in Cairo are: أبوك، أخوك، أخوها and so forth.

تمرين ١٥ **نشـاط قـراءة**

كلمات تساعد على فهم المقالة:

رِوايـة ج. ـات	novel
كاتِب ج. كُتّاب	writer
(هي) اِستهوَتـهُ	= أحبّها

أ ـ القراءة الاولى: الافكار الرئيسية

NUMBER THE PARAGRAPHS IN THE TEXT FOR REFERENCE (THERE ARE 9). SKIM المقـالـة WITH THE GOAL OF FINDING THE ANSWERS TO THESE QUESTIONS:

١ـ عمَّن تتكلم هذه المقالة؟ لماذا هو مشهور؟ اكتبوا ٣ أشياء .

2. Find the paragraphs in the text that give information about and report on:

أ - دراسته　　　　جـ - عمله

ب - كتاباته　　　　د - قراءاته والكتّاب الذين influenced him

ب ـ القراءة الثانية: استراتيجيات للقراءة

THESE EXERCISES ARE DESIGNED TO HELP YOU DEVELOP STRATEGIES FOR READING DIFFICULT TEXTS.

3. Look at the long paragraphs, 2 and 4. Which one is narrative and which one is largely made up of information given in lists? How can you tell? In the narration paragraph, follow the thread of the narration by identifying the main verbs. In the listing paragraph, underline the information that is given in lists. What one word in this paragraph would be helpful to look up?

4. In paragraphs 1, 3, and 7, bracket all prepositional phrases and الذي/التي clauses. Use your knowledge of الإضافة and اسم + صفة to help you figure out where the prepositional phrases begin and end. When you have finished, look again at the non-bracketed words and you should be able to see clearly the main sentence structures. Identify them as اسمية or فعلية and name the parts: مبتدأ + خبر or فعل + فاعل .

5. In paragraph 9, there is only one word you do not know, but the dictionary will not help until you understand the grammar of the sentence. What are the subjects of the two verbs? What does this suggest about the way these two verbs are used here?

جـ ـ القراءة الثالثة: مع القاموس

6. Choose one paragraph to read with the dictionary (paragraph 2 contains a number of verbs of different أوزان if you are interested in working on them). Use القاموس intelligently: have an idea of what you are looking for, and look up only important words.

يعد نجيب محفوظ عبد العزيز السبيلجي الذي حاز على جائزة «نوبل» للأدب لهذا العام، واحدا من اشهر الكتاب العرب، وهو اول عربي يحصل على هذه الجائزة منذ تأسيسها. كتب ٤٠ رواية ومجموعة قصصية، وهو يمارس الكتابة منذ نصف قرن، واليوم وهو في السابعة والسبعين من عمره، ما يزال مواظبا على الكتابة والنشر.

ولد نجيب محفوظ في ١١ ديسمبر (كانون الاول) عام ١٩١١، في حي الجمالية بالقاهرة. التحق بكتاب الشيخ بحيري وعمره ٤ سنوات، وتعلم في مدرسة الحسينية الابتدائية، ثم مدرسة فؤاد الاول الثانوية، وتخرج من قسم الفلسفة بكلية الآداب بجامعة فؤاد الاول عام ١٩٣٤. ثم باشر باعداد رسالة ماجستير عن مفهوم الجمال في الفلسفة الاسلامية باشراف الشيخ مصطفى عبد الرازق، ولكنه انصرف عنها بعد عامين من بدئها، حين استهوته الكتابة وجرفته عن الميدان الاكاديمي. وهو يقول عن هذه المرحلة:

«كنت امسك بيدي كتابا من الفلسفة وفي اليد الاخرى قصة طويلة من قصص توفيق الحكيم او يحيى حقي او طه حسين. وكانت المذاهب الفلسفية تقتحم ذهني في نفس اللحظة التي يدخل فيها ابطال القصص من الجانب الآخر. ووجدت نفسي في صراع رهيب بين الادب والفلسفة، صراع لا يمكن ان يتصوره الا من عاش فيه».

لقد بدأت قراءاته وهو تلميذ في المرحلة الابتدائية، واستهوته اولا الروايات البوليسية، فقرأ روايات سينكلار وجونسون وغيرهما. وكان يترجم لهؤلاء حافظ نجيب ومحمد السباعي ومصطفى لطفي المنفلوطي، ثم انتقل الى الروايات التاريخية التي تأثر بها كثيرا في كتاباته الاولى، كما شغف بالسينما. وفي مرحلة تالية استهوته كتابات طه حسين وعباس محمود العقاد وابراهيم عبد القادر المازني وتوفيق الحكيم ويحيى حقي. وكان الى جانب هؤلاء ينهل من المصادر الاساسية للغة والادب العربيين مثل كتابات الجاحظ وابن عبد ربه وشعر المتنبي والمعري وابن الرومي وغيرهم. وفي مرحلة النضج كان يقرأ الادب الاوروبي.

بدأ بكتابة القصة القصيرة وهو في المرحلة الثانوية من دراسته اي في عام ١٩٢٨، واول قصة قصيرة له كانت بعنوان «ثمن الضعف» وقد نشرها في مجلة «المجلة الجديدة» بتاريخ ٣ اغسطس (آب) عام ١٩٣٤.

صدرت له اول مجموعة قصصية بعنوان «همس الجنون» عام ١٩٣٨ وبعد ٢٥ عاما أي في (١٩٦٣) صدرت له اخر مجموعة من القصص بعنوان «دنيا الله».

عمل طوال حياته في الوظائف الحكومية. فبعد تخرجه من جامعة فؤاد الاول (جامعة القاهرة) عام ١٩٣٤، عمل موظفا في وزارة الاوقاف حتى عام ١٩٥٣ حيث عين مديرا للمكتب الفني ومديرا للرقابة ورقيبا على الافلام في مصلحة الفنون. وفي عام ١٩٦٠ ترأس مجلس ادارة مؤسسة السينما. وكانت آخر وظيفة حكومية له هي مستشار وزير الثقافة في عام ١٩٧٠.

نال وسام الاستحقاق من الطبقة الاولى عام ١٩٦٢، وجائزة الدولة التقديرية. سجلت اعماله في مكتبة الكونجرس الامريكية باعتباره احد الكتاب البارزين في الوطن العربي. كما صدرت موسوعة عن حياته واعماله الادبية مع تحليل لأدبه الروائي باللغة الالمانية.

قدمت عن حياته وادبه عشرات الرسائل الجامعية في العالمين العربي والاوروبي. وترجمت اعماله الى مختلف اللغات العالمية منها: الانجليزية، الفرنسية، الالمانية، الروسية، اليوغسلافية، والايطالية.

من جريدة الشرق الأوسط، ١٦/١٠/١٩٨٨

تمرين ١٦ **نشاط كتابة**

هذا "حنّا" صديق خالد الذي تعرفنا عليه من قبل. ما هي الأشياء التي يجب أن يفعلها حنا ليستعدّ لعيد الميلاد *Christmas* **في هذه الصور؟ اكتبوا القصة.**

ORGANIZE YOUR قصة INTO PARAGRAPHS AND USE CONNECTORS AND COMPLEX SENTENCES.

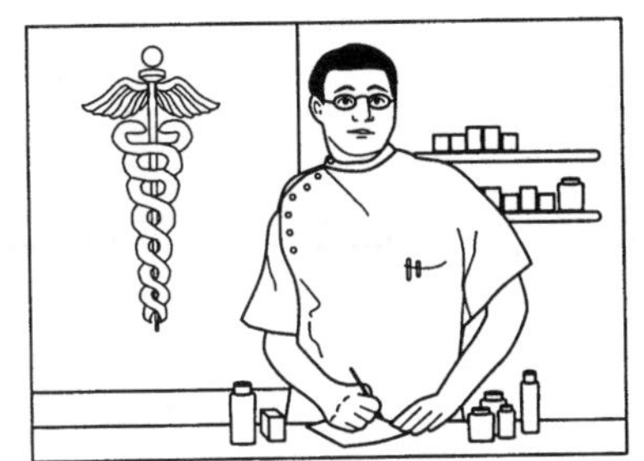

تمارين المراجعة

تمرين ١٧ | الـ + الإعراب

Decide where الـ is needed and write it in, then add إعراب endings to sentences ٥–١ .

١- آه! كم أتذكر ___ أيام ___ شباب وكم أتمنى أن تعود ! كم أتذكر ___ أيام ___ جامعة
و___ أصدقاء و___ ساعات ___ طويلة في ___ كافتيريا و___ تبادل ___ قصص
___ عاطفية .. آه ! ___ أيام جميلة، ذهبت ولن تعود.

٢- بالنسبة لي، ___ طفولة هي ___ أجمل ___ جزء من ___ حياة ___ إنسان
فـ___ أحلام فيها لا تنتهي.

٣- والدتي تستمتع كثيرا برمضان وبطبخ ___ أكلات ___ رمضانية لنا ولكنها لا تحب
___ سحور و___ قيام من ___ نوم في ___ منتصف ___ ليل ولذلك فوالدي هو
الذي يتولّى ___ إعداد ___ سحور لنا.

٤- ___ ربيع هو فصلي ___ مفضل، فـ___ جو فيه لطيف: ___ مطر قليل و___ رطوبة
ليست عالية و___ حرارة تبقى دائما في حدود ٢٧-٢٩ درجة مئوية.

٥- ___ صلاة و___ صوم هما من ___ أشياء الواجبة على كل ___ مسلمين في كل
___ مكان في ___ عالم.

٦- ___ أكل ___ عربي لا يختلف كثيراً عن ___ أكل ___ إيراني ، فـ___ إيرانيون
و___ عرب يحبون ___ لحم و___ أرز و___ خبز.

٧- مشكلة مها أنها تحب ___ بنطلونات أكثر من ___ فساتين ولكن والديها يختلفان
معها في ___ رأي.

٨- ___ موضوع هذا ___ كتاب هو ___ علاقة بين ___ إسلام و___ سياسة و___ شكل
هذه ___ علاقة في ___ بلاد ___ اسلامية اليوم.

٩- ___ موضوع ___ فصحى و___ عامية و___ علاقة بينهما من ___ مواضيع التي
قرأنا عنها في هذا ___ فصل.

تمرين ١٨ — استمعوا الى مها واكتبوا ما تقول DVD

LISTEN TO مـهـا ON DVD AND FILL IN THE BLANKS. WHILE YOU ARE DOING SO, PAY ATTENTION TO THE MEANING AND FUNCTION OF ALL THE PARTICLES, PREPOSITIONS AND PRONOUNS THAT YOU ARE WRITING, ALL OF WHICH ARE ESSENTIAL TO THE TEXT. THINK ABOUT THESE QUESTIONS WHILE YOU WORK: HOW IS THE PUNCTUATION OF THIS TEXT MARKED BY CONNECTORS? WHAT PREPOSITIONS ARE USED? WHAT ROLES DO THE PRONOUNS PLAY IN EACH SENTENCE?

مرّ الوقت ــــ سرعة، سنسافر ــــ أسبوع واحد. أبي يريد ــــ أساعد ــــ ــــ ــــ
اختيار ــــ شراء بعض الهدايا ، ــــ أمي تريد ــــ أساعد ــــ ــــ البيت . ــــ تريد ــــ
مساعدتـ ــــ ــــ بعض ترتيبات السفر. ــــ ــــ الضروري ــــ أقابل أساتذتـ ــــ
ــــ أعرف دروس ــــ أسبوع ــــ سأغيبـ ــــ . سآخذ معي بعض الكتب ــــ مصر
ــــ أكون مستعدّة ــــ اِستئناف الدراسة بعد عودتـ ــــ . ــــ يجب ــــ أشتري بعض
الفساتين ــــ أبي ــــ أمي طلبا ــــ ــــ أشتري بعض الملابس المناسبة ــــ رمضان ــــ
لا أعرف ماذا يقصدان ــــ كلمة «مناسبة»؟! ــــ ــــ البنات ــــ مصر ــــ يلبسن
بنطلونات؟! آه ... ــــ تتوقّف نصائح ابي ــــ أمي ــــ تصرفاتـ ــــ ــــ سلوك
ــــ ــــ القاهرة ــــ ما زلت طفلة !

العامية DVD

- القصة: "يعني ايه كلمة مناسبة؟"

شاهدوا مها تتكلم بالعامية.

كيف تقول «أبي يريد أن أساعده»؟

«من الضروري أن أقابل أساتذتي»؟

«بعض الكتب»؟

Does Maha use feminine plural agreement?

- "اشتريتي ايه؟"

شاهدوا الأم وبنتها تتكلمان بالعامية.

ماذا اشترت البنت؟

ما رأي الأم في الأشياء التي اشترتها بنتها؟

تذكروا هذه الكلمات

رِواية ج. -ات　　كاتِب ج. كُتّاب　　هؤلاء　　اللواتي

٢٠ . يا الله ... ما أحلى القدس !

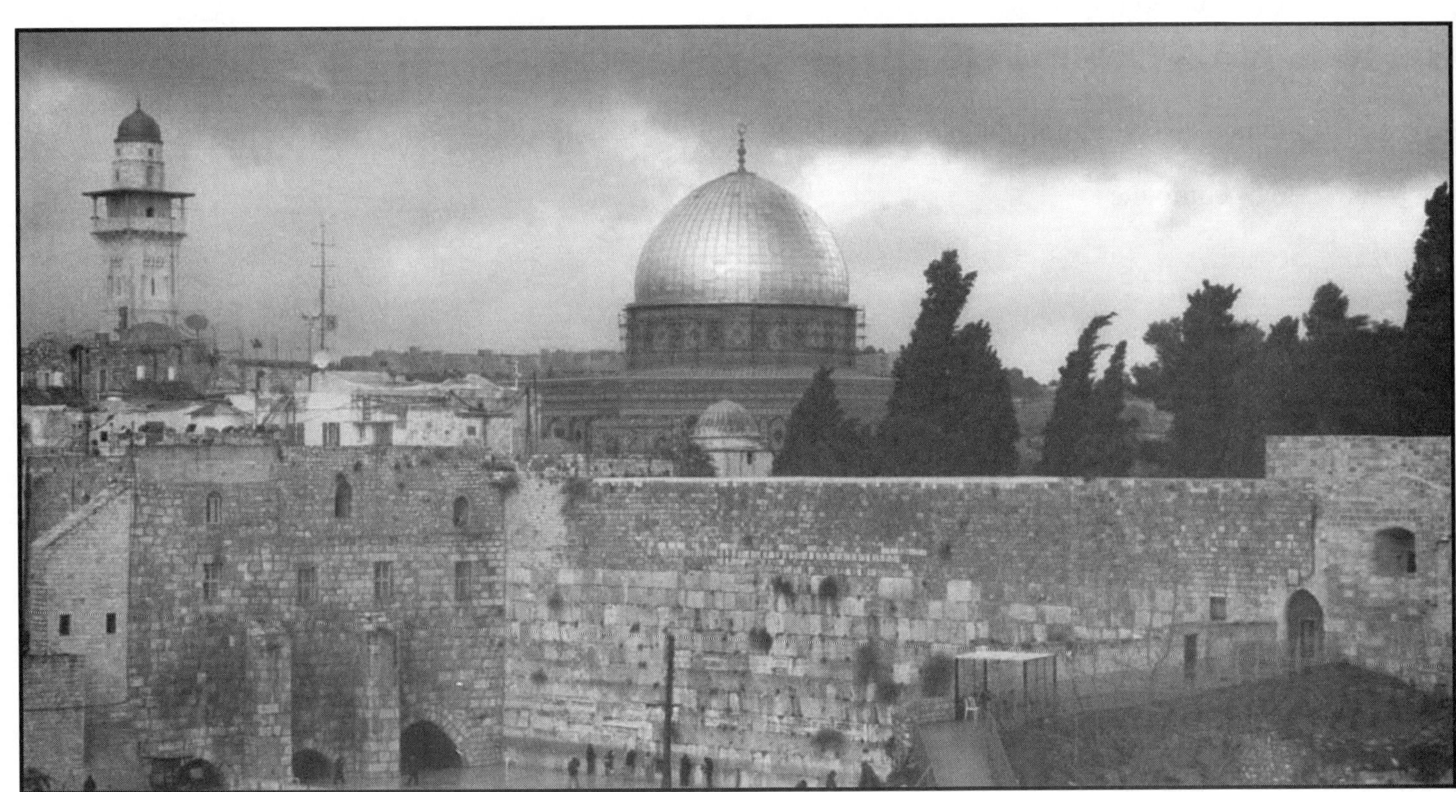

في هذا الدرس:

القصة
- والدة مها ، ملك طاهر درويش

القواعد
- قراءة التواريخ
- المصدر كمبتدأ أو فاعل
- القواعد: ماذا تعلّمنا ؟

القراءة
- كيف تكونت منطقة الشرق الأوسط
- لندن ١٩٣٦ .. وأصدقاء تفرقوا

الاستماع
- مع العائلة والأصدقاء
- حدث في مثل هذا اليوم

العامية
- «قبل ما نتفرق»

المفردات DVD

أُخِذَتْ	it was taken (passive)
أَلْف ج. آلاف	thousand
إنْسان ج. ناس	human being, (plural) people
تَـمَّ ، يَـتِـمّ +المصدر	to be completed
جَرى ، يَجري ، الجَري	to run
جَواز سَفَر ج. جوازات سفر	passport
تَحَدَّثَ عن ، يَـتَـحَـدَّث عن ، التَّحَدُّث /الحَديث عن	= يتكلم عن
ما أَحْلى ... !	how beautiful ... is!
حَمَلَ ، يَحْمِل ، الحَمْل	to carry
الدُّنيا	the world, this world
صَحيح	correct, true
تَـفَرَّقَ ، يَـتَـفَرَّق ، التَـفَـرُّق	to disperse, scatter
القُدس	Jerusalem
نَشَأَ ، يَنشأ ، النَّشأة	to grow up
هاجَرَ ، يُهاجِر ، الهِجرة	to emigrate; migrate
وَطَن ج. أوطان	homeland

تمرين ١ **أوزان الأفعال الجديدة (في الصف)**

USE WHAT YOU HAVE LEARNED ABOUT أوزان الفعل TO COMPLETE THE CHART AND GUESS THE MEANINGS:

ن-ش-ء	ف-ر-ق	ح-م-ل	ح-د-ث	ج-ر-ي	الوزن/الجذر
	-----			to run جرى	I
-----				-----	II
	-----	-----			IV
-----				-----	V

تمرين ٢ **اكتبوا كلمة مناسبة من المفردات الجديدة في كل جملة: (في البيت)**

Practice your إعراب on sentences 1-10.

١- قرأت كتابا جديدا ________ عن التغيّرات الاجتماعية في حياة المرأة العربية.

٢- الحرّية شيء مهم بالنسبة لكل ________ .

٣- شاهدتُ اختي تنزل من الطائرة وهي ________ طفلها الصغير.

٤- صديقتي رياضية جدا تلعب كرة السلة دائما و ________ ميليْن كل صباح .

٥- سمعت أنك توقفت عن التدخين، هل هذا ________ ؟!

٦- هاجر كثير من اللبنانيين والسوريين إلى الولايات المتحدة التي أصبحت ________هم الجديد .

٧- وُلد نجيب محفوظ و________ في منطقة الجمالية في القاهرة .

٨- سنزور عمّان ودمشق إن شاء الله، ومن الممكن أن نزور مدينة ________ إذا سمح لنا الوقت بذلك .

٩- والداي هما أحسن والديْن في ________ .

١٠- كثير من الشباب العرب يرغبون في ________ من بلادهم إلى بلاد الغرب.

١١- كنت أنا وزملائي نقضي معظم أوقاتنا معًا طوال سنوات الدراسة ، ولكننا ________ بعد التخرج .

١٢- إذا أردت الحصول على تأشيرة سفر (فيزا) الى سوريا، فمن اللازم أن ترسل ________ك الى السفارة السورية في واشنطن مع صورتين و ٦٠ دولارا.

١٣- تُرجِمت قصص « ________ ليلة وليلة » إلى لغات عالمية كثيرة .

١٤- الحمد لله ! أخيراً ________ إصلاح الشقة وأصبح من الممكن أن ننتقل إليها.

١٥- يا الله! ما ________ الاجازة بعيداً عن العمل والدراسة والواجبات!!!

تمرين ٣ اسألوا زملاءكم :

1. Where did their ancestors *emigrate* from, and where did they settle?
2. Who *grew up* in a city, and who did not? Who *grew up* in a large family?
3. Who intends to take a trip abroad in the near future?

   Do they have a valid (= صالِح) *passport?*

   How much money do they usually *carry* with them when they travel abroad?
4. Who is always *running* to class because he/she is late?
5. What have they heard or read about the idea of the "Arab nation" (=*homeland*)?
6. Who has had something *taken* from his/her room? What?
7. Who has read or heard stories from *1001* Nights?
8. Who would like to *be spokesperson for* (=*speak* in the name of) the students in this class?

تمرين ٤ (في البيت ثم في الصف)

قبل الصف : THE VERB تَمَّ IS OFTEN USED IN JOURNALISTIC ARABIC TO REPORT THAT AN EVENT *TOOK PLACE/HAS TAKEN PLACE*. IT IS USED IN AN IMPERSONAL CONSTRUCTION WITH المصدر AS ITS SUBJECT:

مثال: تَمَّ اختيارُ مديرٍ جديد للشركة.

YOU ARE WORKING FOR AN AMERICAN COMPANY WITH AN OFFICE IN THE ARAB WORLD. THE NEW DIRECTOR WANTS YOU TO MAKE A SHORT SPEECH TO THE EMPLOYEES IN FORMAL ARABIC OUTLINING WHAT SHE/HE WANTS TO ACCOMPLISH DURING THE COMING YEAR. PREPARE THE SPEECH USING تمّ + المصدر . SOME مصادر YOU MIGHT WANT TO USE:

الاستعداد لـ	الكتابة	التبادل	الإصلاح
الفصل	التعيين	الإعداد	الإرسال
الترتيب	التغيير	الشراء	الاختيار

IMPRESS THE EMPLOYEES WITH YOUR ARABIC BY USING إعراب ENDINGS.

في الصف: اقرأوا ما كتبتم الى زملائكم.

القصة DVD

تمرين ٥ **شاهدوا واكتبوا**

١ـ من يتكلم؟ لماذا لم تتكلم معنا من قبل؟

٢ـ عمَّ تتكلم؟

٣ـ كيف تزوّجت محمد؟

شاهدوا واستمعوا مرة ثانية:

٤ـ ماذا عرفتم عن طفولتها؟

٥ـ ماذا عرفتم عن عائلتها؟ أ ـ

ب ـ

جـ ـ

٦ـ في أي سنة انتقلت اسرة ملك إلى مصر؟ هل تعرفون لماذا؟

٧ـ بِمَ تحلُم ملك؟ أ ـ

ب ـ

استمعوا واكتبوا:

٨ـ اكتبوا الجملة ثم ترجموها الى اللغة الانكليزية:

«صحيح أنّي ______________ مصري و ______________ مصر كثيراً»

= ____

٩ـ اكتبوا ما تقوله ملك عن القدس في آخر جملة:

«ولكن __________ __________ ، __________ __________ __________ !»

القواعد

❁ قراءة التواريخ

date	تاريخ ج. تَواريخ

تعلموا هذه الأرقام: DVD

١٠٠ مِئة (مائة)

٢٠٠ مئتان / مئتيْن

٣٠٠ ثلاثمئة

٤٠٠ أربعمئة

٥٠٠ خمسمئة

٦٠٠ ستّمئة

٧٠٠ سبعمئة

٨٠٠ ثمانِمئة

٩٠٠ تسعمئة

١٠٠٠ ألف

When reading or giving dates (or numbers over 100), note that the order of the numbers is: thousands, followed by hundreds, then ones and finally tens.[1] Remember to say و between each part of the number as in the examples: DVD

١٨٨٣ (عام) ألف وثمانمئة وثلاثة وثمانين

١٩١٤ (عام) ألف وتسعمئة وأربعة عشر

١٩٤٥ (عام) ألف وتسعمئة وخمسة وأربعين

١٩٦٧ (عام) ألف وتسعمئة وسبعة وستّين

٢٠٠٤ (عام) ألفَيْن وأربعة

تمرين ٦ **اقرأوا هذه التواريخ (في الصف)**

١٩٩١	١٩٤٥	١٧٧٦	١٢٥٨
٦٣٢	١٤٩٢	١٨٦٣	١٧٩٨
٢٠٠١	١٩٥٦	١٩١٨	١٩٧٣

ماذا حدث في كل واحدة من هذه السنوات؟

---

[1]This is the modern way of reading numbers. Traditionally, numbers were read right to left as they are written: ones, then tens, then hundreds and finally thousands; however, this style is rarely used now.

❁ المصدر كفاعل أو مبتدأ

You have studied all the basic sentence structures of Arabic, and now it is time to begin focusing on detail and nuance. We will be increasingly concerned with the grammatical choices Arabic provides speakers to express their perspectives. This section on المصدر is not new grammar, but rather is meant to start you thinking about different ways formal Arabic allows you to express infinitive verbs.

You know that المصدر and أنْ + المضارع المنصوب constitute two ways to express an infinitive verb in any given context. You have seen constructions in which المصدر functions as الفاعل *subject* in a جملة فعلية :

١- يمكنني الدراسةُ في المكتبة ساعتين. *Studying in the library for two hours is possible for me.*

٢- يجبُ شراءُ بعض الملايات والفوط. *The buying of some sheets and towels is necessary.*

٣- تَمَّ ترتيبُ كل شيء. *The arranging of everything has taken place.*

The verbs in the first two sentences, يمكن and يجب, are common impersonal verbs in formal Arabic. As you know, these verbs are not conjugated, although يمكن can be personalized with the use of a pronoun object, such as [*for*] *me*. In each sentence, المصدر functions as the subject . In idiomatic English, these constructions are expressed differently, often with impersonal *it*: *it is possible for me to* and *it is necessary to*. But Arabic has no word corresponding to *it*, and needs المصدر to function as the subject of the sentences.

Of course, we can use أنْ + المضارع المنصوب in place of المصدر in these sentences to make them more personal by showing the subject of the action:

١- يمكنني أنْ أدرس في المكتبة ساعتين. *I can study in the library for two hours*

٢- يجب أنْ نشتري بعض الملايات والفوط. *We must buy some sheets and towels*

تمّ + المصدر is another kind of impersonal construction. Example (٣) above shows that this construction is often translated into English using a passive: *everything has been arranged*. The verb تمّ agrees with its المصدر subject: in (٣), تمّ agrees with ترتيب, whereas in (٤) below, تمّت agrees with its subject, المقابلة :

٤- تمّت المقابلةُ بين الرئيسَيْن. *the meeting between the two presidents took place*

The "personalized" alternative to this construction is to use an active voice and an agent:

٣- رتّبت ملك ومها كل شيء. *Malak and Maha arranged everything.*

This choice to use المصدر or أنْ applies to الجمل الاسمية as well. Compare the two alternative sentences in (٥) and (٦), in which the first sentence of each pair shows an impersonal construction and the second a personal one:

٥- من الصعب الكلامُ معهم في أي موضوع سياسي .

من الصعب أن أتكلم /تتكلمي معهم في أي موضوع سياسي .

٦- من الممكن الحصولُ على «فيزا» سياحية لزيارة مصر.

من الممكن أن تحصل/نحصل على «فيزا» سياحية لزيارة مصر.

تمرين ٧ المصدر أو المضارع المنصوب (في البيت)

FOR EACH SENTENCE, DECIDE WHETHER YOU WANT TO EXPRESS THE IDEA PERSONALLY OR IMPERSONALLY AND USE AN APPROPRIATE CONSTRUCTION. ADD TENSE, NEGATION, AND SUBJECT AS YOU WISH. YOU MAY WANT TO USE SOME OF THESE EXPRESSIONS:

من الواجب/يجب	يمكن/من الممكن	من اللازم	من الصعب
من المناسب	من الممتع	من المهمّ	تمّ

مثال: ليس من السهل أن تفَهموا الدرس إذا غِبتم عن الصف. (فهم)

أو: ليس من السهل فَهْم الدرس إذا غبتم عن الصف. (فهم)

١- ____________في الجامعة طوال العطلة بسبب التأخر في الدراسة. (بقي)

٢- ربما ____________عن المحاضرات يوم الاثنين. (تغيَّب)

٣- ____________البيت قبل موعد وصولهم. (رتّب)

٤- أنا مشغول جداً و ____________ إخوتي في المذاكرة. (ساعد)

٥- ____________ رئيس جديد للجامعة. (اختار)

٦- من فضلك، هل ____________ هذه الرسائل معك إلى مكتب البريد؟ (أخذ)

٧- ____________شهر رمضان. (صام)

٨- طفلنا يكبر بسرعة ____________ ملابس جديدة له. (اشترى)

٩- ____________ الهدية بالبريد الجوّي حتى تصل بسرعة. (أرسل)

١٠- ____________العلاقات بين البلدين. (استأنف)

١١- ____________ على الناس في العالم العربي. (تعرّف)

١٢- ____________ إلى مكتب آخر عندما يبدأون في إصلاح بنايتنا. (انتقل)

❁ القواعد : ماذا تعلمنا ؟

!برافو By now you have learned almost all of the basic structures of Arabic. More importantly, you have learned to use these structures to perform the following functions:

— identify yourself and others using الجملة الاسمية , النسبة , المفرد , and الجمع ,
— describe basic physical attributes of humans and non-humans,
— express some feelings,
— obtain information using interrogatives ما , ماذا , من , متى , كيف , لماذا , and أيّ ,
— introduce and specify new entities using الجملة الاسمية and جملة الصفة ,
— describe a specific entity using الاسم + الصفة and الاسم الموصول ,
— refer to entities already known or mentioned using pronouns,
— talk about human, non-human, male, and female groups using appropriate agreement,
— identify and describe a group of two using المثنى ,
— count and state كم ؟ using numbers through 99, and ask about prices using بكم؟ ,
— ascribe association or possession using الإضافة , عند , and لـ ,
— describe spatial relationships using الجملة الاسمية with fronted predicate,
— narrate and describe in the present using المضارع ,
— narrate past events using الماضي ,
— describe past states using the verb كان ,
— relate habitual and continuous activities using verbs like كان and ما زال ,
— talk about the future using سـ , لن , إن شاء الله , أنوي أنْ , أتمنّى أنْ , أريد أنْ ,
— express wishes and hopes using verbs like أريد أن , أرغب في أن , أتمنّى أن ,
— express and report opinions using بالنسبة لـ .. , في رأيـ .. , يظنّ أنّ , and يعتبر ,
— use impersonal constructions such as يمكن , يجب , and من اللازم to express obligations and possibilities,
— make authoritative statements using من الـ ... أنْ ,
— compare and contrast using التفضيل « أفعل » ,
— describe similarity and likeness using مثل , كـ , كما , and كأنّ ,
— give reasons and purposes using بسبب , لـ , لأنّ , and حتى ,
— deny or refute statements and assumptions and answer in the negative using لا , ليس , لم , لن , and ما ,

— report information from another source using sentence complements with أنّ and verbs such as ذكر أنّ , قال إنّ , قرأ أنّ , عرف أنّ ,

— express hypothetical events using إذا ... فـ and لو ... لـ , and

— guess the meaning of new words using context, grammatical clues, الجذر , and a growing awareness of the meanings of أوزان الفعل .

You are learning to:

— read and write narrative prose using Arabic constructions like جملة فعلية , connectors, and parallel structures,

— guess the meaning and pronunciation of new verbs using الجذر والوزن ,

— identify different registers of Arabic and recognize familiar vocabulary in more than one register, and

— read culturally important texts with case endings, and recognize the importance of these endings to meaning and form.

ما شاء الله !

As you continue your study of Arabic, you will:

— expand your knowledge of the verb system, including الأوزان ,

— learn to distinguish between formal and informal situations and to recognize and use language forms appropriate to each,

— learn more details of the case system and sentence structure, and

— expand your vocabulary by reading and listening, both in and outside the classroom.

بالتوفيق إن شاء الله !

تمرين ٨ | نشاط محادثة (في الصف)

YOU ARE STUDYING AT AN ARAB UNIVERSITY, AND A RELATIVE OR FRIEND IS COMING TO VISIT YOU. YOU HAVE A FRIEND HERE WHOSE BROTHER WORKS AT THE AIRPORT AND CAN MEET THE PLANE. GIVE HIM A DETAILED DESCRIPTION OF YOUR VISITOR SO THAT THEY CAN FIND EACH OTHER.

تمرين ٩ أكملوا هذه الجمل

THE FOLLOWING SENTENCES REVIEW MANY OF THE STRUCTURES YOU HAVE STUDIED IN THIS BOOK. FOR EACH, THINK ABOUT WHAT GRAMMATICAL STRUCTURE SHOULD COMPLETE THE THOUGHT, FOR EXAMPLE, IF IT IS AN INDEFINITE NOUN, WHAT KIND OF STRUCTURE DESCRIBES IT? A DEFINITE NOUN? MARK ALL أن AS EITHER أنْ OR أنّ ACCORDING TO WHAT YOU HAVE LEARNED. COMPLETE THE SENTENCES WITH AS COMPLEX A STRUCTURE AS YOU CAN CREATE.

١- لا أفهم كيف ________________ ؟!

٢- مساءَ أمس تذكّرت أن ________________ .

٣- يجب أن أشتري شيئًا ________________ .

٤- اليوم سأعدّ الأكل ________________ .

٥- أين هي الصحيفة ________________ ؟

٦- هل تتمنّين أن ________________ ؟

٧- سيكون من الضروري ________________ .

٨- مَن هم الناس ________________ ؟

٩- يبدو أن ________________ .

١٠- ليس ________________ .

١١- إذا ________________ .

١٢- ما زلتُ ________________ .

١٣- هل طلبتِ من ________________ ؟

١٤- شعرنا كأن ________________ .

١٥- أحسن ________________ .

تمرين ١٠ **اكتبوا الكلمة في شكلها المناسب :**

Put each word in the correct form, and write the case ending on each one:

١ في مجلة «العربي» هذا ______ مقالة ممتعة عن العرب في البرازيل. وقد ذكر

شهر

كاتب المقالة أن معظم ______ ______ تعرف ______ هم ______ من

عربي الذي على برازيلي

أصل عربي جاء آباؤهم و______هم إلى البرازيل قبل ______ طويلة.

جد سنة

وذكر أيضا أنهم لا يتكلمون العربية وأن معظمهم لم ______ أي بلد من ______

زار بلد

العربية ولا يعرفون ______ عن العالم العربي إلا التبولة والحمّص والكبة!

شيء

٢ـ علمت من أختي أن كل ______ في مدرستها ______ ألا ______

طالبة قرر دخل

الصفوف غداً لأن إدارة المدرسة رفضت أن تسمح لـ______ بـ______

(pronoun) اشترك

في مباراة في الكرة الطائرة مع طلاب من ______ «ابن خلدون للبنين». وكان

مدرسة

رأي الإدارة أن هذا ______ ليس ______ .

تصرف مناسب

٣ـ الحمد لله! انتهينا من كل ______ اللازمة لـ______نا إلى الشقة ______

ترتيب انتقل جديد

وبقي فقط أن ______ ______ لغرفة النوم وبعض ______ للحمّام. أما

اشترى ٢ سرير فوطة

بالنسبة لشقتنا القديمة، فوالداي لم ______ حتى الآن ماذا سـ______ بها.

قرّر فعل

الاستماع DVD

تمرين ١١ **مع العائلة والاصدقاء**

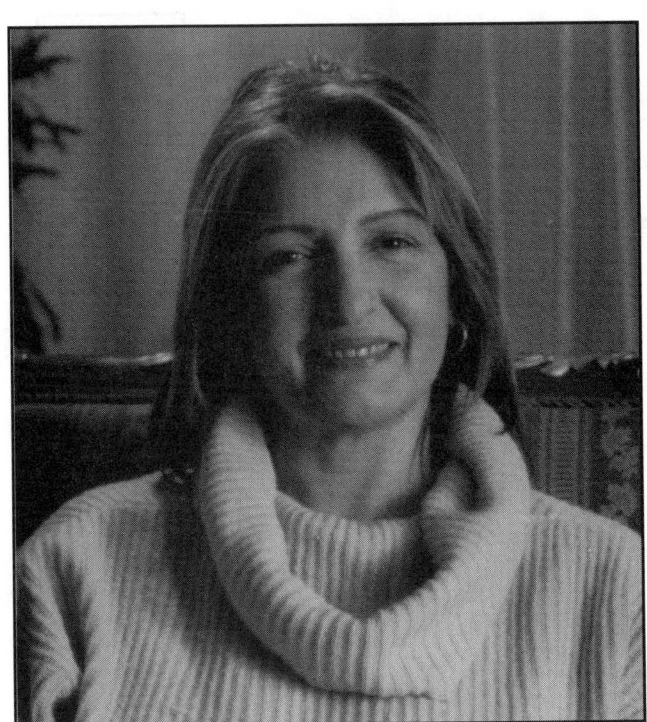

استمعوا أول مرة:

١- ما هي الأشياء الجديدة التي عرفتموها عن ملك من كلامها هنا ولم تعرفوها من قبل؟

أ -

ب -

جـ -

٢- ما هي قصة زواج ملك ومحمد؟

كيف تعرفت ملك على محمد؟ وما كان رأيها فيه؟

٣- ما كان رأي أسرتيْ محمد وملك في زواجهما؟

استمعوا مرة ثانية:

4. Notice that ملك uses verb phrases like كانوا يدرسون and بدأت أكتب to talk about events that took place over a period of time or began in the past. Listen again for more examples of these kinds of verb phrases and write as many as you can:

استمعوا مرة ثالثة: العمل على الاستراتيجيات

5. Listen for و in the text, because it helps you follow the structure of sentences in listening just as it does in reading. You will hear و introducing الجمل الفعلية that constitute the thread of Malak's narrative, and you will also hear it connecting pairs of words and phrases in listing. When Malak describes things, listen for و connecting parallel phrases, and write two examples.

تمرين ١٢　**نشاط قراءة (في الصف)**

للمناقشة قبل القراءة: ماذا تعرفون عن تاريخ الشرق الأوسط؟ قبل بدء الحَرب *war* العالمية الأولى في سنة ١٩١٤، كانت الامبراطورية العُثمانية تحكُم مناطق كبيرة من الشرق الأوسط. ولكن ماذا حدث لهذه المناطق بعد انتهاء الحرب العالمية الأولى في سنة ١٩١٨؟ وكيف تكونت البلاد العربية التي نعرفها اليوم؟ اقرأوا المقالة وأجيبوا عن الأسئلة.

تعلموا هذه الكلمات:

مُحافَظة ج. ـات	province
حَكَمَ ، يَحكُم ، الحُكم	to rule
حُكومة ج. ـات	government
مُستَقِلّ	independent
اِنتِداب	mandate

١ـ أين كانت بريطانيا تحكم في الشرق الأوسط؟ أين كانت فرنسا تحكم؟

٢ـ في أي سنة أصبحت هذه البلاد مستقلّة؟

السعودية ________　سوريا ________　البحرين ________

الأردن ________　الكويت ________　اليمن ________

٣ـ اكتبوا الجذر والوزن وخمنوا المعنى:

أنشأ / أُنشِئَ ________ (فقرة ١)　تَوَحَّدَت (فقرة ٣) ________

4. Find and write the Arabic for:

League of Nations	________	self-rule, autonomy	________
Baath Party	________	holy	________
Sheikhdom	________	to unite	________

كيف تكونت منطقة الشرق الاوسط

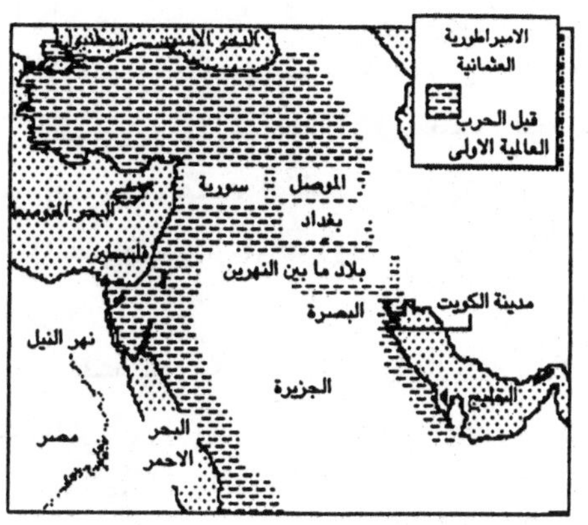

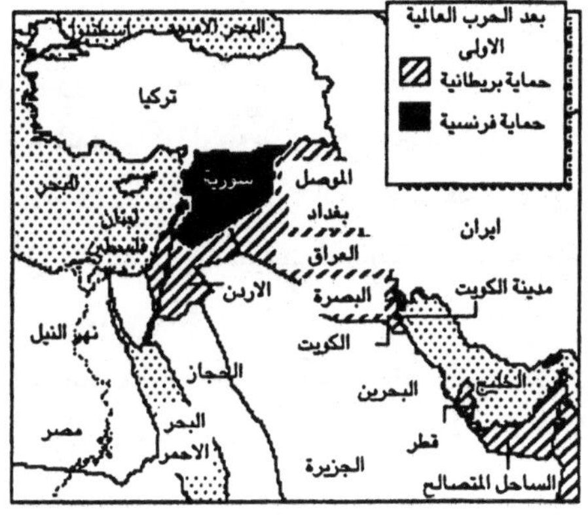

العراق: انشئ في المحافظات العثمانية: بغداد والموصل والبصرة. ووحدت بريطانيا هذه المحافظات بموجب انتداب عصبة الامم عام ١٩٢١ ثم تحولت العراق الى ملكية مستقلة تحت حكم العائلة الهاشمية الموالية لبريطانيا حتى عام ١٩٥٨.

الكويت: كانت مشيخة تتمتع بالحكم الذاتي تحت السيادة العثمانية تحكمها عائلة الصباح. وفي عام ١٨٩٩ طلبت اسرة الصباح الحماية البريطانية وازدادت قوة الحضور البريطاني بعد تفكك الامبراطورية العثمانية مع ان اسرة الصباح بقيت في الحكم. ولم ينسحب البريطانيون حتى عام ١٩٦٢.

سورية: كانت محافظة دمشق العثمانية واحتلها الفرنسيون عام ١٩٢٠ بعد انهيار الامبراطورية العثمانية ومحاولة الاستقلال القصيرة الاجل تحت الاسرة الهاشمية. وحكمتها فرنسا بانتداب من عصبة الامم حتى عام ١٩٤٥. واثر ذلك تلا عهد من الاضطراب والانقلابات ثم توحدت مع مصر الى ان تولى حزب البعث السلطة عام ١٩٦٣.

الاردن: كان جزء من محافظة دمشق العثمانية لكن ضم الى فلسطين تحت انتداب بريطانيا بموجب قرار من عصبة الامم. واستقل عام ١٩٤٦. ويحكمه الآن الملك عبد الله وهو هاشمي.

لبنان: كان يحكمه امراء محليون تحت اشراف عثماني من عام ١٨٦١ حتى عام ١٩١٤. وخضع للانتداب الفرنسي بعد الحرب العالمية الاولى. واصبح لبنان جمهورية برلمانية خلال الحرب العالمية الثانية لكنه وقع في حالة من الفوضى في السبعينات نتيجة الحرب الاهلية.

السعودية: كانت منطقة الحجاز موطن الاماكن الاسلامية المقدسة في مكة المكرمة والمدينة المنورة تحت السيادة العثمانية ثم اصبحت تحت السيطرة السعودية في الدولة الاولى وفي عام ١٩١٦ حكم شرفاء مكة مكة بصفة مستقلة حتى عام ١٩٢٤ عندما اصبحت السيطرة للملك عبد العزيز آل سعود. وكانت الاسرة السعودية تحكم الجزيرة كلها بما فيها الخليج وجنوب العراق. وفي عام ١٩٣٢ اسس عبد العزيز آل سعود المملكة العربية السعودية. ويحكم المملكة الآن ابنه خادم الحرمين الشريفين الملك عبد الله بن عبد العزيز.

البحرين: كانت مشيخة تحت الحماية البريطانية من عام ١٨٢٠ حتى ١٩٧١.

قطر: كانت مشيخة تحت الحماية البريطانية من عام ١٩١٦ حتى ١٩٧١.

الامارات العربية المتحدة: كانت تعرف باسم المشيخات المتصالحة او عمان المتصالحة خلال العهد العثماني حين كانت هذه المشيخات الثماني الصغيرة تحت الحماية البريطانية. ولكن الامارات مستقلة الآن.

اليمن: كان الجزء الشمالي من البلاد تحت السيادة العثمانية حتى عام ١٩١٨ عندما اصبح مستقلا اما الجزء الجنوبي المحيط بعدن فقد احتلته بريطانيا عام ١٩٣٩ ونال استقلاله عام ١٩٦٧ الى ان توحد البلدان اخيرا.

من جريدة الشرق الأوسط ١٩٩٠/٣/١٠ مع تجديد في بعض المعلومات

لندن ١٩٣٦ ... وأصدقاء تفرقوا

نقولا زيادة

قضيت السنوات ١٩٣٥-١٩٣٩ في بريطانيا أطلب العلم في جامعة لندن. في السنة الاولى كان رفيق الدراسة عيسى نخلة (فلسطين) الذي كان يدرس القانون. في سنة ١٩٣٦ انضم إلينا عبد العزيز الدوري وعبد الغني الدلي وعبد الرحمن البزاز (العراق) وفرحات زيادة وموسى عبد الله الحسيني.

كان عبد العزيز الدوري يدرس التاريخ الاقتصادي في دنيا العرب والإسلام. والدلي كان يدرس الاقتصاد والسياسة وعبد الرحمن البزاز انصرف الى القانون كما اتجه فرحات زيادة. موسى الحسيني كان اتجاهه الأدب العربي (وكان قد درس في الأزهر قبلاً). أما انا فكنت أدرس تاريخ اليونان والرومان.

الفترة التي اتحدث عنها (١٩٣٥-١٩٣٩) كانت بالنسبة لعالمنا العربي فترة تتقلب فيها الاحوال على نحو غريب. فلسطين كان وعد بلفور قد تعمقت جذوره فيها. لبنان وسورية كانتا تعانيان مشكلات متنوعة، فيها الكثير من القسوة على أيدي فرنسا. العراق كان يحاول تثبيت اقدامه دولة مستقلة (تحت غطاء بريطاني).

أحسب أن كلامنا كان يدور فرادى وجمعاً حول هذه الصلة بين بلادنا وبريطانيا أولاً (ثم مع فرنسا).

أود اليوم أن أذكر ما آل اليه أمر أولئك الذين ذكرتهم في مطلع المقال اذ اننا تفرقنا كلنا في النهاية عن أوطاننا (إلا موسى عبد الله الحسيني).

كان الأول بيننا الذي بلغ اعلى منصب يمكن ان يصل اليه الذين يحترفون السياسة، هو عبد الرحمن البزاز. بعد ان عاد الى العراق وعمل أستاذاً للقانون آلت اليه عمادة كلية الحقوق في بغداد. واهتمامه المباشر وانغماسه في السياسة حمله الى رئاسة الوزارة. عبد الرحمن اصيب فيما بعد بمرض عضال انتهى به الى الموت (كان الثاني الذي غيبه الموت أما الأول فكان موسى عبد الله الحسيني والثالث عيسى نخلة).

عبد العزيز الدوري انهى دراسة البكالوريوس (١٩٣٩) لكنه تأخر بعض الوقت في العودة، فأتمّ العمل للدكتوراه. ورأيته للمرة الأولى (بعد أيام التلمذة) سنة ١٩٥١ في اسطنبول لمناسبة عقد مؤتمر المستشرقين الدولي. وبعد عمل تعليمي في العراق وعمادة الكلية ترأس جامعة بغداد. وأصابه سيف الغضب الذي أصاب الكثيرين من مثقفي البلاد، فترك العراق وزارنا أستاذاً كريماً في بيروت، ثم استقر في الجامعة الأردنية، وما زال هناك.

عبد الغني الدلي عاد الى بغداد. درّس بعض الوقت لكن السياسة جذبته. عندما زرت العراق للمرة الأولى سنة ١٩٥٦ كان الدلي وزيراً.

علّم الدلي سنة في الجامعة الليبية في بنغازي، ولما آن له ان يعود الى بغداد، عاد الى المجال السياسي وكان سفيراً لبلاده في المغرب. وهو اليوم متقاعد بعد ان استقر في لندن (وقد زارني في بيروت الأسبوع الماضي ما حرك هذه الذكريات).

أنا عدت الى فلسطين وانصرفت الى عملي الأساسي وهو التدريس. كنت مدرساً في الكلية العربية والكلية الرشيدية في القدس. بقيت هناك الى سنة ١٩٤٧، بدأت أبحث عن عمل وكان من حسن حظي انني عثرت عليه في الجامعة الأميركية في بيروت سنة ١٩٤٩. وبقيت في لبنان.

فرحات عاد الى فلسطين. عمل في القضاء بعض الوقت. ثم رحل الى الولايات المتحدة. عمل في جامعة برنستون ثم عهد اليه بادارة (او بانشاء) دراسات الشرق الأدنى في الجامعة الرئيسة في ولاية واشنطن. ولا زال يقيم في الولايات المتحدة.

عيسى نخلة ذهب الى الولايات المتحدة. وهناك عمل في سبيل قضية فلسطين على جبهات كثيرة منها أروقة الأمم المتحدة. وقد توفي قبل زمن قصير.

أما موسى عبد الله الحسيني فلم يغادر لندن قبل الحرب، وبقي هناك بعض الوقت ثم انتقل الى ألمانيا. فضلاً عن عمل سياسي في خصوص فلسطين، فقد حصل على دكتوراه في التاريخ الإسلامي. (وتزوج سيدة ألمانية، وهو الوحيد بيننا الذي تزوج أجنبية). نفي الى سيشل في أحوال لم تتضح لي تماماً، لكنه عاد الى فلسطين وسكن القدس -. وقد التقينا عدداً من المرات في القدس. عندما اتضح انني سأترك عملي في الكلية الرشيدية في القدس سعيت له فعيّن مكاني.

بعد استقراري في بيروت زارني موسى كثيراً، وزرته أنا في عمان.

في سنة ١٩٥١ اغتيل الملك عبد الله ملك المملكة الأردنية الهاشمية. واتهم موسى عبد الله الحسيني بالمؤامرة وحوكم وحكم عليه بالاعدام.

في مساء يوم من أيام شهر آب (اغسطس) سنة ١٩٥١، كنت في زيارة للجزائر وكانت مدينة قسطينة محطتي الأولى في ذلك القطر. مساء ذلك اليوم كنت أجلس في مقهى. تناولت الجريدة لأقرأ فيها خبر اعدام موسى عبد الله الحسيني.

من جريدة الحياة ٢/٦/٢٠٠٤

تمرين ١٣ **نشاط قراءة وكتابة**

اقرأوا المقالة "لندن ١٩٣٦ ... وأصدقاء تفرقوا" واكتبوا:

١- يتحدث الدكتور نقولا زيادة في هذه المقالة عن عدد من أصدقائه.

أ - ما هو الشيء الذي كان هؤلاء الأصدقاء يشتركون فيه؟

ب - ما هي الموضوعات التي كانت تشغلهم؟

٢- في الفِقرة *paragraph* السادسة التي تبدأ بـ «عبد العزيز الدوري»:

عِمادة deanship

خمّنوا المعنى من الوزن والجذر:

أنهى = ____________ أَتَمَّ = ____________ تَـــــرَأَّسَ = ____________

٣- اختاروا ٤ من الأصدقاء واكتبوا فقرة *paragraph* عنهم.

Think of this as an encyclopedia entry of important twentieth-century Arab intellectuals. Include all information you can glean from the article, but phrase it in your own words.

تمرين ١٤	نشاط استماع DVD

استمعوا مرة واكتبوا:

١- ما موضوع هذا البرنامج ؟

2. On the map, circle المناطق والمدن that are mentioned

استمعوا مرة ثانية:

3. Complete:

أي سنة؟	ماذا حدث فيها؟
ديسمبر ١٩٢٥	١- ________________
	٢- ________________ نجد والحجاز
________________	١- أصبح السلطان عبد العزيز ملكاً
	٢- ________________
________________	١- أخذت المملكة العربية السعودية اسمها

٤- كيف قال population ؟ ________ ________ وماذا قال عنه؟ ________________

تمرين ١٥ **استمعوا إلى ملك واكتبوا ما تقول:** DVD

______ ______ كثيرا ______ ______ في ______ ______ .

الحمد لله، ______ ______ كل ______ و ______ ______ إلى ______ .

أنا ملك طاهر درويش، أنا ______ من ______ ، ______ و ______ ______ ،

ثم ______ أسرتي إلى مصر ______ ______ ، و ______ ______ ،

______ ______ إلى أمريكا، ______ توفيق ______ ______ إلى لبنان،

______ ______ ______ إلى امريكا ______ ______ من ______

______ الله يرحمه. بعد ______ ______ الثانوية العامة ______ بجامعة القاهرة،

وهناك ______ ______ محمد و ______ بعد ______ . ______ ______ هي

______ زوجي. ______ أحيانا ______ ______ زوجي ______ طفولته

______ ______ ______ مني. ______ كثيرا بـ ______

التي ______ ______ و ______ فيها، أحلم بـ ______ ______ كل

______ في ______ . ______ ______ أحمل ______ ______

مصري ، و ______ ______ مصر ______ ، ولكن يا الله – ما أحلى ______ !

العامية DVD

– "قبل ما نتفرّق"

شاهدوا ملك ومها تتكلمان بالعامية.

ما هي الصور التي تشاهدها مها ووالدتها هنا؟

كيف تقول ملك «قبل أنْ نتفرّق» بالعامية ؟

تمّ بحمد الله

قاموس عربي-إنجليزي
Arabic-English Glossary

Numbers in italics refer to the chapter in which the word was introduced.
U numbers refer to units in *Alif Baa*.

❄ أ ❄

أب ج. آباء	father ***19***
ابن	*see* ب – ن
اِسْتَأْجَرَ ، يَسْتَأْجِر ، الاِسْتِئجار	to rent ***14***
أَحَد	one of *(m.)* ***18***
لا أحد (مِن)	no one, none (of) ***11***
إحدى	one of *(f.)* ***18***
الأَحَد	Sunday ***6***
أَحَدَ عَشَرَ	eleven ***8***
أَخَذَ ، يَأْخُذ ، الأَخْذ	to take ***12***
أُخِذَ	it was taken *(passive)* ***20***
أَخَّرَ ، يُؤَخِّر ، التَّأخير	to make (someone) late ***18***
تَأَخَّرَ ، يَتَأَخَّر ، التَّأَخُّر	to be late, fall behind ***8***
أخيرًا	finally, at last ***13***
آخَر ج. آخَرون	other *(m.)* ***9***
أُخْرى ج. أُخْرَيات	other *(f.)* ***9***
آخِر ج. آخِرون	last ***12***
مُتَأَخِّر ج. مُتَأَخِّرون	late ***10***
أخ ج. إخْوة	brother ***U-3***
أُخْت ج. أَخَوات	sister ***U-3***

literature **1**	أَدَب ج. اداب
because, since **13**	إذْ
if **8**	إذا
history **2**	التّاريخ
date *(chronological)* **20**	تاريخ ج. تَواريخ
Jordan ***U-9***	الأُرْدُنّ
rice **6**	أُرُزّ
foundation **13**	مُؤَسَّسة ج. مُؤَسَّسات
professor *(m.)* ***U-5***	أُسْتاذ ج. أساتِذة
professor *(f.)* ***U-5***	أُسْتاذة ج. أُسْتاذات
family **2**	أُسْرة ج. أُسَر
Israel ***U-9***	إسرائيل
descent, origin **5**	أَصْل ج. أُصول
of __ descent, origin **5**	مِنْ أَصْل ...
to eat **4**	أَكَلَ ، يَأكُل ، الأَكْل
see أنْ	ألاّ
except **9**	إلاّ
which *(m.)* **15**	الّذي ج. الّذينَ
which *(m., dual)* **18**	اللّذانِ / اللّذَيْنِ
which *(f.)* **15**	الّتي ج. اللّواتي / اللاّتي
which *(f., dual)* **18**	اللّتانِ / اللّتَيْنِ
thousand **20**	أَلْف ج. آلاف ، أُلوف
God *(sometimes used alone as expression of delight)* ***U-6***	اللّه
Thanks be to God ***U-7***	الحَمْدُ لِلّه
May God have mercy on her (=Rest her soul) **7**	اللّه يَرْحَمُها
In the name of God *(said when beginning something)* ***U-6***	بِسْمِ اللّه

God willing ***U-6***	إنْ شاءَ اللّـه
There is no God but God *(said when hearing bad news)* ***U-6***	لا إلهَ إلا اللـه
Whatever God intends *(said when praising someone)* ***U-6***	ما شاءَ اللّـه
to, toward ***U-9***	إلى
mother ***8***	أمّ ج. أُمَّهات
United Nations ***1***	الأُمَم المُتَّحِدة
in front of, before *(spatial)* ***13***	أمامَ
as for... ***9***	أمّا... فَـ...
United Arab Emirates ***U-9***	الإمارات العَرَبيّة المُتَّحِدة
yesterday ***9***	أمْسِ
to *(marks non-finite verb)* ***8***	أنْ + المضارع المنصوب
not to ***13***	ألاّ (أنْ + لا)
that *(introduces sentence complement)* ***13***	أنّ
if ***15***	إن
I ***U-8***	أنا
you *(m.)* ***U-8***	أنْتَ
you *(f.)* ***U-8***	أنْتِ
you *(pl.)* ***2***	أَنْتُم
you *(dual)* ***18***	أَنتُما
you *(f., pl.)* ***19***	أنْتُنّ
feminine ***1***	المُؤَنَّث
English ***1***	إنْجليزي (إنكليزي) ج. إنْجليز (إنكليز)
Miss ***U-4***	آنِسة ج. آنِسات
human being *(pl.= people)* ***20***	إنْسان ج. ناس
people ***11***	ناس
to resume ***19***	اِسْتَأْنَفَ ، يَسْتَأْنِف ، الاِسْتِئْناف

أَوْ	or *9*
أوتوبيس	bus ***U-4***
أوروبا	Europe
أَوَّل ج. أُوَل / أوائِل	first *(m.)* ***4***
أُولى ج. أولَيات	first *(f.)* ***7***
الآن	now ***3***
آية ج. آيات	sign *(from God)* ***16***, verse *(of the Quran)* ***17***
أيْ	i.e. ***16***
أيّ ...؟	which...? ***1***
أيّ / أيّة	any ***15***
إيران	Iran ***U-9***
أيْضاً	also ***2***
أيْنَ ؟	where? ***1***

❄ ب ❄

بِـ	with, by *(things)* ***U-10***
بَحْر ج. بِحار/بُحور	sea ***15***
البَحْرَيْن	Bahrain ***U-9***
بَدَأَ ، يَبْدَأ ، البَدْء	to begin ***9***
اِبْتِدائي	primary ***4***
المُبْتَدَأ	subject of a nominal clause ***2***
تَبادَلَ ، يَتَبادَل ، التَّبادُل	to exchange ***11***
بَدلة ج. بَدَلات	suit ***15***
يَبْدو أنَّ	it appears, seems that *(impersonal)* ***17***
بِدون	*see* د-و-ن
بَرْد	cold *(e.g.: I have a __)*

cold *(e.g.: __ weather)* ***5***	بارِد
cold *(e.g.: I feel __)* ***U-8***	بَرْدان ج. بَرْدانين (عامية)
mail, post ***18***	بَريد
congratulations ***1***	مَبروك
hat ***15***	بُرنَيطة ج. بَرانيط
program ***2***	بَرْنامَج ج. بَرامِج
game, match ***10***	مُباراة ج. مُبارَيات
onions	بَصَل
ticket, card ***18***	بِطاقة ج. بِطاقات
belly, stomach ***18***	بَطن ج. بُطون
after ***8***	بَعْدَ
afternoon ***9***	بَعْدَ الظُّهْر
far, distant (from) ***U-6***	بَعيد (عن)
some of ***9***	بَعْض
to remain ***12***	بَقِيَ ، يَبْقى ، البَقاء
the rest, remainder of ***17***	بَقِيّة
bachelor's degree ***2***	بَكالورْيوس
country ***2***	بَلَد ج. بِلاد/بُلدان
blouse ***15***	بلوزة ج. بلوزات
pullover, sweater ***15***	بلوفر ج. بلوفرات
brown ***18***	بُنّيّ
(a pair of) pants ***15***	بَنْطَلون ج. بَنْطَلونات
purple ***18***	بَنَفْسَجِيّ
son ***3***	اِبْن ج. أَبْناء
cousin *(m., maternal)* ***3***	اِبن خال /ة ج. أَبْناء خال /ة
cousin *(m., paternal)* ***3***	اِبن عَمّ /ة ج. أَبْناء عَمّ /ة

daughter, girl ***U-7***	بِنْت ج. بَنات
cousin *(f., maternal)* ***3***	بِنْت خال /ة ج. بَنات خال /ة
cousin *(f., paternal)* ***3***	بِنْت عَمّ /ة ج. بَنات عَمّ /ة
building ***U-7***	بِنايَة ج. بِنايات
door ***U-1***	باب ج. أَبْواب
house ***U-2***	بَيْت ج. بُيوت
pajamas ***15***	بيجاما ج. بيجامات
white *(m.)* ***18***	أَبْيَض ج. بيض
white *(f.)* ***18***	بَيْضاء ج. بيضاوات
between ***11***	بَيْنَ

❄ ت ❄

commerce, trade ***6***	التِّجارة
below ***14***	تَحْت
museum	مَتْحَف ج. مَتاحِف
translation ***2***	تَرْجَمة
translator ***2***	مُتَرْجِم ج. مُتَرْجِمون
to leave *(something)* ***14***	تَرَكَ ، يَتْرُك ، التَّرْك
Turkey ***U-9***	تُركِيّا
nine ***U-7***	تِسْعة
ninety ***8***	تِسْعون / تِسْعين
tired ***U-8***	تَعْبان ج. تَعْبانين (عامية)
that *(demonstrative pronoun) (f.)* ***6***	تِلْكَ (مذكّر: ذلِك)
to be completed *(subject expressed by maSdar)* ***20***	تَمَّ ، يَتِمّ + **المصدر**
skirt ***15***	تَنّورة ج. تَنانير
Tunisia or the city of Tunis ***U-9***	تونِس

* ث *

culture *1* — الثّقافة

one third *9* — ثُلثْ

three ***U-7*** — ثَلاثة

third *9* — ثالِث

thirty *8* — ثَلاثون / ثَلاثين

Tuesday *6* — الثُّلاثاء

snow, ice *5* — ثَلْج

then *9* — ثُمَّ

eight ***U-7*** — ثَمانِية

eighty *8* — ثَمانون / ثَمانين

two ***U-7*** — اِثْنان / اِثْنَيْن

Monday *6* — الإثْنَيْن

second *4* — ثانٍ / الثّاني

secondary *7* — ثانَويّة

Baccalaureate *7* — الثّانَوِيّة العامّة

the dual *7, 18* — المُثَنّى

garlic — ثوم

* ج *

jacket *15* — جاكيت ج. جاكيتات

grandfather *3* — جَدّ ج. جُدود / أجداد

grandmother *3* — جَدّة ج. جَدّات

very *5* — جِدّاً

new ***U-3*** — جَديد ج. جُدُد

جَذر ج. جُذور	root *8*
المَجْرور	genitive case *(nouns)* ***16***
تَجْرِبة ج. تَجارِب	experience *(life __)* ***11***
جَريدة ج. جَرائِد	newspaper ***9***
جَرَى ، يَجْري ، الجَري	to run; go running ***7***
جُزْء ج. أَجْزاء	part of ***18***
جَزيرة ج. جُزُر	island ***15***
الجَزائِر	Algeria ***U-9***
المَجزوم	jussive mood *(verbs)* ***13***
جِسم ج. أجسام	body ***18***
مَجَلّة ج. مَجَلاّت	magazine, journal ***13***
جَلاّبيّة	traditional gown-like garment worn by both men and women ***15***
جَلَسَ ، يَجْلِس ، الجُلوس	to sit ***9***
جَلْسة ج. جَلْسات	gathering ***10***
اِجْتَمَعَ بِـ/ مع ، يَجْتَمِع ، الاِجْتِماع	to convene, gather ***17***
الجَمع	plural ***2***
الجُمْعة	Friday ***6***
جَميعًا	together *(i.e.: altogether, all of them)* ***12***
اِجْتِماع ج. اِجْتِماعات	meeting ***19***
جامِع ج. جَوامِع	mosque ***10***
جامِعة ج. جامِعات	university ***U-5***
مَجْموعة ج. مَجْموعات	group ***15***
جُمْلة ج. جُمَل	sentence ***1***
جَميل	beautiful ***U-7***
جَنوب	south ***15***
بِجانِب	next to ***14***

foreign, foreigner ***13***	أَجْنَبيّ ج. أجانِب
weather ***5***	جَوّ ج. أَجْواء
to answer	أجابَ عن ، يجيب ، الإجابة
answer	جَواب ج. أجوِبة
good ***U-4***	جَيِّد ج. جَيِّدون / جِياد
well *(adverb)* ***5***	جَيِّداً
neighbor ***U-3***	جار ج. جيران
passport ***20***	جَواز سَفَر ج. جَوازات سَفَر
vacation, leave *(of absence)* ***12***	إجازة ج. إجازات
hungry ***U-8***	جَوْعان ج. جَوْعانين (عامية)
to come ***10***	جاءَ (إلى) ، يَجيء ، المَجيء
skirt ***15***	جيب ج. جيبات
army ***3***	جَيْش ج. جُيوش

❄ ح ❄

to love ***5***	أَحَبّ ، يُحِبّ ، الحُبّ
darling, dear *(m.)* ***U-2***	حَبيب ج. أحِبّاء
so as to ***19***	**حَتّى + المضارع المنصوب**
until *(preposition)* ***17***	حتّى
the main pilgrimage to Mecca ***7***	الحَجّ
pilgrim *(spec.: one who has done the main pilgrimage to Mecca)* ***7***	الحاجّ
to determine, set *(e.g.: __ a curfew)* ***15***	حَدَّدَ ، يُحَدِّد ، التَّحْديد
to happen ***14***	حَدَثَ ، يَحْدُث ، الحُدوث
to talk, speak about ***20***	تَحَدَّثَ عَن ، يَتَحَدَّث ، التَحَدُّث
accident ***7***	حادِث ج. حَوادِث
Hadith *(sayings and deeds of the Prophet)* ***17***	حَديث ج. أحاديث

مُحادَثة	conversation ***1***
حَديقة ج. حَدائِق	garden, park ***14***
حِذاء ج. أَحْذِيـة	*(pair of)* shoes ***15***
حارّ	hot *(e.g.: __ weather)* ***5***
حَرّان ج. حَرّانين (عاميـة)	hot *(e.g.: I feel __)* ***U-8***
حُرِّيّة ج. حُرِّيّات	freedom ***15***
حَرَم	wife ***7***
حَرام	shame *(on you; lit.: not legal)* ***12***
أَحْسَن...	the best... ***5***
حَصَلَ على ، يَحْصُل ، الحُصول	to get, obtain ***6***
حَضَرَ إلى ، يَحْضُر ، الحُضور	to come to, attend ***13***
حَضْرَتَك	you *(formal, m.)* ***U-4***
حَضْرَتِك	you *(formal, f.)* ***U-4***
مُحاضَرة ج. مُحاضَرات	lecture ***6***
حَفِظَ ، يَحْفَظ ، الحِفْظ	to memorize ***4***
مُحافَظة ج. مُحافَظات	province ***20***
حَقَّقَ ، يُحَقِّق ، التَّحقيق	to realize, achieve ***18***
الحُقوق	law ***3***
في الحَقيقة	actually ***3***
حَقيقِيّ	real, actual ***18***
حَكَمَ ، يَحكُم ، الحُكم	to rule ***20***
حُكومة ج. حُكومات	government ***20***
مَحَلّ ج. مَحَلّات	place ***18***
حَليب / لَبَن	milk ***U-6***
حَلَمَ بِـ ، يَحْلُم ، الحُلم	to dream of ***20***
حُلْم ج. أَحْلام	dream ***18***

how beautiful is...! ***20***	ما أَحْلى...!
bathroom ***10***	حَمّام ج. حَمّامات
swimming pool ***14***	حَمّام سِباحة
red ***18***	أَحْمَر (مؤنّث: حَمْراء)
carry ***20***	حَمَلَ ، يَحْمِل ، الحَمْل
lawyer ***13***	مُحامٍ / المُحامي ج. مُحامون
to need, be in need of ***13***	اِحْتاجَ إلى ، يَحْتاج ، الاِحْتِياج
in need of ***8***	بِحاجة إلى
approximately, about ***9***	حَوالَيْ
life ***12***	الحَياة
where *(not a question; also, "in which")* **2**	حَيْثُ
sometimes ***5***	أَحْيانًا

❄ خ ❄

news ***U-3***	خَبَر ج. أَخْبار
predicate of a nominal sentence **2**	خَبَر
experience *(work __)* ***14***	خِبْرة ج. خِبْرات
bread ***U-3***	خُبْز
pita bread ***U-3***	خُبز عَرَبيّ
shyness, abashment ***11***	الخَجَل
shy, abashed ***7***	خَجول
to go out ***9***	خَرَجَ ، يَخْرُج ، الخُروج
to graduate ***6***	تَخَرَّجَ ، يَتَخَرَّج ، التَخَرُّج
outside *(preposition)* ***11***	خارِج
autumn, fall ***5***	الخَريف
special; (its) own, private ***9***	خاصّ

specializing, specialist in **2**	مُتَخَصِّص في ج. مُتَخَصِّصون
green ***18***	أخضَر (مؤنث: خَضراء)
vegetables ***6***	خُضار
she got engaged to ***11***	خُطِبَتْ لِـ
the (Arabian/Persian) Gulf ***14***	الخَليج
to differ from ***17***	اِخْتَلَفَ عَن ، يَخْتَلِف ، الاِخْتِلاف
behind, beyond ***5***	خَلْف
caliph, successor *(note: m.)* ***4***	خَليفة ج. خُلَفاء
different *(from)* ***18***	مُخْتَلِف (عن)
morals ***18***	أخْلاق
five ***U-7***	خَمْسة
fifty ***8***	خَمْسون / خَمْسين
Thursday ***6***	الخَميس
to guess ***1***	خَمَّنَ ، يُخَمِّن ، التَّخمين
scared	خائِف ج. خائِفون
uncle *(maternal)* **2**	خال ج. أخْوال
aunt *(maternal)* **2**	خالة ج. خالات
to choose ***19***	اِخْتارَ ، يَخْتار ، الاِخْتِيار
well, fine *(said of people)* ***17***	بِخَيْر

✻ د ✻

chicken *(collective)* ***U-3***	دَجاج
to enter ***8***	دَخَلَ ، يَدْخُل ، الدُّخول
to smoke ***9***	دَخَّنَ ، يُدَخِّن ، التَّدْخين
degree *(e.g.: of temperature)* ***5***	دَرَجة ج. دَرَجات
to study ***1***	دَرَسَ / يَدْرُس ، الدِراسة

to teach *3*	دَرَّسَ ، يُدَرِّس ، التَّدْريس
lesson ***U-4***	دَرْس ج. دُروس
study (*pf*) studies *3*	دِراسة ج. دِراسات
school *4*	مَدْرَسة ج. مَدارِس
copybook, notebook ***U-6***	دَفْتَر ج. دَفاتِر
minute *9*	دَقيقة ج. دَقائِق
doctor (*m.*) ***U-4***	دُكتور ج. دَكاتِرة
doctor (*f.*) ***U-4***	دُكتورة ج. دُكتورات
Ph.D. *2*	الدُّكْتوراه
blood *18*	دَم
the world *20*	الدُّنْيا
Casablanca *18*	الدّار البَيْضاء
business administration *6*	إدارة الأعْمال
director *12*	مُدير ج. مُديرون / مُدَراء
always *2*	دائِمًا
without *13*	بِدون
religion *3*	دين ج. أدْيان

❄ ذ ❄

that (*demonstrative pronoun*) (*m.*) *6*	ذٰلِك (مؤنّث: تِلْكَ)
also, likewise *13*	كَذٰلِك
so, thus *6*	لِذٰلِك
to recall; mention *14*	ذَكَرَ ، يَذْكُر ، الذِّكْر
to study (*i.e.: review lessons, do homework*) *8*	ذاكَرَ ، يُذاكِر ، المُذاكَرة
to remember *1*	تَذَكَّرَ ، يَتَذَكَّر ، التَّذَكُّر
masculine *1*	المُذَكَّر

smart, intelligent ***18***	ذَكِيّ ج. أذْكِياء
to go ***6***	ذَهَبَ ، يَذْهَب ، الذَهاب
gold ***18***	ذَهَبيّ

❄ ر ❄

head ***18***	رَأس ج. رؤوس
president ***12***	رَئيس ج. رُؤَساء
to see ***13***	رأى / يَرى ، الرُّؤْية
opinion ***8***	رَأْي ج. آراء
God, Lord ***15***	الرَبّ
perhaps ***18***	رُبَّما
one quarter ***9***	رُبْع ج. أرْباع
four ***U-7***	أرْبَعة
forty ***8***	أرْبَعون / أرْبَعين
Wednesday ***6***	الأرْبِعاء
fourth ***4***	رابِع
spring *(season)* ***5***	الرَّبيع
to arrange, prepare ***16***	رَتَّبَ ، يُرَتِّب ، التَّرْتيب
to return ***13***	رَجَعَ / يَرْجِع ، الرُّجوع
man ***U-7***	رَجُل ج. رِجال
foot ***18***	رِجل ج. أرجُل
to hope *(that)*; please... ***16***	رَجا ، يَرجو ، الرَّجاء
to welcome ***18***	رَحَّبَ بِـ ، يُرَحِّب ، التَّرْحيب
deceased ***7***	مَرْحوم ج. مَرْحومون
cheap, inexpensive ***16***	رَخيص
to correspond, exchange letters ***8***	راسَلَ ، يُراسِل ، المُراسَلة

to send *13*	أَرْسَلَ ، يُرْسِل ، الإرْسال
letter *3*	رِسالة ج. رَسائِل
to draw *7*	رَسَمَ ، يَرْسُم ، الرَّسْم
humidity *5*	رُطوبة
to want to, have a desire to *13*	رَغِبَ في ، يَرْغَب ، الرَغْبة
to refuse *8*	رَفَضَ ، يَرْفُض ، الرَّفْض
indicative mood *(verbs)* ***11***; nominative case *(nouns)* ***16***	المَرفوع
dance, dancing *7*	الرَّقْص
number *U-7*	رَقْم ج. أَرْقام
center	مَرْكَز ج. مراكِز
grey *18*	رَمادِيّ
Ramadan *(month in Islamic calendar in which Muslims fast)* ***16***	رَمَضان
comfort, ease *14*	راحة
to want to *8*	أرادَ أنْ ، يُريد ، الإرادة
sports *7*	الرِّياضة
novel *19*	رِوايَة ج. رِوايات

❄ ز ❄

(over) crowdedness *5*	اِزْدِحام
blue *18*	أَزْرَق (مؤنّث : زَرْقاء)
upset; annoyed, angry *U-8*	زَعْلان ج. زَعْلانين (عامية)
skiing *7*	التَزَلُّج
classmate; colleague *(m.)* ***4***	زَميل ج. زُمَلاء
classmate; colleague *(f.)* ***4***	زَميلة ج. زَميلات
pink *18*	زَهريّ
husband *3*	زَوْج ج. أَزْواج

wife *3*	زَوْجة ج. زَوْجات
oil	زَيْت ج. زُيوت
to increase, exceed ***17***	زادَ (عن)، يَزيد ، الزِّيادة
to visit ***12***	زارَ ، يَزور ، الزِّيارة
still, continue to (*lit.*: do not cease) ***13***	ما زالَ ، لا يَزال + **المضارع المرفوع / اسم**

❄ س ❄

(future marker) ***12***	س / سَوْف + **المضارع المرفوع**
question ***U-9***	سُؤال ج. أَسْئِلة
because of, on account of ***5***	بِسَبَب + **اسم في إضافة**
Saturday ***6***	السَّبْت
swimming ***7***	السِّباحة
swimming pool ***14***	حَمّام سِباحة
week ***6***	أُسْبوع ج. أسابيع
seven ***U-7***	سَبْعة
seventy ***8***	سَبْعون / سَبْعين
six ***U-7***	سِتّة
sixty ***8***	سِتّون/ سِتّين
mosque	مَسْجِد ج. مساجِد
meal eaten before dawn during Ramadan ***17***	السُّحور
theater ***13***	مَسْرَح ج. مَسارِح
bed ***11***	سَرير ج. أَسِرّة
quickly ***10***	بِسُرعة
Saudi Arabia ***U-9***	السَّعوديّة
to help ***8***	ساعَدَ ، يُساعِد ، المُساعَدة
happy ***U-5***	سَعيد ج. سُعَداء

to travel ***4***	سافَرَ (إلى) ، يُسافِر ، السَّفَر
ambassador ***11***	سَفير ج. سُفراء
sugar ***U-6***	سُكَّر
to live, reside ***1***	سَكَنَ ، يَسْكُن ، السَّكَن
inhabitant	ساكِن ج. سُكّان
series, serial ***17***	مُسَلْسَل ج. مُسَلْسَلات
salad ***6***	سَلَطة ج. سَلَطات
behavior, manners, way of acting ***19***	سُلوك
my best to ... ***16***	سَلامي لِـ ..
Get well soon! I hope you feel better! ***U-8***	سَلامتَك ! (عامية)
name, noun ***1***	اِسْم ج. أسْماء
to permit *(someone)* to do *(something)* ***15***	سَمَحَ لِـ بِـ ، يَسْمَح ، السَّماح
to listen to ***4***	اِستَمَعَ إلى ، يَستَمِع ، الاِستِماع
dark-complexioned ***18***	أسْمَر (المؤنّث: سَمْراء) ج. سُمْر
fish *(collective)* ***6***	سَمَك
year ***2***	سَنة ج. سَنَوات
to stay up late ***10***	سَهِرَ ، يَسْهَر ، السَّهَر
easy ***12***	سَهل
black *(m.)* ***18***	أسْوَد ج. سود
black *(f.)* ***18***	سَوْداء ج. سَوْداوات
Sudan ***U-9***	السّودان
chapter *(of the Quran)* ***17***	سورة ج. سُوَر
Syria ***U-9***	سوريّا
tourism ***11***	السِّياحة
hour; o'clock; clock ***U-5***	ساعة ج. ساعات
market	سوق ج. أسواق

driver ***13***	سائِق ج. سائِقون
Mr., Sir ***U-5***	سَيِّد ج. سادة
Lady; Mrs. ***15***	سَيِّدة ج. سَيِّدات
car ***U-5***	سَيّارة ج. سَيّارات
cinema ***8***	السّينما

❄ ش ❄

tea ***U-4***	شاي
young man ***18***	شابّ ج. شَباب ، شُبّان
young woman ***U-4***	شابّة ج. شابّات
youth *(abstract or collective)* ***U-4***	شَباب
window ***U-6***	شُبّاك ج. شَبابيك
winter ***5***	الشِّتاء
to encourage (to), cheer (on) ***13***	شَجَّع (على) ، يُشَجِّع ، التَّشْجيع
person ***15***	شَخْص ج. أشْخاص
to drink ***4***	شَرِبَ ، يَشْرَب ، الشُّرْب
soup ***6***	شوربة
Islamic law ***17***	الشَّريعة
street ***U-5***	شارِع ج. شَوارِع
to supervise ***17***	أشْرَفَ على ، يُشْرِف ، الإشْراف
east ***15***	شَرْق
Near East ***2***	الشَّرق الأدْنى
Middle East ***2***	الشَّرْق الأوْسَط
to have in common ***15***	اِشْتَرَكَ في ، يَشْتَرِك ، الاِشْتِراك
company ***7***	شَرِكة ج. شَرِكات
to buy ***16***	اِشْتَرى ، يَشْتَري ، الشِّراء

chess *9*	الشَّطَرَنْج
to feel *(i.e.: an emotion)* *5*	شَعَرَ بِـ ، يَشْعُر ، الشُّعور
hair *18*	شَعْر
work *2*	شُغْل
to be, become occupied with *17*	اِنْشَغَلَ بِـ ، يَنْشَغِل ، الاِنْشِغال
to preoccupy *18*	شَغَلَ ، يَشْغُل ، الشُّغْل
busy with *2*	مَشْغول بِـ ج. مَشْغولون
too busy for *15*	مَشْغول عَن ج. مَشْغولون
apartment *14*	شَقّة ج. شِقَق
blond, fair-skinned *18*	أشْقَر (مؤنّث: شَقْراء) ج. شُقْر
thank you *U-10*	شُكْرًا
form, shape *18*	شَكْل ج. أشْكال
problem *12*	مُشْكِلة ج. مَشاكِل / مُشْكِلات
sun *5*	شَمس
sunny *5*	مُشْمِس
north *15*	شَمال
to watch *4*	شاهَدَ ، يُشاهِد ، المُشاهَدة
degree, diploma *12*	شَهادة ج. شَهادات
month *16*	شَهْر ج. أشهُر / شُهور
famous *16*	مَشْهور ج. مَشْهورون
thing *15*	شَيء ج. أشْياء
grey/white-haired *18*	أشْيَب

to become *10*	أصْبَحَ ، يُصْبِح
morning *U-4*	صَباح

صِحّة	health ***11***
صَحيح	true, correct ***20***
صاحِب ج. أصْحاب	friend *(m.)*, boyfriend ***U-5***
صاحِبة ج. صاحِبات	friend *(f.)*, girlfriend ***U-5***
الصَّحابة	a Companion of the Prophet ***17***
صَحيفة ج. صُحُف	newspaper ***17***
صَحا ، يَصْحو ، الصَّحْو	to wake up ***10***
أصدَرَ ، يُصدِر ، الإصدار	to publish
المَصْدَر	verbal noun ***17***
صَديق ج. أصْدِقاء	friend *(m.)* ***4***
صَديقة ج. صَديقات	friend *(f.)* ***4***
صَداقة ج. صَداقات	friendship ***18***
تَصَرُّف ج. تَصَرُّفات	action *(i.e.: way of acting)*, behavior ***19***
صَعْب	hard, difficult ***U-5***
صَغير ج. صِغار	small ***U-6***
صَفّ ج. صُفوف	class, classroom ***U-6***
صِفة	see under وصف
صَفْحة ج. صَفَحات	page ***U-6***
أصْفَر (مؤنّث: صَفْراء)	yellow ***18***
أصْلَحَ ، يُصْلِح ، الإصْلاح	to repair ***16***
أصْلَعْ	bald ***18***
صَلاة ج. صَلَوات	prayer ***10***
صورة ج. صُوَر	picture ***3***
التَّصْوير	photography ***7***
صامَ ، يَصُوم ، الصَّوْم / الصِّيام	to fast, abstain ***17***
الصَّيْدَلة	pharmacology ***11***

pharmacy ***15***	صَيْدَلِيّة ج. صَيْدَلِيّات
summer ***5***	الصَّيْف
China	الصّين

❄ ض ❄

officer ***3***	ضابِط ج. ضُبّاط
necessary ***19***	ضَروريّ
present/incomplete tense ***4***	المُضارِع
weak ***8***	ضَعيف ج. ضُعَفاء / ضِعاف
pronoun ***2***	ضَمير ج. ضَمائر
iDaafa , possessive construction ***3***	الإضافة
in addition to ***12***	بِالإضافة إلى

❄ ط ❄

medicine ***3***	الطِّبّ
to cook ***17***	طَبَخَ ، يَطْبُخ ، الطَّبْخ
kitchen ***14***	مَطْبَخ ج. مَطابِخ
of course, naturally ***12***	طَبْعًا
floor, story ***14***	طابِق ج. طَوابِق
restaurant ***6***	مَطْعَم ج. مَطاعِم
child ***19***	طِفل ج. أطفال
childhood ***4***	طُفولة
weather ***5***	طَقْس
to ask ***19***	طَلَبَ ، يَطْلُب ، الطَّلَب
student *(m.)* ***U-6***	طالِب ج. طُلاّب
student *(f.)* ***U-6***	طالِبة ج. طالِبات

to be able to *9*	اِسْتَطاع ، يَسْتَطيع ، الاِسْتِطاعة
long, tall ***U-6***	طَويل ج. طِوال
during, throughout *8*	طِوال
table ***U-6***	طاوِلة ج. طاوِلات
delicious *(food)*; good-hearted *(people)* ***U-5***	طَيِّب ج. طَيِّبون
airport	مَطار ج. مَطارات
airplane ***U-9***	طائِرة ج. طائِرات

❄ ظ ❄

to think that, consider *13*	ظَنَّ أنَّ ، يَظُنّ ، الظَنّ
afternoon *9*	بَعْدَ الظُّهْر

❄ ع ❄

wool cloak, wrap *15*	عَباءة ج. عَباءات
to consider *18*	اِعْتَبَرَ ، يَعْتَبِر ، الاِعْتِبار
expression, idiom *18*	عِبارة ج. عِبارات
astonishing, strange ***U-5***	عَجيب ج. عَجيبون
to prepare, make *14*	أعَدَّ ، يُعِدّ ، الإعْداد
to prepare for *16*	اِسْتَعَدَّ لِـ ، يَسْتَعِدّ ، الاِسْتِعْداد
several *11*	عِدّة + جمع indefinite
number *8*	عَدَد ج. أعْداد
preparatory (__ *school = junior high)* *7*	إعْداديّ
prepared, ready *19*	مُسْتَعِدّ ج. مُستَعِدّون
Arab, Arabic *(m.)* ***U-5***	عَرَبيّ ج. عَرَب
the Arabic case system *16*	الإعراب
to know *3*	عَرَفَ ، يَعْرِف ، المَعْرِفة

to get to know ***11***	تَعَرَّفَ عَلى ، يَتَعَرَّف ، التَعَرُّف
getting to know one other ***2***	تَعارُف
Iraq ***U-9***	العِراق
dear ***15***	عَزيز ج. أعِزّاء
ten ***U-7***	عَشَرة
twenty ***8***	عِشْرون / عِشْرين
dinner ***6***	عَشاء
capital *(city)* ***5***	عاصِمة ج. عَواصِم
thirsty ***U-8***	عَطْشان ج. عَطْشانين (عامية)
emotional, romantic ***11***	عاطِفيّ
vacation ***12***	عُطْلة ج. عُطْلات / عُطَل
most of ***11***	مُعْظَم
you're welcome ***U-10***	عَفْوًا
relationship *(pl.: relations)* ***11***	عَلاقة ج. عَلاقات
to learn of, find out about ***12***	عَلِمَ بِـ ، يَعْلَم ، العِلْم
to teach ***16***	عَلَّمَ ، يُعَلِّم ، التَّعليم
to learn *(e.g.: __ a language, a new word)* ***1***	تَعَلَّمَ ، يَتَعَلَّم ، التَعَلُّم
science ***3***	عِلْم ج. عُلوم
anthropology ***3***	عِلْم الإنْسان
sociology ***3***	عِلم الاِجتِماع
psychology ***3***	عِلم النَّفس
political science ***3***	العُلوم السِّياسِيّة
the world ***9***	العالَم
on, on top of ***U-9***	عَلى
high *(m.)* ***5***	عالٍ / العالي
high *(f.)* ***5***	عالِية

عَمّ ج. أعْمام	uncle *(paternal)* ***3***
عَمّة ج. عَمّات	aunt *(paternal)* ***3***
عامّ	general, public ***7***
العامِّيّة	colloquial or spoken Arabic ***15***
عُمْر ج. أعمار	age ***2***
عَمِلَ ، يَعْمَل ، العَمَل	to work ***1***
عامِل ج. عُمّال	worker ***13***
عُملة ج. عُملات	currency ***7***
عُمان	Oman ***U-9***
أعْمى (مؤنّث: عَمْياء)	blind ***18***
عَنْ	on, about ***7***
عَمَّ (عَنْ+ماذا) ...؟	on, about what... ? ***7***
عَمَّن (عَنْ+مَن) ...؟	about whom... ? ***8***
عِنْد	have *(lit.:* at; see عندي) ***7***
عِنْدي	I have (*lit.*: at me) ***U-9***
عِنْدَما + فعل	when *(not a question; e.g.: __ I was young)* ***11***
عُنْوان ج. عَناوين	address ***1***
يَعْني	it means ***13***
مَعْنى	meaning ***8***
عادَ ، يَعود ، العَوْدة	to return ***9***
اِعْتادَ أنْ ، يَعْتاد ، الاِعْتِياد	to get used to ***17***
عادةً	usually ***10***
عيد ج. أعياد	holiday, day of celebration ***16***
عيد الميلاد	Christmas ***16***
مُعيد ج. مُعيدون	graduate fellow, teaching assistant ***6***
عائِلة ج. عائِلات	*(extended)* family ***3***

year *17*	عام ج. أعْوام
to live, be alive *7*	عاشَ ، يَعيش ، العَيْش
living *(e.g.: __ room)* *14*	مَعيشة
I was appointed *(passive)* *12*	عُيِّنْتُ
eye *9*	عيْن ج. عُيون / أعيُن

❄ غ ❄

tomorrow *12*	غَدًا
lunch *9*	الغَداء
to leave *(someone or something)* *17*	غادَرَ ، يُغادِر ، المُغادَرة
west *15*	غَرْب
strange, foreign *U-5*	غَريب ج. غُرَباء
Morocco *U-9*	المَغرِب
longing for one's native land, feeling a stranger in a strange place *13*	الغُرْبَة
room *U-6*	غُرْفة ج. غُرَف
to get angry *15*	غَضِبَ ، يَغْضَب ، الغَضَب
expensive *16*	غالي / غالٍ
to be or remain absent *19*	غابَ (عن) ، يَغيب ، الغِياب
to be absent from, miss *(e.g.: __ school)* *12*	تَغَيَّبَ عن ، يَتَغَيَّب ، التَّغَيُّب
to change *(something or someone)* *16*	غَيَّرَ ، يُغَيِّر ، التَغْيير
to change (intransitive) *18*	تَغَيَّرَ ، يَتَغَيَّر ، التَّغَيُّر
cloudy, overcast *5*	غائِم

❄ ف ❄

thus, so *5*	فَـ...
individual *4*	فَرْد ج. أفْراد

singular *2*	المُفْرَد
opportunity *13*	فُرْصة ج. فُرَص
(blank) space *17*	فَراغ
to be dispersed, scattered *20*	تَفرَّقَ ، يَتَفَرَّق ، التَّفَرُّق
French, French person *2*	فرَنْسِيّ ج. فرَنسِيّون
dress *15*	فُسْتان ج. فَساتين
to fail *13*	فَشِلَ ، يَفْشَل ، الفَشَل
formal or written Arabic *15*	الفُصْحى
to dismiss, fire *(e.g.: from a job)* *13*	فَصَلَ ، يَفْصِل ، الفَصْل
class, classroom ***U-6*** ; season *(e.g.: spring __)* *5*	فَصْل ج. فُصول
comma *(punctuation mark)*, decimal point *9*	فاصِلة ج. فَواصِل
thanks to *8*	بِفَضْل + اسم
favorite *9*	مُفَضَّل
please *(addressing a male)* ***U-10***	مِنْ فَضْلَك
please *(addressing a female)* ***U-10***	مِنْ فَضْلِك
silver *18*	فِضِّيّ
to eat breakfast *9*	فَطَرَ ، يَفْطُر ، الفُطور
breakfast *9*	الفُطور
meal in evening to break Ramadan fast; breakfast *17*	الإفْطار
to do *8*	فَعَلَ ، يَفْعَل ، الفِعل
verb *5*	فِعل ج. أفعال
really! , indeed *2*	فِعْلاً
subject *(of verbal sentence)* *17*	فاعِل
(direct) object of a verb *17*	مَفعول بِهِ
deceased *7*	فَقيد ج. فُقَداء
only *5*	فَقَط

to think about, ponder ***17***	فَكَّرَ في، بِـ ، يُفَكِّر ، التَّفْكير
idea, thought ***18***	فِكْرة ج. أفْكار
fruits ***6***	فَواكِه
money ***U-6***	فُلوس
Palestine ***U-9***	فِلِسْطين
Palestinian ***1***	فِلِسْطينِيّ ج. فِلِسْطينِيّون
philosophy ***3***	الفَلْسَفة
hotel ***11***	فُنْدُق ج. فَنادِق
to understand ***10***	فَهِمَ ، يَفْهَم ، الفَهْم
towel ***16***	فوطة ج. فُوَط
above ***14***	فَوْق
superior, outstanding ***18***	مُتَفَوِّق ج. مُتَفَوِّقون
in ***1***	في

❄ ق ❄

to meet *(in a formal setting)* ***19***	قابَلَ ، يُقابِل ، المُقابَلة
to receive, welcome ***14***	اِسْتَقْبَلَ ، يَسْتَقْبِل ، الاِسْتِقْبال
before ***4***	قَبْلَ
previously, before (now) ***14***	مِن قَبْل
admissions ***2***	قُبول
acceptable, passing ***8***	مَقْبول
future ***8***	المُسْتَقْبَل
particle that emphasizes that action has taken place ***17***	قَد (لَقد ، فَقد) + الماضي
(comprehensive) evaluation, grade ***8***	تَقْدير
Jerusalem ***20***	القُدْس
old, ancient *(for things, not for people)* ***2***	قَديم

قادِم ج. قادِمون	coming, next **12**
مُتَقَدِّم	advanced **2**
قَرَّرَ ، يُقَرِّر ، التَّقْرير	to decide **12**
اِسْتَقَرَّ ، يَسْتَقِرّ ، الاِسْتِقْرار	to stabilize, become settled **13**
قَرار ج. قَرارات	decision **12**
قارّة ج. قارّات	continent **15**
قَرَأ ، يَقْرَأ ، القِراءة	to read **8**
قَريب ج. قَريبون	close **U-6**
قَريب ج. أقارِب / أقْرِباء	family relative **3**
المُقارَن	comparative **12**
قِسْم ج. أقْسام	department **1**
قِصّة ج. قِصَص	story **U-6**
قَصَدَ ، يَقْصِد ، القَصْد	to mean, intend **10**
الاقْتِصاد	economics, economy **3**
قَصير ج. قِصار	short **U-6**
قَضى ، يَقْضي ، القَضاء	to spend, pass *(time)* **12**
قَطَر	Qatar **U-9**
اِنْقَطَعَ ، يَنْقَطِع ، الاِنْقِطاع	to be cut off **11**
القَواعِد	grammar **1**
مُستَقِلّ	independent **20**
قَليلاً	a little **9**
قَلب ج. قُلوب	heart **18**
قَلَم ج. أقلام	pen **U-7**
قَمَر الدين	dried apricots, drink or pudding made from them **17**
قاموس ج. قَواميس	dictionary **8**
قَميص ج. قُمصان	shirt **15**

channel ***9***	قناة ج. قنوات
coffee ***U-7***	قَهْوة
cafe ***17***	مَقْهَى ج. مَقاهٍ / المَقاهي
say ***U-10***	قالَ ، يَقول ، القَوْل
article *(e.g.: newspaper __)* ***13***	مَقالة ج. مَقالات
to get up ***17***	قامَ ، يَقوم ، القِيام
to reside, stay ***10***	أقامَ ، يُقيم ، الإقامة

❄ ك ❄

like, as ***15***	كَـ + اسم
as if ***19***	كَأَنَّ + جملة اسمية
also, likewise ***13***	كَذٰلِك
like, as ***8***	كَما + فعل
important, powerful; big; old ***U-6***	كَبير ج. كِبار
to write	كَتَبَ ، يَكْتُب ، الكِتابة
book ***U-6***	كِتاب ج. كُتُب
Quran school for young children	كُتّاب ج. كَتاتيب
writer ***19***	كاتِب ج. كُتّاب
office ***U-7***	مَكْتَب ج. مَكاتِب
library ***U-7***	مَكْتَبة ج. مَكْتَبات
much, many ***5***	كَثيراً
more ***10***	أكثَر
basketball ***7***	كُرة السَّلّة
volleyball ***7***	الكُرة الطّائِرة
soccer ***7***	كُرة القَدَم
chair ***U-6***	كُرْسي ج. كَراسٍ/الكَراسي

tie (clothing) ***15***	كرافات ج. كرافاتات
all ***4***	كُلّ + الجمع
each, every ***11***	كُل + المفرد
holiday, birthday greeting ***17***	كُل عام وأَنْتُم بِخَيْر
college, school *(in a university)* ***3***	كُلِّيّة ج. كُلِّيّات
word ***U-7***	كَلِمة ج. كَلِمات
to speak ***4***	تَكَلَّمَ ، يَتَكَلَّم ، الكَلام
how many/much? ***7***	كَمْ؟
how much ? *(price)* ***7***	بِكَم ؟
as ***8***	كَما
church ***15***	كَنيسة ج. كَنائِس
a kind of Middle Eastern pastry ***17***	كُنافة
electrical	كَهْرَبائِيّ
to be ***4***	كانَ ، يَكون
to consist of ***14***	تَكَوَّنَ مِن ، يَتَكَوَّن ، التَّكَوُّن
place ***14***	مَكان ج. أَماكِن
Kuwait ***U-9***	الكُوَيْت
fine, good, OK ***U-6***	كْوَيِّس ج. كْوَيِّسين
scarf, Arab headdress ***15***	كوفِيّة ج. كوفِيّات
in order to ***16***	كَيْ = لِـ
how? ***1***	كَيْف؟
How are you? ***1***	كَيْف الحال؟

❄ ل ❄

in order to ***6***	لِـ + مصدر/ مضارع
because ***6***	لِأنَّ + جملة اسمية

why? ***5***	لِماذا؟
for, belonging to ***U-10***	**لِـ + اسم / ضمير**
no ***U-7***	لا
to wear; get dressed ***15***	لَبِسَ ، يَلْبَس ، اللُّبْس
clothes ***15***	مَلابِس
underwear ***15***	مَلابِس داخِلِيّة
milk ***U-7***	لَبَن /حَليب
Lebanon ***U-9***	لُبْنان
to enter, join *(e.g.: school or army)* ***8***	اِلْتَحَقَ بِـ ، يَلْتَحِق ، الاِلْتِحاق
meat ***6***	لَحْم ج. لُحُوم
necessary ***16***	لازِم
tongue ***18***	لِسان ج. أَلسِنة
nice, kind, pleasant ***U-6***	لَطيف ج. لِطاف ، لُطَفاء
to play ***9***	لَعِبَ ، يَلْعَب ، اللَّعِب
language ***2***	لُغة ج. لُغات
but ***U-8***	لـٰكِن
past negation particle ***13***	**لَمْ + المضارع المجزوم**
to hint ***18***	لَمَّحَ (إلى) ، يُلَمِّح ، التَّلْميح
future negation particle ***12***	**لَنْ + المضارع المنصوب**
if *(hypothetical)* ***13***	لَوْ
color ***18***	لَوْن ج. أَلْوان
Libya ***U-9***	ليبيا
is not, are not ***8***	لَيْسَ
night ***10***	لَيْلة ج. لَيالٍ /الليالي
tonight ***10***	اللَّيْلة

❋ م ❋

what? *(in questions without verbs)* ***1***	ما ؟
what/whatever *(non-specific relative pronoun)* ***15***	ما
past negation particle ***8***	ما + **الماضي**
what? *(in questions using verbs)* ***1***	ماذا + **فعل**
why? ***6***	لماذا ؟
still, continue to (*lit.*: do not cease) ***13***	ما زالَ ، لا يَزال + **المضارع المرفوع / اسم**
master's degree ***2***	الماجِسْتير
hundred ***9***	مِئَة (مائَة) ج. مِئات
to enjoy ***10***	اِسْتَمْتَعَ بِـ ، يَسْتَمْتِع ، الاِسْتِمْتاع
fun ***16***	مُمْتِع
when? ***6***	مَتى؟
like, similar to ***8***	مِثْل + **إضافة**
example ***1***	مِثال ج. أمثِلة
test, examination ***U-7***	اِمْتِحان ج. اِمْتِحانات
city ***1***	مَدينة ج. مُدُن
to pass, elapse *(e.g.: the time__es)* ***19***	مَرَّ ، يَمُرّ ، المُرور
once, *(one)* time ***11***	مَرّة ج. مَرّات
woman ***U-7***	اِمْرَأة (def: الاِمرأة/المَرْأة) ج. نِساء
women *(collective)*	المَرْأة
sick ***U-8***	مَريض ج. مَرْضى
drill ***U-10***	تَمْرين ج. تَمارين
Christian ***17***	مَسيحيّ ج. مَسيحِيّون
evening ***2***	مَساء
Egypt ***U-9***	مِصْر

Egyptian ***1***	مِصْرِيّ ج. مِصْرِيّون
the past tense ***8***	الماضي
rain ***5***	مَطَر ج. أمطار
rainy, raining ***5***	ماطِر / مُمْطِر
with *(people)* ***7***	مَعَ
together *(i.e.: with one another)* ***11***	معًا
never mind! don't worry about it! ***U-8***	مَعلِهش / مَعليش!
it is possible to *(impersonal, does not conjugate)* ***10***	يُمْكِن + أنْ / المصدر
boring ***16***	مُمِلّ ج. مُمِلّون
to own, possess ***15***	مَلَكَ ، يَمْلِك ، المُلْك
king ***12***	مَلِك ج. مُلوك
sheet ***16***	مِلاية ج. مِلايات
who?, whom; whoever ***1***	مَن؟
from ***1***	مِنْ
scholarship award, grant ***12***	مِنْحة ج. مِنَح
since; ago ***6***	مُنْذُ
to hope, wish that ***14***	تَمَنَّى أنْ ، يَتَمَنَّى ، التَّمَنّي
to die ***7***	ماتَ ، يَموت ، المَوْت
Mauritania ***U-9***	موريتانيا
music ***7***	الموسيقى
water ***U-7***	ماء
excellent ***8***	مُمْتاز ج. مُمتازون

❄ ن ❄

prophet ***4***	نَبِيّ ج. أنْبِياء
to succeed, pass ***8***	نَجَحَ في ، يَنْجَح ، النَّجاح

we 2	نَحْنُ
club *(e.g.: sports __)* **9**	نادٍ/النّادي ج. نَوادٍ/النّوادي
to descend **9**	نَزَلَ ، يَنْزِل ، النُّزول
the nisba adjective **1**	النِّسْبة
for, in relation to **5**	بِالنِّسْبة لِـ
appropriate, suitable **13**	مُناسِب
women	نِساء (م. اِمْرَأة ، المَرْأة)
to forget **12**	نَسِيَ ، يَنْسى ، النِّسْيان
to grow up **20**	نَشَأَ ، يَنْشَأ ، النُّشوء
activity	نَشاط ج. نَشاطات
text	نَصّ ج. نُصوص
subjunctive mood *(verbs)* **10,** accusative case *(nouns)* **16**	المَنصوب
(piece of) advice **19**	نَصيحة ج. نَصائِح
half **9**	نِصْف
middle, mid-way **16**	مُنْتَصَف
area, region **1**	مِنْطَقة ج. مَناطِق
(pair of) eyeglasses **15**	نَظّارة ج. نَظارات
yes ***U-7***	نَعَم
the same... **1**	نَفْس الـ...
discussion **9**	المُناقَشة (ناقَشَ ، يُناقِش)
to move to **14**	اِنْتَقَلَ إلى ، يَنْتَقِل ، الاِنْتِقال
daytime **2**	نَهار
to finish **13**	اِنْتَهى مِنْ ، يَنْتَهي ، الاِنْتِهاء
to take, have *(a meal)* **9**	تَناوَلَ ، يَتَناوَل ، التَّناوُل
to sleep, go to sleep **10**	نامَ ، يَنام ، النَّوْم
to intend to **15**	نَوى أنْ ، يَنْوي ، النيّة

❋ هـ ❋

this *(m.)* ***U-8***	هـٰذا
this *(f.)* ***U-8***	هـٰذِهِ
those *(human plural)* ***19***	هـٰؤُلاء
these *(m. dual)* ***18***	هـٰذانِ
these *(f. dual)* ***18***	هـاتانِ
thus, so, in this way, that way *7*	هـٰكَذا
telephone *2*	هاتِف
to emigrate ***20***	هاجَرَ ، يُهاجِر ، الهِجْرة
gift, present ***19***	هَدِيّة ج. هَدايا
interrogative *(yes/no?)* particle ***1***	هَل؟
they *2*	هُم
they *(dual)* ***15***	هُما
important, momentous ***18***	مُهِمّ ج. مُهِمّون
they *(pl., f.)* ***19***	هُنَّ
here *12*	هُنا
there; there is/are *7*	هُناك
Indian *(Asian or Native American)*	هِندي ج. هُنود
engineering *3*	الهَنْدَسة
engineer ***11***	مُهَنْدِس ج. مُهَنْدِسون
he ***U-8***	هُوَ
to fascinate, enthrall *19*	اِسْتَهْوى ، يَسْتَهْوي ، الاِسْتِهْواء
hobby *7*	هِواية ج. هِوايات
she ***U-8***	هِيَ

❄ و ❄

واجِب ج. واجِبات	homework ***U-2***
يَجِب أنْ	to be necessary to, must *(expression impersonal and fixed)* ***16***
وَجَدَ ، يَجِد ، الوُجود	to find ***13***
واحِد	one ***U-3***
وِحْدة	loneliness ***5***
وَحيد ج. وَحيدون	only; lonely ***2***
وَرَقة ج. أوْراق	piece of paper ***U-6***
وَراء	behind ***14***
وِزارة ج. وِزارات	ministry ***7***
وَزن ج. أوزان	pattern ***8***
مُتَوَسِّط	intermediate ***2***
واسِع	wide, spacious ***U-5***
وَصَفَ ، يَصِف ، الوَصْف	to describe ***14***
وَصْف ج. أوْصاف	description ***18***
صِفة ج. صِفات	adjective ***5***
وَصَلَ (إلى) ، يَصِل ، الوُصول	to arrive ***16***
اِتَّصَلَ بِـ ، يَتَّصِل ، الاِتِّصال	to contact, get in touch with ***16***
مَوْضوع ج. مَوْضوعات /مواضيع	subject ***15***
وَطَن ج. أوْطان	homeland ***20***
وَظيفة ج. وَظائِف	work, position ***13***
مُوَظَّف ج. مُوَظَّفون	employee *(white collar; m.)* ***2***
مُوَظَّفة ج. مُوَظَّفات	employee *(white collar; f.)* ***2***
مَوْعِد ج. مَواعيد	appointment ***10***
وَفاة	death ***12***

time *(general)* ***9***	وَقْت ج. أَوْقات
to stop ***19***	تَوَقَّفَ (عن) ، يَتَوَقَّف ، التَوَقُّف
was born *(passive)* ***15***	وُلِدَ
son , boy; child ***U-7***	وَلَد ج. أَوْلاد
father ***1***	والِد ج. والِدون
mother ***1***	والِدة ج. والِدات
birth **2**	مِيلاد
to undertake, assume *(e.g.: __ a job)* ***17***	تَوَلّى ، يَتَولّى ، التَّوَلّي
state, province **2**	وِلايَة ج. وِلايات
United States of America ***U-9***	الوِلايات المُتَّحِدة الأمريكيّة

❄ ي ❄

Japan	اليابان
I wonder... *(fixed expression)* ***16***	يا تُرى... + **سؤال**
hand ***18***	يَد ج. أَيادٍ /الأيادي
left *(side)*	يَسار
to wake *(someone)* up ***9***	أَيْقَظَ ، يوقِظ ، الإيْقاظ
Yemen ***U-9***	اليَمَن
right *(side/direction)*	يَمين
day ***6***	يَوْم ج. أَيّام
today ***6***	اليَوْم

قاموس إنجليزي-عربي
English-Arabic Glossary

❄ A ❄

(to be) able ***9***	اِسْتَطاع ، يَسْتَطيع ، الاِسْتِطاعة
about *(to talk ___)* ***7***	عَنْ
about whom... ? ***8***	عَمَّن (عَنْ+مَن) ...؟
about what...? ***7***	عَمَّ (عن+ماذا) ... ؟
above ***14***	فَوْق
(to be) absent or remain absent ***19***	غابَ (عن) ، يَغيب ، الغِياب
(to be) absent from, miss *(e.g.: __ school)* ***12***	تَغَيَّبَ عن ، يَتَغَيَّب ، التَّغَيُّب
(to) abstain, fast ***17***	صامَ ، يَصُوم ، الصَّوْم / الصِّيام
acceptable, passing ***8***	مَقْبول
accident ***7***	حادِث ج. حَوادِث
(on) account of, because of ***5***	بِسَبَب + اسم
(making the mutual) acquaintance (of), getting to know (one other) ***8***	تَعارُف
(to become) acquainted with, get to know ***11***	تَعَرَّفَ عَلى ، يَتَعَرَّف ، التَّعَرُّف
(way of) acting, manners, behavior ***19***	سُلوك
activity ***1***	نَشاط ج. نَشاطات
action *(i.e.: way of acting)*, behavior ***19***	تَصَرُّف ج. تَصَرُّفات
actual, real ***18***	حَقيقِيّ
actually ***3***	في الحَقيقة
(in) addition to ***12***	بالإضافة إلى
address ***2***	عُنْوان ج. عَناوين
adjective ***5***	صِفة ج. صِفات
admissions *(e.g.: office of __)* ***2***	قُبول

advanced **2**	مُتَقَدِّم
(piece of) advice **19**	نَصيحة ج. نَصائِح
after **8**	بَعْدَ
afternoon **9**	بعْد الظُّهْر
age **2**	عُمْر ج. أعمار
ago; since **6**	مُنْذُ
airplane ***U-9***	طائِرة ج. طائِرات
airport **11**	مَطار ج. مَطارات
Algeria ***U-9***	الجَزائِر
all **4**	كُلّ
also **2**	أيْضاً
also, likewise **13**	كَذلِك
always **2**	دائِماً
ambassador **11**	سَفير ج. سُفَراء
Amman *(capital of Jordan)*	عَمّان
angry, annoyed; upset ***U-8***	زَعْلان ج. زَعْلانين (عامية)
(to get) angry **15**	غضِبَ ، يَغْضَب ، الغَضَب
to answer	أجابَ ، يُجيب ، الإجابة عن
answer	جَواب ج. أجوِبة
anthropology **3**	عِلْم الإنْسان
any **15**	أيّ /أيّة
apartment **14**	شَقّة ج. شِقَق
(it) appears, seems that *(impersonal)* **17**	يَبْدو أنَّ
(I was) appointed *(passive)* **12**	عُيِّنْتُ
appointment **10**	مَوْعِد ج. مَواعيد
appropriate, suitable **13**	مُناسِب

Arab, Arabic ***U-5***	عَربيّ ج. عَرَب
Arabic language: formal/written form ***15***	الفُصْحى
Arabic language: colloquial/spoken form ***15***	العامـيّة
area, region ***1***	مِنْطَقة ج. مَناطِق
army ***3***	جَيْش ج. جُيوش
around, approximately ***9***	حَوالَيْ
(to) arrange, prepare ***16***	رَتَّبَ ، يُرَتِّب ، التَّرْتيب
(to) arrive ***16***	وَصَلَ (إلى) ، يَصِل ، الوُصول
article *(e.g.: newspaper __)* ***13***	مَقالة ج. مَقالات
as, like ***8***	كَما + **جملة فعلية**
as, like ***15***	كَـ + **اسم**
as for..., ***9***	أمّا... فَـ...
as if ***19***	كَأنَّ + **جملة اسمية**
(to) ask ***19***	طَلَبَ مِن ، يَطْلُب ، الطَّلَب
(to) assume, undertake *(e.g.: __ a job)* ***17***	تَوَلّى ، يَتَوَلّى ، التَّوَلّي
astonishing, strange ***U-5***	عَجيب ج. عَجيبون
(to) attend, come to ***13***	حَضَرَ إلى ، يَحْضُر ، الحُضور
aunt *(maternal)* ***2***	خالة ج. خالات
aunt *(paternal)* ***3***	عَمّة ج. عَمّات
(to) awaken, wake up ***10***	صَحا ، يَصْحو ، الصَّحْو

❄ B ❄

Baccalaureate ***7***	الثانَويّة العامّة
bachelor's degree ***2***	بَكالورْيوس
Bahrain ***U-9***	البَحْرَيْن
bald ***18***	أصْلَع
basketball ***7***	كُرة السَّلّة

bathroom ***10***	حَمّام ج. حَمّامات
(to) be, is ***4***	كانَ ، يَكون
beautiful, pretty ***U-7***	جَميل ج. جَميلون
because ***6***	لأنَّ + **جملة اسمية**
because, since ***13***	إذْ
because of, on account of ***5***	بِسَبَب + **اسم**
(to) become ***10***	أَصْبَحَ ، يُصْبِح
bed ***11***	سَرير ج. أَسِرّة
before, in front of *(spatial)* ***13***	أَمامَ
before, prior to ***4***	قَبْلَ
before *(now)*, previously ***14***	مِن قَبْل
(to) begin ***9***	بَدَأَ ، يَبْدَأ ، البَدْء
behavior, action *(i.e.: way of acting)* ***19***	تَصَرُّف ج. تَصَرُّفات
behavior, manners, way of acting ***19***	سُلوك
behind ***14***	وَراء
behind, beyond ***5***	خَلْف
belly, stomach ***18***	بَطن ج. بُطون
below ***14***	تَحْت
(the) best... ***5***	أَحْسَن...
between ***11***	بَيْنَ
big *(also: important; old)* ***U-6***	كَبير ج. كِبار
birth ***2***	ميلاد
black *(m.)* ***18***	أَسْوَد ج. سود
black *(f.)* ***18***	سَوْداء ج. سَوْداوات
blind ***18***	أَعْمى (مؤنّث: عَمْياء)
blond, fair-skinned ***18***	أَشْقَر (مؤنّث: شَقْراء) ج. شُقْر

blood *18*	دَم ج. دِماء
blouse *15*	بلوزة ج. بلوزات
blue *18*	أَزْرَق (مؤنّث: زَرْقاء)
body *18*	جِسم ج. أجسام
book ***U-6***	كِتاب ج. كُتُب
boring *16*	مُمِلّ
(was) born *(passive)* ***15***	وُلِدَ
boy, son *(also: child)* ***U-7***	وَلَد ج. أَوْلاد
boyfriend ***U-5***	صاحِب ج. أَصْحاب
bread ***U-3***	خُبْز
breakfast *9*	الفُطور
(to) eat breakfast *9*	فَطَرَ ، يَفْطُر ، لفُطور
brother ***U-3***	أَخ ج. إخْوة
brown *18*	بُنِّيّ
building ***U-7***	بِناية ج. بِنايات
bus ***U-4***	أوتوبيس ج. أوتوبيسات
business administration *6*	إدارة الأَعْمال
busy with *2*	مَشْغول بِـ ج. مَشْغولون
(too) busy for ***15***	مَشْغول عَن ج. مَشغولون
but ***U-8***	لٰكِن
(to) buy *16*	اِشْتَرى ، يَشْتَري ، الشِّراء
by, with *(use with things)* ***U-10***	بِـ

❄ C ❄

cafe *17*	مَقْهَى ج. مَقاهٍ/المَقاهي
caliph, successor *(note: m.)* *4*	خَليفة ج. خُلَفاء
capital *(city)* *5*	عاصِمة ج. عَواصِم

car *U-5* سَيّارة ج. سَيّارات

card *18* بِطاقة ج. بِطاقات

(to) carry *20* حَمَلَ ، يَحْمِل ، الحَمْل

Casablanca *18* الدّار البَيْضاء

center *2* مَرْكَز ج. مراكِز

chair *U-6* كُرْسي ج. كَراسٍ/الكَراسي

(to) change *(something or someone)* *16* غَيَّرَ ، يُغَيِّر ، التَغْيير

(to) change (intransitive) *18* تَغَيَّرَ ، يَتَغَيَّر ، التَّغَيُّر

channel *9* قَناة ج. قَنوات

chapter *(of the Quran)* *17* سورة ج. سُوَر

cheap, inexpensive *16* رَخيص

(to) cheer (on), encourage (to) *13* شَجَّع على ، يُشَجِّع ، التَّشْجيع

chess *9* الشَّطْرَنْج

chicken *U-3* دَجاج

child *19* طِفل ج. أطفال

child; boy, son *U-7* وَلَد ج. أوْلاد

childhood *4* طُفولة

China الصّين

(to) choose *19* اِخْتارَ ، يَخْتار ، الاِخْتِيار

Christian *17* مَسيحِيّ ج. مَسيحِيّون

Christmas *16* عيد الميلاد

church *15* كَنيسة ج. كَنائِس

cinema *8* السّينما

city *1* مَدينة ج. مُدُن

class, classroom *U-6* ; season *(e.g.: spring __)* *5* فَصْل ج. فُصول

class, classroom *U-6* صَفّ ج. صُفوف

classmate; colleague *(m.)* ***4***	زَميل ج. زُمَلاء
classmate; colleague *(f.)* ***4***	زَميلة ج. زَميلات
clock *(also: hour; o'clock)* ***U-5***	ساعة ج. ساعات
close ***U-6***	قَريب ج. قَريبون
clothes ***15***	مَلابِس
cloudy, overcast ***5***	غائِم
club *(e.g.: sports __)* ***9***	نادٍ /النّادي ج. نَوادٍ /النَّوادي/أنْدِية
coffee ***U-7***	قَهْوة
cold *(e.g.: I feel __)* ***U-8***	بَرْدان ج. بَرْدانين (عامية)
cold *(e.g.: I have a __)*	بَرْد
cold *(e.g.: __ weather)* ***5***	بارِد
colleague; classmate *(m.)* ***4***	زَميل ج. زُمَلاء
colleague; classmate *(f.)* ***4***	زَميلة ج. زَميلات
college, school in a university ***3***	كُلِّيّة ج. كُلِّيّات
color ***18***	لَوْن ج. ألْوان
(to) come ***10***	جاءَ ، يَجيء ، المَجيء
(to) come to, attend ***13***	حَضَرَ إلى ، يَحْضُر ، الحُضور
comfort, ease ***14***	راحة
coming, next ***11***	قادِم ج. قادِمون
comma *(punctuation mark)*; decimal point ***9***	فاصِلة ج. فَواصِل
commerce, trade ***6***	التِّجارة
(to have in) common, share ***15***	اِشْتَرَكَ في ، يَشْتَرِك ، الاِشْتِراك
Companions of the Prophet ***17***	الصَّحابة
company ***10***	شَرِكة ج. شَرِكات
comparative ***12***	مُقارَن
(to be) completed *(subject expressed by masDar)* ***20***	تَمَّ ، يَتِمّ + المصدر

congratulations ***1***	مَبروك
(to) consider ***18***	اِعْتَبَرَ ، يَعْتَبِر ، الاِعْتِبار
(to) consist of ***14***	تَكَوَّنَ مِن ، يَتَكَوَّن ، التَكَوُّن
(to) contact, get in touch with ***16***	اِتَّصَلَ بِـ ، يَتَّصِل ، الاِتِّصال
continent ***15***	قارّة ج. قارّات
(to) continue to, still (*lit.:* do not cease) ***13***	ما زالَ ، لا يَزال + المضارع المرفوع / اسم
(to) convene, gather ***17***	اِجْتَمَعَ ، يَجْتَمِع ، الاِجْتِماع
conversation ***1***	مُحادَثة
(to) convince	أقنَعَ ، يُقنِع ، الإقناع
(to) cook ***17***	طَبَخَ ، يَطْبُخ ، الطَّبْخ
copybook, notebook ***U-6***	دَفْتَر ج. دَفاتِر
correct, true ***20***	صَحيح
(to) correspond, exchange letters ***8***	راسَلَ ، يُراسِل ، المُراسَلة
country ***2***	بَلَد ج. بِلاد / بُلدان
(of) course, naturally ***12***	طَبْعًا
cousin *(f., maternal)* ***3***	بِنْت خال /ة ج. بَنات خال /ة
cousin *(f., paternal)* ***3***	بِنْت عَمّ /ة ج. بَنات عَمّ /ة
cousin *(m., maternal)* ***3***	اِبن خال /ة ج. أبْناء خال /ة
cousin *(m., paternal)* ***3***	اِبن عَمّ /ة ج. أبْناء عَمّ /ة
(over) crowdedness ***5***	اِزْدِحام
culture ***1***	الثّقافة
currency ***7***	عُملة ج. عُملات
(to be) cut off ***11***	اِنْقَطَعَ ، يَنْقَطِع ، الاِنْقِطاع

❄ D ❄

dance, dancing ***7***	الرَّقْص (رَقَص ، يَرقُص)
dark-complexioned ***18***	أسْمَر (المؤنّث: سَمْراء) ج. سُمْر

darling, dear *(m.)* ***U-2***	حَبيب ج. أحِبّاء
darling, dear *(f.)* ***U-2***	حَبيبة ج. حَبيبات
date *(chronological)* ***20***	تاريخ ج. تَواريخ
daughter, girl ***U-7***	بِنْت ج. بَنات
day ***6***	يَوْم ج. أيّام
daytime ***2***	نَهار
dear ***15***	عَزيز ج. أعِزّاء
death ***7, 12***	مَوْت / وَفاة
deceased ***7***	مَرْحوم ج. مَرْحومون
(to) decide ***12***	قَرَّرَ ، يُقَرِّر ، التَّقْرير
decimal point, comma *(punctuation mark)* ***9***	فاصِلة ج. فَواصِل
decision ***12***	قَرار ج. قَرارات
degree *(e.g. university)* ***12***	شَهادة ج. شَهادات
degree *(e.g. of temperature)* ***5***	دَرَجة ج. دَرَجات
delicious *(also: good-hearted)* ***U-5***	طَيِّب ج. طَيِّبون
department ***1***	قِسْم ج. أقْسام
(to) descend ***9***	نَزَلَ ، يَنْزِل ، النُّزول
descent, origin ***5***	أصْل ج. أُصول
(to) describe ***14***	وَصَفَ ، يَصِف ، الوَصْف
description ***18***	وَصْف ج. أوْصاف
(to have a) desire to, want to ***13***	رَغِبَ في ، يَرْغَب ، الرَّغْبة
(to) determine, set *(e.g.: __ a curfew)* ***15***	حَدَّدَ ، يُحَدِّد ، التَّحْديد
dictionary ***8***	قاموس ج. قَواميس
(to) die ***7***	ماتَ ، يَموت ، المَوْت
(to) differ from ***17***	اِخْتَلَفَ عَن ، يَخْتَلِف ، الاِخْتِلاف
different *(from)* ***18***	مُخْتَلِف (عن)

difficult, hard ***U-5***	صَعْب
dinner ***6***	عَشاء
diploma ***12***	شَهادة ج. شَهادات
director ***12***	مُدير ج. مُديرون/ مُدَراء
discussion ***9***	المُناقَشة (ناقَشَ ، يُناقِش)
(to) dismiss, fire *(e.g.: from a job)* ***13***	فَصَلَ ، يَفْصِل ، الفَصْل
(to be) dispersed, scattered ***20***	تَفَرَّقَ ، يَتَفَرَّق ، التَّفَرُّق
(to) do ***8***	فَعَلَ ، يَفْعَل ، الفِعل
doctor *(m.)* ***U-4***	دُكتور ج. دَكاتِرة
doctor *(f.)* ***U-4***	دُكتورة ج. دُكتورات
door ***U-1***	باب ج. أبْواب
(to) draw ***7***	رَسَمَ ، يَرْسُم ، الرَّسْم
(to) dream of ***20***	حَلَمَ بِـ ، يَحْلُم ، الحُلْم
dream ***18***	حُلْم ج. أحْلام
dress ***15***	فُسْتان ج. فَساتين
(to get) dressed, wear *(clothes)* ***15***	لَبِسَ ، يَلْبَس ، اللُّبْس
drill ***U-10***	تَمْرين ج. تَمارين
(to) drink ***4***	شَرِبَ ، يَشْرَب ، الشُّرْب
the dual ***7***	المُثَنّى
during, throughout ***8***	طِوال

❄ E ❄

each, every ***11***	كُل + اسم في إضافة
east ***2***	شَرق
easy ***12***	سَهل
(to) eat ***4***	أكَلَ ، يأكُل ، الأكل
economics ***3***	الاقْتِصاد

Egypt ***U-9***	مِصْر
Egyptian ***1***	مِصْريّ ج. مِصْرِيّون
eight ***U- 7***	ثَمانِية
eighty ***8***	ثَمانون / ثَمانين
electrical	كَهْرَبائي
eleven ***8***	أَحَدَ عَشَر
(to) emigrate ***20***	هاجَرَ ، يُهاجِر ، الهِجْرة
emotional, romantic ***11***	عاطِفيّ
employee *(white collar; m.)* **2**	مُوَظَّف ج. مُوَظَّفون
employee *(white collar; f.)* **2**	مُوَظَّفة ج. مُوَظَّفات
(to) encourage (to), cheer (on) ***13***	شَجَّع على ، يُشَجِّع ، التَّشْجيع
(got) engaged to ***11***	خُطِبَت لِـ
engineer ***11***	مُهَنْدِس ج. مُهَنْدِسون
engineering ***3***	الهَنْدَسة
English ***1***	إنْجليزي (إنكليزي) ج. إنْجليز (إنكليز)
(to) enjoy ***10***	اِسْتَمْتَعَ بِـ ، يَسْتَمْتِع ، الاِسْتِمْتاع
enjoyable ***16***	مُمتِع
(to) enter, join *(e.g.: school or army)* **8**	اِلْتَحَقَ بِـ ، يَلْتَحِق ، الاِلْتِحاق
(to) enter ***8***	دَخَلَ ، يَدْخُل ، الدُّخول
Europe	أوروبا
evaluation *(comprehensive)*, grade ***8***	تَقْدير
evening ***2***	مَساء
every, each ***11***	**كُل + اسم في إضافة**
every day ***4***	كُلّ يَوْم
exam, test	اِمتِحان ج. اِمتِحانات
example ***1***	مِثال ج. أَمثِلة

(to) exceed **17**	زادَ ، يَزيد ، الزِّيادة
excellent **8**	مُمْتاز
except **9**	إلاّ
(to) exchange **11**	تَبادَلَ ، يَتَبادَل ، التَّبادُل
expensive **16**	غالٍ /الغالي
experience *(life __)* **11**	تَجْرِبة ج. تَجارِب
experience *(e.g. job ___)* **14**	خِبْرة ج. خِبْرات
expression, idiom **18**	عِبارة ج. عِبارات
eye **9**	عَيْن ج. عُيون / أعْيُن
(pair of) eyeglasses **15**	نَظّارة ج. نَظّارات

❄ F ❄

(to) fail **13**	فَشِلَ (في) ، يَفْشَل ، الفَشَل
fair-skinned, blond **18**	أشْقَر (مؤنّث: شَقْراء) ج. شُقْر
fall, autumn **5**	الخَريف
(to) fall behind, be late **8**	تَأَخَّرَ ، يَتَأَخَّر ، التَّأَخُّر
family *(i.e.: immediate __)* **2**	أُسْرة ج. أُسَر
family *(i.e.: extended __)* **3**	عائِلة ج. عائِلات
famous **16**	مَشْهور ج. مَشْهورون
far, distant *(from)* **U-6**	بَعيد (عَنْ) ج. بَعيدون
(to) fascinate, enthrall **19**	اِسْتَهْوى ، يَسْتَهْوي ، الاِسْتِهْواء
(to) fast, abstain **17**	صامَ ، يَصُوم ، الصَّوْم / الصِّيام
father *(more formal address)* **1**	والِد ج. والِدون
father *(less formal address)* **19**	أب ج. آباء
favorite **9**	مُفَضَّل
(to) feel *(i.e.: an emotion)* **5**	شَعرَ بِـ ، يَشْعُر ، الشُّعور
feminine **1**	مؤنَّث

fifty *8*	خَمْسون / خَمْسين
finally, at last *13*	أخيرًا
(to) find *13*	وَجَدَ ، يَجِد ، الوُجود
(to) find out about, learn of *12*	عَلِمَ بِـ ، يَعْلَم ، العِلْم
fine, OK *(said of people or things)* ***U-7***	كْوَيِّس ج. كْوَيِّسين (عامية)
fine, well *(said only of people)* ***17***	بِخَيْر
(to) finish *13*	اِنْتَهَى مِنْ ، يَنْتَهي ، الاِنْتِهاء
(to) fire, dismiss *(e.g.: from a job)* ***13***	فَصَلَ ، يَفْصِل ، الفَصْل
first *(f.)* *4*	أولى ج. أولَيات
first *(m.)* *7*	أوَّل ج. أُوَل
fish *(collective)* *6*	سَمَك
five ***U-7***	خَمْسة
floor, story *14*	طابِق ج. طَوابِق
football (American) *7*	كُرة القَدَم (الأمريكية)
for, in relation to *5*	بِالنِّسْبة لِـ
for, belonging to; have *7*	**لِـ + اسم / ضمير**
foreign, foreigner *13*	أجْنَبيّ ج. أجانِب
(to) forget *12*	نَسِيَ ، يَنْسى ، النِّسْيان
form, shape *18*	شَكْل ج. أشْكال
forty *8*	أرْبَعون / أرْبَعين
foundation *13*	مُؤَسَّسة ج. مُؤَسَّسات
four ***U-7***	أرْبَعة
fourth *4*	رابِع
freedom *15*	حُرِّيّة ج. حُرِّيّات
French, French person *2*	فَرَنْسِيّ ج. فَرَنسِيّون
Friday *6*	الجُمْعة

friend *(m.)*, boyfriend ***U-5***	صاحِب ج. أصْحاب
friend *(f.)*, girlfriend ***U-5***	صاحِبة ج. صاحِبات
friend *(m.)* ***4***	صَديق ج. أصْدِقاء
friend *(f.)* ***4***	صَديقة ج. صَديقات
friendship ***18***	صَداقة ج. صَداقات
from ***1***	مِنْ
(in) front of, before *(spatial)* ***13***	أمامَ
fruits ***6***	فَواكه
fun ***16***	مُمْتِع
future ***8***	المُسْتَقْبَل

❄ G ❄

game, match ***10***	مُباراة ج. مُبارَيات
garden, park ***14***	حَديقة ج. حَدائِق
(to) gather, convene ***17***	اِجْتَمَعَ ، يَجْتَمِع ، الاِجْتِماع
gathering, meeting ***10***	جَلْسة ج. جَلْسات
general, public ***7***	عامّ
(to) get, obtain ***6***	حَصَلَ على ، يَحْصُل ، الحُصول
(to) get to know, become acquainted with ***11***	تَعَرَّفَ عَلى ، يَتَعَرَّف ، التَعَرُّف
getting to know *(one other)* , making the mutual acquaintance *(of)* ***8***	تَعارُف
(to) get up, rise ***17***	قامَ ، يَقوم ، القِيام
(to) get used to ***17***	اِعْتادَ أنْ ، يَعْتاد ، الاِعْتِياد
gift, present ***19***	هَديّة ج. هَدايا
girl, daughter ***U-7***	بِنْت ج. بَنات
girlfriend ***U-5***	صاحِبة ج. صاحِبات
(to) go ***6***	ذَهَبَ ، يَذْهَب ، الذَهاب
(to) go out ***9***	خَرَجَ ، يَخْرُج ، الخُروج

God ***U-8***	اللّـه
God, Lord ***15***	الرَبّ
gold ***18***	ذَهَبِيّ
good ***U-4***	جَيِّد ج. جَيِّدون / جِياد
good-hearted *(people; also:* delicious) ***U-5***	طَيِّب ج. طَيِّبون
government ***20***	حُكومة ج. حُكومات
grade, evaluation ***8***	تَقْدير
graduate fellow, teaching assistant ***6***	مُعيد ج. مُعيدون
(to) graduate ***6***	تَخَرَّجَ ، يَتَخَرَّج ، التَّخَرُّج
grammar ***1***	القَواعِد
grandfather ***3***	جَدّ ج. جُدود / أجداد
grandmother ***3***	جَدّة ج. جَدّات
green ***18***	أخضَر (مؤنَث خَضراء)
grey ***18***	رَمادِيّ
grey/white-haired ***18***	أشْيَب
group ***15***	مَجْموعة ج. مَجْموعات
(to) grow up ***20***	نَشَأَ ، يَنْشَأ ، النُشوء
(to) guess ***1***	خَمَّنَ ، يُخَمِّن ، التَّخْمين
the (Arabian/Persian) Gulf ***14***	الخَليج

❄ H ❄

Hadith *(sayings and deeds of the Prophet)* ***17***	حَديث ج. أحاديث
hair ***18***	شَعْر
half ***9***	نِصْف
hand ***18***	يَد ج. أيادٍ /الأيادي
(to) happen ***14***	حَدَثَ ، يَحْدُث ، الحُدوث
happy ***U-5***	سَعيد ج. سُعَداء

hard, difficult ***U-5***	صَعْب
hat ***15***	بُرنَيطة ج. بَرانيط
have (*lit.*: at) ***7***	عِنْد
have (*lit.*: for, belonging to) ***7***	لِـ + اسم / ضمير
(to) have, take *(a meal)* ***9***	تَناوَلَ ، يَتَناوَل ، التَّناوُل
he ***U-8***	هُوَ
head ***18***	رَأس ج. رؤوس
health ***11***	صِحّة
heart ***18***	قلب ج. قلوب
(to) help ***8***	ساعَدَ ، يُساعِد ، المُساعَدة
here ***12***	هُنا
high *(m.)* ***5***	عالٍ /العالي
high *(f.)* ***5***	عاليّة
(to) hint ***18***	لَمَّحَ (إلى) ، يُلَمِّحَ ، التَّلْميح
history ***2***	التّاريخ
hobby ***7***	هِوايّة ج. هِوايّات
homeland ***20***	وَطَن ج. أوْطان
homework ***U-2***	واجِب ج. واجِبات
(to do) homework, review lessons, study ***8***	ذاكَرَ ، يُذاكِر ، المُذاكَرة
(to) hope that *(e.g.: I __ you are well; also: please...)* ***16***	رَجا أنْ ، يَرجو ، الرَّجاء
(to) hope, wish that ***14***	تَمَنّى أنْ ، يَتَمَنّى ، التَّمَنّي
hot *(e.g.: I feel __)* ***U-8***	حَرّان ج. حَرّانين (عامية)
hot *(e.g.: __ weather)* ***5***	حارّ
hotel ***11***	فُنْدُق ج. فَنادِق
hour *(also:* o'clock; clock*)* ***U-5***	ساعة ج. ساعات
house ***U-2***	بَيْت ج. بُيوت

how? ***1*** — كَيْف ؟

How are you? ***1*** — كَيْف الحال ؟

how many/much? ***7*** — كَمْ؟

how much ? *(price)* ***7*** — بِكَم ؟

human being *(note: pl. = people)* ***20*** — إنْسان ج. ناس

humidity ***5*** — رُطوبة

hundred ***8*** — مِئَة (مائة) ج. مئات

hungry ***U-8*** — جَوْعان ج. جَوْعانين (عامية)

husband ***3*** — زَوْج ج. أزْواج

❄ I ❄

I ***U-8*** — أنا

ice, snow ***5*** — ثَلْج

i.e. ***16*** — أيْ

idea, thought ***18*** — فِكْرة ج. أفْكار

if ***8*** — إذا ؛ إن

if *(hypothetical)* ***13*** — لَوْ

important, powerful (also: big; old) ***U-6*** — كَبير ج. كِبار

important, momentous ***18*** — مُهِمّ ج. مُهِمّون

in ***1*** — في

in need of ***7*** — بِحاجة إلى

in order to, to ***6*** — لِـ + مصدر / مضارع منصوب

(to) increase, exceed ***17*** — زادَ عن ، يَزيد ، الزِّيادة

independent ***20*** — مُستَقِلّ ج. مُستَقِلّون

Indian (Asian or Native American) — هِندي ج. هُنود

individual ***4*** — فَرْد ج. أفْراد

(to) intend, mean ***10*** — قَصَدَ ، يَقصِد ، القَصد

(to) intend ***15***	نَوَى أنْ ، يَنْوي ، النِّيّة
intermediate ***2***	مُتَوَسِّط
Iran ***U-9***	إيران
Iraq ***U-9***	العِراق
(to) be, is ***4***	كانَ ، يَكون
is not, are not ***8***	لَيسَ
island ***14***	جَزيرة ج. جُزُر
Israel ***U-9***	إسرائيل

❄ J ❄

jacket ***15***	جاكيت ج. جاكيتات
Japan	اليابان
Jerusalem ***20***	القُدْس
job ***13***	وَظيفة ج. وَظائِف
(to) join, enter *(e.g.: school or army)* ***8***	اِلْتَحَقَ بِـ ، يَلْتَحِق ، الاِلْتِحاق
Jordan ***U-9***	الأُرْدُن
journal, magazine ***13***	مَجَلّة ج. مَجَلّات

❄ K ❄

king ***10***	مَلِك ج. مُلوك
kitchen ***14***	مَطْبَخ ج. مَطابِخ
(to) know ***3***	عَرَفَ ، يَعْرِف ، المَعْرِفة
(to get to) know, become acquainted with ***11***	تَعَرَّفَ عَلى ، يَتَعَرَّف ، التَعَرُّف
Kuwait ***U-9***	الكُوَيْت

❄ L ❄

lady; Mrs. ***U-4***	سَيِّدة ج. سيِّدات
language ***2***	لُغة ج. لُغات

last ***12***	آخِر ج. آخِرون
late ***10***	مُتَأَخِّر ج. مُتَأَخِّرون
(to be) late, fall behind ***8***	تَأَخَّرَ ، يَتَأَخَّر ، التَّأَخُّر
law ***3***	الحُقوق
(Islamic) law ***3***	الشَّريعة
(to) learn *(e.g.: __ a language, a new word)* ***1***	تَعَلَّمَ ، يَتَعَلَّم ، التَّعَلُّم
(to) learn, study ***1***	دَرَسَ ، يَدْرُس ، الدِّراسة
(to) learn of, find out about ***12***	عَلِمَ بِـ ، يَعْلَم ، العِلْم
(to) leave ***14***	تَرَكَ ، يَتْرُك ، التَّرْك
(to) leave ***20***	غادَرَ ، يُغادِر ، المُغادَرة
Lebanon ***U-9***	لُبْنان
lecture ***6***	مُحاضَرة ج. مُحاضَرات
left *(side)*	يَسار
foot ***18***	رِجل ج. أرجُل
lesson ***U-4***	دَرْس ج. دُروس
letter ***3***	رِسالة ج. رَسائِل
library ***U-7***	مَكْتَبة ج. مَكْتَبات
Libya ***U-9***	ليبيا
life ***12***	الحَياة
like, similar to ***8***	مِثْل + اسم
like, as ***15***	كَـ + اسم
like, as ***8***	كَما + فعل
likewise, also ***13***	كَذلِك
(to) listen to ***4***	اِستَمَعَ إلى ، يَستَمِع ، الاِستِماع
literature ***1***	أدَب ج. آداب
(a) little *(adverb)* ***9***	قَليلاً

(to) live, be alive **7**	عاشَ ، يَعيش ، العَيْش
(to) live, reside *(e.g.: __ in Egypt)* **1**	سَكَنَ ، يَسْكُن ، السَّكَن
(to) live *(i.e.: to reside or stay ; e.g.: __ in a hotel)* **10**	أقامَ ، يُقيم ، الإقامة
living *(e.g.: __ room)* **14**	مَعيشة
loneliness **5**	وِحْدة
long, tall **U-6**	طَويل ج. طِوال
longing for one's native land, feeling a stranger in a strange place **13**	الغُرْبَة
Lord, God **17**	الرَبّ
(to) love **5**	أحبَّ ، يُحِبّ ، الحُبّ
lunch **6**	الغَداء

❄ M ❄

magazine, journal **13**	مَجَلّة ج. مَجَلّات
mail, post **18**	بَريد
(to) make, prepare **14**	أعَدَّ ، يُعِدّ ، الإعْداد
making the mutual acquaintance *(of)*, getting to know *(one other)* **8**	تَعارُف
man **U-7**	رَجُل ج. رِجال
(young) man **18**	شابّ ج. شُبّان
many, much **5**	كَثيرًا
market	سوق ج. أسواق
masculine **1**	مُذَكَّر
master's degree **2**	الماجِسْتير
match, game **10**	مُباراة ج. مُبارَيات
Mauritania **U-9**	موريتانيا
maybe, perhaps **18**	رُبَّما
(to) mean, intend **10**	قَصَدَ ، يقْصِد ، القَصْد
meaning **18**	مَعْنى ج. مَعانٍ/المَعاني

(*it*) means ***13***	يَعْني
meat ***6***	لحْم ج. لحُوم
medicine ***3***	الطِّبّ
to meet, get together ***17***	اِجْتَمَعَ ، يَجتَمِع ، الاِجْتِماع
meeting ***19***	اِجْتِماع ج. اِجْتِماعات
(*to*) meet (*someone, in a formal setting*) ***19***	قابَلَ ، يُقابِل ، المُقابَلة
(*to*) memorize ***4***	حَفِظَ ، يَحْفَظ ، الحِفْظ
(*to*) mention (*also:* to recall) ***14***	ذَكَرَ ، يَذْكُر ، الذِّكْر
Middle East ***2***	الشَّرْق الأوْسَط
middle, mid-way ***16***	مُنْتَصَف
milk ***U-6***	حَليب / لَبَن
ministry ***7***	وِزارة ج. وِزارات
minute ***9***	دَقيقة ج. دَقائِق
Miss ***U-5***	آنِسة ج. آنِسات
(*to*) miss, be absent from (*e.g.: __ school*) ***12***	تَغَيَّبَ عن ، يَتَغَيَّب ، التَّغَيُّب
Monday ***6***	الاِثْنَيْن
money ***U-6***	فُلوس
month ***16***	شَهْر ج. أشْهُر / شُهور
morals ***18***	أخْلاق
more ***10***	أكْثَر
morning ***U-4***	صَباح
Morocco ***U-9***	المَغْرِب
mosque ***10***	جامِع ج. جَوامِع
most of ***11***	مُعْظَم
mother ***1***	والِدة ج. والِدات
mother ***8***	أُمّ ج. أُمَّهات

(to) move to ***14***	انْتَقَلَ إلى ، يَنْتَقِل ، الاِنْتِقال
Mr., Sir ***U-5***	سَيِّد ج. سادة
Mrs.; Lady ***U-5***	سَيِّدة ج. سَيِّدات
much, many ***5***	كَثيرًا
music ***7***	الموسيقى
must ***16***	يَجِب أن

❄ N ❄

name, noun ***1***	اِسْم ج. أَسْماء
naturally, of course ***12***	طَبْعًا
Near East ***2***	الشَّرْق الأَدْنى
necessary ***19***	ضَروريّ
necessary ***16***	لازِم
(it is) necessary to *(impersonal and fixed)* ***16***	يَجِب أنْ
(to) need, be in need of ***13***	اِحْتاجَ إلى ، يَحْتاج ، الاِحْتِياج
in need of ***8***	بِحاجة إلى
negation ***8***	النَّفي
neighbor ***U-3***	جار ج. جيران
new ***U-3***	جَديد ج. جُدُد
news ***U-3***	خَبَر ج. أَخْبار
newspaper ***9***	جَريدة ج. جَرائِد
newspaper ***17***	صَحيفة ج. صُحُف
next, coming ***12***	قادِم ج. قادِمون
next to ***14***	بِجانِب
nice, kind, pleasant ***U-6***	لَطيف ج. لِطاف / لُطَفاء
night ***10***	لَيْلة ج. ليالٍ / الليالي
nine ***U-7***	تِسْعة

ninety *8*	تِسْعون / تِسْعين
no ***U-7***	لا
no one, none (of) ***11***	لا أحد (مِن)
north ***15***	شَمال
not to ***13***	ألاّ (=أنْ + لا)
notebook, copybook ***U-6***	دَفْتَر ج. دَفاتِر
noun, name ***1***	اِسْم ج. أَسْماء
novel ***19***	رِواية ج. رِوايات
now ***3***	الآن
number ***U-7***	رَقْم ج. أَرْقام
number ***8***	عَدَد ج. أَعْداد

❄ O ❄

(direct) object of a verb ***17***	مَفعول بِهِ
(to) obtain, get ***6***	حَصَلَ على ، يَحْصُل ، الحُصول
(to be, become) occupied with ***17***	اِنْشَغَلَ بِـ ، يَنْشَغِل ، الاِنْشِغال
o'clock (*also:* hour; clock) ***9***	ساعة ج. ساعات
office ***U-7***	مَكْتَب ج. مَكاتِب
officer ***3***	ضابِط ج. ضُبّاط
oil ***6***	زَيْت ج. زُيوت
old (*also:* big; important) ***U-6***	كَبير ج. كِبار
old, ancient *(for things, not for people)* ***2***	قَديم
Oman ***U-9***	عُمان
on ***U-9***	عَلى
once, *(one)* time ***11***	مَرّة ج. مَرّات
one of *(m.)* ***11***	أَحَد
one of *(f.)* ***18***	إحدى

one ***U-3***	واحِد
onions	بَصَل
only ***5***	فَقَط
only; lonely ***2***	وَحيد ج. وَحيدون
opinion ***8***	رَأْي ج. آراء
opportunity ***13***	فُرْصة ج. فُرَص
or ***9***	أَوْ
(in) order to, to ***6***	لِـ + مصدر / مضارع منصوب
origin, descent ***5***	أَصْل ج. أُصول
other *(f.)* ***9***	أُخْرى ج. أُخْرَيات
other *(m.)* ***9***	آخَر ج. آخَرون
outside *(preposition)* ***11***	خارِج
outstanding, superior ***18***	مُتَفَوِّق ج. مُتَفَوِّقون
over crowdedness ***5***	ازْدِحام
overcast, cloudy ***5***	غائِم
(its) own, private; special ***9***	خاصّ
(to) own, possess ***15***	مَلَكَ ، يَمْلِك ، المُلْك

❄ P ❄

page ***U-6***	صَفْحة ج. صَفَحات
pajamas ***15***	بيجاما ج. بيجامات
Palestine ***U-9***	فِلِسْطين
Palestinian ***1***	فِلِسْطينِيّ ج. فِلِسْطينِيّون
(a pair of) pants ***15***	بَنْطَلون ج. بَنْطَلونات
(piece of) paper ***U-6***	وَرَقة ج. أَوْراق
park, garden ***14***	حَديقة ج. حَدائِق
part (of) ***18***	جُزْء (مِن) ج. أَجْزاء

(to) pass, elapse *(e.g.: the time __es)* ***19***	مَرَّ ، يَمُرّ ، المُرور
(to) pass, spend *(time)* ***12***	قَضى ، يَقْضي ، القَضاء
(to) pass, succeed *(e.g.: __ an exam)* ***8***	نَجَحَ في ، يَنْجَح ، النَّجاح
passport ***20***	جَواز سَفَر ج. جَوازات سَفَر
past *(tense)*, past *(week, month, etc.)* ***8***	الماضي
pen ***U-7***	قَلَم ج. أقلام
people *(note: sing. = human being)* ***11***	ناس (م. إنسان)
perhaps, maybe ***18***	رُبَّما
(to) permit *(someone)* to do *(something)* ***10***	سَمَحَ لِـ... بِـ... ، يَسْمَح ، السَّماح
person ***15***	شَخْص ج. أشْخاص
pharmacology ***11***	الصَّيْدَلة
pharmacy ***15***	صَيْدَلِيّة ج. صَيْدَلِيّات
Ph.D. ***2***	الدُّكْتوراه
philosophy ***3***	الفَلْسَفة
photography ***7***	التَّصْوير
picture ***3***	صورة ج. صُوَر
pilgrim *(one who has done the main pilgrimage to Mecca)* ***7***	حاجّ (مؤنث: حاجّة)
(the main) pilgrimage to Mecca ***7***	الحَجّ
pink ***18***	زَهرِيّ
pita bread ***U-3***	خُبْز عَرَبيّ
place ***14***	مَكان ج. أماكِن
(to) play ***9***	لَعِبَ ، يَلْعَب ، اللَّعِب
please *(addressing a male)* ***U-10***	مِنْ فَضْلَك
please *(addressing a female)* ***U-10***	مِنْ فَضْلِك
please... *(e.g.: __ inform him; also: to hope)* ***16***	رَجا ، يَرجو ، الرَّجاء
plural ***2***	الجَمع

political science *3*	العُلوم السِّياسِيّة
position, job *13*	وَظيفة ج. وَظائِف
(it is) possible to *10*	يُمْكِن أنْ
prayer *10*	صَلاة ج. صَلَوات
predicate *2*	خَبَر
(to) preoccupy *18*	شَغَلَ ، يَشْغُل ، الشُّغْل
preparatory (*_ school – junior high)* *7*	إعْدادِيّ
(to) prepare *(i.e.: arrange)* *16*	رَتَّبَ ، يُرَتِّب ، التَّرْتيب
(to) prepare *(i.e.: make)* *14*	أعَدَّ ، يُعِدّ ، الإعْداد
(to) prepare for *16*	اِسْتَعَدَّ لِـ ، يَسْتَعِدّ ، الاِسْتِعْداد
prepared, ready *19*	مُسْتَعِدّ ج. مُسْتَعِدّون
president *12*	رَئيس ج. رُؤَساء
pretty, beautiful *U-7*	جَميل ج. جَميلون
previously, before *(now)* *14*	مِن قَبْل
primary *4*	اِبْتِدائي
private, (its) own; special *9*	خاصّ
problem *12*	مُشْكِلة ج. مَشاكِل / مُشْكِلات
professor *(m.)* *U-5*	أُسْتاذ ج. أساتِذة
professor *(f.)* *U-5*	أُسْتاذة ج. أُسْتاذات
program *2*	بَرْنامَج ج. بَرامِج
pronoun *2*	ضَمير ج. ضَمائِر
prophet *4*	نَبِيّ ج. أنْبِياء
province *20*	مُحافَظة ج. مُحافَظات
psychology *3*	عِلم النَّفس
public, general *7*	عامّ
(to) publish	أصدَرَ ، يُصدِر ، الإصدار

purple *18* — بَنَفْسَجِيّ

Q

Qatar ***U-9*** — قَطَر

(one) quarter ***9*** — رُبْع ج. أَرْباع

question ***U-9*** — سُؤال ج. أَسْئِلة

quickly ***10*** — بِسُرعة

the Quran ***U-9*** — القُرآن

R

rain ***5*** — مَطَر ج. أمطار

rainy, raining ***5*** — مُمْطِر ، ماطِر

Ramadan *(month in Islamic calendar in which Muslims fast)* ***16*** — رَمَضان

(to) read ***8*** — قَرَأ ، يَقْرَأ ، القِراءة

real, actual ***18*** — حَقيقيّ ج. حَقيقيّون

ready, prepared ***19*** — مُسْتَعِدّ ج. مُسْتَعِدّون

really!, indeed ***2*** — فِعْلاً

(to) recall *(also:* to mention*)* ***14*** — ذَكَرَ ، يَذْكُر ، الذِّكْر

(to) receive, welcome ***10*** — اِسْتَقْبَلَ ، يَسْتَقْبِل ، الاِسْتِقْبال

red ***18*** — أَحْمَر (مؤنّث: حَمْراء)

(to) refuse ***8*** — رَفَضَ ، يَرْفُض ، الرَّفْض

(in) relation to, for ***5*** — بِالنِّسْبة لِـ

relationship *(pl.: relations)* ***11*** — عَلاقة ج. عَلاقات

relative, family member ***3*** — قَريب ج. أقارِب / أقْرِباء

religion ***3*** — دين ج. أدْيان

(to) remain, stay ***12*** — بَقِيَ ، يَبْقى ، البَقاء

(the) remainder, rest of ***17*** — بَقِيّة

(to) remember ***4***	تَذَكَّرَ ، يَتَذَكَّر ، التَّذَكُّر
(to) rent ***14***	اِسْتَأْجَرَ ، يَسْتَأْجِر ، الاِسْتِئجار
(to) repair ***16***	أَصْلَحَ ، يُصْلِح ، الإصْلاح
(to) reside, live ***1***	سَكَنَ ، يَسْكُن ، السَّكَن
(to) reside, stay ***10***	أقامَ ، يُقيم ، الإقامة
(the) rest, remainder of ***17***	بَقِيّة
restaurant ***6***	مَطْعَم ج. مَطاعِم
(to) resume ***19***	اِسْتَأْنَفَ ، يَسْتَأْنِف ، الاِسْتِئْناف
(to) return ***13***	رَجَعَ ، يَرْجِع ، الرُّجوع
(to) return ***9***	عادَ ، يَعود ، العَوْدة
(to) review (lessons; i.e.: do homework, study) ***8***	ذاكَرَ ، يُذاكِر ، المُذاكَرة
rice ***6***	أَرُزّ
right (side)	يَمين
(to) rise, get up ***17***	قامَ ، يَقوم ، القِيام
romantic, emotional ***11***	عاطِفيّ
room ***U-6***	غُرْفة ج. غُرَف
root ***8***	جَذر ج. جُذور
roughly, around ***9***	حَوالَيْ
(to) rule ***20***	حَكَمَ ، يَحكُم ، الحُكم
(to) run ***7***	جَرَى ، يَجْري ، الجَري

❄ S ❄

salad ***6***	سَلَطة ج. سَلَطات
(the) same ***1***	نَفْس الـ...
Saturday ***6***	السَّبْت
Saudi Arabia ***U-9***	السَّعوديّة
(to) say ***U-9***	قالَ ، يَقول ، القَوْل

scared	خائِف ج. خائِفون
scarf, Arab headdress **15**	كوفيّة ج. كوفيّات
scholarship award, grant **12**	مِنْحة ج. مِنَح
school **4**	مَدْرَسة ج. مَدارِس
school, college *(in a university)* **3**	كُلِّيّة ج. كُلِّيّات
science **3**	عِلْم ج. عُلوم
sea **15**	بَحْر ج. بِحار
season *(e.g.: spring __ ; also: class)* **5**	فَصْل ج. فُصول
second *(e.g.: the __ lesson)* **4**	ثانٍ /الثّاني
secondary (__ *school = high school)* **7**	ثانَويّة
(to) see **13**	رأى ، يَرى ، الرُّؤْية
(it) seems, appears that *(impersonal)* **17**	يَبْدو أنَّ
(to) send **13**	أرْسَلَ ، يُرْسِل ، الإرْسال
sentence **2**	جُمْلة ج. جُمَل
series, serial **17**	مُسَلْسَل ج. مُسَلْسَلات
(to) set, determine *(e.g.: __ a time)* **15**	حَدَّدَ ، يُحَدِّد ، التَّحْديد
(to become) settled, to settle down **13**	اِسْتَقَرَّ ، يَسْتَقِرّ ، الاِسْتِقْرار
seven ***U-7***	سَبْعة
seventy **8**	سَبْعون / سَبْعين
several **11**	عِدّة + **جمع**
shame *(on you; lit.: not legal)* **12**	حَرام
(to) share, have in common **15**	اِشْتَرَكَ في ، يَشْتَرِك ، الاِشْتِراك
shape, form **18**	شَكْل ج. أشْكال
she ***U-8***	هِيَ
sheet *(bed___)* **16**	مِلاية ج. مِلايات
shirt **15**	قَميص ج. قُمصان

(pair of) shoes ***15***	حِذاء ج. أَحْذِية
short ***U-6***	قَصير ج. قِصار
shy ***7***	خَجول
shyness ***11***	الخَجَل
sick ***U-8***	مَريض ج. مَرْضى
silver ***18***	فِضِّيّ
since; ago ***6***	مُنْذُ
singular ***2***	المُفرد
sister ***U-3***	أُخْت ج. أَخَوات
(to) sit ***9***	جَلَسَ ، يَجْلِس ، الجُلوس
six ***U-7***	سِتّة
sixty ***8***	سِتّون / سِتّين
skiing ***7***	التَّزَلُّج
skirt ***15***	تَنّورة ج. تَنانير / جيب ج. جيبات
(to) sleep, go to sleep ***10***	نامَ ، يَنام ، النَّوْم
small ***U-6***	صَغير ج. صِغار
smart, intelligent ***18***	ذَكِيّ ج. أَذْكِياء
(to) smoke ***9***	دَخَّنَ ، يُدَخِّن ، التَّدْخين
snow, ice ***5***	ثَلْج
so as to ***19***	حَتّى + المضارع المنصوب
so, thus ... ***5***	فَـ...
so, thus ***6***	لِذٰلِك
so, thus ***7***	هٰكَذا
soccer ***7***	كُرة القَدَم
sociology ***7***	عِلم الاِجتِماع
some of ***9***	بَعْض

sometimes *5*	أحْيانًا
son *3*	ابْن ج. أبْناء
son, boy *(also:* child*)* ***U-7***	وَلَد ج. أوْلاد
song *17*	أُغنية ج. أغانٍ/الأغاني
soup *6*	شوربة
south *15*	جَنوب
spacious, wide ***U-5***	واسِع
(to) speak, talk (about) *4*	تَكَلَّمَ (عن) ، يَتَكَلَّم ، الكَلام
(to) speak, talk about *20*	تَحَدَّثَ عن ، يَتَحَدَّث ، التَّحَدُّث
special; (its) own, private *9*	خاصّ
specializing, specialist in *2*	مُتَخَصِّص في ج. مُتَخَصِّصون
(to) spend, pass *(time)* *12*	قَضى ، يَقْضي ، القَضاء
sports *7*	الرِّياضة
spring *5*	الرَّبيع
state, province *2*	وِلاية ج. وِلايات
(to) stay, remain *12*	بَقِيَ ، يَبْقى ، البَقاء
(to) stay, reside *10*	أقامَ ، يُقيم ، الإقامة
(to) stay up late *10*	سَهِرَ ، يَسْهَر ، السَّهَر
still, continue to *(lit.:* do not cease*)* *13*	ما زالَ ، لا يَزال + **المضارع المرفوع / اسم**
stomach, belly *18*	بَطن ج. بُطون
(to) stop *(doing something)* *19*	تَوَقَّفَ (عن) ، يَتَوَقَّف ، التَّوَقُّف
story ***U-6***	قِصّة ج. قِصَص
story, floor *14*	طابِق ج. طَوابِق
strange, foreign ***U-5***	غَريب ج. غُرَباء
(feeling a) stranger in a strange place, longing for one's native land *13*	الغُرْبَة
street ***U-5***	شارِع ج. شَوارِع

student *(m.)* ***U-6***	طالِب ج. طُلاّب
student *(f.)* ***U-6***	طالِبة ج. طالِبات
study (of), studies ***3***	دِراسة ج. دِراسات
(to) study *(i.e.: review lessons, do homework)* ***8***	ذاكَرَ ، يُذاكِر ، المُذاكَرة
(to) study, learn ***1***	دَرَسَ ، يَدْرُس ، الدِّراسة
study (of), studies ***3***	دِراسة ج. دِراسات
subject ***15***	مَوْضوع ج. مَوْضوعات / مَواضيع
subject *(grammar: _ of verbal sentence)* ***17***	فاعِل
(to) succeed, pass ***8***	نَجَحَ في ، يَنْجَح ، النَّجاح
Sudan ***U-9***	السّودان
sugar ***U-6***	سُكَّر
suit ***15***	بَدلة ج. بَدَلات
suitable, appropriate ***13***	مُناسِب
summer ***5***	الصَّيْف
sun ***5***	شَمس
Sunday ***6***	الأحَد
sunny ***5***	مُشْمِس
superior, outstanding ***18***	مُتَفَوِّق ج. مُتَفَوِّقون
(to) supervise ***17***	أشْرَفَ على ، يُشْرِف ، الإشْراف
sweater ***15***	بلوفر ج. بلوفرات
swimming ***7***	السِّباحة
swimming pool ***14***	حَمّام سِباحة
Syria ***U-9***	سوريّا

❄ T ❄

table ***U-6***	طاولة ج. طاولات
(to) take ***12***	أخَذَ ، يَأْخُذ ، الأخْذ

(it was) taken *(passive)* **20** — أُخِذَ

(to) take, have *(a meal)* **9** — تَناوَلَ ، يَتَناوَل ، التَّناوُل

(to) talk, speak about **20** — تَحَدَّثَ عَن ، يَتَحَدَّث ، التَحَدُّث

tall, long ***U-6*** — طَويل ج. طِوال

tea ***U-4*** — شاي

(to) teach **3** — دَرَّسَ ، يُدَرِّس ، التَّدْريس

to teach **16** — عَلَّمَ ، يُعَلِّم ، التَّعليم

teaching assistant, graduate fellow **6** — مُعيد ج. مُعيدون

telephone — هاتِف

ten ***U-7*** — عَشَرة

test, examination ***U-7*** — اِمْتِحان ج. اِمْتِحانات

thank you ***U-10*** — شُكْرًا

thanks to 8 — بِفَضْل

that *(after a verb; e.g.: to think __)* **13** — أنَّ

that *(demonstrative pronoun) (m.)* **6** — ذٰلِك (مؤنّث: تِلْكَ)

that *(demonstrative pronoun) (f.)* **6** — تِلْكَ (مذكّر: ذٰلِك)

theater **13** — مَسْرَح ج. مَسارِح

then **9** — ثُمَّ

there; there is/are **7** — هُناك

they **2** — هُم

they *(dual)* **15** — هُما

they *(pl., f.)* **19** — هُنَّ

thing **15** — شَيء ج. أشْياء

(to) think about, ponder **17** — فَكَّرَ في، بِـ ، يُفَكِّر ، التَفْكير

(to) think that, consider **13** — ظَنَّ أنَّ ، يَظُنّ ، الظَنّ

third *(e.g.: the __ lesson)* **9** — ثالِث

(one) third ***9***	ثُلْث
thirsty ***U-8***	عَطْشان ج. عَطْشانين (عامية)
thirty ***8***	ثَلاثون / ثَلاثين
this *(m.)* ***U-8***	هٰذا
this *(f.)* ***U-8***	هٰذِهِ
those *(human plural)* ***19***	هٰؤُلاء
thought, idea ***18***	فِكْرة ج. أفْكار
thousand ***20***	أَلْف ج. آلاف / أُلوف
three ***U-7***	ثَلاثة
throughout, during ***8***	طِوال
Thursday ***6***	الخَميس
thus, so ... ***5***	فَـ...
thus, so ***6***	لِذٰلِك
thus, so ***7***	هٰكَذا
tie (clothing) ***15***	كرافات ج. كرافاتات
time *(e.g.: I have __)* ***9***	وَقْت ج. أَوْقات
(one) time, once ***11***	مَرّة ج. مَرّات
tired ***U-8***	تَعْبان ج. تَعْبانين (عامية)
to, in order to ***6***	لِـ + مصدر / مضارع
to, toward ***U-9***	إلى
today ***6***	اليَوْم
together *(e.g.: with one another)* ***11***	مَعًا
together *(e.g.: altogether, all of them)* ***12***	جَميعًا
tomorrow ***12***	غَدًا
tongue ***18***	لِسان ج. أَلسِنة
tonight ***10***	اللَّيْلة

topic *15* — مَوْضوع ج. مَوْضوعات / مواضيع

tourism *11* — السِّياحة

towel *16* — فوطة ج. فُوَط

toward, to *U-9* — إلى

trade, commerce *6* — التِّجارة

translation *2* — تَرْجَمة

translator *2* — مُتَرْجِم ج. مُتَرْجِمون

(to) transmit, convey *17* — نَقَلَ ، يَنْقُل ، النَّقْل

(to) travel (to) *4* — سافَرَ (إلى) ، يُسافِر ، السَّفَر

trip, flight *10* — رِحْلة ج. رِحلات

true, correct *20* — صَحيح

Tuesday *6* — الثُّلاثاء

Tunisia or Tunis *U-9* — تونِس

Turkey *U-9* — تُركيّا

twenty *8* — عِشْرون / عِشْرين

two *U-7* — اِثْنان / اِثْنَيْن

❄ U ❄

uncle *(maternal)* *2* — خال ج. أخْوال

uncle *(paternal)* *3* — عَمّ ج. أعْمام

(to) understand *10* — فَهِمَ ، يَفْهَم ، الفَهْم

(to) undertake, assume *(e.g.: __ a job)* *17* — تَوَلّى ، يَتَوَلّى

underwear *15* — مَلابِس داخِلِيّة

United Arab Emirates *U-9* — الإمارات العَرَبِيّة المُتَّحِدة

United Nations *1* — الأُمَم المُتَّحِدة

United States of America *1* — الوِلايات المُتَّحِدة الأمريكِيّة

university *U-5* — جامِعة ج. جامِعات

until *(preposition)* ***17*** — حَتَّى

upset; annoyed, angry ***U-8*** — زَعْلان ج. زَعْلانين (عامية)

usually ***10*** — عادةً

❄ V ❄

vacation, leave *(of absence)* ***12*** — إجازة ج. إجازات

vacation, holiday ***12*** — عُطْلة ج. عُطْلات / عُطَل

vegetables ***6*** — خُضار

verb ***5*** — فِعل ج. أفعال

verse *(of the Quran)* ***20*** — آية ج. آيات

very ***5*** — جِدّاً

(to) visit ***12*** — زارَ ، يَزور ، الزِّيارة

volleyball ***7*** — الكُرة الطّائِرة

❄ W ❄

(to) wake up, awaken ***10*** — صَحا ، يَصْحو ، الصَحْو

(to) wake (someone) up ***9*** — أيْقَظَ ، يوقِظ ، الإيْقاظ

(to) want to ***8*** — أراد أنْ ، يُريد ، الإرادة

(to) want to, have a desire to ***13*** — رَغِبَ في ، يَرْغَب ، الرَّغْبة

watch *(also clock, hour)* ***U-5*** — ساعة ج. ساعات

(to) watch ***4*** — شاهَدَ ، يُشاهِد ، المُشاهَدة

water ***U-7*** — ماء

we ***2*** — نَحْنُ

weak ***8*** — ضَعيف

(to) wear *(clothes)*, get dressed ***15*** — لَبِسَ ، يَلْبَس ، اللُّبْس

weather ***5*** — جَوّ / طَقْس

Wednesday ***6*** — الأرْبِعاء

week ***6*** — أُسْبوع ج. أسابيع

(to) welcome **18**	رَحَّبَ بِـ ، يُرَحِّب ، التَّرْحيب
(you're) welcome **U-10**	عَفْوًا
well, fine *(said of people)* **17**	بِخَيْر
well *(adverb)* **5**	جَيِّدًا
west **15**	غَرْب
what? *(in questions using verbs)* **1**	ماذا + **فعل**
what? *(in questions without verbs)* **1**	ما ؟
whatever **13**	ما + **فعل**
when *(not a question)* **11**	عِنْدَما
when? **6**	مَتى ؟
where *(not a question; also, ≠ "in which")* **2**	حَيْثُ
where? **1**	أيْن ؟
which, that *(m.; relative pronoun)* **15**	الَّذي ج. الَّذين
which, that *(f.; relative pronoun)* **15**	الَّتي ج. اللَّواتي/اللاَّتي
which...? **1**	أيّ ...؟
white *(m.)* **18**	أبْيَض ج. بيض
white *(f.)* **18**	بَيْضاء ج. بيضوات
white/grey-haired **18**	أشْيَب
who?, whom; whoever **1**	مَن ؟
why? **5**	لِماذا ؟
wide, spacious **U-5**	واسِع
wife **3**	زَوْجة ج. زَوْجات
wife **7**	حَرَم
window **U-6**	شُبّاك ج. شَبابيك
winter **5**	الشِّتاء
(to) wish, hope that **14**	تَمَنّى أنْ ، يَتَمَنّى ، التَمَنّي

with *(people)* ***7***	مَع
with, by *(things)* ***U-10***	بِـ
without ***13***	بِدون
(a) woman *(note: def. form is also collective)* ***U-7***	اِمْرَأة (def: المَرْأة) ج. نِساء
women	نِساء (م. اِمْرَأة ، المَرْأة)
(I) wonder... *(fixed expression)* ***16***	يا تُرى... + **سؤال**
word ***U-7***	كَلِمة ج. كَلِمات
(to) work ***1***	عَمِلَ ، يَعْمَلَ ، العَمَل
work ***2***	شُغْل / عَمَل
worker ***13***	عامِل ج. عُمّال
(the) world ***9***	العالَم
(the) world ***20***	الدُّنْيا
(to) write	كَتَبَ ، يَكْتُب ، الكِتابة
writer ***19***	كاتِب ج. كُتّاب

❄ Y ❄

year ***17***	عام ج. أعْوام
year ***2***	سَنة ج. سَنَوات
yellow ***18***	أصْفَر (مؤنّث: صَفْراء)
Yemen ***U-9***	اليَمَن
yes ***U-7***	نَعَم
yesterday ***9***	أمْس
you *(m.)* ***U-8***	أنْتَ
you *(f.)* ***U-8***	أنْتِ
you *(pl.)* ***2***	أنْتُم
you *(f., pl.)* ***19***	أنْتُنّ
you *(polite form, f.)* ***U-4***	حَضْرِتِك

you *(polite form, m.)* ***U-4***	حَضْرِتَك
you *(pl.)* **2**	أنْتُم
you *(dual)* ***15***	أنْتُما
you *(fem. pl.)* ***19***	أنْتُنَّ
young person ***18***	شابّ ج. شُبّان
youth *(abstract or collective)* ***18***	الشَّباب

جدول الضمائر Pronouns

الضمائر المنفصلة Independent	ضمائر الملكية Possessive	مع الماضي	مع المضارع	ضمائر النصب Object
هُوَ	كِتابـ ـهُ	فَهِمَ	يَـ ـفْهَمُ	فَهِمَ ـهُ
هُما	كِتابـ ـهُما	فَهِمـ ـا	يَـ ـفْهَمـ ـانِ	فَهِمَ ـهما
هُمْ	كِتابـ ـهُم	فَهِمـ ـوا	يَـ ـفْهَمـ ـونَ	فَهِمَ ـهُمْ
هِيَ	كِتابـ ـها	فَهِمَ ـتْ	تَـ ـفْهَمُ	فَهِمَ ـها
هُما	كِتابـ ـهُما	فَهِمـ ـَتا	تَـ ـفْهَمـ ـانِ	فَهِمَ ـهُما
هُنَّ	كِتابـ ـهُنَّ	فَهِمْـ ـنَ	يَـ ـفْهَمْـ ـنَ	فَهِمَ ـهُنَّ
أَنْتَ	كِتابـ ـكَ	فَهِمْـ ـتَ	تَـ ـفْهَمُ	فَهِمَ ـكَ
أَنْتُما	كِتابـ ـكُما	فَهِمْـ ـتُما	تَـ ـفْهَمـ ـانِ	فَهِمَ ـكُما
أَنْتُم	كِتابـ ـكُم	فَهِمْـ ـتُم	تَـ ـفْهَمـ ـونَ	فَهِمَ ـكُم
أَنْتِ	كِتابـ ـكِ	فَهِمْـ ـتِ	تَـ ـفْهَمـ ـينَ	فَهِمَ ـكِ
أَنْتُما	كِتابـ ـكُما	فَهِمْـ ـتُما	تَـ ـفْهَمـ ـانِ	فَهِمَ ـكُما
أَنْتُنَّ	كِتابـ ـكُنَّ	فَهِمْـ ـتُنَّ	تَـ ـفْهَمْـ ـنَ	فَهِمَ ـكُنَّ
أنا	كِتابـ ـي	فَهِمْـ ـتُ	أَ فْهَمُ	فَهِمَ ـني
نَحْنُ	كِتابـ ـنا	فَهِمْـ ـنا	نَـ ـفْهَمُ	فَهِمَ ـنا

تصريف فعل " كتب "

الوزن: فَعَلَ — المصدر: الكتابَة

الضمير	الماضي	المضارع المرفوع	المضارع المنصوب	المضارع المجزوم	الأمر
هو	كَتَبَ	يَكْتُبُ	يَكْتُبَ	يَكْتُبْ	———
هما	كَتَبا	يَكْتُبَانِ	يَكْتُبا	يَكْتُبا	———
هم	كَتَبوا	يَكْتُبُون	يَكْتُبوا	يَكْتُبوا	———
هي	كَتَبَتْ	تَكْتُب	تَكْتُبَ	تَكْتُب	———
هما	كَتَبَتا	تَكْتُبانِ	تَكْتُبا	تَكْتُبا	———
هنَّ	كَتَبْنَ	يَكْتُبْنَ	يَكْتُبْنَ	يَكْتُبْنَ	———
أنتَ	تَكْتُب	تَكْتُبُ	تَكْتُب	تَكْتُبْ	أُكْتُب
أنتما	كَتَبْتُما	تَكْتُبانِ	تَكْتُبا	تَكْتُبا	أُكْتُبا
أنتم	كَتَبْتُمْ	تَكْتُبون	تَكْتُبوا	تَكْتُبوا	أُكْتُبوا
أنتِ	كَتَبْتِ	تَكْتُبين	تَكْتُبي	تَكْتُبي	أُكْتُبي
أنتما	كَتَبْتُما	تَكْتُبا	تَكْتُبا	تَكْتُبا	أُكْتُبا
أنتنَّ	كَتَبْتُنَّ	تَكْتُبْنَ	تَكْتُبْنَ	تَكْتُبْنَ	
أنا	كَتَبْتُ	أَكْتُبُ	أَكْتُبَ	أَكْتُب	———
نحن	كَتَبْنا	نَكْتُب	نَكْتُبَ	نَكْتُبْ	———

تصريف فعل " بدأ "

الوزن: فَعَلَ

المصدر: البَدْء

الضمير	الماضي	المضارع المرفوع	المضارع المنصوب	المضارع المجزوم	الأمر
هو	بَدَأَ	يَبْدَأُ	يَبْدَأَ	يَبْدَأْ	———
هما	بَدَآ	يَبْدَآنِ	يَبْدَآ	يَبْدَآ	———
هم	بدأوا	يبدأون	يبْدأوا	يَبْدأوا	———
هي	بَدَأَتْ	تَبْدَأُ	تَبْدَأَ	تَبْدَأْ	———
هما	بَدَأَتا	تَبْدَآنِ	تَبْدَآ	تَبْدَآ	———
هنَّ	بَدَأْنَ	يَبْدَأْنَ	يَبْدَأْنَ	يَبْدَأْنَ	———
أنتَ	بَدَأْتَ	تَبْدَأُ	تَبْدَأَ	تَبْدَأْ	اِبْدَأْ
أنتما	بَدَأْتُمَا	تَبْدَآنِ	تَبْدَآ	تَبْدَآ	اِبْدَآ
أنتم	بَدَأْتُمْ	تَبْدأون	تَبْدَأوا	تَبْدَأوا	اِبْدَأُوا
أنتِ	بَدَأْتِ	تَبْدَأين	تَبْدَأي	تَبْدَأي	اِبْدَأي
أنتما	بَدَأْتُمَا	تَبْدَآنِ	تَبْدَآ	تَبْدَآ	اِبْدَآ
أنتنَّ	بَدَأْتُنَّ	تَبْدَأْنَ	تَبْدَأْنَ	تَبْدَأْنَ	اِبْدَأْنَ
أنا	بَدَأْتُ	أَبْدَأُ	أَبْدَأَ	أَبْدَأْ	———
نحن	بَدَأْنَا	نَبْدَأُ	نَبْدَأَ	نَبْدَأْ	———

تصريف فعل " عاد "

الوزن:فَعَلَ

المصدر:العَوْدة

الضمير	الماضي	المضارع المرفوع	المضارع المنصوب	المضارع المجزوم	الأمر
هو	عَادَ	يَعودُ	يَعودَ	يَعُدْ	———
هما	عَادا	يَعودانِ	يَعودا	يَعودا	———
هم	عَادوا	يَعودونَ	يَعودوا	يَعودوا	———
هي	عَادَتْ	تَعودُ	تَعودَ	تَعُدْ	———
هما	عَادَتا	تَعودا	تَعودا	تَعودا	———
هنَّ	عُدْنَ	يَعُدْنَ	يَعُدْنَ	يَعُدْنَ	———
أنتَ	عُدْتَ	تَعودُ	تَعودَ	تَعُدْ	
أنتما	عُدْتُما	تَعودا	تَعودا	تَعودا	
أنتم	عُدْتُم	تَعودون	تَعودوا	تَعودوا	
أنتِ	عُدْتِ	تَعودين	تَعودي	تَعودي	
أنتما	عُدْتُما	تَعودا	تَعودا	تَعودا	
أنتنَّ	عُدْتُنَّ	تَعُدْنَ	تَعُدْنَ	تَعُدْنَ	
أنا	عُدْتُ	أعودُ	أعودَ	أعُدْ	———
نحن	عُدْنا	نَعودُ	نَعودَ	نَعُدْ	———

تصريف فعل "جاء"

الوزن: فَعَلَ

المصدر: المَجيء

الضمير	الماضي	المضارع المرفوع	المضارع المنصوب	المضارع المجزوم	الأمر
هو	جاءَ	يَجيءُ	يَجيءَ	يَجِئْ	——
هما	جاءا	يَجيئانِ	يَجيئا	يَجيئا	——
هم	جاءوا	يَجيئون	يجيئوا	يَجيئوا	——
هي	جاءَتْ	تَجيء	تَجيءَ	تَجِئْ	——
هما	جاءَتا	تَجيئان	تَجيئا	تَجيئا	——
هنَّ	جِئْنَ	يَجِئْنَ	يَجِئْنَ	يَجِئْنَ	——
أنتَ	جِئْتَ	تَجيء	تَجيءَ	تَجِئْ	تَعالَ
أنتما	جِئْتُما	تَجيئان	تَجيئا	تَجيئا	تَعالا
أنتم	جِئْتُم	تَجيئونَ	تَجيئوا	تَجيئوا	تَعالَوا
أنتِ	جِئْتِ	تَجيئينَ	تَجيئي	تَجيئي	تَعالَي
أنتما	جِئْتُما	تَجيئان	تَجيئا	تَجيئا	تَعالا
أنتنَّ	جِئْتُنَّ	تَجِئْنَ	تَجِئْنَ	تَجِئْنَ	
أنا	جِئْتُ	أَجيءُ	أَجيءَ	أَجِئْ	——
نحن	جِئْنا	نَجيءُ	نَجيءَ	نَجِئْ	——

تصريف فعل "قضى"

الوزن: فَعَلَ

المصدر: القَضاء

الضمير	الماضي	المضارع المرفوع	المضارع المنصوب	المضارع المجزوم	الأمر
هو	قَضى	يَقْضي	يَقْضِيَ	يَقْضِ	———
هما	قَضَيا	يَقْضِيانِ	يَقْضِيا	يَقْضِيا	———
هم	قَضَوا	يَقْضونَ	يَقْضوا	يَقْضوا	———
هي	قَضَتْ	تَقْضي	تَقْضِيَ	تَقْضِ	———
هما	قَضَتا	تَقْضِيانِ	تَقْضِيا	تَقْضِيا	———
هنَّ	قَضَيْنَ	يَقْضِينَ	يَقْضِينَ	يَقْضِينَ	———
أنتَ	قَضَيْتَ	تَقْضي	تَقْضِيَ	تَقْضِ	اقْضِ
أنتما	قَضَيْتُما	تَقْضِيانِ	تَقْضِيا	تَقْضِيا	اِقْضِيا
أنتم	قَضَيْتُم	تَقْضون	تَقْضوا	تَقْضوا	اِقْضوا
أنتِ	قَضَيْتِ	تَقْضين	تَقْضي	تَقْضي	اِقْضي
أنتما	قَضَيْتُما	تَقْضِيانِ	تَقْضِيا	تَقْضِيا	اِقْضِيا
أنتنَّ	قَضَيْتُنَّ	تَقْضين	تَقْضين	تَقْضين	اِقْضِينَ
أنا	قَضَيْت	أَقْضي		أَقْضِ	———
نحن	قَضَيْنا	نَقْضي	نَقْضِيَ	نَقْضِ	———

تصريف فعل ”بقي“

الوزن: فَعِلَ

المصدر:البَقاء

الضمير	الماضي	المضارع المرفوع	المضارع المنصوب	المضارع المجزوم	الأمر
هو	بَقِيَ	يَبْقى	يَبْقى	يَبْقَ	———
هما	بَقِيا	يَبْقَيانِ	يَبْقَيا	يَبْقَيا	———
هم	بَقُوا	يَبْقون	يَبْقُوا	يَبْقَوا	———
هي	بَقِيَت	تَبْقى	تَبْقى	تَبْقَ	———
هما	بَقِيَتا	تَبْقَيانِ	تَبْقَيا	تَبْقَيا	———
هنَّ	بَقِينَ	يَبْقَينَ	يَبْقَينَ	يَبْقَينَ	———
أنتَ	بَقيتَ	تَبْقى	تَبْقى	تَبْقَ	اِبْقَ
أنتما	بَقيتُما	تَبْقَيانِ	تَبْقَيا	تَبْقَيا	اِبْقَيا
أنتم	بَقيتُم	تَبْقَونَ	تَبْقَوا	تَبْقَوا	اِبْقَوا
أنتِ	بَقيتِ	تَبْقَينَ	تَبْقَيْ	تَبْقَيْ	اِبْقَيْ
أنتما	بَقيتُما	تَبْقَيانِ	تَبْقَيا	تَبْقَيا	اِبْقَيا
أنتنَّ	بَقيتُنَّ	تَبْقَينَ	تَبْقَينَ	تَبْقَينَ	اِبْقَينَ
أنا	بَقيتُ	أَبْقى	أَبْقى	أَبْقَ	———
نحن	بَقينا	نَبْقى	نَبْقى	نَبْقَ	———

تصريف فعل " ظنّ "

الوزن: فَعَلَ المصدر: الظَّنّ

الضمير	الماضي	المضارع المرفوع	المضارع المنصوب	المضارع المجزوم
هو	ظَنَّ	يَظُنُّ	يَظُنَّ	يَظُنَّ
هما	ظَنّا	يَظُنّانِ	يَظُنّا	يَظُنّا
هم	ظَنّوا	يَظُنّونَ	يَظُنّوا	يَظُنّوا
هي	ظَنَّت	تَظُنُّ	تَظُنَّ	تَظُنَّ
هما	ظَنَّتا	تَظُنّانِ	تَظُنّا	تَظُنّا
هنَّ	ظَنَنَّ	يَظْنُنَّ	يَظْنُنَّ	يَظْنُنَّ
أنتَ	ظَنَنْتَ	تَظُنُّ	تَظُنَّ	تَظُنَّ
أنتما	ظَنَنْتُما	تَظُنّانِ	تَظُنّا	تَظُنّا
أنتم	ظَنَنْتُم	تَظُنّونَ	تَظُنّوا	تَظُنّوا
أنتِ	ظَنَنْتِ	تَظُنّينَ	تَظُنّي	تَظُنّي
أنتما	ظَنَنْتُما	تَظُنّانِ	تَظُنّا	تَظُنّا
أنتنَّ	ظَنَنْتُنَّ	تَظْنُنَّ	تَظْنُنَّ	تَظْنُنَّ
أنا	ظَنَنْتُ	أَظُنُّ	أَظُنَّ	أَظُنَّ
نحن	ظَنَنّا	نَظُنُّ	نَظُنَّ	نَظُنَّ

تصريف فعل " غيّر "

الوزن: فَعَّلَ

المصدر: التَّغْيير

الضمير	الماضي	المضارع المرفوع	المضارع المنصوب	المضارع المجزوم	الأمر
هو	غَيَّرَ	يُغَيِّرُ	يُغَيِّرَ	يُغَيِّرْ	ـــــ
هما	غَيَّرا	يُغَيِّرانِ	يُغَيِّرا	يُغَيِّرا	ـــــ
هم	غَيَّروا	يُغَيِّرون	يُغَيِّروا	يُغَيِّروا	ـــــ
هي	غَيَّرَت	تُغَيِّرُ	تُغَيِّرَ	تُغَيِّرْ	ـــــ
هما	غَيَّرَتا	تُغَيِّرانِ	تُغَيِّرا	تُغَيِّرا	ـــــ
هنَّ	غَيَّرْنَ	يُغَيِّرْنَ	يُغَيِّرْنَ	يُغَيِّرْنَ	ـــــ
أنتَ	غَيَّرْتَ	تُغَيِّرُ	تُغَيِّرَ	تُغَيِّرْ	غَيِّرْ
أنتما	غَيَّرْتما	تُغَيِّرانِ	تُغَيِّرا	تُغَيِّرا	غَيِّرا
أنتم	غَيَّرْتُم	تُغَيِّرونَ	تُغَيِّروا	تُغَيِّروا	غَيِّروا
أنتِ	غَيَّرْتِ	تُغَيِّرينَ	تُغَيِّري	تُغَيِّري	غَيِّري
أنتما	غَيَّرْتُما	تُغَيِّرانِ	تُغَيِّرا	تُغَيِّرا	غَيِّرا
أنتنَّ	غَيَّرْتُنَّ	تُغَيِّرْنَ	تُغَيِّرْنَ	تُغَيِّرْنَ	غَيِّرْنَ
أنا	غَيَّرْتُ	أُغَيِّرُ	أُغَيِّرَ	أُغَيِّرْ	ـــــ
نحن	غَيَّرْنا	نُغَيِّرُ	نُغَيِّرَ	نُغَيِّرْ	ـــــ

تصريف فعل " شاهد "

الوزن: فاعَلَ المصدر: المُشاهَدة

الضمير	الماضي	المضارع المرفوع	المضارع المنصوب	المضارع المجزوم	الأمر
هو	شاهَدَ	يُشاهِدُ	يُشاهِدَ	يُشاهِدْ	———
هما	شاهَدا	يُشاهِدانِ	يُشاهِدا	يُشاهِدا	———
هم	شاهَدوا	يُشاهِدونَ	يُشاهِدوا	يُشاهِدوا	———
هي	شاهَدَتْ	تُشاهِدُ	تُشاهِدَ	تُشاهِدْ	———
هما	شاهَدَتا	تُشاهِدانِ	تُشاهِدا	تُشاهِدا	———
هنَّ	شاهَدْنَ	يُشاهِدْنَ	يُشاهِدْنَ	يُشاهِدْنَ	———
أنتَ	شاهَدْتَ	تُشاهِدُ	تُشاهِدَ	تُشاهِدْ	شاهِدْ
أنتما	شاهَدْتُما	تُشاهِدانِ	تُشاهِدا	تُشاهِدا	شاهِدا
أنتم	شاهَدْتُم	تُشاهِدونَ	تُشاهِدوا	تُشاهِدوا	شاهِدوا
أنتِ	شاهَدْتِ	تُشاهِدينَ	تُشاهِدي	تُشاهِدي	شاهِدي
أنتما	شاهَدْتُما	تُشاهِدانِ	تُشاهِدا	تُشاهِدا	شاهِدا
أنتنَّ	شاهَدْتُنَّ	تُشاهِدْنَ	تُشاهِدْنَ	تُشاهِدْنَ	شاهِدْنَ
أنا	شاهَدْت	أُشاهِدُ	أُشاهِدَ	أُشاهِدْ	———
نحن	شاهَدْنا	نُشاهِدُ	نُشاهِدَ	نُشاهِدْ	———

تصريف فعل " أرسل "

الوزن: أَفْعَلَ — المصدر: الإِرْسال

الضمير	الماضي	المضارع المرفوع	المضارع المنصوب	المضارع المجزوم	الأمر
هو	أَرْسَلَ	يُرْسِلُ	يُرْسِلَ	يُرْسِلْ	——
هما	أَرْسَلا	يُرْسِلانِ	يُرْسِلا	يُرْسِلا	——
هم	أَرْسَلوا	يُرْسِلونَ	يُرْسِلوا	يُرْسِلوا	——
هي	أَرْسَلَت	تُرْسِلُ	تُرْسِلَ	تُرْسِلْ	——
هما	أَرْسَلَتا	تُرْسِلانِ	تُرْسِلا	تُرْسِلا	——
هنَّ	أَرْسَلْنَ	يُرْسِلْنَ	يُرْسِلْنَ	يُرْسِلْنَ	——
أنتَ	أَرْسَلْتَ	تُرْسِلُ	تُرْسِلَ	تُرْسِلْ	أَرْسِلْ
أنتما	أَرْسَلْتُما	تُرْسِلانِ	تُرْسِلا	تُرْسِلا	أَرْسِلا
أنتم	أَرْسَلْتُم	تُرْسِلونَ	تُرْسِلوا	تُرْسِلوا	أَرْسِلوا
أنتِ	أَرْسَلْتِ	تُرْسِلينَ	تُرْسِلي	تُرْسِلي	أَرْسِلي
أنتما	أَرْسَلْتُما	تُرْسِلانِ	تُرْسِلا	تُرْسِلا	أَرْسِلا
أنتنَّ	أَرْسَلْتُنَّ	تُرْسِلْنَ	تُرْسِلْنَ	تُرْسِلْنَ	أَرْسِلْنَ
أنا	أَرْسَلْتُ	أُرْسِلُ	أُرْسِلَ	أُرْسِلْ	——
نحن	أَرْسَلْنا	نُرْسِلُ	نُرْسِلَ	نُرْسِلْ	——

تصريف فعل " أراد "

الوزن: أَفْعَلَ　　　　المصدر: الإِرادة

الضمير	الماضي	المضارع المرفوع	المضارع المنصوب	المضارع المجزوم
هو	أَرادَ	يُريدُ	يُريدَ	يُرِدْ
هما	أَرادا	يُريدانِ	يُريدا	يُريدا
هم	أَرادوا	يُريدونَ	يُريدوا	يُريدوا
هي	أَرادَتْ	تُريدُ	تُريدَ	تُرِدْ
هما	أَرادَتا	تُريدانِ	تُريدا	تُريدا
هنَّ	أَرَدْنَ	يُرِدْنَ	يُرِدْنَ	يُرِدْنَ
أنتَ	أَرَدْتَ	تُريدُ	تُريدَ	تُرِدْ
أنتما	أَرَدْتُما	تُريدانِ	تُريدا	تُريدا
أنتم	أَرَدْتُم	تُريدونَ	تُريدوا	تُريدوا
أنتِ	أَرَدْتِ	تُريدينَ	تُريدي	تُريدي
أنتما	أَرَدْتُما	تُريدانِ	تُريدا	تُريدا
أنتنَّ	أَرَدْتُنَّ	تُرِدْنَ	تُرِدْنَ	تُرِدْنَ
أنا	أَرَدْتُ	أُريدُ	أُريدَ	أُرِدْ
نحن	أَرَدْنا	نُريدُ	نُريدَ	نُرِدْ

تصريف فعل " تكلّم "

الوزن: تَفَعَّلَ　　　　المصدر: التَكَلُّم

الضمير	الماضي	المضارع المرفوع	المضارع المنصوب	المضارع المجزوم	الأمر
هو	تَكَلَّمَ	يَتَكَلَّمُ	يَتَكَلَّمَ	يَتَكَلَّمْ	ـــــ
هما	تَكَلَّما	يَتَكَلَّمانِ	يَتَكَلَّما	يَتَكَلَّما	ـــــ
هم	تَكَلَّموا	يَتَكَلَّمونَ	يَتَكَلَّموا	يَتَكَلَّموا	ـــــ
هي	تَكَلَّمَت	تَتَكَلَّمُ	تَتَكَلَّمَ	تَتَكَلَّمْ	ـــــ
هما	تَكَلَّمَتا	تَتَكَلَّمانِ	تَتَكَلَّما	تَتَكَلَّما	ـــــ
هنَّ	تَكَلَّمْنَ	يَتَكَلَّمْنَ	يَتَكَلَّمْنَ	يَتَكَلَّمْنَ	ـــــ
أنتَ	تَكَلَّمْتَ	تَتَكَلَّمُ	تَتَكَلَّمَ	تَتَكَلَّمْ	تَكَلَّمْ
أنتما	تَكَلَّمْتُما	تَتَكَلَّمانِ	تَتَكَلَّما	تَتَكَلَّما	تَكَلَّما
أنتم	تَكَلَّمْتُم	تَتَكَلَّمونَ	تَتَكَلَّموا	تَتَكَلَّموا	تَكَلَّموا
أنتِ	تَكَلَّمْتِ	تَتَكَلَّمينَ	تَتَكَلَّمي	تَتَكَلَّمي	تَكَلَّمي
أنتما	تَكَلَّمْتُما	تَتَكَلَّمانِ	تَتَكَلَّما	تَتَكَلَّما	تَكَلَّما
أنتنَّ	تَكَلَّمْتُنَّ	تَتَكَلَّمْنَ	تَتَكَلَّمْنَ	تَتَكَلَّمْنَ	تَكَلَّمْنَ
أنا	تَكَلَّمْتُ	أتَكَلَّمُ	أتَكَلَّمَ	أتَكَلَّمْ	ـــــ
نحن	تَكَلَّمْنا	نَتَكَلَّمُ	نَتَكَلَّمَ	نَتَكَلَّمْ	ـــــ

تصريف فعل " تبادل "

الوزن: تَفاعَلَ — المصدر: التَّبادُل

الضمير	الماضي	المضارع المرفوع	المضارع المنصوب	المضارع المجزوم	الأمر
هو	تَبادَلَ	يَتَبادَلُ	يَتَبادَلَ	يَتَبادَلْ	———
هما	تَبادَلا	يَتَبادَلانِ	يَتَبادَلا	يَتَبادَلا	———
هم	تَبادَلوا	يَتَبادَلونَ	يَتَبادَلوا	يَتَبادَلوا	———
هي	تَبادَلَت	تَتَبادَلُ	تَتَبادَلَ	تَتَبادَلْ	———
هما	تَبادَلَتا	تَتَبادَلانِ	تَتَبادَلا	تَتَبادَلا	———
هنَّ	تَبادَلْنَ	يَتَبادَلْنَ	يَتَبادَلْنَ	يَتَبادَلْنَ	———
أنتَ	تَبادَلْتَ	تَتَبادَلُ	تَتَبادَلَ	تَتَبادَلْ	تَبادَلْ
أنتما	تَبادَلْتُما	تَتَبادَلانِ	تَتَبادَلا	تَتَبادَلا	تَبادَلا
أنتم	تَبادَلْتُم	تَتَبادَلونَ	تَتَبادَلوا	تَتَبادَلوا	تَبادَلوا
أنتِ	تَبادَلْتِ	تَتَبادَلينَ	تَتَبادَلي	تَتَبادَلي	تَبادَلي
أنتما	تَبادَلْتُما	تَتَبادَلانِ	تَتَبادَلا	تَتَبادَلا	تَبادَلا
أنتنَّ	تَبادَلْتُنَّ	تَتَبادَلْنَ	تَتَبادَلْنَ	تَتَبادَلْنَ	تَبادَلْنَ
أنا	تَبادَلْتُ	أتَبادَلُ	أتَبادَلَ	أتَبادَلْ	———
نحن	تَبادَلْنا	نَتَبادَلُ	نَتَبادَلَ	نَتَبادَلْ	———

تصريف فعل " انقطع "

الوزن: انْفَعَلَ

المصدر: الانْقطاع

الضمير	الماضي	المضارع المرفوع	المضارع المنصوب	المضارع المجزوم
هو	اِنْقَطَعَ	يَنْقَطِعُ	يَنْقَطِعَ	يَنْقَطِعْ
هما	اِنْقَطَعَا	يَنْقَطِعَانِ	يَنْقَطِعَا	يَنْقَطِعَا
هم	اِنْقَطَعُوا	يَنْقَطِعُونَ	يَنْقَطِعُوا	يَنْقَطِعُوا
هي	اِنْقَطَعَتْ	تَنْقَطِعُ	تَنْقَطِعَ	تَنْقَطِعْ
هما	اِنْقَطَعَتَا	تَنْقَطِعَانِ	تَنْقَطِعَا	تَنْقَطِعَا
هنَّ	اِنْقَطَعْنَ	يَنْقَطِعْنَ	يَنْقَطِعْنَ	يَنْقَطِعْنَ
أنتَ	اِنْقَطَعْتَ	تَنْقَطِعُ	تَنْقَطِعَ	تَنْقَطِعْ
أنتما	اِنْقَطَعْتُمَا	تَنْقَطِعَانِ	تَنْقَطِعَا	تَنْقَطِعَا
أنتم	اِنْقَطَعْتُمْ	تَنْقَطِعُونَ	تَنْقَطِعُوا	تَنْقَطِعُوا
أنتِ	اِنْقَطَعْتِ	تَنْقَطِعِينَ	تَنْقَطِعِي	تَنْقَطِعِي
أنتما	اِنْقَطَعْتُمَا	تَنْقَطِعَانِ	تَنْقَطِعَا	تَنْقَطِعَا
أنتنَّ	اِنْقَطَعْتُنَّ	تَنْقَطِعْنَ	تَنْقَطِعْنَ	تَنْقَطِعْنَ
أنا	اِنْقَطَعْتُ	أَنْقَطِعُ	أَنْقَطِعَ	أَنْقَطِعْ
نحن	اِنْقَطَعْنَا	نَنْقَطِعُ	نَنْقَطِعَ	نَنْقَطِعْ

تصريف فعل " التحق بـ "

الوزن: افْتَعَلَ

المصدر: الالْتحاق بـ

الضمير	الماضي	المضارع المرفوع	المضارع المنصوب	المضارع المجزوم	الأمر
هو	الْتَحَقَ	يَلْتَحِقُ	يَلْتَحِقَ	يَلْتَحِقْ	——
هما	الْتَحَقا	يَلْتَحِقانِ	يَلْتَحِقا	يَلْتَحِقا	——
هم	الْتَحَقوا	يَلْتَحِقونَ	يَلْتَحِقوا	يَلْتَحِقوا	——
هي	الْتَحَقَت	تَلْتَحِقُ	تَلْتَحِقَ	تَلْتَحِقْ	——
هما	الْتَحَقَتَا	تَلْتَحِقانِ	تَلْتَحِقا	تَلْتَحِقا	——
هنَّ	الْتَحَقْنَ	يَلْتَحِقْنَ	يَلْتَحِقْنَ	يَلْتَحِقْنَ	——
أنتَ	الْتَحَقْتَ	تَلْتَحِقُ	تَلْتَحِقَ	تَلْتَحِقْ	الْتَحِقْ
أنتما	الْتَحَقْتُما	تَلْتَحِقانِ	تَلْتَحِقا	تَلْتَحِقا	الْتَحِقا
أنتم	الْتَحَقْتُم	تَلْتَحِقونَ	تَلْتَحِقوا	تَلْتَحِقوا	الْتَحِقوا
أنتِ	الْتَحَقْتِ	تَلْتَحِقينَ	تَلْتَحِقي	تَلْتَحِقي	الْتَحِقي
أنتما	الْتَحَقْتُما	تَلْتَحِقانِ	تَلْتَحِقا	تَلْتَحِقا	الْتَحِقا
أنتنَّ	الْتَحَقْتُنَّ	تَلْتَحِقْنَ	تَلْتَحِقْنَ	تَلْتَحِقْنَ	الْتَحِقْنَ
أنا	الْتَحَقْتُ	أَلْتَحِقُ	أَلْتَحِقَ	أَلْتَحِقْ	——
نحن	الْتَحَقْنا	نَلْتَحِقُ	نَلْتَحِقَ	نَلْتَحِقْ	——

تصريف فعل " استقبل "

الوزن: اسْتَفْعَلَ | المصدر: الاسْتِقْبال

الضمير	الماضي	المضارع المرفوع	المضارع المنصوب	المضارع المجزوم	الأمر
هو	اِسْتَقْبَلَ	يَسْتَقْبِلُ	يَسْتَقْبِلَ	يَسْتَقْبِلْ	ــــ
هما	اِسْتَقْبَلا	يَسْتَقْبِلانِ	يَسْتَقْبِلا	يَسْتَقْبِلا	ــــ
هم	اِسْتَقْبَلُوا	يَسْتَقْبِلُون	يَسْتَقْبِلُوا	يَسْتَقْبِلُوا	ــــ
هي	اِسْتَقْبَلَتْ	تَسْتَقْبِلُ	تَسْتَقْبِلَ	تَسْتَقْبِلْ	ــــ
هما	اِسْتَقْبَلَتا	تَسْتَقْبِلانِ	تَسْتَقْبِلا	تَسْتَقْبِلا	ــــ
هنَّ	اِسْتَقْبَلْنَ	يَسْتَقْبِلْنَ	يَسْتَقْبِلْنَ	يَسْتَقْبِلْنَ	ــــ
أنتَ	اِسْتَقْبَلْتَ	تَسْتَقْبِلُ	تَسْتَقْبِلَ	تَسْتَقْبِلْ	اِسْتَقْبِلْ
أنتما	اِسْتَقْبَلْتُما	تَسْتَقْبِلانِ	تَسْتَقْبِلا	تَسْتَقْبِلا	اِسْتَقْبِلا
أنتم	اِسْتَقْبَلْتُم	تَسْتَقْبِلونَ	تَسْتَقْبِلوا	تَسْتَقْبِلوا	اِسْتَقْبِلوا
أنتِ	اِسْتَقْبَلْتِ	تَسْتَقْبِلينَ	تَسْتَقْبِلي	تَسْتَقْبِلي	اِسْتَقْبِلي
أنتما	اِسْتَقْبَلْتُما	تَسْتَقْبِلانِ	تَسْتَقْبِلا	تَسْتَقْبِلا	اِسْتَقْبِلا
أنتنَّ	اِسْتَقْبَلْتُنَّ	تَسْتَقْبِلْنَ	تَسْتَقْبِلْنَ	تَسْتَقْبِلْنَ	اِسْتَقْبِلْنَ
أنا	اِسْتَقْبَلْتُ	أَسْتَقْبِلُ	أَسْتَقْبِلَ	أَسْتَقْبِلْ	ــــ
نحن	اِسْتَقْبَلْنا	نَسْتَقْبِلُ	نَسْتَقْبِلَ	نَسْتَقْبِلْ	ــــ

تصريف فعل " استطاع "

الوزن: اسْتَفْعَلَ — المصدر: الاسْتطاعة

الضمير	الماضي	المضارع المرفوع	المضارع المنصوب	المضارع المجزوم
هو	اِسْتَطاعَ	يستَطيعُ	يَسْتَطيعَ	يَسْتَطِعْ
هما	اِسْتَطاعا	يَسْتَطيعانِ	يَسْتَطيعا	يَسْتَطيعا
هم	اِسْتَطاعوا	يَسْتَطيعونَ	يَسْتَطيعوا	يَسْتَطيعوا
هي	اِسْتَطاعَت	تَسْتَطيعُ	تَسْتَطيع	تَسْتَطِعْ
هما	اِسْتَطاعَتا	تَسْتَطيعانِ	تَسْتَطيعا	تَسْتَطيعا
هنَّ	اِسْتَطَعْنَ	يَسْتَطِعْنَ	يَسْتَطِعْنَ	يَسْتَطِعْنَ
أنتَ	اِسْتَطَعْتَ	تَسْتَطيعُ	تَسْتَطيع	تَسْتَطِعْ
أنتما	اِسْتَطَعْتُما	تَسْتَطيعانِ	تَسْتَطيعا	تَسْتَطيعا
أنتم	اِسْتَطَعْتُم	تَسْتَطيعونَ	تَسْتَطيعوا	تَسْتَطيعوا
أنتِ	اِسْتَطَعْتِ	تَسْتَطيعينَ	تَسْتَطيعي	تَسْتَطيعي
أنتما	اِسْتَطَعْتُما	تَسْتَطيعانِ	تَسْتَطيعا	تَسْتَطيعا
أنتنَّ	اِسْتَطَعْتُنَّ	تَسْتَطِعْنَ	تَسْتَطِعْنَ	تَسْتَطِعْنَ
أنا	اِسْتَطَعْتُ	أَسْتَطيعُ	أَسْتَطيعَ	أَسْتَطِعْ
نحن	اِسْتَطَعْنا	نَسْتَطيعُ	نَسْتَطيعَ	نَسْتَطِعْ

قواعد الإعراب
Summary

الاسم		
المرفوع	المنصوب	المجرور
المبتدأ الخبر الفاعل	المفعول به: direct object متى؟ كيف؟ الاسم الذي يجيء بعد إنْ وأنّ	الاسم الذي يجيء بعد: – حرف جرّ – أول كلمة في الإضافة

الفعل المضارع		
المرفوع	المنصوب	المجزوم
main verbs بعد سَـ/سوف	الفعل الذي يجيء بعد : – أنْ – لَنْ – لِـ ، كَيْ – حتّى	الفعل الذي يجيء بعد : – لمْ

Grammar Index فهرست القواعد

المصطلحات العربية Arabic Terms

COMPONENTS OF THE *AL-KITAAB* LANGUAGE PROGRAM

Alif Baa

Alif Baa with DVDs: Introduction to Arabic Letters and Sounds
Second Edition
ISBN 978-1-58901-102-1, paperback with 2 DVDs bound in
(All audio and video materials combined on DVD)

Answer Key to Alif Baa with DVDs
Second Edition
ISBN 978-1-58901-036-9, paperback

....

Part One

Al-Kitaab fii Ta^{c}allum al-^{c}Arabiyya with DVDs
A Textbook for Beginning Arabic, Part One
Second Edition
ISBN 978-1-58901-104-5, paperback with 3 DVDs bound in
(All audio and video materials combined on DVD)

Answer Key to Al-Kitaab, Part One with DVDs
Second Edition
ISBN 978-1-58901-037-6, paperback

....

Part Two

Al-Kitaab fii Ta^{c}allum al-^{c}Arabiyya with DVDs
A Textbook for Arabic, Part Two
Second Edition
ISBN 978-1-58901-096-3, paperback with 3 DVDs bound in
(All audio and video materials combined on DVD)

Answer Key to Al-Kitaab, Part Two with DVDs
Second Edition
ISBN 978-1-58901-097-0, paperback

....

Part Three

Al-Kitaab fii Ta^{c}allum al-^{c}Arabiyya with DVD and MP3 CD
A Textbook for Arabic, Part Three
With New Video Material!
ISBN 978-1-158901-149-6, paperback with DVD and MP3 CD bound in

....

Audio On the Go
These CDs contain MP3 files of the audio only from the Alif Baa and Al-Kitaab volumes. Perfect for those students who want the portability of MP3 files for practice, these files can be transferred to an MP3 device, played on a computer, or played on some home CD players.

Alif Baa Audio On the Go ISBN 978-1-58901-152-6
Al-Kitaab Part One Audio On the Go ISBN 978-1-58901-150-2
Al-Kitaab Part Two Audio On the Go ISBN 978-1-58901-151-9

For price and ordering information, visit our website at www.press.georgetown.edu or call 800-537-5487.
For more information on teaching the *Al-Kitaab* language program, visit www.alkitaabtextbook.net.